Ink, Dirt and Powder Smoke: The Civil War Letters of William F. Keeler, Paymaster on the USS *Monitor*

edited by
Charles W. McLandress

Copyright © 2023 Charles W. McLandress

Seal River Publishing, Toronto, Ontario, Canada

www.sealriverpublishing.com

All rights reserved.

ISBN: 978-1-7387269-0-5

For Cora and Matthew

My father was the son of a New York merchant, and was a merchant himself part of his life, but he was of a roving disposition, and, partly on this account, and partly through heavy losses by fire, he left but a small property at his death. He served as Paymaster in the U.S. Navy during the civil war, and afterwards moved to Florida, where he lived until his death, some six years ago. He was an active and highly cultivated man and I acquired from him my liking for scientific matters.*

— James Edward Keeler

---

* Portion of James E. Keeler's letter to his future father-in-law W. Wilson Matthews asking for his daughter's hand in marriage. Original letter is in the possession of the editor; a photocopy of the letter is in the James E. Keeler Papers (MS 271), Special Collections and Archives, University Library, University of California, Santa Cruz, CA.

Contents

Acknowledgments viii
Editorial Method ix
Preface x
Introduction 1
Part 1: Early Years 5
Part 2: Civil War Years 13
   USS *Monitor* (1862) 16
      New York Navy Yard (January to March 1862) 18
      Hampton Roads (March to May 1862) 41
      James River (May to August 1862) 120
      Off Newport News (August to October 1862) 221
      Cape Hatteras (November to December 1862) 249
   USS *Florida* (1863-1865) 287
      Off Wilmington (March to September 1863) 290
      Norfolk Navy Yard (September to October 1863) 371
      Cruising (October to December 1863) 390
      Off Wilmington (December 1863 to March 1864) 415
      Norfolk Navy Yard (April to May 1864) 450
      Off Wilmington (May to August 1864) 466
      To Halifax (August to November 1864) 495
      Gulf of Mexico (March to November 1865) 509
Part 3: Mayport Years 571
   Final Letters 576
Epilogue.. 589
Appendices 591
Biographical Notes 601
Selected Bibliography... 625
Index 627
Abbreviations.. 647
About the Editor... 648

Acknowledgments

I would like to thank the following people for helping to make this book a reality: Patrick Lohier, friend and writer, for his encouragement, advice and comments on earlier drafts of the manuscript. Tracy Logan, senior curator of the United States Naval Academy Museum, for kindly photographing pages from Keeler's letter book that were partially illegible or missing in the 55-year old photocopies I was using to transcribe the letters. John Quarstein, Civil War historian and USS *Monitor* expert, for answers to questions about the vessel and her crew, and for an excellent tour of the Hampton Roads area in the spring of 2019. Tina Gutshall, conservation administrator for the USS *Monitor*, for a fascinating tour of the USS *Monitor* Center, including the conservation facility where the *Monitor*'s turret and guns are being restored. Henry Dutton Foster, my distant cousin from Minneapolis, for so generously lending me the Henry Dutton Family Letters which are quoted a number of times in this book. Those letters have since been donated to Yale University. Julie Lewis of the First Congregational Church of La Salle for providing me with copies of church records pertaining to the Keelers. The late Dorothy Schaumberg, curator of the Mary Lea Shane Archives of Lick Observatory at University of California Santa Cruz, for providing me with a photocopy of Keeler's wonderful *Mayport Journal*. The late Dorothy Turmail, elder of the First Presbyterian Church in Brooklyn, New York for records of that church. Abigale Mumby, reference assistant at the Bentley Historical Library in Ann Arbor, Michigan, for records of the First Presbyterian Church of Pontiac, Michigan. I am also grateful to my friend and writer Adam Haviaras for help and advice on self-publishing. Last, but not least, a very big thankyou to my wife Diane Pendlebury for listening to my seemingly endless outpourings about my great-great grandfather and for helpful comments on an earlier draft of the manuscript.

Editorial Method

William Keeler's letters were written rapidly and often under adverse conditions. Despite that they flow smoothly and contain remarkably few crossed-out or inserted words. Not wanting to waste space, and with much to say, his letters are devoid of paragraphs and often wrap into the margins. For ease of reading the letters are broken into paragraphs. Text that appears in the margin is placed at the end of the letter and is identified as marginalia. The intrusive [sic] is not used to identify misspelled words. Square brackets denote editorial insertions; round brackets and the text therein are Keeler's. Keeler frequently misspelled proper nouns (e.g., McClelland instead of McClellan, Staunton instead of Stanton, Fort Sumpter instead of Fort Sumter). The correct spelling of proper nouns is given at the first occurrence and omitted thereafter provided the intent is clear. When a word mistakenly appears twice in succession, the repeated word is silently omitted. Keeler had his own particular style of punctuation, making frequent use of the dash and consistently misusing the apostrophe. In cases where a period is more appropriate than a dash, a period is silently used. Misspelled contractions (e.g., do'nt instead of don't) are silently corrected and missing possessive apostrophes added. For clarity, missing question marks, commas and periods after abbreviations are also silently added. Superscripts following numbers or in abbreviations are lowered. Names of ships, newspapers and books, which he sometimes put in quotes, are italicized, and the quotes, if used, omitted. Words that are underlined are also changed to italics, while words that are double underlined are changed to underlined italics. Words that Keeler has crossed out, which are very few, are retained. Footnotes provide the reader with additional information. An asterisk after a person's name in a footnote indicates that a brief sketch of that person is given in the Biographical Notes.

Preface

In November 1962 my grandmother received a letter from Robert W. Daly, a history professor at the United States Naval Academy, asking for information about her grandfather, William F. Keeler, who had served as paymaster on the legendary Union ironclad the USS *Monitor* during the American Civil War. Six years earlier Daly had begun editing Keeler's wartime letters from the *Monitor* for publication in commemoration of the hundredth anniversary of the start of the Civil War. While he could build a complete picture of Keeler's life during the war, Daly knew virtually nothing about the rest of his life and had been searching for his descendants in hopes they could flesh out the bare bones of what he had learned about the Paymaster. He had been drawing blanks until he learned of the whereabouts of my grandmother, who was living in San Antonio, Texas with my grandfather, a retired U.S. Army colonel. Daly explained to her the importance of Keeler's "superbly vivid letters" and apologized for any seeming impertinences, stating that he felt like a friend of the family, having been "shipmates with your fine grandfather for so long." My grandmother, unfortunately, was unable to furnish him with much information, since she had never known her grandfather, who died before she was born, and would probably have remembered little about him from her astronomer father who died when she was six. Moreover, fire had destroyed almost all of the family records in her mother's house in Berkeley, California, in 1923. All she could provide him with was a handful of meagre crumbs: three of her grandfather's business cards, a family tree drawn by her father, and excerpts from a journal her father kept as a teenager in Mayport, Florida where Keeler and his family settled after the war. In Daly's second letter to my grandmother he laments that

> *fire absolutely haunts the Paymaster. All the back copies of the La Salle newspaper for his era (he contributed letters at the height of his* Monitor *fame) vanished in a fire in the 1880's. A single file was somehow preserved in the State Library at Albany, and that building, too, wisped away in smoke. Fire struck at Bridgeport and Utica, wiping out leads, and time has eroded away all traces of his presence at Mayport, Florida. And now I hear from you about the 1923 fire at Berkeley. He was a very modest man, and I have an uneasy feeling that he may be covering his tracks.*

The correspondence between Daly and my grandmother continued intermittently for the next six years until the two volumes of her grandfather's letters were published: *Aboard the U.S.S. Monitor, 1862: The Letters of Acting Paymaster William Frederick Keeler, U.S. Navy, to His Wife, Anna* and *Aboard the U.S.S. Florida, 1863-1865: The Letters of Paymaster William Frederick Keeler, U.S. Navy, to His Wife, Anna*. After my grandmother's death in 1986, her papers found their way to my parents' home in Winnipeg, Manitoba. These included her correspondence with Daly, copies of the two volumes of letters, photocopies of the original letters, Keeler's business cards, a gold nugget he had brought back from the California Gold Rush, and a silver fork he had had made after the Civil War on which was engraved "Paymaster United States Steamer Monitor."

My grandmother's papers sat untouched until a few years ago when I decided to read the letters, not from Daly's books but from the somewhat grainy photocopies of Keeler's letter book. Finding the original letters far more compelling than the abridged ones in Daly's books, I realized that a revised and updated version of Keeler's letters would be a valuable contribution to Civil War literature which would bring his vivid writing and keen observations to a new generation of readers. And so, with the photocopies of the original letters, I set out to transcribe my great-great grandfather's letters in their entirety and delved deeply into his remarkable life. I reached out to several leading Civil War historians who affirmed the importance and historical significance of the letters and the value of a complete and unabridged version of them. This book is the culmination of those efforts.

By the spring of 2019 I had nearly completed a first draft of the book, I made a trip to the James River area with my great-great grandfather's letters in hand and visited the places he so vividly wrote about nearly 160 years ago. My amiable and knowledgeable tour guide, Civil War historian John Quarstein, took me to the Monitor Overlook to see where the USS *Monitor* and her foe, the Confederate ironclad CSS *Virginia*, battled it out on March 9, 1862 on the second day of the Battle of Hampton Roads. Gazing out over the wide expanse, I imagined the smoke-covered waters, the roar of the big guns, and the hundreds of Union soldiers on shore cheering on their little ironclad. As I stood there reading the short note Keeler wrote to his family two hours after the battle, in which he stated that his hands were "all dirt & powder smoke as you will discover by the paper," his letters sprung to life. That vivid quote epitomizes the beauty of his writing and inspired the title of this book.

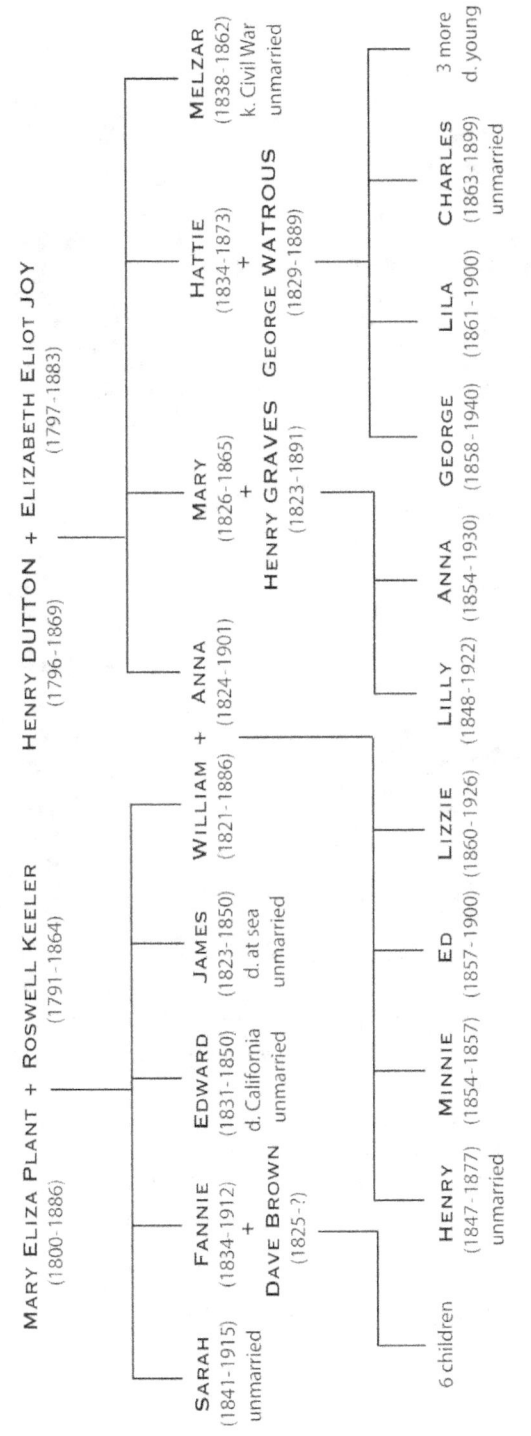

William and Anna Keeler, wartime photographs. The top two photos, which are from Keeler's letter book, were taken while he was serving on the USS *Florida*. When asked by his sister whether he occupied the same position on the *Florida* as he did on the *Monitor* he replied that "I have a higher one & am entitled to indulge in the expensive luxury of *two* gold bands on my sleeves, instead of one. This I was not aware of till Capt. B. informed me a few days since. He told me that ordering me to this vessel placed me in a position not given to any other volunteer Paymaster in the navy. Unfortunately the pay is not increased in proportion." Note that the uncropped version of the photo at top right that is in the letter book shows Keeler with two bands on his sleeve. Courtesy U.S. Naval Academy Museum (top); Mariners' Museum (bottom left); Mark Ewing (bottom right).

Officers of the USS *Monitor* in front of the turret (July 9, 1862). (Top) Back row, left to right: Albert Campbell, Mark Sunstrom, William Keeler, Lieutenant L. Howard Newman, executive officer of the USS *Galena*. Middle row, left to right: Louis Stodder, George Frederickson, William Flye, Daniel Logue, Samuel Dana Greene. Front row, left to right: Robinson Hands and Edwin Gager. (Bottom) Same officers as in top photograph but with the addition of Isaac Newton (back row, right). Courtesy Library of Congress.

Sailors on the USS *Monitor* (July 9, 1862). In the foreground is former slave Siah Carter who escaped from Shirley Plantation and enlisted as a first-class boy on May 19, 1862. Keeler described him as "one of the most useful men on board, a good carpenter, a shoemaker, fisherman, can wash & iron." Courtesy Library of Congress.

Sailors on the USS *Monitor* (July 9, 1862). The caption of this photo in Keeler's letter book reads: "Deck of the *Monitor* aft of the turret—The crew in the first dog watch off duty." In his letter of October 28, 1863, Keeler identifies Acting Master's Mate Peter Williams as the one "sitting reading a paper" behind one of the smokestacks at center left. A dog watch is half the length of the standard four-hour watch. Courtesy Library of Congress.

Turret and pilot house of the USS *Monitor* (July 9, 1862). The caption of this photo in Keeler's letter book reads: "Deck of the *Monitor* looking forward—shewing shot marks received from the *Merrimac*." Included in his letter of July 25, 1862 is a description of this photo: "To the left & on a line with the lower lip of the port is a couple of shot marks from the *Merrimac*. . . . A part of another shot mark can be seen on the right edge of the turret about half way below the gun & the deck. The circle in the foreground is an opening into the coal bunkers below closed by an iron opening. In the background is the pilot house, this side of which are some of the iron plugs fitting into our deck lights. Mr. Flye & Mr. Campbell stand near the side. A little this side of them you can see the side armour started off by one of the *Merrimac*'s shot." Courtesy Library of Congress.

Lieutenant John Worden, commanding officer of the USS *Monitor*. Keeler's first impressions of their new captain, who had recently been released from a seven-month stint in a Confederate prison: "He is tall, thin & quite effeminate looking, notwithstanding a long beard hanging down his breast. He is white & delicate probably from long confinement & never was a lady the possessor of a smaller or more delicate hand. But if I am not very much mistaken he will not hesitate to submit our iron sides to as severe a test as the most warlike could desire. He is a perfect gentleman in manner." Wartime photograph from Keeler's letter book courtesy U.S. Naval Academy Museum.

Lieutenant Commander William Jeffers, commanding officer of the USS *Monitor*, with the *Monitor*'s turret as background (July 9, 1862). "A rigid disciplinarian, of quick imperious temper & domineering disposition," according to Keeler, "he is one of the best ordnance officers in the service, of undoubted courage, cool & calculating in action, well fitted for the command of a vessel like ours that is to lead the van. I have nothing to do with the working or management of the vessel & so am not brought into so close contact with him, but I have heard him talk to some of the officers as I should not want anyone to talk to me." From a photograph identical to that in Keeler's letter book but cropped in size. Courtesy Library of Congress.

Commander John Bankhead, commanding officer of the USS *Monitor* and USS *Florida*. Keeler described him as "a strict disciplinarian, exacting obedience & respect from both officers & men and according to each their due. But while he was a model officer he never forgot he was a gentleman. His officers he always expected to do their duty & while they did, were always treated with the greatest courtesy & consideration. To those of us who stood by him on the *Monitor* he seemed particularly attached. For myself I have nothing but the most pleasant recollections while under his command." Wartime photograph from Keeler's letter book courtesy U.S. Naval Academy Museum.

Lieutenant Samuel Dana Greene, executive officer on the USS *Monitor* and USS *Florida*. "Generous, impulsive, excitable, somewhat reserved & unsocial in his disposition," according to Keeler. He died by suicide in 1884 as a result, it was believed, of accusations of cowardice during the fight with the CSS *Virginia* levelled at him after the war. The year after his death, Keeler commented on the bravery of his old friend: "I saw Greene in more trying circumstances than these where greater coolness & presence of mind were required if possible — it was when the *Monitor* went down. . . . After most of the crew had been swept off the deck or carried off in the boats, Greene approached me as he crossed the top of the turret in the darkness — 'Is that you, Pay?' 'Yes.' 'Well why don't you get into the boat? Now's your chance, jump in.' Forgetting himself in his anxiety to get all others safely out of the sinking vessel." Wartime photograph from Keeler's letter book courtesy U.S. Naval Academy Museum.

William Flye, acting volunteer lieutenant on the USS *Monitor*. He joined the vessel immediately after the fight with the CSS *Virginia*, which he observed from the USS *Roanoke*, and was detached in late October 1862. For the remainder of the war, he and Keeler exchanged letters and the two had the occasion to meet in North Carolina in 1863. Keeler described him as "a very pleasant easy writer & a well educated person [who] was formerly a Prof. of Mathematics in the navy." Wartime photograph from Keeler's letter book courtesy U.S. Naval Academy Museum.

Louis Stodder, acting master on the USS *Monitor*. He received a commendation from Capt. Bankhead, as well as a promotion to acting volunteer lieutenant, for his actions when the *Monitor* sank off Cape Hatteras, one of which was cutting the towline connecting the vessel to the USS *Rhode Island*, "a task involving almost certain destruction" according to Keeler who observed the scene from the turret. After two sailors had tried and failed and were swept off the deck to their deaths, Stodder "seized a hatchet & going cautiously forward holding on the life line, which was stretched around the deck, with a few blows severed the connection while the waves were rolling high over his head & returned in safety to the turret." Wartime photograph from Keeler's letter book courtesy U.S. Naval Academy Museum.

Albert Campbell, acting second assistant engineer on the USS *Monitor*. The day before Christmas 1862 he received a hefty care package from back home in Brooklyn, the consumption of which Keeler described as follows: "Following the call of the Master at Arms at my room with his 'six bells' &c last evening came Mr. Campbell with a big mince pie & a pitcher of cider, so instead of obeying the hint just rec'd we hung our blankets over the sky lights & other openings making the officer of the watch believe the report made to him by the Master at Arms of 'lights all out sir.' Campbell had just rec'd a large box from home filled with a variety of cakes, candies, some very fine mince pies & six gallon cans, filled with mince meat. He is one of that sort who will never eat such things by himself so, as I said, he brought one of his pies, some real nice crullers & a pitcher of cider in to my room & himself, the M.D. & myself had a time till 12 o'clock." Wartime photograph from Keeler's letter book courtesy U.S. Naval Academy Museum.

Peter Williams, quartermaster and later acting master's mate on the USS *Monitor* and acting ensign on the USS *Florida*. Promoted for bravery and valor during the Civil War, he is shown here wearing the Medal of Congress which he was awarded for gallantry in the fight with the CSS *Virginia*. In regards to the fight, Keeler remarked that "it would take a man of more than ordinary nerve to look steadily & cooly into the muzzle of a ten inch rifled gun & see it loaded, trained & fired within 15 feet of his head. He did it without any apparent emotion, cooly saying to Capt. W., 'take care, sir, they are going to try us now.'" Wartime photograph from Keeler's letter book courtesy U.S. Naval Academy Museum.

Samuel Crafts, acting ensign and later acting master on the USS *Florida*. He was "a very pleasant companion," according to Keeler, but with "no polish or refinement whatever about him—very fond of argument, with a little smattering, superficial knowledge of everything from the latest improvement in tin whistles to the most approved method of frying an egg." He was promoted to acting volunteer lieutenant for gallant conduct during the second battle of Fort Fisher in January 1865. Wartime photograph from Keeler's letter book courtesy U.S. Naval Academy Museum.

Acting Lieutenant Edgar Merriman, executive officer on the USS *Florida*. Keeler described him as "full of fun & frolick & music & I think we shall get along first rate. He keeps a guitar & melodion in his room & every night before I 'turn in' he sends a note by one of the messenger boys for 'Pay to come up & take a smoke.' So I go up & smoke while he sings. He is a capital singer & is the best hand at telling a comic story that I ever saw. He has dark curling hair, a pleasant face with fun in every lineament." Wartime photograph from Keeler's letter book courtesy U.S. Naval Academy Museum.

John McGowan Jr., acting master on the USS *Florida*. His sea-captain father commanded the commercial vessel *Star of the West* which attempted to provision Fort Sumter shortly before the start of the Civil War. His uncle was "the notorious Ned McGowan of California," the Philadelphia lawyer turned Confederate army officer who was captured and then escaped from the prison ship *Maple Leaf*. John joined the regular Navy after the war and rose to the rank of rear admiral. Wartime photograph from Keeler's letter book courtesy U.S. Naval Academy Museum.

Hiram James, acting assistant surgeon on the USS *Florida*, whom Keeler aptly described as "very tall, his lower limbs long drawn out." He suffered from debilitating sea sickness on the *Florida* and was transferred to the Mississippi Squadron where he was forced to resign five months later due to chronic diarrhea. He remained an invalid for the rest of his life and died in a sanatorium in upstate New York where he had gone for relief. Wartime photograph from Keeler's letter book courtesy U.S. Naval Academy Museum.

Robert Brooks, acting assistant surgeon on the USS *Florida*. Keeler described him as "the greenest & most homely specimen of the genus homo that I have seen in a long time," although the photo does not convey that impression. The son of an Irish immigrant, he was raised on a farm and graduated at the top of his class at Miami University in Oxford, Ohio. He was described as "a man of fine taste, public spirited and very liberal toward and considerate of the poor."[*] Wartime photograph from Keeler's letter book courtesy U.S. Naval Academy Museum.

---

[*] *The Biographical Record of Jasper County, Missouri*, Malcom G. McGregor, Lewis Publishing Co., Chicago, 1901.

Edwin Vose, acting assistant surgeon on the USS *Florida*. "A very pleasant appearing young man," he cared for Keeler after he was wounded in February 1864. He resigned in April 1864 when the vessel was at the Norfolk Navy Yard. According to Keeler, he "got sick of the service, having been in it only four or five months." Wartime photograph from Keeler's letter book courtesy U.S. Naval Academy Museum.

John Ziegler, acting chief engineer on the USS *Florida*. He served on the *Florida* until December 1863. He was subsequently ordered to the ironclad USS *Monadnock* on which he served for two years. In August 1865 he was ordered to make the experimental trip to the Pacific Ocean, which had never before been attempted by an ironclad. In a letter to the Navy Secretary in 1870 he proudly stated that "although Naval officers expressed their opinion of her inability to make the voyage around Cape Horn, I successfully steamed the *Monadnock* 16,000 miles to San Francisco, Cal. without costing the Navy Department one cent for repairs on shore, doing all the work of the vessel in the Engineers department."* Wartime photograph from Keeler's letter book courtesy U.S. Naval Academy Museum.

---

* J. Q. A. Ziegler to George M. Robeson, 26 August 1870, Navy Officers' Letters, 1802-1884, NARA M148.

William McLean, acting first assistant engineer on the USS *Florida*. "He is a still, quiet man," wrote Keeler, "& I think will make a pleasant messmate." He first served on the U.S. Army Steamer *George Washington*, which was sunk by Confederate batteries near Beaufort, South Carolina in April 1863. Under fire from the rebels, the men fled to the marshes to safety. Wartime photograph from Keeler's letter book courtesy U.S. Naval Academy Museum.

Quarterdeck of USS *Florida*, New York Harbor. Keeler is seated in front row center. Photograph from Keeler's letter book courtesy U.S. Naval Academy Museum.

Two views of the USS *Florida:* (top) in Newport Harbor, Rhode Island and (bottom) coaling at the New York Navy Yard. Photographs from Keeler's letter book courtesy U.S. Naval Academy Museum.

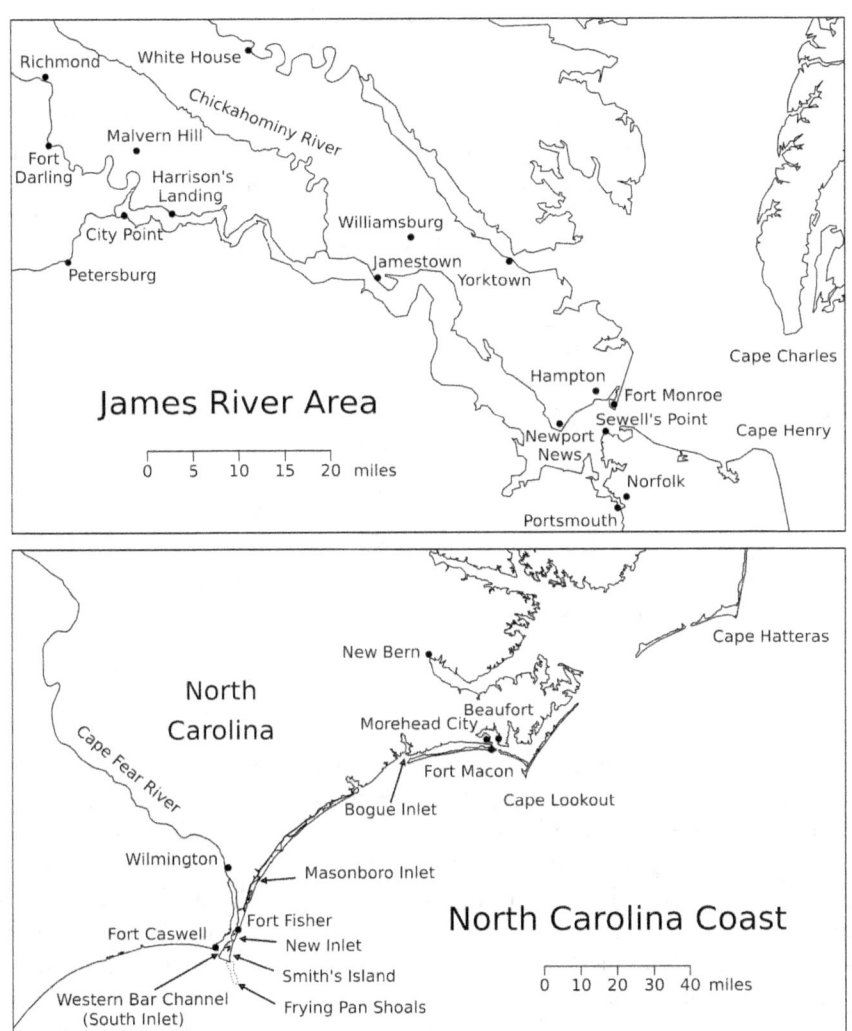

Maps showing the principal places mentioned in Keeler's letters.

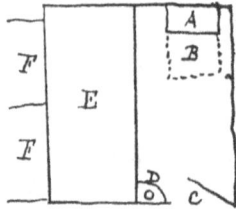

Sketch No. 1 – Keeler's stateroom on the USS *Monitor*: desk (A), fold-down door of desk (B), door (C), shelf for wash bowl (D), berth (E), and closets (F, F). See March 5, 1862 letter. Reprinted, by permission, from *Aboard the USS Monitor: 1862* . . . by William F. Keeler, edited by Robert W. Daly (Annapolis, MD: United States Naval Institute, (c) 1964).

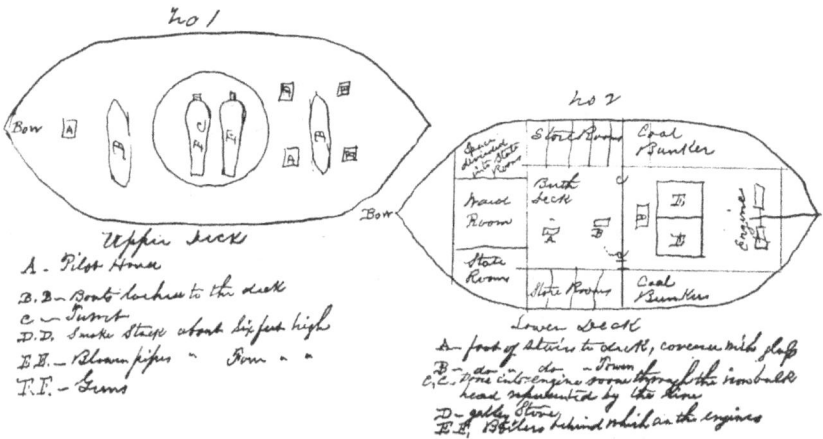

Sketch No. 2 – Upper and lower decks of the USS *Monitor*. Upper deck (left): pilot house (A); boats locked to the deck (B, B); turret (C), smoke stacks, about six feet high (D, D); blower pipes, about four feet high (E, E); guns (F, F). Lower deck (right): foot of stairs to deck, covered with glass (A); foot of stairs to tower (B); doors into engine room through the iron bulk head represented by the line (C, C); galley stove, located just aft of the bulk head (D); boilers (E, E), behind which are the engines. On either side of the engine room are the coal bunkers, adjacent to which are the store rooms. The staterooms are on either side of the wardroom. The berth deck where the crew slept is aft of the wardroom. See March 6, 1862 letter. Reprinted, by permission, from *Aboard the USS Monitor: 1862* . . . by William F. Keeler, edited by Robert W. Daly (Annapolis, MD: United States Naval Institute, (c) 1964).

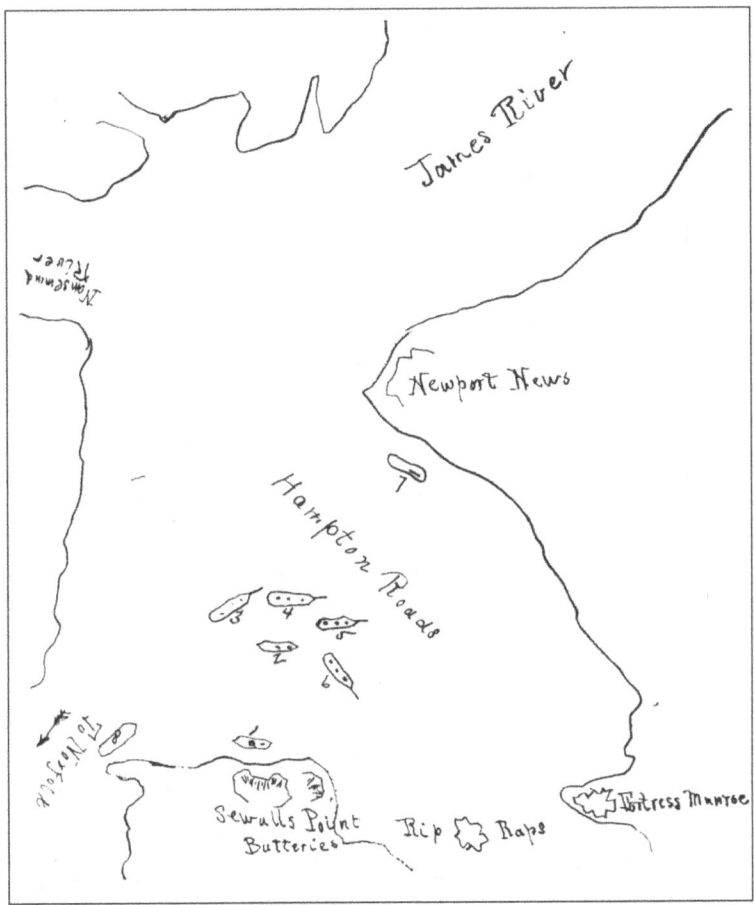

Sketch No. 3 – Position of Union gunboats during the shelling of the rebel batteries at Sewell's Point on May 8, 1862: First position of the USS *Monitor* while firing (1); second position of the *Monitor* while witnessing the fight of the gunboats (2); USS *Seminole* (3), USS *Dacotah* (4), USS *Susquehanna* (5), USS *San Jacinto* (6) and USS *Naugatuck* (7). See May 8, 1862 letter. North is to the right. Reprinted, by permission, from *Aboard the USS* Monitor: *1862* . . . by William F. Keeler, edited by Robert W. Daly (Annapolis, MD: United States Naval Institute, (c) 1964).

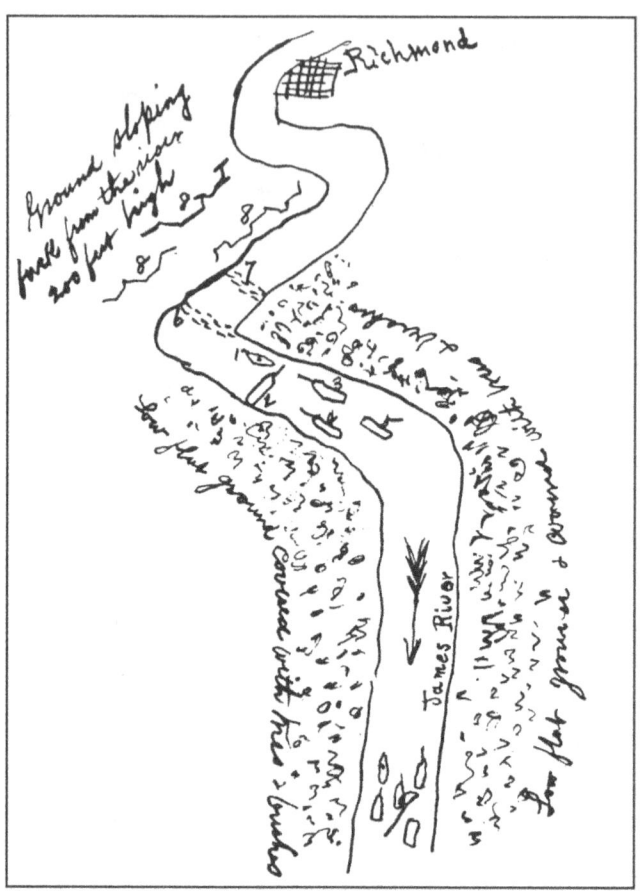

Sketch No. 4 – Position of Union gunboats during the attack on Fort Darling on May 15, 1862: USS *Monitor* (1), USS *Galena* (2), USS *Aroostook* (3), USS *Port Royal* (4) and USS *Naugatuck* (5); first and second lines of obstructions in the river (6, 7); rebel batteries, on ground sloping back from the river, rising to a height of 200 feet (8, 8, 8); position of gunboats while they were at anchor the morning before the attack (9). On either side of the river is low flat ground covered with trees and bushes. See May 12, 1862 letter. Reprinted, by permission, from *Aboard the USS* Monitor: *1862* . . . by William F. Keeler, edited by Robert W. Daly (Annapolis, MD: United States Naval Institute, (c) 1964).

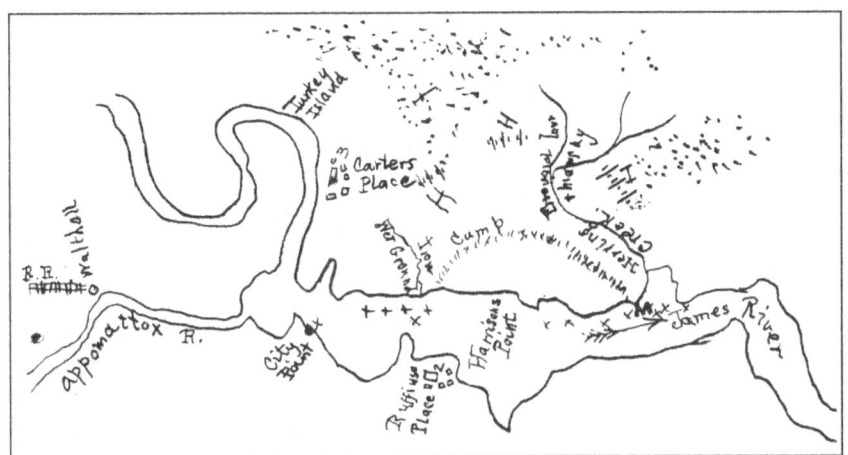

Sketch No. 5 – Army of the Potomac camp at Harrison's Landing. The curved dotted line labelled "Camp" denotes the front line of the Union army. The left and right flanks are protected by Kimages Creek ("low wet ground") and Herring Creek ("ground low and marshy"), respectively. The speckling denotes rebel troops; the H's and I denote their batteries. Union gunboats are denoted by the X's. The USS *Monitor* is denoted by the hard-to-see letter M (located near the mouth of Herring Creek). On the south side of the river to the east of City Point is "fire-eater" Edmund Ruffin's house (2). Hill Carter's Shirley Plantation (3) is north of City Point, just below Turkey Island. See June 30, 1862 letter. Reprinted, by permission, from *Aboard the USS Monitor: 1862 . . .* by William F. Keeler, edited by Robert W. Daly (Annapolis, MD: United States Naval Institute, (c) 1964).

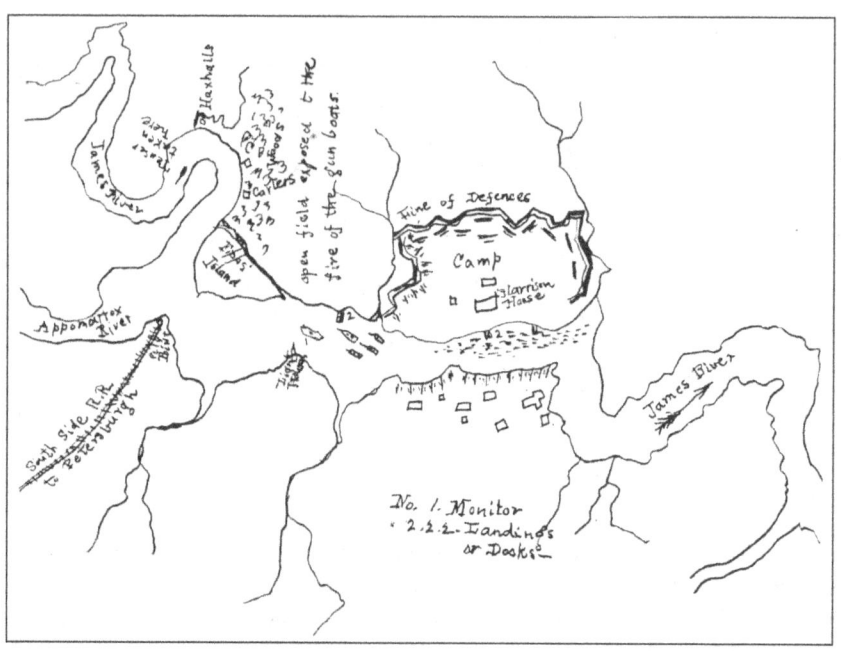

Sketch No. 6 – Army of the Potomac camp at Harrison's Landing. The USS *Monitor* (1) is just off Light House Point; behind her are the other Union gunboats. Harrison's Landing (2) is directly below Harrison's House. On the south side of the river directly opposite Harrison's Landing is rebel artillery. Between the left flank of the Union defences and "Carter's" (Shirley Plantation) to the west lies open field exposed to the fire of the gunboats. To the west of Carter's, just south of Haxall's plantation ("Haxall's"), is where the CSS *Teaser* was captured on July 4, 1862. See July 30, 1862 letter. Reprinted, by permission, from *Aboard the USS Monitor: 1862* . . . by William F. Keeler, edited by Robert W. Daly (Annapolis, MD: United States Naval Institute, (c) 1964).

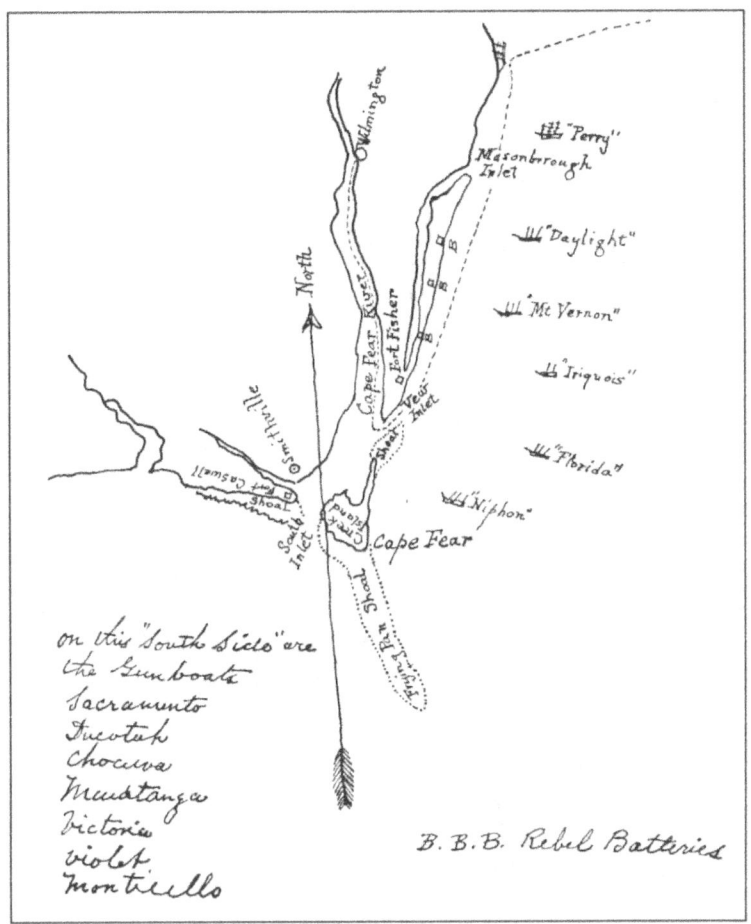

Sketch No. 7 – Location of the Union blockading vessels off Wilmington. The USS *Florida* is shown on the north side of Frying Pan Shoals. The rebel forts guarding the two entrances to Cape Fear River are Fort Fisher at New Inlet and Fort Caswell at South Inlet. Wilmington is shown near the top of the map. Smith's Island is mistakenly labelled Creek Island. The dashed line (red ink in the letter book) denotes the inward path of the blockade runner that Keeler discusses in detail in the April 18, 1863 letter. The place where she ran ashore and was unloaded is denoted by the tiny ship symbol near the top of the map. Note that this map and the discussion pertaining to it, which appear in the April 11, 1863 letter, were bound out of sequence in the letter book. Reprinted, by permission, from *Aboard the USS* Florida: *1863-65* . . . by William F. Keeler, edited by Robert W. Daly (Annapolis, MD: United States Naval Institute, (c) 1968).

> U.S. Steamer Monitor
> Hampton Roads
> March 9th 1862
> 2 o'clock P.M.
>
> My Dear Wife & Children
>
> I have but a few moments to spare just to say that I am safe — we have had an engagement with the Merrimac continuing for three hours & have driven her off, we think in a sinking condition — We have three men disabled among them & the worst is our noble Captain who has lost his sight, I hope only temporarily — The first opportunity I get you shall have full details & my own experience — With my best & kindest love to you all
>
> William
>
> We fought her at 20 feet distance a part of the time, the two vessels even touching. My hands are all dirt & powder smoke as you will discover by the paper.

"My hands are all dirt & powder smoke as you will discover by the paper." Keeler's letter to his wife and children written two hours after the fight with the CSS *Virginia*. Three dirty fingerprints are faintly visible at bottom left below the word "paper," as is a dirty smudge mark at top left. Courtesy U.S. Naval Academy Museum.

Introduction

"Another chapter has been added to my eventful life. The *Monitor* is no more. What the fire of the enemy failed to do, the elements have accomplished." And thus opens William Frederick Keeler's letter to his wife Anna written a week after the Union Navy's most famous ironclad slipped below the waves in a violent gale off Cape Hatteras on December 31, 1862. Ten months earlier the USS *Monitor* had fought the Confederate ironclad CSS *Virginia* to a standstill at Hampton Roads, Virginia in a four-hour battle that revolutionized naval warfare and electrified the North. Over the course of his twelve months as paymaster on the *Monitor*, Keeler wrote 87 vividly detailed letters to Anna. For the remainder of the war he served on the side-wheel steamer USS *Florida* doing blockade duty off the Confederate port city of Wilmington, North Carolina. Those experiences are described in 83 equally vivid letters.

William Keeler's letters from the *Monitor* provide the most complete picture of life on board a Civil War ironclad. His riveting accounts of the battle with the *Virginia*, naval expeditions up the James River, the Peninsula Campaign, and the sinking of the *Monitor* bring an immediacy to events that makes the 21st century reader feel part of the action. His equally colorful letters from the *Florida* provide one of the most compelling pictures of life on board a vessel on the Union blockade, a hugely important, but largely overlooked, chapter of the war. Pulitzer-Prize-winning Civil War historian James M. McPherson considers Keeler's letters to be "among the very best of naval letters."[*] Distinguished naval historian Craig L. Symonds says that of "the many collections of Civil War letters, both published and unpublished, few of them are as vivid and pertinent as Keeler's."[†]

The abridged versions of Keeler's letters that were edited by Robert W. Daly and published in the 1960s have been a staple for scholars for two

---

[*] Email correspondence (July 22, 2019).
[†] Email correspondence (August 2, 2019).

INTRODUCTION

generations.* Starting with William C. Davis' *Duel Between the First Ironclads* written more than four decades ago, through to David A. Mindell's *War, Technology, and Experience aboard the USS Monitor*, and up to John V. Quarstein's more recent *The Monitor Boys: The Crew of the Union's First Ironclad*, Keeler's graphic prose has taken a front-row seat. William Keeler himself plays a starring role at the USS *Monitor* Center at the Mariners' Museum in Newport News, Virginia where a life-size model of the be-spectacled Paymaster can be seen seated in his cabin writing a letter to "Dear Anna," while in another part of the museum he can be overheard reading from his nail-biting last letter as the clank of chains, the crash of waves, and the frantic cries of sailors can be heard in an exhibit depicting the sinking of the ironclad.

Since Daly's primary focus was on the naval aspects of the letters, many of the passages pertaining to personal matters were omitted. Not only does this render the letters disjointed and difficult to read, which is compounded by editorial notes that break up individual letters, it also leaves the reader with an incomplete picture of William Keeler, the husband, father and friend. Daly also paid scant attention to many of the people mentioned in the letters. These include not only Keeler's family and friends, but also navy and army officers he encountered along the way, many of whom are interesting characters and unsung heroes of the Civil War. Daly also provided little contextual information about the military situation, making it difficult for all but the expert reader to easily follow the letters. All of this is remedied in this book which is a complete and unabridged version of Keeler's letters from the *Monitor* and the *Florida*, as well as a more in-depth story of the Paymaster's fascinating, adventure-filled and eclectic life.

In Part 1 Keeler's life up to the Civil War is discussed. This includes a discussion of his "yankee parentage, pure and unadulterated," as he proudly referred to it, his growing up in Brooklyn and Michigan, his days as a dry-goods merchant in Bridgeport, Connecticut, his ill-fated trip to the gold fields of California in 1849, and his life in La Salle, Illinois. Family members and friends who are frequently mentioned in his letters are introduced here. Additional information about these people and others mentioned in the letters is provided in the Biographical Notes at the end of the book. The bulk of the book is found in Part 2 which covers the Civil War years and includes all of his letters from the *Monitor* and the *Florida*. The letters are divided into subsections, with each subsection commencing with a short introduction to provide the reader with the necessary information to follow the story. Part 3 delves into Keeler's life in Mayport, Florida where he and his family moved

---

* *Aboard the USS Monitor: 1862: The Letters of Acting Paymaster William Frederick Keeler, U.S. Navy, to his Wife, Anna*, ed. Robert W. Daly, U. S. Naval Institute, Annapolis, MD, 1964; *Aboard the USS Florida: 1863-65: The Letters of Paymaster William Frederick Keeler, U.S. Navy, to his Wife, Anna*, ed. Robert W. Daly, U. S. Naval Institute, Annapolis, MD, 1968.

INTRODUCTION

to after the war. Included here is Keeler's short-lived correspondence with Connecticut collector Frank H. Pierce who was gathering information about the *Monitor* in the 1880s. These previously unpublished letters contain Keeler's final thoughts on the battle with the *Virginia*, the sinking of the *Monitor*, and his friend and messmate, the *Monitor*'s executive officer, Samuel Dana Greene who had tragically committed suicide the year before. Keeler's last letters also serve to round out his life story, for they were written while he was dying of heart disease. Although none of Anna's letters from the Civil War have survived, her voice is briefly heard when she takes up the pen and continues the correspondence with Pierce when her husband was too ill to write. Her last letter to him was penned several weeks after Keeler's death.

Scattered throughout Keeler's letter book are photographs of some, but not all, of the officers Keeler served with on the *Monitor* and *Florida*. He enclosed those photographs in his letters to Anna and pasted them into his letter book when he had it bound after the Civil War. In keeping with this book's attention to the personal side of the letters, copies of those photos are included at the beginning of the book, along with Keeler's descriptions of those officers. Also found in the letter book are group photos of the *Monitor*'s officers and crew which were taken in July 1862 by Civil War photographer James F. Gibson. For those photos, the high-resolution digital images from the Library of Congress are reproduced here instead of Keeler's poorer quality ones. Keeler annotated his letters with a number of sketches. Shown here are reproductions of those sketches from Daly's two books, which are identical to those in the letter book but without the distraction of the ink which has bled through from the reverse side of the letter.

Part 1
Early Years

Tho' not yankee born I pride myself upon my yankee parentage, pure & unadulterated. My mother (still living) being a native of old Branford & related to the Plants & Frisbees of that region, & my father from near Danbury. Mr. Watrous & myself married sisters, daughters of the late Gov. Dutton. I was born in Pearl Street, New York City some 60 odd years ago & lived there & in Brooklyn the first 13 years of my life. There's my pedigree — you know all about me now. (15 November 1885)

William Frederick Keeler was born on June 9, 1821 above his father's dry goods store at 398 Pearl Street in the heart of Manhattan's dry goods district and baptized a few blocks away at the Brick Presbyterian Church at the corner of Beekman and Nassau Streets. He traced his name to an English carpenter named Ralph Keeler who immigrated to Hartford, Connecticut in the 1630s and settled in southwestern Connecticut in the town of Norwalk. Ralph's son Samuel fought at the Great Swamp Massacre in Rhode Island in 1675, a brutal lop-sided victory for the New England colonists during a bloody Indian uprising known as King Philip's War. Thirty-four years later, Samuel and a group of Norwalk residents founded the town of Ridgefield located 14 miles north of Norwalk on land they purchased from the Ramapo Indians for one hundred pounds. Four generations of Keelers down to William's father Roswell were born and raised there. They lived a short distance north of the town in the tiny parish of Ridgebury. Most were farmers, none were famous. The only interruption to their quiet and uneventful lives appears to have been during the American Revolution when in 1777 a force of 1,800 British redcoats marched past the tavern of William's great grandfather Ensign Samuel Keeler on their way to Ridgefield where they skirmished with 700 militia commanded by Benedict Arnold. Later in the Revolutionary War

Early Years

Ensign Keeler was reputed to have hosted two distinguished guests: George Washington, who was on his way to meet French general le Comte de Rochambeau in Hartford in 1780, and Rochambeau himself, when he celebrated his 56th birthday at the tavern on his way to meeting Washington and the Continental Army at Yorktown in 1781.

Keeler's mother Mary Eliza Plant also descended from solid Yankee stock. Her 4th great grandfather was an Englishman named John Potter who was one of the first settlers of New Haven, Connecticut. Her great-great grandfather John Plant and his descendants hailed from Branford, Connecticut. In the 1790s, her father Benjamin Plant, a farmer, and her grandfather Stephen Potter, also a farmer, as well as a deacon of the Presbyterian Church and a captain of a Connecticut militia company during the Revolutionary War, settled in Utica, New York. Benjamin Plant's house, where Keeler's mother was born and raised, was located at the corner of State and Genesee Streets. Nearby Plant Street is presumably named in his honor. Captain Potter's house was one mile north of Benjamin's at the corner of Potter and Whitesboro Streets. His only son William Frederick Potter, who inherited his farm, was Keeler's namesake great uncle.

Keeler's parents probably met at the First Presbyterian Church in Utica, where the Plants were members and where his father taught Sunday school after moving there from Ridgebury in 1815. They were married at the church in 1820 and settled in New York City where Roswell Keeler had been working for the past year. In 1825 they moved to Brooklyn, a bedroom community of New York City. They lived on Cranberry Street near Willow Street in a part of the village now called Brooklyn Heights. By then they were a family of four, for Keeler's brother James was born in 1823 in Utica, presumably at his grandparents' home. Roswell Keeler continued his work as a dry goods merchant in Manhattan, commuting there on the Fulton ferry which docked a short distance from their house. A short way up their street was the First Presbyterian Church, which William's parents joined and where his father later served as deacon. William and his brother James probably received their early schooling at the Classical Hall, a schoolhouse on Washington Street a five-minute walk from their house, which opened in 1831. That same year Edward Keeler, the youngest of the three brothers, was born.

In 1834 the Keelers moved to Auburn, Michigan, a tiny village about five miles north east of the town of Pontiac. Although the reasons for moving to this seemingly remote outpost have long since been forgotten, something of their life there can be pieced together. Roswell and Mary Keeler joined the First Presbyterian Church of Pontiac (then located in Auburn), where Roswell served as a church elder. He also opened a general store which sold an assortment of fancy and staple dry goods, groceries, hardware, and crockery. There, young William Keeler would have honed his skills as a bookkeeper and storekeeper, skills he put to good use later in life, and helped look after his baby sister Frances (Fannie) who was born in Auburn in 1834. In the spring of 1837 Roswell retired from the dry goods business and sold off his merchandise. Included in the list of items for sale was also "a good pair of horses, harness, waggon and sleigh" and "a first rate cow."* Following that, he purchased land in several nearby counties, some of which was sold off at a sheriff's sale in 1841. However, by then the Keelers had moved to Utica, New York, and were living on Genesee Street, a half mile from downtown and close to the farm of Keeler's uncle James Plant where his mother had grown up. The fact that the Utica city directories do not mention Roswell Keeler's occupation suggests that he was still retired. In 1841, Sarah Emma, the last of Roswell and Mary's five children, was born. In 1846 the Keelers (minus William) moved to Newtown, Connecticut where they lived for eight years.

In the early 1840s William Keeler struck out on his own and headed to Bridgeport, Connecticut where he followed in his father's footsteps and went into the dry goods business. In 1845 he formed a partnership with Hiram Olmstead and opened the Empire Store at the corner of Bank and Water Streets in the city's downtown. Their merchandise ranged from "plain and fancy beaver and pilot cloths" and the "latest and most fashionable styles of Ladies' Dress Goods " to "fans in great variety, warranted, if well used, to blow a perfect hurricane."† The ads, which no doubt were penned by Keeler, reveal his flare for words, and one, in which he warns a customer about an unpaid bill, reveals the offbeat sense of humor seen in the journal he kept in Mayport, Florida in the 1880s: "That lame man who came with tears in his eyes to borrow $1.50, to pay for mending a wagon, Sept. 13th 1844, is notified that his *three* weeks was up about 18 months ago."‡ However, misfortune struck in December 1845, only six months after the launch of their business, when a fire swept through downtown Bridgeport, destroying their store and most of their merchandise. Although they were back in business two months later at a new location, fire struck again the following year. In 1847 they threw in the towel and dissolved the partnership. Following that, Keeler dealt in "wharfage" and "storage for articles of every description" at the "old steam-boat dock" near the bridge crossing the Pequonnock River.§

It was in Bridgeport that Anna Eliza Dutton came into his life. Where they met is lost to time, but it was probably at the Second Congregational Church, a short walk from Keeler's dry goods store, where he would have attended Sunday services to hear the church's eloquent minister Nathaniel Hewitt preach about moral reform and temperance. There he would have met Anna and her parents who were distinguished members of the church.

---

* *Pontiac Courier*, Pontiac, MI (March 13, 1837).
† *Republican Farmer*, Bridgeport, CT (October 28, 1845; July 1, 1845; June 24, 1845).
‡ *Republican Farmer*, Bridgeport, CT (June 9, 1846).
§ *Republican Farmer*, Bridgeport, CT (April 1, 1847).

They were married on October 5, 1846. The following year their first child, Henry Dutton Keeler, was born.

Anna Keeler was the eldest of four children of Henry and Eliza Dutton. She was born on October 15, 1824 in Newtown, Connecticut where her father had started practicing law the year before. She spent her childhood in Newtown, and moved to Bridgeport with her family in 1837. By the time she and William met, her father was one of Bridgeport's leading lawyers, as well as a seasoned politician, having been elected four times to the Connecticut House of Representatives. In 1847 her parents and two youngest siblings[*], 12-year-old Hattie and 8-year-old Melzar, moved to New Haven, where her father had been appointed a professor of law at Yale College. His star still rising, Henry Dutton went on to become a one-term governor of Connecticut from 1854 to 1855 and a judge on the Connecticut Supreme Court from 1861 to 1866.

By the late 1840s William Keeler's business ventures in Bridgeport were doing poorly. And so, with the discovery of gold at Sutter's Mill in January 1848, he decided to try his luck and head to California, leaving behind Anna and 16-month-old son Henry. Joining Keeler were his younger brothers James and Edward, who were living in Newtown, Connecticut with his parents and two sisters. In January 1849 the three Keelers and 48 other men from Connecticut formed the New Haven and California Joint Stock Company. They purchased an old sailing bark, the *Anna Reynolds*, hired an old sea captain to sail her, and set sail from New Haven on March 12, 1849. A newspaper advertisement undersigned by Keeler two months before their departure spelled out the type of man they were after: "The Association goes out on strict temperance principles — gambling is forbidden, and the sanctity of the Sabbath is to be observed . . . references will be required as to good moral character."[†]

Although none of Keeler's letters to Anna from the Gold Rush have survived, his brother James' diary[‡], as well as the journal of fellow Forty-Niner Nelson Kingsley[§], help to fill in some of the gaps. James' diary covers the voyage to San Francisco in which he notes the weather, the ship's coordinates, and places they visited along the way. Kingsley's journal covers both the voyage and their time in California.

Their grueling 256-day trip to San Francisco took them as far east as Cape Verde off the west coast of North Africa and from there south westward to

---

[*] Anna's other sister Mary married in 1847 and was living in Litchfield, CT in 1850.
[†] *Republican Farmer*, Bridgeport, CT (January 16, 1849).
[‡] *James P. Keeler Diary*, 1849-50, California Historical Society, San Francisco, CA. The journal was donated to the historical society in 1935 by Mrs. T. F. Trumbull, namely William Keeler's niece Elizabeth (Lida) P. Brown.
[§] *Diary of Nelson Kingsley, A California Argonaut of 1849*, Publications of the Academy of Pacific Coast History, ed. Frederick J. Teggart, Vol. 3, University of California, Berkeley, CA, 1914.

the Falkland Islands where they encountered the huge storms of Southern winter. James' diary and Kingsley's journal describe those dreadful conditions, which would have made life on board the *Anna Reynolds* not only miserable but also terrifying. On July 11, 1849 when they were about 180 miles north of the Falkland Islands, James wrote:

> *Have been hove to ever since 4 o'clock this morning in the heaviest Gale of wind we have yet had. Shipped several seas. A most tremendous sea running. 9 o'clock at night. A most dismal night, drear & dark as pitch, & nothing to be heard but the roar of the angry elements & the shrill whistling of the wind through the rigging, the groaning of the timbers & bulkheads and the swashing of the water across the deck & every sea that strikes her makes her tremble from Truck to Keel.*

Around Cape Horn, the bitter cold froze the ocean spray onto the masts, sails and rigging, and huge seas rocked the vessel. Describing their passage around the Horn on August 20, 1849 Kingsley penned:

> *Last night is a most memorable night. The wind increased at night so that they were obliged to take in the Main Sail but notwithstanding the frequent heavy squalls and heavy wind they kept double reefed top sails and fore sail & stay sail, and it seemed at times as if the vessel must certainly be torn in pieces, but our bark stands it well yet and why we carry sail is that we may not make to[o] much lee-way and get foul of land. The rigging is hard to look upon being cover[ed] with nearly its own weight in solid ice and where the spray has come over forward leaves a huge quantity of ice on deck ... we shall soon get her pointed North ...*

After rounding the Horn the remainder of their trip was smooth sailing, although it took them another three months before they reached San Francisco, which they did on November 22, 1849.

The men remained in San Francisco for several weeks before heading up the Sacramento River. Having decided to go into the wood and timber business before heading to the gold fields in the spring, they set up camp along the river about forty miles downstream of Sacramento City. The winter of 1849-50, however, proved to be a very wet one. The river rose above its bank, flooding the camp. Many of the men, including Keeler*, fell sick with dysentery and other diseases, five of them died. One of those who perished was Keeler's 18-year-old brother, whose death on January 28, 1850 Kingsley noted as follows:

> *This morning about 8 oclock Mr Edward Keeler died after about 10 days illness of a sort of brain fever. At first he was entirely deranged and was not at times all through his sickness in his right mind. His loss will be*

---

* A newspaper advertisement in the *Sacramento Transcript* (May 28, 1850, Sacramento, CA, p. 2) lists Keeler as having been cured by "Dr. Dow's Dysentery Cordial."

EARLY YEARS

> *deeply felt by his two brothers William & James, and not a little among many of the company. He was of steddy good habits, and on the voyage displayed considerable ingenuity in the way of tinkering. He the youngest of the brothers was the first to be taken away from dear parents whome he had left at home to come to this country. Went to work this morning and made the coffin and commenced a skiff to take the corpse down to the mound where we have good dry ground to use as a burrying place.*

By the time spring arrived, the company had been dissolved and the men had gone their separate ways. Kingsley briefly mentioned working with Keeler at Roses Bar on the Yuba River in early June 1850 but gave no particulars. Kingsley's final mention of Keeler concerned his suspicion that he had stolen money from the company safe, an accusation based solely on his observation that Keeler appeared to have had "plenty of money by him of late," and had left for home not long before the robbery was discovered. Based on Kingsley's flimsy evidence and the picture one draws of Keeler from his Civil War letters, it is extremely unlikely that he was the guilty party.

On June 13, 1850 Keeler and his brother James had had enough and set sail for home on the *Samuel Russell*, a clipper ship used in the China trade that was making its maiden voyage around the world. Tragedy befell Keeler once more when his brother died the day after their departure from San Francisco. Although James' death notice in the *New York Daily Tribune* does not name the ship he sailed on, it was no doubt the *Samuel Russell* since the two brothers would have been travelling together.

Although little is known about James Plant Keeler's short life, Kingsley's journal indicates that he was a well-educated young man. Not only did he serve as the company secretary, he also taught the men logarithms and geometry, read sermons at prayer meetings, and led the debating club during their long voyage to California. A talented artist, James' diary is filled with pencil sketches and watercolors of people, ships and places seen along the way, including one small sketch depicting their camp along the Sacramento River, with a tent and a stack of firewood in front, an axe buried in a log and a small boat pulled up upon the bank, and the grim caption: "The lower camp at which Edward lived till he was taken sick." Placed loose in the journal is also a clipping from an unnamed newspaper (dated 1851), with a poem written by a person identified only as "E." Entitled *Lines: On the death of J. P. Keeler, who died at sea, on his passage from San Francisco to the Sandwich Islands*, the poem expresses the grief felt by his loss: ". . . Sleep sweetly in thy dreamless rest upon the ocean's bed, there ne'er again will aught disturb till it gives up its dead. . . . Sleep sweetly now, tho' parents' hearts with grief are rent in twain, no more on Earth will come to them their darling boy again. . . ."

At the California Historical Society are cartes de visite of James and Edward Keeler, which were taken in Brooklyn shortly before they sailed for

Early Years

California. Although the images are tiny and the facial features therefore hard to clearly see, both are clean-shaven and nattily dressed in jacket and tie.

Keeler's voyage home on the *Samuel Russell* took him by way of Singapore and Hong Kong where they stopped for three months taking on teas and silks, and finally to New York City where they arrived on January 28, 1851, a trip of more than seven months. He returned to Bridgeport and reunited with Anna and his young son after an absence of nearly two years. Although the Gold Rush was a personal tragedy for him, he appears to have been moderately successful based on the comments of the captain of the *Samuel Russell*, Charles P. Low, with whom Keeler and the five other passengers passed their evenings in conversation on their long voyage home.[*] In his reminiscences of his sea-faring days written more than 50 years later, Captain Low stated that Keeler was "very successful" after his arrival in California and had made "quite a little 'pile'" and "was going home by the way of China on business."

Not long after his return, Keeler got itchy feet again. With little chance of business success in Bridgeport, he looked elsewhere for opportunities, and set his sights on northern Illinois where New Englanders had been settling since the 1820s. In 1853 he and his family headed to La Salle, a recently incorporated city of several thousand on the Illinois River at the terminus of the Illinois and Michigan Canal. Business opportunities arising from the development of canals and railways were likely what brought him there. Keeler probably went first, followed by Anna and Henry, and not long after by his parents and sisters Fannie and Sarah. Between 1853 and 1855 he purchased five lots of land in the city. Their house was located at the corner of Seventh and Gooding Streets, a little north of downtown. They appear to have been moderately self-sufficient, for out back of their house was a barn with a milk cow, a hen roost, and an extensive garden containing vegetables, strawberries, grapes, cherry and plumb trees, and numerous ornamental plants. Anna stayed at home and raised the children, which by the eve of the Civil War numbered three: 13-year-old Henry (Hen), 3-year-old James Edward (Eddie) who was named after his two dead uncles, and 9-month-old Elizabeth (Tibbie) Eliot. They had a fourth child, Mary Ann (Minnie), who was born in 1854, but died several months before James Edward's arrival. Living with them was Keeler's youngest sister Sarah. In 1856 his sister Fannie married a grocer named David Brown, and raised a family of her own. They lived on Wright Street just north of Fourth, a few blocks away from the Keelers. Living next to Fannie and Dave were Keeler's parents.

In 1853 Keeler opened up a watch and jewelry shop at the corner of First and Wright Streets opposite the Hardy House, the largest hotel in the city. In 1857 he sold that business to one of his employees and opened the La Salle

---

[*] *Some Recollections by Captain Charles P. Low, Commanding the Clipper Ships* Houqua, Jacob Bell, Samuel Russell, *and* N. B. Palmer, *in the China Trade, 1847–1873*, Charles P. Low, Boston, MA, 1906, pp. 113-14.

Iron Works, a foundry and machinist operation located on the steamboat basin. Anna joined the First Congregational Church, as did Keeler's parents and sisters. The independent-minded Keeler, however, appears never to have been a member of any church, preferring it would seem to keep his options open. The church's first pastor William Collins was a friend of the Keelers and later an infantry captain in the Civil War. Present at Collins' first sermon in June 1854 and taking an active part was Reverend Owen Lovejoy, who had organized dozens of anti-slavery Congregational churches across northern Illinois in the 1850s. The First Congregational Church of La Salle was presumably one of those churches. Lovejoy was also instrumental in helping to organize the Republican Party in Illinois and was elected to the U.S. House of Representatives from Keeler's district in 1857. It was thanks to him that Keeler got his commission in the Union Navy.

The Keelers closest group of friends in La Salle, which he referred to as "our little circle," included David and Elizabeth Hough, and John and Anne Rockwell. A native of Vermont, Hough was a lawyer for the trustees of the Illinois and Michigan Canal, and Keeler's business partner at the La Salle Iron Works. A graduate of Yale College in New Haven, Rockwell was a banker in La Salle. His father was Charles Rockwell, the wealthy land developer and banker from Norwich, Connecticut who in 1836 founded the town of Rockwell, Illinois located a mile east of La Salle on the Illinois River (the town was abandoned two years later due to disease).

Keeler had more than watchmaking and iron founding to keep him busy in La Salle. Although his formal education did not extend beyond grade school, he was well read and an excellent writer. He was also mechanically gifted and had a deep and abiding interest in science and the natural world, which he passed on to his two sons, one of whom became one of America's leading astrophysicists. His work as a machinist led him to devise an improvement to the device that regulated the speed of a steam engine, which he patented in 1865. He was an avid reader of *Scientific American* and published several short letters in that magazine over the years. His detailed description of a meteor in the *Chicago Press and Tribune* (October 10, 1860) reveals those supreme powers of observation that make his Civil War letters so riveting:

> *A very brilliant meteor was observed from here last Tuesday afternoon, the 2d inst., at about a quarter past five, of which I have as yet seen no published account. It was observed in the northeast, and when first seen was about 39 degrees above the horizon, and descending rapidly, at nearly right angles with it. The nucleus was a clear, intense white light, leaving a scintillating train behind of the same color, the whole having some resemblance to a rocket. No report was heard on its disappearance, which took place just before reaching the horizon. Notwithstanding the sun was shining brightly at the time, it was distinctly visible; had it occurred a few hours later, its brilliancy must have attracted general observation.*

Part 2
Civil War Years

We were quite surprised yesterday at finding William Keeler in our parlor when we returned from the breakfast hall. He spent the sabbath and went back to New York this morning. I suppose your father told you about his appointment. He expects to come up again as he does not know when they will leave. He appeared very well. He felt sad of course at leaving his family but he says all kinds of business is very dull in La Salle. He thinks he has got one of the most amiable and best of wives. He said she felt badly to have him go but with her characteristic good sense she went to work to get him ready. She has had the trial before when he went to California. (Keeler's mother-in-law Eliza Dutton to her son Melzar, a lieutenant in the 5th Connecticut Infantry, 13 January 1862)*

By the early 1860s William Keeler's iron works was doing poorly. His timing could not have been worse, for the Panic of 1857 had brought the country's economy to a standstill. In 1859 one of his partners sold out and a commercial reporting agency rated the business as doubtful. The Confederate bombardment of Fort Sumter on April 12, 1861 provided the change he needed. Viewing Confederates as traitorous, villainous souls and slavery as a hideous deformity, he saw the war as an opportunity to put down treason and stamp out slavery. And so, with the aid of his Republican Congressman Owen Lovejoy, he obtained a commission in the Union Navy. On December 17, 1861 he was appointed Acting Assistant Paymaster and Clerk, and three weeks later ordered to the New York Navy Yard in Brooklyn to await assignment. In early January 1862 the 40-year-old father of three packed his bags and headed East to an uncertain future.

---

* Henry Dutton Family Letters.

Civil War Years

The date Keeler was assigned to the USS *Monitor* has not been found. According to Daly it would have been in the second or third week of January. Keeler served on the *Monitor* until the vessel sank off Cape Hatteras on December 31, 1862. Having proved his worth, he was asked by the *Monitor*'s last captain, John Bankhead, to serve with him on the USS *Florida*. He served on the *Florida* from March 1863 to several months after the end of the war. A neophyte when he first arrived at the New York Navy Yard, he was unsure whether he needed to wear a uniform. A year later he was an "old salt" and clear as to what his responsibilities were. As the war dragged on, he yearned to be back home, but unlike many of his fellow volunteer officers refused to resign, telling Anna that he meant to stay until he received an honorable discharge.

Well-liked by the many captains under whom he served, he was often invited to join them for dinner in their cabin. When they were transferred to other vessels or sent home on sick leave they would often write to him, inviting him to come visit. His way with words was why the *Monitor*'s first captain, John Worden, asked him to transmit verbal messages between the pilot house and the turret during the fight with the *Virginia*, why he was asked by one of his captains to help draft official correspondence, and why he was designated the *Monitor*'s unofficial tour guide for the multitude of generals, politicians and foreign dignitaries who visited the vessel. On their trip down to Hampton Roads on March 6-7, 1862, it was his mechanical ability that enabled him to man the *Monitor*'s engines until the engineers recovered from smoke inhalation. Several days after the fight with the *Virginia* he was even promised a more active role in the next fight: operating the machinery that turned the turret. And it was his machinist's eye that enabled him to suggest an improvement to the *Monitor*'s turret that was approved by the Admiral and acted on. Although he was an Acting Assistant Paymaster and Clerk, he was clearly much much more.

A man of strong opinions, he ranted about issues he felt strongly about. A tea-totaler, he railed against the evils of alcohol, which he believed was the ruin of many a good officer. A hater of red-tape, he fumed against the inefficiencies of the regular Navy and many of its aged and ineffective commanders, whom he referred to as "old fogies," and praised the officers in the volunteer Navy, "whose well earned laurels have in most cases been appropriated by the "*nobility*" of the [regular] service." He chafed at the rose water war that was being waged by the Union forces on the Virginia Peninsula in 1862, which left the James River planters' crops and animals untouched, stating "Let these wealthy rebels bear the penalty of the war they have brought upon them & be made to feel its pressure & presence in the severist possible manner." In 1862 he was a strong defender of George McClellan, the commander of the Army of the Potomac, but like most was unaware of the general's failings. Two years later when McClellan ran as a Democrat against Lincoln and lost, he viewed the general as a traitor, stating that he respected him "when he led our armies against the armed foes of the country, but when he comes to marshall the secret foes of the country against it he has my utter loathing & contempt." Although he was an abolitionist and yearned for the end of slavery, like virtually all white Americans at that time he was racially prejudiced and viewed African-Americans as socially inferior.

Since none of Anna's letters to William have survived, the reader is left to imagine the hardships she must have endured. Glimpses of her state of mind can be gleaned from Keeler's letters and to some extent from those of her mother. His bellicose words and his desire to see action must have filled her with dread. In a letter to her mother she stated that she feared that if the *Monitor* and *Virginia* had another engagement that the *Monitor* would not fare so well.* In addition to her constant worry for his safety, she also had to contend with raising their three young children (two of whom were under four years old when the war started), which was compounded by the ever-rising price of consumer goods. As the war dragged on with no end in sight, her letters grew more despondent in spite of the comforting words of her eternally optimistic husband. Although William returned home safely, Anna suffered two huge losses during the war: Her brother Melzar was killed at the Battle of Cedar Mountain in Virginia in August 1862. Her sister Mary died of cancer in Litchfield, Connecticut in February 1865.

---

* Eliza E. Dutton to H. Melzar Dutton (May 2, 1862; Henry Dutton Family Letters).

USS *Monitor* (1862)

> *Sir: In accordance with your request, I now submit for your approbation a name for the floating battery at Greenpoint. The impregnable and aggressive character of this structure will admonish the leaders of the Southern Rebellion that the batteries on the banks of their rivers will no longer present barriers to the entrance of the Union forces. The iron-clad intruder will thus prove a severe monitor to those leaders. But there are other leaders who will also be startled and admonished by the booming of the guns from the impregnable iron turret. "Downing Street" will hardly view with indifference this last "Yankee notion," this monitor. To the Lords of the Admiralty the new craft will be a monitor, suggesting doubts as to the propriety of completing those four steel clad ships at three and a half million apiece. On these and many similar grounds, I propose to name the new battery* Monitor. (John Ericsson to the Assistant Secretary of the Navy Gustavus V. Fox, 20 January 1862)*

Five days after the fall of Fort Sumter on April 12, 1861 and President Lincoln's call three days later for 75,000 troops to put down the rebellion, Virginia seceded from the Union and joined the seven other states that had already left. Fearing that the Virginia militia would seize the Gosport Navy Yard at Portsmouth, the yard's commander ordered the buildings burned, the cannons spiked and the warships laid up there scuttled. However, the hull of one of those ships, the steam frigate USS *Merrimack*, survived intact. Undaunted by the damage to the vessel and lacking a navy of their own, the Confederates set about fashioning an ironclad warship from the burned hulk. By early summer the carpenters had cut away the charred timbers of the *Merrimack* and had begun building the wooden frame that would house the iron casemate. Progress was slow because they had to rummage through scrap yards and rip up miles of unused railroad track to secure the 800 tons of iron needed to clad the vessel. The vessel's broadside battery included six IX-inch Dahlgren smoothbores (two of which fired hot shot) and two 6.4-inch rifled guns, while at the bow and stern were placed two 7-inch rifles, which served as pivot guns. On the deck was a pair of howitzers. The final touch was a 4-foot long 1,500-pound iron ram at the bow. When finally completed the ironclad was a fearsome looking thing: iron sides sloping upward at an angle of 36 degrees to deflect shot, 263 feet from bow to stern, twelve powerful guns and a massive battering ram—a destroyer of wooden warships. On February 17, 1862 she was commissioned the CSS *Virginia*.

By the summer of 1861 the Secretary of the Navy Gideon Welles had realized that the Union Navy had to develop its own ironclad warships to counter the threat posed by the *Virginia*. In early August Welles received $1.5

---

* *Battles and Leaders of the Civil War*, Vol. 1, New York, NY, 1887, p. 731.

Civil War Years: USS *Monitor* (1862)

million from Congress to build three ironclads and immediately started soliciting bids. He also set up a board of three senior naval officers to select the designs. By early September sixteen proposals had been submitted to the Ironclad Board. Of those sixteen, two were given serious consideration. The first proposal was for a huge armoured frigate mounting sixteens guns in broadside batteries that would become the USS *New Ironsides*. The second was for an egg-shaped vessel with rounded iron-plated sides to deflect shot that would become the USS *Galena*. The board, however, had serious concerns about the buoyancy of the *Galena*. To address that issue, the *Galena*'s financial backer, a wealthy entrepreneur named Cornelius Bushnell, went to New York City to ask naval engineer John Ericsson whether his vessel would float. The brilliant Swedish-born inventor did the necessary calculations and assured him it would. Ericsson, who had not submitted a proposal because of a bad experience with the Navy two decades earlier, then asked Bushnell whether he would like to see his design for a "floating battery." Bushnell agreed and was shown a scale model of a curious-looking vessel with a rotating cylinder on top of its deck. Greatly impressed, Bushnell told Welles about it, and also arranged for a meeting with the President. Lincoln, who was fond of gadgets and new technologies, was so taken with the design that he attended the meeting of the Ironclad Board the next day. With the help of Lincoln's endorsement and a brilliant presentation by Ericsson two days later, the Board adopted his design. Of the three proposals that were chosen, Ericsson's radical design was by far the riskiest, and for that reason the vessel was deemed an "experiment" by the Board.

Ericsson's floating battery was built at the Continental Iron Works at the Greenpoint Ship Yard in Brooklyn, New York. Construction began in late October 1861. Components of the vessel were subcontracted to various firms and shipped to Greenpoint. The 120-ton turret had to be disassembled and re-constructed on site. As the vessel was being put together, problems were encountered that Ericsson had to remedy on the fly in the mad rush to completion. On January 30, 1862 the vessel was launched, 28 days after the promised 100-day completion date (still a remarkably short time). Three weeks later she was delivered to the New York Navy Yard, and on February 25 was commissioned the USS *Monitor*.

Measuring 173 feet from bow to stern and 41 feet 6 inches abeam, the *Monitor* looked more like a submarine than a warship since her deck was only 18 inches above the water line. Sitting atop the deck was the 21-foot diameter, 9-foot high, 8-inch thick turret which housed the two guns, giving the vessel the appearance of a cheese box on a raft, as she was derisively called. What was revolutionary about the ironclad, however, was that the turret rotated, enabling the vessel to fire in almost any direction without having to change course. Moreover, her shallow draft (10 feet 6 inches) and light displacement (987 tons) meant that she was much more maneuverable than her sluggish opponent, the *Virginia*. Two XI-inch smoothbore Dahlgrens were mounted side-by-side in the turret. Protecting the interior of the turret when the guns were being reloaded were two pendulum port shutters. To aim the guns, a small steam engine rotated the turret. Near the bow stood the pilot house where the captain commanded the vessel and the quartermaster steered her. From within the pilot house, the captain's only view of the outside world was through narrow slits in the armour plate.

Aside from the turret and the pilot house, everything else was located below the waterline. An iron bulkhead which supported the turret divided the interior of the vessel in two. The stern half contained the ship's machinery, the galley and flush toilets. Forward of the bulkhead and directly below the turret was the berth deck where the enlisted men slept. The powder magazine and shell room were located on either side of the berth deck. Further forward were the officers' quarters (or staterooms) and the wardroom where the officers ate and socialized. Closest to the bow and directly below the pilot house were the captain's cabin and stateroom. Fresh air pumped by blowers at the stern of the vessel kept the men from suffocating while below deck. Not one to leave things out, Ericsson fitted out the wardrooms and staterooms at his own expense, lining them with hardwood paneling.

New York Navy Yard (January to March 1862)

> *Well here I am, dear Anna, on ship board at last in my little cubby hole of a state room, small but nicely furnished. My boy has made my bed but it has a full wheelbarrow load of books, blanks, paper, bundles, boxes, bottles of ink, &c, &c deposited on top which has got to be removed to their proper places before I can turn in, for there is no place to lay them outside till morning.* (25 February 1862)

By the second week of January 1862 Commodore Joseph Smith, one of the members of the Ironclad Board, had found the right man to command the *Monitor*. He was 28-year Navy veteran Lieutenant John Worden, who had recently returned from seven months in a Confederate prison cell in Montgomery, Alabama, having been arrested at the start of the war after delivering secret orders to the Pensacola Squadron for the reinforcement of Fort Pickens, Florida. On January 12 Worden received a letter from the Commodore asking him to command the yet unnamed ironclad. After visiting the vessel at Greenpoint, Worden replied that he believed the vessel would prove a success and accepted the command. On January 16 he reported for duty at the New York Navy Yard and began securing his officers and crew, all of whom voluntarily served on the vessel.

Two days before Worden was given formal command of the *Monitor*, William Keeler arrived at the New York Navy Yard after a three-day train trip from La Salle. Not yet assigned to a vessel, and with time on his hands,

New York Navy Yard (January to March 1862)

he purchased a uniform and dress sword, had his photograph taken, and made trips to New Haven to visit Anna's parents and to New York City to visit her uncle Franklin Joy and his family. He boarded a short distance from the Navy Yard at his uncle Jarvis Brush's house on Henry Street, and reported for duty once a day. While awaiting assignment, he would have heard of the ironclad floating battery that was being built at Greenpoint. Wanting to be a part of the history that he knew that that vessel would write, he would no doubt have asked to serve on her, and was assigned to the *Monitor* sometime before February 9 when he first mentions the vessel.

By the time the *Monitor* arrived at the Navy Yard, Keeler was well versed in his duties as paymaster. He was in charge of all the provisions, clothing, stationary, and small stores (tobacco, soap, candles, thread, buttons, needles, jack knives, etc.). He had a steward who would give out the men's rations, as well as a personal servant, a young African-American (probably an escaped slave), who would make his bed, tidy his room and lay out his clothes. He was also happy to learn that he did not need to serve as the captain's clerk, as his appointment letter states, since Worden's 24-year-old nephew Daniel Toffey served in that regard.

By mid-February most of the *Monitor*'s officers had been assigned, and Keeler was getting to know them. He was particularly impressed with Worden, whom he described as "tall, thin & quite effeminate looking, notwithstanding a long beard hanging down his breast," a "perfect gentleman" who would "not hesitate to submit our iron sides to as severe a test as the most warlike could desire." Worden's executive officer was an intense 22-year-old Navy lieutenant named Samuel Dana Greene, who was serving in the China Station when the war broke out. Keeler was drawn to his "eyes that look through a person." The two men became friends and later served together on the USS *Florida*. In the room next to Keeler's was the *Monitor*'s 29-year-old surgeon Daniel Logue. "The life & fun & wit of the ship," he bored Keeler to death by reading to him his correspondence with his "lady love," but was "a good, genial, warm hearted fellow" and Keeler humored him when he was not too busy.

The *Monitor* became Keeler's home on February 25, the day the vessel was commissioned. His stateroom measured a cozy six feet by eight. In addition to a bed, his room also had a writing desk, two closets, and a set of drawers under the bed, all constructed of black walnut. His only complaint was that the room was too dark, and he had to do all his writing by candle light. Since the rooms were open at the top for ventilation and the doors were blinds, sound travelled freely through the officers' quarters and the wardroom, making letter writing difficult, as he would soon discover.

Five days before the *Monitor* was commissioned, Worden had received orders to proceed to Hampton Roads. Reliable information had it that the *Virginia* (or "*Merrimac*" as Keeler referred to her) was nearing completion and Navy Secretary Gideon Welles was getting nervous. He wanted the *Monitor* down there to protect the Union fleet. However, a steering malfunction and heavy seas along the coast delayed her departure by a week.

Letters of special note: February 9 (duties as paymaster; first impressions of Worden and Greene); February 13 (visits the *Monitor* at Greenpoint); February 28 (trial run; first impressions of man-of-war life); March 4 (the wardroom steward's escapades); March 5 (layout of his cabin).

New Haven
Jan'y 12, 1862

Dear Anna,

You will see by the above date where I am spending Sunday & in direct violation too of your command not to make my appearance un till I had my uniform &c, but of this more by & by.

To begin at the beginning. I took a sleeping car at the Rock Island depot, got a good double berth to myself, in a few minutes heard them call out Ottawa, have a very indistinct recollection of something being said about Morris & the next thing of which I was concious was a vigourous shake from our contraband* chamber*maid*, or rather man, with the announcement the [that] we were 'most to Chicago, accompanied with the modest demand of ten cents for blacking the gentleman's boots. I got up feeling much refreshed, & at 1/2 past 5 found myself in Chicago. I took a ticket for N.Y. via Lake Shore & Erie R.R. paying $24.00, making the fare through $27.00. At six we had started for New York. In the evening we were at Toledo where we changed cars & went on to Cleveland, changed again. Took a narrow top shelf in a sleeping car & in the morning found myself in Buffa[l]o after a good night's sleep, just half an hour after the train for N.Y. had left for N.Y. Went to the hotel & got breakfast. Staid at the hotel to dinner & continued staying there to supper, a slow drizzling mist keeping me in the house most of the day. At 7 P.M. was aboard the train for N.Y. At Hornelsville laid myself away on a shelf for the night. At 1/2 past 12 the next day found myself crossing the Jersey City ferry for N.Y., the boat grinding her way through masses of floating ice with which the harbor was filled.

As soon as we landed I made my way across the city for the Fulton Ferry & from there to the Navy Yard, leaving my baggage (which was checked through from Chicago) to the tender mercies of the R.R. Co., whose checks I carried off in my pocket. At the entrance to the Yard I was stopped by the guard who demanded my business. I told him I was ordered to report to Commodore Paulding† & was referred to the sergeant of the guard who told me to pass in & directed me to the Commodore's office which I found filled with men & officers, getting orders, signing papers, &c.

---

* The slang term for a slave who crossed Union lines to freedom.
† Hiram Paulding, commandant of the New York Navy Yard.

NEW YORK NAVY YARD (JANUARY TO MARCH 1862)

I made my business known to one of the clerks who entered my name in two or three different books, then turned me over to another who entered my name again in as many more, then endorsed the time of my reporting on the back of my dispatch, then sent me back to clerk No. 1 who told me that the Commodore's signature was needed to my papers, but as he was absent to find Commander Almy* & dispatched a contraband with me in search of him. Found him in one of the other offices, a frank, blunt sort of a sailor man. He took my papers, looked them over,

"Ah Paymaster Keeler glad to see you Sir. Where are you from Sir?"

Told him from Illinois.

He looked a little surprised. "Well," said he, "we don't get a great many sailors from the prairies out there."

"No," I told him, "folks there were doing their duty on land."

"Yes, glad to hear it. Ever been to sea?"

Told him I had.

"Well," said he, "are you ready to start right off?"

I told him that I was not quite.

Asked me if I had a uniform.

Told him that I had not, that I thought perhaps they would let me go as I was.

"Not at all, not at all, get a uniform before you go to sea," said he in a queer blunt sort of way, continuing, "we will let you rest a while before you go."

He signed my papers & I returned to clerk No. 1 who told me that there was one ahead of me who had not been assigned to duty & that after him my turn would come. He then gave me an order on the Navy Agent in N.Y. for my travelling allowance at the rate of 10 cents per mile. As the distance cannot be less than 1000 miles it will make quite a sum.

I was introduced to quite a number of the officers in the different offices I went into & was much pleased with their looks & appearance. "First impressions" are good at any rate. There appeared to be more real earnestness of purpose & less of that swagger & bluster & rowdyism about them than among many of the land officers I have met with.

Getting through with my business there I started for Uncle Brush's & found Uncle & Aunt B.† & Aunt Burton‡ just sitting down to dinner. Of course they were much surprised at seeing me & gave me a warm welcome. It occurred to me while eating that I might go to New Haven & spend Sunday, so I swallowed a few mouthfuls hastily & left before the others were through. Got to 47th street just as the express train was leaving, reached New

---

* John J. Almy, second in command at the New York Navy Yard.
† Jarvis Brush*, a retired inventor and businessman. His wife Sarah was Keeler's father's sister. They lived in Brooklyn at 99 Henry Street, a short distance from the Navy Yard.
‡ Keeler's father's sister Rachel Burton.

Civil War Years: USS *Monitor* (1862)

Haven little after dark when it occurred to me for the first time that I did not know where your Father boarded nor where Geo. lived.* I went into a store & found a directory & with the assistance of that & a few inquiries found Geo.'s with but little trouble. He came to the door, shook hands &c, but I saw did not recognize me & told me so. I told him that was of no consequence [as] I thought his wife would, but she had heard my voice & came rushing out accompanied by Nettie who was there with her husband.† They were just sitting down to tea & you may imagine we had a merry tea party.

After tea I went down with Geo. to see your Father & Mother but they were out. After breakfast this morning I went down to the hotel again & found your Father sitting alone in his parlour. Of course he was much surprised to see me, as was your Mother who came in soon after. I can't see that they have altered much & Hattie‡ is just [the] same affectionate, warm hearted creature she always was. Your Mother went to church & I spent the whole forenoon with your father. What him & Geo. have told me in relation to some thing I will write you some other time. Your Father & Mother are coming up to tea to night. All have gone to church this P.M., leaving me alone to write to you & it has been hastily done I assure you. Little Geo. is a quiet well behaved little fellow & the baby is a real pretty little thing, fat & plump as can be.§

I have orders to report at the Navy Yard every day, so shall go back to morrow for that purpose, try & hunt up my baggage, get a uniform &c &c &c &c &c &c &c. Uncle Brush has invited me to stay there till I get ready to start & I shall probably do so.

Don't circulate this [letter] but you can read such parts as you see fit.

10000000 thanks to Mr. Hough** for his energetic endeavours to get rid of me. Tell him I had no difficulty in getting my *ball* checked through from Chicago. Speaking of the Ohio R.R., I would say "from all such evils good Lord deliver us." I think I have made my last trip over it. The folks have just ret'd & I must leave off. I am so sorry that I neglected to bid Henry†† good bye. I hope he did not feel worse than I did. I will write him in a few days. Love to all. Good bye.

William

---

* Anna's parents lived at the corner of Crown and Temple Streets, but had closed their house for the winter on account of her father's frequent trips as a judge on the Connecticut Supreme Court. They were boarding one block away at the New Haven House, a hotel on Chapel Street across from the New Haven Green. Keeler's brother-in-law George H. Watrous*, a respected New Haven lawyer, lived a half mile further west on Chapel.
† Henrietta (Nettie) Tuthill, Anna's first cousin on her mother's side. Nettie's husband John Dutton* was Anna's first cousin on her father's side.
‡ Keeler's sister-in-law Harriet Joy Watrous*.
§ Hattie's and George's children: 3-year old-George and 7-month-old Elizabeth.
** David L. Hough*, a close friend of Keeler's. He was a lawyer in La Salle.
†† Keeler's eldest son.

New York Navy Yard (January to March 1862)

[Marginalia] (Hat[tie] has only given me half a sheet, must get some more.) Monday morning [January 13] Geo.'s office. McAllister* spent the evening with us. Had a grand time talking over old times.

Brooklyn
Sunday, Feb'y 9, 1862

Dear Anna,

Instead of going to church this morning I will spend the time in writing to you. This afternoon I am going to Birdsey's† & shall stay to tea & spend the evening. I suppose you will not feel bad if I say that I have taken quite a fancy to his wife. She is a very pleasant intelligent woman & without being realy handsome appears well.

I have easy times now & shall have till our vessel gets into the yard, when I shall have more to do, as there is a great anxiety to get her off & have her metal‡ tested.

I find it very pleasant at Uncle B.'s. We have breakfast at 8 o'clock & I get down to the yard at 10, see what is going on there & improve my chances in getting posted in my duties. I do not know enough about them yet to give you much of an idea of what they will be.

I have charge of all the provisions, clothing, stationary, what are called small stores, such as tobacco, soap, candles, thread, buttons, needles, jack knives, & all the thousand & one little things a sailor will stand in need of, besides the money. The arms, ammunition & ship stores, such as sails, cordage & the like, I have nothing to do with. My steward's business is to give out the men's rations daily & render me an a/c [account]. Clothing, small stores & everything but the daily rations I issue myself. I give my requisition upon the government stores in the yard here for such stores as I deem necessary, making my calculations from tables furnished me by the department. That you may see just what every one is allowed for each day of the week I send you a copy of the table of rations, issued each day to every one, officers as well as men. Anything more must be provided at our own expense. Any one not drawing these rations is allowed 20 cents per day in lieu. The officers usually form messes & buy such provisions before leaving port as the majority of them decide.

I have not yet seen my iron home & know nothing more about it than what I hear from others, but I conclude it is a novel looking craft. The impression prevails here that our destination is the Potomac & our business

---

* Alexander McAlister*, a New Haven banker. "Old times" refers to Bridgeport where they first met.
† Birdsey Blakeman*, book publisher in New York City and close friend of Keeler's from Bridgeport. He lived on Hanson Place about a mile south of the Navy Yard.
‡ The *Monitor*'s guns.

will be to *dust* the rebel batteries off its banks.* At any rate if the boat proves a success we shall see as much if not more service than any vessel yet fitted out from here.

Our officers are not yet all assigned. Capt. Worden† is in the regular service. He is tall, thin & quite effeminate looking, notwithstanding a long beard hanging down his breast. He is white & delicate probably from long confinement & never was a lady the possessor of a smaller or more delicate hand. But if I am not very much mistaken he will not hesitate to submit our iron sides to as severe a test as the most warlike could desire. He is a perfect gentleman in manner. Mr. Green‡, our lieutenant, is a young man, also in the regular service, black hair & eyes that look through a person & will carry out his orders I have no doubt. The two masters are volunteers from the merchant service, good steady men.§ The master's mate, a good honest Dutchman.** These are all the officers that have yet been assigned. Capt. Worden told me that it was the desire of the Department to have the officers & crew all picked men. He has his choice of all in the yard to select from.

I am glad that I left you so well provided with coal since it has been so cold with you. We hardly know what cold is here in a house warmed by a furnace. I do not miss the warmth of a bedfellow nor do I find it cold dressing in the morning. I could just as well have remained at home another month as to have spent the time here.

I perfectly coincide with you in your opinion of my photograph.†† I wanted to select my own attitude & put on spectacle *frames* but the *artist* said it was unnecessary. I am sorry now that I did not insist upon having my own way. Other men waiting & he was in a hurry. If I have a good opportunity I will get a larger one before I leave.

Bright handsome uniforms are so common here that scarcely any notice is taken of them. I felt awkward enough at first in mine. It seemed as if every one was looking at me, but I am getting used to it now.

I stand corrected in my [spelling of] *icicle*. It did not look right after I had written it, but I got confused after studying over it a little while & I let it go.

I am glad that Father & Mother are with you. I wish for the sake of you all that the house could be expanded a little. No one shall impugn the Dea[con]'s generosity after this. I sent him a paper a few days ago.

---

* In the summer of 1861 the rebels constructed a series of forts on the Virginia side of the Potomac River in an attempt to isolate Washington. The blockade ended in early March 1862 after Confederate forces withdrew from their position near Washington to south of the Rappahannock River.
† John L. Worden*.
‡ Samuel Dana Greene*.
§ Louis N. Stodder* and John J. N. Webber*.
** George Frederickson*.
†† The letter enclosing this photograph is missing from the collection. That letter would have presumably informed Anna of his assignment to the *Monitor*.

New York Navy Yard (January to March 1862)

I see that Laning's boat has met with a terrible mishap.* I hope he is not one of the sufferers. Our boilers will not be so easily reached as they are entirely below the water line. In fact almost the entire boat is under water, but the tower.

I am glad to hear that Capt. Pratt has found something to do. I see his name as 2nd Master on one of the boats at the taking of Fort Henry.†

I have not been up to your Uncle Frank's‡ yet but shall try & do so sometime this week.

Capt. Limeburner's ship has been chartered again by government & is now preparing for sea.§ It is a monstrous ship. A good deal of the work is done with a steam engine which they carry on board and an engineer at $60. per month to run it. He is just the same bluff sort of a sailor he used to be.

Monday morning [February 10]—I went to church with Birdsey yesterday afternoon & heard Dr. Storrs**. Took tea with him & spent the remainder of the evening very pleasantly with Joseph†† who lives but a short distance from Birdsey's. Mother's cousin, Mrs. Warner‡‡, also lives near there. She is in very poor health.

Say to Henry that I will try & write him before I leave & send him a draft of the fence as he wanted. How I would like to step in & see you all this

---

* Keeler's friend from La Salle, James Laning*, was second master on the USS *Essex*, one of the four brown-water ironclads that participated in the attack on Fort Henry on February 6, 1862. One of the shells that struck the *Essex* exploded the boiler and scalded twenty men to death. Laning, who was commanding one of the bow batteries and was not hurt, described the gruesome scene: "As soon as the scalding steam would admit the forward gun deck was explored. The pilots who were both in the pilot house were scalded to death. Marshall Ford who was steering when the explosion took place was found at his post at the wheel standing erect his left hand holding the spoke and his right hand grasping the signal-bell rope. A seaman named James Coffey who was shot man to the No 2 gun was on his knees in the act of taking a shell from the box to be passed to the loader. The escaping steam and hot water had struck him square in the face and he met death in that position." (*Battles and Leaders of the Civil War*, Vol. 1, New York, NY, 1887, p. 364).
† La Salle steamboat captain Oscar H. Pratt* served on the USS *Cincinnati*, one of the ironclads involved in the attack on Fort Henry. He was seriously wounded in the attack when a spent musket ball shattered his leg.
‡ Joseph Franklin Joy*, half-brother of Anna's mother. He was a railroad executive in New York City.
§ Joseph Limeburner, captain of the *Great Republic* the largest clipper ship ever built for the China trade. His ship was transporting 5,000 men, 500 horses and 1,000 tons of coal to Ship Island on the Gulf Coast for the Butler Expedition. Keeler met Limeburner in 1850 on his way home from California on the *Samuel Russell* when Limeburner was the ship's mate.
** Richard S. Storrs, minister of the Congregational Church of the Pilgrims at Henry and Remsen Streets in Brooklyn. He was an active member of the abolitionist movement in the years leading up to the Civil War and preached civil disobedience to the Fugitive Slave Law of 1850.
†† Joseph B. Brush, Keeler's first cousin. He was a merchant in Brooklyn.
‡‡ Helen Warner, daughter of Keeler's namesake uncle William Frederick Potter.

morning. 'Tis cold here but clear & pleasant. How do Dave's* eyes get along & how does business prosper with him? How does he like the idea of Treasury notes being made a legal tender? There is a diversity of opinion here, but the great majority I think are favourable.

With the best of love to yourself, the children & all our kind friends,

Yours truly,
William

Brooklyn
Feb'y 13, 1862

Dear Anna,

On my return from the "Yard" this noon I found your welcome letter of the 8th waiting me & was glad to learn by it that you are all well at home. I hope you will have some warm weather by & by to thaw you out.

I rec'd a letter yesterday from your Father saying that he thought of coming down Friday or Saturday to see the Battery†. I hope nothing will prevent him.

Last Tuesday evening I spent at your Uncle Frank's & had a *capital time*. Nothing was wanting but your company. I went up with your uncle from his office & took dinner with them at 4 o'clock & spent the evening till nearly 10. Uncle Brush's folks were alarmed as I had not been there since breakfast & were beginning to think that I had been started off in the Battery at very short notice.

Mary is the very life of your Uncle Frank's house.‡ No one would have time to be dull or gloomy where she is. Without being handsome, she is intelligent, lively & animated & the greatest talker & mimic. But there is a vein of good sense running through the whole of it. Something was said about her Father [and] she asked me if I didn't think him a good looking man. I replied that I certainly did, that I always considered him good looking but that with his heavy beard he looked better now than I had ever seen him, that he was one of the very few who didn't seem to grow old. "Well," says she, "I knew you would think so & I am going to love you for it. We shall be first rate friends, you see if we ain't." She took her own & Henry's§ photographs out of her album & gave me them in exchange for mine. You will find them enclosed. But she is one of those you can never photograph unless you could contrive to animate it after taking it. But she rules the house. Her mother** grows old & the silver hairs begin to shew.

---

* David Brown*, Keeler's brother-in-law in La Salle.
† Short for ironclad floating battery. In this case the *Monitor*.
‡ Uncle Frank's 16-year-old daughter Mary Eliot Joy*.
§ Mary's older brother Henry DeWitt Joy*.
** Uncle Frank's wife Anna.

New York Navy Yard (January to March 1862)

Your Aunt Mary* looks *50 years* older than when I last saw her. Old maids do grow old fearfully fast. Ain't you glad you are married, even if your husband does flirt with pretty cousins. Another old maid I called on recently has also grown old at about the same rate, but this is private, as I suppose Mr. Hough does not want his relations slandered.

Yesterday I saw my iron home for the first time, but I shall not attempt a description of it now. But you may rest assured your *better half* will be in no more danger from rebel compliments† than if he was seated with you at home. There isn't even danger enough to give us any glory. Thick heavy plates & bars of iron on all sides above & below, with two of the largest sized Columbiads‡ in the tower. Our quarters for eating & sleeping are quite small & will not be *uncomfortably comfortable*. Not a man is exposed in action, our boilers & our entire machinery are completely & effectually protected. Two guns still larger than those we have are making to throw 300 lb. balls. When we get those I think we could cope with the English *Warrior*§, for we should have a large mark for our heavy pieces while she would have a mere speck as it were to fire at.

I think we are fitting out for the Potomac forts & the *Merrimac*, if the rebels contrive to get her out, but this is all surmise. Two steamers will accompany us when we go to sea as a precaution. When we shall be ready I can't tell. She is not yet in the yard & the work seems to go on slowly. If we don't get off soon I fear nothing will be left us to do.

Have you given my message to Capt. Woodson?

The Department has given Captain Worden a clerk** which will serve to make my duties still lighter, & more, they give me a *servant*. So I have spent a portion of two or three days in hunting up a contraband & finally found a good looking young darkey that came to me well recommended, but he wasn't of age & it was uncertain if his mother would let him go. I shall know tomorrow when I go aboard of the *North Carolina*†† (where the men are all sent when they enlist) & if I don't find him shall have to make another hunt.

I formed the acquaintance of our M.D.‡‡ who was appointed yesterday & think I shall like him. He is from New York where he has an office & has invited me up to spend the evening with him. Mean to accept *sometime*.

---

* Uncle Frank's unmarried sister Mary Pyncheon Joy*.
† Shells.
‡ Keeler was mistaken. The *Monitor*'s guns were Dahlgrens.
§ The British Navy's first iron-hulled warship was 420 feet in length and carried forty guns.
** Daniel Toffey (1837-1893). Son of a cattle broker and a nephew of Captain Worden, he was a clerk in Hudson, NJ at the start of the war, and served on the *Monitor* until April 17, 1862. His 17-year-old younger brother John later enlisted in a New Jersey infantry regiment and was awarded the Medal of Honor at the Battle of Missionary Ridge in November 1863.
†† A receiving ship at the Navy Yard.
‡‡ Daniel C. Logue*.

Civil War Years: USS *Monitor* (1862)

How strangely we sometimes run upon old acquaintances. The countenance of one of the officers I met daily in the yard seemed familiar & I studied over [it] for a long time. I finally asked him one day if his name was Taylor. "Yes," he said. "Did you go to California in the *Anna Reynolds*?" He said he did & so it turned out to be one of my fellow sufferers on that tedious voyage.*

Has Ham Brown† got the place he was after? I felt very much interested & hope he will succeed.

Saturday evening [February 15]—Your Father came down last evening & after I got through my business at the Yard this morning & found he had not come in I went back to the house & found he was not there. From there I went down to the Wall St. ferry & crossed to Mr. Joy's‡ office & found your Father had left Mr. J.'s house in the morning with the intention of going into the Yard for which purpose I had sent him a pass. I hurried to the Fulton ferry, across & down to the Yard where the guard told me he had not been in, at least he had taken no pass of that kind. So I waited till nearly dinner time expecting he would come in & finally went back to Uncle B.'s & found him there. He had got into the cars which had taken him a long distance past the Yard & had taken another car back to it, had gone in (the guard returning him his pass) and had looked around enquiring for me, & all the time I was in one of the offices waiting. Well we got our dinner, & by the way Uncle B. had a capital beef steak which it would have done you good to see your Father eat, & started of[f] to Greenpoint, where the boat still lies,§ in the midst of the hardest snow storm your Father said he ever saw. We reach it by one of the horse rail roads which lands us within a very short distance of it. Your Father was quite pleased and seemed to think we were in no danger from shot or shell, but thought the trip in her not quite so safe. He saw it under very unfavourable circumstances as everything was covered with snow above & fresh paint below. Besides, men were at work at every part of the boat where it was possible for a man to work. However he saw enough to give him a tolerable idea of what it is.

As soon as we get in the Yard I shall have lots of visitors & I fear but little time to receive them. Your Uncle Frank & Mary [Joy], Birdsey & his wife,

---

* Dudley E. Taylor (~1831-1866). At the age of 18 he joined the company of 51 men from Connecticut who sailed to California in the *Anna Reynolds*. A sailor in the merchant marine before the war, he was appointed acting master in the Union Navy the month before Keeler encountered him at the Navy Yard. He served on the USS *Mercedita* in the blockade off Wilmington. In May 1866 he was placed on sick leave, and returned home to New Haven where he died two months later.

† Brother of Keeler's brother-in-law, who was looking for a place in an Illinois cavalry regiment.

‡ Uncle Frank.

§ The Continental Iron Works was two miles north of the Navy Yard on the East River at Greenpoint.

NEW YORK NAVY YARD (JANUARY TO MARCH 1862)

Uncle & Aunt B., Joseph & his wife & a good many others want to see it there. I wish I could add your name & some of our good LaSalle friends to the list. But we shall not have much time for visitors as we shall take in our stores & be off.

Well we had a good look at the Battery & your Father got warmed up in the engine room, for he was chilled through after his long ride in the cars, & started for Mr. Joy's [Uncle Frank's] & reached there just as they were sitting down to *dinner*, 6 o'clock. I spent the evening very pleasantly & have just got back, 10 o'clock. I told Mary I would be over & go to Church with her tomorrow if it was pleasant, but it is still storming & judging from the past the storm will continue. I asked Mary if she rec'd my picture. "Yes," she said, "but it wasn't good a bit. It makes you a real old fellow, when you are a nice young man." She says just what comes first. But it is late, the folks are all in bed, so good night.

Sunday evening 10 o'clock [February 16]—I have just ret'd from Mr. Joy's where I have spent the evening very pleasantly. It had stopped snowing this morning & the day has been passably pleasant. They all sent much love to you & have often spoken of you & wished you were with us. Your Father returns to morrow.

I have just bought a paper with the first dispatch of the capture of Fort Donelson.[*] Ain't it glorious news. It makes me impatient to be off & do something, [even] if it is in ever so humble a way. I do hope it will fall to our lot to clear the bank of the Potomac of those rebel batteries which have so long disgraced the vicinity of the Capital. If that work is set off to us & we can do it, it will be glory enough. Do not imagine that in the midst of all this excitement, home & its dear ones are forgotten. By no means. The farther I am from you, the more precious you all seem.

You say that "Capt. Pratt broke his leg." I don't understand you as I see by the papers that a Capt. Pratt had his leg broken by a spent ball [at the Battle of Fort Henry]. How is it? So much good news coming now will keep old Mr. Chapin[†] traveling all the time to carry it. What is the matter of Capt. Coates[‡]?

You must have fine times sliding down hill & wish I was there to take a part. I told Aunt B. of Fan's[§] mishap. Well, says I, [I] was just imagining her shut up with three children with the whooping cough, & was going to write her a letter of condolence, but I don't see as she needs any. I sympathise with your hips & would advise you to take a *part* better *cushioned* the next time you fall.

---

[*] The Confederate fort on the Cumberland River was captured by Ulysses Grant on February 16.
[†] Julius F. Chapin*, the Keelers' neighbor in La Salle.
[‡] James H. Coates*, a La Salle merchant and captain in the 11th Illinois Infantry. His regiment suffered huge casualties at the Battle of Fort Donelson.
[§] Keeler's sister Frances (Fannie) E. Brown*.

I am sorry that the house in Ottawa was sold for taxes, as it has just doubled the original sum. I asked Mr. Hough to attend to it for me & he assured me he would & for fear he might forget it I wrote Prescott requesting him to pay it & deduct it from the rent. I do not blame Mr. Hough as he has so much to do for himself & others. 'Tis nothing strange that he should forget sometimes. It is possible he may get some reduction by making proper representations to the person who bid it off.

Hen, the little scamp, why don't he write to me? Tell him I have a letter partly finished to him but am a great mind not to send it. But as I do not like to loose all my labour I will try & complete it in a day or two. I have tried to remember what I did with his [ink] powder but can think of no other place than the top of my desk. If you don't find it there I can't tell where you will. He *must be very careful with it.*

I am sorry to hear so bad an account from the hen roost. I don't know any other way than to eat them, to save their lives.

Who should I run against Saturday when I was at the Battery with your Father but my particular friend Finch, of Punderford & Finch memory.* I did not recognise him till your Father told me it was him.

Monday morning [February 17]—I left my sheet late last night expecting to have time to finish it this morning & I do not like to send it away with any blank space but must do so as it is time I was at the Yard. You must imagine the remainder of the sheet filled with lots of love & kisses to yourself & the children, as well as kind remembrances to all our friends. Henry will probably get a letter from me in a day or two. I hope to spend the next Sunday at sea or what would be better in the Potomac. Before I sail I will write you. Till then good bye.

William

Tell Eddie† that I was real glad to get his nice little letter. It was very nice & interesting.

Brooklyn, Feb'y 22, 1862
Saturday Night 10 o'clock

Dear Anna,

Yesterday & to day have been two busy days with me, not so much manual labor, as being continually on my feet & constantly stirring about. Our vessel is in the Yard taking in stores, & as I am responsible for those under my charge I have felt obliged to keep a close watch of them.

---

* Lucius R. Finch and James Punderford were New Haven merchants who in 1849-50 were the agents of the New Haven and California Joint Stock Company, which Keeler and his two brothers joined before sailing to California.
† Keeler's 4-year-old son James Edward*.

New York Navy Yard (January to March 1862)

To day has been an exciting one in the Yard. Besides our Battery, which has attracted hundreds, there was the launch of the new screw steamer *Adirondack* & every one who could get passes came to see. I furnished them to all my friends here who desired to go. All the vessels in the Yard were hung with flags & streamers. The *North Carolina, Sabine,* & *Savannah* fired salutes at intervals & a fine brass band on the *North Carolina* gave us our favourite national airs.

Our vessel has been visited by hundreds of ladies whose heartily expressed good wishes we shall carry with us. The duty devolved upon me to shew most of them around the vessel. You can imagine your polished & accomplished husband *shining* in this new sphere. I believe I got along well enough. I rubbed up my antiquated & somewhat indistinct ideas of etiquette, & bright buttons & shoulder straps made up any deficiency. I find that they (buttons &c) are a sure passport to the notice of the weaker sex & I rather enjoy the idea of handing those around who, if I was dressed in other clothes, would scarcely notice me. It's real fun. Don't get jealous. I thought often of you & our friends at home to day & wished you might have been among the gay crowd. Among others whom I had the pleasure of shewing around was Mr. Wales, one of the editors of the *Scientific Am[erican]*.* He brought a person with him to take a sketch which he will [have] published soon. Also Mr. Pike†, an ex consul from Lisbon.

The greatest treat to me was the launch [of the *Adirondack*]. I was one of the privileged ones admitted on board (buttons again) & it was an exciting scene as she slid gently of[f] the ways into her future home amid the roar of cannon, the music of the band, the waving of flags & the cheers of thousands.

Capt. Worden told me to day that he thought we should go into commission on Monday, which consists of the formal delivery of the vessel by the officers of the Yard to those in command of her. She is then considered our home & we are expected to live on board of her. If she should be put in commission Monday we shall probably sail Tuesday if nothing happens & I hope before long you will hear a good account of us on the Potomac, as I have a number of reasons for thinking that that is our destination. One is that in buying our provisions we went to some extra expense as we were told that the Asst. Sec'y of the Navy Mr. Fox‡ & some other of the dignitaries at Washington were going up the Potomac with us. I hope Mr. Lovejoy§ will be one of them.

Just let me say here that if after we leave you hear of dreadful storms &c don't let it trouble you as I have no fear but what we shall reach there safely.

---

* Salem H. Wales, managing editor of *Scientific American*.
† Nicolas Pike.
‡ Gustavus V. Fox.
§ Owen Lovejoy*, the Republican member of Congress who got Keeler his naval commission.

Civil War Years: USS *Monitor* (1862)

At any rate after you hear of our danger it will be time to be alarmed. Steamers will accompany us to assist us if we need. Good night.

Sunday evening [February 23]—I have just returned from your Uncle Frank's where I went to tell them good bye & was very glad I did so as I met Harry who was at home spending a short vacation.[*] He is a real fine young fellow. They all sent you their best love & lots of it. I had a *splendid kiss* from *Aunt* Mary on parting, not to mention one from Cousin Mary. Harry is coming to the boat to morrow to see it.

Your letter of the 14th reached me & was as ever welcome. What a cold spell you have had. Here it has just been cold enough to freeze nights & that is all. I am glad you are so well provided with coal. Harry says it has been very cold in Williamstown. Ther. at one time 20° below.

I hope to be here long enough to get your next letter. After that I shall receive them through another channel. I enclose an envelope to shew how they should be directed. It is important that they be directed very plainly, especially the name of the vessel. I would suggest that you let Father direct them as he writes a heavier hand.

Hen wasn't far from right in telling Sarah[†] about my counting the pins & needles, for the "red tapism" manifested in our system of keeping accounts is very well expressed by Hen's remarks. It is not so much the labor as the great complication & the responsibility.

If we go to Washington I shall call on Mr. Lovejoy. I believe I have no other acquaintances there. I am glad that Mr. Rockwell takes so much interest in me. I hope he will hear a good account of us on the Potomac or wherever we are sent. Remember me to him & Mr. & Mrs. John[‡] — have you seen that baby yet?

I should like some of Mother's doughnuts first rate. Suppose you send me some.

I suppose you rec'd my letter to Carter[§]. I hope it will stir him up. I am very glad you mentioned the thing to me & hope you will do so if you find any further difficulty from that or any other source. I think if his notes are not promptly met you had better get Dave to advise you what to do with them.

I sent Mary [Joy] none of my photographs so you had better send her the one you have. I mean to have some more taken, if not now, by & by & will then give Mother & Sarah theirs.

Hen wanted to know if I wear a sword. Tell him I do, the regulations require it. So I had to go to the expense of $16.00 for one of those useless

---

[*] Uncle Frank's son was studying at Williams College in Williamstown, MA.
[†] Keeler's 20-year old sister.
[‡] John Rockwell* and his wife Anne were close friends of the Keelers. The Mr. Rockwell referred to earlier in the paragraph is presumably John's father Charles, a wealthy banker in La Salle.
[§] Samuel B. Carter*, a friend of Keeler's from La Salle.

toys, for it is nothing else. For service we use a ship's cutlass. This [the sword] is for mere dress. My expenses have been enormous. I dare not figure it up myself.

The scraps you sent were very *readable*. I hope to see more. I send Hen a Pictorial enclosing the seeds of a very fine squash that Aunt B. cut a few days ago, but not equal to a Hubbard.

It seems as if I wrote you a good many more letters than I receive. I send the usual number of kiss[es] & love to you & the children & kind remembrances to all our friends. I have no room to name each one. You shall hear again before we go.

William

[Marginalia] Don't let baby* forget me & I must have a letter from Eddie when you write & if Hen don't write I shall send "Uncle Sam's *Foote*" after him.† I wish I could take him on board the *North Carolina* with me to morrow. He would enjoy it so much.

Tell Father that Aunt Brush found a letter to day from Uncle Elihu's‡ son — he died June 16th 1853. Please alter the list I sent home.

Don't fail to write often. If we are sent to the Potomac I shall get letters regularly. Mails are made up in the Yard for all the different vessels & sent as often as practicable.

U.S. Steam Battery *Monitor*
Monday Evening, Feb'y 25, 1862

Well here I am, dear Anna, on ship board at last in my little cubby hole of a state room, small but nicely furnished. My boy has made my bed but it has a full wheelbarrow load of books, blanks, paper, bundles, boxes, bottles of ink, &c, &c deposited on top which has got to be removed to their proper places before I can turn in, for there is no place to lay them out side till morning.

I am full of *write* but unfortunately the time is wanting as we are to start to morrow morning & I have nearly a night's writing to do. This is merely to let you know that we are going and when. I shall write you at length the first opportunity or rather I will endeavor to keep a sort of journal & send home every opportunity. Very fortunately your third welcome letter reached me to day, one day earlier than usual, & glad was I to get it & hear that all were well at home. I shall hope to hear from you every opportunity & you may rest assured I shall not fail to write. You already have my directions. Follow them strictly & be careful to give the name of the vessel plainly.

---

* Keeler's 18-month-old daughter Elizabeth (Tibbie) Eliot*.
† A play on the words "Uncle Sam's foot" (America's military might), but in this case in reference to the Union naval commander Andrew H. Foote, whose gunboats were crucial to Grant's victories at Forts Henry and Donelson.
‡ Keeler's paternal uncle Elihu Keeler.

Civil War Years: USS *Monitor* (1862)

I sincerely hope our passage will be a short one. I do not expect a pleasant one. A powerful steam tug accompanies us to Fortress Munroe [Monroe]* from which place I hope you will hear from me soon.

Tell Henry I will answer his letter as soon as I can find time. My best love to all. I just begin to realise now that I am leaving home for I hardly know what, but I hope that a few months at furtherest will bring me back. It seems as if I could fill two or three sheets but my till will not allow [it] so must say good bye. With love to yourself & all the dear ones.

William

[Marginalia] Tell Henry I think he will find the powder on the top of my *desk* not on the book shelves.

New York,
Feb'y 28th, 1862

Dear Anna,

Here I am at *anchor* in Birdsey's store. When I last wrote you everything was hurry & confusion on board expecting to start immediately. Powder, shot, shell, grape & canister were taken on board in abundance & I had made, as I suppose, my last visit ashore as we were under sailing orders & were to leave the same day. But our preparations were so numerous we were delayed till the next morning (yesterday), when our hawsers were cast loose & we were on our way to Hampton Roads in the midst of a terrible snow storm. We ran first to the New York side then to the Brooklyn & so back & forth across the river, first to one side then to the other, like a drunken man on a side walk, till we brought up against the gas works with a shock that nearly took us from our feet. We found she would not answer her rudder at all & it was of no use to go further, so we took a tow back to the Yard & are now waiting for alterations in her steering apparatus, which we hope will be completed by tomorrow night so that we hope to try once more either Sunday of Monday evening.

All are getting impatient & want to get alongside the *Merrimac*. Still I should not be at all surprised if we met with further delays & eventually were obliged to have a new rudder. When we left yesterday morning we intended to come to anchor at Quarantine† & remain till the storm was over, so I hurried down to my state room to write you the last letter & had got it nearly finished when the collision with the gas works ended the matter & the letter remains in my desk on board.

I suppose you will ask, how I like man of war life. Well I havn't tried it long enough yet to tell, but I have made the discovery that there are some things about it not very romantic, such as getting up as we did this morning

---

* The Union controlled fort at the mouth of the James River.
† A small island in Lower New York Bay about two miles east of Staten Island.

New York Navy Yard (January to March 1862)

& eating breakfast with the Ther. in the ward room at *35°*, shivering so that one can hardly find the way to his mouth. My first night on board was spent between a pair of linen sheets. If I have an enemy I wish him no greater ill than to be similarly situated with the surrounding temperature at freezing. I didn't sleep a wink all night, but lay & shivered & shook till I thought the frame work of my berth would be shaken apart.

Morning brought relief in the form of my darkey with a wash bowl of warm water. I made short work of my toilette & hurried into the engine room to thaw out, an operation I have hardly got accomplished. As you may suppose, the next night I discarded bed *linen* & substituted *cotton* & piled on top every movable thing in my room except the iron safe, that I could not lift. The shrill sound of the bo'sun's whistle & "all hands up hammocks" the next morning brought me to a realising sense of having had a night's first rate sleep & I turned out when my boy informed me that breakfast was 'most ready, feeling quite comfortable.

No fires are allowed on board except in the engine room & to cook with, which in the cold weather we are now having is more safe than comfortable. We live well, that is we have the best of food provided by our caterer, which if well prepared will be all that we can desire.

All the commissioned officers, numbering eleven, are in our mess & eat in the ward room. We provide all our own dishes & table furniture as well as provisions. One of our number is chosen as caterer, who makes all the purchases & sees that the food is properly prepared. The cost to each of us for our dishes &c & provisions for two months is *$70.00* — not very cheap board.

As far as I know my fellow officers I am very well pleased with them & hope everything will pass pleasantly while we are shut up together. When we are once at sea & everything is reduced to a system I will give you all the details of this new sphere of existence. With the exception of Capt. Worden, I am the oldest person in the ward room.

I rec'd the [*La Salle*] *Press* this morning. Was sorry to see so many of my acquaintances among the killed.* Such things brings the war home to us & we feel it to be a sad reality. I hope your *spell* of *weather* will be over before long, but as long as it does continue, take my advice & don't put on *linen sheets*, unless you make a good coal fire on top. You shall hear from me again before we leave, or if we should happen to anchor off Quarantine. I have a letter all ready.

---

* At least 19 men from the city of La Salle were killed at Fort Donelson. Many of them were from the 11th Illinois Infantry which suffered the most casualties of all Union regiments participating in the battle. Among those killed was 17-year-old Edwin H. Carter, a private in the 11th, who was the brother of Keeler's good friend Samuel.

Civil War Years: USS *Monitor* (1862)

I have just heard a rumor that Gen. Banks* has crossed the Potomac & is marching upon Centreville. If this is true Melzar is probably with them.† Your Mother will feel anxious as well as all the rest of us.

I hope I shall get another letter from you before sailing. Capt. Worden told me that I should have had my letters directed to Hampton Roads, but I believe I shall let the direction remain as it is for the present. I can alter it when I get there if I desire to.

Give me all particulars from home however trifling as everything from there is interesting. Tell Eddy I got his picture & it was real nice. He is a good little boy to think of papa. With a kiss to yourself & the dear children.

I am yours truly,

William

[Marginalia] My love to Father, Mother, Sarah, Dave, Fan, Mrs. & Mr. Hough & all friends. Tell Hen to look on the top of my *desk* for his powder, not on the book shelves.

U.S. Steamer *Monitor*
New York Navy Yard
March 4, 1862

Dear Anna,

We are finally all ready for a start & are now only waiting for a favourable wind, not to fill our *"billowing"* sails, but to give us smooth water. Perhaps I had better said waiting for a calm, which would be much preferable, though we cannot expect it at this season of the year.

We got our steering apparatus fixed & made another trial trip yesterday which proved quite satisfactory to all. I send Henry a paper containing a short notice of it. It was a dismal rainy day & our wet iron decks were anything but comfortable to stand upon. We had an awning fitted over the top of the turret, running up to a point in the center like a tent & under this we managed to keep pretty dry, going down below occasionally to warm.

Commodore Gregory‡ & other notables from the Yard were with us & arrangements were made on board to give them a dinner suited to the occasion. The preliminaries were all right, but unfortunately we found upon seating ourselves at the table that "the wisest plans of mice & men gang aft

---

* Nathaniel P. Banks, a division commander in the Army of the Potomac and soon-to-be commander of the newly created V Corps of that army.
† Banks' army crossed the Potomac River on March 3 and marched up the Shenandoah Valley to Stonewall Jackson's headquarters at Winchester, which they occupied without a fight. Anna's brother Henry Melzar Dutton*, a lieutenant in the 5th Connecticut Infantry, was with them.
‡ Francis H. Gregory. The 72-year-old was recalled from retirement at the start of the war and placed in charge of gunboat construction at New York.

New York Navy Yard (January to March 1862)

aglee"* (I don't know as the quotation is right, you may correct it if it isn't) for to sum it all up in one short sentence, the Steward, upon whom it all depended, was drunk.† I suppose he had been testing the brandy & champaine before putting it upon the table. As may be suppose[d] it was a decided failure. The fish was brought in before we had finished the soup, & champaine glasses were furnished us to drink our brandy from & vice versa. However everything passed off as well as we could make it. Our visitors made all due allowance for our Steward's weakness & returned home satisfied with our good intentions at any rate.

Of course in speaking of liquors you will not suppose that I made any use of them. At first I was always asked to join when they were brought upon the table but excused myself so that now it is "Paymaster I don't ask you, as you don't drink, but will you please pass the bottle."

Upon our return, about 5 o'clock, Mr. Steward was put in irons & kept so till 9. He yelled & hollowed [hollered] & begged and plead, but t'was of no use. He was pretty well sobered before he was released & appeared a good deal humbled & mortified. But this morning he had got some liquor from the ward room store room of which he keeps the keys & was drunk again, I think to drown his feelings, so I have had an opportunity to see a little more man of war discipline. To day he has been ironed & shut up in one of the chain lockers. The lieutenant [Greene] this morning told the officers that those who had liquor in the store room must put it away where the servants could not get it or he should throw it overboard.

I see no reason why everything should not pass very pleasantly on board. Some of the officers as I get better acquainted with them I like better, others not as well. There are eleven of us, when all are present to sit at the table. Usualy there is company, as any of us who has a friend on board at meal times invites him to the table. The caterer of the mess (Mr. Newtown‡) sits at one end of the table & Capt. Worden when present at the other. I am seated at the Capt.'s left, & Lieut. Green at his right. At my left is the first Master Stodder, then Master Webber & so on. Each of us has our seat which we always occupy unless we choose to give it up to company. Our table is an extention & will reach the length of our cabin & accommodate quite a little company.

I think in my last I told you how cold & uncomfortable it was in the ward & state rooms. Since then we have had steam heaters put up in the ward room, taking steam from the boilers, which makes it very comfortable.

I sleep soundly nights till the shrill whistle of the bo'sun about 5 in the morning & his loud hoarse call of "a-l-l hands up hammocks" wakes me for

---

* Robert Burns' *To a Mouse* (1785).
† Wardroom steward Lawrence Murray (~1828-1862). He drowned six months later after another drinking binge.
‡ First Assistant Engineer Isaac Newton*.

37

a short time when I turn over & take another nap till my darkey comes in to tell me "8 o'clock Sir, breakfast 'most ready Sir." After breakfast I usually take one of the boats & go ashore to get fresh provisions for the crew for the next day & get letters from the Lyceum Post Office*. If I have leave of absence till afternoon I go to Uncle Brush's & get my dinner, as I must confess it tastes a little better there than on board. Our evenings are usually spent in reading or conversation — card playing is not allowed on board a man of war so we cannot make us[e] of that to kill time. I generally take the evenings to do my writing. Whenever I write, day or night in my state room, I have to use a candle, it is so dark. My little deck light lets in light enough for all purposes except reading & writing. Your suggestions as to having my boy black my boots is very good but was unnecessary for I find a pair of well blacked boots in my room every morning when I get up. As to shaving I have pretty much given it up. Uncle & Aunt Brush, George† & Joseph all advised me too & I am inclined to take their advice, at sea at any rate.

I shall be glad for your sake when this long cold winter is at an end. I can imagine you all shut up in our little rooms, the poor children hardly daring to stick their noses out of doors. But spring will be all the pleasanter when it comes.

I took dinner at Birdsey's last Sunday & saw Abijah's wife who had just come on from Minnesota.‡ She looked very much as she used to, had grown old but little. The day before we went into commission Birdsey & his wife, Mrs. & Mr. Snow & one or two other ladies paid me a visit on board. I escorted them into the turret. They are the only ones of the female sex who have ever been there.

We are preparing to start in the morning & will in all probability get off, so you will next hear from me at Hampton Roads. You must remember me to all our friends with as much love as you feel able to spare. It is 12 o'clock & I want to write a few lines to Henry, so good night. Sincerely & affectionately,

Yours, William

[Marginalia] Our arrival at Hampton Roads will probably reach you by telegraph before you hear from me. I hope you have sent your signature to Uncle Brush as I requested. Don't neglect it as the money will be of no use to you without it.

---

* The New York Naval Lyceum at the New York Navy Yard. Established in 1833 as a museum, it also forwarded the mail for the Navy.
† Uncle Brush's youngest son George, a professor of minerology at Yale College.
‡ Abijah Blakemen, brother of Keeler's friend Birdsey.

NEW YORK NAVY YARD (JANUARY TO MARCH 1862)

Supplementary

Wednesday Morning
March 5th, 1862

Capt. Worden has just come on board & says the Commodore has just had a dispatch saying that a heavy storm was raging on the coast & it was not safe to go to sea. So here we shall remain till to morrow & probably longer as we have every indication of a gathering storm.

I made my last visit on shore this morning as I suppose, to bring off the mail matter for the ship. I found among others your good long one of the 1st & I need not assure you how eagerly it was opened & read, though it was more than two hours before I had time to read it through. It seemed as if the Paymaster never was in such demand. I had shut myself in my state room for the sake of being alone & quiet. First came my boy to make my bed & clean up the room. I dismissed him without ceremony. Then came the Surgeon, just as I had fairly commenced, & seated himself to read the morning paper & have a chat. One of the masters followed to hear the news. "Ah," says the M.D., "a letter from your *girl*, hey?" "Yes," says [I], "& I wish you would let me read it." I had no sooner disposed of him than my Steward presented himself to know something about the day's rations. Then came the lieutenant to get some information of some men who deserted day before yesterday. I got through with him & had taken up your letter once more when I heard Capt. Worden enquiring for the Paymaster & found he wanted some papers made out for the Department. Through with this & some of the men wanted some money which involved an examination of their accounts. Then I had to go on board of the Frigate *Sabine* to see her Paymaster*, from there to the *North Carolina* & when I got back to my state room once more I found my darkey had been putting my room to rights &, as is always the case at such times, turned every thing upside down & loosing your letter. I blowed him up, found your letter, read that & felt better natured. So you see the effect of a good long letter. I know you don't regret writing it & I am sure that I felt decidedly better after reading it for I felt rather bad at the idea of leaving without hearing from home once more (as I expected to at the time) when I knew that your letter was due to day.

Perhaps you would like to know just how my room looks. I wish you could look into it & see for yourself. As you can't & as I have none of "Porte Crayon's"† skill, I must perforce use pen & ink. Here is a plan that will give you a little idea.‡ A is my desk, D [B] is the door let down to write on, the iron chest is placed underneath, C is the door, D is the shelf in which is my washbowl, underneath is another shelf in which are holes cut (remember that

---

* J. George Harris (1809-1891).
† Pseudonym of illustrator and writer David H. Strother whose articles appeared in *Harper's Weekly*.
‡ See Sketch No. 1 at the beginning of the book.

at sea nothing is placed *on* a shelf, but *in* it) for my slop jar, tumbler, water pitcher, soap dish &c &c, all of nice white ware with "Monitor" on each in gilt letters. Over the wash bowl is a small shelf for hair brush, comb &c. Over this shelf, & the bottom resting on it & reaching nearly to the top of my room, is a large looking glass in a gilt frame. The floor of my room is covered with oil cloth on which is a tapestry rug & on this again is a fine, soft goat's hair mat. E is my berth, wide enough to be comfortable, & just so long that when my head touches one end, my feet touch the other. In front of it is a handsome rail, 8 or 9 inches high, turning down on hinges when I wish, the top of the rail being about on a level with my chin, so I have something of a climb to get into bed. F.F. are two closets, 3 shelves each, back of the berth, but they are so high up & so far back that it is unhandy to get at them. Under the berth are four drawers. The berth, drawers, & closets are all of black-walnut, the curtains are lace & damask, or an imitation I suppose. For a seat I have a camp stool covered with a piece of tapestry carpet.

Capt. Ericcson* fitted our rooms up at his own expense & has been very liberal. I have been on board of nearly all the vessels that have left the Yard since I have been here & have seen no rooms as handsomely fitted up as ours. The only objection is they are too dark. I have all my writing to [do] by candle light & lamps are always burning in the ward room. If the sun ever shines again it may light us up a little better. The room is about a foot higher than I can reach. A register is in the floor for the purpose of admitting fresh air when we desire it, so you see we are provided against suffocation. The air is forced under the floor by the blowers in the engine room.

I should think from your account there would soon be war in La Salle. I hope you nor none of my friends will get mixed up in it. Nothing would pain me more than to see our pleasant little circle broken up from some such foolish thing. It seems as if everything Mrs. Hitchcock had anything [to] do with ended in a quarrel, though she may not be to blame.

I fear my letters do not sound so well to the public ear as they do to your partial one. You must bear in mind the circumstances under which they are written. Our rooms are all open at the top, for ventilation, & the doors are blinds, so that as far as sounds are concerned we might as well be in one room. While writing now, every word spoken by the circle around the ward room table is as audible as if they were seated at my elbow. This does not assist one to concentrate his thoughts & very likely is the occasion of not a very few mistakes.

Tell Mr. Hough that I had no desire to slander the fair sex, especialy those who I have no doubt would warmly welcome me even in old clothes. You know there are some flies that you can't always catch with molasses & water.

---

* Ericsson joined the Swedish army in 1820 at the age of 17 and was promoted to captain in 1826 while he was living in England. He resigned from the army the day he received his promotion, but used the title of Captain for the rest of his life.

New York Navy Yard (January to March 1862)

I am sorry that Miss Woods' school is deteriorating. If Henry is so dissatisfied I should think you had better take him out as soon as his quarter expires as there is no use in paying money for nothing. Henry can pursue his studies at home till there is an opening.

Yours, William

[Marginalia] My love to Fan & Dave. Will write to them soon. Here are 4 sheets. I hope to receive one as long.

Hampton Roads (March to May 1862)

> *I have but a few moments to spare just to say that I am safe. We have had an engagement with the* Merrimac *continuing for three hours & have driven her off, we think in a sinking condition. We have three men disabled, among them & the worst is our noble Captain who has lost his sight, I hope only temporarily. . . . We fought her at <u>20 feet</u> distance a part of the time, the two vessels were touching. My hands are all dirt & powder smoke as you will discover by the paper.* (9 March 1862)

On March 6, after a week's delay resulting from loading coal and ammunition, faulty steering and a storm in the Atlantic, the *Monitor* departed for Hampton Roads under tow of the tug USS *Seth Low*. Accompanying them was Ericsson's right-hand man in the Navy, 34-year-old Chief Engineer Alban Stimers, who served as an official observer and was responsible for operating the turret in the upcoming battle with the *Virginia*. Their trip down was nearly disastrous. On the second day they encountered a gale that nearly sank the vessel. To compound matters, seas poured down the blower pipes, causing the ventilator fan belts to stretch and slip, depriving the furnaces of draft. This caused smoke and gas to fill the vessel, which suffocated the men in the engine room. However, by next morning the storm's fury had abated, the blowers were working again, and the gas cleared out. While the men overcome by the fumes were recuperating in the top of the turret, Keeler, the ever-versatile paymaster, took charge of the engines until morning when the engineers were sufficiently recovered to attend to their duties. They muddled through and reached Fort Monroe around 9 pm on March 8.

The scene before them was one of utter chaos and destruction. Off in the distance lay the sunken 24-gun USS *Cumberland*, the burning and about-to-explode 50-gun USS *Congress*, the grounded 47-gun USS *Minnesota* with her crew frantically throwing heavy items overboard in a futile attempt to get her afloat, and dozens of smaller craft scurrying back to the protection of Fort Monroe. Earlier in the day the *Virginia* had steamed out of the Elizabeth River and over to Newport News where the *Cumberland* and *Congress* lay anchored. With their guns ablaze, they rammed the *Cumberland*, sending the big wooden ship to the bottom of the river. They then turned their attention to the *Congress*, which had been purposely run aground to avoid the same fate as the *Cumberland*, and forced her surrender. When they boarded their prize, federal infantry on shore began shooting. Enraged at this breach of naval etiquette, the *Virginia*'s captain ordered the *Congress* destroyed. Hot shot and incendiary shells then set the *Congress* ablaze. When the fires reached the powder room six hours later she exploded in a thunderous boom. In imminent danger of destruction were also the *Minnesota* and two other Union frigates which had run aground while coming to the aid of the *Congress* and *Cumberland*. However, with darkness falling and the tide receding, the *Virginia* called it a day and steamed over towards Sewell's Point to await the next morning. News of the stunning attack shocked Lincoln and his cabinet. Secretary of War Edwin Stanton even feared that after destroying the entire Union fleet at Hampton Roads the rebel ironclad would steam up the Potomac and shell out the capital, before heading north along the Atlantic coast, laying waste to cities along the way. The *Monitor*'s arrival could not have come at a more opportune time.

Upon arriving in Hampton Roads, the *Monitor* was ordered to protect the *Minnesota* which lay stranded on a shoal three miles away. Shortly after dawn on March 9, the *Virginia* steamed towards her prey, unaware of the *Monitor*'s presence. It was not until Worden ordered the first shot fired that the *Virginia* took notice. The two ironclads circled each other for two hours, probing each other's weaknesses with their heavy guns. However, neither vessel's fire was effective in penetrating the iron hide of the other. By this time the supply of shot in the *Monitor*'s turret was exhausted and Worden broke off action and withdrew to shallower water. After replenishing her supply of ammunition, the *Monitor* approached the *Virginia* and fired several shots at close range. Unable to inflict any damage on the Union ironclad in return, the *Virginia* then attempted to ram the *Monitor*, her captain unaware that the ram had fallen off the day before and was lodged in the hull of the sunken *Cumberland*. The far more maneuverable *Monitor* avoided the brunt of the blow by veering off to the side. When the two vessels were again in close proximity the *Virginia* fired point blank at the *Monitor*'s pilot house just as Worden was peering through the observation slit. The shot blinded him. Bleeding profusely from the wounds to his face, Worden was carried down the ladder to his cabin where Surgeon Logue began removing iron splinters from his eyes. Greene rushed down from the turret to confer with Worden and was placed in command of the vessel. With the tide falling fast, the *Virginia* called it a day and steamed back towards Sewell's Point, believing that the *Monitor* had broken off the engagement. By this time Greene had assessed the damage to the *Monitor* and ordered the vessel back into action. But seeing that the *Virginia* was leaving, he ordered the *Monitor* back to the *Minnesota* in compliance with their orders. Thus, ended the Battle of Hampton Roads.

While neither vessel could claim a decisive victory, it was considered a tactical victory for the *Monitor* since the rest of the Union fleet at Hampton

HAMPTON ROADS (MARCH TO MAY 1862)

Roads had been saved from destruction, but a strategic victory for the *Virginia* whose continued presence on the James River impeded the Union army's upcoming operations on the Virginia Peninsula. Northern newspapers, of course, reported it as a brilliant victory for the *Monitor*, whose officers became instant celebrities and were treated like royalty wherever they went.

The day after the battle, command of the *Monitor* passed to 26-year-old Thomas Selfridge, a lieutenant on the *Cumberland*, who two days earlier had narrowly escaped his sinking ship. His tenure was short-lived (two days) until a more senior officer could be found. That man was Lieutenant William Jeffers, a 21-year veteran of the Navy and a specialist in ordnance and gunnery, whom Keeler described as "an easy, fluent talker, a jolly, devil may care kind of way & a man of fine acquirements," but also "a rigid disciplinarian, of quick imperious temper & domineering disposition."

Under strict orders from President Lincoln that the *Monitor* "be not too much exposed,"* the ironclad lay off Fort Monroe with her steam up day and night. During those days of inactivity, visitors flocked to see the famous ironclad and to shake the hands of the heroes inside her. One of the first to come on board was the Assistant Secretary of the Navy Gustavus Fox, who had made the trip down from Washington. After witnessing the *Monitor*'s stellar performance on March 9, he sent a verbal order to Ericsson to build six new monitors. Two other visitors who played important roles in the weeks to come were Major General John Wool and Commodore Louis Goldsborough. Wool, who at 78 was the oldest serving general in the Civil War, had come out of retirement in June 1861 when asked to command the Union garrison at Fort Monroe. Goldsborough, at 57, and no spring chicken either, was commander of the North Atlantic Blockading Squadron. "Monstrous in size, a huge mass of inert matter," according to Keeler, he was appropriately nicknamed "Old Guts."

As the purchaser of the provisions, Keeler was one of the lucky ones on board the *Monitor* who got the chance to stretch his legs on shore, and, as a celebrity, doors were wide open to him. He became fast friends with William Kimberly, the owner of the provision store at Old Point Comfort just outside the main gate of Fort Monroe, and for the next four years would be a welcome guest at his house. Strolling around the fort and its surroundings, Keeler also observed the build-up of the huge Union army and encountered some of the officers who served in it, one of whom was Jim Beecher, the half-brother of the famous author Harriet Beecher Stowe. The two had first met on the clipper ship *Samuel Russell* on their way to China in 1850, and would meet up several times over the course of the war.

With the Union Navy in control of the mouth of the James River, George McClellan's long-awaited advance on Richmond could go ahead. One week

---

* ORN, I:7, p. 83.

Civil War Years: USS *Monitor* (1862)

after the Battle of Hampton Roads, elements of the Army of the Potomac began arriving at Fort Monroe, followed by the 35-year-old general himself on April 2. By the time the operation was complete several weeks later more than 120,000 men, nearly 15,000 horses and mules, and hundreds of cannon and siege guns had been shipped to the fort. However, McClellan's advance up the Virginia Peninsula did not get off to a good start. With the Confederate Navy still in control of most of the James River, McClellan needed control of the York River in order to supply his army as it moved towards Richmond. With rebel batteries at Yorktown and Gloucester Point closing that river, and Goldsborough unwilling to provide the warships needed to silence them, McClellan was forced to attack the Confederate army defending Yorktown. Vastly overestimating the strength of his opponent, the overcautious general spent one month investing the Confederate line, only to find it had been held by a small force when the rebels slipped away on May 4.

For the month after the Battle of Hampton Roads, the *Virginia* underwent repairs at the Gosport Navy Yard in Portsmouth. On April 11 she reappeared in Hampton Roads in the company of five other gunboats. With the *Monitor* under strict orders not to engage the *Virginia* unless she entered the open waters of Chesapeake Bay, which the *Virginia* refused to do, the two ironclads steamed back and forth until late afternoon and exchanged no shots. For the remainder of the month a stalemate prevailed in Hampton Roads, with no side wanting to risk their precious ironclad. All this changed on May 6 when President Lincoln arrived at Fort Monroe to "stir up dry bones." With Norfolk still in enemy hands and the *Virginia* still a threat, Lincoln took matters in hand and met with Goldsborough and Wool to discuss his plan. He ordered the *Monitor* and five other gunboats to shell out the batteries at Sewell's Point which guarded the entrance to the Elizabeth River. He then ordered Wool's troops to land at Willoughby's Point on the south side of Hampton Roads and march to Norfolk. This they did without a fight since the Confederates had already withdrawn from Norfolk and were regrouping near Richmond. Left behind was the *Virginia*. With a draft too deep to get up the James River to Richmond and certain death awaiting them if they attempted to pass the gauntlet of big guns at the mouth of the James River, they had no choice but to destroy the vessel to prevent her capture. And so, early on the morning of May 11 the ironclad was run ashore, set on fire and exploded with a tremendous boom.

Letters of special note: March 6 (trip down to Hampton Roads; fight with the *Virginia*); March 26 (boarders and visitors); April 11 (reappearance of the *Virginia*); April 29 (handing out small stores); May 3 (visit to Camp Hamilton); May 7 (Lincoln visits the *Monitor*); May 8 (shelling of Sewell's Point batteries); May 9 (Lincoln stirs up dry bones); May 11 (short note stating that the *Virginia* had been destroyed — details given in May 12 letter).

HAMPTON ROADS (MARCH TO MAY 1862)

U.S. Steamer *Monitor*
Hampton Roads
March 9th, 1862*
2 o'clock P.M.

My Dear Wife & Children,

    I have but a few moments to spare just to say that I am safe. We have had an engagement with the *Merrimac* continuing for three hours & have driven her off, we think in a sinking condition. We have three men disabled, among them & the worst is our noble Captain who has lost his sight, I hope only temporarily. The first opportunity I get you shall have full details & my own experience. With my best & kindest love to you all.

William

We fought her at *20 feet* distance a part of the time, the two vessels were touching. My hands are all dirt & powder smoke as you will discover by the paper.†

U.S. Steamer *Monitor*
Off Sandy Hook
March 6th, 1862

    4 o'clock P.M. We have just parted with our pilot & may consider ourselves at sea. We have a fine westerly wind, a smooth sea & as fair a sky as we could expect in the month of March. We are in tow of the tug *Seth Low* & convoyed by the U.S. Steam Gun Boats *Currituck* & *Sachem*, who are ordered to accompany us the whole distance. Our boat proves to be much more buoyant than we expected & no water of consequence has yet found its way on deck. Our hatchways are covered with glass hatches battened down & the only means of access to the deck is up through the top of the tower & then down to the deck.

    9 P.M. I have just returned from the top of the turret. The moon is shining bright, the water smo[o]th & everything seems favourable. The green lights of the gun boats are on our lee beam but a short distance off & the tug is pulling lustily at our big hawser, about 400 feet ahead. A number of sail are visible in different directions, their white sails glistening in the moon light. Not a sea has yet passed over our deck, it is as dry as when we left port. We had a merry company at the supper table, the Captain telling some of his experience as a Midshipman.

    Friday, March 7th. When I awoke this morning I found much more motion to the vessel & could see the green water through my deck light as

---

* This letter is bound out of sequence in the letter book since it was received before the letter dated March 6 which describes in detail the Battle of Hampton Roads.
† Keeler's fingerprints adorn the bottom left corner of the page as can be seen in the photograph of the letter at the beginning of the book.

the waves rolled across the deck. A number were complaining of seasickness, among them Capt. Worden & the Surgeon.

The water had worked under the tower during the night & drowned out the sailors whose hammocks were hung on the berth deck immediately below. The water was coming down this morning from under the tower & from the hatches & deck lights & various other openings making it wet & very disagreeable below. In the engine room it was still worse. From the top of the tower, where our seasick ones were laid out, a number of sail were in sight, our companions the gun boats maintaining about the same relative position to us they had last night. They were rolling badly.

Towards noon the wind, which blew quite fresh in the morning, increased, blowing a gale from the no'west & of course getting up quite a heavy sea. The gun boats would occasionally roll the muzzle of their guns under & as far as motion was concerned they were much more uncomfortable than ourselves. To form a correct idea of our position you must bear in mind that our deck is a flat level surface barely a foot above the water in still calm weather, with nothing whatever to keep the seas off our deck. Now the top of every sea that breaks against our side rolls unobstructed over our deck, dashing & foaming at a terrible rate.

The wind continued to increase after dinner with a heavier sea pouring across our deck with an almost resistless force, every now & then breaking against our smoke pipes, which are only about six feet high, sending a torrent of water down on our fires. Our decks are constantly covered with a sea of foam pouring from one side to the other as the deck is inclined, while at short intervals a huge green sea rolls across with terrible force, breaking into foam at every obstruction offered to its passage. Now we scoop up a huge volume of water on one side &, as it rolls to the other with the motion of the vessel, is met by a sea coming from an opposite direction, the accumulated weight seeming sufficient to bury us forever.

The steady & monotonous clank, clank of the engines assure us that they are still at work & the tug ahead is still pulling at the hawser, but as the day advances some anxious faces are seen. Things continued in this way till about 4 o'clock when on turning to go down from the turret I met one of the engineers coming up the steps, pale, black, wet & staggering along gasping for breath. He asked me for brandy & I turned to go down & get him some & met the sailors dragging up the fireman & other engineers apparent[ly] lifeless. I got down as soon as possible & found the whole between decks filled with steam & gas & smoke. The sailors were rushing up stifled with the gas. I found when I reached the berth deck that it came from the engine room, the door of which was open. As I went to shut it one of the sailors said he believed that one of the engineers was still in there. No time was to be lost, though by this time almost suffocated myself. I rushed in over heaps of coal & ashes & fortunately found the man lying insensible. One of the

Hampton Roads (March to May 1862)

sailors who had followed me helped pull him out & close the door. We got him up to the top of the tower but he was nearly gone.

To understand correctly the nature of our troubles you should get a correct idea of the boat. I enclose a draft of the deck & space below the deck which may assist you some.* Immediately under the blower pipes E.E., which are about 2 ft. by 2 1/2 ft. sqr. on the upper deck, are the blowers which take the air down through the pipes & force it into the room aft of the bulk head C.C. This room is tight, the openings to the deck being kept closed. Communication is had with the other part of the ship through small oval openings closed by iron doors about where the letters C.C. are. The air being forced into this room by powerful blowers & having no other outlet goes into the ash pit of the boilers, & up through the fires & so out of the smoke stacks D.D., supplying a strong draft & keeping up combustion. So much water found its way down the blower pipes E.E. that it wet the belts with which the fans were driven & so stretched them as to make them so loose they would not work. This deprived the furnaces of their draft & of course the engine room was soon filled with carbonic acid gas, mingled with the steam of the water which ran down the smoke pipes into the fires. As long as the doors through the iron partition was closed there was no escape for the gas. But as soon as they were opened by the men who were trying to escape the engine room, the gas & steam rushed through & completely filled the whole lower part of the vessel.

We got all the men who were in the engine room stretched out on the top of the turret & put up an old piece of sail as an awning or a protection from the wind & spray which occasionally reached us. It was a sorry looking company which crowded the only *habitable* spot on our vessel. Our colors were set union down to bring the gun boats to our assistance, but they rolled so on the heavy sea, they could help us none. Things for a time looked pretty blue, as though we might have to "give up the ship."

We succeeded finally in getting the ventilation started once more & the blowers going. The M.D. in the meantime attending to the sick ones on top of the turret. Evening had now come on & we managed to get the gas out so that we got below once more with the sick. Our supper was crackers & cheese & water. My mechanical genius came in play, as I took charge of the engines till morning when the engineers were sufficiently recovered to attend to their duties. Of course there was no sleep on board that night.

Towards morning the wind moderated & the water became more smooth. Breakfast tasted good I assure you. Weather was a little more pleasant & the water smoother through the day, still it continued to roll over the deck. It seemed singular to sit in my room & hear the huge waves roll over my head & look up through the little deck light at the mass of water [that] darkened the few straggling rays.

---

* See Sketch No. 2 at the beginning of the book.

Civil War Years: USS *Monitor* (1862)

A little after noon Cape Charles was seen & about 4 P.M. Cape Henry. About the same time we imagined we heard heavy firing in the distance. Of course all began to speculate as to the cause. As we neared the land, clouds of smoke could be seen hanging over it in the direction of the Fortress[*] & as we approached still nearer little black spots could occasionally be seen suddenly springing into the air, remaining stationary for a moment or two & then gradually expanding into a large white cloud. These were shells & tended to increase the excitement. As the darkness increased, the flashes of guns lit up the distant horizon & bursting shells flashed in the air.

We soon took a pilot & then learned that the *Merrimac* was out & making terrible havock among the shipping. How slow we seemed to move, the moments were hours. Oh, how we longed to be there. But our iron hull crept slowly on & the monotonous clank, clank of the engine betokened no increase of its speed. No supper was eaten that night as you may suppose.

As we neared the harbour the firing slackened & only an occasional gun lit up the darkness. Vessels were leaving like a covey of frightened quails & their lights danced over the water in all directions. We stopped by the *Roanoke* frigate & rec'd orders to proceed at once to Newport News to protect the *Minnesota* which was aground there, so we went up & anchored near her. Capt. Worden went on board & on his return we heard for the first time of the havoc made by the *Merrimac* & the terrible excitement prevailing among the shipping in the harbour & among the troops ashore.

Everything on board of us had been prepared for action as far as possible as we came up the harbour & the report every little while through the night that the *Merrimac* was coming kept all hands to quarters through the night. No one slept.

The first rays of morning light saw the *Minnesota* surrounded by tugs into which were being tumbled the bags & hammocks of the men & barrels & bags of provisions, some of which went into the boats & some into the water, which was covered with barrels of rice, whiskey, flour, beans, sugar, which were thrown overboard to lighten the ship. One of the little tugs alongside had the engine & the whole inside blown out by the explosion of a shell in the previous day's fight.

After getting up our anchor we steamed slowly along under the towering side of the *Minnesota*. The men were clambering down into the smaller boats. The guns were being thrown overboard & everything seemed in confusion. Her wooden sides shewed terrible traces of the conflict.

As a light fog lifted from the water it revealed the *Merrimac* with her consorts lying under Sewall's Point[†]. The announcement of breakfast brought also the news that the *Merrimac* was coming & our coffee was forgotten.

---

[*] Fort Monroe.
[†] The rebel battery on the south shore of Hampton Roads across from Fort Monroe.

Hampton Roads (March to May 1862)

Capt. Worden inquired of the *Minnesota* what he intended to do. "If I cannot lighten my ship off I shall destroy her," Capt. Van Brunt[*] replied. "I will stand by you to the last if I can help you," said our Capt. "No Sir, you cannot help me," was the reply. The idea of assistance or protection being offered to the huge thing by the little pigmy at her side seemed absolutely ridiculous & I have no doubt was so regarded by those on board of her, for the replies came down curt & crispy. As the *Merrimac* approached, we slowly steamed out of the shadow of our towering friend no ways daunted by her rather ungracious replies.

Every one on board of us was at his post, except the doctor & myself who having no place assigned us in the immediate working of the ship were making the most of our time in taking a good look at our still distant but approaching foe. A puff of smoke arose from her side & a shell howled over our heads & crashed into the side of the *Minnesota*. Capt. Worden, who was on deck, came up & said more sternly than I ever heard him speak before, "Gentlemen, that is the *Merrimac*, you had better go below." We did not wait a second *invitation* but ascended the tower & down the hatchway, Capt. W. following. The iron hatch was closed over the opening & all access to us cut off. As we passed down through the turret the gunners were lifting a 175 lb. shot into the mouth of one of our immense guns. "Send them that with our compliments, my lads," says Capt. W.

A few straggling rays of light found their way from the top of the tower to the depths below which was dimly lighted by lanterns. Every one was at his post, fixed like a statue. The most profound silence reigned. If there had been a coward heart there its throb would have been audible, so *intense* was the stillness. I experienced a peculiar sensation. I do not think it was fear, but it was different from anything I ever knew before. We were enclosed in what we supposed to be an impenetrable armour. We knew that a powerful foe was about to meet us. Ours was an untried experiment & our enemy's first fire might make it a coffin for us all. Then we knew not how soon the attack would commence, or from what direction it would come, for with the exception of those in the pilot house & one or two in the turret, no one of us could see her. The suspense was awful as we waited in the dim light expecting every moment to hear the crash of our enemy's shot.

Soon came the report of a gun, then another & another at short intervals, then a rapid discharge, then a thundering broadside & the infernal howl (I can't give it a more appropriate name) of the shells as they flew over our vessel was all that broke the silence & made it seem still more terrible. Mr. Green says, "Paymaster, ask the Capt. if I shall fire." The reply was, "Tell Mr. Green not to fire till I give the word, to be cool & deliberate, to take sure aim & not waste a shot." O, what a relief it was when at the word the gun over

---

[*] Gershom Van Brunt.

my head thundered out its challenge with a report which jar[r]ed our vessel, but it was music to us all.

The fight had been opened by the *Merrimac* firing on the *Minnesota* who replied by the broadside we first heard. As we lay immediately between the two, we had the full benefit of their shot — the sound of them at least, which if once heard will never be forgotten I assure you. It would not quiet the nerves of an excitable person I think.

Until we fired, the *Merrimac* had taken no notice of us, confining her attentions to the *Minnesota*. Our second shot struck her & made the iron scales rattle on her side. She seemed for the first time to be aware of our presence & replied to our solid shot with grape & canister which rattled on our iron decks like hail stones. One of the gunners in the turret could not resist the temptation when the port was open for an instant to run out his head. He drew it in with a broad grin. "Well," says he, "the d----d fools are firing canister at us." The same silence was enforced below that no order might be lost or misunderstood.

The vessels were now sufficiently near to make our fire effective & our two heavy pieces were worked as rapidly as possible, every shot telling. The intervals being filled by the howling of the shells around & over us, which was now incessant. The men at the guns had stripped themselves to their waists & were covered with powder & smoke, the perspiration falling from them like rain.

Below, we had no idea of the position of our unseen antagonist, her mode of attack, or her distance from us, except what was made known through the orders of the Capt.

"Tell Mr. Green that I am going to bring him on our starboard beam close along side."

"That was a good shot, went through her water line."

"Don't let the men expose themselves, they are firing at us with rifles."

"That last shot brought the iron from her sides."

"She's too far off now, reserve your fire till you're sure."

"If you can elevate enough, try the wooden gun boat."

"You struck her." (We learned afterward that that shot killed four men & wounded the Captain.)

"They're going to board us, put in a round of canister."

"Can't do it," replies Mr. Green, "both guns have solid shot."

"Give them to her then."

Bang goes one of the guns. "You've made a hole through her. Quick give her the other." Snap goes the primer.

"Why don't you fire?"

"Can't do it, the cartridge is not rammed home."

"Depress the gun & let the shot roll overboard."

"It won't do it."

In the meantime two or three more primers snap.

Hampton Roads (March to May 1862)

"How long will it take to get the shot out of that gun?"

"Can't tell, perhaps 15 minutes" & we hauled off, as the papers say, "to let our guns cool."

We were soon ready for her again as the order from Capt. W. indicated. "Port bow close aboard, load & fire as fast as possible."

"A splendid shot, you raked them there."

"Look out now they're going to run us down, give them both guns."

This was the critical moment, one that I had feared from the beginning of the fight. If she could so easily pierce the heavy oak beams of the *Cumberland*, she surely could go through the 1/2 inch iron plate of our lower hull. A moment of terrible suspense, a heavy jar nearly throwing us from our feet, a rapid glance to detect the expected gush of water. She had failed to reach us below the water & we were safe.

The sounds of the conflict at this time were terrible. The rapid firing of our own guns amid the clouds of smoke, the howling of the *Minnesota*'s shells, which was firing whole broadsides at a time just over our heads (two of her shot struck us), mingled with the crash of solid shot against our sides & the bursting of shells all around us. Two men had been sent down from the turret who were knocked senseless by balls striking the outside of the turret while they happened to be in contact with the inside.

At this time a heavy shell struck the pilot house. I was standing near, waiting an order, heard the report which was unusually heavy, a flash of light & a cloud of smoke filled the house. I noticed the Capt. stagger & put his hands to his eyes. I ran up to him & asked if he was hurt. "My eyes," says he, "I am blind." With the assistance of the Surgeon I got him down & called Lieut. Greene from the turret. A number of us collected around him. The blood was running from his face, which was blackened with the powder smoke. He said, "Gentlemen, I leave it with you. Do what you think best. I cannot see, but do not mind me. Save the *Minnesota* if you can."

The quartermaster at the wheel*, as soon as Capt. W. was hurt, had turned from our antagonist & we were now some distance from her. We held a hurried consultation & "*fight*" was the unanimous voice of all. Lieut. Greene took Capt. W.'s position & our bow was again pointed for the *Merrimac*. As we neared her she seemed inclined to haul off & after a few more guns on each side, Mr. Greene gave the order to stop firing as she was out of range & hauling off. We did not pursue as we were anxious to relieve Capt. W. & have more done for him than could be done aboard. Our iron hatches were slid back & we sprang out on deck which was strewn with fragments of the fight. Our foe gave us a shell as a parting fire which shrieked just above our heads & exploded about 100 feet beyond us.

In a few minutes we were surrounded by small steamers & boats from Newport News, the Fortress, the various men of war, all eager to learn the

---

* Peter Williams*.

extent of our injuries & congratulate us on our victory. They told us of the intense anxiety with [which] the conflict was witnessed by thousands of spectators from the shipping & from the shore & their astonishment was no less on learning that though we were somewhat marked we were uninjured & ready to open the fight again.

The Merrimac had a black flag flying during the fight. This was the Commodore's flag. She was crowded with men, accounts varied in number, some placing it as high as 400 & from that down to 200.

The battle commenced at 1/2 past 8 A.M. & we fired the last gun at 10 minutes past 12 M.

Capt. W. was taken off in a tug boat, in charge of an acquaintance to go to Washington. Our Stewards went immediately to work & at our usual dinner hour the meal was on the table, much to the astonishment of visitors who came expecting to see a list of killed & wounded & a disabled vessel, instead of which was a merry party around the table enjoying some good beef steak, green peas, &c.

"Well, gentleman," says Sec'y Fox[*], "you don't look as though you was just through one of the greatest naval conflicts on record."

"No Sir," says Lieut. Greene, "we havn't done much fighting, merely drilling the men at the guns a little."

Never was a set of men more completely sold than those on board the *Merrimac*. She came out in the morning evidently expecting to find an easy prey in the *Minnesota* without any idea of finding a new antagonist. At first she would scarcely condescend to notice us till we gave her a taste of our quality from our 11 inch Dahlgrens, when she replied with grape & canister, probably thinking that would demolish her puny looking foe.

I believe I have already told you the compliments paid us by Gen. Wool[†] & Sec'y Fox. All regarded us as their deliverers nor doubt could the rebels have succeeded in their designs it would have been a disastrous thing for the country. They could have destroyed & driven off the shipping in the harbour, shelled out the Rip Raps[‡], & Fortress Munroe itself would have been at their mercy as Gen. Wool afterward told us. The[y] would have attacked Gen. Mansfield's[§] army at Newport News in front while Magruder[**] took them in the rear. This & still more extensive plans of operations had been laid by them when our appearance blocked the game.

---

[*] The Assistant Secretary of the Navy had come down to Hampton Roads to witness the battle.
[†] John E. Wool, the 78-year-old commander of the Department of Virginia. His headquarters were at Fort Monroe.
[‡] The Union-controlled fortified man-made island in Hampton Roads, one mile from Fort Monroe.
[§] Joseph J. K. Mansfield, brigadier general in the Department of Virginia in command at Newport News.
[**] Confederate Major General John B. Magruder.

Hampton Roads (March to May 1862)

The night after the fight I stood watch for one of the officers who I thought needed rest more than I did till 12 o'clock when I turned in & had the first sleep for three nights.

The night we arrived I was on deck & witnessed the explosion of the burning *Congress*, a scene of the most terrible magnificence. She was wrapped in one sheet of flame, when suddenly a volcano seemed to open instantaneously, almost beneath our feet, & a vast column of flame & fire shot forth till it seemed to pierce the skies. Pieces of burning timbers, exploding shells, huge fragments of the wreck, grenades & rockets filled the air & fell sparkling & hissing in all directions. It did not flash up & vanish in an instant, but seemed to remain for a moment or two, an immense column of fire, one end on the earth the other in the heavens. It soon vanished & a dense thick cloud of smoke hid every thing from view. We were about two miles from the wreck & the dull heavy explosion seemed almost to lift us out of the water.

I think we get more credit for the mere fight than we deserve, any one could fight behind an impenetrable armour — many have fought as well behind wooden walls or behind none at all. The credit, if any is due, is in daring to undertake the trip & go into the fight, in an untried experiment & in our unprepared condition. We were all exhausted before the fight commenced, for want of food & rest. The men had never been drilled at the guns & were not prepared to act in concert. We were unacquainted with our own powers, offensive & defensive & knew nothing of our antagonist except the terrible exhibition of her destructive powers given the previous day. Before we left Brooklyn we heard every kind of derisive epithet applied to our vessel. She was called a "silly experiment," an "iron coffin for her crew" & we were styled fool hardy for daring to make the trip in her, & this too by naval men. But we did dare & we have won & what is more none of us were ordered to the vessel till we had expressed our willingness to go, or in other words we volunteered.

We have had a letter from Capt. Worden's wife. She says that he is very weak & nervous, but the doctors say he will recover his sight, though he may be confined for some time. The old quarter master [Williams] who had the wheel by his side has been promoted to a master's mate. It would take a man of more than ordinary nerve to look steadily & cooly into the muzzle of a ten inch rifled gun & see it loaded, trained & fired within 15 feet of his head. He did it without any apparent emotion, cooly saying to Capt. W., "take care, sir, they are going to try us now."

The day after the fight the English war steamer *Rinaldo* came in, & her Capt. went ashore. When in conversation with Gen. Wool he first noticed the *Monitor* & enquired of the Gen. if that was a machine for raising wrecks. No says the Gen. "that is for making them!"

Civil War Years: USS *Monitor* (1862)

Sunday March 25—We have been overrun with visitors to day. Among others Gen. Van Vliet* & Gen. Heintzleman† & Staff & _lady_, the first one I have seen since I left Brooklyn. Yesterday we were visited by Prince de Joinville‡, son of Louis Philippe. We have also rec'd a letter from Sec'y Welles§ covering the thanks of Congress to officers & crew. Fifteen more steamboats arrived this afternoon crowded with soldiers. Each in turn steamed around us & gave us three cheers, their bands striking up some of our favourite airs. "Onward to Richmond" I think will soon commence from this point, taking Norfolk in the way. I hope we may be "counted in."

Your letter mailed the 18th I rec'd yesterday the 22nd. It was the first I had had since the 4th & I began to think I had been forgotten. The great event of the day is the arrival of the boat with our mail & you cannot imagine how eagerly letters are devoured. Don't fail to write often.

[No signature]

[Marginalia] I fear this will scarcely be intelligible. It has been written while listening to discussions & conversations — sense & nonsense more distracting to me than the *Merrimac*'s guns. If read to any out of the family you must apologise. I send lots of love & kisses to you all. Direct to Hampton Roads instead of Fortress Munroe.

U.S. Steamer *Monitor*
Off Fortress Munroe
March 11th, 1862

Dear Anna,

I am full of business & have no time to write in detail. I want to say that I am well & to request you to direct my letters to Fortress Munroe, Va., as I shall get them much sooner.

For the first time I have been ashore & have just ret'd. You cannot conceive of the feeling there. The *Monitor* is on every one's tongue & the expressions of gratitude & joy are varied as they are so numerous. Says one gentleman to me after taking me by the hand & inquiring if I "was from the *Monitor*." "My insurance is worth $2000. You can draw on me at any time for that amount & it shall be honoured." It was told from one to another as I passed along, "he's an officer from the *Monitor*" & they looked at me as if I was some strange being. At the store where I went to get fresh provisions for the crew the gentleman told me, "Tell your ward room officers to come and

---

* Stewart L. Van Vliet, chief quartermaster of the Army of the Potomac.
† Samuel P. Heintzelman, commander of the III Corps of the Army of the Potomac.
‡ François d'Orléans, third son of the King of France Louis Philippe and a vice-admiral in the French Navy in the 1840s. At the start of the Civil War he came to America and offered his services to President Lincoln, serving on McClellan's staff during the Peninsula Campaign.
§ Secretary of the Navy Gideon Welles.

see me whenever they come ashore. I have first rate quarters & they are allways welcome without expense. The safety of all I have is due to them."*

At the close of the action our deck was covered with fragments of shell. I enclose a few small pieces to Henry in a paper. How anxious you must all have been when the telegraph first brought you news of the terrible conflict.

We shall remain here as *guardians of Fortress Munroe* & the small amount of shipping which will remain in harbour. All have been ordered off in apprehension of the reappearance of the *Merrimac*. We shall remain here to meet her. We are *ready, willing* & *anxious* for another interview.

We are now commanded by Lieut. Selfridge† from the sunken frigate *Cumberland*. His description of the fight as we were at the supper table last night was intensely interesting. 130 men were lost.

Yesterday I had the pleasure of shaking hands with Gen. Wool, who came aboard with his staff (Mr. Cannon‡ was not with them). As he was about leaving he turned to us (the officers) who stood in a group & taking off his hat said, "gentlemen you have made heroes of yourselves." Asst. Sec'y Fox also paid us a visit. The officers were called together to be introduced & he said while shaking hands, "gentlemen I want you to remember that millions [of dollars] of property is entrusted to your care."

During the action I acted as aid to Capt. Worden, conveying his orders to different parts of the vessel & although I played a humble part I had all [I] could do, but I did it well I know, for I had both Capt. Worden's & Lieut. Greene's emphatic declarations to that effect. I am writing a detailed account of the whole thing which I will send home as soon as complete.§

With the kindest love to yourself, the children & all friends.

William

[Marginalia] We think the *Merrimac* left us in a sinking condition. If that be the case it will be some time, if ever, before we see her again. Write me as often as possible. You have no idea how anxious I am to hear from you all.

Iron Clad Battery *Monitor*
Off Sewal's Point
March 13th, 1862

My Dear Wife & Children,

Your threefold welcome letters of March 4th reached me via the N.Y. Navy Yard this morning & you cannot imagine the pleasure with which they were read. The events of a life time seem crowded into the last few days & I

---

* Keeler's soon-to-be-friend William H. Kimberly*, owner of a provision store at Old Point Comfort.
† Thomas O. Selfridge, Jr.*
‡ Le Grand B. Cannon*, Wool's chief-of-staff and a relation of Keeler's by marriage.
§ The letter dated March 6.

can hardly convince myself at times that the past week has not been an exciting ~~shell~~ (they are talking about shell in the cabin) dream.

We are now at anchor right off Sewall's Point within easy range of their guns but they do not seem disposed to notice us. What little shipping has dared to remain, lie below us under the guns of Fortress Munroe & the Ripraps, while singly & alone we lie much further up the stream, a Monitor to the rebel batteries & boats.

Our steam is kept up day & night & a most vigilant watch is maintained that our old foe do[es] not attack us unawares. Yesterday we had got as far as soup in our dinner programe when "the *Merrimac* is coming" was reported. Dinner of course was soon done, our cable was slipped & in just three minutes we were steaming up to Craney island.* We took a nice turn up that way to give the rebels a good view of us, but "nary" *Merrimac* did we see & returned to our anchorage with good appetites for supper.

Commodore Goldsborough† was on board yesterday & complimented us very handsomely. To day we had a note from Gen. Wool inviting the officers to dine with him & his staff any day we would name as most convenient. Of course we were obliged to decline for the present, as the orders are that none shall go ashore from our vessel except on the most urgent business as everyone must be in his place should our *friend* make his appearance. It seems hard that we should be cooped up here so closely, but it shews the importance they attach to our service. I have been ashore but once & then I thought folks would devour me before I could get away.

I have not the least idea that the *Merrimac* will make her appearance for some time to come. We all think she was so badly injured that many repairs will be needed before she will be fit for another fight.

In the meantime we are making some slight repairs ourselves, particularly in the pilot house, which proved, as I thought, to be the weakest & I might say the only vulnerable spot about us. As soon as they are completed should the *Merrimac* not be on hand I think we will make a search for her & beard the lion in his den. My greatest aspiration now is that we may be the ones to take or sink her & if we ever meet again we will not part till one or the other succumbs. We are being furnished with every possible instrument of destruction which it is supposed can be of service to us — shot, shell, schrapnell, hand grenades, & wrought iron shot, which we now have permission to use, besides Enfield rifles with sword bayonets & plenty of small arms. We have gained a reputation we do not mean to lose.

The day after the fight Asst. Sec'y Fox sent a commission on board to get the name & rank of each officer with the post he occupied during the fight

---

* The Confederate-controlled fortified island near the entrance to the Elizabeth River.
† Louis M. Goldsborough, the corpulent commander of the North Atlantic Blockading Squadron.

Hampton Roads (March to May 1862)

& the manner in which he performed his duties. As the report was given me to copy I am able to say what mention was made of the Paymaster. "Acting Asst. Paymaster W. F. Keeler, acted as aid to Capt. Worden, carrying the orders between the pilot house & the turret, giving them always in a cool distinct manner that added greatly to the complete understanding between these two important positions." This report is to be laid before a cabinet meeting, for what purpose of course I can't say.

The proudest moment of my life I believe was when Gen. Wool & his staff visited us the day after the fight. The officers were all called around him & introduced. Lifting his hat to us he said, "gentlemen, you have made heroes of yourselves." Asst. Sec'y Fox, who also came on board, as he was leaving turned to us & said, "gentlemen, I want you to remember that millions of [dollars of] property are entrusted to your care." Are not these things to make one feel vain? You can appreciate these enconiums [ecomiums] from such sources & understand my feelings at such a moment.

Col. Cannon was with the General's staff. I introduced myself & was very cordially received & invited to visit headquarters whenever I had an opportunity & I would be furnished with passes to go whenever I desired. We were also visited by Gen. Mansfield & staff & by any quan[ti]ty of foreign nobles, counts, &c who are serving in our army. Among them quite a number of Swedes, who being countrymen of Capt. Ericsson's, naturaly feel a pride in his invention & its triumphant success.

Yesterday on our return from our search for the *Merrimac* we passed along close to Newport News. The whole army came out to see us. Thousands & thousands lined the shore, covered the vessels at the docks & filled the rigging. Their cheers resembled one continuous roar. Each regiment had its band, the nearest of which as we approached struck up "See the conquering Hero comes," then the "Star Spangled Banner," & so it passed from one band to another as we slowly steamed along in front of them. All our national airs were given when a lull in the tumultuous cheering would allow them to be heard. It was laughable to hear the great variety of names applied to us by the soldiers, for we passed so near we could readily converse. Says one, "You're the boys," another "Bully for you," "No sand bag batteries there," "You're our saviours," "Iron sides & iron hearts," "No back down to you," "You're trumps every one," &c &c &c.

I sent by Col. Cannon the end of an exploded shell I picked up off our deck at the close of the fight to Pres't Lincoln "with the respects of the officers of the *Monitor*." Our deck was covered with fragments of shattered shells of which I have kept a small box full as mementoes. While I was gathering them up one of the *Merrimac*'s shells went about 20 feet over my head, bursting about 100 feet beyond me. One of the men who had been working the guns, touching his hat, said very cooly, "Paymaster, there's some more pieces." I confess I looked rather anxiously to see if any more were coming. I saw two shells to day while I was standing on deck, thrown from the big gun at the Rip raps to Sewall's point just abreast our ship, one striking in the sand & exploding close in front of the rebel batteries, the other passing over them & exploding in the water.

The English war steamer *Rinaldo* came into the harbor the day after the fight & before her Captain had ascertained our character he went ashore & saw Gen. Wool. In a conversation with the Gen. he asked what kind of a machine they had out there, pointing to the *Monitor*, & asked if it was for raising wrecks. "No," says the Gen., "that is not for raising wrecks, it is for making them."

Government has chartered a little tiny steamboat for a tender for us, to run around the bay on errands, go after our mail in the morning, for fresh provisions &c. I only wish they would let us go ashore in her once in a while.

Now that you have heard of our arrival I think you need no longer feel any anxiety as to the danger of our being sunk at sea, though when you get my a/c which I am going to send home as soon as I get time to write it[*], you will see that your apprehensions were well founded, for a time we thought we should have to give up the ship. That however is now all past & our safe arrival here has been *reported* to the country. I suppose the realities of the dangers we have passed through are not half as dreadful as those your imagination conjured up. I would rather go through the same thing every week for a year than take another ride in Carter's infernal machine[†] — I never think, "horse," without a shudder.

You all seem to make quite merry of my experiences in linen sheets. I expected to enlist your warmest sympathies & not to be quite so cooly treated. Never mind, my turn to laugh may come next. You see your suggestions as to heating by steam were anticipated. It has made our ward room quite comfortable, though since we have been here we have hardly needed it. It seems Dave's prophecy in regard to the *Merrimac* has proved true. We have partly accomplished the task he assigned us and hope to complete it before long. I feared she [the *Monitor*] might be a failure, but hoped not, that we might "find a foeman worthy of our steel,"[‡] & she is, there is no denying that.

You want to know how we light the vessel. Well I will tell you. In the ceiling of my state room is a hole about six inches in diameter into which is fitted a thick heavy glass set in an iron frame, which opens downward on a hinge to give air & ventilation in warm weather. It closes with a screw water tight, the cup above this formed by the thickness of the deck is often full of water, but none of it comes into the room, neither does it seem to diminish the quantity of light. When the sun shines bright it is sufficiently light to read

---

[*] Keeler is referring to his long letter of March 6 which was not completed until March 25.
[†] An invention perhaps of his friend in La Salle, Samuel B. Carter, who aspired to become a civil engineer and railway man.
[‡] Sir Walter Scott's *The Lady of the Lake* (1810).

and write without difficulty but in cloudy thick weather I have to burn a candle, but it is always light enough for all other purposes. Into this hole a heavy iron plug is placed every night to be ready in case of a sudden attack & this is always kept in in action. Our iron hatches are placed on every night & the most vigilant watch is kept that we may not be taken unawares nor our *friend* slip by unnoticed. Each state room is lighted in the way I have described. Over the dining table in the ward room are three or four such lights which are sufficient in bright clear days.

As to our manner of living, one day will answer for all now that the excitement is over and things are settling down to one monotonous round. The first thing I hear in the morning about day light is the Bo'sun's whistle & "all hands up hammocks." As "all hands" don't refer to me, I roll over & take another nap till my boy comes in to leave my boots & tell me "'tis half past 7 sir." He has previously taken the iron plug out of my deck light & let in a glimpse of day.

I dress & get ready & at just 8 breakfast is ready. No one is in a hurry, so that usually occupies an hour when all hands are mustered to quarters, that is each one takes the position assigned him in action & upon being questioned in turn relates the particular duty devolving upon him. Then the turret division (those who fight the guns) are drilled for an hour or so.

The Surgeon & Paymaster, who are the drones, as we have no watch duties to perform, pass our time as we see fit. I find considerable writing to do & shall till I get fairly posted in all the details of my work. The Dr., whose room joins mine, bores me to death by wanting to read me all his correspondence with his lady love & the newspapers, in which of course I take no special interest. But he is a good, genial, warm hearted fellow & I humour him when I am not too busy.

Dinner at two. We have a regular course, soup, fish, meats, puddings, fruits & nuts, winding up with a cup of strong coffee. This takes an hour or an hour & a half. Then those who choose take a cigar on deck.

Supper at six which is usually bread & butter, dried beef, cheese, crackers, coffee & tea.

------ An excitement, 11 o'clock at night, dark & foggy, cant see two feet, must go on deck & see what's up. The *Merrimac*'s coming. All hands turned out & prepare to go to quarters. It has turned out to be as we think a boat full of rebel deserters crossing over to our side when they were fired at by the batteries on Sewall's point just abreast of us. Blue lights were burned & canon fired apparently to no purpose. So we'll return to every day life.

At 7 o'clock the bo'sn's whistle again & all hands down hammocks. In the evening all gather around the ward room table & "fight their battles o'er again," each one relating his individual experience, stories are told & jokes cracked, till 10 when all on board must be quiet & still. It is usual on men of war to have all lights extinguished at 10 but this is not enforced in our case

— we appear to be an exception to ordinary men of war. Card playing is prohibited in the Navy, so we have none of that.

In this manner I suppose day after day will pass with us, with but little variation. Still we are all hoping to be sent up to Norfolk before long.

Tell Father we have 59 souls on board, all told. Stories vary as to the number the *Merrimac* had on board the day of the fight, none put less than 200 & from that to 800. In the next paper Hen gets he will find some of the splinters from our deck torn up by the *Merrimac*'s shell. I sent him some pieces of shells a few days since in a paper & hope they reached him. I have a nice piece of one I am going to send to Mr. Lovejoy at Washington.

Leslie's pictorial of the 22nd has a picture of the fight. If I can get one I will send it to you. It is not entirely correct, still it is about as near as they ever get. It is laughable to hear how the newspaper accounts vary. Some are entirely false, some simply ridiculous, some nonsensical & a few in the main correct. One statement I want to correct, that is our hauling off an hour to allow our guns to cool. We were obliged to stop firing twice for a few minutes at a time to get shot up in the turret & also when Capt. Worden was hurt, when a little confusion ensued in the changing around of men to fill other places. These are the only times when our firing ceased & for the reasons mentioned. In the next fight I am partly promised a better position, one in the turret, having charge of the machinery which turns the tower.

We have one splendid man on board, Alban C. Stimers, Chief Engineer of the Navy. He was ordered to the vessel to report the effect of shot upon us. He worked the whole time as cool as a cucumber. In fact it is hard to make any distinction when all did well.

We have had a number of changes since the fight. After Capt. Worden was hurt Mr. Green, our first Lieut., was ordered to take command. The next day Lieutenant Selfridge was ordered to command us. He staid three days when Lieut. Jeffards [Jeffers]* was sent on board. He will probably remain, at least till Capt. Worden is able to take command again. Lieut. Jeffards has been in most of the fights along the coast & it is very interesting as we sit at the table to hear him give his experience[s] in the different fights. Some of them he sets out in a very amusing light.

But if I keep on I shall use up all the writing now & have nothing left to fill future sheets. I shall try & answer Henry's letter soon, as well as Fan's note. Tell Mrs. Hough I sympathise with her in all her troubles real & imaginary. How I long to get your next letter to see what you all say at home about the fight. Remember me to Mr. & Mrs. Rockwell, Mr. & Mrs. Sisson† & especially to Mr. & Mrs. Hough, as well as all other friends. From what all tell us here our services have not been overestimated. I hope spring will shew himself in your region soon. The winter must have been a long & dreary one

---

* William N. Jeffers*.

† Edward Sisson, a soap manufacturer on the Steamboat Basin in La Salle.

to you. I would like to dig a little while in the garden. How I want to see you all. When shall we meet again? Good night & my best kiss to yourself & the dear children.

William

[Marginalia] We fired 41 shots during the action — *shooting over three & a half tons of iron. Let Mrs. Chapin do the sewing & you do the writing by all means.*

U.S. Steam Battery Monitor
Hampton Roads
March 18, 1862

Dear Anna,

I cannot resist the temptation of chatting awhile with you this evening though I do not know that I have much to say that will be new or interesting.

There is but little use to attempt to send news by mail for you are sure to be headed off by telegraph. Movements here indicate a gathering storm, but in what part of rebeldom it will burst is more than I can tell. Since morning no less than 13 vessels have arrived here loaded with mules & the cry is still they come. Large steamers are also coming in with troops & it is reported that 65,000 are to be landed here.* It is very evident that Gen. Wool is about making an important movement. Before you read this the telegraph may inform you that an advance has been made on Yorktown & Norfolk. When that comes about we hope to have a hand in.

Mechanics are at work on us day & night fixing & strengthening our pilot house which without doubt was our weakest point. When that is done we hope to have the fun of shelling out Sewall's Point. I say fun, for such it will be to destroy that plague spot just under the nose of Fortress Munroe, though I think if it is let alone for a short time, it will be evacuated, if it is not already.

It is realy amusing to listen to the great variety of ingenious expedients said to emanate from the rebels to destroy or capture us. The latest was in a letter read to us at dinner to day by our Captain (Jeffers). They proposed to take a long stout chain, make each end fast to a steamboat, the steamboats to separate as far as the chain would admit, in which way they would come upon us, a boat on each side. The chain would catch across our turret & in this manner they would bear us in triumph to Norfolk. The letter was rec'd by Gen. Mansfield & by him sent to Gen. Wool with the remark that he considered the source reliable. Gen. Wool turned it over to Com. Goldsborough, who refered it to our Captain. We unanimously voted it a capital thing & hoped they would make the attempt.

We fear being boarded more than anything else by large bodies of men in small boats or fast steam boats in some thick dark night. Every precaution is taken to prevent it. Our iron hatches are put on every night & a vigilant watch

---

* These were the first arrivals of McClellan's troops.

is maintained. In case of an attempt to board, our watch will retreat to the top of the turret where the hatch is open, draw up the ladder & retreat inside where an abundance of hand grenades is always in readiness. Then on an agreed signal the men of war whose guns will reach us will sweep our decks with grape & canister. All these things are duly discussed at our table.

Chief Engineer Stimers & Capt. Jeffers are both men of scientific attainments, well educated & intelligent. Capt. Jeffers is said to be one of the best ordnance officers in the navy. The discussions between them is often very interesting. Ordnance, all kinds of projectiles, the build & shape of ships, & strength of materials are all brought in, interspersed with various incidents of the war, of which Capt. J. has seen a good deal, having just ret'd from Hatteras inlet.

We have had a number of changes since the fight. After Capt. Worden was hurt, Mr. Green, our Lieut., was ordered to take command till relieved. The next day Lieut. Selfridge, 2nd Lieut. of the sunken *Cumberland*, was ordered to take command. Then when the Commodore returned* he ordered Lieut. Jeffers, our present Captain, to take charge. Lieutenants Selfridge & Jeffers, though energetic thorough seamen & able commanders, still lacked that noble kindness of heart & quiet unassuming manner to both officers & men which endeared Capt. Worden to all on board. He was nearly worshiped by us all. That he was a lion in the fight is known wherever a news paper finds its way.

I send you his (Worden's) autograph & one of *another distinguished* officer of the *Monitor*, which you will find at the end of the letter. Our autographs are getting to be valuable, we have almost daily applications for them. I had another of Capt. Worden's which I was going to send to Mrs. Hough but have mislaid it. Will send it the next time I write. The last request of the kind was from Dr. Rawlings†, the correspondent of some of the N.Y. papers. I got quite well acquainted with him. He is a very entertaining funny fellow.

We are perfectly over-run with visitors. So many were coming that orders were issued that no one would be allowed on board unless by special invitation of one of the officers.

I suppose you have seen a short letter from me in the *Sci. American*.‡ I formed the acquaintance of Mr. Wales before I left N.Y. He was quite anxious I should write to him. His paper contains the only good representation of our boat I have seen. I send Henry *Harper's Weekly*. The picture of Capt. Worden is not at all good though it looks some like him.

---

* Goldsborough had been overseeing naval operations in the North Carolina Sounds when the Battle of Hampton Roads took place and only returned on March 13.
† Augustus Rawlings, a 29-year old English-born medical doctor who was formerly an artist for *Frank Leslie's Illustrated Magazine*.
‡ *Scientific American* (March 22, 1862, Vol. 6, No. 12, p. 181). Keeler's short letter describes the effect of the *Virginia*'s shot on the *Monitor*. See Appendix A.

Hampton Roads (March to May 1862)

Sunday, the naval committee from Congress made us a visit. The only striking thing about them was they were not dressed in uniform. Everything you see here is epauletts, shoulder strap, buttons & swords.

I do so long to hear from home. The last letter rec'd was dated the 4th. I know you must have written but suppose they have not reached me yet, but I shall get them. I expected to have rec'd letters from all my LaSalle friends male & female congratulating their distinguished fellow citizen of *Monitor* renown &c &c but begin to fear that I shall be disappointed. Remember me to all who enquire. Tell Mr. Hough that I sent Mr. Lovejoy a piece of shell picked up from our deck after the fight as a memento.

My letters must be a confused, jumbled up, disconnected mass of almost nonsense. I hope you polish them up before reading them to others. Every word spoken in the ward room or in any other of the state rooms is distinctly heard by me & when the officers are discussing some interesting subject, as they are just now, it is impossible to keep my thoughts from wandering. You will probably find many repetitions in my letters from time to time as I cannot always remember when writing what I touched upon in my last. If I could go ashore occasionally I should have something to say but now it is difficult to find anything to write about.

Remember me to Father, Mother & all friends. Tell Henry I send him papers very often & that he must write to me. A kiss & lots of love to yourself & the children.

William F. Keeler
(the autograph)

Iron Clad *Monitor*
Hampton Roads
March 26th, 1862

Dear Anna,

Little if anything new has turned up since I last wrote you that is of itself interesting. Troops in large bodies are continually arriving. Some fifty thousand are here now and one hundred thousand more are to come. Important movements are on the tapis, of which we on board here are well posted—much better than the troops themselves—but we are strictly forbidden to communicate what we may know to others. There is no danger of our transgressing orally, inasmuch as we are never allowed to go ashore to find confidants for our dangerous secrets & as to commiting them to paper, that is not to be thought of when implicit obedience is paramount to every thing else. Sec'ys of the War & Navy, Generals, Cols., Commodores & all intermediate ranks & grades assemble in our cabins to discuss the pros & cons & every word is distinctly heard in all our state rooms, so that we become possessed of knowledge which would send some of our editors to Fort Lafayette* if they were so indiscreet as to publish it.

Yesterday, the artist of *Harper's Weekly* spent the day on board & took sketches of the *Monitor*, inside & out, cabins & cook room, with the likeness of each of the officers. This is to be prepared to issue immediately after our next fight, with the likeness of such of us as are so fortunate as to distinguish ourselves. Nothing like taking time by the forelock. How the Paymaster would look as the figure head for Harper's W*ea*kly. Commodore Goldsborough was on board to day & told us we must be in readiness for another fight at anytime.

I thought at one time that Melzar might possibly be among the troops arriving here but I learned that none of Gen. Banks' command are to be brought here. I am inclined to think that he has taken part in the recent fight at Winchester [Kernstown].† I feel anxious to hear from there.

I have pretty much done writing letters to any one but you. I have written to a number of my friends since I have been here but have had no reply & even your letters are like angels' visits — few & far between but ever welcome.

Things don't go as smoothly & pleasantly on board as when we had Capt. Worden. Our new Capt. [Jeffers] is a rigid disciplinarian, of quick imperious temper & domineering disposition. But he is one of the best ordnance officers in the service, of undoubted courage, cool & calculating in action, well fitted for the command of a vessel like ours that is to lead the van. I have nothing to do with the working or management of the vessel & so am not brought into so close contact with him, but I have heard him talk to some of the officers as I should not want anyone to talk to me. My business is more particularly with the Department who I suppose will inform me when I am in error. So far I have got along smoothly enough with Capt. Jeffers but I am expecting every day that I may forget to touch my hat, or give him the deck in passing, or greviously offend him in some little point of etiquette, when I shall get a blast. I keep my seat next to him at the table but do not find it as pleasant as when Capt. Worden filled his place.

For the gratification of my inquisitive friends I will say here that I rank as Paymaster, nothing more, nothing less. In the navy a Paymaster is a Paymaster, a Captain is a Captain & a cook, a cook, just as much as a shoemaker in civil life is a shoemaker. As to other officers whom I rank with, my copy of "General Orders" says "Paymasters of more than 12 years will rank with Commanders. Paymasters of less than 12 years will rank with Lieutenants."

---

* The fort in New York Harbor where political prisoners were kept.
† The Battle of Kernstown (March 23), the opening salvo of Stonewall Jackson's Shenandoah Valley Campaign. On March 22 Melzar's regiment had been sent east to reinforce McClellan, but was ordered back to the Shenandoah Valley after the battle to guard against a possible backdoor strike on Washington by Jackson.

HAMPTON ROADS (MARCH TO MAY 1862)

This is verbatim & hope it will prove entirely satisfactory. My rank brings me on an equality with Lieut. Greene, except that being the executive officer of the ship he has the precedence.

Thursday evening, 27th. The fearful calamity which we have all thought possible, but not at all probable & which in your last letter you hoped would not happen, has at last taken place — we were carried by boarders to day & for a time our ship was completely in their possession. The matter has been carefully kept from all the reporters, so that this will in all probability be the first intimation you will have of another exciting scene on our gallant little craft. I trust you will be careful that this does not find its way in print. Ever since the fight our precautions against a surprise have been increasing & we hoped effectual. This I suppose gave us a feeling of security which at last proved fatal. What is more astonishing, it took place in broad daylight, with numerous vessels lying on all sides of us, our steam tender along side, the officer of the deck pacing his usual rounds, a vigilant old quartermaster was at his station on the top of the turret, a spy glass in hand, with a liberal supply of hand grenades prepared for instant use close by. A full head of steam was up & we could have slipped our moorings in a moment & been off if we could have done nothing better. The surprise was complete.

It was just at noon when the crew were at dinner — the time selected probably for that very reason — when they made their appearance. I was talking with Capt. Jeffers in his cabin when the officer of the deck came rushing in with the announcement that they were on us — a whole boat load, close along side. The order was instantly given to prepare for boarders. The Capt. was making some hasty preparations mingled with numerous orders as I left him & hurried to my state room to prepare myself the best I could for the coming trial. Sword, revolver & all are kept in constant readiness & a moment sufficed to arm me for the emergency. As I hurried through my preparations I could not help but think of the future & I must confess that I felt a little nervous as the noises on deck increased. T'was no time now to hesitate, so with desperate energy I rushed up the steps just after the Capt. & at the first step encountered the foe armed to the teeth with --------- smiles & flowers & perfumed handkerchiefs. We all did the agreeable to the best of our ability & our fair — excuse me, female (for none of them were troubled with an excess of beauty) — boarders retreated much pleased with the attentions they received. They were Mrs. Majors & Cols. & Generals & Captains & we received many urgent invitations to call at their quarters. T'was a pleasing interruption of the present monotony of our man of war life which I hope is not to continue long. I think work is being cut out for us as soon as other preparation are complete.

A boat has just come aboard from the flag ship bringing your letter mailed the 13th via the N.Y. Navy Yard. I had to laugh when I came to where you hope I will be allowed to read it in quiet, for in the cabin were Capt. Jeffers, Engineer Stimers & one or two more discussing iron clad ships. In the Dr.'s room, from which I am separated by only a blind door, are half a dozen, alternately spouting Shakespeare, criticising the Opera, Theater, & other places not quite as reputable, while another in a room at my side is exercising his lungs by reading in a loud tone the "personals" of the *N.Y. Herald* interspersed with intended witticisms. If all that don't help one to read & understand, then I think it useless to tender any other assistance. But come to write, I think some of my letters will be curiosities, for I find it almost an impossibility to finish completely one connected train of ideas. They must sound sadly disjointed.

With your letter of the 18th [13th] I rec'd one from Uncle Brush congratulating us on our victory. How glad I was to get your letter. I felt disappointed this morning when our tender came off without one for me, as I should have had one to day, but the evening compensated for it, though it was old & I have rec'd one written since. Yes, I should like to run in & tell you all about our fight, for the tongue moves a good deal faster than a pen & is not half so troublesome to use. You see, I have no fixed regular time for writing to you, but take it along piece meal at a time as I find time & disposition & a partial lull in the *distracted elements* by which I am surrounded will admit. I am glad you can compliment the length of them if nothing else. Poor Tibbie I fear is neglected on such occasions. The best time I have is after the master at arms knocks at our state room doors proclaiming "10 o'clock, gentlemen, lights must all be out." Mine seldom goes out I notice much before 12. That's the only good quiet time I get out of the 24 hours & that is frequently broken in upon by the M.D. intruding his head to read me one of his love letters. Of course I listen patiently but advise him to marry the first thing he does on his return.

Last night an empty wine bottle came sailing over the top of the partition into my room about 12 o'clock & its crash echoed all over the ship. As I blew out the light & sailed into bed I heard Capt. J. calling to the Master at Arms to know what that noise was. Every one looked very innocent at the breakfast table this morning. The youngsters are full of tricks.

As to l[a]ying a bed I acknowledge the corn, but then I have no garden to dig & besides I have improved now that the weather is more pleasant & these pleasant mornings find me on deck at 7 o'clock. On deck, yes. I'd give a good pair of boots to tread on something besides iron—to enjoy the delightful sensation of sticking my feet in the mud again. I am tired of everlasting iron. The clank, clank, clank, while I am writing this, of the officer of the deck as he paces back & forth on the iron plates over my head, although suggestive of security, is not a good opiate.

Friday, 28th. No letter from home today. It has been a clear, warm, pleasant spring day & the harbour has presented an exciting seen [scene] as steamer after steamer came in loaded with troops. Tugs are puffing about, towing schooners, barges, canal boats, & other water craft, loaded with horses, mules, hay, army wagons, pontoon bridges, artillery & army stores, while the almost unending line of soldiers as they debark from the steamers & march for the interior look from where we lie like a long black snake creeping along the white sandy shore, their muskets glittering in the bright sunshine.

Of course with every fresh arrival of troops, & which are now almost continuous, we have fresh irruptions of visitors. We are hardly up from the breakfast table before they commence & do not cease till dark. I proposed at supper to night to get up a guide book for the *Monitor* & hand a copy to each visitor as he arrives to read after this fashion — "This is the turret, gentlemen, & is made to revolve on a central spindle by means of engines placed below the deck. It contains our armament which consists of two, eleven inch Dahlgren guns, weighing eight tons each & throwing balls of 175 pounds. It is eight inches in thickness, made of plates of the best quality of rolled iron & weighs with the guns about 150 tons. These are the marks of the *Minnesota*'s shot & here is where we were hit by a 100 lb. percussion shell from the *Merrimac*. This bruise in our side was made by her bow when she attempted to run us down, it does not affect us in the least. None of the balls on our sides hurt us at all except in appearance. [We] do not leak any more now than before the fight." This is a specimen of what the book will be, it will be copyrighted.* As soon as published you shall have a copy. The above is a very small fraction of what we all go over with 40 times a day, day after day.

This day opened by a visit from Gen. Keys† with a lot of Cols., Majors, Capts. &c &c. He was followed by Gen. Benham‡ with a train of a similar kind. Then Gen. Wool & a portion of his staff & Asst. Sec'y of War§ came on board, including Col. Cannon. You may tell Fan that I do not think the Col. is a very distinguished looking person in military dress. In the afternoon the Col. of the regiment called the Ellsworth avengers** (I can't think of his name just now) came to see us. There were about a dozen in the company. I was introduced to him & requested to shew him around the ship. He introduced me to his companions & among others Chaplain Beecher of the Long Island 1st.†† I thought I had seen him before & asked if he was a brother of Henry Ward & if his name was James. That was it he said, but he could not fix me till I reminded him of the trip of the *Samuel Russell* from California to China. We had a good chat before he left, of old times. The Col. with him

---

* Keeler was of course joking about the guide book.
† Erasmus D. Keyes, commander of the IV Corps of the Army of the Potomac.
‡ Henry W. Benham, commander of the Northern District of the Department of the South.
§ John Tucker.
** Stephen W. Stryker, colonel of the 44th New York Infantry, nicknamed the Ellsworth Avengers in honor of Elmer Ellsworth, the first Union officer killed in the Civil War.
†† James C. Beecher*, chaplain of the 67th New York Infantry. He was a half-brother of Henry Ward Beecher, the famous anti-slavery advocate, and Harriet Beecher Stowe, the author of *Uncle Tom's Cabin*. He was serving as a ship's officer in the East India trade when Keeler first met him on his trip from San Francisco to Canton, China in 1850.

told me that he made a reconoisance with his regiment to Great Bethel yesterday & the troops will occupy it to morrow. A larger body are now advancing on Yorktown.

I do not believe there is a place in the United States where we could see as many of the noted men of the country—naval, military & civil—as just where I am. Even in Washington you would have to hunt them up. But here they all center at this point.

I was ashore for a few minutes to day to get fresh provisions for the men. The soldiers were landing from the numerous steamboats & forming in large columns. They were mostly young looking men, hardy & bronzed from constant exposure, but dusty & dirty & most of them had a tired & weary look with a heavy knapsack, blanket, tent sticks strapped to their backs, canteen & tin cup slung over their shoulder & a heavy musket. I could think of nothing but a lot of overloaded pack horses as they passed along with their shoulders stooping under their loads. Their clothing in many cases was getting ragged & shoes down at the heel & out at the toes. They hadn't that lively air & mien & the military gait you see in soldiers on parade. Some of them looked thin, pale & sickly notwithstanding their bronzed cheeks. My heart realy ached for some of the poor fellows. They looked as though they should be at home under the kind care of a wife, sister or mother. This is war in reality, divested of its paint & feathers & I must say viewed in this light it looses much of its poetry & romance.

Military & naval men of all ranks & grades covered the docks & filled the streets & buildings. Long trains of artillery were starting off with baggage wagons, camp equipage &c. In some respects it was a stirring & exciting scene. Do not infer from what I say that I think our men will not fight. On the contrary the deep seated resolution manifested in almost every countenance will overcome every obstacle as they "forward to Richmond."

The quartermaster [Williams] who had the wheel during our fight with the *Merrimac* rec'd his promotion to day as Master's Mate & well deserved it was. It increases his pay from 24 to 40 dollars per month.

We do not lack for reading matter on board, though but little besides the newspapers are read. We get the N.Y. papers of the previous day every morning in time to discuss their contents at the breakfast table. We havn't the amusement of card playing as that is forbidden on men of war.

You ask me what I think of Gen. McClelland's resignation.* I'll tell you just what I think. It was brought about by that set of miserable, gloomy, discontented, never satisfied race of disappointed politicians who are resolved to ruin because they cannot rule, of whom Alex Hitchcock† is a fit type & representative. The filth which they have been throwing at others is soiling no one but themselves. Of such things I prefer to think & judge for

---

* Keeler is presumably referring to McClellan's removal as General in Chief on March 11.
† A La Salle grain merchant and mayor of La Salle in the late 1850s.

Hampton Roads (March to May 1862)

myself. This thing of shaping your ideas to suit another's prejudices is not characteristic of an independent mind. Isn't it better to think, speak & act for yourself, even if you are wrong sometimes, than to piddle out another's crude & erroneous ideas as your own. It's no credit to any one. I regard McClelland as a man of pure, high minded & patriotic motives &, mark my word, although his enemies may for a time prevail, his name will be handed down by history without a stain. Every day brings fresh evidence that his is the controlling mind in all the important movements of the war, in many cases even to the minutest details. The sun moves on, although the reptiles who bask in his rays do sometimes croak. I knew by the tone of your letter that you had been talking with Hitchcock or some of his class. If such are to constitute the republican party I should be tempted to join hands with the South, for if they are to rule we fight for nothing.

I see even Capt. Worden has not escaped his slime because his [Hitchcock's] brother is connected with the *Chicago Times*. Many a good republican has a brother in the rebel army but is true to his country nevertheless & has the respect of [the] community. One of the heroes of the *Cumberland* [*Congress*], who fought till their guns went down with the ship, was a brother of the Commander of the *Merrimac*.* He told some of the officers during the fight, "gentlemen, you can imagine my feelings when I tell you my brother commands that ship," but he was none the less a true brave man. You see I speak rather feelingly on this subject. I speak from what I see & hear & know & do not feel disposed to favour those who stay at home & croak.

You need have no fear of my becoming tainted with pro Slavery doctrines. The more I see of the hideous deformity the more I hate it. If any of our naval men are of that way of thinking they have the good sense to keep it to themselves. They are enough of gentlemen not to intrude sentiments they know are distasteful & odious to the companions they associate with. Capt. Worden is not a pro Slavery man, I *know* from his own lips. But enough of this. When I change it will be for a good reason & you will know it.†

It is amusing to see the cool, matter of fact, business way in which the naval men (in the regular service) view this contest. Capt. Jeffers has been with the Burnside‡ expedition at Hatteras. He has a peculiar manner of telling a story which few possess — an easy, fluent talker, a jolly, devil may care kind of way & a man of fine acquirements. He does most of the talking at the table & it is laughable as well as interesting to hear him at times.

Saturday Morning, 29th—Our mail has just come on board bringing yours of the 22nd (mailed at that time). Notwithstanding you seemed to think it so

---

* McKean Buchanan, paymaster on the USS *Congress* and older brother of Franklin Buchanan who commanded the *Virginia* on the first day of the Battle of Hampton Roads.
† It is unclear what Keeler is referring to here. However, it would not have been a change in his views on slavery, which were rock solid.
‡ Ambrose E. Burnside.

much trash, it was interesting to me as your letters always are. I shall not wait to reply to it but will finish my sheet & send if off.

I am glad you regarded my feelings & refused to allow any of [my] letters to be published in the [*La Salle*] *Press*. If the editors desire me for a correspondent, I would rather write an occasional letter to them than any other paper as it would be seen by more of my friends, but it would have to be done under a different state of feeling than the one at present existing. I am perfectly willing to meet them half way if they desire a reconcilli[a]tion. You may say this much to O. N.* who seems to be a kind of go between for the parties. Under no other circumstance whatever will I allow an extract, even from one of my letters, to be published in their paper.

The reports you see in the papers about the *Monitor* watching the *Merrimac* & all that is very unreliable — mere floating rumours & need give you no uneasiness. One thing, we are ready for her when she does come. What I consider the most reliable information, we rec'd this morning from one of the mechanics who is at work on our pilot house, who formerly lived in Norfolk & is well acquainted there. He says he saw two contrabands last night who came down from Norfolk yesterday. He knew them when he lived in Norfolk & believes what they tell him. One says he was a servant in the hospital when she got up there after the fight, that [he] helped to put 30 of them in coffins, that the *Merrimac* had six feet of water in her lower hold when she got up there, that we killed 14 at one shot, the ball striking one of their guns on the muzzle shattering it to fragments [and] that she had one or two large holes below her water line & a very large one in her roof. They say further that she was still in dock on Monday last. My impression is that she will not come out of her hole to attack us. We will have to follow her up if we want to fight.

[No signature]

[Marginalia] More boats with troops, music & cheering. I send Capt. Worden's autograph to Fan & Mrs. Hough.

Iron Clad *Monitor*
Hampton Roads
March 30th, 1862

Dear Anna,

Here it is evening, after a dull, dismal, gloomy Sunday, rainy, windy & rough, the sea rolling over us continually. Our deck light covers are in, hatches down & candles burning, & in this way we have been living in our submarine cellar for the last two or three days. This is a species of sea life of which it is possible for a person to get a surfeit. However we have plenty to eat, good cheerful company & try to have a contented mind, although the old

---

* Keeler's friend Orville N. Adams*, a merchant in La Salle.

Hampton Roads (March to May 1862)

flag officer (Goldsborough) gets an occasional anathema for compelling us to remain in our present unpleasant anchorage.

The fact is the Government is getting to regard the *Monitor* in pretty much the same light as an over careful house wife regards her ancient china set — too valuable to use, too useful to keep as a relic, yet anxious that all shall know what she owns & that she can use it when the occasion demands, though she fears much its beauty may be marred or its usefulness impaired. We are kept here waiting for [our] old foe while she is repairing & fitting up to meet [us] with renewed vigour. The whole harbour is filled with old hulks of steamers, all of them with orders to run into the *Merrimac* the moment she makes her appearance with a full head of steam & at their utmost speed. At the same time, although they evidently distrust our power to whip our antagonist again, they compel us to remain in constant readiness for her. They say "the moral[e] effect on the country is so great." They fear to have us attack her for fear we may be used up, when if we should be used up the consequences would be terrible. So here we are compelled to remain inactive, while as I have said our old foe is allowed quietly to use all her energies to prepare more efficiently to meet us again. If they would only let us go up the river & get the rat in his hole it would suit us exactly, much better than doing blockading duty in a diving bell.

I think you have asked me why we let her escape. In the first place, when Capt. Worden was hurt, which for a short time occasioned some confusion, we felt the want of a head, one who was willing to take the responsibility of our further movements. Of courage & willingness to continue the fight there was no want, the only fear was one of *red tape*. When after a short consultation it was decided among us to return & renew the fight (for we had retreated some distance from her in the meantime), we found after firing a few guns that she had enough & was anxious to leave. We did not know how badly she was hurt, nor did we know the extent of our own injuries. Besides, Capt. Worden needed better medical attention than we could give him on board. But more than all, our orders were to defend the *Minnesota* but not to follow up the *Merrimac*. Our first Lieut., Mr. Greene, was too young to be willing to take the responsibility of disobeying orders, however good his reasons may have been for doing so.

The pretty little stories you read in the papers of the officers adjourning occasionally to take a drink during the fight & stopping once in a while to let the guns cool & all that, although it may sound very nice & funny, is nevertheless entirely untrue. Once during the fight I opened the spirit room by order of Capt. Worden & dealt out to each man half a gill of whiskey*, & if liquor ever does good to any one & is ever useful it must be on some such occasion. The person who concocted such a yarn could have but little idea of the rigid discipline maintained on board a man of war at all times &

---

* Half a gill is two ounces.

especially during action. Our guns were fired so slowly that they did not heat. The only stoppages we made was to get nearer our foe [so] that our aim might be more sure, & twice we stopped to get shot up in the turret from below, as there is room in the turret for but a few at a time & we will always have to replenish occasionally during action.

It is well for the Commander of the *Minnesota* that the whole facts connected with his ship are not made public. They would not be much to his credit. His brother officers here seem disposed to throw a vail of charity over that day's deeds on board his vessel. But you will notice that there is but little mention made of them in the papers, except their own puffing. Her Capt. (Van Brunt) says in his report that he gave us orders to make the attack. He did no such thing. Capt. W. had his orders from a higher source (Capt. Marston*). As I have written you before I believe, as we passed close along under his side on our way to meet the *Merrimac*, in reply to Capt. Worden, he said he had decided to destroy his vessel & the scene of utter confusion & destruction that we witnessed on board is beyond description—the fright & panic was complete. Another thing which is but little known & which has been denied by some of the officers—some of her guns were spiked the evening we arrived. This we know, for one of our lieutenants was on board in the evening & not only saw the spikes in the vents of the guns but to be certain put his finger out & felt them. Even after the fight was over & the *Merrimac* moving off, he [Van Brunt] repeated his declaration that he should burn his ship if he could not get her off. It certainly is not much to Capt. Van Brunt's credit to try & detract from us, or to try & build himself up at our expense.

But of those noble fellows on board the *Cumberland* too much cannot be said. They deserve much more credit than ourselves. Her 2nd Lieut. (Selfridge) was on board of us for a day or two after the fight as commanding officer & t'would make your blood run cold to hear him describe some of the scenes he witnessed on board during that eventful day.† A Capt. of one

---

* John Marston, commander of the USS *Roanoke*. On March 8 and 9 he was the senior Navy officer at Hampton Roads since Goldsborough was still off the North Carolina coast.
† Two decades later Selfridge described the horror on board the USS *Cumberland*: "The second shell from the [*Virginia*'s] murderous 7 inch rifle burst among the crew as they were running out, destroying literally the whole crew except the powder boy . . . The captain of this gun, a splendid seaman named Kirker . . . had both arms taken off at shoulder as he was holding his handspike and guiding the gun. He passed me as he was carried below but not a grown escaped from him. . . . The dead were thrown over [to] the other side of the deck, the wounded carried below. No one flinched but went on loading and firing, taking the place of some comrade killed or wounded as they had been taught to do. But the carnage was something awful, great splinters torn from the side wounded more men than the shell. Every 1st and 2nd captains of the guns of the first division was killed or wounded, and the writer [Selfridge] with a box of cannon primers in his pocket went from gun to gun firing them as fast as the decimated crews could load them." Selfridge escaped the sinking ship by jumping through one of the gun ports. (*From an Address on the* Cumberland

of the guns of which Lieut. S. had command, lost both legs at the knee by a shell which in exploding took off one of his arms at the shoulder. After he fell he contrived to get hold of the lockstring with his remaining hand & fired his gun. "Don't mind me boys, stand by your gun to the last," he said while the ship was rapidly sinking. Epauletts & gold lace don't cover all the true brave hearts, nor do they conceal all the coward ones.

Monday evening [March 31]—It cleared off this morning & we have had a bright, clear, beautiful, still day, one of excitement, of pleasant excitement. A whole steamboat load from Washington paid us a visit & remained about two hours. There were so many that we did not have a formal introduction as is usual, nor did we seem to need one, for we were all well acquainted in a very short time—Vice President Hamlin* & lady, Senator Hale† [&] lady &, I believe, two or three daughters, Sherman of Ohio‡ & lots of others, then Gen. Wool came aboard from the Fortress. We had a jolly time I assure you.

As soon as the steamboat approached us near enough, Sen. Hale sprang on board with hat in hand exclaiming, "here I stand on the iron deck of the noblest vessel in the world." I went up to Mr. Hamlin & told him that I was attached to the *Monitor* as Paymaster & wanted to shake hands with the Vice President. He grasped my hand very cordially saying, "My dear Sir you do me honor, your country regards you with pride." By the way, he is the very last man you would pick out as Vice President of the United States. He is very "ornary" to look at, to say the least. Any amount of enthusiasm & patriotism was expended. How sincere & deep felt it was of course I do not know. But some speeches were made which, though they sounded immensely patriotic at the time, leave rather laughable recollections.

A Mr. Wall§ connected with the Navy Department in Washington introduced me to his wife, with the request that I would take charge of her for a time. As she was young, handsome & intelligent, of course I couldn't refuse. I asked her if she had been in the turret to see the guns. "Oh yes," she said, "& kissed them too. I feel as if I could kiss the deck we stand on," &, continued one of her female friends who was standing near, "I would like to kiss all who were on board during the fight if I thought they would let me." I don't know but that I should have taken advantage of this fit of enthusiasm if I hadn't thought it might by some accident have reached your ears.

I distributed among them about half a peck of old fragments of cast iron—pieces of the *Merrimac*'s shells—cut splinters of wood from our side & chipped out pieces of iron for them as mementoes of their visit, to say

---

prepared by Rear Admiral Selfridge, Jr., 1885, National Archives, Naval Record Collection of the Office of Naval Records and Library, Washington, DC).
* Hannibal Hamlin.
† John P. Hale, U.S. senator and chairman of the Committee of Naval Affairs.
‡ John Sherman, U.S. senator from Ohio.
§ William E. Wall, a clerk in the Bureau of Yards and Docks and his 25-year old wife Mary, daughter of a New York City inn keeper.

nothing of half a dozen autographs. A splendid brass band (or I could say more appropriately, silver band) accompanied them. They came on board of us & played Hail Columbia, Star Spangled Banner, Yankee Doodle, &c &c. Then Senator Hale made a complimentary speech to Gen. Wool & proposed three cheers for him which were lustily given. He then proposed three more for the "brave, gallant & victorious band of Monitors." I cannot repeat the multitude of complimentary speeches made to us individually & collectively—you would have some reason to think I was getting vain & egotistical.

One lady said to me, "you cannot think how pleased I am to stand on the deck of this ship that I have heard so much about & have felt so proud of, you have saved us all. You may think it strange I should talk so when I tell you I am from the South, but the North is right & may God protect her."

I was quite disappointed that I did not find Mr. Lovejoy & some of his family among them, but hope to see them yet before we leave here. Salutes were fired from the Fortress, the Rip Raps, Newport News & the different men of war. The party dined with Gen. Wool & then returned to Washington. How much I wished you could have been with them. Your company was all that was wanting to complete my happiness.

Steamers have been arriving with troops through the day. How many have been landed here within the last few days I do not know, but a Col. of one of the Penn. regiments stationed at Newport News told me that over one hundred thousand men have passed there within the last few days. Just before dark to night I noticed a huge balloon rearing it[s] head among the tents, trees & houses ashore. So I suppose we are to have a balloon reconoisance to morrow or as soon as the weather permits.

We still vainly watch the mouth of Elizabeth river. No *Merrimac* makes her appearance, nor in my opinion will she.* I hope we shall be allowed to leave here before we get so enveloped with red tape & old fogyism as to rust through & sink where we are. The powers that be are so exceedingly choice of us that they have made us anchor so near the mouth of the harbor that we might about as well be in New York. Two Frenchmen & a Johnny Bull† are directly in the line of our fire to Sewall's Point, & schooners, steamers & other craft envelope us on all other sides, so that it would be almost impossible to extricate ourselves in case of a sudden attack.

Never before did I so fully realise the truth of the old axiom that "large bodies move slowly" as when watching the movements of these immense bodies of troops with their vast quantities of material. It seems like an endless procession, continually arriving. They disappear as if swallowed up, but no movement is heard of. If a mountain is under the hands of the accouche[u]r‡

---

* The *Virginia* had been undergoing repairs at the Gosport Navy Yard since March 10.
† A British warship.
‡ A midwife.

HAMPTON ROADS (MARCH TO MAY 1862)

I hope something will be produced beside a mouse. We should certainly have some little mole hills to say the least.

Tell Mary Brown* that I have never instituted a very particular examination among our younger officers as to affections of the heart, but the close contiguity of our ward rooms makes me the unwilling repository of some things which lead me to suspect that most if not all of them are afflicted with a disease of that nature, though having never been troubled in that way myself I hardly know what its symptoms are. However I always make it a point to speak in terms of highest praise of all our Sucker girls†, to all the good looking young Navy and Army officers who visit us. Who knows but what some of them influenced by my glowing descriptions may take a notion to see for himself—nil desperandum.

How I wish I could set down & have a good chat with you all to night. Have you any questions to ask? I can think of lots I would like to say that I can't get on paper — the Department has'nt furnished me with enough. I can imagine our pleasant little circle in Mrs. Hough's sitting room by the side of the stove having one of our old fashioned chats. Would that be *grand*, though if I continue writing I don't know as I could find much that would be new to say. My kind remembrances to all that pleasant circle individually & collectively. I shall send off these two sheets without waiting to add to them. I shall be busy for the next few days on my quarterly reports to the Department, which will shorten my letters for a little while.

It makes me feel sad to think that baby has forgotten me. If Eddy does I will spank him when I get home. When you can have some <u>good</u> photographs taken of yourself & the children get them. Don't mind the expense if they are <u>good</u>. I think they had better be taken carte de visites. With love & kisses, yours

William

[Marginalia] Will account to Sarah for the hose entrusted to my care shortly. One of the *Merrimac*'s shells came within three feet of filling them—just one foot too many.

Iron Clad Monitor
Hampton Roads
April 3rd, 1862

Dear Anna,

This has been a bright beautiful warm day, almost summer. I have been pretty busy for the last two or three days, or rather I have tried to do something, but have had so many interruptions that I have accomplished but little. It is now evening & before going to bed, or nautically speaking, turning

---

* The 21-year-old unmarried sister of Keeler's brother-in-law from La Salle.
† Illinois girls.

in, I cannot resist the impulse of scratching off a few lines to the loved ones at home.

I rec'd a letter from your Father yesterday, congratulating me on my connection with the *Monitor* & her rising fame. He stated also that he had just rec'd a letter from you containing some portions of my letters home, which together with a letter I had written him, he had caused to be published in the *N.Y. Times*.* Of course I cannot doubt his motive—it was good—but it has caused me the *greatest uneasiness*. I have no idea what I wrote him, nor what you wrote him & do not know what parts he published. From some unexplained cause the edition of the paper containing that letter has not been seen here, though a number of copies are taken on board every day, but I tremble lest every mail should bring one. In the first place, it may contain things the publicity of which would place me in a very unpleasant predicament indeed, to say the least — & again I am now on pleasant, friendly terms with our Capt., but newspaper correspondence [correspondents] are his abhorence & a sight of this letter would bring those friendly relations to a close & make it exceedingly unpleasant for me on board. Besides, it would be most unmercifully criticised by my fellow officers, though this I should not mind so much. All others to whom I have written, I have requested them emphatically not to allow any portion of it to appear in print, but did not deem it necessary in your Father's case. Please don't send copies to any one in future unless this is made a sine qua non. Since the rec't of your Father's letter I have imagined every boat that has come alongside of us to contain a messenger from Gen. Wool desiring to see me at the Fortress.

Yesterday a large steamer came in bringing Col. Duryea's zouaves† — blue coats, red breeches, brown leather leggins, white cap with a large red tassel hanging down behind. They were an odd looking set of mortals but have the reputation of being a fine regiment of soldiers, physically & morally. More soldiers are coming but I think that the most of them are here as the Gen. [McClellan] himself came yesterday. His staff were on board of us this morning, including two of Prince de Joinville's sons. We expected the Gen. himself but he did not come with them. Three or four had ladies with them.

While we were at dinner the Quarter Master came down & reported Gen. McCleland just arrived in a *small boat*. "Well," says Capt. Jeffers, "the best goods always come in small packages." He staid with us an hour or more. We were all introduced & of course complimented. He left in the small dingy looking boat in which he arrived with only one attendant, besides two seedy looking men to row. He made the 19th General who has visited us since we have been here.

---

* The letter appears on the front page of the March 30, 1862 edition of *The New York Times*. Entitled *Interesting Particulars by one on Board the Monitor*, it contains enough information to easily identify Keeler as the author. See Appendix B.
† Hiram Duryea, lieutenant-colonel of the 5th New York Infantry.

Hampton Roads (March to May 1862)

Prince de Joinville was here in the afternoon with a few friends & I had the pleasure of shewing them about. This "doing the ship" for the numbers who daily come to see it is getting to be quite a task & most of the officers when they see a boat coming retreat to their state rooms to avoid it. Still we try & receive all with politeness & shew each what attention we can. Capt. Jeffers has given orders (jokingly) that he mus'nt be called for anything less than a Maj. Gen.

Our ship is a perfect magazine of destructive missiles. I don't believe that one ever before had such a variety, although they may have had a larger quantity. Besides the ordinary cast iron shot, shell, grape, & canister, we have been furnished with hollow wrought iron shot, hollow composition shot (made by casting brass around a 9 in. shell), schrapnell *each one of which contains 500* bullets (enough to destroy a regiment if properly exploded) & hand grenades. As if this was not enough we rec'd to day from the Department 50 "incendiary 11 in. shells" filled with an inflammable substance which, when the shell is exploded, burns for 20 minutes without the possibility of being quenched. Capt. Jeffers told the officer who brought them that he didn't object to killing all he could in the old fashion way, but this stewing, frying, & burning human beings seemed to him rather barbarous, but as the Department had ordered it he supposed he would be obliged to use them. They will be a terrible thing if we can manage to get one in the *Merrimac*.

One of Gen. McCleland's aids told me that the army would begin to move tomorrow morning. So if nothing happens you may look for news before long & there are indications also that we shall act a part in the great drama approaching. Let me say here lest I may forget it, that if you hear of our being in another fight don't believe any reports of my being hurt, as I shall make arrangements to telegraph immediately to you in case of accident.

Did I tell you that my steward's name is Hubbell* from St. Louis, a grand son of Ben Hubbell of Bridgeport?

Wasn't I a true prophet when I said that King & Loomis wouldn't remain together for a year?† I think that King regrets now that he didn't keep Dave with him. How does Dave get along in business? Tell him when his eyes get [better] so that he can write to let me hear from him.

Your Father says that you have consented to let Henry go to school there for a year.‡ I am glad of it, though I can appreciate & honor you[r] feelings in

---

* Robert K. Hubbell (1841-1878). Born in Bridgeport, CT, he enlisted as a first-class boy in September 1861. He was transferred to the *Monitor* in early March and promoted to acting ensign in October 1862. He subsequently served in the Mississippi Squadron where he was commended for bravery for rescuing a wounded comrade on shore while coming under heavy fire.
† Wholesale grocers in La Salle.
‡ The Keelers were worried that their eldest son was not getting a good enough education in La Salle and wanted him to attend school in New Haven, which he did in in September 1862.

parting with him while I am away. How is Father & Mother? Ask them to write to me. How does Henry like the idea of going to New Haven to school? It will be a good chance for him & I hope he will improve it. I often wish he was here to look around. He would see much that would interest & please him.

I hope myself to be allowed to go ashore & see how it looks one of these days. As it is I go semi weekly to buy fresh provisions for the crew, with orders to be back as soon as possible. The store where I buy is about 100 feet from where I land, so that is the extent of my walk.

I shall send off this short letter without waiting to add to it. Don't be surprised to hear at any moment that we have made a move.

William

Iron Clad Monitor
Hampton Roads, Va.
April 8th, 1862

Dear Anna,

In the letter I wrote Henry Sunday night I told him of the bright beautiful day we had, but it changed in the night & it has been storming & raining ever since with a heavy east wind bringing the rollers in from the sea. Of course we have been living with hatches on & all *corked* up, close, wet & disagreeable & decidedly unpleasant.

Yours of April 3rd reached me to day. I enclose a little note which you can hand to Dave & let him do as he thinks best. There are two "bills payable" books, in my desk I think, in which you will find the date of the note. I have tried to call to mind the details of the fence, but am unable to do so & consequently am unable to give draft or directions that will enable Graham[*] to build it as I would like it. Hadn't he better fix up the old one so that it will last through the summer or till I return? Do as you think best.

I am still of the opinion that your letters are like angels' visits, inasmuch as they are ever welcome. Make them as frequent as you can. I will find no fault. The finale of your prayer meeting I think must have been interesting.

I do not care about your reading my letters to our friends when you think them suitable, but I *do object* most decidedly to your lending them. I was sorry you lent them to Mr. Rockwell[†], though I suppose you could not well avoid it. A letter of that kind don't amount to much when a person has to study it out word by word, whereas it might sound tolerably well, read off glibly by a person familiar with the writing who would give it the proper intonation. I want all to unders[t]and that my letters are not written with the expectation of having them criticised. They are merely familiar scratches to the dear ones

---

[*] Gardener and handyman Thomas Graham who did work around the Keelers' house.
[†] Presumably Charles Rockwell, the venerable father of Keeler's good friend John.

at home, written as I have said before amid confusion enough sometimes to distract a ship load of mules. While I am writing this our M.D. is reading a letter just rec'd from some cousin to a crowd in his room, which a few open slats separate from mine. You can readily imagine how much it assists me to fix my thoughts upon your letters

If Gen. McClelland is not governed by patriotic motives but is working from mere policy he certainly has a very queer way of shewing it. What his success as a commander will be, a very few hours probably will determine. The elements just now seem to be against him. His troops must be having a miserable time in the incessant rain. His siege train is stuck in the mud so that it is of no use to him.*

All kinds of stories are afloat in regard to the two armies. We heard to day by Sec'y Fox, who spent the aftern[o]on on board, that the probability was that Magruder had over 50,000 men. Gen. McClelland has double that I think if he can make them all available. Of his ul[t]imate success I cannot doubt.

I was prepossessed with him [McClellan] when he first came on board. He shook hands with us all, complimented us in a few very concise words & looked hastily around the ship in a thorough business like way, comprehended everything as soon as he saw it. He seemed thoroughly self reliant & was the only one of all who have been on board who spoke decidedly of what "*I*" was going to do, though not in an offensive or egotistical manner. He certainly cares but little for shew, as his dress which was very plain & his manner of coming aboard of us in a little dingy row boat indicate. He did not go ashore to receive the attentions & compliments of the officers there but remained on board the steamboat which brought him, sending his orders ashore in small boats which were going back & forth to him all night long.

Well, a fight is on the tapis for to morrow & I am glad, not so much that we are to fight, but it is another step towards bringing this abominable war to a close. Besides this is a portion of our work & "if 'twere done, 'twere well it were done quickly."† The *Merrimac*, we are told, is at Craney island (only 5 or 6 miles off) waiting for favourable weather for another fight. If it moderates it will come off to morrow. I hope so, still I can hardly believe it yet, though it may be before this reaches you the telegraph will tell you of the conflict. They are probably anxious to get out of here in order to go up York river to the assistance of Magruder, but they can't do it.

You may tell Mr. Hough & all my friends that I am not going to "write long letters" to any one in LaSalle but you. I think as long as they have the benefit of them they should be satisfied. My will is good — I would like to write each one a letter every day, but I have neither time, material or patience.

---

* McClellan had started marching his army up the Virginia Peninsula on April 4, but was soon stymied by Magruder's tiny force of 12,000 which was entrenched behind the Warwick River which traverses the Peninsula at Yorktown.
† William Shakespeare's *Macbeth*.

I shouldn't have any brains left, they'd be *writ* out, or I would have to draw largely upon imagination & invention & give them a Baron Munchausen* colouring.

I am neglecting my returns to the Department to write you this. I find it no small task to make out my returns correctly this first time, as I have it all to learn with few or no facilities.

I will except Mrs. Hough & will try & answer a letter from her if she will give me time enough. I will be right glad to receive letters from any others who will write but they will have to accept my letters to you as a reply. Tell Mr. Hough I have a bag full (a small one) of fragments of the *Merrimac*'s shells reserved for friends at home when I can send them & expect to get more to morrow.

I am glad the prospect of fruit is so good with you. I only wish I could help you eat it, but my chances for fruit with you or any where else this year is small I think. I think the strawberries will do better if they are thinned out *well*.

Don't fear the result of the coming fight to the country. As for myself I shall try & do my duty & that is all that any one can do. I shall try & give my friends no cause to be ashamed of me.

There are 7 steamers waiting for us with the *Merrimac* but there are gun boats here to attend to them. This grappling & piercing & all that is not so easily accomplished. If one of our incendiary shell[s] gets into the *Merrimac* she is done for.

I am going to get photographs of all the officers when an opportunity presents. Will send one of myself home the first chance.

W

[Marginalia] Your cake is to be eaten on the *Merrimac* or in Fort Sumpter [Sumter] if possible. My best love to all, yourself & the children included. Good night.

William

Iron Clad *Monitor*
Hampton Roads, Va.
April 11th, 1862

Dear Anna,

You will find below a sort of jotting down of events from day to day. If the days pass in the same way this one has I shall have but little time to give much in detail. When paper enough is filled I will fold it up & start it on its way westward.

---

* The larger-than-life fictional German nobleman who, among other things, could ride a cannonball and travel to the moon.

Hampton Roads (March to May 1862)

To begin this morning, Friday April 11th, the sun rose bright & clear with a light cool wind from the north. It is the first pleasant day we have had since last Sunday. From that day till this morning we have been living with hatches down & deck lights in, the top of a wave every few minutes rolling over our heads. It was crowded, dark & confined below, cold, wet & cheerless above. However, when I feel at all discontented I call *Anna Reynolds** to mind & memory silences all complaint.

Well, as we expected, the *Merrimac* made her appearance this morning in company with 5 other steamers & gun boats, including the *Yorktown* & *Jamestown*. In anticipation of the event our breakfast was ready half an hour earlier than usual, but before we were through the qua[r]ter master on watch informed us that five or six steamers were to be seen coming around Sewall's point. *We finished our breakfast* & on going on deck, sure enough there was our old acquaintance with her satellites dimly seen by aid of our glasses through the fog which covered the water in the vicinity of Craney island. But a few minutes were required to "prepare ship for action" as we have lived in a constant [state] of preparation for the last month. A stroke of the hatchet loosed us from our moorings & the *Monitor* stood ready for the fight. The thunder of one of our eleven inch guns waked the echoes of the shores & gave the first notice to the large fleet behind us of the approach of the foe.

Not being directly concerned in the preparations going on below, I remained on deck to obtain a good view of our antagonist as she slowly steamed towards us over the smooth waters of the harbor. As she slowly approached in advance of her attendants she seemed like some huge gladiator just entering the vast watery arena of the amphitheater, while on the opposite side the *Monitor* steamed forth her defiance with her attendant fleet as spectators in her rear. There they stood on the edge of the arena, each hesitating to advance, neither caring to retreat, each desiring the fight to come off on their side of the house that the assistance of their friends might be called in if necessary. She had no desire to come under the fire of the Fortress & all the gunboats, to say nothing of the rams, while engaged with us. Neither did the *Monitor* with her two guns desire to trust herself to the tender mercies of the gun boats & Craney island & Sewall's point batteries while trying the iron hide of the monster. I had a fine view of her at the distance of about a mile through a good glass & I tell you she is a formidable looking thing. I had but little idea of her size & apparent strength till now. She carries four guns on a side, a pivot gun on the bow & stern & two smaller rifled guns on the ridge of her roof (if you can call it so) which is wide & flat & was covered with men.

While we lay in the position I have described the *Jamestown* steamed up to the edge of the schooner fleet just over the bar & cooly took possession of three of them, towing them off, the secession rag floating at their mastheads.

---

* The ship in which Keeler made his long and tedious trip to California in 1849.

The vessels were light & of no great value, but it made my blood boil with indignation to see it done with such impunity right under our very nose & not the least attempt made on our part to prevent it. When I say "our" I don't mean the *Monitor*, as she drew too much water to go to their assistance. Besides, our orders compelled us to remain where we were.* But there were plenty of light draught gun boats which were just what was wanted. They however were kept back till the catastrophe was complete & then how they hurried up & locked the door with a slam after the horse was gone.

Well, each party steamed back & forth before their respective friends till dinner time, each waiting for the other to knock the chip off his shoulder, when the *Merrimac* withdrew & we hurried up & got our dinner. About three o'clock she again steamed up towards us when a duel at long range took place between her & the *Naugatuck* (Steven's one gun battery).† Half a dozen rounds were fired by each when the *Merrimac* withdrew. The last shot from the *Naugatuck*'s gun (a 100 lb. rifled Parrott) was thrown a good four miles & a half & fell within a few rods of the *Merrimac*. Neither vessel was struck.

The same comedy I suppose will be enacted day after day for I don't know how long, though how soon it may be turned to tragedy none of us can tell. Capt. Jeffers prophecies "a regular straight out fight" to morrow. The *Merrimac* can make it so if she chooses but our orders from Commodore Goldsborough are not to move above our present position to make the attack. His object is to get the *Merrimac* in deeper water where the large steamers fitted up as rams can have a chance at her, but I don't think she will venture too much as the very existence almost of the rebels here are staked on her success.

I have so nearly filled my sheet I will send it off to morrow without waiting for more. Possibly it might fall into rebel hands & so be published for the edification of the butternut‡ gentry.

We had a weak decoction of English nobility on board yesterday in the form of Lords Cecil & Cavendish.§ What good news we get from No. 10 & Corinth & yet so sad.** Capt. Carter I see is among the killed.†† I trust the

---

* The order came from Gideon Welles' telegram of March 10 which stated that "It is directed by the President that the *Monitor* be not too much exposed; that in no event shall any attempt be made to proceed with her unattended to Norfolk . . ." (ORN, I:7, p. 83). Since then Goldsborough had kept the ironclad in the channel between Fort Monroe and the Rip Raps, and forbade her from entering Hampton Roads without his explicit orders.

† See footnote on the USS *Naugatuck* in the letter of April 15, 1862.

‡ Slang term for a Confederate soldier.

§ Adelpert P. Cecil (1841-1889) and Edward Cavendish (1838-1891), officers in the Rifle Brigade in the British Army who were serving in Canada and were visiting America.

** Union victories at Island No. 10 on the Mississippi River and at Shiloh in Tennessee. The latter opened the way to the strategic railway junction at Corinth, Mississippi.

†† Henry H. Carter of 11th Illinois Infantry, the 24-year-old brother of Keeler's friend from La Salle. He was killed early on the first day at Shiloh. His regiment's commanding officer's report states that "The noble, lamented Captain Carter, commanding Company K,

families of such men will not be forgotten by their country. I expect a letter from you to morrow. Hope I shall not be disappointed.

Sunday morning, 13th.* Yesterday the *Merrimac* & her attendants were steaming back & forth along Craney island but did not advance towards us. Till 12 last night they were still there burning blue lights & signalising the shore. This morning they are not to be seen. We all wish we knew their plans. They are conco[c]ting something. What it is we shall probably find out before long. Yesterday the roar of cannon could be distinctly heard in the direction of Yorktown. There is no doubt but what the enemy are there in large force. The "onward to Richmond" battle might be fought there.

Tuesday afternoon [April 15]. No boat in from Baltimore to day. Consequently no mail. So we are without our letters or papers, but have an opportunity of putting on an additional postscript. We had a deserter on board to day, just in from Norfolk. He brings considerable news if it is to be relied upon. He says that the *Jamestown*, *Yorktown* & two or three other vessels have come down from Norfolk & gone up James river to Richmond for coal, that one of them had in tow a schooner loaded with R.R. iron taking to Richmond to be rolled into plates to cover another iron battery they are building at Norfolk†, that the *Merrimac* is making some alterations to her ports & will probably be down again in three or four days. He gave us some information in regard to the details of her construction which was altogether new to us & may prove of advantage. One of our balls he said passed through her just a foot over her boiler. Capt. Jeffers seems disposed to believe what he says. He cross questioned him for almost all the forenoon & his stories seemed very consistent.

Capt. J. immediately sent down to the Commodore for permission to go up James river & take the vessels when they come down. If no measures are taken to seize them as they pass down it will shew a want of energy & management on the part of the commanding officer here for which the country should condemn him. It is a gross shame that the rebels should be allowed to hold uninterrupted water communication between Norfolk & Richmond, their vessels passing under our very eyes & no effort made to prevent it. It is no fault of ours that the *Merrimac* lay all day aground in plain sight of us and no attempt made by us to seize her. We all have the will & think we have the power if we were only allowed to use it.

Capt. Jeffers is a cool, cautious, careful, brave man & if he could be allowed a little discretion I honestly believe the Stars & Stripes would now be waving over the *Merrimac* or she would be quietly resting at the bottom of the

---

who, with his company, so bravely cut his way through the rebel cavalry at Donelson, was among the first to fall on this bloody field mortally wounded—a good man and a true soldier, his loss is irreparable." (ORA, I:10, p. 138).

* The text in this paragraph was written on a separate piece of paper with the word "Private" written on the back.

† This was the CSS *Richmond*.

harbour. It is a great mistake that superannuated old men are given the control of such important measures. They no doubt have been good men in their day but their day is past & they should be allowed to rest. We need younger men, quick & skillful to plan, energetic & resolute to execute.

Wednesday noon [April 16]. Have spent the whole forenoon ashore in a vain hunt for a barrel of grog (whiskey) sent us from the storeship *Brandywine* to deal out to the men. It is a warm pleasant day. Happened to run against Chaplain Beecher again, just in from Yorktown. Brought nothing new, though I think from what I can gather that we may look for some important movement in three of four days. Good bye once more.

William

[Marginalia] The telegraph will tell you the news sooner than I can get it to you, but I will follow it up with details. Remember me to all friends. With love & kisses to yourself & children. "Ten o'clock gentlemen, please put out your lights," so good night.

William

Iron Clad *Monitor*
Hampton Roads
April 15th, 1862

Dear Anna,

I am in good writing mood & feel like writing a good long letter to you all, but a sad scarcity of material will I fear frustrate all my good intentions. I can't fill a sheet of paper when I have nothing to say. To be sure I can talk about myself but that subject will soon wear out. It will tire me & disgust my friends. But hold, I have it — congratulate me, I have been ashore this afternoon & as prima facia evidence (don't let Hough criticise my legal phraseology) I enclose in a paper to Sarah some flowers & live oak leaves picked from Gen. Wool's garden inside the Fortress.

I found the shore to consist of a promiscuous collection of sand, contrabands in every stage of growth & variety of costume, fierce bearded men secured to clattering swords, trig* uniforms on horseback and plainer ones on foot, big siege guns hurrying to McClelland to enter their protest against Magruder's advance, huge eight mule wagons loaded with pills & powders to assist said guns in maintaining a proper tone of voice, nice polished muskets with attachments of wide awake sentinels, loose faded uniforms containing sick soldiers & clumsy go-carts carrying off dead ones.

All this "pomp & circumstance of glorious war"† was interspersed with a few consumptive looking live oaks rooting for subsistence in the loose dry

---

* Smart.
† William Shakespeare's *Othello*.

Hampton Roads (March to May 1862)

sand, a disorderly collection of has[t]ily constructed shanties (style of architecture a la La Salle), a few, more substantial looking, brick ones, a big stone fort & the once famous Hygiea Hotel*, now no longer filled with Southern wit & chivalry but used for the more noble purpose of a hospital for our sick & wounded soldiers.

My first care after getting a footing in the sacred, sandy soil was to place my cranium under the tonsorial care of an intelligent looking contraband within the walls of the Hygea. I left a splendid crop of capillary tubes to be collected & treasured as mementoes of the *Monitor's* Paymaster by the fair damsels of the sunny south, when the base mud sills & low born, greasy mechanics† of the north give way to Southern chivalry, & Southern hoops & petticoats take the place of sword, soldier & sentinel.

I realy felt concerned when upon weighing myself I found that I had fallen away from 145 (my usual weight) to 157. I felt consoled however when I thought that it was an unanswerable argument against hard work (which you know I never liked) & in favour of a more easy way of living. Capt. Jeffers explain[e]d the phenomena very satisfactorily at the supper table by saying that he supposed I had never been weighed with so much brass on before. Don't be alarmed at this falling away. If I continue to decline I will advise you in time to send down a health committee & examine me.

The *Norfolk Day Book* of to day was shewn me, just brought down by our flag of truce. It was about the size of this sheet, printed on dirty brown paper with type which looked as if they had seen long & hard service. Nothing of interest was in it save the intelligence that the yankees had lost their boasted confidence in the *Monitor*, as their fleet had been down & defied her to meet them in fair fight & they cowardly declined. It also contained a jubilant article on Bureagard's great victory at Pittsburg landing [Shiloh], where "he mowed down the yankees by thousands."‡ An article on "The future of the South," whose writer must have been troubled with a constipation of ideas, filled nearly one column & an abortive attempt at poetry headed the next. The remainder of the sheet was peppered over with a variety of advertisments.

---

* The sprawling resort hotel was located at Old Point Comfort outside the main gate of Fort Monroe. Deemed a threat to the fort's defenses, the hotel was torn down in December 1862.

† Mudsill was a derogatory term used by antebellum Southerners for a white Northerner who performed manual labor. Northern working-class men used the term as a badge of honor, and in the lead up to the war formed "Mud Sill Clubs" and urged working men to vote Republican. "Greasy mechanic" was another derogatory term for a white Northern working-class man.

‡ Confederate General Pierre G. T. Beauregard led the massive attack on the first day of the Battle of Shiloh that drove Ulysses Grant's beleaguered troops back to Pittsburg Landing on the Tennessee River. Confident of victory the next day, he telegrammed Richmond of his "complete victory." The Confederate War Department immediately released that information to the press, which is what Keeler read. Beauregard never bothered to send a follow-on telegram the next day notifying his superiors of his defeat. (*Crossroads of Freedom: Antietam*, James M. McPherson, New York, NY, 2002, p. 23).

Civil War Years: USS *Monitor* (1862)

John Bull* was accused of standing on his dignity in refusing some of the *Merrimac*'s officers permission to come on board the *Rinaldo* the day she was down here & carried off the three schooners.

My liberty was for only two hours, from 1/2 past 3 to half past 5, but short as it was I enjoyed it, the more perhaps from being so long confined on ship board.

I met Chaplain Beecher just in from Yorktown. He told me that McClelland was constructing large defences out there & mounting heavy guns evidently preparing for hard work, that when he had them ready the country need not be surprised to hear of his sudden appearance before Norfolk with troops enough to make his appearance effectual. He did not say where he got his information, but I imagine it to be mere camp rumour. It may however prove to be the case. If McClelland does so he will have to transport a large army across the James river for which he must be prepared, judging from the number of pontoon bridges landed here. The banks of the river however are wet & swampy which is unfavorable for his purpose. Whatever his plans are he has wisdom enough to keep them to himself & not make them the subject of newspaper gossip & criticism & I think he has the ability to carry them out without the aid or assistance of either the *New York* or *Chicago Tribune*. If he should out general Magruder & bag him & his whole army his opposers would grumble still, because he didn't demolish Fort Sumpter, crush out Corinth & conquer New Orleans at the same time.

When the crisis approaches at Yorktown [and] if there is no prospect of a fight here, I shall try & get two days leave of absence & go out there with the hope of witnessing the battle. A horse has been offered me for the purpose by a Col. acquaintance of one of the Penn. regiments.

I think the policy of the rebels to be to keep the *Merrimac* at Norfolk threatening us occasionally by appearing down here & in this manner neutralise the whole fleet in the harbour. How long it will continue is uncertain, probably till some decisive movement is made at either Yorktown or Norfolk.

The *Naugatuck*, about which so much is said, does not resemble us at all. She was presented to the Treasury Department by Mr. Stevens who built her for the purpose of testing some of the principles involved in the old Stevens battery.† She carries a hundred pounder rifled Armstrong gun, which though

---

* England.
† Naval engineer and inventor Edwin A. Stevens, who along with his brother Robert, pioneered the development of ironclad warships in the 1840s and built a large vessel known as the Stevens Battery at their estate in New Jersey. The Navy lost interest in the project in the late 1850s and the battery was never completed. When the Civil War began, Stevens purchased an iron-hulled steamer named the *Naugatuck* and added a 100-lb Parrott rifle amidships. He donated the vessel to the Revenue Cutter Service (under the authority of the Treasury Department) after the Navy refused the gift. The USS *Naugatuck*, however,

Hampton Roads (March to May 1862)

of long range is not accurate. This gun is completely exposed on the deck. It is loaded from below by depressing the muzzle. But the persons training & firing it can easily be picked off by rifles before she is near enough to render her fire effective against such an enemy as the *Merrimac*, while her sides would be crushed like an egg shell by such an opponent's fire.

Whoever or whatever conquers the *Merrimac* will have to do it at very short range & nothing has yet been built which will stand the hammering of her heavy guns but the *Monitor*. All we want is that our fleet here should engage the rebel gun boats & leave the *Merrimac* to us. Not that we consider ourselves entirely invulnerable but nearer to it perhaps than anything yet built. We have weak points. A shell from a thirteen inch mortar, such as Com. Foote used at [Island] No. 10, would go through us, top & bottom, but the rub would be to land one on our decks. Then the bursting of one of our own guns would be fatal, or the explosion of a cartridge would fire our magazine. All these things must be taken into calculation. Then too our guns are just as liable to be disabled by a well aimed shot as our opponent's. If however we can get one of our incendiary shells inside her iron hide, her hours are numbered. I wish this task was finished, it is not a pleasant one. The result, "Quien Sabe?"

Wednesday, 16th. A fine beautiful day. We had a very pleasant visit to day from Capt. Hewitt* of the English War Steamer *Rinaldo*. He brought with him one or two English Army officers. The paragraph in the *Norfolk Day Book* was explained when he told us that when the *Merrimac* lay alongside of him last Friday some of her officers came off in a boat & he sent them word that he did not whish [wish] to see them on his decks & they returned in high dudgeon. From Capt. H.'s conversation he evidently had his fill of chivalry while he had Slidell & Mason on board.† "Blast their impudence," said he, "I just sent them (the *Merrimac*) word by my first Lieut. that I wanted to hold no communication with them whatever." He is in constant communication with Lord Lyons‡ & this I think may be considered some evidence that old Bull is disposed to moderate down somewhat. He gave us some valuable information in regard to the construction of the *Merrimac* which will be of service in our next encounter. He settled one thing which we had supposed to be the case, that her sloping sides were covered with grease to glance off our balls more easily.

---

proved to be a failure when the 100-lb gun exploded during the Union Navy's attack on Fort Darling, which Keeler describes in his letter of May 12, 1862.

* William N. W. Hewett.

† Five months earlier, Confederate diplomats James M. Mason and John Slidell were taken prisoner by the Union Navy frigate USS *San Jacinto* as they were on their way to England on board the Royal Mail packet *Trent*. The Trent Affair, which nearly resulted in war between the United States and Great Britain, was resolved by the release of the two commissioners, who were transported to the Caribbean on the HMS *Rinaldo* and finally to England on board another vessel.

‡ Richard B. P. Lyons, British Ambassador to the United States.

Civil War Years: USS *Monitor* (1862)

Capt. Jeffers & Eng. Stimers went to see Gen. Wool & Com. Goldsborough to day & used every argument & entreaty they could think of to persuade them to allow us to go up York river to the assistance of McClelland, but 'twas of no use.* Their reply was that the interest at stake here was too great & that for the safety of the vast amount of property here they relied solely upon us. They may be right but none of us "can exactly see it." They said we might be injured. Capt. J. told them that that was just what we were built for, to be hammered & punched & we were able to stand it. They have no less than four large steamers here with steel plated bows, as rams, to run the *Merrimac* down, & speak confidently of their being able to do it. If so, they can certainly spare the *Monitor* for a few hours. The shoe pinches just here — Com. Goldsborough looks to the safety of the Navy first, the Army next & Gen. Wool is jealous of McClelland. This is the whole story in a few words. I believe the Department are going to build a big glass case to put us in for fear of harm coming to us.

Your favour of the 11th inst. reached me to day with Mother's & Henry's. All were very acceptable & have been read & reread without any of the yawning you seem to fear.

Thursday evening, 17th. It has been a bright clear day. The sun shining uncomfortably warm & reminding me that I have to get summer clothing, though what we are to be allowed to wear I don't know, but our present uniform will soon be too thick & warm. I suppose blue flannel will be used. Good cool linen pants would be preferable, though probably not allowed. Still they will not be as particular on board of us as on large ships where all are in the regular service.

Time passes slowly. One day is much like another. These bright pleasant mornings I am up at 1/2 past six, pace our iron pavement till 8 when I go down to breakfast. Before we get through, the morning New York papers of the previous day are brought down & their contents discussed with our coffee. Army & Navy movements [are] discussed & when Capt. Jeffers joins in it is done with ability & is at times very interesting. By the time our papers are well digested our steam tender is dispatched for the mail which is the great event of the day. When fortune or correspondents don't favour me with a letter, the M.D. generally lets me read one of his. My writing then usually occupies my time till noon. If not, we watch for a smoke behind Sewall's point as an indication of the *Merrimac*, or a boat load of army officers come on board to "do the *Monitor*." Or perhaps a foreign man of war comes in, runs the Stars & Stripes up to the fore & fires a salute of 21 guns which is returned from the Fortress. Then some of the men of war bang away at a

---

* McClellan had been urging Goldsborough to open the York River by reducing the rebel batteries at Yorktown and Gloucester Point that sealed that river. Arguing that his orders were to remain at Hampton Roads to neutralize the threat of the *Virginia*, Goldsborough refused to provide the necessary naval support.

Hampton Roads (March to May 1862)

target & we watch the shot & shell as they ricochet over the water or burst in pieces. Then the Fortress takes a notion to stir up the "butternuts" on Sewall's point & the 15 in. shells from the Union gun go tearing directly over our heads like an untamed steam engine. Firing at Yorktown—Smoke at Pig Point—Rebel tug under Craney island—Union steamer loaded with troops—Flags of truce—all tend to vary the monotony somewhat & excite speculation. Lunch at 12, of whiskey & crackers of which I don't partake, but am sorry to say *all* the rest do. Dinner at 2 which we draw out as long as possible, after which we loaf around deck (those who have cigars smoke them) & wish for the *Merrimac*. In the evening we chat in the Ward room or write in our state rooms as we prefer till 10 o'clock when the lights are all *supposed* to be put out. So it passes day after day with little varyation.

Tell Mother that her note was welcome. She need not worry about the *Merrimac* — we can take care of her, if we can have her alone.

Do you get any milk yet? I do not like the way Mr. Brown* has served me about the hay. I paid him in advance for it, with the distinct understanding that I was to have good sweet Hungarian hay he had in his barn. It seems that he has been drawing little batches of prairie hay & one thing and another from different places just as it happened. I do not like it at all. You may tell Dave so. I do not like to have my absence taken advantage of.

I wish Dave had his stock of goods here as he would have enough to do to satisfy even him.

My love to all.

              William

              Iron Clad *Monitor*
              April 21st, 1862
              Hampton Roads

Dear Anna,

Yours of the 15th inst. reached me to day. You say very truly when you say that the sight of your handwriting will do me good. Your letter must have left a rainy region for one still more stormy. We have been doing penance for the last 48 hours with closed hatches & the waves surging over our heads — the rain pouring in torrents & the wind roaring with old fashioned Cape Horn fierceness & the storm still continues with no prospect of a close. No comfort to be found above water & "cabined, cribbed, confined"† below. But when I think of our poor land forces and the additional hardships which this terrible weather is occasioning them I cannot find it in my heart to complain.

But why McClelland tolerates such weather as this surprises me. If it interferes with his operations why don't he dry up the mud & like old King

---

* No relation to Keeler's brother-in-law Dave.
† William Shakespeare's *Macbeth*.

CIVIL WAR YEARS: USS *MONITOR* (1862)

Canute forbid the further flow of the watery flood. It is becoming more evident to the country every day that his first step was a wrong one. Why didn't he come to me to consult before venturing so rashly into the enemy's country? He ought to have known that the windows of heaven were going to be opened & that the floods of course would descend, and then any reasonable man might have known it would have been muddy.

But then as long as he [McClellan] would persist why didn't he follow his artillery & baggage trains with a rail on his shoulder to pry them out of the mud. If he had applied to me for advice, as was his duty, I should have said just go to work now & build a good macadamised road right out to your enemies entrenchments, or perhaps better, a rail road or a canal. How much easier it will be to transport your heavy batteries this way than haul them out by mules & men. Nonsense, the enemy won't interfere with any of these operations. If they do why just shell them out, you musn't let them interfere. Where will you get mortars to do this shelling? Why, make them of course, you don't suppose they grow do you. You must hurry up for you only have 30 minutes to get 150,000 men with their few equipments & the small amount of material they will need in front of the enemy. Don't stop to entrench. If you want entrenchments use the enemy's.

It's all nonsense for you to say you've had to gather, equip & drill an army & they don't need any drilling. Let every man fight on his own hook, it's altogether the best way & what better arms does he want than those nature has furnished him with. But they havn't clothes or tents. Serves them right if they expected to come here & be clothed & sheltered at the expense of the country. You should have accomplished this long ago. Don't put in the plea that you have been plan[n]ing victories for Foote, Mitchell, Burnside, Grant & others. That won't go down. You should have done all that yourself. Any stupid fool could have done all the plan[n]ing.

There now you see what II* would have done!!!!!! Wouldn't II make a good figure head for the *N.Y. Tribune* or some other organ of free love, fourierism & anarchy. But then I suppose that I am not the only II to be found.

I think if some of these stay at home, easy chair, would be critics would come down here & let me shew them, first a harbor filled with shipping waiting to disgorge their contents of army stores into warehouses & onto wharves already full, then go ashore & look at the vast piles of cannon & ammunition, the droves of horses and mules, let them see the almost endless trains of large army wagons loaded to their utmost capacity continually starting off from the various docks & store houses.

Let them think of an army of 100 or 150,000 men to be fed, clothed & cared for. Let them make a calculation to see how much it will take to furnish *one* meal for this number of men, then multiply it by days & weeks & months. Let them realise if they can that all this has to be taken over roads almost

---

* Keeler has written "II", here and in the next two sentences, in large capital letters.

impassible with mud, across morasses & through streams whose bridges have been destroyed. I think their criticisms would have a more kindly tone, to say the least, when they came to reflect upon the Herculean task of reducing all this apparent disorder & confusion to a well fed, well armed, efficient body of troops, well supplied with all the material of war. Whose is the master mind that controls & directs all this, if not McClellan's. Did it ever occur to you to abuse the main spring of a clock which quietly & silently but surely & effectually furnished the power that kept the whole machinery in motion because it did not appear on the face to assist the hands in marking the flight of time.

When McClelland's officers & men begin to distrust his capabilities as a general, then it will be time for others. I have conversed with hundreds both of officers & men & I have yet to find the first one to speak unkindly of him. They all speak of him in terms of highest praise, both as a man & an officer. I am convinced he has the entire confidence of his army & am just as sure that he will keep their confidence by leading them to victory.

I did not mean to fill my whole sheet with McClelland when I began, but having taken a dose of *N.Y. Tribune** was forced to regurgitate & find it has covered my sheet. However, as I hadn't much else to write about it has helped to fill up the space.

How sad it makes me feel to read over the long list of killed & wounded at Pittsburgh [Landing].† How many homes have been made desolate & how many hearts made sad by that one battle.

One needs to go through the hospital & see the sick and wounded, as I have done, to realise fully what our soldiers undergo. Then they can better estimate too, the value which should be placed upon their services. Some 75 wounded men were brought to the hospital here from Yorktown the other day. It was a sad, sad sight I assure you. Some of the poor fellows will never see home again.

This long continued storm will delay operations before Yorktown & increase ten fold the labours of our army. It will be a splendid opportunity for the *N.Y. Tribune* to pitch in. Its impotent howls would extort a bray of laughter from a cast iron donkey.

[No signature]

---

* Horace Greeley's staunchly Republican newspaper was highly critical of McClellan, who was a Democrat.
† With a combined total of nearly 24,000 casualties, which included nearly 3,500 killed, the Battle of Shiloh (also known as Pittsburg Landing) was the bloodiest battle of the war up to that point.

Civil War Years: USS *Monitor* (1862)

Iron Clad *Monitor*
Hampton Roads, Va.
April 25th, 1862

Dear Anna,

Your welcome messenger of the 18th reached me yesterday with the good news that you were all well at home & that after such a long wet spell of dismal weather you have a promise of some sunshine. Farmers must be nearly discouraged at the prospect, as the season is so late & help is so scarce it will be very difficult to get their crops in in season to get them started early enough to be out of the way of the early fall frosts. I suppose our garden, under Father's & Hen's *tuition*, "is being put to rights" in first rate style. I fear you will have to eat my share of fruit for me, unless I should get home sooner than the warlike aspect of things at present promise.

Troops are still arriving here, though the most of them going up York river we do not see, but an occasional boat load is landed here. From the best information I can get Burnside has been heavily reinforced & has now an army of 40,000 men. A rumor reached us this morning that he was within a short distance of Norfolk, but it does not look probable, though he may take that on his way to Richmond to which place I believe he is bound.* In fact a number of the divisions of our army seem to be converging there. We hear heavy firing every day in the direction of Yorktown, some days but a few guns, on others a heavy & continued cannonade.

How we long to take a part in the game being played there, but we are so enveloped in red tape that we cannot leave our moorings. Capt. Jeffers gets almost frantic at times & goes down to see the old Flag (as the Commodore is called)† but it does no good. The *Galena* & *Naugatuck* are both here but would be totaly unable to cope with the *Merrimac*. However as Capt. J. says, "the moral[e] effect of having them here is great." They could be used to good effect against the *Yorktown* & *Jamestown*.

Evening. Gen. Van Allen‡ has been on board all the afternoon. He came from McClelland to get the *Galena* to go up York river. Some of her machinery is broken & will take three or four days for repairs. He came on board of us & Capt. J. shewed him all around the vessel, setting forth all our good qualities & how effective we would be up York river. The result was that the Gen. sat down in our ward room & wrote a letter to the Sec'y of War stating that it was absolutely necessary for us to go to McClelland's assistance,

---

* Burnside's capture of Roanoke Island, NC two months earlier gave the Union Navy control of Albemarle Sound and the waterways linking it north to Norfolk. However, instead of heading to Norfolk, Burnside marched south to attack New Bern and Fort Macon. After the successful conclusion of the North Carolina campaign in June 1862, his army was sent to Fort Monroe and merged into McClellan's Army of the Potomac.

† Goldsborough.

‡ James H. Van Alen, soon-to-be military governor of Yorktown and Gloucester.

as we could enable him to maintain certain positions there, which otherwise he could not do. I hope it will result in our being ordered up there, though I consider it far from certain.

As to my letters already sent home being published I shall leave that with you. You know they were not intended for anything of that kind & as I cannot have them to polish them up myself must leave it for you, if Father chooses to copy such parts as you think best to publish, making such corrections & improvements as you deem proper. I don't want any typographical errors as there will be enough of my own. I want them dated from the "Iron Clad *Monitor*" Hampton Roads over my own signature as I don't believe in anonymous correspondents. If the editors express publicly any desire for further communications after the first is in print, you can furnish more, & I will write when I have anything to write about, otherwise I will let it drop. You can say so to Adams*. Don't let any loose, badly expressed sentences get into print. The editors should furnish each of us with a copy as the least thing he can do. Keep my reputation in sight & use your own judgement in the matter.

I shan't attempt to fill the other half sheet but tear it off & send it along, hoping to find something more to write about soon. Rec'd Sarah's thunder this P.M. Will get up an echo soon. Love to all, especially to yourself & children.

William

[Marginalia] Sent a paper to Henry & one to Eddy with this. Please excuse the half sheet. You shall not have one often. Saturday morning [April 26]. Cold, rainy & gloomy, just as the whole week has been.

[Continuation of the remainder of the first sheet]

Yes, I would like a piece of pie & cake & a cup of your coffee & would even be willing to take it off our kitchen table without "William" for a waiter. But what's the use of setting the table out in that tantalising way when you know I can't help clear it off. It is all very funny no doubt, but I can't exactly see where the laugh comes in. We have plenty of all that is good in our store rooms but it undergoes some strange metamorphosis before it reaches our mahogony, which by the way happens [to] be black walnut.

Hadn't you better write to your Father to know when he wants Henry to come? That he expects him I know, for he wrote so to me. I have a good deal of confidence in Henry's judgement & discretion for one so young, but he has had so little experience in travelling that I never could consent to his starting off on such a journey alone. I have no doubt he thinks he could get along very well & he would quite as well as most boys of his age & experience but he has but little idea of what an undertaking it would be. Just think of the poor fellow being dumped into such a wilderness as N.Y. [City] without a friend or acquaintance & in total ignorance of all the streets. I wish he was

---

* Keeler's friend Orville Adams, who apparently had a connection with the *La Salle Press*.

ready to go with Mrs. Treat*. He would be no trouble to her & might make himself useful a little. Use what money you want in fitting him out, though perhaps it would be best not to give him too many clothes as your Mother might not think them fashionable enough for refined New Haven. It would cost more I know, but perhaps it would be better to send the money & let your Mother get them for him. Hadn't you better write to your Father telling him of the opportunity you have of letting Henry have company & asking if it would be convenient to have him come then? I don't see how I could consent to his going alone, though some arrangement might be made with the Express Co. to look to him a little in changing cars & see that his baggage went through safely. I fully appreciate your feelings in allowing him to go. You will feel lonesome I know but as you say it will be for his good & it would seem selfish to keep him with you for the sake of his company and assistance when he can be benefitted so much by leaving.

Nothing has made me feel so indignant for a long time as the manner in which Mr. Brown has served us about the hay. I spoke to Mr. Dean before I left about pasturing the cow but agreed upon no terms. Whatever they are you had better pay as I suppose you can do no better elsewhere, though you may find pasture nearer where Father can drive the cow back & forth if he wants to.

I am glad Hen has at last found the [ink] powder. I have no recollection of burying any grape vines in the middle of the garden but think they must be Clintons. The strawberries from Mr. Rockwell are buried in a row in one of the beds among the currant bushes. They can be set out in one of those beds that has but few other vines in it—one of the south ones I think. Where was Snow's vine put? That was Campbell's† autograph on the back of his likeness. I believe I have answered all your enquiries.

Tuesday morning [April 29]. Clear & pleasant with the sun shining brightly & a cool westerly wind. I believe the *Merrimac* has retired without any idea of again making her appearance till forced out by our army taking possession of Norfolk.

This storm is going to retard the operations of our army very much.

There are three great evils in both our army & navy which if corrected would render them much more efficient. The first is whiskey, the second is whiskey & the third is whiskey. If this evil spirit was banished entirely from our land & sea forces it would add ten per cent to their strength & efficiency, while it would decrease in a much greater ratio the number in the hospitals.

Last Saturday we had quite a number of visitors on board, among others Mr. Cozzens, better known as "Sparrowgrass."‡ It is very difficult now for

---

* Wife of La Salle hardware merchant Edward Treat who had family in New Haven.
† Albert B. Campbell*, second assistant engineer on the *Monitor*.
‡ Frederick S. Cozzens, American humorist and author of the *Sparrowgrass Papers* (1856).

Hampton Roads (March to May 1862)

civilians to get papers from Washington to visit here. We consequently see but few of them, though army officers continue plentiful as ever.

We still continue to receive the most absurd suggestions for destroying the *Merrimac*. One of the latest, emenated from some fertile brain in Mass., and cooly proposed that we should board & then let some of our men drop three or four of our eleven inch shells into her smoke stack which would have the effect to explode her boiler. The writer did not tell how our men were to climb up her greased roof, on an incline of 45 degrees, carrying shell of 175 lbs. weight, nor how when they were up there they were to reach up 10 or 12 feet more to drop their loads into the desired place. Nor did he say how our men were to escape the fate laid out for the enemy.

Another proposition from some brilliant personage in N.Y. was that we should all board the *Merrimac* each carrying a vial filled with cloroform & ammonia which we were to break among the enemy who were to be speedily asphyxiated, though what was to prevent our sharing the same fate he didn't say. We replied to this letter requesting the author to come down with a lot of Spaulding's glue & rub it over the *Merrimac*'s decks. When they were well covered & all her crew stuck fast, we would go on board & hold a sponge filled with cloroform under the nose of each one. This we thought a humane improvement upon his original plan.

I was yesterday shewn an English paper stating that Mr. W. F. Keeler, Paymaster of the *Monitor* who had charge of the powder division during the action, had made a report stating — & then went on to copy my letter to the *Scientific American*.

Mr. Stimers has left us. He has been ordered to the New York Navy Yard to superintend the building of more ~~Monitors~~ iron batteries, but there *never* can be but one *Monitor*.

The Capt.'s clerk was recently sent to Washington on business. He staid two or three days at Willard's [Hotel] & returned without having spent a cent. The *Monitor* was enough.

Our letter bag is being made up so I must say good bye once more.

William

[Marginalia] I hope to hear from you again soon. I find it hard to write when I know others are to see it. I could fill three sheets for you easier than I can one for them.

Sent a paper to Eddy yesterday. Will send another in a day or two. Eddy must write me another letter.

How about coming east when I get ready to come home? Persuade Mrs. Hough to accompany you.

It is late & I must close with my best love to yourself & kind remembrances to all. Kiss the dear children.

Civil War Years: USS *Monitor* (1862)

Iron Clad *Monitor*
Hampton Roads, Va.
April 29th, 1862

Dear Anna,

Your package of the 23rd inst. has just been rec'd containing one letter from you, Helen Plant's* with mother's, Henry's & last but not least dear little Eddie's. In regard to rainy weather, I can sympathise feelingly with you for we have had nothing else for a long time past but raw easterly winds bringing in a heavy sea which washes constantly across our decks. A heavy shower serves to vary the monotony.

Last Sunday afternoon I got liberty ashore, but the day was bleak & raw, threatening momentarily to rain. Still I took advantage of the opportunity for a little pedestrian excursion, both to gratify my curiosity & exercise my pedal extremities. The incidents of the tour were duly recorded in a letter to Sarah the same evening.

I was very glad Mother sent me Helen's letter, the reading afforded me much pleasure. When Mother writes tell them Mr. Knox or any of their friends coming on board the *Monitor* will receive every attention I can shew them. A letter of introduction would be advisable, as civilians find it difficult to get from the shore to the boat without some one on board to vouch for them & of course I should always pass any one with a letter from any of my friends. Any of our friends coming to Washington, by all means have them come down here. I should be very glad to see them.

I have been hoping to see Mr. Lovejoy. I wrote to him just after the fight & sent him a large piece of one of the *Merrimac*'s shells but its rec't has never been acknowledged. I care nothing about it, any further than I don't want him to think that I have forgotten his kindness. Sometime when Mr. Hough is writing [to Lovejoy] I wish he would mention it.

Our M.D.'s letters are not *quite* as interesting as your own, so please continue till further notice. His [her] letters are the voice of a fond loving heart, as well as a good sensible girl, & I think sometimes he does not appreciate her as he ought. I am glad that you *read* my letters instead of passing them 'round, which latter I don't think I could consent to.

Just at present, 4 P.M., there is a quiet in the usual *disorderly* state of *disordered* elements aboard. The rain is quietly pattering on the iron deck, a dim light diffusing itself through my little room from the small opening over my head. The M.D. (the life & fun & wit of the ship) thank fortune is enjoying his siesta. Other officers are either reading, writing or attending to their duties. The crew have just seated themselves to supper on the berth deck & the confused hum of their voices & the clatter of their spoons & tin cups & plates are about the only audible sounds.

---

* Keeler's 20-year-old first cousin from Utica, NY. See Biographical Notes.

Hampton Roads (March to May 1862)

Notwithstanding the rain just now a portion of the forenoon was warm & pleasant & was spent by all longingly watching Sewall's Point for the expected appearance of the *Merrimac*, but in vain. We hear from her about every day & know, or think we do, just what they are doing. But have got to wait for further advices to find out what keeps them now, as the last news was that she was all ready to come out, this time to *fight*, spurred up by the accusations of cowardice from Norfolk folks for their retreat when last out. Let them come, we are ready.

I am glad that the time your Mother has set for sending for Henry suits you. It may be that you will want to go at the same time. I hope so, it would be very pleasant. I think with Henry you would get along very well. If Miss Cavenaugh has scholars & classes suitable for Henry I think he had better go if you can spare him, [even] if he does nothing more than review his former studies. But by all means have her pay the strictest attention to his reading & *spelling*. I cannot emphasize the last too much as it is my particular request.

I do not want you to go to New York till you have been "rejuvinated," & if all that is required is a set of teeth have them in as soon as possible. I have been desiring you should have some for a long time & I don't believe you will have a better time than the present if you can find a good dentist. I suppose Dr. Kelsey is still in LaSalle. You had better see him & find out what he will put them in for & do it *well*. I have talked with him about it a number of times & he has always recommended gutta percha. If he still inclines to that opinion you had better use it, as it will be much less expensive than gold. See him at once as it will probably be necessary to have the old stumps extracted *now* in order that the gums may shrink all they will. If you think best to take chloroform you had better consult Dr. Bry & get him to go to Kelsey's with you, or better still, have them both go to the house.* Perhaps you had better get Dave to make a bargain for you. You can tell him that the money will be ready as soon as the work is completed to your satisfaction. He will probably be glad to do something for money in these times. If you mean to have it done don't put it off.

Mr. Gager†, of whom you inquire, is an acting Master & is an able, active, & energetic officer. He was not on board at the time of the fight but was ordered to us soon after. For some years past he has commanded a steamer running to different places on our southern seaboard with which he is familiar & was ordered to us with special reference to his qualifications as a pilot. He has been in the service since the commencement of the war. He was in the *Monticello* when she saved an Indiana regiment at Hatteras that had been left on a naked strip of sand all night & were about being cut off by the rebels,

---

* Physician Francis M. Bry and dentist Alvin M. Kelsey, both from La Salle. Bry was married to Keeler's brother-in-law's sister, which would explain why Anna might have got a bargain.
† Edwin V. Gager*.

CIVIL WAR YEARS: USS *MONITOR* (1862)

when he came up & began shelling them (the rebels) & they attempted to retreat in a large flat boat which he blew up with a shell, killing most of them. You will find a picture of it in one of the *Leslie's* you have at home.

I was not at all surprised to hear of Clay's cowardice. I always considered him as one of those barking dogs who are never dangerous.

I would really like to know if Melzar is at Yorktown.[*] When you write to your Father tell him to ask Melzar to write to me, if he is there, as it is not impossible but what I may go out there. I have the offer of a horse & a pass from Gen. Wool any time I want to go. If the *Merrimac* comes out & we dispose of her we shall be started for Yorktown before our powder smoke is fairly blown away.

Your Uncle Frank's address is 287 Second Avenue N.Y. When you write tell Mary Elliott[†] that my address is Iron Clad *Monitor* & ask her if she is good at taking hints.

If you can have three or four shirts made for me without bosoms & sent to New Haven as you propose & from there by Express I shall get them. Direct them as you do my letters. There is no use of putting bosoms in them now as I wear my vest buttoned close up in my neck & it would only be wearing out a good linen bosom for nothing to put them in now. But if they can be so *built* as to have bosoms put in some other time if I want them 'twould be just the thing.

The language ascribed to Capt. Worden in the Utica paper Mother sent me is false in toto. He is too much of a gentleman ever to stoop to use such language, to friend or foe. Not a word passed between the commanders of the two vessels during the fight & I doubt very much if either knew who was in command of his opponent.

Capt. Jeffers went up in the flag of truce a few days since with Capt. Millward[‡] (the Capt. of the Port), who always commands the boat that takes the flag up[§]. It is in fact, in nine cases out of ten, nothing more than a contrivance to spy out the enemy & learn what you can of his movements. You will see by some of the maps I have sent home about the place where the two flags meet. Beyond this spot, which is marked by a buoy, neither boat must pass. The spot is much more favourable for us to spy out their movements than for them to see what is going on among us. The boat first arriving at the buoy makes fast to it & awaits the arrival of the other, sometimes a period of four or five hours. In this case our boat waited about three hours, Capt. J. improving the time & opportunity with a good pair of opera glasses.

---

[*] Anna's brother was still in the Shenandoah Valley with Banks' army chasing Stonewall Jackson.
[†] Uncle Frank's daughter.
[‡] James Millward*.
[§] To near Craney Island.

Hampton Roads (March to May 1862)

Capt. Millward went on board the rebel steamer when she came alongside carrying his dispatches & accepted an invitation to "imbibe." He then returned to his own boat followed by the rebel captain after making up *his* dispatches, when of course they "imbibed" again, & remained at the table for some time conversing. Capt. M. inquired the news & was informed of the capture of New Orleans in what was intended as a joking, careless manner but it came out to[o] hard for a joke. He told Capt. M. that they were coming down from Norfolk to tow the *Monitor* up in a few days. Capt. M. hoped they would have a pleasant time. We would do all in our power to make it so if they would only let us know when they were coming. There was an endeavour to have the conversation appear easy & unconstrained but there was a stiffness & want of cordiality to[o] apparent to pass unnoticed. *While they were thus engaged one of the hands on the rebel boat managed to pass some of their papers on board of us unnoticed*— this is the way we get rebel news. Yesterday the flag [of truce] brought down Parson Brownlow's son & family.*

May 1st. This sheet should have been filled & sent off before now. The last two or three days of the month & the first two or three days of the next [are] rather busy ones with me, as at those times I deal out the clothing & small things the sailors need for the coming month. To give you a little idea of the machinery of a man of war I will try & go through the routine attending the giving out these things. In the first place, two or three days before the month expires I give my steward a blank for clothing & one for small stores (such as needles, thread, buttons, blacking, tobacco, soap & the numerous little things the sailor wants) for each mess. The ship's crew for convenience are divided into messes of ten or twelve men each, four in our case. Each of these messes as I have said are furnished by my steward with a blank for clothing & one for small stores. The name of each one in the mess is on the blanks & each one places opposite his name & in the appropriate column the number or amount of what he wants. These are then given to me by my steward & I have them to look over to see that no man is calling for more than I think he needs. I then copy them off on another blank & return the originals to the men through my steward. I then carry the copies to the Capt. & he approves them as being necessary for the health & comfort of the men. Then I go to the store rooms, have the boxes containing the different things taken out by the Capt. of the Hold & the boxes opened by my steward. The head men of each mess, or cooks as they are called, come up & get what the men of his mess had put down on the blank. My duty is to stand by with the requisition (as it is termed) & see that the things are properly dealt out. One of the officers of the ship must be with me & sign his name to the requisition as having seen the articles delivered, after which it is of no use for any of the

---

* William G. "Parson" Brownlow, Methodist minister and newspaper editor from Tennessee, who was a vocal opponent of secession in the years leading up to the Civil War. After being jailed briefly at the start of the war, he and his family were exiled to the North.

men to complain of mistakes as they will not be listened to. The articles each one has had is then copied on a rec't book & he signs his name, an officer signing as witness. Nothing is dealt out at any other time (except provisions which are served every day) so that if one gets out of tobacco in the middle of the month he must wait till the first of the next for a supply.

We rec'd an order from the Department to day forbidding any one on board giving information to any one in regard to the vessel, of her armament, repairs, intended destination, or any of the details of construction & no one must be allowed on board except the personal friends of the officers, in whom they have the fullest confidence. This applies to all vessels.

I went on deck to day after finishing my dinner just as a small boat came along side with a number of army officers & among them a lady. This was before the order referred to above had been read. I was the only officer on deck except the one on watch (whose duty is to receive visitors, but is not allowed to shew them around) so I volunteered to shew them around. One of them (a Col.) introduced the lady to me as his wife, Mrs. Howland[*], & one of his companions, as Gen. Morrill[†]. As the lady was young & pretty & withal intelligent I took special pains to shew them everything worth seeing. Before the party left I was told that she had expended over one hundred thousand dollars of her private fortune in chartering the steam ship *Dan'l Webster* as a hospital ship & fitting it out with every kind of hospital stores for the use of the sick & wounded in the brigade to which her husband is attached & she was to remain to superintend the nursing. She said it was a terrible necessity that compelled men to fight in this way but it was a woman's duty to alleviate the sufferings of the sick & wounded as far as possible. Her husband is a son of Mr. Howland of the late firm of Howland & Aspinwall.

But it is late at night & I have a severe head ache & must bid you good night.

William

[Marginalia] Friday morning, May 2nd. A clear pleasant morning for a wonder. I think you will find this a particularly stupid letter & had better consider it private for that reason. My love to all, especially to yourself & children.

William

---

[*] Eliza N. Howland (1826-1917). From a wealthy New York City family of social reformers and anti-slavery activists, she and her two sisters and mother served as nurses during the war. Her husband, Joseph Howland, the son of a New York shipping magnate, was colonel of the 16th New York Infantry.
[†] George W. Morell, a brigade commander in the III Corps of the Army of the Potomac.

Hampton Roads (March to May 1862)

No. 1—

Iron Clad *Monitor*
Hampton Roads, Va.
May 2nd, 1862

Dear Anna,

It fell to my lot to send off to you this morning a couple of extremely stupid sheets of paper, or rather the matter contained in them, for I won't libel the paper, but rather the matter. It is the only time since I left home that I have written merely as a duty. At all other times it has been a real pleasure. But for the last few days I have had a dull, heavy headache which I find is not very conducive to brilliant ideas or suggestive of any very interesting trains of thought. So if you find the letter dull & insipid you must take the above as an apology.

This has been rather an eventful day with us. In the first place we have taken a jump from raw chilly easterly winds to the middle of summer. The sun rose bright & clear & soon after breakfast a shelter from his rays was a desideration. The water of the harbour was as still & smooth & placid as the surface of a mirror, a great contrast to the heaving surges amid which we have existed nearly ever since we have been here. At noon a soft, pleasant, southerly breeze sprung up, just enough to cover the surface of the watery mirror with gentle ripples & refresh us with its welcome coolness.

Event No. 2. Before we were up from the breakfast table we were honored with a call from a new married couple — a brother of Lieut. Greene & his wife, who were on their wedding tour.[*] We all had a very pleasant time & enjoyed their visit exceedingly. She took dinner with us, being the first lady who has ever dined on board the *Monitor*. After leaving us Lieut. G. went with them to Gen. Wool's head quarters in the Fortress. The Gen. received them very cordially, shewed them his quarters, took Mrs. G. into his garden & picked a bouquet for her & then detailed *Col. Cannon* to escort them around the Fort. Capt. Jeffers remarked at the dinner table, "that he [Jeffers] was an old married man of 12 or 15 years standing & held his wife in great estimation. He honored her above all other women & he didn't know of any better way of manifesting his esteem than by shewing ladies all proper attention when they were so placed as to make those attentions desirable. He thought he was manifesting his regard for his wife by honoring the sex." That's good doctrine isn't it?

Well, to event No. 3. Of course such an extraordinary physical phenomena as a pleasant day would draw out crowds of visitors. They came in swarms, of all ranks & grades, from Brig. Gen. Franklin[†] down. Of course at such times I have an opportunity of forming many pleasant acquaintances,

---

[*] George S. Greene, Jr., a civil engineer in New York City, and his wife Susan Dana from Charlestown, MA.
[†] William B. Franklin, a division commander in the Army of the Potomac.

but ten chances to one if I ever see them again. Those who are located in camps in this vicinity I sometimes meet when I go ashore, but the most of them are on the move to different distant localities & their stay here is but a few days. I generally manage to get posted up by them in the war news & movements, past & to come. But in regard to future movements it is a good deal of surmise with most of them, or a matter of opinion, so that after hearing them talk you are as much in the dark as before.

I asked Gen. Franklin this afternoon about McClelland's operations. He said he thought another week would tell the story. Afterward the Col. of a Penn. regiment told me that McClelland was commencing regular siege operations which it would take six months to complete. But after hearing all of them talk I am inclined to the opinion that McClelland is attracting their attention in front till Banks or McDowell[*] can take them in the rear & thus bag the whole army. There is no grumbling here at McC.'s want of energy or slowness. Every one is perfectly satisfied thus far & thinks he has done all that could be expected. We have heard occasional heavy firing in that direction all day.

All the officers were ashore this afternoon, except the few on duty & Capt. J. had turned in for his siesta, so it devolved upon myself to do the honors to our numerous visitors & you can imagine I was kept busy enough. No sooner was one boat load disposed of than another arrived, sometimes two or three at a time. All expressed themselves much pleased, at leaving, very profuse in their thanks &c. You may think it strange but my hand is actualy lame from the shaking & squeezing it has rec'd. You know my right hand can't bear much squeezing. Towards the latter part of the day I used my left.

I heard from my letter in the [*New York*] *Times* this morning in a singular way. One of our vessels came in this morning from Fort Macon bringing the news of its capture[†] & the Paymaster came on board to see me. While I was shewing him the ship he began to compliment me on my letter, saying it was the best account of the fight he had read. I thought at first he was mistaken & it was only after he had repeated some portions that I called to mind my letter to your Father. Strange that the first I should hear of it should be from Fort Macon.

Saturday noon [May 3]. Yours containing one from Fanny Dikeman[‡] mailed the 29th April has just been rec'd. I fear from some of your enquiries that you do not get all my letters, as you want a description of the *Galena* & you should have rec'd some little a/c of her in a letter I sent you some time ago. You should also have a letter by this time in regard to having my letters

---

[*] Irwin McDowell, commander of the I Corps of the Army of the Potomac. His troops were in northern Virginia guarding Washington from a possible attack by Stonewall Jackson from the Shenandoah Valley. Banks' army was still in the Shenandoah Valley.

[†] The fort guarding the North Carolina port cities of Beaufort and Morehead City had fallen to Burnside's forces on April 26, 1862 after a one-month siege.

[‡] Eldest daughter of Anna's aunt Nancy Tuthill from Utica, NY.

published in the press. Yes, by all means tell me all about the garden. Next to yourself & my friends I want to hear about that even if I can't enjoy walking in it & tasting the fruit. Sarah should be in rec't of her letter before this time. Fanny Dikeman has gott to learn some common sense yet & have some of her false ideas of life changed.

Is everybody in LaSalle going to fight? It must be a pleasant state of society there.

I am going ashore this afternoon to *straw hat* the crew. The sun comes down hot & a shade is grateful. We are trying to get an artist on board & have our photographs taken. Hope we will be successfull.

As you propose I could send you two or three sheets of news every day if I did not know that the telegraph would anticipate me. If it were not for that you could have it from me two or three [days] before you see it in the papers. As it is it is useless to fill my sheets with it. Hereafter I will number my letters so you will know when one misses. This will be No. 1. Sending letter for letter I shan't keep this to make two sheets of it but send it as it is.

Love to all,

William

[Marginalia] "Latest news from Fortress Munroe — All quiet at Hampton Roads."

No. 2—

Iron Clad *Monitor*
Hampton Roads, Va.
May 3rd, 1862

Dear Anna,

I went ashore & mailed a letter to you after dinner & then started for a stroll among the soldiers' quarters at Camp Hamilton*. I got as far as the quarters of the 16th Mass. when I came across Capts. Banks† (brother of Gen. B.) & Richardson‡, both of the 16th. Of course I could go no further, for a Monitor isn't often picked up in their camp, so we all turned in to Capt. Richardson's quarters — a good snug comfortable log house, green blind door & windows, tasty fence made of the limbs & branches of trees interwoven, surrounding nice, well filled & carefully cultivated flower beds &

---

* The camp was located 100 yards from the causeway connecting Fort Monroe and the mainland.
† Gardner Banks (1830-1871), captain of Company H of the 16th Massachusetts Infantry and a younger brother of Major General Nathaniel Banks. His regiment did garrison duty at Fort Monroe until May 8, occupied Norfolk on May 10, and joined the Army of the Potomac at the Battle of Fair Oaks on June 13. They fought at all the major battles in the East. His youngest brother Hiram, a second lieutenant in his regiment, was killed at his side at the Second Battle of Bull Run in August 1862.
‡ Samuel W. Richardson (1824-1884), captain of Company A of the 16th Massachusetts Infantry.

gravel walks. A well laid but rather narrow brick walk led by the door & continued on to the neighboring quarters. His single room was well furnished with chairs, table, &c, & photographs of his family graced the walls.

We had a very pleasant chat of an hour or more without the annoyance of being asked *to drink*. The Capt. got me a glass of water upon my asking for some, displaying unusual good sense in offering no apology for not asking me to take something stronger. His actions said, I am a temperance man & I take it for granted all my guests are.

They shewed me around the Camp, pointing out all worth seeing. We visited their bakery, where they had 1400 loaves of nice looking bread all baked to day. The gymnasium, quite a roomy building, all the material for which, except the floor, were obtained by the soldiers from the woods. Until our fight with the *Merrimac* they had 25 or 30 ladies (wives of the officers) in the camp & this building furnished facilities for many pleasant balls & parties. From their account time must have passed pleasantly so long as the ladies remained, but now they long for active service.

Their chapel tent was large & roomy with a good board floor. They were using for a hospital a commodious & comfortable looking house, surrounded by a handsome garden, roses in full bloom & peeping in at the windows, formerly the residence of one of the F.F.V.'s*. Here was the dark side of the picture — though the regiment being in a healthy locality but few were sick, only two severely so, one had been wounded by an accidental shot through the foot.

In passing around the camp I remarked to Capt. Banks the incongruous appearance of the green blinds, lattice work & occasionaly some tastily carved wood work ornamenting the rough looking log houses of the men. Well, said he in reply, when we first came here there were a good many secesh houses scattered around through the country. A vacant house would be pointed out to the "boys" as a secesh, with a hint that it was of no special benefit to the country in its present location, when a few hours sufficed to distribute it around the camp & in this way the boys have added many comforts to their quarters. In the enclosure around one house I saw 4 beautiful peacocks — secesh plunder.

In some former letter I have mentioned how singularly we sometimes come across old acquaintances. An instance of the kind occurred to day. About the middle of the forenoon a boat load of Army officers came on board &, as in nine cases out of ten, I was detailed to escort them through the *Monitor*. One was introduced to me as Col. Mix[†] of one of the N.Y. cavalry

---

[*] First Families of Virginia.
[†] Simon H. Mix (1825-1864), colonel of the 3rd New York Cavalry and a newspaper editor in Schoharie, NY before the war. He was killed near Petersburg on June 15, 1864. After the war his younger brother, who had been searching for Simon's grave, received a letter from a former Confederate officer, portions of which were published in the *Schoharie Union* on December 21, 1865: "At half past twelve, the enemy commenced a charge, which

regiments & his brother as Lieut. Col.* of the same Reg. In my school boy days I attended school with two brothers of this name & upon comparing notes found them to be the persons. They were on their way to reinforce Burnside & I made an appointment with them to meet in Norfolk. Hope to be able to keep it. Burnside I think is being largely reinforced.

Ten o'clock & I must to bed. The roar of heavy guns at Yorktown for the last few minutes has been almost incessant.

Sunday morning. Just done breakfast. Tug alongside with Sec'y Fox, Frank Blair†, M. [Henri] Mercier (the French minister), a brother of Sec'y Welles & about twenty other notables, including one of the Blows from St. Louis (I believe an acquaintance of Dave's). Also two remarkably homely looking females of an age uncertain. Half an hour later and a boat load of army officers comes, & few minutes after, another & another & another. So here is business for the forenoon without even time to read the papers.

We have just rec'd news of the evacuation of Yorktown. I do not know the particulars but hope the rebels have not left if there is none of our forces in their rear to cut off their retreat.

Later—Our boat has just arrived from shore while I am writing with McClelland's dispatch to Gen. Wool saying simply that he was in Yorktown. We shall have particulars soon.

There would be some satisfaction in sending you the various items of news if I were not sure that the telegraph would give them to you three or four days in advance of my letters. The surrender of Fort Macon at that particular time was owing to a fortunate shot of a rifled gun from our forces, which dismounted three of their barbette guns, then richoched & dismounted another, killing eight men in its passage & wounding nineteen others. Two of the guns disabled were rifled pieces which had annoyed our forces the most.

---

was led in gallant style by your late brother, across a piece of woods which had been cut down in front of our Battery. When about three hundred yards from our Battery, your brother was shot down, with several of his men, when the line gave way. We then charged in turn, and I passed by where your brother was lying. Supposing by his uniform he was a Captain, I thought nothing more about the matter until we returned, when I went to him. He asked for water, which I gave him. . . . He was shot in the breast by a small grenade[?] which went through him. He died in about fifteen minutes after he was wounded, with his head on my knee, seemingly very easy. He only spoke once while I was with him, and that was to ask for water. . . . You have the consolation to know that your brother died as a brave man should die, with his face to the enemy, and fully ten feet in advance of his command."

* John Mix (1834-1881). Born in Chautauqua County, NY, he served ten years as a dragoon in the regular army before the Civil War. He was commissioned a major of the 3rd New York Cavalry in September 1861. In December 1862 he resigned from the volunteer service and was commissioned a captain in the 2nd U.S. Cavalry. At war's end he was transferred out West where his regiment fought the Plains Indians. He died on board a Santa Fé train bound for Fort Cummings, NM, where he was headed on sick leave. No evidence could be found supporting Keeler's claim that John and Simon Mix were brothers
† Republican Congressman from Missouri.

Civil War Years: USS *Monitor* (1862)

On the last appearance of the *Merrimac* Com. Tatnall[*] was in command. He left Norfolk with sealed orders to be opened off Sewall's point. When opened they instructed him to pass the blockade at all events & go up York river.[†] He returned to Yorktown [Norfolk] & resigned rather than be dismissed. Capt. Buchanan is now in command.[‡] He was probably not as severely wounded in the fight with the *Cumberland* as was reported. What effect the taking of Yorktown will have upon the *Merrimac*'s future movements we cannot tell, but a few days will probably shew what policy she will pursue.

Don't believe all the thousand & one rumours you hear & will hear of our being taken by driving wedges under our turret, throwing hot water on our decks &c &c. We all laugh at it & you may too for we cannot be injured in that way. The attempt to board us would be the very extreme of folly — a blank cartridge from our own guns would sweep our decks to say nothing of hand grenades &c. They never will attempt it.

Special love to yourself & the children & kind regards to all.

William

[Marginalia] Send Hen a paper to day with one of my vest buttons as I thought he would like to see a naval button. Coat buttons are the same but larger.

1/2 past one P.M. *Merrimac* just in sight around Sewall's point. Crew going to quarters & company leaving like frightened chickens.

No. 3—

Iron Clad *Monitor*
Hampton Roads, Va.
Sunday Evening, May 4/62

Dear Anna,

I had a letter just finished as the cry, the "Big Thing" (as we have nicknamed the *Merrimac*) is coming, started me from my state room to the deck. Sure enough there she was just emerging from behind Sewall's Point, the black cloud from her bituminous coal hovering over her like the genius of evil omen. She steamed over towards Newport News a piece & then came to a stand.

In the meantime down came our awnings. Off came the smoke stacks following the bo'sun's whistle & the hoarse & prolonged call of "a-l-l h a n d s prepare ship for action." Odds & ends were gathered up & stowed away.

---

[*] Josiah Tattnall, commander of the defenses of Virginia's waters.
[†] Tattnall received no such orders.
[‡] Franklin Buchanan commanded the *Virginia* on the first day of the Battle of Hampton Roads and was shot in the thigh after having come on deck to fire a musket at Union infantry who had refused to recognize the surrender of the *Congress*. He did not resume command of the *Virginia* after his injury.

Hampton Roads (March to May 1862)

The iron hatches placed in readiness to cover the openings. Magazine opened. Additional hand grenades filled. Everybody seemed to step with a livelier gait & countenances which had been clouded with discontent for the past six weeks, now fairly radiated with satisfaction. Our decks which had been crowded with visitors was speedily vacated. One female who happened to be among the number nearly fainting upon learning that the dreaded *Merrimac* was actually coming. I rushed back to my state room, added a hasty P.S. to your letter & dispatched it by a tug, which happened to be along side, expecting to be able to date my next from the interior of the "Big Thing."

A few minutes of apparent confusion to the uninitiated but in reality of the strictest order & discipline & we were ready. So was our dinner, on which we immediately commenced a vigorous attack, carrying everything before us by assault, passing the outer works (soup) without difficulty & carrying the stronghold of roast beef at the point of the fork. Capt. Jeffers (who by the way loves a good dinner & can tell just how one should be cooked) declaring that as we had tried her before on an empty stomach he would fight her this time on a full one.

On returning to the deck she lay just where we left her. An increased volume of smoke soon indicated a renewal of her fires & in a little time she was slowly floating off to her lair. She probably came down on a sort of Sunday excursion as we thought we could distinguish females on board. When they learn of the evacuation of Yorktown, which they must on their return to Norfolk, they must soon decide upon the course they will pursue. I think a day or two will shew what they intend to do. I see but two things left them — to stay in their hole & be nabbed there as they surely will or come out into the Roads & fight as a last desperate resort.

The "Old Flag" (the Commodore) is anticipating an attack to night, but we have watched the "beast" closer than he has & think we know its habits better. Although its deeds are manifestly evil, still it evidently prefers light to darkness. At any rate I shall make my usual toilette for the night, confidently expecting to slumber undisturbed till "Billy"* makes his entree with, "half past seven sir."

We are all waiting anxiously to hear the details of the evacuation of Yorktown. We hear now that the enemy left everything in his haste — artillery, camp equipage, stores & in fact pretty much everything & that "George"† was after them with all his cavalry, light infantry & field artillery. For half an hour this afternoon we could hear one continuous roar of cannon — we suppose the rear guard of the rebels & our advance. The firing I mentioned as having heard last night was to conceal their retreat. Sec'y Fox, who was on board this morning, slept with "George" last night & left there this morning

---

* Keeler's African-American servant William Scott. He survived the sinking of the *Monitor* but later deserted.
† McClellan.

at 5, knew nothing of the evacuation. It could not have been discovered till after that.

Capt. Jeffers has sent down to the "Old Flag" for permission to shell out Sewall's Point tomorrow. Of course we shan't get it. The supineness & want of energy exhibited in keeping the two hundred guns that are afloat here, silent & useless when they could render effective service, is disgraceful & shameful & it is no wonder that the people are beginning to ask why something is not done. Day after day the emblem of rebellion flaunts in our very faces, & day after day we remain torpid & inactive. On board the *Monitor* we begin to feel that, like the turtle, we would like to draw in our head, go to the bottom & burrow into the mud out of sight.

'Tis no fault of our Captain you may rest assured. Half his time is spent in contriving plans for crippling the rebels, cutting out a vessel, shelling a battery or destroying the *Merrimac*. His plans are no boyish schemes. He is a person of sound judgement & large experience & as an ordnance officer is second to no one in the Service but Dahlgren.[*] The fact of his being ordered to the *Monitor* shew[s] the confidence the Department have in his ability. At Hatteras he had charge of getting the whole fleet over the bar & it was only through his untiring energy that our fleet was taken safely over & so few of the vessels lost. I honestly believe if his advice had been followed, Norfolk & the *Merrimac* would now be in our possession.

In one of your letters you enquired about the *Galena*. I won't venture an opinion of my own but will give you Com. Goldsborough's. The Department, after she arrived her[e], wrote him asking him to examine her & give his opinion. The "Old Flag" came down one day (she lies just alongside of us) & after looking through her wrote to them just these words, "I consider her beneath naval criticism." Other vessels are building on a similar plan to our own which will be larger, stronger & more perfect in detail, *but there never will be but one Monitor.*

Lieut. Greene's father has just been promoted to a Brig. Gen.[†] The Gen. Smith[‡] whose death you may have noticed a few days since is a brother of Capt. Jeffers' wife.

---

[*] John A. Dahlgren, the Navy's ordnance expert. He designed the muzzle-loaded cannon bearing his name that was used with such deadly effect by both sides during the Civil War.
[†] George S. Greene, Sr. A West Point graduate, he resigned his commission in the army in 1836 following the death of his first wife and their three young children. He remarried, had six more children, one of whom was Keeler's messmate, and worked as a civil engineer. In January 1862 he was appointed colonel of the 60th New York Infantry. He was promoted to brigadier general of volunteers on April 28, while serving on Nathaniel Banks' staff in the Shenandoah Valley. The next year the 61-year old general gained nationwide fame on the second day at Gettysburg when his brigade defended the Union right flank against an entire Confederate division.
[‡] Major General Charles F. Smith. He died of disease in Savannah, TN on April 25.

Hampton Roads (March to May 1862)

Monday morning [May 5]. As I anticipated, I slept undisturbed even by a dream of our foe. She is not in sight. 'Tis raining hard & we shall probably have an unpleasant day. We have had *three* day[s] of pleasant weather.

Monday noon. Have just rec'd a paper from Mary [Brown]. Thanks & love to her & Dave. I believe you[r] offer was letter for letter. I shall hold you to it, so look out.

[No signature]

No. 5—

Iron Clad Monitor
Hampton Roads
May 6th, 1862

Dear Anna,

Have you any serious objections to the issue of edition No. 5 from this prolific press? If so, please write & let me know. By the way, I will not insist upon your rigidly fulfilling your part of the contract but will let you off with one or two letters a week if they are good long ones. I know very well that I have twenty four leisure hours when you have one & I know just as well that that is all that would prevent me from getting a letter by every mail. I sent off sheet No. 4 to Henry by to day's mail. I believe it contained no particular news, nor anything very interesting, but I contrived to fill the sheet with something, I hardly know what. Hope you will have the patience to read it.

I find your letters are accumulating on my hands & am in a quandary what to do with them. Most of our folks destroy their letters as soon as rec'd so as to leave no trophies of that kind to fall into rebel hands in case we should not always come out conquerors. What shall I do with yours? I do not like the idea of destroying them & have kept them so far, intending if we ever got into a tight spot to throw them into one of the furnaces.

From the thousand & one rumours afloat here in regard to the evacuation of Yorktown by the rebel forces, we hardly know how to separate facts from fancies, to know what to believe & what to discredit. I fear McClelland has to some extent been out generaled.* Still his friends here claim that he has all the fruits of a great victory, excepting prisoners. He has all the enemy's cannon, camp equipage, and material of war. Still he has not the prestige which perhaps is important as anything else. Then on the other hand he has no fearful list of killed & wounded, of broken hearts & homes made desolate. That the evacuation was entirely unexpected by every one & by no one more than "George" himself I have by the best authority.

---

* Indeed he had. Commanding only a small force at Yorktown, Magruder marched his troops back and forth along the Warwick-Yorktown line, making McClellan believe he had a much larger force. They slipped away undetected on the night of May 3-4, the day before McClellan's planned grand bombardment on May 5.

Civil War Years: USS *Monitor* (1862)

On Sunday forenoon, as I have before written you, Sec'y Fox was on board of us at the time that the intelligence of the evacuation [of Yorktown] first reached here. The news was brought on board & he could not believe it — 'twas impossible he said. He had left McClelland's tent at four o'clock that morning & nothing was know[n] of it then. The rebels up to two o'clock that morning had kept up a steady & heavy firing. After that it was as still as a country village. He came down for the purpose of taking the *Galena* up York river the same day (Sunday) & running her past their batteries in the night to have her ready to open her fire on their rear early Monday morning. Asst. Sec'y of War, Mr. Tucker, was on board this morning. He left McClelland's tent in company with Mr. Fox & came off with him. At that time nothing had occurred to excite their suspicions.

The fear of our gun boats was probably the real cause of this sudden movement. Why they [the rebels] did not commence sooner & thus gain time to take with them their material is surprising. It has been know[n] that they have been occupied for some weeks past in throwing up intrenchments around Williamsburg. They commenced about the time McClelland began to move his army this way. The position they now occupy cannot be reached by our gun boats except by their long range guns, while their gun boats on James river will probably prove very annoying to our troops around this new position of the enemy.

The *Galena* goes up James river to morrow morning & I presume will be accompanied by other of our gun boats, enough I hope to sink the rebel fleet or drive it up to Richmond. It is expected that as soon as our boats get started up the river the *Merrimac* will be after them, in which case we will go too & the "Big Thing" will probably find her self in a trap, for there is not sufficient depth of water to carry her to Richmond & her retreat down the river will be cut off by ourselves, so that nothing will be left but to fight for it. Almost any way you look at it, warm work must come in a few days, it cannot be much longer delayed.

It cannot be that they will passively see our gun boats go up the river to destroy their fleet & shell out their batteries on Jamestown island. What sort of infernal machines they are contriving for our destruction we don't know, but we caught sight to day of a singular looking craft with something on top that looked & turned like the arms of a windmill. It came out from behind Sewall's point for a few moments & then darted back again. We are putting in two more engines to drive a large pump intended to free us from water in case the "Big Thing" succeeds in getting a hole in us under water, either with her ram or shot. When this is done she cannot sink us.

I went ashore to day for an hour or two & having nothing else to do took a stroll around the Fort [Monroe]. It looked very pleasant. The green velvety slopes of the ramparts & glacis (you see I am getting scientific) were spangled with bright yellow daisies, while inside, the dark green of the live oaks mingled with the livelier foliage of the willows. In some parts companies of soldiers were on drill, others were playing ball, wrestling & amusing themselves in a variety of ways.

As I passed by Gen. Wool's quarters, which are surrounded by a beautiful garden, he stood at the gate bareheaded & recognizing me invited me in, an invitation I was forced to decline as I was not dressed to regulation. As I stood admiring the flowers he picked a sprig or two of migonet (*Webster* for spelling) & handed it to me with the remark that it was a sweet smelling flower. I told him if he would allow me I would send it to my wife. "Oh no," he said & started off, "I will pick her a nice boquet." I told him that as you lived on the western prairies it would be impossible for me to get it to you, but with his permission I would send this to you from him. "Certainly," he said, "send it to your lady with my kind regards. Tell her that I wish she was here that I could pick her a nice boquet." You will find it enclosed.

[No signature]

[Marginalia] Wednesday morning [May 7]. Clear, cool & pleasant. No *Merrimac* to be seen. Her last Sunday's excursion was for Sen. Mallory* who was on board of her.

1/2 past one—Pres't Lincoln & suite just left.† *Merrimac* coming down. Clearing ship for action. 1/2 past 3—Just done dinner. *Merrimac* in sight under Craney island.

No. 6—

Iron Clad *Monitor*
Hampton Roads, Va.
May 7th, 1862

Dear Anna,

My last was mailed to you to day with one or two hurriedly added postscripts. One about noon to the effect that the "Big Thing" had again made her appearance & another just after dinner while she was in status quo under Craney island, apparently chewing the bitter cud of reflection & ruminating sorrowfully upon the future. She remained there smoking, reflecting & ruminating till nearly sunset when she slowly crawled off nearly concealed in a huge murky cloud of her own emission, black & repulsive as the perjured hearts of her traitorous crew. The water hisses & boils with indignation as like some huge slimy reptile she slowly emerges from her loathsome lair with the morning light, vainly seeking with glairing eyes some mode of escape through the meshes of the net which she feels is daily closing her in. Behind

---

* Stephen R. Mallory, the Confederate Secretary of the Navy.

† Lincoln arrived at Fort Monroe on May 6, accompanied by Secretary of the Treasury Salmon Chase and Secretary of War Edwin Stanton. The purpose of their visit was to prod the slow-moving McClellan into action.

her she already hears the hounds of the hunter & before are the ever watchful guards whom it is certain death to pass.

We remain in the same position we have occupied since the fight, a sort of advance guard of the fleet. A little astern & to one side is the *Galena*, then the *Octororo* & scattered along at intervals are the light draught but heavily armed gun boats of the fleet. Behind all these & at the entrance of the harbour are congregated the steam rams, Frigates, transports & other vessels, large & small, composing the "North Atlantic Blockading Squadron." The tri color of France & the cross of St. George indicate the representatives of other nations & to day a Danish man of war was added to the number. Here we all lie waiting the progress of events, though we incline to the opinion that events progress very slowly as far as we are concerned, so slowly in fact that we begin to fear a state of utter stagnation.

We received a visit to day from President Lincoln, in company with Secretaries Chase & Staunton [Stanton] & other dignitaries, attended by Gen. Wool & staff in full uniform. Mr. Lincoln had a sad, care worn & anxious look in strong contrast with the gay cortege by which he was surrounded. As the boat which brought the party came along side every eye sought the *Monitor* but his own. He stood with his face averted as if to hide some disagreeable sight. When he turned to us I could see his lip quiver & his frame tremble with strong emotion & imagined that the terrible drama in these waters of the ninth [eight] & tenth [ninth] of March was passing in review before him. As the officers were introduced I was presented as being from his own state. He was very happy he said to find one from Illinois on board the *Monitor*. He examined everything about the vessel with care, manifesting great interest. His remarks evidently shewing that he had carefully studied what he thought to be our weak points & that he was well acquainted with all the mechanical details of our construction. Most of our visitors come on board filled with enthusiasm & patriotism, ready, like a bottle of soda water, to effervesce the instant the cork is withdrawn. But with Mr. Lincoln it was different. His few remarks as he accompanied us around the vessel were sound, simple & practical. The points of admiration & exclamation he left to his suite. Before he left he had the crew mustered on the Spar deck & passed slowly before them hat in hand. It gives me pleasure to say, & I record it to his credit, that he declined the invitation to whiskey but took a glass of ice water.

Gen. Wool recognised me & enquired if I had sent his flowers to you & seemed much pleased when I told him that I had.

As the President & his party left us we gave them three hearty cheers.

Another tug was soon alongside with a company of congressmen, some twenty or more, to see the *Monitor*. Sen. Latham of Cal.[*] & Howard of Michigan[†] with two or three others were assigned to me. Of course, all

---

[*] Milton S. Latham.
[†] Jacob M. Howard.

expressed themselves much pleased with all they saw, but their sight seeing was suddenly interrupted by the bo'sun's whistle & cry of "all hands prepare ship for action." As they beat a hasty retreat the *Merrimac* was seen slowly coming around Sewall's Point, apparently bound straight for us, but as I stated in the commencement of my letter she soon came to a stand.

In the afternoon [we] received a visit from a number of the officers of the Danish man of war which a[n]chored here in the morning. Among them was a Flag Officer & the Captain of the vessel. All of them conversed in english very readily & appeared much pleased with the attentions we shewed them. They were a fine appearing, intelligent looking set of officers, appearing better both morally and physically than any from our own or from foreign ships of war who have visited us.

Capt. Jeffers upon an invitation has gone ashore to Gen. Wool's to meet the Pres't, the Gen., Mr. Chase & others for the purpose I suppose of planning some work for our vessels which are now lying here utterly useless. I feel confident that Capt. J. with his restless energy will persuade them to do something but fear that he will be defeated by our superannuated "Old Flag." Mr. Lincoln evidently respects Capt. J.'s opinions & I am inclined to think will give him his support if his plans appear at all reasonable or feasible.

I enclose an article from the *Baltimore American*, the publishing of which will send the editor to the Rip Raps the next time he makes his appearance here.

What are you all doing at home? We are having beautiful weather here & hope you are sharing it. I can imagine you busy planting the garden, admiring the flowers & wishing that I could see them. It is late, so a kiss & good night.

William

No. 7—

Iron Clad *Monitor*
Hampton Roads
May 8th, 1862

Dear Anna,

I will commence where I left you in my last, which ended with last evening.

Capt. Jeffers returned late in the evening, having spent the time in consultation with Messrs. Lincoln, Chase, Staunton & Gen. Wool & Com. Goldsborough. He gave us to understand that work was on hand for the morning, though it was possible we might not take any active part.

This morning in good season I turned out & found the *Galena* just getting under way, followed soon after by the *Port Royal* & *Aroostock*. They proceeded up James river, followed by our hearty wishes for their success. They had not gained the mouth of the river when we saw a dense cloud of black smoke coming down. Imagination at once conjured up the *Jamestown* & *Yorktown* (who had gone up the river in the night) as coming down to meet them. Others would have it the "Big Thing," others again some infernal machine for blowing us up. On it came enveloped in its smoky vail which disclosed just enough to allow us free play for our imaginations. Every moment we expected to see the *Galena* (who lead) open her fire, but no. The cloud drove past the *Galena* apparently unnoticed, then past each of the other two in succession, still not a shot was fired. Then it must be a flag of truce, but what could it want in this unusual place. Our doubts were soon solved, for out of the cloud of smoke fairly skimming over the smooth waters of the bay came a little tug as if the evil one was after it. Our hail as she passed us brought her to, where we found she had been sent from Norfolk last night to tow up a schooner from some small creek in this vicinity. But the crew, coming to the conclusion that they were towing on the wrong end of the line, thought they would try the other. So instead of fastening onto the schooner they came over to Gen. Mansfield's Camp at Newport News & let the soldiers fasten onto them.

They brought us the gratifying news that Norfolk was about being abandoned. They continued on to the Fort & in a short time word came to Capt. J. that the Pres't & Flag Officer [Goldsborough] wanted to see him. He returned in a short time with orders to go up & feel of Sewall's Point. We were soon under way followed by the *Naugatuck* & four other of our gun boats.

I remained on deck till we got well around the point & in full sight of the rebel rag floating from the center of their earth works. All our men were at quarters & Capt. J. deeming it unsafe to remain on deck any longer, I went below.

Capt. J. sent the order to Mr. Gager to take her as close in as the water would allow. There followed a short period of deathlike silence — then an order to Mr. Greene to load with ten second Birney shell (incendiary) — then to elevate his tangent sight for four hundred yards — then to take deliberate aim & fire. Bang went the gun, echoed in a few seconds by the exploding shell.

"Give her the other, Mr. Greene," & the gun responds.

'Round goes the turret to bring the ports away from the fort to load which did not take long."

"Can't you take us in a little closer, Mr. Gager?"

"I will try sir."

"Tell Mr. Greene to lower his tangent to three hundred yards," & bang, bang go the guns again. As yet no response from the fort. Their rag still flies but nothing living is to be seen.

We are now within about three hundred yards of the entrenchments & our guns are served as rapidly as possible using Birney shells with five second fuses. Capt. J., [who] has left the pilot house & has slid back one of the iron

Hampton Roads (March to May 1862)

hatches of the turret, stands with his head out to have a good view of the effects of our shot.

Our gun boats had now come within shooting distance, 3/4 of a mile, & the rapid firing of their guns told of an iron storm around the rebel works which had now woke up & replied by an occasional shot. We continued till our guns were well warmed up when we withdrew from position No. 1 on the accompanying diagram to position No. 2 & ceased our fire.* Capt. J. here told me if I was good at dodging I might go on deck, a permission I gladly accepted & witnessed a scene never to be forgotten.

In front of us was the battery with the flag still bidding us defiance. On the other side, four of our gun boats drawn up in a half circle were sending an almost uninterrupted storm of iron over our heads & into the rebel defences. You will understand our relative positions by refering to the accompanying rough diagram. No. 1 is our first position while firing — No. 2 our second while witnessing the fight of the gunboats — No. 3 the *Seminole* — No. 4 *Dacotah* — No. 5 *Susquehanna* — No. 6 *San Jacinto* — No. 7 the redoubtable *Naugatuck* as far out of harm's way as she could well get & whose chief exploit consisted in sending a shot through the *Susquehanna*'s spanker & exploding a shell over our decks, one of the pieces coming not ten feet from Capt. J. & myself who were standing together. "Why the beggar," says Capt. J., "we are in more danger from him than the enemy."

One of our incendiary shells had fired the buildings inside the defences & they were blazing up fiercely, sending up dense volumes of black smoke. The shells from the gun boats were bursting in, around, overhead & on all sides, some ricocheting in the water in front, then plunging full into the defences. Others bursting in the air & sending their fragments in a deadly shower below. Others again bury themselves in the sand in front — their explosion sends a huge column of it into the air. Now a splendid shot from the *Seminole* & down comes the emblem of rebellion with three hearty cheers from all our vessels.

Still the iron storm ceases not & we look anxiously as we see the fallen flag just shewing itself above the earth work ready to rise once more & bid us defiance, but a shell explodes apparently in its very folds & again it falls. But they manage to get it up once more, though some lives must have been lost in doing it. They fire but seldom, no one appearing willing to expose himself to our fire in loading, but they made some good shots, some of their shells going but a few feet above our heads, but strange to say not one of our vessels was struck. I could not but admire their pluck, rebels though they were, in putting up their fallen flag amid the burning of their buildings & the iron storm we were raining down upon them. What further damage we did them we could not tell.

---

* See Sketch No. 3 at the beginning of the book.

Civil War Years: USS *Monitor* (1862)

The *Merrimac* made her entree upon the stage about this time & our orders being not to bring on an engagement of the vessels at this time & having accomplished our object, we obeyed the Commodore's signal to "resume moorings."

We returned about six o'clock, got our supper or dinner & I went ashore [and] found tugs, steamers, barges, canal boats & in fact everything that could carry a soldier crowded with them. They are to effect a landing on the opposite side to night & to morrow will be a day big with events. The whole fleet are to move up & there will be a general pitching into the forts, the *Merrimac*, & everything wearing the "Stars & bars" & to morrow night is to see us in Norfolk. This is the programme according to report, so mote it be.*

I hope you will give me credit for this letter. It is nearly twelve o'clock, I am tired & sleepy besides having a severe headache, the effect of the excitement & an empty stomach. I hardly know what I have written, but have endeavoured to give you a faint description of the events of the day. To do it justice would require an abler pen than mine. But I must bid you good night with love to yourself & all.

William

[Marginalia] Friday Morning, 9th. No movement yet. Mr. Lincoln & Sec'y Staunton have just left us for the flag ship. They are stirring up the dry bones.

No. 8—

Iron Clad *Monitor*
Hampton Roads
May 9th, 1862

Dear Anna,

Notwithstanding all the array of troops crowded on the different boats & the report that a landing was to be made last night, & which no doubt was contemplated, nothing was done. For some reason, a good one no doubt, the plans were changed or at least delayed, so that everything when I turned out this morning was just as I left it last night except that the blue coated soldiers had disappeared from the boats, seeking & I hope not vainly for a comfortable spot to spend the night. I believe they were marched back to their quarters.

A little while after breakfast the President came on board & after a short talk with Capt. J. we let go our moorings & steamed up the river to our position of yesterday in front of the battery. We threw a couple of shell into the works without eliciting a reply, sounded out the channel and steamed about awhile & returned to our moorings about two o'clock. But few persons could be seen about the batteries which presented the same appearance they

---

* A ritual phrase used by Freemasons meaning "so be it," suggesting that Keeler was a Mason.

Hampton Roads (March to May 1862)

did yesterday. The *Merrimac* was just off the battery when we started but retired towards Norfolk as we approached.

A good deal of fault has been found with Capt. Jeffers by the officers on board for not attacking the *Merrimac* as we had her in a very favourable spot that would have given us every advantage we desired. He has always complained that he could not get permission to attack her from the Flag Officer, but we have reason to think that he had the consent of the President to "pitch into her" if a favourable opportunity offered. Still, if his orders were simply to make a reconnoisance to discover if the batteries had been strengthened or reinforced with men or guns, he accomplished his object.

All that were on board of the *Monitor* during the fight with the *Merrimac* consider her our game & are anxious for another chance at her. The *Galena* & our other gun boats have the *Jamestown*, *Yorktown*, *Teazer* & one or two other of the rebel's vessels penned up in James river, so that now we could try the "Big Thing" single handed, which is all we ask. We want it as a crowning glory to our career so finely commenced.

It is extremely fortunate that the President came down as he did. He seems to have infused new life into everything. Even the superannuated old fogies begin to shew some signs of life & animation. He has been busy to day visiting different points. First the Com're, then us, then to the Rip Raps, then to the Fortress. Not a place has escaped him where he thought his presence could do any good.

To night we have five thousand troops afloat ready to land on the opposite shore to morrow morning at day break, whence they start for Norfolk under Max Webber.* It was a beautiful sight to see them this evening as the long files marched down to the boats to embark. Just at dusk the Rip Raps opened on Sewall's Point and are still keeping it up, landing their shells with astonishing accuracy at a distance of three & three quarter miles.

We have amused ourselves all the evening watching the bursting of the shells around the battery & now the heavy boom of the guns & hoarse howl of the shells are the music to which I write. The Baltimore boat was not allowed to leave to night, probably that the intelligence of this movement might not be made public.

Our troops will have 12 miles to go after landing to reach Norfolk. Good roads now that the mud has pretty much dried up, though they will probably find some obstructions. There is also Tanner's Creek to cross which will be difficult especially if they should be opposed by rebel forces. Whether we are to take any part in the programme I do not know. Anything that will give us the *Merrimac*. She is the summit of our wishes, the height of our ambition.

---

* Gen. Wool commanded the landing at Willoughby's Point with troops under Generals Mansfield and Weber. Unbeknownst to Wool, the rebels had already evacuated Norfolk and were on their way to Richmond to join the main army.

Civil War Years: USS *Monitor* (1862)

I shall leave the remainder of my sheet to fill to morrow. As the mail has been delayed in consequence of stopping the boat you will miss one day in getting my letters. I thought as long as I had any material I would endeavour to manufacture one a day, especially after getting your offer of letter for letter. Good night.

Saturday morning [May 10], 6 o'clock. Our troops are now landing just opposite the Rip Raps on Willoughby's point. I think you will find the place on some of the maps I have sent home.

It is a clear beautiful morning. A cool westerly wind blowing. Everything seems auspicious. If they are to attack the Sewall's Point batteries in the rear we shall probably be ordered up again to day to shell them in front.

The *Baltimore American* of yesterday which I send you contains a highly exaggerated & incorrect account of the shelling of Sewall's Point. The batteries were not, & I think are not, evacuated. The *Naugatuck* did not take the lead, but ran off under the Newport News shore at a much greater distance from the batteries than the tug containing the President who accompanied us into range & witnessed the fight. Neither was the firing from the enemies batteries as heavy as represented, for ours was so incessant that they could not work the guns.

After we hauled off I was on deck the whole time & witnessed the whole, being *inside* of all our fleet who maintained an incessant fire over our heads. It was a grand an[d] awful sight. I was incorrect in saying that none of our vessels were hit. The *Seminole* I have since been told received one shot, doing no harm.

I send you a paper nearly every day. Hope you get them. I send the [*New York*] *Herald* as I suppose you get the [*New York*] *Times* regularly. I mail[ed] a pictorial to Eddy this morning, also a *Herald* to Henry.

1/2 past 11 A.M. All our troops were disembarked some time ago, quietly not a gun being fired. *Pres't Lincoln made a reconnoisance last evening in a little tug, where the party was to land.* Women & children came to the shore waving white flags.

A rumour has reached us that the "old Flag" has been put under arrest & is in the fort.* I don't credit it, although his pennant is down from the Flag Ship. 'Tis too good to be true.

[No signature]

---

* A false rumor.

Hampton Roads (March to May 1862)

No. 9—

Iron Clad *Monitor*
Hampton Roads
May 10, 1862

Dear Anna,

Here it is 10 o'clock at night & I have just set down to commence my letter for to morrow's mail. It is a lovely evening & I have been enjoying it to the fullest extent seated on deck in "the clear silvery light of the moon" thinking of the dear ones at home & speculating with my brother officers upon the coming events of the next few hours. The gentle ripples as they dance over the surface of this bay in the soft moon light seem like tiny waves of liquid silver murmering in gentle music, as they kiss our iron sides, the praises of the *Monitor* (sentimental).

A cool refreshing breeze breathes quietly over our decks bringing with it the softened music of a splendid band from the distant Fortress. Now the heavy rumble of Artillery & baggage wagons, the tramp of horses & the quick decided orders of the officers comes faintly over the water — & now the tones of mirth & fun from the jolly tars on board some man of war are more distinctly heard.

Landward, a long dark line silently & quietly winding towards the dock & the bright glitter of its thousand bayonets shew us many strong arms & warm hearts starting to join their comrades already on their march to Norfolk. Astern are the numerous lights of the fleet interspersed with the blue & red ones of the steamers carrying reinforcements to our brave soldiers landed on rebel ground this morning.

On this side, that low dark mass on the water is the Rip Raps, now still & silent, but a few hours since the thunder of its guns bid defiance to rebellion as their flashes lit up the shore. Still farther in the distance the horizon is lighted up, as we all suppose, with the flames of Norfolk, lighted by a rebel torch for a purpose that rebels only can define.* Its flames however will serve as a beacon light for our forces who we hear are only four miles from the rebel stronghold. With Norfolk in our possession what is to become of the *Merrimac*? She has been laying in sight of us all day at Craney Island.†

---

* The flames were from the Gosport Navy Yard which the rebels had set on fire before departing.
† As Keeler was writing this letter, the *Virginia*'s crew were frantically trying to lighten their vessel in order to take her up the shallow waters of the James River to Richmond. However, unfavorable wind conditions, which produced insufficiently high enough water levels upstream, prevented the ironclad from attempting the trip. So instead of facing the big guns of Fort Monroe and the Rip Raps with her exposed unarmoured hull if she tried to escape into Chesapeake Bay, they blew her up.

Civil War Years: USS *Monitor* (1862)

[The following short note appears at the bottom of Letter No. 9.]

> Iron Clad *Monitor*
> the first vessel into
> *Norfolk, Va.*
> Sunday Morning 9 o'clock
> May 11th, 1862

The Stars & Stripes wave over the Sewall Point batteries. *Merrimac* blown up. Norfolk Navy Yard destroyed by the rebels & the place in full possession of our forces. *Monitor* the first vessel into Norfolk. Enclosed is the first trophy from the place. Will write you in full to morrow.

> William

11 o'clock A.M. The *Susquehanna, San Jacinto, Mount Vernon, Dacotah* & *Seminole* are coming up. Stars & Stripes flying & bands playing Hail Columbia & Yankee Doodle.

11:30. Steamboat just coming up with the Pres't, Sec'ys Staunton & Chase, Gen. Wool & the Flag Officer.

James River (May to August 1862)

> *There [at City Point] we had at times some little excitement, something to talk about or something to look at — a flag of truce would come up occasionally & be met by one from Petersburg, an exchange of prisoners would be made, we would see some of the folks from below & learn the news, get an occasional mail & now & then a paper, contrabands would pay us stolen visits with stolen edibles. But here — bah — nothing but a widening of the river with low marshy banks, not even a contraband in sight, unless frogs, snakes, & mud turtles can be classed as such & as to mails,* the *males we already have on board are all we expect to see for some time to come.* (14 June 1862)

With the *Virginia* out of the way, Lincoln believed that Richmond was now within the Union Navy's grasp. On May 11 while still at Hampton Roads after his successful foray into generalship, the commander in chief urged Goldsborough to act quickly. And so, on May 12 the *Monitor* and four gunboats headed up the James River with orders to destroy all Confederate works along the way and shell the rebel capital to a surrender. Leading the flotilla was the USS *Galena*, one of the three ironclads selected by the Ironclad Board back in September 1861. The mission was a defeat, for standing between them and Richmond was Fort Darling, a powerful Confederate battery perched 90 feet above the river on Drewry's Bluff. When the vessels got within 600 yards of the fort the rebels opened fire. The plunging shot tore through the iron sides and wooden deck of the *Galena*, killing 14 men and

James River (May to August 1862)

wounding 7. Unable to silence the battery or force their way past the fort due to obstacles placed in the river by the rebels, they returned to City Point.

For the remainder of May and all of June the *Monitor* remained idle, most of the time off City Point, with the exception of ten hot and miserable days in a stretch of the James River known as Devil's Reach about 18 miles upstream of City Point. While at City Point or in the narrow confines of the river above, constant vigilance was kept for rebel sharpshooters hidden in the dense undergrowth. The men suffered intensely from the sweltering summer heat, which was compounded by the vessel's faulty ventilation system which saw temperatures soar to a roasting 165°F in the galley and a somewhat cooler 140°F in the engine room. Letters from home and newspapers carrying the day's news reached them infrequently. Boredom was the order of the day. The monotony was broken by flags of truce bringing Union prisoners from Petersburg and rebel spies from Washington. A new experience for the men was the boat loads of slaves escaping from nearby plantations who were arriving at the *Monitor*. With no extra room to hold them, they were turned away or told to head downstream to Fort Monroe where freedom awaited them. One young African-American who remained on board was Siah Carter. He escaped from Shirley Plantation and enlisted for a three-year term as a first-class boy. According to Keeler, he was one of the most useful men on the vessel.

As May turned to June, the sounds of heavy artillery in the direction of Richmond could be heard from the deck of the *Monitor*. McClellan had started his long-awaited assault on Richmond. From May 31 to June 1 the armies clashed in the first major engagement of the Peninsula Campaign, the Battle of Fair Oaks. Among the 11,000 casualties was Confederate General Joseph Johnston, who was injured by a shell fragment and replaced by Robert E. Lee. Realizing the futility of continuing the battle, Lee withdrew his forces and for the next three weeks set about strengthening the defenses around Richmond and probing McClellan's lines for weaknesses. On June 26 Lee launched his offensive after discovering McClellan's right wing north of the Chickahominy River exposed and vulnerable to turning. In a series of bloody engagements known as the Seven Days Battles, Lee drove McClellan from the doorstep of Richmond to Harrison's Landing on the James River. Despite being outnumbered, Lee's knowledge of the weakness of McClellan's position and character enabled him to beat back his timid opponent.

On the same day Lee launched his offensive the *Monitor* and eight gunboats were sent up the Appomattox River in a night time raid to destroy a railroad bridge over Swift Creek about five miles from City Point. The purpose of their mission was to cut off one of the routes of retreat of the rebel forces had McClellan been able to push them from their defenses around Richmond. The mission was abandoned after several of the vessels ran aground and sharpshooters harried the lead boats. For two days they

Civil War Years: USS *Monitor* (1862)

remained precariously perched in the narrow confines of the Appomattox trying to get the grounded vessels off when word arrived that McClellan had been defeated at the Battle of Gaines' Mill on June 27 and was retreating to Harrison's Landing. The vessels were all ordered back down the Appomattox to the James River to cover McClellan's retreat. The *Monitor* lay off City Point to protect the transports that were carrying soldiers and supplies, while the rest of the gunboats headed to Harrison's Landing to protect the growing army camp there. The last of the Seven Days Battles took place on July 1 at Malvern Hill, a mile north of the James River.

For the next two months the *Monitor* lay above the rest of the fleet half way between City Point and Harrison's Landing as a guardian of McClellan's army and as a lookout for the rebel ram CSS *Richmond* which was being built in Richmond. Construction of the ironclad had started in March 1862 at the Gosport Navy Yard. When the Confederates evacuated Norfolk in May 1862, the unfinished vessel was towed to Richmond where it was completed. Although the *Richmond* never ventured far down the river and never encountered the *Monitor*, her presence was nevertheless felt, for she put the Union ships on the James River on constant alert and many of the senior officers in a state of fear, a condition Keeler derisively referred to as "ram fever," which he remarked was "raging furiously, especially among those inclined to old fogyism."

One of those old fogies was no longer around, at least not on the James River. Goldsborough's unwillingness to coordinate with McClellan during the early days of the Peninsula Campaign had made Lincoln question his ability to protect the Union army at Harrison's Landing. As a result, in early July the James River Flotilla, which had been under Goldsborough's control, was placed under the separate command of Charles Wilkes. Insulted by this change, Goldsborough asked to be relieved of command of the North Atlantic Blockading Squadron. When Samuel Phillips Lee arrived in early September to replace him, Goldsborough left for a desk job in Washington. A far more welcome change was the departure of their captain, William Jeffers, who by then was despised by all on board the *Monitor*. In mid-August Jeffers resigned due to chronic rheumatism and left for Washington where he was made an inspector of ordnance. His replacement was Commander Thomas Stevens, a 25-year veteran of the Navy and "a quiet modest man" according to Keeler.

The Peninsula Campaign ended on August 3 when Henry Halleck, Lincoln's new general in chief, ordered McClellan's army to withdraw to Aquia Creek on the Potomac River where they would unite with John Pope's Army of Virginia for a combined attack on Lee. However, McClellan dragged his feet, and it wasn't until early September that the last of his troops left the Peninsula. While McClellan dallied, Lee acted. On August 9 he defeated a portion of Pope's army at Cedar Mountain. Two weeks later he crushed Pope at the Second Battle of Bull Run. At the first of those two battles, Keeler

James River (May to August 1862)

suffered a tragic loss: his beloved 24-year-old brother-in-law Melzar Dutton, a lieutenant in the 5th Connecticut Infantry, was killed in an infantry charge.

Letters of special note: May 12 (first Union naval vessel into Norfolk; attack on Fort Darling); May 22 (evades capture at City Point); May 23 (Captain Millward's flag of truce); June 3 (rebel spies; an exchange of prisoners;); June 14 (life among the bullfrogs); June 21 (Sunday inspection of the crew); June 30 (night time raid up the Appomattox; stragglers from the Seven Days Battles); July 4 (capture of the CSS *Teaser*); July 14 (a virtual tour of the Union army camp at Harrison's Landing); July 25 (a visit to Norfolk and Portsmouth); July 30 (Captain Jeffers' brutality); August 16 (departure of the Army of the Potomac; another visit to Norfolk); August 24 (news of Melzar Dutton's death).

No. 10—

> Iron Clad *Monitor*
> James River, Va.
> May 12th, 1862

Dear Anna,

Events have so closely crowded for the last few hours that I have almost forgotten where I left you. I think it was on Saturday evening [May 10] after our reconnoisance of the Sewall Point batteries & then sent you a very brief & hasty summary of the events of Sunday. I will now go back to Sunday morning May 11th & try & give you as connected & intelligible a history of events since then as I can with the ward room full of officers laughing & talking.

A lurid glare in the direction of Norfolk continuing the whole of Saturday night, taken in connection with the fact that our soldiers were on their way to that place, led us to the belief that the rebels had applied the torch & then (to use a phrase more expressive than elegant) "skedaddled."

A little after midnight a bright light was seen over Sewall's Point which continued increasing till about four o'clock in the morning when a sudden flash & a dull heavy report brought us all on deck to conjecture & surmise till the morning light should reveal the mysteries of the night. Morning came & with it the expected intelligence that our forces were in possession of Norfolk & that the *Merrimac* was blown up.

This latter information was not so gratifying to us as we had ever since the fight looked upon the "Big Thing" as our exclusive game & were hoping in a short time to be able to gratify our curiosity by an inspection of her construction & internal arrangement. Her career was as short & infamous as her end was sudden & unexpected. We knew her days were numbered but felt confident that she would die game rather than fall by her own hand.

The boat that brought us the news also brought us the welcome orders to proceed at once up the river & endeavour to force our way through to

Norfolk. In five minutes we were on our way. As we neared the Sewall's Point batteries the flag which waved so defiantly during the fight two days before could not be seen & a close inspection with our glasses shewed no human being within or about the works.

A small tug with a flag lieutenant which was following some distance astern after reconnoitering for a while sent a boat ashore with five men who marched without interruption over the earth works & the Stars & Stripes soon waved over these formidable rebel batteries. They proved much larger, stronger & more extensive than we had supposed, mounting about twenty five guns, most of them of heavy caliber.

We left the works manned by our *five* sailors & continued on till two rebel flags could be distinguished floating from as many tall flag staffs from the works on Craney island. All hands went to quarters as we passed. The cannon peered out [at] us through casemates & embrasures & over parapet grim & threatening but silent. We passed on without receiving a shot & found every favourable point on both banks occupied by batteries, most of them of a very formidable character both as to construction & armament.

When nearly within sight of Norfolk we found the [Elizabeth] river obstructed by a double row of piles. In the middle of the row was a narrow opening, on one side of which was moored the hull of the old *United States* frigate in such a manner that she could be swung across the opening & sunk & very effectually block up the channel. The traitorous scoundrels had left in such haste that they neglected to do this & we passed up without trouble.

The banks of the river where not occupied by batteries looked dreary & uninviting being sandy & covered with a sparse growth of stunted pines till we were near Norfolk where the country began to wear a more inviting aspect — a cultivated field now & then & a house with barns & outbuildings. But everything looked as if it had been levied on by the recent occupants of the batteries — fields without fences, houses minus doors & windows and pastures without cattle. We approached Norfolk with shotted guns & men at quarters till a bend in the river disclosed the glorious old stars & stripes waving in triumph above the Naval hospital.

It was a quiet beautiful Sunday morning, the bells ringing for Church as we slowly passed along by large warehouses, beautiful residences & finely cultivated gardens & made fast to the *Merrimac*'s old moorings. A large crowd of rough looking specimens of the genus homo congregated on the docks to witness our arrival & a female could now & then be seen on the verandahs or at the windows of the buildings fronting on the river, but not a handkerchief was waved nor a cheer given to welcome us. The only flag floated from the top of the Naval hospital, placed there by our soldiers who arrived about four o'clock the preceding day. Another was run up soon after our arrival on the court house. We were told however that there was a very strong union feeling prevaling which would manifest itself as soon as the citizens felt assured of our ability to hold possession of the place.

JAMES RIVER (MAY TO AUGUST 1862)

The rebels before leaving had burned everything about the Navy yard that was combustible & blown up the costly dry dock, though strongly opposed by the citizens. Shortly after our arrival the stately *Susquehanna* came steaming up followed by the *San Jacinto, Dacotah* & other of our guns boats till we had a fleet formidable in number & batteries.

The last of the fleet was scarcely at anchor when a small steamer came up with the President, Sec'ys Chase & Staunton, Commodore Goldsborough & Gen. Wool & staff. The President, as the boat passed by us, had his hat off bowing, appearing highly pleased at the successful result of *his plans*.*

Our Captain was signalised by the Commodore to come on board & soon returned with orders to return at once to Hampton Roads & be ready to start the next morning for Richmond. As we slowly steamed down the river an inspection of the batteries as we passed them led us to realise the nature & extent of the defences of the water approach to Norfolk. Not one foot of the way after getting in range of the Sewall's Point batteries could be passed without being under a heavy fire & nothing but the advance of McClelland upon Yorktown & driving the traitors from the peninsular could have compelled the abandonment of this formidable series of works mounting over one hundred & fifty guns, most of them rifled pieces or smooth bores of heavy caliber. One of the h[e]aviest of this chain of defences was a water battery just before coming to Norfolk. The guns were casemated, the walls fifteen feet thick, the casemates formed of heavy timbers & lined with railroad iron.

The same might be said of the batteries on Craney Island. This island is a sand bank about ten acres in extent & is entirely covered with the works of the rebels on which they have vainly expended much money, time & skill. The two rebel rags that were flying there when we went up had been taken down & presented to Mr. Lincoln & Our Flag now occupied their place. At the upper end of the island a blackened sunken wreck was pointed out as all that remained of our old foe, the *Merrimac*. I obtained a piece of her & some mementoes from the batteries both interesting & amusing which I shall send home the first chance.

We returned to our moorings at four o'clock, coaled & at half past four the next morning we were "forward to Richmond" in company with the *Naugatuck*. The morning was clear & pleasant, the water smooth & the river quite wide. We passed two or three deserted batteries, [with] nothing of note occurring till a sudden bend of the river revealed the rebel flag flying from a battery on a projecting tongue of land known as Day's point†. As soon as we

---

* In a letter to his daughter, Treasury Secretary Chase wrote: "So has ended a brilliant week's campaign for the President; for I think it quite certain that if he had not come down, Norfolk would still have been in possession of the enemy, and the *Merrimac* as grim and defiant and as much a terror as ever." (*Tried by War: Abraham Lincoln as Commander in Chief*, James M. McPherson, New York, NY, 2008, p. 90).
† On the south shore of the James River, across from Newport News.

got within easy range they opened fire & kept it up very slowly till we were past the works. One shot whistled over us two or three feet above our decks but none struck. We passed on without giving them the compliment of a shot as the work was about as good as abandoned, being manned by only ten or a dozen men who would run from one gun to another & train & fire it at us as we came within its range.

About noon we arrived at Jamestown & found the *Galena, Port Royal* & *Aroostock* lying at anchor. Just abreast of them was the ruins of the old Jamestown Church around which cluster so many historic associations connected with the early settlement of the country. About thirty feet of the tower is still standing & the foundation walls of the main building remain to shew its outline. Joining it was a deserted rebel earth work bringing in strong contrast the deep toned piety of the early settlers & the perjured villany of their degenerate offspring.

The river up to this point was quite wide, appearing more like an arm of the sea. Here it narrowed somewhat but was still wide & deep. The banks in some places were low & level & laid out in cultivated fields. In others they were slightly elevated & quite heavily timbered, the dark foliage of the evergreen being interspersed with the lighter green of deciduous growth & an occasional dog wood mingling its white blossoms presenting a pleasing & never tiring panorama as we steadily steamed along.

At intervals we could see the "great house" of the wealthy owner of the soil & laborers, half hidden in beautiful groves, the extensive grounds surrounding them laid out with great taste & carefully cultivated. Barns & out buildings were large & well kept, but the slave quarters which always formed the background or outskirts spoiled the effect of what would otherwise have been a beautiful picture. In some instances the plantations were of large extent, stretching for a long distance along the river bank. But very few persons were visible & these were mostly blacks & poor whites. The aristocracy if at home studiously kept out of our sight, not manifesting any curiosity to see us. No sign of welcome was given us & we felt that we were threading our way through an enemy's country.

We came to anchor just at sundown in a beautiful bend of the river opposite the celebrated Brandon estate*, one of the largest on its banks. About a mile & a half above us a slight elevation jutted out into the river forming a most favourable point for a battery which we expected to shell out the next morning. At four o'clock the following morning we were under way slowly, steaming up in line of battle in preparation for the expected battery. As soon as we could command a view of the place with our glasses we found it in full possession of a couple of negro women who were planting corn, where we supposed was covered with rebel entrenchments.

---

* Upper Brandon Plantation on the south shore of the James River about 17 miles upstream of Jamestown.

James River (May to August 1862)

Towards noon we came within sight of City Point, a place of a few small buildings & the terminus of a rail road to Petersburg. As soon as we hove in sight a huge column of smoke & blaze was seen rising from a cluster of buildings standing by the river side. Upon coming to an anchor just off the dock we found that a small guard of rebel soldiers had fired the rail road depot & ware house & started off with the train as soon as we made our appearance. The buildings contained two hundred & fifty hhds. of tobacco belonging to a house in Bremen, Europe. Those who remained made a prodigious display of white flags, using for that purpose, I should think, all the clothing of a suitable color to be had in the place.

I went ashore for a few minutes & found a strange commingling of poor white trash, ignorant & uneducated, a happy mass of ragged blacks of all grades of color, happy because "Massa Lincoln's ships be comin," deserted tumble down looking houses, an ocean of hot dry sand & a big pile of burning tobacco. The whites all professed to be strong Union men but in conversing would get off their guard & talk of *our* army & *your* army, *our* flag & *your* flag. They were not to be trusted.

We went ashore well armed & the guns of the fleet were trained on the place. Some of the men told me that corn which is the main crop here is just being planted, that the season had been very wet & backward & that most of the slaves had been taken off by the army to work in the entrenchments, making labour very scarce.

The banks of the river presented much the same pleasing variety they did yesterday. The wooded knolls, cultivated fields, aristocratic mansions & fisherman's huts were disclosed one after another as we turned successive bends of the river. At this place it receives the waters of the Appomatox after which it becomes much narrower, so much so that all the afternoon we were obliged to keep a close lookout in the bushes & timber which fringe the banks to see that they contained no concealed riflemen to pick us off the deck for we were all the afternoon with in good shooting distance of both banks. We anchored a little after sundown in a wide expanse of the river, with low marshes on each side, called Devil's reach. On one side of us a schooner had been run ashore & set on fire by the rebels on our approach & was still burning when we let go our anchor.

Our anchor came up betimes Wednesday morning [May 14] with the expectation of an exchange of compliments with the batteries on Ward's Hill[*] (about eight miles from Richmond) in a few hours but after running a few miles the *Galena*, who was leading & who drew the most water, unfortunately ran aground. The tide was on the ebb so we had nothing to do but wait with patience till it should change & float her off. This did not take place till after two o'clock when we ran up a short distance where the banks were destitute of bushes to conceal sharp shooters & anchored for the night. We were fired

---

[*] Fort Darling on Drewry's Bluff.

at a number of times during the afternoon from both shore[s] which were so close we could easily throw a stone on them, but fortunately no one was hurt, although we all remained about the decks as usual. All suspicious looking clumps of trees & bushes along the shore were probed by canister & schrapnell from the twenty four pound howitzers of the gun boats.

While the *Galena* was aground a small company of cavalry made their appearance on the top of a smooth round hill in the midst of a wheat field some three miles off, apparently reconnoitering. Their observations were cut short however by a shell from the *Naugatuck*'s rifled gun & they left with more haste than I supposed Southern chivalry would use.

Early in the morning we passed about a dozen negroes at the mouth of a wild ravine who waved their old hats & shook their rags to us & bowed & gesticulated, some even getting on their knees. About three o'clock we espied a man ashore dodging & peering through the bushes & were upon the point of calling to one of the gun boats to give him (or them as we supposed it to be) a charge of canister when a darkey came out to the bank of the river & asked to be taken on board. A boat was sent & he proved to be one of the party we had passed in the morning. He had followed us the whole day & was trembling with excitement or fear when brought aboard. When questioned he could give us no information of consequence but wanted we should take him & his party on board of "Massa Lincoln's ship." He said they would work hard for us & seemed much disappointed when told that he must go ashore again as we had no room for him. To soften his disappointment the Capt. told him to wait a few days till other large ships came up when they would help him. I felt sorry for the poor fellow as dejected & downcast he returned to "chains & slavery," not however till he had visited each of the other vessels in succession with his vain application. He had not been gone long before he returned & informed us that a "lot of soger men" were in a piece of woods about half a mile off. The *Port Royal* threw a schrapnel which exploded just over the trees when the fellows, whom we had not seen before, broke & ran, making time it would be safe to bet on.

The river has been covered all the afternoon with sawdust, chips, logs of wood, lumber, tops of piles, charred fragments of steam & sailing vessels, indicating that the rebels were busy filling the river with obstructions.

During the night we kept pickets posted on the banks of the river abreast of the vessel & I had the *pleasure* of standing a four hour watch in charge of four blue jackets*. It was a dark dismal night & the rain pattered on the roof on the old cow shed where I established my *head quarters* insinuating itself through a hundred crevices in an extremely damp & disagreeable manner. The idea that we were in the heart of the enemy's country, only ten miles from Richmond & their sharp shooters on all sides of us, did not add a great

---

* Union sailors.

James River (May to August 1862)

deal to the pleasure of my meditations during my four hour watch. However as I volunteered for the service, I could find not fault.

Thursday morning [May 15] we got under way in good season in the midst of a heavy rain storm & an occasional ball from the rifles on shore. Not a man could shew himself on the decks without a ball whizzing by him. A man on the *Galena* who was sounding was badly wounded & one passed between my legs & another just over Lieut. Greene's head.

We moved up, the *Galena* (the flag ship) taking the lead, the *Monitor* following. Two miles brought us to the obstructions in the river & they opened upon us from the batteries which were a series of hastily constructed earth works on a side hill rising from the water. The river was so narrow that the vessels could not manoeuvre without running into each other so that we were obliged to run in and anchor. The *Galena* lay across the stream, her broadside to the batteries. We anchored under her stern, the *Port Royal* & *Aroostook* a little further down stream & the *Naugatuck* still further down & in this position we lay from 1/2 past 7 to 1/2 past 11, a perfect tempest of iron raining upon & around us to say nothing of the rifle balls which pattered upon the decks like rain. But three shot struck us making deep indentations but doing no real harm. No one on board was hurt but all suffered terribly for the want of fresh air. It was one of those warm muggy days with a very rare atmosphere which, shut up closely as we were, made ventilation very difficult. At times we were filled with powder smoke below threatening suffocation to us all. Some of the hardiest looking men dropped fainting at the guns.

Being unable to change our position, the batteries soon got the range & their shot began to tell fearfully on the *Galena*, against whom they seemed to concentrate their fire. Her iron sides were pierced through & through by the heavy shot, apparently offering no more resistance than an egg shell, verifying the Commodore's opinion that "she was beneath naval criticism." We soon began to see that she was being roughly used as shot & shell went crashing through her sides. Still she held out & the thunder of her guns pealed out from the sulphurous cloud that enveloped her, sending their iron messengers with remarkable accuracy.

We could see large clouds of dirt & sand fly as shell after shell from our vessels exploded in the rebel works, & no sooner was a gun silenced apparently in one portion of the batteries than they opened from some other part or from some new & heretofore unseen battery. Their guns were manned by sailors, probably from the *Merrimac* & the *Jamestown* & *Yorktown*, which last two had been sunk with the other obstructions. It became evident after a time that it was useless for us to contend against the terrific strength & accuracy of their fire.

Suddenly volumes of smoke were seen issuing from the *Galena*'s ports & hatches & the cry went through us that she was on fire, or a shot had penetrated her boiler. Her men poured out of her open ports on the side opposite the batteries, clinging to the anchor, to loose ropes, and dropping into the boats. We at once raised our anchor to go to her assistance but found she did not need it. Her Capt. (Rogers*) hailed us & said that he should have to leave as he had expended all his ammunition, having fired 360 rounds. The smoke proceeded from a shell exploding & setting fire to a cartridge which one of the powder boys was carrying to a gun, burning him badly.

We all started down the stream, followed on the banks by sharp shooters cracking away at every man who exposed himself.

The *Galena* had fourteen men killed & twenty five wounded, some of whom will die. The wooden vessels fought well but were not as badly injured as the *Galena*, on whom & on ourselves the enemies fire was concentrated. All our vessels combined could bring but ten guns to bear, but they were heavy & well served & the fire from them was almost incessant. There was the same heavy howl of the shells, the screech of solid shot, the shrill whistle of the rifle balls as in my *Merrimac* experience. The captain, occupying a position where he could communicate directly with the pilot, made me an idler in the fight & left me at liberty to observe more closely the various incidents of the battle. The shot would strike us with a heavy thud & the *Monitor* would shiver as if she were a sensitive being, shrinking from the blow.

We do not regard the matter in the light of a defeat, as we accomplished our purpose, which was to make a reconnoisance, ascertain the nature & extent of the obstructions, the position & strength of the batteries.† We found them of such a nature that it was an impossibility to force them with the means at our command & the river is so narrow it is equally impossible to bring a much larger force to bear. We could have remained there & let them hammer away but it would have done no good & it was a matter of prudence on the part of a good commander to withdraw. I suppose the secession sheets are shrieking with delight at the defeat of the Lincoln gun boats. Our turn will come soon when we can act in conjunction with McClelland who is forcing his way toward the Rebel capital.

We came down the river in the evening & are now (Friday morning) [May 16] lying at anchor off City Point. One of the vessels is to leave soon for Hampton Roads to communicate with the fleet & I shall take the opportunity to send you the few pages I have written. If you see fit to publish any portion of it you can do so except that relating to the nature & extent of our injuries which has been forbidden. The most of it has been written in haste & without any idea of its being published. You will have to polish it up if it is to be printed. I shall continue to write as I find opportunities. In the meantime don't credit any reports you may hear of us through secession sources. We shall probably keep up a weekly if not a daily mail with Hampton Roads.

---

* John Rodgers, captain of the USS *Galena* and commander of the James River Flotilla.
† It was in fact a defeat since their orders were to shell out Richmond.

James River (May to August 1862)

The matter below the lines on the opposite page* was written with the expectation of sending it down the river by one of our gun boats. But I found she was going down no further than Jamestown, from which place our mail matter was to go across the country to McClelland's army by contraband. I did not fall in love with this mode of conveyance, or rather the safety of it, so sent only a note which I hope will reach you safely.

I went on board the *Galena* at the termination of the action & the scene that I witnessed there is beyond the power of language to describe. To say that she looked like a slaughter house would convey but a faint idea of the appearance of her decks. They were literally & without exageration a slaughter house of human beings. Here was a body with the head, one arm & part of the breast torn off by a bursting shell. Another with the top of his head taken off, the brains still steaming on the deck. Partly across him lay one with both legs taken off at the hips & at a little distance was another completely disemboweled. The sides & ceiling overhead, the ropes & guns were spattered with blood & brains & lumps of flesh while the decks were covered with large pools of half coagulated blood & strewn with portions of skulls, fragments of shells, arms, legs, hands, pieces of flesh & iron, splinters of wood & broken weapons were mixed in one confused, horrible mass. Twenty five wounded were groaning in agony. The sight was awful, horrible in the extreme, too fearful to look at & impossible to describe.

The shell though performing its errand with such murderous accuracy would sometimes commit strange & even laughable freaks. The performances of the bull in the crockery shop is nothing to the antics of a shell in the *Galena*'s china closet. If it wasn't "a wreck of matter & a crush of worlds"† it was a general smash of all the crockery on board, leaving the ward room a decidely broken concern in the way of table ware. Another shell made the galley stove its "base of operations," the result of said operations being the reduction of the cooking apparatus to sundry & numerous fragments. Another after exploring a passage through the side of the ship effected a lodgement in the berth of one of the master's, where disgusted with its quarters it exploded leaving the master to settle the rent. One took a fancy to go to the spirit room on a "bust," but got tight before reaching the "[illegible word]."

As we passed down the river after the fight, the sharp shooters followed us along the banks popping away with their rifles at our persons, & with their tongues at our feelings, using no small amount of lead & a vast quantity of decide[ed]ly ungentlemanly language not to be mentioned to ears polite. We returned their leaden compliments to the best of our ability with our rifles when they were singly or in pairs, but when there was enough to make it an object we treated them to about a peck & a half of iron balls about the size

---

* Keeler is referring to the text after "We came down the river in the evening . . ."
† Joseph Addison's *Cato, A Tragedy* (1712).

of a horse chestnut to which forcible argument many of them had to succumb.

We made our way down to City point & anchored & the next day the dead were taken on board the *Naugatuck* to the old Jamestown church yard & buried. The *Naugatuck*, I should have said, burst her 100 pounder rifle at the 10th round.

You may be able to get some little idea of the position of the vessels & batteries during the fight from the following rough plan.* No. 1 *Monitor*—2 *Galena*—3 *Aroostock*—4 *Port Royal*—5 *Naugatuck*—6 First line of obstructions—7 Second do—8.8.8. Rebels Batteries—9 Our anchorage of the morning before going into action. The batteries are on one bank sloping back from the river, which is about 200 feet high. The first battery is about 50 feet above the river, the others from 75 to 100. They were incomplete & we think they mounted one gun while the fight was in progress. The position we took was from 800 to 1000 yards from the batteries but we were forced to drop further back in order to get sufficient elevation for our guns. The obstructions in the river are made of piles, canal barges loaded with stone, crib work, lots of old vessels & canal boats besides two or three good steamers & the *Yorktown* & *Jamestown* & all sunk & forming two lines of obstructions. It is very evident that we took them unawares, coming upon them sooner than they expected.

Being in an enemy's country it behoves us of course to be on the alert, especially nights, as our low, easily accessible deck offers inducements to desperate persons ready to attempt any daring deed. Our night watch are armed, with instructions to hail every boat coming in sight & fire immediately if no answer is returned. The first night after getting here I was upon the point of turning in when, "boat ahoy," followed by a musket shot led me to conclude that something had turned up. The shout of "boarders" from our worthy captain & valorous first Lieut. was followed by a stampede from all the state rooms for the deck. Anxious to distinguish myself by some desperate deed of valor I grasped my ever ready revolver & made a rush determined to "do or die." My first effort resulted in bringing up against the broadside of our nag of an M.D. who stood rubbing his eyes by the side of his berth declaring he "didn't think there was going to be much of a shower after all." Tacked ship & came full against the edge of the ward room door. Finding said door, determined to act strictly on the defensive, hauled off, made a dive under the hammocks on the berth deck, & was boarded by a blue jacket as he tumbled out of his hammock, disposed of boarder & forged ahead, bringing my head full into the *stern sheets* of our gouty captain who was just going up the ladder, backed off & essayed an outlet through the turret, found the passage obstructed by a spit box & a collision unavoidable, thrown over on my beam ends & shin badly skimmed. Tried again, successfully,

---

* See Sketch No. 4 at the beginning of the book.

James River (May to August 1862)

receiving reinforcements on the way in the form of a hand grenade. Gained the deck, right flank strongly defended by a Colt's revolver, the left by a hand grenade. Found the vast array of Monitors armed to the teeth drawn up confronting the enemy — a poor trembling contraband. We very magnanimously concluded to retire, having made such an imposing demonstration.

The darkey was from some of the neighboring plantations & is now acting as first assistant to the cook.* He was pretty thoroughly frightened by being shot at by our guard & soon found his voice, crying at the pitch of his voice, "O, Lor' Massa, oh don't shoot, I'se a black man Massa, I'se a black man." The account he gave of himself was that his master was a colonel in the rebel army, that he with other slaves had been taken to work on the defences at Yorktown, then to cut a road from that place to Williamsburg. That his master had gone off with the army to Richmond & he had returned to the plantation. "The yankee sogers," he said, "came to Yorktown with a great cutting machine & had cut up 3000 Southern soldiers in ten minutes," that "their horses were all covered with iron so they couldn't be shot." He said his master called all his slaves together & told them that if any of them went on board of the yankee ships, the yankees would carry them out to sea, tie a piece of iron about their necks & throw them overboard. They have probably been forbidden to visit us as none come off during the day but will steal alongside at night, bringing a few fish or eggs or poultry.

Monday, May 19th—Yours written the 9th was rec'd yesterday by some of the gun boats which came up the river & was more than ever welcome. With this I send two or three amusing love letters from the Craney Island Batteries, also some Secesh papers. Let me know if they reach you safely. I sent some time ago some old papers, were they rec'd?

There is some talk of sending us to the Washington Navy Yard for alterations when we get through here. If we do I shall try & go to New York & New Haven. How I would like to meet you there.

I fear the Deacon's ten days will be lengthened out indefinitely. *Your* garden must be looking pretty now. I would like very much to see it. If Mrs. Treat will send the bundle from either New York or New Haven I shall get it.

Richmond must fall before long & I expect we shall take a part in it. We have already penetrated to within eight miles of it by water or about six by land. It must have set them to thinking in the rebel capital to hear such a vigorous knocking at the door. You need not fear but what I shall write every opportunity & shall hope to hear from you frequently. If I get hurt or am sick you shall hear of it. My best love to you all.

William

---

* The escaped slave was Siah Carter*. See letter of August 16, 1862 for a wonderful description of the young man.

Civil War Years: USS *Monitor* (1862)

[P.S.] If you furnish any part of this for publication you need pay no attention to what I have said about withholding a portion as that is already public. Use any portion you choose.

Iron Clad *Monitor*
James River
May 16th, 1862

Dear Anna,

Here we are off City Point at anchor. We have just returned from a *pleasure* excursion from eight miles this side of Richmond. I have a good long letter for you with a detailed account of my doings & goings for the last few days but dare not send it to you from this place for fear it may not reach you, as it will have to pass the gauntlet of the enemy & it is too *valuable* a document & has cost me too much labour to be lost.*

We have had another severe fight with the batteries just this side of Richmond [Fort Darling]. The particulars you will get when I can safely send them to you. I am unhurt & well but have seem some awful sights.

We hope soon to have an uninterrupted communication with Hampton Roads & get our mails with regularity. Write as you have done heretofore, the letters will be for'd to me. I shall keep on writing & send when an opportunity offers. Don't let any accounts you may hear from rebel sources cause you any uneasiness. We have the enemy above & below us, but shall soon clear them out below & I hope soon to be able to write to you from Richmond. My love to all.

William

When you write to Utica tell Helen [Plant] that I rec'd her letter & will answer when I can do so without a probability of its being perused by the rebels. I have also rec'd a letter from Mary Joy which I have yet to reply to. You see what a correspondence I have opened with the young ladies. Don't scold, for you know that the <u>old</u> ones are not neglected.

I shall be glad when this war is over for I am free to acknowledge that I have seen enough of it. Not that I am homesick, nor frightened, but such scenes as I have witnessed would make any humane person desire the peace & quiet of a pleasant home in preference to bursting shells & burning ships & mangled bodies, but I shall remain with the *Monitor* till she goes out of commission if I am alive & well. I believe I counted the cost before I entered the service & do not feel now as if I had a right to leave.

I think often of you all at home & long to see you. I hope to hear frequently from you & that you all continue well. Remember me to all our

---

* He is referring to the letter dated May 12, 1862 which was completed and mailed a week later.

James River (May to August 1862)

friends & acquaintances & to Father, Mother, Sarah, Fan, Dave, Mr. & Mrs. Hough & all. A kiss to yourself & the dear children.

William

[Marginalia] City Point is about 75 miles above Hampton Roads & at the terminus of the Rail Road from Petersburg, about 9 miles distant. We have penetrated to within 8 miles of the rebel capitol.

No. 11—

Iron Clad Monitor
Off City Point, Va.
"Out of humanity's reach"
May 22nd, 1862

My dear Wife,

An unexpected opportunity has presented itself of sending a letter & I hasten to write a few lines, though with but very little of consequence to say, further than one or two items that may interest you. In the first place then I remain well & hearty. We still lie here "out of humanity's reach"* where we anchored after our attack on the Richmond batteries [Fort Darling].

Since coming here I have seen civil war in a new phase & came very near having taste also. Last Monday [May 19] I took one of the boats with a crew & went ashore to stretch my legs & look around a little. A boat from one of the gun boats (the *Wauchusett*) had preceded me an hour or more, containing quite a number of officers & men.

At the landing there [City Point] are a number of small buildings & shanties beside a brick & a wood Rail Road ware houses with the R.R. track running in front. Back of these a short distance rises a bluff about 75 feet high, beyond & on top of which are the better buildings of the place. Altogether it has something of the appearance of La Salle around the R.I. [Rock Island] depot, except the bluff here is not as high.

I had been ashore but a few minutes & was looking for the officers of the *Wachusett*, some of whom I had agreed to meet on the dock, when a darkey came running to me saying the "Sojer men are coming jus' on the bluff dar."

I started for my boat, only a few rods off & ordered the men to shove off, shouting to the crew of the other boat to look out for their officers as I believed the "Secesh" were coming. None of their officers were in sight. They waited a few moments & shoved off also, but had got but a short distance when a smart fire of rifles was opened on us from the brick ware house spoken of before. Half a dozen or so were all that were directed at us, as we were the furtherest off, but a shower of them fell around the other boat & I saw two men fall. They kept firing as fast as they could load till but one man was left in the *Wauchusett* boat to row, consequently her progress was slow.

---

* William Cowper's *The Solitude of Alexander Selkirk* (1782).

Civil War Years: USS *Monitor* (1862)

By this time I had got pretty much out of their range, one ball going through the boat about 18 inches from me, but they still kept firing at the other boat. They were now seen from the vessels & the *Monitor* was just getting under way when I got aboard.

One of our 11 inch guns was charged with canister & fired into the warehouse but not till the scoundrels had cleared. The *Wauchusett*'s boat was now picked up. One officer was found dead, two were fatally wounded, one badly so & one unhurt. These were those who had remained by the boat. The others who had gone up the bluff were taken prisoners, with one exception & he escaped & got off in a little skiff he found on some other part [of] the beach. The Paymaster, Surgeon, Chief Engineer, & Signal officer & five seamen were made prisoners & sent immediately on to Petersburg. All of the officers had side arms only & the men had muskets but were taken completely by surprise by over fifty of the scoundrels. Even if they had had a chance to fight it would have been of but little use.

My first thought was to stay on the beach till the others came, but as I had nothing but side arms & my men were entirely unarmed, I shoved off immediately & it was fortunate that I did, as the other officers did not come down the bluff & I could not have given them any assistance if they had. I don't know as I have any particular desire to attend another "secesh" *ball*.

Our vessels ranged up before the town but did not like to fire into it as many innocent persons might be killed. But few men were in the place besides the negroes. The *Galena* commenced throwing shells over the town, falling beyond hoping to cut off the retreat of the scoundrels.

We fired two shells & a stand of canister through a beautiful house stan[d]ing on a point of the bluff formed by the junction of the Appomattox.[*] The house & grounds I had often looked at from the ship with a very covetous longing. It seemed like a little paradise & was just such a spot as I had often wished might be mine. It belongs to [a] Col. in the rebel army[†] & the soldiers when they retreated went towards it & as we thought went into it. We intended to set fire to it with our shells but they went through before exploding. An old man & quite a pretty looking young woman (his daughter) came off to us to beg us to spare the place, as they supposed we intended to destroy it & were terribly frightened. Capt. J. very properly told them that he considered them as accessory to the murder of our men as if they had been Union folks, as they represented themselves to be, they would have sent us word that the soldiers were skulking around the place, which they could easily have done. Capt. J. sent the inhabitants word that he did not come to make war on unarmed men or women & children. They seemed however to be more afraid of their own soldiers than ourselves, whom they said would return & abuse them for holding communication with us. The result was that

---

[*] Appomattox Manor, which later served as Ulysses Grant's headquarters.
[†] Richard Eppes* was a surgeon in the Confederate army, not a colonel.

James River (May to August 1862)

they commenced leaving the place in haste, each one carrying what he could most readily get hold of. The boats on the beach were soon loaded with bundles of bedding & household goods & shoved off for the opposite shore or rather an island, where there was a nice farm house & plantation. There they are at present encamped under the trees.

What we will do with the town [City Point] I believe is not yet determined. Probably the R.R. buildings will be burned so that they may not shelter any more of the numerous ruffians. The place now is entirely deserted & our vessels throw a shell over it occasionally to wake up the enemy's pickets which we know are in the outskirts.

The Surgeon [of the *Wachusett*] went up the bluff to see a sick woman at the request of her sister & was accompanied by the other officers. They had no sooner got into the house than it was surrounded & they were made prisoners. We are inclined to think it was a plot laid to trap them but cannot be sure. At any rate we do not feel that any of the people around here are to be trusted — unless it be the black ones — and those have been forbidden by their masters to come off to us, so that we but seldom see them, except it be stolen visits at night when a little skiff will steal alongside with two or three slaves bringing a few eggs or chickens or perhaps wanting to remain on board themselves. It was a sad sight to see the inhabitants of this place so suddenly abandoning their homes, humble though they were, the most of them.

McClelland's army we hear is within a few miles of Richmond & we occasionally hear heavy firing which we suppose to be from him. All feel satisfied that the place cannot hold out long. It is rumoured that they are now preparing to evacuate it, but we hardly give it credit, as they certainly will make a fight first.

We are expecting to be ordered to Washington for repairs where if I can get leave of absence for a short time I intend to go to New York & New Haven. How I wish I could meet you there.

Outside news I know nothing of as I have not seen a paper for more than a week. If I can obtain a Sesech paper I will send it to Mr. Rockwell, but they are very difficult to obtain. When you see him give him my kind regards, as all my other friends.

I wrote a long letter to Helen Plant a few days since as she seemed so anxious to hear from me in a letter I had from her. I wrote some time since to Mary E. Joy. In her reply she said that my letter was read at their dinner table at the Spingler institute* by Mrs. Abbott & very much complimented. My letters I think must have a pretty large circulation.

Friday Morning, 23rd. I have just been reading the Petersburg paper of yesterday lent me by Capt. Millward (our flag of truce officer). It contains the official report of the fight at the Richmond batteries† & acknowledges to the

---

* The girls' school in New York City that Keeler's 16-year old niece attended.
† Fort Darling on Drewry's Bluff.

loss of 7 killed & 8 wounded. From the tone of the editorials the[y] have a big scare on.

It is getting to be very tedious staying here — no papers & very few letters. I hope we will get to Richmond or Washington pretty soon. Continue to write as often as possible, they will turn up some time or other. Love to all.

William

No. 12—

Iron Clad Monitor
James River, Va.
May 23rd, 1862

Dear Anna,

Yours of the 14th has just reached me & how welcome it was only those who have been similarly situated can tell. In it you speak of having "sent a long letter yesterday" but it has not yet reached me yet. It will probably come round in time. I sent off No. 11 to day by a steamboat that came up with a flag of truce to communicate with the rebels from this point. They used to meet our flag of truce, from Norfolk. Now [that] they have been driven from there, we are obliged to come up to this place & they come out from Petersburg.

Capt. Millward has just ret'd having been out on the road towards Petersburg with a flag of truce in search of some of the rebel pickets by whom to send a dispatch to Petersburg. He says after being landed on the dock he took his flag & started up the R.R. track expecting at every step to meet some of their men. He had proceeded nearly a mile without meeting anyone when he saw a sentinel lazily pacing along the Rail Road bank, musket on shoulder. He was nearly upon the man before he was discovered. Capt. M. told him he was in search of one of the outer pickets & inquired if he was one.

"Well," he said slowly & carelessly, "I believe I am but don't know."

"Well," said Capt. M., "didn't you see me as I came along?"

"Yes."

"Did you see my flag of truce?"

"No."

"Why didn't you fire then?"

"I hadn't any orders to fire on anybody," the picket continued in the same indifferent tone he had maintained during the whole of the conversation.

Capt. M. said he was evidently an unwilling servant & he thought would gladly have come away with him (Capt. M.) if he had thought it safe. The picket accompanied Capt. M. to the commanding officer & Capt. M. sent his dispatch to Petersburg.

Saturday, 24th—A flag of truce came in on the cars this morning from Petersburg and Capt. Millward went ashore to meet it. We moved up right abreast of the dock on which the two officers stood, one of our guns loaded

James River (May to August 1862)

with cannister, the other with shell, ready to fire on the first appearance of treachery.

The rebel officer was a Capt. Preston*, a fine looking fellow, who had always been the bearer of the flag from Norfolk before that place came into our possession. They shook hands with great apparent cordiality, delivered their dispatches, stood & talked nearly an hour, & separated. Capt. M. gave him a copy of the *N.Y. Herald* & he in return gave Capt. M. the latest Richmond paper. This is a scene we shall probably frequently witness while we lie here.

You ask if I get any fresh vegetables or fruit? NO most emphatically — we don't even get fresh meat while lying here. There is plenty of secesh beef walking around ashore but we are forbidden to forage. The rebels must still be handled with silk gloves. At Jamestown there is a barn full of sweet potatoes taken there to feed the rebel soldiers of the battery near by — but nary [a] potato can we have.

Capt. Jeffers proposed to go to a plantation near by, owned by Col. Carter† in the rebel service, & secure the Col. as a prisoner & confiscate one or two of his fat cattle. But, no, that couldn't be done. It does seem as if men were selected to lead these expeditions notorious for their want of activity & enterprise, to call it by no worse name.

We have not been able to get any of the slaves off to trade with us till to day [when] a boat came to us containing two contrabands who furnished us with plenty of fine fresh shad, at ten cents apiece. A short time after they were gone another came on board telling a sad tale. His story was that in the fall his master took him down to work on the defences on Craney island & after working four or five weeks there his master went off to join some other portion of the army, sending his slaves home. A little while after he got home his master returned in a great fury declaring "the d----d yankees had licked them like h--l." He gave all his slaves a cruel flogging as it were out of spite & this one he threatened to hang. The fellow run [ran] away, living in the woods for three months & fed by the slaves of the adjoining plantations. He was very anxious to remain on board but Capt. J. told him he had no room, which was very true. We gave him a good hearty breakfast & sent him ashore with the assurance that he would be able to get away before long.

The slaves on the plantations along the river seem to have the idea that "Massa Lincoln's" ships & soldiers are somehow to effect their deliverance — to which I say Amen. I wish you would ask Mr. Hough if Congress did not pass an act liberating all slaves who had been employed on the rebel

---

* John S. Preston (1836-1880), son of a wealthy planter from Columbia, SC. He was a staff officer for his father-in-law Major General Benjamin Huger and later for his uncle Major General Wade Hampton.
† Hill Carter*, the owner of Shirley Plantation.

entrenchments, or in aiding the rebellion in any way. We had quite a discussion in the Ward room to day on the subject, I maintaining that it had.

We have been listening to day to the distant roar of cannon, hoping it was McClelland knocking at the doors of Richmond for admission.* Whether we shall make another effort that way or not I do not know. I would like very much to take a stroll through the streets of the rebel capital before I return.

This warm weather is making it very uncomfortable on board our vessel. There is not sufficient ventilation. Three men were sent down to the hospital at Norfolk yesterday. The quarters of the men are not as well ventilated as the officers' State rooms.

Since the blowing up of the *Merrimac* we hear numbers of stories of her preparations to meet us. Among them a forlorn hope of 100 picked men with scaling ladders to mount our turret with buckets of turpentine & petroleum to pour through the openings, wedges to drive in & prevent its turning, sheets of iron & canvas to cover over the openings in our decks giving access to air below & egress to smoke & gas from the furnaces. This plan if carried out would have succeeded but it seems they had not confidence enough in it to give it a trial.

My love to yourself & the children & kind regards to all.

William

No. 13—

Iron Clad Monitor
City Point, James River
May 27th, 1862

Dear Anna,

Since my last I have hardly been able to scrape together enough to fill a letter. I am very much surprised to see in an occasional paper that reaches us, our fight with the Drury's [Drewry's] Bluff batteries (near Richmond) termed a repulse. It was only intended as a reconnoisance, to ascertain where the obstructions & batteries (which we knew were somewhere between ourselves & Richmond) were, & the nature & extend [extent] of them. This we accomplished. We ascertained also that the obstructions were of such a nature that we could not pass them, and the batteries so placed that we could not take them without the assistance of land forces. I do not give this as any surmise of my own, but have it from the best authority — from Capt. Rogers, the commander of the expedition. Had we found the river clear of obstructions the *Monitor* would undoubtedly have gone to Richmond regardless of batteries, but this we could not expect. The *Galena* was roughly

---

* The distant roar was skirmishes between the two armies in the lead up to the Battle of Fair Oaks.

handled — it was desired by the Department that Capt. Rogers would test his new iron clad vessel* — the result I have already given you.

Capt. Jeffers has written to the Department that if they will send up land forces he will shell out the batteries. Let the land forces drive the riflemen out of their pits & then spike or destroy the guns in the batteries when the obstructions in the river could be removed. What is going to be done we don't know but are waiting impatiently to find out.

It is disgusting to see how largely the *Naugatuck* figures in the papers. She has simply been used as a tug since we have been up here & for sounding out the channel, her light draught fitting her for that purpose. In the late fight, as in every other, she was far in the background firing an occasional shot. Her gun burst at the tenth fire & she has nothing now but a couple of howitzers. How such monstrous lies can be published of her in the papers I can't conceive unless it be as we suppose that the papers have been bought up by Stevens to puff her in order to get an appropriation from Congress to complete his battery, which all naval men declare will be a failure.

I see the papers also make a mistatement in regard to the shooting & taking prisoners a boat crew at this place a few days ago, an account of which I have already sent you. The boat passed our ship on its way to the shore & one of the officers hailed me to "come along" which I did a little while after. I saw no flag of truce in the boat as the papers represent & I know I carried none in mine. We simply went ashore for the fun of the thing & that is all. The Surgeon after landing was persuaded to go up the bluff to see a sick woman. The other officers accompanied him & were all taken prisoners.

Yesterday morning at daylight we sent a boat ashore & brought off a couple of deserters who we saw there waving a small white flag. They represented themselves as Virginia conscripts & posted here on picket duty. They know but little of Richmond but say that a good many sick are being sent to Petersburg from that place. They say that there is a force of two or three thousand at Petersburg & about 300 are kept in the vicinity of this place as pickets. They represent that the conscript law is extremely distasteful to all & will ultimately be the cause of much trouble.† In case of a retreat of the rebel forces, the Virginia troops, they say, will not leave the state, but if there is no prospect of a successful fight the majority will disperse & go to their homes.

The flag of truce which came up yesterday brought up, among others, the wife of a Col. in the rebel army. He was in the different fights on the peninsular & when their army retreated he was forced to leave his wife behind to the care of our forces. She was now on her way to Richmond in search of her

---

* Disgusted with the performance of the *Galena*, Rodgers derisively stated in his report to Goldsborough that "we demonstrated that she is not shot proof." (ORN, I:7, p. 357).
† The Confederate Conscription Act of April 16, 1862 made all white males between 18 and 35 years old eligible to be drafted for three years.

husband. She spent the afternoon on board of us & was shewn over the *Monitor.* To day she left on the cars for Petersburg.

We are getting quite a fleet up here, numbering now some 14 or 15 vessels, among them the *Stepping Stones* of the Potomac flotilla, so famous in the newspapers during the Potomac blockade. Some of the smaller vessels started to day to go up the Appomattox but were fired upon by Sharp shooters after getting up three or four miles & returned.

We have news to day through the Richmond papers that Banks has been defeated with the loss of 4000 prisoners. I fear we have met with some disaster there but it can't be as bad as is represented. I feel anxious for Melzar. If you hear from him let me know.*

10 o'clock P.M. A clear, still, miald [mild] evening which I have spent seated on deck listening to the roar of cannon in the direction of Richmond, & to the more agreeable concert of myriads of frogs & whip-poor-wills along the banks of the river. So far we have had but very few days when the heat of the sun has been uncomfortable. Yesterday the flag of truce brought a quart or two of strawberries to Capt. J. I had a taste of them, the first of the season. Good night.

Friday evening, 30th. I have kept my letter unfinished till now hoping to find something of interest to fill it with while waiting for an opportunity of sending it to Hampton Roads — a tug leaves for that place to morrow morning, the first for a week. We have had no mail for about two weeks & are about reduced to desperation, as may well be supposed. Here we are within 20 miles of Richmond, in a direct line, & don't know as much about it as you do at home. We heard the rumour that McClelland has taken it but do not give it credence. We hear also the painful news of Banks' defeat with a loss of 4000 — it can't be as bad as that.

Here we lie, day after day & week after week, prisoners to all purposes, no going ashore — no nothing, but eat, drink & sleep, & while away the tedious hours as best we may. I have made various efforts to sleep away a portion of the day, but can't do it. Write often, they will come around in time. My best love to yourself, children & all.

William

[Marginalia] Sent Mr. Rockwell a *Norfolk Day Book* a few days ago.

---

* The First Battle of Winchester on May 25, which saw Banks soundly beaten by Stonewall Jackson. Those who escaped, which included Anna's brother, retreated 40 miles north to the Potomac River and back across into Maryland. The number of prisoners was less than 4,000, more in the neighborhood of 800. Banks' defeat had serious repercussions for McClellan, for McDowell's corps would remain at Fredericksburg to guard Washington against a possible backdoor attack by Jackson, and so did not reinforce McClellan.

James River (May to August 1862)

No. 14—

>Iron Clad *Monitor*
>James River
>June 2nd, 1862

Dear Anna,

An unexpected opportunity has just presented itself for sending a letter & I haste to write a few lines just to let you know of my continued good health if nothing more.

This has been a bright day in my callender, made so by the arrival of our mail, the first one we have had for two weeks. I rec'd by it yours of May 23rd. There are still two of which you have made mention which I have not rec'd, but hope they will come around by & by. I hope you have got my long letter before this as there was a good deal in it which I think would be interesting to you & which I could not no[w] re-write. I believe it contained the account of our shelling out the Sewall's Point batteries, our visit to Norfolk, trip up James river & attack of the Richmond batteries [Fort Darling].

Each letter (not sheet) of mine is numbered so that you can easily tell when any are missing. I wish you would number yours if not too much trouble. If you will adopt my plan I think you will find it easy. It is to take a half quire of paper & number each sheet on the first page commencing on the outside. Use that half quire for nothing else & your letters will always be numbered right. If more than one sheet is needed, take some other paper & leave the numbered sheets for the next letter.

Yesterday was a hot uncomfortable day & we lay broiling on or in our iron box, or cage as it has now become, out of humour with ourselves & the world generally, but more particularly with the slow moving functionaries of the war department. Not a mail, letter or paper had blessed our eyes for two weeks, except a stray copy of the *New York Herald* which was read to tatters before it had gone half 'round. I had read & re-read your old letters out of sheer desperation till I had committed them to memory & if bear like I could have hybernated for a time I would have blessed the man who invented sleep.

About eleven o'clock at night (last night) a tug came up from Hampton Roads with orders to go at once to McClelland's assistance as he had commenced the fight & now our assistance would be valuable. We had heard heavy firing in the direction of Richmond all day long.* No mail however was on board the tug. She was sent off in such haste that they would not even let him go to the Post office. You may imagine the manner of the *thanks* the Commodore received.

Early this morning in accordance with orders our anchor was up & we were "forward to Richmond" once more, accompanied by the remainder of

---

* The Battle of Fair Oaks (May 31 to June 1).

the fleet.* Despite the Commodore's orders however the engine concluded it wouldn't go to Richmond & in proof of its obstinacy after going about eight miles got sulky & finally broke down. Nothing was left us but to stop also. So down went the anchor & we had the mortification of seeing all the fleet of which we had heretofore had the lead pass by us, "bound up."

Well we lay at anchor all day close by a bank covered with a heavy undergrowth of bushes, a good cover for sharp shooters who we knew were in the neighborhood. We kept one of our guns trained on a fine white house a little distance off, intending if we were fired at to make it a target for our shells. However we passed the day undisturbed, broiling in the sun & watching for sharp shooters.

Our engineers could not repair the engine & we are now (8 o'clock P.M.) on our way back to City Point from which place a tug will be dispatched to Hampton Roads to have us ordered there for repairs. From there we expect to go to Washington, or rather we hope to go, so you may expect my next from one of those places.

We were very much disappointed that we could not go up the river with the rest of the fleet. There will be work to do there, soon, if not just now. How I would like to visit the rebel capitol before going to Charleston, but from present appearances I do not think it will be.

Should we go to Washington we shall probably remain there for a fortnight or more. If possible I shall get leave of absence & visit our friends in New York & New Haven. Wouldn't you like to be along? I would like to have you.

Do you remember Jeb Lockwood of Bridgeport? I rec'd a letter from him to day congratulating me as one of the officers of the *Monitor*.

But our letter bag is closing & I must say good night. Love to all.

William

No. 15—

Iron Clad *Monitor*
James River,
Off City Point, Va.
June 3rd, 1862

Dear Anna,

One of the gun boats came up last evening having on board the *Monitor*'s letter bag, its *sole contents* being your letter of the 27th May. A flag of truce also came up, bringing the pirates or privateersmen whom we have had

---

*Early on the second day of the Battle of Fair Oaks (June 1), McClellan asked Goldsborough to send the James River Flotilla up river toward Richmond to distract the enemy. Upon receiving the order on June 2, the gunboats headed upstream, but were blocked by obstructions in the river three miles downstream of Drewry's Bluff and could go no further.

imprisoned so long, expecting to make an exchange for Col. Corcoran* & others.

This morning another [flag of truce] made its appearance, having the celebrated Mrs. Greenhow, accompanied by Mrs. Morris & Mrs. Baxley & two children.† This afternoon the rebel flag of truce from Petersburg came on to the dock abreast of the *Monitor* & the women & children were turned over to it, to all appearance highly pleased. The party were set ashore in one of our boats, which after taking them from the steamer that brought them up, stopped along side of the *Monitor* a few minutes on their way to the land. Capt. Jeffers was formerly well acquainted with Mrs. Greenhow & the scene as they came alongside of us was decidedly a funny one.

Says one female voice, "Oh here's the Yankee Cheese Box."

"How do you do, Capt. Jeffers," says Mrs. M. [Greenhow] to Capt. J. who was standing a few feet off looking into the boat. No reply from our usually very polite captain. Perhaps he didn't hear. Then followed a volley from the female tongues — "What a funny looking boat." "Where can they all sleep?" "Where do you cook?" "Wish we could go aboard." "Wonder where they keep their guns?" "Where's the holes the *Merrimac* made in you?" "Captain, was all these men on board in the fight?"

"Yes," from Capt. J.

"Well where did they all keep themselves?"

Capt. J., "In their holes."

By this time Mrs. G., finding the Capt.'s tongue loosed, put in again, "Capt. Jeffers, how do you do?", but with no better result than before, our gallant Captain becoming unaccountably deaf all at once.

"Can't we come on board?" "Oh yes, do let us get aboard." "I should so like to see it," chimed in all at once.

---

* Michael Corcoran, the Irish-born colonel of the 69th New York Infantry. Captured at the First Battle of Bull Run in July 1861, he gained national recognition after he was selected by the Confederate government as one of 14 high-ranking Union prisoners to be executed if the Federal government carried out its threat to execute 14 Confederate privateers who had been convicted of piracy. Demonstrations for Corcoran's release swayed public opinion and caused the Federal government to reclassify the privateers as prisoners-of-war. While in prison Corcoran's stature rose further when he refused to accept the parole offered him if he promised not to take up arms against the Confederacy. He was eventually exchanged on August 15, 1862 and was given a hero's welcome in Washington, as well as a promotion to brigadier general.

† Rose O'Neal Greenhow, Washington socialite and Confederate spy. She headed a spy ring that passed along military secrets that she and her collaborators, which included Augusta Morris and Catherine Baxley, gleaned from politicians and high-ranking officers. She was caught in August 1861 and confined to house arrest where she continued her activities. Arrested a second time she was imprisoned for five months before being exiled to the Confederacy, which is where she and her entourage met up with the *Monitor*. In 1863 she went to Europe on a diplomatic mission for the Confederacy, but on her way back the following year, weighed down by $2,000 worth of gold sewn into her clothing, drowned when her boat overturned at the mouth of the Cape Fear River.

Civil War Years: USS *Monitor* (1862)

"Look in *Harper*. It's all pictured out there," says Capt. J.

"Yes, but we want to see how you look inside."

"You'd be telling the rebels how to build one as soon as you get back."

"We're not rebels sir."

"What then?"

"Confederates," (with a great display of virtuous indignation) "& the Confederates want just such a boat & we'll send them to come & take it."

Capt. J. thinking the interview sufficiently prolonged waved his hand to the coxswain & ordered him to shove off which he did as the females were telling how the confederates would get the *Monitor* yet & use her in a better cause. The concluding paragraph being from one of the children about 12 years old, "Yes the confederate soldiers will come & take the *Monitor* away from you damned yankees," (right smart child that).

Well they were put on shore with another boat load of their baggage & the last we saw of them they were stowed away in a crazy looking old freight car bound for Petersburg. Mrs. Greenhow, I do not think, would be a standard for female beauty. I should call her quite "*ornary.*" Mrs. Baxley resembles *your* particular friend Mrs. Morris of Peru* in her style of beauty. In fact there wasn't good looks enough in the boat to keep it afloat if two or three of our blue jackets had been taken out.

June 4th. It has not only rained but poured all last night & to day till evening, making it very uncomfortable on board as we have to keep *corked* up & feel the want of ventilation in the close confined atmosphere which has been almost stifling. We fear it will affect our health.

8 P.M. I have just ret'd to my sheet which I left for the deck an hour ago on hearing "boat ahoy" from our watch. I found a boat just coming alongside with three contrabands from "Massa Carter's" plantation.† They had in the boat a sheep, a couple of chickens, & some eggs, all of which we gladly bought, asking no questions as to proprietorship. They begged hard to stay on board but it was impossible for us to take them for we have no room. We dismissed them, telling them to bring us all the pigs, calves, sheep, chickens, eggs &c that they could find & tell all the other boys on the other plantations to do the same & we would pay them well, cautioning them however not to let it be known to the *pretended* owners of this description of property who, having might on their side, might set up a counter claim with an unpleasant result to the poor darkies. Such things come off more plenty to us now than they did at first, the slaves finding in the present unsettled state of affairs that they are not liable to be detected & the trade is a profitable one to them.

10 o'clock—"Boat ahoy," again. This time a boat full of men, women & children that had been driven out of City Point when it was shelled by our vessels & had taken refuge with a good many others on the opposite side of

---

* The town near La Salle.

† Shirley Plantation, located on the north shore of the James River across from City Point.

the river where they had been living under a tree. But even this poor refuge was denied them [for] they were driven off by the overseer of the plantation. They were in a most miserable plight, having no shelter from the pouring rain of last night & to day. What few clothes they had was soaked through & muddy. No homes, no friends, nothing to eat, no where to go, their few earthly possessions were tied up in bundles & appeared to be nothing but a few ragged clothes. Capt. J. sent them on board the *Stepping Stones* which lay near us, to spend the night & get something to eat.

We see a good many such sights which although they excite our sympathy & compassion we cannot to any extent relieve. Most of the contrabands appear bright & intelligent & many of them seem to be well posted in the events of the war in this vicinity. One of them said Massa Carter had told all his slaves that they might go with the Yankees if they wanted to, [but] they would be taken off to Cuba & sold, & advised them to stay on the plantation where there was land enough for them all, & raise their children.

Thursday, 5th. Our flag of truce has been able to effect no exchange of prisoners & returned to day with the privateersmen, as villanous a looking set of cut-throats as is often [ever] seen. Col. Whipple* & Capt. Millward who had charge of the flag went ashore in the afternoon in search of the rebel officer to get a final answer. They hunted all over town & finally came upon a *picket* guard of 20 or 30 in one of the deserted houses smoking & playing cards. The guard were not aware of their presence till our two officers walked into the door. They found no decided reply had been sent from Petersburg in relation to the proposed exchange of prisoners & having nothing more to feed them on & it being so uncertain when the exchange would be made, concluded to return. Capt. J. sent one of the gun boats down in company with the flag to give them assistance in case the pirates made any resistance to being taken back, as they had threatened they would.

Friday, 6th. A flag of truce in from Petersburg this morning bringing the French Consul from Charlestown (an old French Count), his young No. Carolina wife, her child 7 months old & nurse, all on their way to France, perfectly disgusted with this country.†

The *Mrs. Count* set next me at the dinner table but was not very communicative in regard to matters south. She complained much of the fatigues & hardships of their journey & the round-about way, when formerly they used to go aboard of a fine steamer in Charleston harbor & in a few hours were landed in New York. I told her that we intended to make the passage between the two places just as easy & pleasant as it used to be, in a very short time.

Her nurse woman was more talkative. She gave a hard account of matters in Charleston. Some kinds of provisions were not to be had. Coffee they had

---

* William D. Whipple, Wool's assistant adjutant general at Fort Monroe.
† Count Joseph Marie Gabriel St. Xavier de Choiseul, French consul in Charleston from 1831 to 1856.

not seen for some time, butter was one dollar a pound, tea, ten dollars. Shilling callico one dollar per yard & other things in like proportion.

Besides these persons the flag brought down three of our officers taken prisoners at Pittsburg Landing [Shiloh] — Col. Stone, Maj. Miller, & Capt. Gregg — one from Rock Island & one from Iowa. They were on parole for 40 days & were on their way to Washington to effect an exchange for themselves & fellow prisoners.*

Maj. Miller was a very agreeable & intelligent man & gave a most stirring description of the first day's fight at Pittsburgh landing at which time he was taken prisoner. They had been taken from one place to another on their way here, passing through 12 different slave states. They were two days in Richmond & represent the feeling there as one of confidence in their ability to resist & drive back McClelland.

The rebels they say must have about two hundred thousand troops in & around Richmond. Portions of Bureaugard's† army are just beginning to arrive. I do not see why McClelland is not reinforced. He cannot have over one hundred thousand men. They are the very flower of the army to be sure, still it does not make him strong enough to attack the rebels in their strong defences. Even if McDowell unites his forces he will still be deficient in strength, for the attacking party always needs the strongest force.

The officers‡ do not complain of very bad treatment in general, but their food sometimes was miserable, though often the same as the rebels had themselves. It did me good to see them eat when our dinner was ready. The first good meal they had had since being taken, they said. The newspapers we were able to furnish they devoured quite as eagerly as the dinner.

Capt. J. got into a fever, fearing he would have to keep the whole party, women, baby & all, all night. T'would have been nearly equal to friend Hough's & my own experience in Livingston Co. had they been obliged to remain, but one of our gun boats coming down the river Capt. J. sent them on their way rejoicing. You can't imagine how queer it seemed to hear a baby crying on board.

Saturday, 7th. Two boats came alongside early this morning with four men, three women & four children. The men said they were going to be taken

---

* Major William M. Stone (3rd Iowa Infantry), Colonel Madison Miller (18th Missouri Infantry) and Captain Patrick Gregg (58th Illinois Infantry) were captured at the Battle of Shiloh on April 6, 1862. Having been authorized to effect a general exchange of prisoners, they met with President Lincoln who told them that a general exchange was in the works. Stone and Miller were offered exchanges for themselves, which Gregg refused. He had a private meeting with Lincoln who ordered one-month's pay to be delivered to each of the imprisoned officers. With the bag of gold in hand, Gregg, a physician from Rock Island, IL, returned to a hero's welcome at the Confederate prison in Alabama. The 2,200 Union soldiers captured at Shiloh, including Gregg, were exchanged in October 1862. Stone and Miller negotiated their own release during their second trip to Washington in July.
† Confederate General Pierre G. T. Beauregard.
‡ Stone, Miller and Gregg.

James River (May to August 1862)

off to work on batteries & so run away bringing they [their] wives & children. We have anchored near us two very large barges or flat boats which floated down a few days ago probably brought from Richmond by the present great freshet. We sent them to one of these & as they had nothing to eat but a little corn meal, told the men that they must go off at night & steal all the calves, sheep, pigs &c that they could find. I won't say steal for I don't think it would be stealing.

An hour or so after we had got them comfortably disposed of a boat came alongside containing three villainous looking scoundrels, one of whom represented himself as an overseer of one of the neighboring plantations in search of some of his hands who had run away & he had been told had come on board of us.

Capt. J. had a twinge of rheumatism which kept him in the cabin in a not very amiable & pleasant frame of mind. Mr. Overseer was walked down to see him. Capt. J. (very short), "What do you want?"

"I am after some run away hands sir."

"What's your name?"

"Osborn."

"Whose negroes are these?"

"Dr. Eppes."

"Where's Dr. Eppes?"

"In the Confederate army sir."

"What's he doing there?"

"He's a Surgeon."

"So you want me to give these folks up to you?"

"Yes sir I would like to have you."

"Well I have a good mind to put you in double irons & send you down to Fortress Munroe, you can't have the negroes."

"Can I have the boat they stole to come off in?"

"No, you may consider yourself fortunate in being allowed to leave here at all. Master at Arms shew this man to the deck," & Mr. Overseer departed smothering his wrath I doubt not.

We have had another heavy storm this afternoon. Heavy firing was heard in the direction of Richmond a little while before the storm came up & continued all the afternoon & even now, 10 o'clock, the occasional report of a heavy gun is heard. Judging from the sounds a hard battle must have been fought there this afternoon in the midst of a pouring rain.[*]

You see by the *Home Journal* you rec'd how near newspaper scribblers get to the actual fact & how little they are to be relied on. Mr. Willis[†] did not see

---

[*] The heavy firing was coming from Confederate batteries that were trying to prevent McClellan from bridging the Chickahominy River as he prepared to shift his forces to the James River side of the Virginia Peninsula.
[†] Nathaniel P. Willis, editor and founder of the weekly magazine *The Home Journal*.

Civil War Years: USS *Monitor* (1862)

Capt. J. at all & took it for granted that Mr. Greene (who introduced him to me with the request that I would shew him the *Monitor*) was the commander. His whole letter is a mass of absurd inconsistencies, reading smoothly & nice to be sure, but giving the reader after all but little idea of the place he visited. He very evidently sacrifices facts to style.

Sunday, 8th. Last evening & to day has been quite cool. If this weather extends to Illinois you will have some frosts I fear. We hope to have a chance to send a mail down to morrow & receive one in return. Our expectations of going to Washington for alterations & repairs have been nipped by the refusal of the Commodore to allow us to leave here for the present. Though of what use we can be will take a wiser head than mine to tell. I hope we will have Richmond pretty soon so as to let the *Monitor* get away from here.

Remember me to Dave & Fan. Tell Fan not to help you fill your sheets but fill one for herself. How are Mr. & Mrs. Hough, Mr. & Mrs. Rockwell & all other friends? Remember me to all & to Father, Mother & Sarah. With much love.

Yours,
William

[Marginalia] Tell Eddy we have got a pretty little lamb tied up on our deck. I send him an old pictorial; it may amuse him. Also a couple of papers to Hen. I don't get many papers now to read or send away.

No. 16—

Iron Clad *Monitor*
City Point, James River
June 9th, 1862

Dear Anna,

I started off a couple of sheets for you this morning filled with something, I hardly know what, for I find it a difficult matter to manufacture letters from no material & there is but little prospect of our having any as long as we remain here idle. The *Stepping Stones* got here at 5 o'clock this morning from Old Point bringing about four bushels of mail matter for the fleet which are all up the river but ourselves. The officer of the deck came down & woke me up & between us we sorted it over, picking out quite a pile for the *Monitor* but my share of it was small — your letter that has been lying so long at Old Point for postage & two LaSalle papers. However that was better than none. Your letters even if old are always acceptable.

A flag of truce came in to day from Petersburg bringing dispatches to General Wool. They gave us a Richmond paper of to day containing no news of importance. I noticed a long list of prices of various articles in Richmond. Among them was cap papers $25.00 per Ream, Quinine $15.00 per oz., Coarse Boots $6.00 per pair, Hoop Skirts $6.00 to $11.00, Coffee $1.00 lb., Pork $40.00 per Bbl., Black Tea $6.00 per lb., Kerosene Oil $5.00 per gall.,

James River (May to August 1862)

Calico 50 to 75 cents per yard, Spool Cotton 25¢ & a long list of other articles bearing prices in about a like proportion, though even those prices might be cheap if paid for in Secesh rags.

I have been trying to get hold of a Confederate Treasury note to send you. They resemble in general appearance our Treasury notes but are much more coarsely engraved & *redeemable six months after a treaty of peace with the U.S.* I will be able to obtain one by & by & will send it. I enclose with this a document from the Rebel War Department with Sec'y Benjamin's* autograph. You will see by the imprint on the paper that it (the paper) has been stolen from the United States. (Please preserve it.)

Our captured scows with their tenants started for Hampton Roads this afternoon in tow of the *Stepping Stones*.† A short time before they left they rec'd an addition of ten or a dozen more contrabands, sent on board by us. Last night some of the first party we sent on board went out on a foraging expedition & returned with ten sheep which they distributed among the vessels (receiving in return bread, sugar, coffee, &c), reserving a couple for themselves to feed them going down the river.

What a beautiful thing the Dilytra must be. I believe it will be pretty much as you say [that] everything will blossom this year. How is it with the Bear Grass? I supposed there would be quite a number of blossom stalks shoot up from them. Does the Fringe tree shew any signs of sprouting from root? I do not believe it will be as well to let the Benton grape perfect too much fruit. How are the two plumb trees & my *favourite* cherry? Does the Pie Plant grow any larger in size than last year? Is that pretty little vine (well I can't think of the name, yes I have) coradlice [corydalis] living & growing & promising to blossom & the Japan quince will that blossom full this year? How is the Twining Honeysuckle & the vine close by with the blue bean shaped blossom? Do the lilachs blossom full? You see I do not forget all my old acquaintances in the midst of *Monitor* excitement. You or Henry must give me the history in detail of each & every old acquaintance in the garden, present & prospective.

You will have to divide my share of berries with my friends. Tell Mrs. Hough that I mean to be home in time to eat my own share of grapes, though I am under obligations to her for her kind intentions. Are you going to make wine this season? Have you used up what we made last? Now I have given you the text I shall expect you to enlarge upon it & not complain for the want of something to fill your letters.

You do not mention Mr. & Mrs. Nixon in your letters.‡ What kind of folks are they? How do you like them? Where do they live & where is his office?

---

* Confederate Secretary of State Judah P. Benjamin.
† These were the slaves from Eppes' plantation that were mentioned in the previous letter.
‡ A banker in La Salle.

Civil War Years: USS *Monitor* (1862)

Tell Dave to send me his [*La Salle*] *Press* every week when he is through with it. I find a good many little items in them that are new to me. If Dave wants to make some money he can go east, charter a schooner, load it with provisions & take them to Norfolk or after we get possession of Richmond, up there. It will pay.

Where is Ham*? Did he get the place he was trying to, in Col. Dickey's cavalry†? What has become of Capt. Woodson?

Tuesday, 10th. This has been a cold, rainy, gloomy, disagreeable day. I hope you have none of it at home as you would surely have a frost when it cleared off. I certainly expected to find different weather from this in Virginia. What a terrible time our troops must have in the cold & wet & mud. We hear firing in the direction of Richmond every day but know nothing of what is going on.

Early this morning a boat came alongside with two men & the same number of women from two miles below fort Darling. They could give us no information however. They were wet through with the cold chilling rain & were allowed to spend the forenoon in the engine room to dry their rags & warm themselves. The men ran away because their master was going to whip them, & the women for fear of abuse from the rebel pickets who were in the neighborhood. The women were young & quite light colored. One who was quite intelligent said she could sew, wash & iron & cook & had very pleasing manners. If I had been going home I should have been tempted to have taken her with me & not have to rely any more upon St. Patrick for servants.

Capt. J told them that we could not keep them on board & they would have to go back home. I had a private interview with them before they left & told them if they did not want to go home to keep on down the river in their boat till they reached Fortress Munroe, where they could find work they would be paid for doing & be their own masters, that they could go ashore as soon as it came night & get what they could find to eat from any of the plantations. We have such parties coming off very frequently & when they cannot be taken on board any of the vessels, I always tell them, when I have an opportunity, to make their way down the river, hoping they may find their way to a land of freedom. The more I see of the "Patriarchal . . .

[The next several pages of the letter are missing.]

Friday Noon, 13th. A boat came up early this morning bringing the mail. I rec'd yours & Hen's of the 4th. To day is quite warm, as much so as any day we have had, still in the evening & morning woolen clothing is not uncomfortable. I am wearing my blue shirts without any[thing] under them. They are just the things. I wish I had more of them. Paper collars are very con-

---

* Hamilton Brown, brother of Keeler's brother-in-law.
† Theophilus Lyle Dickey, 4th Illinois Cavalry.

James River (May to August 1862)

venient as I can wear one of them a week (we don't use bituminous coal here*) costing about two cents & then throw it overboard.

A boat leaves here for down the river soon & I shall avail myself of the opportunity to send this. I think you will hear from me at least once a week, as we shall probably have opportunities to send as often as that & I shall avail myself of every chance to write you.

Heavy firing was heard in the direction of Richmond commencing at daylight this morning & for an hour the roar of cannon was incessant. Since then only occasional discharges have been heard. Of course only cannon & not the small arms or musketry are heard except when muskets are fired by large divisions. We hope something decisive will take place soon, if it has not already.

With this I send a pictorial for Eddy & a paper for Henry & my very best love to you all. I shall commence another letter to you to night & keep writing as I find anything to say & send it off the first chance. I find it is the best way to have a letter ready as now & then an unexpected opportunity offers to send. I shall write to Hen soon. Don't forget to answer my questions about the garden.

What is Darrow† doing this summer & O. N. Adams? Is Carter still at the Shaft? Who has the store there now? How is Father's health? Tell Hen in answer to one of his enquiries that he must make a close calculation as to whether corn or oats are the cheapest to feed the hens & then go to work economically. But I must close by bidding you all good bye with lots of love. Kiss the children & remember me to Father, Mother, Dave & Fan & all.

Yours,
William

P.S. A flag of truce just in from Petersburg. Can't tell their errand as our boat has not ret'd.

No. 17—

Iron Clad Monitor
James River, Va.
Among the Bullfrogs
June 14/62

Dear Anna,

"Out of the frying pan into the fire" was never more fully exemplified than it has been to day with us. We have for weeks been anxiously longing for a change & we got it to day with a vengeance, having been ordered from City Point up to this place, which I believe is nameless. It is about eighteen

---

* Bituminous coal, which burns dirty, would have resulted in a more frequent change of collar! The *Monitor* burned anthracite coal.
† Sidney Darrow, a grain merchant in La Salle.

miles above City Point by way of the river & only four in a straight line, such is the tortuous course of the river above the place where we have been lying for some weeks.

There [at City Point] we had at times some little excitement, something to talk about or something to look at — a flag of truce would come up occasionally & be met by one from Petersburg, an exchange of prisoners would be made, we would see some of the folks from below & learn the news, get an occasional mail & now & then a paper, contrabands would pay us stolen visits with stolen edibles. But here — bah — nothing but a widening of the river with low marshy banks, not even a contraband in sight, unless frogs, snakes, & mud turtles can be classed as such & as to *mails*, the *males* we already have on board are all we expect to see for some time to come.

Who wouldn't be a sailor? Half a dozen of us took a boat to night to indulge in a bath, rowed up a sort of creek some distance from the vessel, found the banks beautifully diversified with pond lillies & coarse rushes & thickly populated with frogs &c &c — disrobed & found the water about knee deep — mud bottomless —withdrew disgusted. On our return to the vessel struck a snag, capsized & took bath number two — water being a little deeper & somewhat cleaner, the mud remaining from our first effort was partly rinsed off. Came on board in a very happy frame of mind & have been cooling off in a pair of pajammes, perfectly satisfied that the James river is a somewhat turbid stream & that capsizing a boat is a damp operation.

Gov. Wise has turned up again.* He is in our neighborhood, a few miles distant, with 5000 men. His experience thus far in the war will learn him the expediency of having ample means of retreat. Capt. Jeffers says that the last time he saw the Gov. he was making the biggest kind of time at Roanoke island with a schrapnel from one of Capt. J.'s howitzers travelling after him. Whether the schrapnel or the Gov. came out ahead the Capt. don't say.

A commission of two Danish officers sent out by their Government to inspect our iron clad vessels have spent the afternoon on board taking drawings, sketches &c of the *Monitor*. They go from us to the *Galena*. They will have a good opportunity to note the power of resistance & the penetrating force of shot by inspecting the two vessels.

Your question of "what is the *Monitor* doing" is more easily asked than answered, though it is very evident that she is doing nothing. But then the question comes up, why is she kept up the river if she is of no use, nor can be of none.

The prevailing opinion among the ships in the river here is that the old Commodore [Goldsborough] has a large fleet of vessels on his hands which, as the *Merrimac* is out of the way, Norfolk disposed of, York river clear &

---

* Henry A. Wise, governor of Virginia from 1856-60. He was appointed a brigadier general in the Confederate army, and first served at Roanoke Island in North Carolina. He returned to Virginia and commanded a brigade during the Seven Days Battles.

James River (May to August 1862)

James river open nearly to Richmond, he has no use for & don't know what to do with & fearing if he kept them all about him in Hampton Roads the public would begin to ask why it was. He has sent them up here as a convenient hiding place, hoping that the simple minded public would imagine that their services here are of vast benefit & importance, when in reality two or three light draft gun boats kept running up & down the river are all that are needed & would be of more real service than all the huge unwieldy iron clad in the world.

Not a newspaper reporter has been allowed to come up the river since it has been opened & orders have been sent to all on board the vessels to write nothing for publication that would give any information of our movements. The gullible public are duped into believing that we are shelling batteries, making reconnoisances, supporting McClelland (of whose movements we don't know as much as yourself) & using every exertion to carry the war into the enemy's country. They are very little aware that we are having a nice little game of hide & seek. So far the Com[modor]e has the best of the play, but I hope the people will begin to look around by & by & enquire what all this means, what all their ships are doing.

What disposition will be made of us when we are allowed to come out of our hiding places up the river here I don't know, but it is certain that the *Monitor* will be obliged to have some alterations made before she will be fit to go to sea or lie in any of the Southern seaports through the hot weather. For nearly five months, ever since we went into commission our steam has been kept up night & day & at no period of this time has there been a time when we could not get underway at five minutes' notice.

Of course there are many repairs needed. Our ventilation wants attending to. The officers' quarters are tolerably comfortable, [but] the men suffer a good deal for the want of pure fresh air. In the galley where our cooking is done the thermometer stood to day at *165°*. Of course a cook don't last but a few days before he is cooked himself & gives out. In the engine room the thermometer ranges from 130° to 140°. But it is in action when our air ports & hatches are closed that we suffer the most.

These things have all been represented to the Commodore but nothing is done to relieve us. The fact is, & it is the opinion of all the officers, that the Commodore is not the man for the position he occupies — real merit never placed him there. He is coarse, rough, vulgar & profane in his speech, fawning & obsequious to his superiors, supercilious, tyranical, & brutal to his inferiors. He hasn't the first qualification of an officer or a gentleman & I don't know of an officer under him who respects him in the least. He is monstrous in size, a huge mass of inert animal matter & is known throughout his whole fleet by the very significant appellation of *"Old Guts."*

See how we were kept lying in Hampton Roads, doing nothing but watching the *Merrimac* which time & again came out & offered us battle, but because she wouldn't come down to the Fortress where the whole fleet could pitch into her, we were forbidden to make a move to meet her. I am satisfied that we should have remained there till this time had it not been for the President's visit producing a few spasmodic throes of vigorous activity which as quickly subsided into the former state [of] imbecility & old fogyism. I wish the public could see all these things just as we do who are actors in them. There would be such a howl raised that it would set some of the superannuated old grannies, who undertake to manage these things for the dear people, to thinking.

The fact is I am getting to regard the navy as a most stupendious & costly humbug. Now & then some actors in this expensive play happen by good luck to stumble upon a good thing & they sparkle above the warlike horizon like a rocket. Sensation writers make them a text for numberless items. They receive the thanks of Congress & the credulous public accept them as heroes of the first water, while the real heroes who have done the work & occupy subordinate positions are passed by unnoticed.

In all these criticisms I refer to the *regular* navy in distinction of the *volunteer* service. There is not life enough in it (the regular) to preserve it from putrefaction & were it not for the volunteer navy, or rather the officers, our naval operations would have been remarkable for nothing but inefficiency & stupidity. These remarks are meant to have a general application, but to apply to no particular ones.

Sunday, 15th. The forenoon has been very hot & the shade of our awnings feel grateful. About noon a heavy thunder storm came up, raining heavily & continuing till evening when it cleared off cool & comfortable.

Monday, 16th. I have found a name for our locality. Upon reference to our pilot I find that we are at last in the "Devil's Reach," not his infernal majesty I hope, but rebel devils in our neighborhood I find are plenty, [and] in their reach we may yet find ourselves. The names along on the river must have been selected by persons of taste & refinement. The straight portions of it between the bends or elbows are termed reaches. After passing through "Pull & Be Dam'd Reach" we come to "Dead Man's Reach," from there into "Graveyard Reach," out of that into Reach of the devil in which unfortunate position we happen to be just at present, but we intend to follow up the injunctions of the good Book & resist the old boy, expecting he will flee from us. We are pretty sure he will if he comes in the form of Gov. Wise, as that appears to be his forte. This portion of the infernal regions I find is not so bad after all & will take back a small portion of what I have previously said concerning it.

A party of our more enterprising officers (of which your *better half* made one) got a boat & started on an exploring expedition this forenoon & succeeded in discovering a narrow strip of dry sandy land skirting the river nearly abreast of the vessel, covered with stunted bushes, briers, dwarfed tulip trees, small pines & a few raspberry bushes (black cap) on which I found one ripe berry & a diminutive patch of emaciated corn.

James River (May to August 1862)

A portion of our iron deck has been converted into a stock yard containing just at present, one homesick lamb, one tough combative old ram, a consumptive calf, a fine lean swine, an antediluvian rooster & his mate, an old antiquated setting hen. The soil on our deck not producing sufficient pasturage for all our stock it became necessary in the course of animal events to procure something for their subsistence, which we did by confiscating the aforesaid corn & transfering it to our barn yard.

Of course it would not do to venture from under the cover of our guns so our rambles were confined to a stretch of half a mile up & down this narrow strip of sand. Even this was splendid, or seemed so, as it was the first time since our shooting scrape at City Point that we have been ashore.

In the afternoon we started to make more extensive explorations with a view to forage. After skirting along the marshy banks of the stream for some distance we selected a landing spot on the narrow strip I have previously described & waded ashore through the mud. We had hardly reached terra firma & forced our way into a tangled thicket of briers when, "ough, ough," & out started a drove of 40 or 50 hogs. I happened to be ahead with nothing but a revolver which I fired & lamed one a little & we started off on a race but a few more shots brought him down.

Our last shot was echoed from the other side of the river which is here quite narrow & accompanied by what is now quite a familiar sound, the whiz of a rifle ball. We looked across & could see a little cloud of smoke rising among the bushes where the [rebel] pickets were concealed. But as more porkers were not far off we concluded we would not go back empty handed & so kept at it, the pickets getting an occasional shot at us & we at the pigs, till we had bagged five (pigs I mean), which we carried down to our boat where we could shove off without molestation from the pickets. We knew our turn would come & felt contented to wait.

As soon as we got on board we sent word to the *Mahaska* (who carries a number of howitzers), pointing out the locality of the pickets. One or two shells started them from their hiding place & we had the satisfaction of seeing about a dozen of the fellows making a 2.40 gait across a wheat field for the timbers with shell & schrapnell bursting over their heads. When they were out of sight the *Mahaska* turned her guns on a large farm house & out buildings from near which the scoundrels had been firing. How much the buildings were injured we do not know, as they were nearly concealed by trees which prevented our seeing the effects of the shot upon them. It is well understood along the river that if we are fired upon from the banks, the buildings, if there are any upon the premises from which the firing proceeds, will be shelled. Our big guns are seldom fired for such purposes as the above — the game is too small for the amount of ammunition required for a load.

The most valuable event of the day & by far the most welcome & cheering was the arrival of your letter mailed the 11th with Henry's, Melzar's & Eddie's — the dear little fellow how I wish I could see him.

Civil War Years: USS *Monitor* (1862)

Wednesday Morning, 18th. The *Port Royal* has just come up from City Point & set her signal, "an opportunity for sending letters," so I will close this & send it off hoping it may reach you safely & find you all well.

The Capt. of the *Port Royal* brings the news that the rebels yesterday brought down a battery of field pieces from Petersburg & opened on our vessels from City Point, a thing I have often wondered they didn't do. What the result was I have not yet learned, but will inform you in my next. The gun boats must have driven them back.

The usual hour's cannonading was heard from Richmond this morning. What these frequent cannonadings portend we don't know but hope it augurs good. Gen. McClelland has been busy the last few days bringing up his commissary & ordnance stores from the rear, so it is rumoured & we judge from that that the attack cannot be delayed much longer & it is very evident if all the rumours are true that he has no idea of being compelled to fall back.

It is cool & cloudy this morning, just good fighting weather. The heavy rains that have fallen lately must have caused a good deal [of] additional hardship in the army.

I was very much interested in Melzar's letter & was glad to hear he came off safely.* Lieut. Greene's father, Gen. Greene, is with Gen. Banks.

Remember me to all friends. With lots of love & kisses to yourself & the dear ones.

William

[Marginalia] Tell Henry I am going to write him & Eddy next. Good bye.

Saturday Morning 21st. My letters did not go Wednesday morning as I expected, the *Port Royal* leaving before we had an opportunity to send our letters to her.

Nothing new since the sheets accompanying this, or I can give a sentence which had better be stereotyped all quiet in the Devil's Reach. Just below us however in the next bend of the river there we discovered yesterday a battery of [rebel] field pieces and an encampment of about a regiment of troops. The *Jacob Bell* was fired at & struck twice coming up. Whether we shall go down & shell them out or allow them to remain to fire at us at their leisure is as yet undecided. Probably the former [latter] as it would correspond very well with the way in which this rose water war is carried on.

I have just learned from a Washington paper the astonishing *fact* that the *Monitor* had succeeded in getting up to Richmond where she had been taken & her crew made prisoners. The fact however is not very apparent to us. If they had said surrounded by bullfrogs & threatened by turkey buzzards they would have hit it. I have told you before not to let all these rumours trouble

---

* Keeler is referring to his brother-in-law's narrow escape back across the Potomac River to Maryland after the First Battle of Winchester, which Melzar described in detail in a letter to his mother (May 27, 1862; Henry Dutton Family Letters).

James River (May to August 1862)

you & I hope they don't. I wish those starting them was obliged to swallow one of our 11 inch shot & go without eating till it was digested.

I think you cannot complain about the quantity of matter in my budget this time, though I will not boast about the quality.

This is going to be a hot day. I wish I was laying off under a certain piazza in an arm chair with my feet up on the railing & you know who by my side.

Once more good bye.

William

> Iron Clad *Monitor*
> Devil's Reach, James River, Va.
> June 21, 1862
> Saturday night

Dear Anna,

"Sweethearts & wives"[*] is a pleasant subject to let one's thoughts dwell on, coupled with the picture of a quiet pleasant home & its dear inmates. As my sweetheart is not present our chat must be with pen, ink & paper.

I have just been reading over your last (No. 1 of the date of June 8th) for the tenth or twelfth time. You seem to think in it that my health is not very good. Quite the contrary I assure you. It never was better, as my extraordinary weight (157 lbs.) would indicate. My old troubles seem to have disappeared altogether — once or twice I have had a slight dull headache, nothing more.

It seems sometimes as if you did not write in very good spirits. If anything goes wrong let me know. I shall feel better for sharing your troubles with you as far as I can at this distance. As far as money is concerned don't let that worry you, use all you have need of. As soon as we get back to Hampton Roads I shall place $200 more to your credit in the bank. You must look forward to meeting me in the fall in New York where we will try & have a good time & enjoy ourselves if possible. Remember what I have told you about sewing — hire it done as far as possible.

How I would enjoy a dish of strawberries & cream with you to night. I fear that is a luxury I shall not be able to indulge in this season.

There is nothing that pleases me so much as to find that Henry is such a good steady reliable boy. I hope your father will adhere to his intention of having him go to New Haven this summer.

How fast the summer is passing away. Here is the longest day of the year & though time has passed slowly it seems but a few days since we were lying shivering in the New York Navy yard.

I have spent an hour or two to day looking over all your letters & I judge from the dates that I have rec'd most if not quite all of them.

---

[*] The British Navy's wardroom toast that was made at Saturday's dinner.

Civil War Years: USS *Monitor* (1862)

I fear our chances of going to a Navy Yard for alterations, & consequently my chances for a leave of absence, are very slight as Capt. Jeffers' request has been refused. He was wrathy enough and wrote immediately to the Sec'y of the Navy asking to be relieved of his command & ordered to a wooden gun boat. Mr. Gager sent in his resignation but it was not accepted. All on board are getting tired of this life of inactivity.

I certainly feel under many obligations to Dave for his kindness & trouble in securing that claim against Locklin*. For L. I felt but little sympathy, as I had frequently given him an opportunity & urged him to work it out. The fact is he is lazy.

How is Dave getting along in business? Is business looking up any in LaSalle so that there will be a prospect of something for me to do when I get back? I do not desire to leave there but shall unless I can find some business to give me a living.

Have I told you that my shirts reached me in good order. They were very nicely packed indeed & are just the things I wanted. The bosoms of my nicer shirts are of but little use the way we dress & would soon be worn out the way they are washed down here. Tell Alice I wish she had my clothes to wash & do up every week — they would look a little nicer than they do now I think. Unless we get back to Hampton Roads pretty soon my clean clothes will begin to run short & I shall have to give the dirty ones a second wear. Of course there is no such thing as getting washing done here. "Billy" washes a towel or a pair of stockings occasionally but the ironing is minus.

Sunday Morning [June 22]—It is a good deal as you say about Sunday. It is but little known on ship board, except that everything is a little more quiet. The usual routine of daily work, of men drilling & at quarters, of painting & scraping &c is not carried on. After breakfast everything is cleaned up nice & at ten o'clock the men are all "mustered for inspection." Each one is expected to be dressed in his Sunday best & at exactly four bells (10 o'clock) the bo'sun's call musters all hands for inspection. The seamen & petty officers are drawn up on one side of the deck, the firemen & coal heavers on the other. Each man answers to his name as the Lieut. calls the roll. The Capt. is then informed that the men are ready for inspection. He passes slowly along in front of the lines of men looking closely at their dress, appearance &c.

"Jones, why are your shoes not blacked?"

Jones having no good excuse, the Paymaster's steward is ordered to stop his grog for a day or two.

"Lieut., what is this man's name?"

"Smith sir."

"Well, have his grog stopped for a week for coming to inspection without a cravat."

"Do you belong to the ship?"

---

* Samuel W. Locklin, a millwright in La Salle.

James River (May to August 1862)

"Yes sir."

"Well, you are a filthy beast, a disgrace to your shipmates. The dirt on you is absolutely frightful. If I see you so again I will have the Master at Arms strip you & scour you with sand & canvas," & so the inspection goes on.

After the men, the ship is inspected by the Capt. to see that all parts are neat, clean & in order. The men are then released & pass the day as they choose, reading, mending, fishing &c &c. We officers are expected to appear in undress uniform with sword.

How I would enjoy a good stroll on shore just now, devoid of all fear or expectation of meeting a rebel musket in every clump of bushes in your path or behind every log or stump. More than that, how I would like a drink of good cool water from *our well*, for our river water is too muddy & the condensed water made on the ship is *rather warm* & ice is not to be thought of here.

I hope you will have no more of those colds. I wish you were as free from such things as I am. Be careful of the children. I tremble every time I open a letter lest some of you may be sick.

Kiss the dear children for me & accept as many from myself as you desire.

William

No. 18—

Iron Clad *Monitor*
Devil's Reach, James River, Va.
June 22, 1862

Dear Anna,

We have had a warm Sunday & now 9 o'clock Sunday evening the thermometer in the Ward room stands at 86°. You say I never feel the heat. It may be so but I certainly have not felt it as severely here yet as I have sometimes at home. Those acquainted with the country say the summer thus far has been uncommonly cool. A large field of wheat about two miles from us is just beginning to look yellow, as if it would soon be fit to harvest. Capt. J. this morning was proposing to try one of our Berney (incendiary) shells upon it & harvest it for the owner who is a rank secessionist.

What a dismal hole we are in. The contrast makes even City Point seem almost a paradise. We hope to be ordered back there again soon but have pretty much given up the idea of going to Washington for repairs, Capt. J.'s request for that purpose having been refused. If the Department send us down the coast in our present condition they will be guilty of murder. I am perfectly willing to risk my life in the discharge of my duty, but it does not seem to be my duty to throw it away to conceal the willful negligence of the Department.

I saw in a Washington paper recently that they were preparing to receive us there with great honor, no doubt but we should have been lions for a time.

Civil War Years: USS *Monitor* (1862)

However we shall miss [all] of that as well as our dinner with Gen. Wool & Staff, he having removed from Fortress Munroe. But for these things I care but little, thought [though] it is pleasing to know that your services, when realy valuable, are appreciated.

Monday evening [June 23]—We had a narrow escape last night from destruction. The vessel was discovered to be on fire where the galley pipe passes through the deck. It was burning within six feet of one of the shell rooms when first seen. It was quickly put out by those on watch & none of the rest of us knew anything about it till morning. The discipline of the ship prepares every one for all such emergencies, consequently there is no noise or confusion at such a time. The fire burned through the wooden deck to the iron plating, rendering our galley stove unsafe to use. So this morning our breakfast was a scanty one, crackers & coffee, the latter being made in the fire room, in one of the furnaces. A rude fireplace was afterward improvised on the deck, of bricks & plates of iron which served to cook our dinner in.

At ten o'clock this morning our anchor was up & we were under way for City Point once more having laid here for ten days — a young eternity seemingly. We had watched & gazed at the shores in that "slough of despond"* till we knew every crook & turn in its miry bank. Every stump & log, every clump of weeds & rushes were familiar to us. We were acquainted with the croak of every frog & the notes of all the birds. The two old cranes who flew over us every evening homeward bound, stretched their long necks & seemed finally to look with complacency upon our intrusion upon their haunts & even the buzzards as they hovered over us appeared to look down upon us as a fixture in the midst of the mud & slimy water.

Well here we are at last at City Point which important place has undergone but little change since we left it except that some of the buildings bear the rough marks of the shells thrown through them by our ships at the time we were fired upon by their field battery spoken of in my last. But little harm was done to us although we were taken entirely by surprise. The first that was know[n] of the presence of an enemy was a hail storm of musket balls flying across the decks of our vessels followed by a rapid fire from their battery of four twelve pounder field pieces. No one was hurt although the vessels were struck by a large number of musket balls & a schooner loaded with ordnance stores received one ball from their field pieces.

As we came down the river to day we passed large fields of wheat, some harvested, others ready to harvest, the owners of it know[n] to be rebels, some of them bearing arms in the rebel army. Of course we can expect but one use to be made of all this bread stuff — to feed our enemies. Still nothing is done to take possession of it ourselves or to destroy it & the rebels go on with their harvest right under the muzzle of our guns [with] no one to molest

---

* John Bunyan's *The Pilgrim's Progress* (1678).

them or make them afraid. It is high time that more severe measures were inaugurated & the rebels made to feel the heavy hand of war.

The *Monitor* under her present commander will never be what she was under Capt. Worden. We have all been greatly disappointed in our present Captain. He will sit at the table & entertain us with plans of the most magnificent conceptions, but he is most sadly deficient either in ability or power to carry them out. With him the navy (that is the regular navy in distinction of the volunteer) is the pivot of pretty much all of creation & himself is the very center of that point. For the volunteer officers he entertains the most supreme contempt. Still he is a person of intelligence & scientific attainments, but these do not compensate for his extreme selfishness & his want of decisive energetic action.

We have had another severe thunder storm to day, raining heavily & of course delaying McClelland's hourly expected attack. I hope you hear something from him. We do not, but we feel assured of one thing: when he fights it will be to win.

We have an opportunity to send off letters early to morrow morning & I must wind up my scrawl. I hope you will find something readable in it but I doubt very much whether it will be worth the postage. Give my love to all friends.

Did Mr. Rockwell receive the Norfolk paper I sent him? Remember me to him & Mr. & Mrs. Hough.

William

[Marginalia] Tuesday morning [June 24]—McClelland has sent over to us wanting us to destroy a rail road bridge crossing a creek between Richmond & Petersburg, to cut off the rebels' retreat south.* Our vessels will go up the Appomatox to the mouth of the creek & from there up in boats. I am not acquainted with all their plans but these are the main features. If the expedition takes place you shall have all the details soon as possible.

McClelland was to have commenced his attack yesterday, but it has been delayed from some unexplained cause, probably rain — it rained hard all last night.

No. 19—

Iron Clad Monitor
City Point, James River
June 25th, 1862

Dear Anna,

How provoking. We have had six boats up the river in the last seventy two hours but none of them brought any mail. It is now over a week since we have received letters. This abominable negligence is caused by the

---

* The expedition up the Appomattox River is described in the letter of June 30, 1862.

Civil War Years: USS *Monitor* (1862)

Commodore. All vessels which leave here are obliged to go to him to report. His vessel, the *Minnesota*, lies at Norfolk & he will not allow the vessels to go to Old Point for the mail before coming back up the river. We are usually indebted to the army boat (the flag of truce) when we get a mail. We hear the old brute has the gout very severely. He softens it down by calling it rheumatism. Whatever it may be he has no sympathisers here among the fleet. I believe most of his officers would be glad to see the place vacated that it might be filled by a more worthy man.

It rained hard all yesterday afternoon, as it has done for several preceding days. Such weather must add very much to the toils & hardships of our army before Richmond. Between the peals of thunder, while the shower was coming up yesterday, we thought we could hear the almost constant roar of heavy artillery in the direction of Richmond & imagined we could see the "sulphurous canopy" hanging over a hard fought battle field. We have heard firing in that direction all day & even while I write the distant explosion of a gun comes booming up occasionally.*

Among the arrivals to day has been a sub-marine battery, intended to work beneath the water. It resembles in appearance & is about the size of a large steam boiler pointed at both ends, with a row of small glass lights along the top & a man hole for entrance. It is sunk by admitting water into one of the water tight compartments with which it is furnished & is propelled by means of a screw turned by the men inside. What use is intended to be made of it up here I don't know, unless it be to blow up the obstructions at Fort Darling which if they attempt I prophesy will be a failure.†

We have also had the arrival of one of McClelland's officers, four hours from head quarters, with dispatches to Com. Rodgers. Of their contents or import I have no knowledge, neither did the officer who brought them. He seemed to think it would be a week or more before McClelland would be ready for the final struggle. McC. was busy bringing up his heavy artillery & attending to many little details, each perhaps trifling in itself but adding to the completeness & perfection of his plans & all aiding to give him success when the hour of trial arrives.

We have also had an irruption of newspaper reporters, the first of their species who have found their way up here. They came up in the flag of truce.

I am sorry to see by some of the late papers I have been reading that much is expected of our fleet in the river here & especially of the *Monitor* in the

---

* The roar of artillery that Keeler was hearing was from the Battle of Oak Grove (June 25), the first of the Seven Day's Battles in which Lee pushed McClellan to Harrison's Landing on the James River. Lee launched his offensive on June 26 after discovering that McClellan's right flank north of the Chickahominy River was exposed and vulnerable to turning.

† The hand-propelled submarine USS *Alligator* participated in the raid up the Appomattox River to destroy the railway bridge over Swift Creek on June 26. The bridge was to have been blown up by the two torpedoes carried by the *Alligator*, but the mission was aborted before they ever reached the bridge.

attack upon Richmond. Without the assistance of a powerful land force we can be of no use whatever in an attack upon the river batteries owing to their peculiar position & the extreme narrowness of the river. Since our attack on Fort Darling we are told that other forts have been built this side & a powerful submarine battery sunk. Notwithstanding this I think it is our duty to try, but I doubt if the imbecility of our naval powers will permit us even to fire a gun that way. I hope I shall be mistaken.

I think the boat expedition I mentioned in my last will come off to morrow night, though from the little knowledge we have been able to obtain of the locality I fear it will be a failure. It is intended to run our vessels (all but one or two) up the Appomatox, eight or nine miles, to Port Walthall, from which place we are to send out our boats up Swift Creek three miles to the rail road bridge we design to destroy. Ten boats carrying about 100 men will comprise the expedition. None of the *Monitor*'s crew go & and only two officers, Mr. Greene & Mr. Gager. In order to distract the attention of the enemy who will no doubt have discovered us, one of the small vessels will keep on up the Appomatox as if intending to attack Petersburg, only 8 or 9 miles distant. The others will commence a fire on the buildings at Port Walthall, burning whatever they find combustible. At the same time the vessels left behind at City Point will fire that place & keep up a cannonade generally, dropping their shells all over the country. The men in the boats will pull swiftly & silently up the creek, furnished with combustibles which they will place on the bridge, fire them & retreat as soon as possible. I hope the enterprise will be successful as it cuts off the retreat of the rebel army south. The Sec'y of War, we are told, is very anxious it should be done, deeming it of very great importance. I hoped to be allowed to accompany the expedition, but cannot get Capt. J. to consent. I even offered to shoulder a musket & go as a private.

Monday evening [June 30]—Hurrah. The *Southfield* has just come up bringing the mail. I have your letter of the 15th & the [*La Salle*] *Press*. It did seem good to hear from home once more.

Our engine, I should have told you before, we have patched up after a fashion, but it is liable to give way at any moment.

You must be anxious at home hearing so many false reports of our capture &c & getting letters so seldom. I write every opportunity.

I enclose you a wild rose picked for me during our hog hunt, [which] I have written you about, by a rebel bullet, though I have been obliged to shorten the stem considerably.

If our boat expedition comes off you shall have the particulars as soon as possible.

Don't believe in the stories of our capture &c that are published. We are lying lazily & quietly at anchor here. The only fear I have is of getting eaten through by rust.

Civil War Years: USS *Monitor* (1862)

Tell Mrs. Rockwell I will keep her invitation in reserve hoping to be able to accept it at some future time.

The darkeys are coming off to us again with chickens, eggs &c. They brought us a few quarts of cherries to night — little, sour things but good for puddings.

My kind remembrances to all friends & love to yourself & the children.

William

[Marginalia] By special favor I am writing this at midnight, having permission to burn a light after the forbidden hour of ten. Don't feel sleepy as I contrive [to] sleep away two or three hours every afternoon.

No. 20—

Iron Clad *Monitor*
James River, Va.
June 30th, 1862

Dear Anna,

On Thursday evening, the 26th, we left City Point just at sundown on our expedition up the Appomatox to destroy the Rail Road bridge over "Swift creek." The destruction of this bridge would cut of[f] the railroad communication between Petersburg & Richmond & destroy the great artery of the rebel army leading south from their capital.

Some of the small boats followed by the *Port Royal* (the flag ship) took the lead. The *Maritanza* came next, followed by the *Monitor* & then came the others in the order laid down by Flag Officer Rogers.* In crossing the bar at the mouth of the Appomatox the *Maritanza* got aground, completely stopping the narrow channel. In endeavouring to pass her we were obliged to let go an anchor to prevent running into her. Vessel after vessel kept coming up, each anxious to cross the bar & get on their way up the river before it should be too dark & each one as they came up only added another to the now tangled & confused mass of boats & shipping lying at the mouth of the river.

Darkness came on while they were backing & filling & turning this way & that endeavouring to find their way through the narrow & crooked channel across the bar. The *Port Royal* which was now some ways ahead commenced firing, answered by the *Galena* which remained behind at City Point. Their shells were thrown indiscriminately over the land in all directions, it being our object to divert & distract the enemy's attention from our real object. The mass of vessels on the bar now opened & gun followed gun in quick succession, the shells tore howling through the air exploding miles inland. It was realy wonderful that some of us were not hurt. As we set so low in the water,

---

* John Rodgers.

the guns from the tangled mass of shipping flashed across our decks their hot blast nearly sweeping us into the water.

With the aid of some tugs we finally got straightened out & proceeded up the river in our designated order. The Appomatox is quite narrow, the banks muddy & marshy for a short distance, when they rise into bluffs some 40 or 50 feet high & covered with timber of moderate growth, mostly pine. Of course nothing could be seen in the darkness but two long parallel lines of black wall between which wound the narrow stream we were navigating. The dancing light of myriads of fire flies sparkled in strong relief against the dark back ground, startled from their leafy covert by the heavy concussion of our guns. The scene was one of the most terrible magnificence & will remain forever impressed upon my memory. It was a sight I had often desired to see, a bombardment in the night. I could look up the river & note a succession of dark island like spots denoting our vessels & behind the same. From one side of one of these dark spots would suddenly jet out a volume a [of] flame, then one from the other & so from side to side & from vessel to vessel, ahead & behind. From our own turret, look which way we would & the dark spots were belching forth jets of fire.

The thunder of the guns was intensified by being confined between the narrow walls. It would roll from side to side & then the echo would return to us from the distance with startling force & distinctness mingled with the heavy explosion of our bursting shells. The echo was certainly remarkable for the force, distinctness & number of times with which it was repeated & added tenfold to the magnificence of the spectacle.

The guns were elevated sufficiently to carry the projectiles over the tree tops & must have swept over the country like a hurricane. Woe to the unfortunate dwelling when these terrible miss[i]les sought a landing or over whose roofs they exploded. I imagine there were few who slumbered undisturbed on the line of the river this night.

In this way we proceeded up the river some seven or eight miles, sowing our shells broadcast over the land. When about a mile & a half below the mouth of Swift Creek, we found the Flag Ship & her attendant boats had come to a stand. We ran up as near as we deemed prudent & let go an anchor. We waited here till nearly midnight in suspense as to the fate of the small boats which were to row up the creek to destroy the bridge. We expected every moment to see the signal rocket rise which would bid those who remained behind at City Point [to] apply the torch (for this was a part of the programe) to the buildings there, but we were still more anxious to see the flames denoting the destruction of the bridge. Moments seemed hours. At last a boat came alongside & Mr. Greene, who was to have charge of one of the boats of the expedition, jumped out & all crowded around him to hear the news. It was brief & discouraging. The *Port Royal* had been opened on from the shore by sharp shooters & the *Maratanza* had run aground in e[n]deavouring to run up the river towards Petersburg which was nine miles further up. Of course the boat expedition was given up.

The tide was on the ebb, so we had nothing but to summon our patience & wait till the next flood tide should float her off. Our situation was not particularly pleasing. The dark walls on either hand rose close by our sides & we might at any moment have our decks swept by a storm of rifle balls or even by artillery, but the night passed quiet[l]y & undisturbed, except by the discharges of our own guns which maintained their fire at intervals through the night.

The morning revealed our position anchored in the middle of the narrow stream. The bluffs on each side covered with a thick growth of trees & underbrush making a fine cover for sharp shooters. Houses were scattered along the edge of the bluff on one side for some distance above & below us. Our vessels lay at anchor up & down the stream & the *Maritanza* aground behind a bend of the river & out of our sight. No sign of an enemy was to be seen & not a gun had been fired at us since the attack of the sharp shooters last night.

A dense black smoke was rising in the direction of Port Walthall, a mile & a half above us, supposed to be from a large pile of bituminous coal that lay on the dock there. I felt extremely mortified at the unsuccessful result of our expedition, at being detered & driven off by a mere handful of sharp shooters, for I am satisfied there were but few of them & they fled after firing a few rounds. In fact the whole country seemed to be completely panic stricken & I doubt very much if a soldier was nearer us than Petersburg & it was possible that the force there had retreated towards Richmond, supposing our object to be to land a large body of troops & advance upon the place. Of our real object I think they were in total ignorance.

The failure of the expedition can be traced to two causes. First, a total want of a preconcerted plan of action & a want of understanding between the persons who were to be placed in command of the different boats. The expedition was plan[n]ed by the Commanders of the different vessels here, but they seemed to have failed to give definite instructions to the persons who were to be in charge of the boats. These persons were lieutenants & masters selected from the different vessels. They did not meet to agree upon any plan of action till the *Port Royal* started up the river when they went on board with their boats & crews. But one person went from the *Monitor*, Lieut. Greene. As soon as they assembled on the *Port Royal*, the second cause of the failure manifested itself — *whiskey*. They got around the Ward Room table & drank till every shot fired by the sharp shooters sounded like a thirty two pounder & the reports were multiplied indefinitely. Under these circumstances the expedition was given up & they returned on board their respective vessels with fearful stories of narrow escapes from the myriads of sharp shooters.

James River (May to August 1862)

During the remainder of the night & all the next day not a shot was fired from the shore & I feel confident that twenty good men could have rowed up to Port Walthall, a mile & a half, & marched from there to the bridge, four miles further, without interruption. At any rate I would willingly & gladly have made one of the number to make the trial & take the chances.

We remained here all day, Friday [June 27], the tide not rising sufficiently high to float off the *Maritanza* & the different commanders began to talk seriously of destroying her, as we could not expect to remain long where we were without an attack from the enemy. We were looking every moment for them to open on us with artillery & musketry. The position we occupied was very favourable for an attack without our being able to make much of a defense.

During the day a man came off to the flag ship from somewhere back in the country to claim pay for damages to his house which had one of the corners knocked off by one of our shells. I don't think he got much satisfaction.

Saturday morning [June 28] we found the *Maritanza* had been got off during the night but the *Island Belle* was now ashore. I should have said her captain had been suspended during the bombardment Thursday night for getting drunk & running into the Commodore [Rodgers], producing a fearful crush of carpenters' work.

About noon on Saturday a little tug came puffing up the river at a prodigious rate bringing the painful intelligence of McClelland's retreat* & orders for the whole fleet to proceed at once up the river to our old anchorage in Devil's Reach. The guns & some few other things were hastily removed from the *Island Belle*, she was set on fire, & we steamed down the Appomatox & before sun down were at anchor midst the familiar scenes & sounds of this *romantic?* locality.

I think our expedition up the Appomatox would form a disgraceful page of our country's history & I only wish some truthful historian with a powerful pen had been with us to give to the public a plain unvarnished tale of facts. 'T will bring a blush to the face of the nation if it is capable of blushing. Four or five thousand dollars worth of ammunition expended, one steamer (not very valuable) burned, a large quantity of whiskey drank, with what result? A number of people badly frightened & the corner of a house knocked off — that I believe is about the way the account foots. This however does not detract from the terrible magnificence of a night bombardment. How often I wished Henry stood by my side as we went up the Appomatax that night. No one but the gunners were at quarters so I stood on the deck the whole time & had a good view of the whole scene with no great danger from enemy's shots.

---

* McClellan abandoned his advance on Richmond after his defeat at the Battle of Gaines' Mills on June 27 and commenced his retreat to Harrison's Landing on the James River.

Civil War Years: USS *Monitor* (1862)

Early Sunday morning [June 29] the *Galena* signalised to follow her down the river. We followed close after the *Mahaska*. In turning a bend in the river I noticed a few little jets of smoke from the bank just abreast of her, quickly followed by the sharp reports of rifles, answered by two or three rapid discharges of her howitzers. One man, I afterward learned, was killed on board of her by that fire of sharp shooters. You may imagine the pleasure of sailing up & down the river when every bush or log or stump may conceal sharp shooters ready to fire the moment your person is exposed.

We came to anchor about the middle of the forenoon at Turkey island, 8 or 9 miles above City Point. Here we picked up a Signal officer of the Army with dispatches from McClelland. He was unable to give a very clear idea of the state of things with the army & we were left to surmise & imagine the worst. He told us the army would soon be down to the river under cover of our guns.

About the middle of the afternoon a huge, dense column of thick white smoke suddenly sprang up from the ground in the direction we supposed the army to be. It continued gradualy rising & expanding till its top was lost in the clouds. Of course we could only guess at its origin & purpose. We supposed it to be our troops blowing up one of the bridges, to cut off pursuit, across the Chicahominy.

In the evening we were gladdened by the arrival of a mail. Your No. 3 was rec'd & devoured. I need not say how eagerly & with what satisfaction to hear you were all well at home. (I am now up to Monday morning & will continue from day to day in the form of a journal.)

Monday morning June 30—At early light a rapid & heavy fire was heard a few miles inland continuing for three hours, indicating the pursuit of our flying forces. The rapid boom, boom of field artillery sounded clear & distinct above the long & continuous smothered roar of musketry. How I wish our big guns were where they could pour their contents into the rebel ranks, but that cannot be & we have nothing to do but watch & wait, but this state of suspense is awful.

About 8 o'clock A.M. the advance stragglers made their appearance along the banks of the river & about the same time we received orders to go further down the stream opposite City Point to protect that portion of the army coming in there. We passed slowly down. The banks on our left in many places now lined with our men. Hundreds of them were in the water enjoying a bath & hailed us with jocular remarks, seemed in no ways dispirited.

As we passed Hill Carter's fine house* I saw one of our sentrys pacing back & forth in front of his door to keep our men from entering, while at the dock before the house was the *Stepping Stones* loaded with our sick & wounded laid on her decks in the full glare of a broiling sun. This Carter is one of the rankest rebels in this section of the country & has a son, a colonel, just

---

* At Shirley Plantation.

returned home wounded from the Rebel army at Richmond. If I could have had my way Mr. Rebel Carter & family should have taken up their quarters with their negroes & our wounded soldiers should have enjoyed his mansion for a while. This is a sample of the way this "rose water war" is carried on in this part of the country & it will continue to be carried on till more severe measures are allowed to be taken by our officers in command here. Let these wealthy rebels bear the penalty of the war they have brought upon them & be made to feel its pressure & presence in the severist possible manner.

We reached City Point a little after noon. The rail road buildings & docks of which I have spoken in some of my former letters had been burned in our absence by some of our vessels & are now nothing but a smoking mass. Dr. Epps' fine place on the point, of which I have spoken before, was spared, for what reason I can't imagine, though it is tolerably well riddled by shot & shell.

About 3 o'clock P.M. firing commenced again, musketry & artillery & the roar was constant for upward of two hours.* But it appeared to gradually recede from which we argue that our forces are driving the rebels back.

Scooners loaded with army stores are now continually arriving in tow of steamers & the river here will soon be thickly covered with them, over one hundred are on the way up.

5 o'clock P.M. I have just ret'd from one of our steamers that left White House on the York river Saturday night [June 28].† The Capt. told me that the scene there was frightful. Vessels were being hurried off by everything that could tow them. Large quantities of stores were being burned & the confusion there, as he said, was "infernal." This dreadful change brings us at once in the very center of the theatre of the war & we may now consider ourselves as located for the season. It will be more comfortable than being off Charleston however, which I suppose was to have been our fate. That can be postponed till cooler weather.

This will be the base of McClelland's operations for future operations on Richmond & there is but little doubt but what we shall be kept busy, that is if our rattling old engine holds together of which there is strong doubts.

The feeling in the fleet here is one of the greatest bitterness & indignation against Sec'y Staunton for refusing McClelland the troops he desired. For McClelland the deepest sympathy. Of the details we know nothing, not even as much as yourself, & of course are unable to form a decided definite opinion.

It is now nine o'clock. All the afternoon, one continuous cannonade has been kept up. The roar has been incessant & without intermission, now advancing & now receding as the tide of battle waved back or forth. Not in the remote distance but so near that we could distinctly see the shells

---

* The inconclusive Battle of Glendale, eight miles north of City Point.
† White House Plantation, McClellan's supply base on the Pamunkey River, which he abandoned on June 28 when he retreated to Harrison's Landing on the James River.

exploding in the air. Far in the distance, relieved against a dark back ground & more distinctly seen for that reason, has been passing all day one continuous line of army wagons, miles & miles & miles in length, like a long line of white dots passing rapidly along.

1/2 past nine—The firing still continues at intervals. A dispatch boat has just come down the river from the Commodore [Rodgers] from our anchorage of the morning, saying that our gun boats had been engaged all the afternoon & bringing orders for all the gun boats below here to go up the river to the assistance of the army there, the *Monitor* to remain here & protect the fleet of transports.

We expect McClelland will fall back to Dancing Point (formed by the junction of the Chicahominy with the James river) to commence operations anew. As I said before, I think this will occupy most of the summer, but this is merely a surmise of mine. You will probably get news — general news — sooner than I will so I shall not attempt to send you that but will try & give you such details as I think will be interesting.

I don't want you to think after reading some portions of my letter that I feel as Dave would say, "blue." That is not the case. But I frequently feel pained & disgusted to see such a want of energy & enterprise as is frequently manifested in the Navy. The novelty of the service has worn off & I can now criticize its movements cooly & with better judgement.

Of course much that I have written will not do to publish. In fact none of it was written for that purpose. Surrounded as I have been most of the time while writing with almost every element of discord, I have found it exceedingly difficult to concentrate my thoughts on the sheet before me & much of it has been scratched off in such haste that I fear you will find it a difficult matter to read it. My friends are welcome to all you choose to read to them, but I fear it will not sound as well in print. As heretofore I shall keep a quantity of matter on hand ready to send off every opportunity which I hope will now be more frequent.

Tell my kind friend David L. [Hough] if he thinks I have nothing to do but write, that the most prolific brain will get exhausted. Not that I mean to call mine one of that kind, but after writing you three or four sheets of facts, if I was to commence three or four more to him, it would be of *fancies* & that I suppose would not suit his fancy. In the place of asking me to write to him, if he & all my other friends could form any idea how welcome letters are to us away from friends & home I feel fully satisfied that each & every one of them would write me at least every other day. Tell Mrs. Hough that I have been looking for that letter from her for a long time.

Why don't Dave write me here? I have been writing to them all — to all our circle I mean — for the letters to you are to all — week after week & not a line have I had from any one of them but you. Not but what your letters are interesting & valuable, more so than all the others combined, but I would like to see a line from them occasionally. Tell Dave that I would like to have some ocular demonstration that his eyes are of some practical use.

I wish you could see the group of eager anxious faces that surround our Ward Room table as a newly arrived mail is being sorted over & distributed. No one would ever say it was any trouble to write after once watching the pleased smiling countenances of the circle of happy recipients of the welcome paper messengers.

Tell my friends at your strawberry party that their kind wishes are reciprocated. I would like to make one of their number over a dish of your strawberries. I still hope to eat some grapes with them in the fall & discuss the respective merits of Dianas, Concords &c. Will we have many more than we did last year?

Tuesday morning, July 1st—All is quiet this morning, not a sound is heard. One would hardly think that two hostile armies numbering thousands were so near us. If you have a good map of this part of the country, & I hope you have, you can see McClelland's position. His army stretches across the peninsular from this river to the Chicahominy. His left wing, on which the attack has been made, resting on the James river abreast of where we now lie, City Point. We have just heard that he succeeded in driving them back yesterday, but nothing of the particulars.

Do you still receive the *Sci'c American*? If not let me know as I do not wish it stopped. I suppose you continue *Harper* & Father the *Agriculturalist*.

10 o'clock A.M. The *S. R. Spaulding* has just passed us on her way up to get the wounded from yesterday's battle field & carry them, such as can be moved, immediately to New York. She is in the employ of the U.S. Sanitary Commission.

The roar of battle has again begun, to day further towards the Chicahominy, on McClelland's center. The continuous fire from field artillery resembles the distant roar of thunder.

4 P.M.—The battle still rages. The roar of the guns increases in rapidity & distinctness. The conflict is surging over towards the river on the left wing.[*] Oh if our gun boats could only plunge their shot into the rebel ranks. It is terrible indeed to be compelled to sit & listen to such fearful sounds & not be able to give assistance.

Where the long line of army wagons were passing yesterday, a cloud of dust is hanging over the road, shewing our troops hurrying in their retreat.

A Col. in the commissary department was aboard last evening. He said that at no time since McClelland left Yorktown has he had more than 80,000 men. The rations issued from that department would give him a very correct

---

[*] Malvern Hill, the last of the Seven Days Battles. The 130-foot hill was located two miles north of the James River. The Confederates suffered heavy losses from multiple failed assaults against the Union forces positioned on the hill.

idea of the number of troops. The rebels are said to number over 200,000*, including all the choicest of B[ea]uregard's troops.

5 P.M. Firing on the left wing has pretty much ceased but a distant cannonade is still audible. Schooners are constantly arriving loaded with ordnance & commissary stores. Reinforcements are beginning to arrive — two steam boat loads are now passing us, going up the river to Carter's landing.

Ten thousand rumours are afloat regarding McClelland's movements, policy & intentions. He was on board the *Galena* yesterday but if he made know[n] any of his plans they have not reached me. We are still at anchor at City Point guarding the fleet of transports which is hourly increasing in numbers. Our guns loaded with shell & canister are trained on the Point where a battery of field pieces may be expected at any moment from Petersburg, ready to open on them as soon as they shew themselves.

I have just heard, among many other rumours, that our forces took four batteries of guns yesterday, that Stonewall Jackson has been killed & that our forces are advancing up James river on the opposite side. This last is doubtful.

Wednesday morning, [July] 2nd. Raining hard with a prospect of continuing through the day. Yesterday it was cool & cloudy with a cool pleasant wind. The day before was excessively hot, the sun shining bright & clear.

8 A.M. The *Galena* has just passed us on her way down with McClelland on board where he spent a portion of the night to get some rest. We are now on our way up to Turkey island once more as a sort of rear guard of this wing of the army. This wing fell back last night & now rests on the river opposite Harrison's bar, a few miles below City Point, for the sake of being nearer & more convenient to his supplies. Where he now is are good docks and facilities for discharging vessels.

We hear that day before yesterday (Monday) our troops were severely handled but yesterday the enemy were repulsed at every point, loosing many prisoners. They (the prisoners) represented that they had not tasted food for 48 hours & begged for something to eat as soon as taken.

Noon—Here we are at Turkey island, just on the outskirts of the battle field of the two or three previous days & the scene is truly distressing. The *Spaulding* has passed down with her load of wounded, gathered up from the battle field & the gun boat *Delaware* lies just under our stern. The rain is still pouring down.

Come up to the top of our turret & stand under the awning with me & take a look ashore. The bank you see slopes gently down to the water's edge, covered with fine large trees. Over & between their tops, you get a glimpse of the "great house" of one of the "F.F.V.s." Scattered along on the shore are some of the wounded & stragglers from the battle field. Here a fallen tree

---

* The number of Confederate troops was far less by roughly a factor of two.

forms a seat for a long line of poor dejected looking fellows, some with ragged blankets drawn over their head & shoulders as a slight protection to the beating rain. There another group has sought the shelter of that cluster of young pines.

A tall stalwart fellow stands exposed to the rain on the end of the dock moodily leaning on his musket as though he were bidding defiance to both the elements & enemies. Here a sick one lies stretched out on a cast away plank, not even a blanket to shelter him from the rain. Here one limps painfully along through the mud & water by the aid of an old branch, with a wounded foot from which he has discarded the shoe, the suffering member tied up in a bloody, dirty rag, sinks deep in the mud at every step.

Another is using his musket as a crutch. There one is up to his armpits in the river vainly endeavouring to wade off to the *Delaware*. There one pale, weak & dejected makes a faint effort to seek a better shelter, but after a few tottering steps through the mire is forced to give up the attempt & sinks exhausted on a rock.

There on the beach is one of the *Delaware*'s boats, the crew are gathering up the debris of the battle. Here comes a blue jacket with his arms full of muskets which he deposits in the boat, another follows with a drum, a saddle, some swords & here is another with a flag, some overcoats & blankets & another comes staggering through the mud under a load of cartridge boxes, canteens, bayonet belts & sheaths & so they come one after another loaded with a confused mass of the wreck of the battle field.

Take my glass & look along up the marshy bank. There they come straggling along singly & in pairs, tracing their weary way through mire & marsh, over rocks & stumps & fallen trees, & through masses of tangled briers & young pines drenched with the water shaken from their foliage & the pouring rain. Do not think I am exaggerating. The scene is beyond exageration & bids defiance to the most fertile imagination.

A pile of provisions lies piled up in boxes ashore which the slaves are carrying off. They are also scattered around through the woods busily gathering up the thousand & one useless articles cast aside by the sick, wounded & weary. Strict discipline evidently prevails for amidst this scene of suffering & confusion the slaves of the wealthy rebel near by are quietly leading down his sleek fat horses to drink. Flocks of hens are scratching around the grass plots & the whole domestic machinery moves smoothly on in its usual routine. Would this be the case if their own army had occupied the place? I think not.

Here we lay till three o'clock P.M. when just before getting under way our boat was sent ashore & brought off three poor sick fellows who had been left there by their comrades in an outbuilding of the rebel mansion. Another trip was made & three more well ones were brought off who made their appearance after these three sick ones were brought aboard. These three last were carried down the river quarter of a mile where Capt. Jeffers with the cold hearted brutality of a fiend ordered the boat manned & the men sent on shore. You may be surprised at these expressions. I will explain in my next as I have no time now as the mail is about to leave & I want to give you all the items up to the last minute.

In front of Hill Carter's [Shirley Plantation] the dock was covered with the poor fellows & by the orders of Capt. J. her [the *Delaware*'s] capt. ran up to the dock & took them on board. Many had to be carried on board on stretchers. Before all were on board the artillery of the rebels could be heard a short distance off & the boat shoved off leaving numbers running along the bank in the vain hope to reach her. Many of the sick & wounded too were left lying in the mud where they had been placed waiting to be taken on board. Poor fellows, the rebels were soon upon them.

One of the three we set ashore just after we started, was a boy but little larger than Henry. He had come into the camp he said to see his brother & then staid to cook for one of the officers. They were hungry they said & wanted something to eat but were brutally ordered into the boat. They begged hard to be allowed to remain [on board the *Monitor*], but they might as well have talked to a stone.

We are now on our way to Harrison's Point from which place I hope to be able to send my hastily written sheets. I would like to fill this page but will not have time I fear. You cannot complain for want of length in this — five sheets & a half!!! However, 'tis a pleasure to write when I find anything to write about. You shall hear from me every opportunity.

If you can get a *Harper's Weekly* of May 31 you will find quite a good map of this section of country. I have one I would send you but I fear I cannot easily replace it. You can probably get one easier than I can.

But the mail is about to close so I must say good bye with love & good wishes to all.

Yours, William

[Marginalia] 8 o'clock P.M. At anchor on Harrison's bar. A city of tents ashore stretching for miles along the river & way back as far as we can see, through woods & openings, over corn & wheat fields, are tents & soldiers. The river is full of steamers, gun boats & sail vessels. Another Hampton Roads, only the vessels are not as large.

Your No. 4 enclosing Henry's has just been rec'd & read with the greatest satisfaction. Tell Henry he shall hear from me soon. You must have had a fine time at your strawberry party. I would [have] liked right well to have been there.

We are now in the very center of the war & I will try & pick up something interesting for you.

W—

Wednesday evening 3rd [2nd]. As I did not have an opportunity to send off my sheets as I expected I will continue them. I think if I keep continuing in

James River (May to August 1862)

this way much longer you will begin to cry "hold enough," though I believe you to be possessed of as good a stock of patience as usually falls to the share of us poor mortals.

The day has been cool & cloudy & without rain & has been favourably for our poor soldiers. That you may form some one idea of our respective positions I send you a rough kind of a sketch of the river & adjacent ground now occupied by our troops & gun boats.* The dotted line in pencil represents the outer line of our camp, the right [wing] resting on the river & protected by Herring Creek & the low marshy ground, & our gun boats which are represented by crosses XXX. M is the *Monitor*. The left wing is protected by a small creek & low marshy ground & by the gun boats. The ink dots represent the rebel army which you will see swarm on all sides & are only kept back by the impassible nature of the ground & fear of the gun boats. Expecting McClelland would retreat to the point made by the juncture of the Chicahominy & James rivers, a large body of them pushed rapidly ahead to cut him off, but finding that he has made a stand here they have made a retrograde movement & with a battery of field pieces, I, have been shelling McC.'s camp to day, replied to by the gun boats on the right wing. H.H. also represent batteries from which they have been firing through the day.

We regard McC.'s position as a strong one & think he will undoubtedly be able with our assistance to hold it till Buell & Pope, who are each advancing with 50,000 men, reaches him.† The rebels have followed our army up with a persistence & courage which must have been given them by the confidence of having overwhelming numbers. From the best information I can get I am inclined to think that McClelland has not now over 50,000 effective men. It is impossible to separate truth from falsehood or mere guesses from positive facts in the numberless stories & rumours that we hear. I give it to you as I get it. Much of it I suppose will prove erroneous. I fear our losses have been appalling in this disaster. It will be some time before we learn the full extent of them.

Some officers of the N.Y. 92nd [98th] was on board to day. They told me that your Cousin Wm. Dutton had been obliged to leave on account of his health.‡ They were in the midst of the retreat & say our losses are heavy, especially in camp equipage. They thought the rebels lost quite as many if not more men than ourselves. They saw our batteries of artillery§ mow them down when advancing in full column & they fell like grass. On one of our batteries eight regiments charged at different times & were swept off. The[y]

---

* See Sketch No. 5 at the beginning of the book.
† John Pope commanded the newly formed Army of Virginia which was gathering in northern Virginia, while Don Carlos Buell's Army of the Ohio was advancing towards Chattanooga, TN. Neither came to McClellan's assistance on the Peninsula.
‡ Anna's first cousin William Dutton* contracted typhoid fever at the Battle of Fair Oaks and was taken to a friend's house in New York City where he died on July 4.
§ At the Battle of Malvern Hill.

represent the rebels to have plenty to eat of good plain food — flour & beef, & the canteens of most of them who were taken prisoners had whiskey in them.

A constant skirmish has been going on all day in front of the lines. Our guns could not be elevated enough to reach the rebels so I have interested myself by watching the effects of the fire from the gun boats which lie around us on the enemy. Infantry, cavalry & artillery would come out in sight in a large field of wheat or rather wheat failed. A few shells would be sent howling through the air & they would soon disappear. Whether our fire was effective or not we could not tell. If our enemies didn't suffer our friends did, for a tug came down in haste with orders to "stop firing as we were killing & driving our own troops." Even with the firing of our vessels ringing every few moments in our ears it was difficult to believe that a battle, or call it a skirmish if you please, was going on.

McC's effective force was drawn up as represented by the dotted line, while inside it was full of stragglers, idlers, sick & hordes of followers which are always found around a camp. Tents, wagons, artillery &c seemed to cover the ground. Vessels lined the shore wherever they could get sufficiently near for the purpose, discharging their cargoes of supplies of all kinds, employing whole droves of contrabands as labourers.

In the very center of the camp stands Mr. Harrison's fine residence. His large fields of wheat & corn so green & promising the day before are now beat hard & brown. On the opposite side of the river is the princely mansion and extensive grounds of the perjured villain Ruffin* who boasts of having fired the first gun at Sumpter. No attempt is made to disturb it & it stands surrounded with large fields of grain which I suppose will go to feed the rebels at Richmond — such is our policy.

But the Master at Arms has just informed us that it is ten o'clock at which time all lights must be out, so good night. I will fill the next page in the morning if I have time.

W.

[Marginalia] 10 P.M. [July 2] Another mail — a paper from Dave & a letter [from] Helen [Plant]. Dear little Nellie [Helen], she's a trump, she is.

---

* Virginian fire-eater Edmund Ruffin, who was one of the South's strongest advocates of states' rights and secession in the years leading up to the Civil War. His plantation was at Coggin's Point on the south side of the James River across from Harrison's Landing.

JAMES RIVER (MAY TO AUGUST 1862)

No. 21—

Iron Clad *Monitor*
James River
July 4, 1862

Dear Anna,

After a number of fruitless attempts I finally succeeded in getting No. 20, consisting of five or six sheets, started off this morning & hope it will reach you safely.

Things seem to remain about as they were when I wrote you last evening. McClelland, we hear, is throwing up entrenchments in his front & actively preparing for defence. The rebels are said to be in great force in his front. His wings in his present position are well protected by the gun boats.

It was rumoured this morning that last evening the Irish brigade made an attack on the left wing of the rebels, capturing a battery of artillery & six hundred prisoners. It may however be one of the thousand idle reports which are constantly being circulated through the camp & fleet. We hear so much that is absurd & improbable, mixed with what seems plausible, that we are at a loss how to separate it & tell what to believe & what to reject & wish we could get the *papers to learn the news*. From some of the late papers I got hold of to day I find they are trying to make this retreat out as "a piece of strategy," "a masterly movement," "a change of front by which we get possession of Richmond in a few days" &c. This may sound very well to those at distance but it don't go down here.

McC. probably foresaw great difficulty in maintaining his position amidst the swamps around Richmond & keeping up an advance against such a vastly superior force as the rebels were concentrating against him & attempted a change of front of which the rebels took advantage & threw upon him an overwhelming force. He has probably made a masterly retreat, loosing in killed, wounded & missing, as is now estimated here, *20,000* men. No one is disposed to blame him in the least. All feel as much confidence in him as ever. But I am sorry to see the papers giving a false colour to the matter, for it is nothing less than a retreat before a vastly superior force. The blame falls where it should on the Sec'y of War.

Fifty thousand of Halleck's army are coming up.* If the Ill. 11th is among them I hope to see some of our La Salle folks. The Irish Brigade are here. Can you tell me the Co. & Reg. & State of our neighbor O'Kam? Tell his wife when she writes him to tell him where I am & to come on board & see me if he has an opportunity, as he would find me much easier than I would him.

With the exception of a salute from the batteries at noon it has been very still & quiet — not a gun to be heard except an occasional musket. The sun

---

* Believing he was greatly outnumbered, McClellan sent urgent messages to Washington for more troops following his defeat at Gaines' Mill. Lincoln's request to Halleck that he send McClellan 25,000 men was refused because they were needed out West.

has shone out bright & clear but accompanied with a fine cool wind tempering the heat.

We had a fine "pleasure excursion" for the Fourth. We got under way at noon in company with the *Maratanza* & proceeded up the river to Turkey bend or island. As we turned the bend we saw the small rebel gun boat *Teazer* some distance ahead. A shell from the *Maratanza* went screeching just over her smoke pipe, followed by a stand of grape when her bow was turned shorewards & a boat load of rebels "skeedadled" just as the second shell from the *Maratanza* struck her boiler, exploding it & knocking the machinery & upper works as the saying is "into a cocked hat." She was bringing down a load of rebel army officers to join some of their regiments around McClelland when we so suddenly interrupted their trip & intruded upon their pleasant little dinner party, for they had just set down to dinner when the first shell from the *Maratanza* heralded our approach.

Dispatches, officers' clothing & a large quantity [of] confederate notes fresh from the mint was found on board of her. The nature of the Dispatches I do not know but understand them to be very important, revealing many of their government secrets & is in this respect considered one of the most important captures of the war.

Among other things [on the *Teaser*] was a balloon with the cord, a long coil of insulating wire for firing the submarine batteries they have sunk in the river near Richmond [and] a large quantity of nitric acid to use in their electro magnetic batteries. The most interesting thing to us however was the private memorandum book of Hunter Davidson who was in command [of the *Teaser*].* He was one of the officers of the *Merrimac* & in this book was drafts of the *Monitor* & sketches of the mode of our capture, as they intended to attempt it. It was minute in all its details. We were to be boarded from four tugs at the same time (one of them the *Teaser*) by men carrying turpentine, ladders, fire balls, wedges, sheets of metal, chloroform &c. The names of the men were given, just what article each one was to carry, to what part of the *Monitor* he was to go &c. It even gave the men who were to carry the matches & sand paper to rub them on.

We got hold of a very amusing letter from Davidson's wife. She addresses him as "My Splendid Hunter" & goes on to say that "you thought I never was good for anything but to spend money, now I want to tell you that I am making up that lawn dress I bought in Richmond to prove that I can do something else when I set out." She tells him that she has sent him a tin pail

---

* Two years later Davidson led a daring raid down the James River against the USS *Minnesota* using a torpedo boat. Although he detonated the mine, the big wooden warship did not go down, and he and his crew escaped in their boat back to Richmond. His last command was the CSS *City of Richmond*, the consort for the ironclad CSS *Stonewall* which was launched in early 1865. Unable to accept the defeat of the Confederacy he travelled abroad for several years before returning to Maryland where he commanded the Maryland Oyster Navy, tracking down oyster pirates in Chesapeake Bay.

filled with fried chickens & butter, a delicacy she thinks he hasn't tasted for a long time, but wants him to be sure & return the pail as she was obliged to borrow it &, as no more are to be had there, a fuss will be made if it is not returned.*

Among other papers was a detailed account of the position, number &c of the submarine batteries sunk in the river by Lieut. Maury, also plans of some new batteries which have been erected below fort Darling.†

What my share of the prize money will be I am unable to say but I think I shall have no difficulty in counting it. Did I ever tell you that in case we had captured or destroyed the *Merrimac* our prize money would have been about one million of dollars to divide among us? That was something worth while.

We are now (in the evening) lying off the camp, the numerous lights looking at the distance like the gas lights of a large city. I want to write a little to Henry & so will close with best love to you & all the folks.

William

[Marginalia] We have been informed by the Department that we are to be ordered to Washington for repairs as soon as our services can be dispensed with here.

July 8th—Your No. 5 & the B[ridge] Port paper reached me last evening. Have been through the camp ashore & will give you particulars when I write again. Don't believe McC. has over 50,000 effective men exclusive of those joining him after he came here.

Monitor
James River, Va.
Fourth of July 1862

My Dear Boy‡,

How are you spending this glorious Fourth? I hope you have as pleasant & cool a day as we have here on the "sacred soil." Here there is no excitement, no stir. Everything is as still & quiet as a country village. There is nothing to indicate its being the anniversary of our independence except that the numerous vessels lying around us are wearing an unusual quantity of bunting, having hoisted their holiday flags & streamers. Contrary to the usual custom there is hardly the sound of gunpowder to be heard except the occasional discharge of a musket by some of the troops on shore.

---

* By 1872 Davidson had had enough of his wife Mary, the daughter of a Navy surgeon from Annapolis, MD, and left her and his five children and moved to Argentina where he served in the Argentine navy. Thirteen years later he moved to Paraguay, married a woman 45 years his junior, and had another brood of kids.
† Matthew F. Maury, former chief of the Bureau of Coast, Harbor and River Defenses in the Confederate Navy. In the summer of 1862 he perfected the electric torpedo and began mining the stretch of the James River just below Drewry's Bluff.
‡ Henry Keeler.

CIVIL WAR YEARS: USS *MONITOR* (1862)

If you are not busy, supposing we take a look into McClelland's camp* which is right abreast of the *Monitor*. As I cannot leave the vessel, we must stand on the top of the turret. We are quite near the bank & by taking this glass you can see very distinctly. You see the shore just opposite to us slopes gently up from the water's edge & was probably a beautiful lawn before beaten down by feet of our troops, the hoofs of horses & wheels of wagons. Farther along both up and down the stream you see low banks, their edges fringed with bushes which partly intercept the view, but we can see between them & over their tops. The ground stretches smooth & level for a long distance back where it is bordered by timber. Remember we are in the rear of our army & are consequently looking into their back yard & so see them differently employed from what we should if we were in front of them where they are probably at work throwing up entrenchments & otherwise preparing to defend themselves against the enemy.

Midway up this slope I have shewed you see that fine large house called Harrison's house. It is said all the inmates left it on the approach of our forces except one young lady, 20 years of age, who refused to go with the rest & now our troops refuse to allow her to leave unless she will take the oath of allegiance, which she declines to do. She is furnished with a guard to prevent any of our troops from disturbing her. Look at the top of the house & you see that out folks have cut a hole through the roof so as to get on the top & keep a look out for the enemy. Many of our officers probably have their head quarters there as you can see them passing out & in.

The shore along there you see is lined by hundreds of our soldiers enjoying the luxury of a bath. They have probably been hard at work on the entrenchments in front & are glad to wash off the dirt & dust. Here large numbers of horses & mules are being led down to water. What droves of them there are. You see they are all branded U.S. A little back from the water [is] a large cluster of tents with smoke rising from the numerous camp fires where the soldiers are doing the cooking. You see the groups of sick & wounded, those of them who are able to be about, lying around in the shade of clumps of trees & bushes. That long black line winding along so snake like in the distance is a large body of infantry marching to the front. You see their muskets glitter in the sun.

See what lots of big heavy army wagons with their round canvas tops. They seem to cover acres. In these all the army stores are carried in the march. Here is a long line of them just going out, four & six mules to each. The driver rides one of the wheel horses.

That is a long column of lancers riding by with small red flags fastened to the end of the long lance each one carries. These are followed by a body of cavalry & off to the right is a train of artillery wagons. There, a large cluster of tents are grouped under those large trees. The tired soldiers have stacked

---

* At Harrison's Landing.

their muskets & stretched themselves on the ground to sleep, glad to get a little rest after the constant fighting & marching of the last week.

Those half a dozen light black top wagons are ambulances bringing in the sick & wounded. There are more of them coming from that direction & there comes another long string. Yes, they come from all quarters & seem to center at the large building before us* which is probably to be used for hospital purposes. To the right beyond those bushes is another melancholy sight — a small party burying the dead.

Here & there you see officers galloping hurriedly in different directions, probably conveying orders to different portions of the army. There's a body [of troops] in gay uniform. Yes, those are some of Duryea's zouaves. If you could get close to them you would find their uniform[s] don't look as bright & clean as when we saw them landed from the *Spaulding* at Fortress Munroe where they commenced their march up the peninsular.†

There's a gun, yes artillery, near that flag where Gen. McClelland has his head quarters. There's another way off to the right & another to the left & here is another right down by the river, you can see the smoke rising from it. There they go again, bang, bang, bang in all directions. See the clouds of smoke rising up. There must be a battle. No, you have forgotten it's the 4th of July & now it is just noon & these are the salutes fired from different parts of the camp. For a few minutes you have the cannonade of a battle without any of the fearful results.

Do you see that man on the top of the house we have been looking at waving that flag in such [a] singular way & without any apparent object? Well, that is a semaphore signal & is the way they talk between distant portions of the army. Let's look around & see who he is talking with. Here we have it, close by us, on board the *Galena*. Now the man on the house is done with his flag & the one on the *Galena* is at work. Messages are transmitted between different portions of the army in a very rapid manner in this way. At night they use torches instead of flags. Now the vessels are talking. You see the string of flags being hoisted to the *Galena*'s mast head. The first one is white with a red cross in it. That means she is going to talk to the *Monitor* & Capt. J. sends for the signal book. The flags read No. 3684 & that no. in the book is "the enemy are in sight, get under way immediately." So we must go & I must tell you good bye. With love to yourself, little Eddy & baby.

Your Father

---

* Harrison's House.
† See letter of April 3, 1862 for a description of Duryea's zouaves when they arrived at Fort Monroe.

Civil War Years: USS *Monitor* (1862)

No. 22*—

Monitor
James River, July 14th, 1862
Off Harrison's Landing

Dear Anna,

It seems a long, long time since I wrote you & to you I suppose it seems longer still. I have in the meantime sent home a couple of little notes to let you know that I was still in existence & had not forgotten "the old folks at home," nor the young ones either. What has been wanting in letters I have endeavoured to make good in papers, of which I have sent quite a number, some of them pictorials to Eddy. I continue to receive your letters regularly & read them as you may well suppose with the greatest satisfaction.

If this sweltering weather continues it will curtail letter writing as you will find, for our state rooms are nearly as bad as the black hole of Calcutta & I find a letter is written at the cost of a large amount of perspiration, the mental exertion is nothing. But this is not to the point. You want the news & as perhaps it would come the best in the form of a connected narrative as far as concerns myself.

We will go back to my proposed walk through the camp on Sunday the 6th inst. It is Sunday to be sure but there is no church & the time would be no better spent if we remained on board. If you desire to accompany me just step into the captain's gig. Take a seat on the cushions &—shove off men—we're off for the camp. See what four stout fellows we have to pull the oars. They're Norwegians, each one the model of a sailor. We will land here at the end of this long dock. Harrison's landing it is called. How the steamboats & smaller vessels cluster about it. Most of the steamboats are to be hospitals for the sick & wounded & the somewhat antiquated females you see about their decks are the Florence Nightingales—that are to be. After seeing the sights I think you will agree with me that it is no place for a modest female, a lady.

Now we are at the end of the dock. You see the ground slopes gently upward for some distance till you reach the house which is approached by what has been a finely gravelled walk through clumps of trees & a beautiful lawn. But now how different. These portions of the grounds are attached to the hospital department & are covered with tents in which are those not severely sick.

Look into the tents as we pass along towards the house. Be careful where you step for as yet no sanitary regulations are enforced in the camp. Here are three or four poor fellows in this tent pale, that is a[s] pale as their leather like skin can be pale. Cheeks fallen in & eyes sunken. They have a pitiful tale to tell of their privations & sufferings during the six days' retreat. Too sick to fight, too well to be left behind they straggled along, now in the hands of the

---

* The sheet marked No. 23 was included in this letter.

enemy, now with our own forces. Here is one with his head bandaged up, one with his arm in a sling, another hobbling along with a rudely constructed crutch. Each has a tale to tell of horror & of blood for they were among the fighting men.

See lying on the ground in the shade of that ragged blanket stretched on the tops of a few small bushes that boy but little larger than our Henry. He tells you he was a drummer boy & was ridden down by a charge of cavalry, breaking his ribs. His thin pale face shews how he suffers. Still he talks cheerfully & points with pride to the two or three bullet holes that decorate his ragged clothes.

There is one lying on an old bit of cloth in the partial shade of that bush. How miserably he looks. He is from Michigan where he has a wife & children whom he says he never expects to see again, as he knows he must die. What must be his feelings as he lies there alone and unattended. But his is only a single case out of thousands.

From this tent on the right they are bringing out the corpse of one whose fighting days are o'er. Tent after tent as we pass them are filled with their care worn faces, weak sickly frames & bandaged limbs. Many are strewn around in the shade of the bushes & trees which line our path. All seem glad to rest, to rest in the glad conciousness of safety & security to which they have for so long a time been strangers.

Here we are at the house which you see is a large two story brick one with a wide hall running through it in the middle. Our signal corps have added two rudely constructed stages on the ridge of the roof for the purpose of signalising at a distance. The building bears evident marks of age, the bricks of which it is constructed having been brought from England. It also has an additional interest from having been the birth place of Pres't Harrison.

The large wooden *stoop* in front weakened by decay has broken down by the weight of our soldiers & the floor now rests upon the ground. Step into the wide hall. The large square room on our right is used by the surgeons for medicines & stores. A large handsome table stands in the middle covered with instruments, bandages, bottles &c, many of the latter filled with liquor for the sick. Seems to be common to every one who enters, many of whom by their straps you recognise as Cols., Majs. &c &c, & some of whom have already had too much, but this has become so common it ceases to excite remark. The only wonder is that our folks at home will send out such persons to serve out these delicacies to the sick & needy. I heard an officer remark the other day that he would consider a person as no gentleman who did not ask him to drink with him when he called upon him.

Let's complete our survey of the building. The room has two deep old fashioned recesses, one on each side of a modern marble mantle & grate, & the cornices & ornaments on the walls are of the fashion of years gone by. Pictures hang on the walls. Books are piled upon the mantle. A costly sofa occupies that corner upon which is stretched at full length a cavalry officer booted & spurred. The room on the opposite side of the hall looks very much like the one we have just left, with pictures & handsome furniture. It is used for an operating room. Nearly a wagon load of books are piled upon the floor. The other rooms upon this floor, as are the rooms above, are used for the more severely sick & wounded. The kitchen as is the fashion at the South seems to be detached from the main building & is used now to prepare food for the sick.

We will go out the back door & continue our walk towards the front. The ground is covered with old rags & tattered garments. Here a broken sword, there a bayonet, there a cartridge box. All half trodden into the stiffening clay, which lies hardening in deep ruts & ridges as it has been left by the heavy wheels of artillery & baggage wagons. Here in this mud hole is the wreck of an ammunition wagon. The boxes still full & half buried in the stiff clay form stepping stones for crossing. One of the boxes has been broken open & minie balls, wet, broken cartridges & dissolving gun powder are tramped into the clayey soil by the hoof of every passing horse. There is a dead mule & near it a horse & a little further on the entrails of cattle killed for food, & here we pass more & still more, all lying putrifying on the ground, mingling their odors with other unbearable smells which might naturally be supposed to arise from a newly made camp where proper sanitary regulations are not yet enforced.

Here we meet a long line of soldiers (a regiment) coming into camp with their guns slung on their backs, some with axes on their shoulders, others with spades & shovels. They have been at work through the day on the defences in front. Now we are passed by a large body of cavalry bound on picket duty. This is an ambulance coming in with sick & wounded men.

On the other side of this large cleared field across which soldiers are passing & repassing in all directions is Gen. Meagher's brigade*. The men look tough & hardy as we pass through them & their tents occupy a large piece of ground. This large collection of tents & men we are now passing through is Gen. McCall's who is reported to be a prisoner.† The men are variously occupied, cooking, washing, mending, reading, sleeping &c. These large guns passing us are a portion of McClelland's heavy siege artillery & are on their way to the front to be placed in position. See what a long train of heavy baggage wagons, each drawn by six mules.

We must now be nearly three miles from where we landed & must be nearing the defences in front of the left wing. Yes, here we are. This long wooden wall, breast high, looking like the continuous wall of a log house is a

---

* Brigadier General Thomas F. Meagher's famed Irish Brigade, which fought at all the major battles of the Peninsula Campaign and suffered enormous losses at the Battle of Antietam on September 17, 1862.

† George A. McCall, division commander in the V Corps of the Army of the Potomac. He was captured at the Battle of Glendale on June 30, 1862.

portion of the entrenchments. A ditch is dug some little distance in front of this wooden wall, the earth from it being thrown up against the logs. Spaces are left at short intervals from which peer out field pieces & howitzers charged for the foe. A sentry is at each gun. The remainder of the Co. lying around in the shade but ready for duty on the first notice from our pickets.

Let's talk awhile with this sentry who gives us the military salute as we approach. His story savours of romance. Still we cannot doubt its truth when he tells us of the fatigues & hardships of six days of constant fighting & marching & how his face lights up when he tells how his gun mowed down whole columns of the enemy as they charged desperately upon his piece. How proud he is of the ball hole through his cap & another through his pants, & here comes his comrade to exhibit his canteen smashed by the fragment of a shell. You cannot doubt their story, strange though it may seem; there is too much earnestness in their manner. They tell us we can go a little further on where we will find pickets we cannot pass without the countersign which not having we will retrace our steps towards our starting point.

We take a somewhat different route but everything has the same general look. We pass regiment after regiment & brigade after brigade. The tents in long rows & the bright muskets stacked in front of each. The drum beats for evening muster & each idler springs for his piece & falls into the ranks. Here is a whole brigade on review & see what a large body of cavalry & there a long, long line of light field artillery. How densely populated this small area of country has suddenly become these last few days & what changes they have made in its surface. Large tracts of woodland have been levelled, earth works zig zag through the pastures, artillery in the place of the plough passes through the corn fields & the ripening wheat is beat down by the tramp of ten thousand horses. White men labour now where slaves have heretofore & the slaves I hope are free & call no man master.

Hear the troops cheering off on the right. You may be assured that Gen. McClelland is there to call forth such a manifestation of enthusiasm. He is almost worshiped by his officers & men. Not another person in the Union can command their confidence & respect as he does. These are his head quarters we are now passing, a simple tent, nothing to distinguish [it] from others but its size. While some of his generals take up their quarters in comfortable houses & assume some style, he chooses a tent & is plain & unostentatious in dress & manner. He can be reached by any one.

Now you can see a balloon ascension as we pass head quarters. The car was lost in the retreat & you see they merely have a small square box suspended from the bag capable of holding two persons standing. It is kept at a proper elevation by means of four stout cords which serve to pull it down when desired. It is raised & lowered nearly every hour of the day.

Here we are at last at our starting point. You have taken a walk of some six miles with me through the camp & have seen through my eyes. I wish it had been through your own for much of it cannot be described by a pen, mine at any rate. So good bye.

Monday 7th—Gen Meagher visited us on board & remained some time. He appeared like a plain good hearted well educated irishman & no doubt is a good officer.* His description of the firing of our field artillery at white oak swamp on Monday [June 30] was truly interesting. The enemy as he said were mowed down like grass & lay in front of our guns in long winrows. They came up in solid column & each discharge of our guns cut a lane through them, which however was quickly filled up. His brigade must have fought nobly. Gen. M. is a good talker & an admirable story teller but I fear like too many others he likes good liquor occasionally. That is the bane of both army & navy & will prove the ruin I fear of many a good officer.

Good night. Will send another sheet in a day or two.

William

[Marginalia] I send a little piece of the rebel balloon captured on the *Teaser*, also a photograph given me by Gen. McC's photographer taken on the spot. I have more & will send them occasionally, one at a time. Did you get the *Monitor* pictures?

No. 24—

Monitor
James River
July 22/62

Dear Anna,

To continue my disconnected sort of a medley we will go back to 8th when we went up the river to Haxall's† in company with the *Maratanza* to make a reconoisance of the river banks. On our return we stopped at Carter's‡ & took on board (or rather the *Maratanza* took them) 40 sick & wounded of

---

* Born in Ireland, educated in England, and a political activist by the age of 22, Meagher was arrested in 1848 on charges of sedition and banished for life to Tasmania. He escaped in 1852 and made his way to New York City where he became a lawyer and newspaper editor. When the Civil War broke out, he gave rousing speeches to recruit his fellow countrymen to the 69th New York State Militia and was elected captain of a company of Zouaves. After the First Battle of Bull Run, where the 69th suffered heavy losses, he returned to New York City and organized the Irish Brigade. A newspaper reporter who was visiting Meagher at his headquarters on the Virginia Peninsula in 1862 described him as having "the richest and most musical of brogues . . . large, corpulent and powerful of body . . . piercing blue eyes . . . and liable to fluctuations of pevishness, melancholy and enthusiasm." (*The Fighting 69th: A History*, Richard Demeter, Pasadena, CA, 2002, p. 80) After the war he was made Acting Governor of the Montana Territory and drowned in the Missouri River after falling drunk off a steamboat.

† A plantation on the north side of the James River two miles upstream of Shirley Plantation.

‡ Shirley Plantation.

our men. Many were able to get down to the boats themselves, others hobbled along with a little aid & others were obliged to be brought down in litters. They said Carter's folks did what they could for them & were very kind.

Gen. Lee sent a note to Gen. McC. saying he would afford him every facility in his power to get his sick & wounded as we had many more comforts for them than he had & I suppose too he was glad to get them off his hands, for they must have been a heavy incumberance, besides the rebels had more of their own sick & wounded than they could properly care for. One of our surgeons who remained to take care of these folks was taken prisoner by some of the rebel pickets upon his refusal to give his parole, which coming to Gen. Lee he had him released & an apology sent him & his case of instruments which had been taken from him returned. The wounded men were brought down here (off the camp) & placed in one of the hospital ships.

The next morning [July 9] as I was dressing I heard a tug come alongside & upon going on deck who should I see then but Pres't Lincoln, the Asst. Sec'y of War, & Frank Blair. The Pres't had come on board to see Capt. J. who was not yet up. Hearing that Commodore Goldsborough was in the *Dacotah* near us, he [Lincoln] wished us to send a boat for him which of course we did. The old Com. stormed & swore awfully at such a breach of etiquette but finally condescended to come on board the *Monitor* to see the President. (It is said his dignity received such a shock that it has required a wet nurse ever since.)

The party remained on board but a short time when they left for the camp. The President seemed to be in better spirits than I supposed he would be. His visit here has been a good thing, serving to give more confidence to the army by his presence among them, also giving him an opportunity for personal observation & a conference with McClelland & must result in a better & more complete mutual understanding with the leader of our armies. Busy bodies & meddlesome politicians have been at work to produce a breach between them but I doubt now if their influence will amount to much. Gen. McC. will, I think, have the earnest support of the President.*

[July] 10th—This morning I started in one of the old North river steamboats for Old Point, on business connected with the fleet here. The boat coming up yesterday having been fired into by a battery of light field pieces from some of the bluffs, we were convoyed down to the mouth of the Chickahominy by two of the gun boats. I am free to say that the sensation of standing behind slight wooden bulwarks & impenetrable iron ones to be fired at was somewhat different. However we passed down unharmed.

---

* Not so. Although Lincoln was reassured of the army's safety at Harrison's Landing, the first thing he did upon returning to Washington was to appoint Henry Halleck as General in Chief, the lofty position McClellan once held.

Civil War Years: USS *Monitor* (1862)

Government controls all the boats running on the river. No fare is charged but no one is allowed to go up or down without a pass, obtained from the Quartermaster at McClelland's head quarters & to get it from him a leave of absence has to be shewn from your commanding officer. This rule is strictly observed with all army officers, many of whom I am told would gladly absent themselves for a time without leave if they could. With naval officers the rule is not so strictly adhered to. I found no difficulty in procuring my pass without written leave & then was not required to shew it on board. With civilians it is an utter impossibility to go up or down, no passes are given them. Quite a number of military officers & men went down, most of them out of health & going home to recruit.

We had quite a pleasant trip. Having been so long on board the *Monitor* she had with me become a common place thing & I supposed had in a great measure lost her prestige, but I found it quite otherwise. People seemed to regard her as a sort of irresistable war monster & any one from her as something more than human.

On arriving at Old Point I found the *Hygiea* (is it spelt right?) full & was wondering where I was to pass the night, when I stumbled upon an acquaintance* (who has always been chock full of Monitor).

"Where are you stopping?"

"Just got in & the hotel's full," says I.

"Glad of it," says he, "don't want a Monitor to go to a hotel while I have a house." Told him that just suited me.

I had left him but a few rods when I met an officer from the Fortress who insisted that I should go to his quarters inside the Fort. There I was met by the Captain of one of our gun boats with, "Hullo Paymaster, when did you come down? Come aboard & stay with me."

I found I would be well provided for in almost any event but preferred the accommodations of my first acquaintance, Mr. Kimberly, who gave me very comfortable accommodations while I staid.

You may imagine the grateful change from the hot air of the river & close stifling atmosphere of the bowels of the *Monitor* to the cool fresh sea breezes of the old ocean. What a night's sleep I had with the wind sweeping across my bed, & what an appetite next morning.

It rained hard all the next day [July 11] (but my kind friend lent me the only umbrella he had (a splendid silk one)) & I started for Norfolk on the Government boat, the only boat running. Paddled round there for a time through deserted streets, mud, water & rain & finally returned to Old Point with the determination to wait till it had rained out. The next day [July 12] was delightfully cool & pleasant of which I took advantage & made another trip to Norfolk. Business took me on board the Flag ship (the *Minnesota*). She looked as neat as a pin, very different from what she did when we anchored

---

* William Kimberly.

James River (May to August 1862)

alongside her just after the *Merrimac*'s raid. Returned to Old Point & spent the evening in the Fortress listening to a splendid brass band playing in front of Gen. Dix's head quarters.*

[No signature]

Monitor
James River
July 25/62

Dear Anna,

I sent Henry a letter day before yesterday & enclosed in it a photograph for yourself, hope it will come safe to hand. With this I send a group of our Officers & a deck view shewing a portion of the turret.† The officers are (the turret for a back ground)

No.	1 S. D. Greene	1st Lieut. & Ex. Officer
"	2 Geo. Frederickson	Master's Mate
"	3 L. N. Stodder	Master
"	4 M. F. Sunstrom‡	3rd asst. Engineer
"	5 E. V. Gager	Master
"	6 W. F. Keeler	Paymaster
"	7 Wm. Flye§	Act. Lieutenant
"	8 Isaac Newton	Senior Engineer
"	9 D. C. Logue	Surgeon
"	10 R. W. Hands**	3rd asst. Engineer
"	11 A. B. Campbell	2nd do do

The other view shews a portion of the turret with both ports, one gun run out.†† To the left & on a line with the lower lip of the port is a couple of shot marks from the *Merrimac*. (A portion of one made by the *Minnesota* in the same fight can also be seen on the other picture just below Mr. Newton's right shoulder.) A part of another shot mark can be seen on the right edge of the turret about half way below the gun & the deck. The circle in the foreground is an opening into the coal bunkers below closed by an iron opening. In the background is the pilot house, this side of which are some of the iron plugs fitting into our deck lights. Mr. Flye & Mr. Campbell stand near the side. A little this side of them you can see the side armour started off by one of the *Merrimac*'s shot.

---

* John A. Dix, commander of the Department of Virginia after Wool's departure.
† A cropped version of the group photograph is shown at the beginning of the book.
‡ Mark F. Sunstrom (1844-1875).
§ See Biographical Notes.
** Robinson W. Hands (1838-1862). The Baltimore native drowned when the *Monitor* sank.
†† This photograph appears at the beginning of the book.

Civil War Years: USS *Monitor* (1862)

Let me know if you get them safely. All is quiet here, & probably will be for some time to come. Remember me to all with much love. Many kisses to yourself & the children.

William

No. 25—

Monitor
James River
July 25/62

Dear Anna,

I sent you a letter by to day's mail (for we have a mail regularly now every day) winding up with my return from Norfolk Saturday evening [July 12]. The next day, Sunday, I went up [to Norfolk] again, having nothing to do but take a look at the place. Passing the Custom House, a fine granite building, Gen. Viele's* head quarters, I went in & made the acquaintance of Capt. Ludlow† the Asst. Qtr. Master. All the offices in the large building are finely furnished with Sesech furniture taken from the warehouses where it had been sent for shipment south. Capt. L. had a beautiful tapestry carpet on his two office floors, fine table, chairs, sofas &c — all rebel plunder. Learning that I was from the *Monitor* & desirous of visiting the Navy Yard on the other side of the river he placed one of his tugs at my disposal.

The Yard is very much as you see it described but it is difficult to realise the vast amount of property destroyed there without looking over the ruins.‡ The Yard, which is a very large one, must have been filled with large expensive buildings & machinery of which nothing now remains but long rows of brick walls windowless, doorless & roofless — heaps of burned & ruined machinery forming piles of warped, twisted & useless iron — broken cannon & anchors & the charred wrecks of Gov. vessels. It forms a sad memento of the Civil War & will remain, I think for a long time, a monument of the insane folly of the "Old Dominion."

The streets of the town [Portsmouth] were deserted except by blacks & the only two well dressed white females I saw passed over to the opposite side of the street, evidently to avoid me. I returned to Norfolk with my tug just as the boat left for Old Point. As Capt. L. had left his office & I had no

---

* Egbert L. Viele, the military governor of Norfolk.
† Edwin Ludlow (1824-1894). Born and raised in New York City, he graduated from the University of the City of New York in 1843. From 1852 to 1858 he was the New York City-based manager of the Ohio Life Insurance and Trust Company, one of Ohio's largest banks. Over a period of several years he embezzled the company's entire capital base, causing the company to fail in 1857. Despite his unsavory past, he was commissioned assistant quarter master with the rank of captain in April 1862.
‡ The rebels did a much more thorough job of destroying the Gosport Navy Yard when they evacuated Norfolk on May 9 than the federals had done the year before.

James River (May to August 1862)

authority to make further use of his tug & as it was necessary for me to be at Old Point the next morning, I hired two men to take me down in a small sail boat. One of them, I found on conversing with him, was a sailor on board the *Merrimac* in her fight with us & was also in the Sewall Point batteries when we shelled them & was on board the *Merrimac* when she was fired & blown up. His account of things was interesting & amusing. Of course I did not let him know that I had anything to do with the *Monitor* or had hardly heard of her. I told him I had heard that the *Monitor* did not make much of a fight. "Yes she did," he said, "they were bully men to fight." "How was it that the *Merrimac* came to back out?" "Well we got enough."

The batteries constructed by the rebels on the banks of the river looked very much as they did the Sunday we came down from Norfolk in the *Monitor* expect the rebel flag no longer waved over them. A few blackened timber heads of the *Merrimac* were visible above the water as we passed the upper end of Craney island. The wind was very light & we did not get down to Old Point till nearly nine o'clock. Mr. Kimberly's good natured old irish woman, Rosa, got me my supper with a pitcher full of delicious iced milk & I spent the remainder of the evening till nearly twelve o'clock sitting on the roof of the house enjoying the cool fresh breeze & listening to the murmur of the waves over the smooth pebbly beach.

The next morning [July 14] I was homeward bound (I wish it were so in fact) on board the Gov't boat *John A. Warner*. I found quite a number of pleasant companions, among them Gen. Gorman* on his way to join his brigade in Gen. McClelland's camp. As an officer of the *Monitor* I received much attention, this I am getting so accustomed to I look upon it as a matter of course. We ran the gauntlet of rebel sharp shooters & batteries unharmed & I reached the *Monitor* about five o'clock.

Found in my absence a new Commodore (Wilkes†) had been appointed to the command of the James river fleet [Flotilla] which has now become a separate command, so that we are now independent of Com. Goldsborough though I fear in some respects we have made nothing by the change.‡ A great mistake is made in appointing superannuated old fogies whose life & energies are used up to these important commands when a younger man of life, energy & enterprise is so much needed.

---

* Willis A. Gorman, a brigade commander in the II Corps of the Army of the Potomac.
† Charles Wilkes, whose long and tumultuous career with the Navy included the massacre of 80 Fijians during his South Seas Expedition in 1840 and the arrest of the Confederate envoys Mason and Slidell from the British mail ship RMS *Trent* in November 1861, which nearly brought on war with Great Britain.
‡ Lincoln's dissatisfaction with Goldsborough had grown since his first visit to Hampton Roads in early May. Concerned that Goldsborough would not provide the naval support that McClellan needed at Harrison's Landing, the Navy Secretary relieved him of command of all Union warships on the James River on July 6.

CIVIL WAR YEARS: USS *MONITOR* (1862)

"New Lords bring new laws." An order has been issued making it imperative for every one to be on board his vessel half an hour before sun down & at no time to be out of signal distance of his ship. The next day we rec'd an order to proceed up the river above the fleet & come to an anchor. So here we now lie, half way between City Point & Harrison's landing, both in plain view from our deck, waiting the appearance of *Merrimac* No. 2, or the *Richmond* as she is to be called.* We have a complete description of her from deserters from Richmond. She is about ready to come out but I doubt very much if she ever comes down the river to attack us. I think she will be kept for home defence. She might succeed in destroying a few of our vessels if she were to make the attempt, but it would result in her own destruction — a hazardous experiment they would not be justified in attempting.

Last Tuesday P.M. [July 22] I went on shore & made a call on Col. Van Wyck† (of the investigating committee) at his head quarters, as a small inconvenient canvass tent was called. He is a very fine appearing man & I was much pleased with him, the more so that he told me he was a temperance man & consequently had nothing but water to offer his visitors. Very different from many officers, he seemed to regard his men as his children, speaking very pleasantly with them when they had occasion to come to his tent on business. He was dressed in a coarse flannel shirt, no coat or vest, coarse blue pants & said he made his aim to live & eat just as his men to prevent any feeling of dissatisfaction. He is strongly opposed to the administration in the conduct of the war.

The Lieut. Col. of the N.Y. 98th‡ was on board a day or two since. He said your Cousin Wm. [Dutton] was very popular among his men & had the reputation of a brave man & a good officer.

[No signature]

---

* Construction of the Confederate ironclad had started in March 1862. When Norfolk fell, the unfinished vessel was towed to Richmond where she was completed in July. The CSS *Richmond* never ventured far down the James River and never encountered the *Monitor*.
† Charles H. Van Wyck (1824-1895). A lawyer by profession, he was elected to the U.S. House of Representatives as a Republican in 1858. In July 1861 he organized the 56th New York regiment in Newburgh, NY, doing double duty as a congressman and a colonel. He was wounded at the Battle of Fair Oaks when his sword was driven into his leg by an artillery shell that had ricocheted off the ground. However, shortly before the start of the war he experienced a much closer brush with death: Late one night as he was passing along the north wing of the Capitol building on his way to his lodgings he was assaulted by three men brandishing Bowie knives. His life was saved by a triple-folded copy of the *Congressional Globe* and a thick memorandum book in his pocket that absorbed the thrust of the knife. The attack was believed to have been motivated by the anti-slavery speech he delivered on the House Floor in March 1860 in which he vehemently denounced the Southern states for "crimes against the laws of God and nature."
‡ Charles Durkee.

James River (May to August 1862)

No. 26—

Monitor
James River
July 28, 1862

Dear Anna,

Last Friday in a stroll through the camp [at Harrison's Landing] who should I stumble upon by [but] my fighting parson acquaintance "Jim Beecher" wearing captain's straps. I think he must resemble very closely in some things to a man you wot of.* He said he was doing both the praying & fighting, using both sword & bible. The Capt. of the company was sick & he had taken his place for the nonce, though he had sent in his resignation as Chaplain & was expecting an appointment as Capt., which latter I think would become him quite as well as he is one of the fighting sort. I passed a very pleasant hour in his company. He accompanied me along the front quite a distance pointing out the natural advantages of their present position & also the vast amount of labour expended in strengthening it.

I do not believe it is in the bounds of possibility for the rebels to make a successful attack upon the left wing. The defences are erected along the edge of a bluff some 30 or 40 feet high, at the bottom of which is a small stream running through a wide marshy bottom. Crossing this there are what were corn & wheat fields for half or three quarters of a mile when you enter a strip of timber. This strip of cleared level land could be swept by the fire of the gun boats in one direction & by the fire from the batteries in another, so that the rebels the moment they emerged from the timber would be exposed to the cross fire of the gun boats & batteries in crossing the open fields for half a mile or more. Then they would have to descend the bluff & cross a miry bottom covered in many places with an almost impassable mass of briers, brush & fallen timber & cross the stream in the face of the fire from rifle pits on the opposite bluff & musketry from the entrenchments to say nothing of the storm of grape & canister which would be poured upon them from the light field pieces with which the batteries are numerously studded. An enemy that would attack there would be courageous indeed, or fool hardy.

Beecher is the first one in the army whom I have heard speak against Gen. McC. He is bitter enough, but I imagine it arises from some imaginary slight, at least I could not find why he had any good grounds for his ungenerous criticisms of McClellan's conduct. Beecher has had some narrow escapes & gave me an interesting & thrilling description of some of the battles.

As I left his tent I fell in with a good natured, half drunken, Lieut. of Regan's Battery†. He insisted upon my going to his tent with him where he further insisted upon my joining him in a glass of whiskey which of course I

---

* Keeler was referring to their friend William H. Collins*, who was chaplain of the 10th Illinois Infantry before becoming a captain in the 104th Illinois Infantry.
† The 7th New York Independent Battery.

positively refused. Thereupon he insisted that I should take his horse & ride down to the boat, though I much prefered walking I consented. Just as I was fairly in the saddle, four more of our officers hove in sight. The Lieut. declared we must all have horses, so sending off one of his men we were all soon mounted. I had a fine looking but a hard riding beast that struck off at once into a rapid gallop & *I havn't got over it yet.*

The wounded are being send [sent] down to us from Richmond by the way of City Point, a long train of 16 or 20 cars coming in every day, sometimes twice a day. Our large hospital steamers go up to the latter place & receive them on board. The poor fellows must be glad to get back among friends once more & the rebels must be glad also to be rid of them, for from all accounts they have more of their own sick & wounded than they can properly attend to.

Last night we were aroused by a glare of light some distance below us in the river. We found it proceeded from a schooner loaded with corn which some of the enterprising rebels had boarded from the opposite shore, made prisoners of the crew, helped themselves to such of her rigging, sails, chains &c as they wanted, then set her on fire & cleared out. I honor them as an enterprising set of scoundrels. Had we shewn one tenth part of the energy, activity & enterprise in proportion to the means at our command that they have, there wouldn't be enough of the rebellion left to make a newspaper item.

Pope's order in regard to the property of the rebels is hailed with joy & will do more towards recruiting our army than all the public meetings in our large cities.* It shews that we are getting to be in earnest & if an iron hand can be laid upon the wealthy rebels through the country where our armies are & where they (the rebels) are luxuriating in idleness & plenty & they be made to drink the cup they have helped to fill to the bitterest dregs, the effect will be good.

Now as soon as a portion of our army encamps near the plantation of some rich scoundrel, who perhaps himself may be in the rebel army, sentinels are placed around his house, barns, buildings & fields. His cattle rove about undisturbed though our soldiers are feeding on hard bread & salt beef. Soldiers have the faculty of writing letters as well as other human beings, & such things are heard of at home. Their friends hear of it, the public hear of it & those who would enlist hear of it too. They are not going to starve on miserable food & scanty at that when they are living in a land flowing with milk & honey. The fact is Government has not taken the care of its soldiers [that] it should have done, neither the sick or well, & the soldiers know & feel it. I have seen sights that for the time has made me feel perfectly indifferent

---

* The commander of the Army of Virginia, John Pope, believed that the South should be punished for starting the war and therefore instructed his troops to live off the land and confiscate food and supplies from civilians.

James River (May to August 1862)

as to the result, as though we were contending for "a string of glittering generalities" not worth the second thought. That if we ceased to exist as a nation it was a matter of the smallest consequence, in fact of none whatever. I felt ashamed of the name of an American. But I don't know when to stop when I get on this topic so I shall just break off by saying good bye.

　　　　　　　　　　　　　　　　　　　　　　Will

No. 27—

Monitor
James River
July 30th, 1862

Dear Anna,

To day I have been strongly reminded of *old* times in Hampton Roads. About the middle of the forenoon a small smoke was discovered over the tree tops way up the river which was decided at once to be the *Richmond* coming. Fires were crowded, steam increased, the intelligence sent to other vessels who were immediately in an active state of preparation, boats were pulling about from ship to ship, signals were flying from every mast head & waving from every army station, tugs puffing about the river. Fifteen or twenty gun boats large & small rushed up the river & formed in line of battle behind the *Monitor*. By this time the single cloud of black smoke like the three black crows had increased in magnitude & numbers till there were six huge volumes of smoke (invisible to my naked eye) & a proportionate number of Merrimacs. Of course the excitement increased in the same ratio. The Commodore [Wilkes] was rushing around in his tug suggesting here, ordering there, changing the position of this ship, sending a tug to reconnoiter. Well, we waited all day & here we are, 9 o'clock P.M., & the cloud of smoke has produced nothing but a big scare. Much ado about nothing.

Some of us will die off one of these days with Merrimac on the brain. The disease is raging furiously, especially among those inclined to old fogyism. Hereafter there is to be no more going ashore for us as the *Richmond* might come down & find some poor Surgeon, Paymaster or Lieut. absent from his post & ungenerously taking advantage of such officer's absence capture his vessel. Now we are to live in a state of continued preparation, us Monitors especially, as upon our shoulders rests the salvation of the whole navy. So you may imagine us close prisoners in the bowels of our iron monster, not a very enviable situation I assure you in the present hot weather. However I try & console myself with the reflection that I am serving my country hugely, besides weaving a crown of glory for my own brow & earning a few pennies for my family, though this last is of small consequence.

To add to the enjoyments of this patriotic disposition of our time & energies we have come to the bottom of our larder, so that calling upon our Steward for edibles is like calling spirits from the vasty deep — they don't answer the call. A piece of salt beef regularly makes its appearance with the call for dinner. It reappears in the form of hash for supper, & is re-hashed for breakfast the next morning. If vegetables exist in any portions of the civilised world they are intangible to us. You may imagine me walking in & asking for some cucumbers and bread & butter before saying how do, [how] do. I have hardly had a taste of anything green this summer. When I came up from Old Point I brought up with me a bbl. filled with a mess or two of well ripened, well wilted peas, a few cucumbers, some cabbage, lettuce & beets. These for a mess of sixteen did not last long. This is the extent of my vegetarian experience this summer. It would do me good to live out of the garden for a week or two. I should think with the rains you have had this summer the vegetable portion of the garden must flourish finely. I only wish I could go to it every morning.

But I must tell you for Sarah's benefit, the disposition I made of her stockings. The Wednesday [July 2] after the battle at Malvern Hills we went up to Carter's [Shirley Plantation] & took off from there six of our soldiers. Three of them were sick, two of whom could not walk without assistance. One of them seemed partly insane & unable to give a clear account of himself. He had nothing on but a pair of muddy drawers. His feet were sore & bleeding from walking through the brush & over the stones & altogether he was about a[s] pitiable an object as you ever saw. On my way down to Harrison's landing we dressed him up. I contributed Sarah's stockings & a pair of my pants. Others gave him other articles so that when he left the vessel he was comfortably clothed. Sarah may rest assured that if I had made it my sole purpose to hunt up a deserving object for her stockings a more worthy & needy one could not have been found. The poor fellow would undertake to express his gratitude but his mind would wander off on something else. I never heard of him afterward. He had a hard fever & our M.D. said it was very doubtful if he lived unless he had the best of nursing, a thing I know he did not have in camp. One of the other three was quite sick & had to be carried off the vessel, in all probability to die.

The place from which we took these men was a short distance above Carter's in a small deserted house or barn standing near the river bank. We were lying there all day in company with one of the gun boats. Numbers of our soldiers constantly passing along, many of the sick & wounded stopping at this building as if expecting assistance from us. No notice was taken of them however except to send a boat ashore & bring off three or four officers who shamelessly deserted their crippled men who clustered around the boat to the number of thirty or more as it left the shore vainly hoping to be taken on board. I think I have described in one of my previous letters their miserable plight, but my indignation was so great at that time I did not dare to give it vent.*

---

* See letter of June 30, 1862.

JAMES RIVER (MAY TO AUGUST 1862)

We lay here as I have described till nearly sundown by which time all but two or three of the wounded soldiers had disappeared, where I do not know & probably never shall. No dou[b]t most of them fell into the clutches of the rebels & ended their existence in a Richmond prison. Well, just before sundown we were preparing to get under way, two or three of the poor fellows standing or rather sitting anxiously watching us, one of our officers asked the Captain [Jeffers] if he was going to leave those men. "Certainly, they're a lot of damned used up beggars of no use, what do we want of them." I had learned our Capt. as devoid of nearly every feeling of humanity but I must say I was not prepared for an exhibition of fiendish brutality that would have disgraced a pirate. Of course we could not argue the point, but no doubt the monster read our disapproval in our faces for he finally gave an evidently unwilling order to have the boat manned & the men brought off. The first boat brought off the three sick ones I have referred to, also three more who were well, at least they were able to move about very well. They reported one more lying on the ground behind the building who they believed was dying. "Shall I go for him," says the officer in charge of the boat. "No," was the reply.

We had got down the river about half a mile when all at once the Capt. ordered the boat manned & the three well ones set ashore. No reason was given, no explanation was deigned. It was done apparently to revenge himself on his officers whom he saw were enjoying the pleasure of being able to save a few of our soldiers who for the last five or six days & nights had been fighting for our common country. Mr. Gager, who took them ashore, said that one of them, a pale sickly looking little drummer boy, not much larger than Henry, begged most pitiously to be allowed to go back on board. He was sick & his legs ached so that he couldn't walk. Said he would do any kind of work for us we wanted if we would only let him stay [and that] the rebels would kill him if we put him ashore.

Tell of rebel barbarities to our dead at Manassas [Bull Run]. They were out Heroded here by our Capt. in his atrocious inhumanity to the living. How I wanted their positions reversed & our Captain placed on the bank with a dozen or more rebels charging at him with their bayonets. The sight I believe would have pleased me & his cries for help would have been sweet music.

What a picture this would be to exhibit at the patriotic meetings now being held in all our large cities for the purpose of getting volunteers. No wonder men hold back & need large bounties to get up their patriotism. Had I not seen this transaction it would have seemed incredible that an officer of the Navy fighting for the same cause as our soldiers, & whose lives had been imperilled for him as well as others, could treat them with such cold blooded inhumanity.

It is, I find, characteristic of the man (if he can be called a man). He is selfishness intensified. So long as his own selfish ends are brought about & personal comfort secured, it is not of the least possible consequence to him who suffers or how much. I truly believe that he remains with the north from no other motives than those of policy. He very evidently sides with the south in all their aristocratic tastes & manners, & a person who labors is, with him, a mere machine for the purpose of aiding his selfish ends & adding to his pleasures. With him the Navy is the very essence of all that is true & manly & honorable & noble (just the reverse with me) & he is the center around which the very navy revolves — outside of it there is nothing worthy the attention of a gentleman. You may be surprised to hear me speak of him in such a manner after sometimes alluding to him in a more honorable way, but I know him better now. I entertain no personal ill will, for I have had no cause. I have received as good treatment at his hands as any of the officers, better than most of them, but I am thoroughly disgusted with his cold selfish brutality exhibited almost daily in many different ways. I will dismiss him, only hoping that he may see the time when he will plead like the little drummer boy for mercy & with no better success.

Aug. 1st—Last night was one of pitchy darkness. All of a sudden about one o'clock the opposite shore from the camp for some distance up & down the river was lighted up with the flash of artillery & shot & shell came raining into the camp & among the crowded shipping lying in front of it. Our gun boats replied with their heavy pieces & we had a merry time of it for about an hour & a half. The scene was described by those who witnessed it as a magnificent spectacle. Large jets of flame fringed the opposite shore & fiery balls sped through the air bursting over or among our vessels or in the camp among the soldiers. Our gun boats seemed like small volcanoes pouring out fire & smoke & the discharge of their heavy guns lit up the air for miles around. I say it was a grand sight for those who witnessed it. Unfortunately I did not, as I slept soundly through the whole, no one thinking to call me. The first I heard of it was when it was discussed at the breakfast table the next morning. Some few of our vessels were hit but as far as I can learn no one on them was seriously injured. The camp however fared worse. The number killed there I have heard variously estimated at from five to twenty & a number wounded.

We lay up the river at the head of the fleet, "*in constant preparation for the* Merrimac" [*Richmond*] & so a short distance above the fire. I enclose a rough diagram to give you a little better idea of just where we are.* No. 1 is the *Monitor* with some of the gun boats behind her. The river against the camp is filled with vessels of all kinds. On the opposite side from the Camp is the cannon in position as they were used by the rebels last night. It is seldom that they attempt to fire into us now as they have found it is only a waste of ammunition.

This afternoon some steamers took a regiment of troops over the river who effected a landing under the cover of some of the gun boats & set fire

---

* See Sketch No. 6 at the beginning of the book.

to the buildings on the bank of the river along where the artillery was placed the night before. I believe, but am not sure, that the old villain Ruffin's house was among the number burned. If so, it is a most righteous retribution. It is only a pity he was not in it.

The small squares on the diagram back of the artillery represent the buildings, though not correct as to number or exact locality. Some of them were very fine buildings. One in particular was a large, beautiful, modern built house with towers & verandahs & from our vessel made a conspicuous object in the landscape. They blazed up furiously as our soldiers applied the torch to one after another. I have heard no particulars but suppose their contents went with them, as it would be a disgrace to our army to make any show of pillage.

At present one regiment remains encamped on that side protected by the gun boats to prevent any more night attacks. It is hard to tell in what direction our move will be made, or when. I do not know positively that any has yet been decided upon, but think preparations are being made which will end our present inactive state. Some of our boats have been employed a few nights past in sounding out the opposite shore & there are other moves which seem to indicate that a large body of troops will be thrown over there.

Love to all.

W.

[Marginalia] No. 9 with Henry's, Lilly's* & John Dutton's has just reached me. Also a La Salle paper — Aug. 2nd.

No. 28—

Monitor
James River
Aug. 3rd, 1862

Dear Anna,

No mail arriving for us last night I did not get a letter from you & which as it was due I knew was not far off. The mail for the squadron is brought on board the flag ship & is distributed to the different vessels from there by one of the Commodore's tugs, but after getting their own mail on board the Flag ship they are sometimes rather neglectful of the rest of us.

I mistrusted a letter from you was waiting there for me so about half past 4 this morning I was called at my request & taking one of our boats with six good men to row pulled down to the Flag ship, about two miles, & there found a package of mail matter for the *Monitor* which we should have had last night. In it was your No. 9 with one from Henry, Lilly & John Dutton. Also a paper from Henry. Had I known that Wm. Dutton's friends were desirous of ascertaining any of the particulars of his first sickness I would have made

---

* Keeler's 13-year old niece Mary Elizabeth Graves from Litchfield, CT.

some inquiries of the Lieut. Col. of his regiment who was on board a few days ago & could probably have learned some things of interest from him. He urged me very strongly to come to his quarters & see him but as we are not allowed to go ashore now I don't know when we way meet again.

I am sorry that Henry could not go east with Hatch as I think he would do more to help Hen along than Rosenberg.* If we go to Washington as I think we shall in a few weeks I shall go to New Haven if I can get leave. Wish I might meet you there too. You don't say anything about your teeth. How do they get along?

As to the abuse you speak of "heaped upon McClelland" by Brewster & other "Sir oracles"† I am content to take the opinion of such men as Gens. McCall, Meagher, Gorman, McCook, Burnside & the unanimous voice of all his subordinate officers & men & adopt their opinion as my own, satisfied that these men who accompanied & assisted in the movements of the army during the retreat are more competent to judge of McClelland's skill & ability than either myself or the writers of the newspaper articles, nine tenths of whom never heard a gun fired. No one claims him to be a Napolean but he is acknowledged by competent judges to be superior as a leader to any one yet in the field. If this be so is it not better to hold on to him till a greater than he arises. Does any one of these Street corner oracles realise anything of the number of men in an army of 100,000 or of the material attached to them & the amount of brains required to direct & use all this vast multitude of men & mass of material to the best possible advantage? The criticisms of such egotistical ninnies fools (I was going to say) would be about as valuable as Pete Gibbons or a Hebrew Bible.

I _know positively_ beyond all dispute that McClelland's original plans were to come up this river, in which case City Point would probably have been his base of operations as he would have advanced on Richmond from Petersburg, which would have been done in a country much more favourable for military operations & the health of his men than the Chickahominy swamps. The existence of the *Merrimac* compelled a change of his plans, & the existence of that bugbear at that time was owing altogether to Com. Goldsborough. I send you a newspaper slip to the truth of which I can subscribe.

There are some indications at present that seem to point out the plan I have just mentioned as the one to be followed, 5000 infantry, 2000 cavalry & 5 or 6 batteries of artillery are now across the river entrenching themselves a few miles below City Point. Whether they are to be followed by still larger forces destined to operate on Richmond, or are merely as a protection to the camp on the opposite side & the fleet in the river against future artillery attacks I cannot say.

---

* Volney G. Hatch and Charles Rosenburg were La Salle dry goods merchants who were travelling East to purchase their merchandise.
† Persons of supposed great wisdom.

JAMES RIVER (MAY TO AUGUST 1862)

McClelland did wrong in going into the Chickahominy swamps relying upon the Department to furnish him with men as he needed, enough to be equal to any emergency. See with what an overwhelming force he was attacked, how successfully he held them at bay, till with consumate skill he provided for the safety of his men.

The correspondence between Staunton [Stanton] & McClelland will see the light one of these days, when the public will be at no loss who to blame. McC. kept vainly urging more & more strongly for reinforcements till the correspondence with Staunton took a personal turn & to conclude it Gen. McC. wrote to the Sec'y of War that it was not himself that he (the Sec'y) was injuring by his repeated denials, but his country. Staunton was determined to kill him off but I think has met with but poor success. I set political considerations aside in all this & I think they should be in our present emergency. Chandler in his traiterous lying speech* has done more to injure our cause than many who are now confined in Fort Henry. It is based upon falsehood & is a tissue of lies from beginning to end.

I was as anxious to see slavery wiped out of existence as any one can be & I *know* from [what] I have seen that the present course of things is accomplishing it as rapidly as any one could desire. The army is a mill for manufacturing abolitionists & it is turning them out with a rapidity that would astonish the greatest radical. Pro slavery democrats in it are speedily transformed to strong anti slavery men who will yet be felt. I am content to bide my time feeling assured that it is coming.

Two of our gun boats went up the river this morning on a reconnoisance & not returning at noon another was sent up after them. At sundown two small tugs were sent up to see what had become of those that had preceded them. As they got opposite City Point they were opened on by a rebel battery & one of the missing gun boats coming down the river to their assistance got aground & the firing back & forth has been kept up till to[o] dark to see. The *Galena* is also up having a hand in.

Wish I had some of your currant wine. I do not give up the idea of having some of *your* grapes this fall, but do not feel as confident as I did a few weeks ago.

Remember me to all friends. Love to yourself & the children.

W.

---

* Radical Republican Zachariah Chandler, U.S. Senator from Michigan, a vocal critic of McClellan's conduct of the war.

Civil War Years: USS *Monitor* (1862)

No. 29—

Monitor
James River
Aug. 5th, 1862

Dear Anna,

Since my last, which has just left, nothing of moment has occurred. The gun boat *Southfield* still remains aground off City Point. We heard to day that in her firing Sunday evening [August 3] she killed a number of the rebels, among them the Captain of one of the batteries firing at her.

The past two days have been very hot & to add to our discomforts the bowels of our iron monster are densely populated with flies & mosquitoes. You may imagine me writing this with a towel in one hand brushing off mosquitoes & wiping off perspiration, my brains in a sort of mix with the buzzing of the mosquitoes, the hum of the flies, the trickling of sweat & the amount of mental labour necessary to express my thoughts on this sheet. So you need not be surprised if my letter should be a medly of nonsense.

I had the forethought when at Old Point to buy me a mosquito bar (the only one on board) so that I can sleep at night undisturbed at night by the pestiferous vermin, that is when the heat will allow of it. To night we will have a scorcher. All of the men & some of the officers have gone on deck to sleep, but I fear the heavy dews which fall at night & so far have remained below.

My health so far has been remarkably good. With the exception of one or two slight headaches I have not had an ache or pain & what is a remarkable fact I am the only one on board the ship among the officers and men who has not been obliged to take medicine & am the only one among the whole number on board who makes no use of liquor. Whether my good health is attributable to that or not I do not know, but I have sometimes thought it had something to do with it.

According to an Act of Congress the liquor ration will be abolished after the 1st of next month & no liquor will be allowed on board our men of war except for medical purposes. This great good has been brought about by Sen. Grimes of Iowa[*] & if strictly followed up will add very much to [the] efficiency of the Navy.

Artillery firing has been heard at intervals through the forenoon. A portion of the time it has been very rapid, indicating sharp work. This evening we hea[r]d that Gen. Hooker[†] had taken Malvern Hills, capturing 300 of the rebels, coming upon them unawares. No further particulars have reached us.

A boat was up to day from Old Point with fresh beef & vegetables. I had a dinner of tomatoes & cucumbers which I assure you I ate with a relish. I

---

[*] James W. Grimes, who introduced the Congressional bill allocating $1.5 million to build the three ironclads (*Monitor*, *Galena* and *New Ironsides*) in the summer of 1861.
[†] Joseph Hooker, a division commander in the III Corps of the Army of the Potomac.

shall be able to appreciate such things when I get back to our garden once more.

What Porter's Mortar fleet is coming up here for is more than I can imagine as I do not see what good result they can accomplish. If they expect to shell out Fort Darling I fear they will find another Vicksburg.*

Thursday, 7th—Hot, hotter, hottest. Could stand it no longer, so last night I wrapped my blanket 'round me & took to our iron deck — if the bed was not soft it was not so insufferably hot as my *pen*. I have a good mosquito bar around my berth but others have suffered terribly with them & what with heat, mosquitoes & a gouty Captain have nearly gone distracted.

Another 300,000 men called for. Good. The greater the number of labourers the more speedily the work will be accomplished, but the war looms up in gigantic proportions. Now let them use the negroes where they can be employed to the best advantage, whether with musket or shovel & let the country occupied by our troops be made to subsist there & a large stride will be taken towards the desired end.

Ruffin's house was not burned a few evenings since as I supposed but it has been pretty thoroughly cleaned out by some one to the serious damage of splendid mirrors & furniture generally.

I took a boat's crew early this morning & went ashore on Epp[e]s island & brought of[f] a boat load of green corn. Perhaps the fact of its having been planted by the rebels added to its flavour for it certainly went with a relish. We shall have it now for a week or two to come.

I some expect to go down to Old Point again in a day or two, so you need not be surprised to hear from me from there.

I don't know what I am writing or how for it is *so hot* & mosquitoes & flies are so troublesome I cannot keep my wits on my paper.

Evening—Your No. 10 has just come to hand enclosing a copy of Melzar's which I read with much pleasure. Poor fellow he is having a hard time. From what I see in camp ashore here I can imagine his situation & feel for him. If I knew how to direct I would write to him.

One thing you alluded to which I cannot pass without notice. Your surmise of an article in the *Independent* is I think correct as to the authorship.†
From what Jim Beecher told me I found he was very bitter against McClelland, arising I think from some private pique. I know of my own

---

* Following the capture of New Orleans in April 1862, David Porter's mortar fleet headed up the Mississippi River to Vicksburg only to discover that the rebel stronghold could not be taken without the support of ground forces. His fleet was then ordered to Hampton Roads, but arrived after the end of the Peninsula Campaign and so was never used in an attack against Richmond.

† The author of the article was presumably James Beecher. The *Independent* was an anti-slavery newspaper published by the Congregational Church and edited by Henry Ward Beecher, James' famous half-brother.

knowledge that what the writer says about his [McClellan's] being on one of the gun boats drinking champaine &c is false.

The facts are these & I *know* them to be such. Early Monday morning [June 30] Capt. Rogers of the *Galena* took McC. on board for the purpose of taking him down the river to select a new position for his army. It was Gen. McC.'s intention to go down to Dancing Point (formed by a junction of the James & Chicahominy) but upon Capt. Rogers' recommendation of his present place he stopped & looked at it & concluded to halt his army there. When he came on board, notwithstanding he had had no sleep for 36 hours, he was busy looking over maps & charts confering with Capt. R. Capt. R., of course, gave him his breakfast & he may have taken a glass of wine. I don't know that he did or did not [but] in his exhausted state he may have done so, 'twould be nothing surprising. On his trip up the river to join his army he turned in & went to sleep, the first he had had for 36 hours. These are the facts of the case & I know them to be such but of what use are facts to that class of persons you mention who think they know as much at a distance of these things as we who are on the ground or who choose to pin their faith to every foolish newspaper report which favours their views, 'tis only casting pearls to swine. Ask Dave to give my respects to Campbell* & tell him what I have said in regard to this foolish lie. It is not only an insult to McClelland but a libel on Capt. Rogers who is not the man to drink wine with *any one* when there is *work* to [do]. My love to you all.

William

[Marginalia] The photographs of the *Monitor* were taken on board by an attache of Gen. McClellan's Staff on Secret Service. Of course they are correct. He has told me some things which will astonish folks if they ever come to light.

U.S. Steamer *Mount Washington*
Bound down James River
Aug. 12th, 1862

Dear Anna,

Here I am bound for Old Point once more & hope for a few days to be out of the roasting broiling sun of James river & enjoy the cool breezes of Old Point. (The jar of the machinery shakes the boat like an ague fit as you may judge by the looks of the writing.)

Your No. 11 reached me last evening & was read with as much pleasure as yours always are. When I wrote you last I can't say but it was some days since. Since then the weather has been so awful hot I have had to succumb & give up writing except my official business with the Department — the spirit indeed was willing but the flesh was weak. For the first time I have

---

* La Salle politician Alexander Campbell*.

James River (May to August 1862)

found weather too hot for me & you know it has to get pretty well warmed up for that. The "innards" of our iron box was hot as a dutch bake oven & about as endurable to live in. When the heat moderates a little I am going to write long letters almost every day, but you must spare me now. None of us pretend to sleep below now. All camp out on deck prefering the night air there to the suffocating heat & mosquitoes below. My health is good & I hope it will continue so.

I have with me a small box which I shall for'd by Express & pay all charges from Old Point. I hope it will reach you before Hen leaves for New Haven as one or two things in it are for him. There is nothing in it of special value save as mementoes of the past fights &c I have been in. As such I value them & would like to have them preserved. Pretty much all are labeled though it was done in haste. The revolver is one of our U.S.N. pistols taken from the *Teaser**. I would like to have Hen clean, oil it, & put it away. The fragments in the bag, of shot & shell, will give you some idea of the appearance of our decks after the fight with the *Merrimac*. I hadn't the heart to destroy your letters so send them all back. Don't feel bad at having your correspondence returned. You may discover some of my correspondence with young ladies among them — murder will out.

Hen gave me his [ac]count as I was coming away. I send him one in return from the Paymaster's stores of the *Monitor*, that & the box & soap for Eddy are such as I serve out to the men on board. I am sorry I had nothing for baby but a man of war is a poor place for children's playthings.

Hen must write me as soon as he reaches New Haven. I shall feel very anxious about him till I hear of his safe arrival. I have sent him no photographs as I hope to see him in the course of a month or so & have saved two or three for him.

Important movements are about being made here. What they indicate I hardly know. From what has already transpired it looks as if the whole army were going to leave the river & the peninsular & were going up the Rapahannock.† I can hardly convince myself that it is so & I hope I may be mistaken but there are certainly indications of that kind. Large transports filled with troops went down the river last night towing schooners filled with artillery & appliances *packed for long transportation* & when I left this morning cavalry horses were being loaded up, vessels filled with knapsacks were going down the stream & the docks were filled with army stores waiting shipment.

If my surmise is right the move is a sudden one & will raise a howl over the whole country. The object is probably to have the cooperation of Pope & McDowell & at the same time not leave Washington to[o] much exposed as would be the case if they were to come this way. It will have the appearance

---

* The Confederate gunboat that was captured on July 4, 1862.
† On August 3 General-in-Chief Halleck ordered McClellan to withdraw his forces to Aquia Creek on the Potomac River and unite them with Pope's army in northern Virginia.

of the labour of a whole season spent for nothing, not to mention the vast amount of property lost & lives sacrificed & can only be compensated for by a series of rapid & successful movements from the new base of operations wherever it may be. Don't let this get into the papers. You may read it to Dave & others, but it would not do to let it get into print.

I am no blind worshipper of McC. but go with him just so far as I see he does as well or better than any one else with the forces government has placed under his command. But I must say that a move like the one just named will weaken my confidence in him, unless something happens which I cannot now forsee.

How I hope some of the Masons* will be drafted. They were always very free with their criticisms, claiming to be oracles & I presume they have not altered now. 'Twould be of vast benefit to give such persons a little practical experience of matters which they speak so knowingly. It won't hurt any of Dr. Brown's children to serve their country in this emergency.† Others have children, just as good & just as much loved they have gladly sent forth. I am glad to hear you say that you are glad I went as I did. I do not regret it myself.

I was going to write a long letter but fear you cannot read what I have already written, there is such a jar to the boat. I carry Gov. dispatches & hoped to go to Washington, but shall not. Love to all.

William

[Marginalia] I feel anxious from what you said about Eddy. Do write me.

No. 30—

Monitor
James River
Aug. 15th [1862]

Dear Anna,

I returned from my trip down the river this morning having had a very pleasant time & had just set myself down to commence this letter to you giving an account of my trip, experiences in Norfolk &c when Capt. J. came on board from the Flag ship with the news that after this evening, no mail was to be allowed to leave here for fifteen days.‡ So don't think that you are forgotten or that I am sick should you not hear from me in that length of time. Continue to write me as frequently as possible as mails will be brought up the river though none will be taken down. I will keep on writing so that I will have a good long letter finished for you by the time I am allowed to send

---

* Freemasons.
† Vermont-born physician James Brown, who was presumably a Mason. He had two sons in their early 20s who in 1863 were not serving in the military.
‡ This was an attempt to keep the movements of the Army of the Potomac hidden from the enemy as it withdrew from the Peninsula.

James River (May to August 1862)

it. I wrote you on my way down to Old Point, the jar of the boat making the letter look as if I had a severe attack of the *joggles*. Hope you will be able to decypher it.

Capt. Jeffers has been detatched from the *Monitor* & Capt. Stevens* of the *Maratanza* takes his place. I don't know Capt. S. but we can't be any worse off for the exchange.

Great movements in the army are taking place. What they portend I do not know. I only hope they will lead to good results. I can hardly believe that the whole army will leave here. But enough remain to hold this position & threaten Richmond from this quarter. This is only a surmise of mine. I may be wrong.

With this mail I send a Richmond paper. The box by Express from Old Point I hope you will get to you safely. I only wish that there was something in it of more value to the children. When the time is fixed for Henry to start for New Haven let me know & he must be sure to write me when he gets there as I shall feel very anxious to hear from him.

The weather for the last day or two has been cooler & more comfortable.

I write in haste as the mail will soon close & will probably remain closed for some time to come. Remember me to all — Father, Mother, Sarah, Fan, Dave & all our circle. If Mrs. Hough don't write to me I shall cut her acquaintance *till* I get back.

How anxious I feel to hear from Melzar since the fight. All that I have yet heard is that his regiment was badly cut up.† Hope to hear particulars soon. Let me know what you hear.

Kiss the children. Take good care of them as well as yourself. With much love & many kisses,

                   Yours, William

---

* Thomas H. Stevens, Jr.*

† Anna's brother was killed in an infantry charge across a stubble wheat field at the Battle of Cedar Mountain in northern Virginia on August 9. In that charge, and in the ensuing fight in the woods beyond, every field officer in his regiment, all but two of the line officers, and 224 men were killed, wounded or captured, a little over half of those engaged. Melzar was reported to have fallen when his regiment entered the woods on the far side of the wheat field after having taken command of his company after the captain had been shot down. Melzar was said to have more than once "seized the colors from some fallen hero, and to have borne it along from a fallen color bearer, carrying it along to another." (Memorial to Lt. Henry M. Dutton, *Connecticut War Record*, New Haven, CT, Vol. 2, No. 9, April 1865, p. 384.) Newspaper reports first listed him among the wounded, but since his name never appeared on the lists of prisoners he was given up for dead.

Civil War Years: USS *Monitor* (1862)

No. 31—

Monitor
Off Light House Point[*]
Aug. 16th, 1862

Dear Anna,

I wrote you a hasty note last evening saying that in all probability it would be some time before you could hear from me again, orders having been given that no mail matter should leave here for fifteen days. Such orders seem rather arbitrary but I presume are necessary for the safe keeping of the plans for the movements of the army.

This morning when I rolled out of my blanket on deck I found the river vacated by the great number of schooners, steamers, & various kinds of vessels which had filled it for some weeks past. The forest of masts had disappeared, nothing remained but 10 or a dozen of our gun boats & one solitary steamer which seemed to be busy burning docks & making a general finishing up of everything left behind by our forces.[†]

In the camp nothing living was to be seen, neither man, horse nor mule. The village of white tents which for weeks past had dotted the yellow, dusty slope of the river bank & peeped out in pleasant relief from the bushes & trees on its margins had all disappeared. Contrabands, wagons, & artillery, all were gone & nothing left to mark the spot till now occupied by McClelland's large army with its immense amount of material, but a smooth, extensive plain of yellow dust. Nothing to disturb it now but the wind which blew in strong fitful gusts carrying with it large clouds of the sacred soil in a very *fine* condition.

The smoke from the burning wharves (which had been fired by the steamer remaining behind) rose in dark columns & mingled with the dust as it flew over the water towards the shipping, as if loath to be shaken off our feet. The long line of earth work on the opposite side so recently put up, shewed no warning sentinel & a glass revealed no guns from the embrassures, not even quakers[‡].

So this large army have gone, disappeared in a night apparently. Not so to us however who knew for some days past that they were generally withdrawing, but the change this morning seemed almost magical. A great skeedadle the rebels no doubt will call it when it reaches their ears, though McClelland may reach their senses before this news reaches their ears.

All going ashore from any of the vessels is now positively prohibited, but I cannot believe that our vessels are to remain long inactive, the country

---

[*] Jordan's Point on the south side of the James River, two miles west of Harrison's Landing.
[†] The Army of the Potomac had departed in the dead of night. Part of the army marched to Yorktown, the rest were shipped by steamer to Newport News and Fort Monroe.
[‡] Wooden logs painted black to look like cannons.

demands something to be done. My last visit ashore was just before I went down to Old Point.

I am always up early in the morning & on hand for anything to vary our dull routine of life, so I got permission from the Capt. to take a boat's crew & go ashore on Epps island & get a boat load of green corn & a calf, sheep or anything else I could find that was good. I shoved off from our vessel at daylight, cool, clear & perfectly delightful (the air not myself). We landed & got what corn we wanted in the boat & were driving down a drove of cattle to the boat, among which were half a dozen calves, with the intention of shooting one as near the boat as possible, when a couple of our soldiers made their appearance with the information that they were a portion of the Provost guard who had charge of the island & all on it, with instructions to arrest any one from the army or navy that they might find on the island. I asked them if their instructions applied to officers, they said they did. I told them I had orders also to take from the island a load of corn & a calf & intended to execute them, as I had the power to do it, & turned to my boat's crew of six good men, well armed, adding that if they undertook to make any arrests they might find themselves the arrested parties. I stepped one side in front of the cattle, told the soldiers & my men that I was going to shoot the calf, adding to my men that if the soldiers interfered to disarm them & put them in the boat. I shot the calf without any interference from the soldiers who when they found I was bound to carry out my orders agreed to compromise the matter by taking a receipt from me stating it had been killed for the use of the *Monitor*. This I agreed to & is the last I have heard of it. The Capt. when I told him of it said I did right.

While the men were skinning & dressing the calf I made an unsuccessful "reconnaisance" to see if I could find vegetables of any kind. You will find the island on some of the maps, opposite City Point. It is quite a large one, that is to have but one owner, being some three miles one way & two the other. It is nearly all under cultivation — a corn field of some three hundred acres, a large field of wheat ungathered & another put up in shocks, pastures & meadow lands all fenced off with the osage orange, a fine road running lengthwise of the island, the overseer's house, negro quarters, barns, sheds, tool houses & other outbuildings making quite a village. It is entirely deserted however by its former occupants — the owner [Eppes] being in the rebel army, a surgeon, the overseer having left after all the negroes (over one hundred) had made a practical application of their right to life, liberty & the pursuit of happiness. The persons driven from City Point occupy the buildings & horses, cattle, mules, sheep & hogs roam unrestrained through corn & wheat fields, meadows & pastures. A Provost's guard of some forty men are placed on the island, in charge of the cattle &c.

This Dr. Epps must have been a man of considerable wealth & was probably one of the F.F.V.'s. His fine house on City Point of which I have previously spoken is pretty much demolished by our shells. He must have lived there in princely style, his domains exceeding in extent those of many of the European princes. From his residence on the high bluff he could overlook his three large plantations, each a principality of the eastern world — one of them back of City Point on the South side of the Appomatax, one on the opposite side of the same river at Bermuda hundreds, & the third, Epps island, opposite his residence across James river. His house, grounds, & location were picturesquely beautiful. Art had assi[s]ted nature in developing the beauties of the place. His position here, aside from the curse of slaving, must have been all that one could desire — just far enough removed from the confusion & bustle of the world to give him quiet & retirement [and] at the same time within easy daily communication with it. He could almost be said to be the "monarch of all he surveyed." What a fool such a man must be to forsake such a place for the purpose of aiding a causeless and futile rebellion. I suppose his case is but one of thousands of similar ones to be found on the sacred soil. He returns at the end of the war, if so fortunate as to return at all, to find his home destroyed, his plantations confiscated & his *bone* & *muscle* working for its own support.

We have on board of us one of Hill Carter's negroes who came off to us one night soon after we first came up here — the one who was fired at & called out not to shoot as he "was a black man, massa."* He is one of the most useful men on board, a good carpenter, a shoemaker, fisherman, can wash & iron, & for a slave is remarkably intelligent. He is a favourite among us all for his honest simplicity & docility. I overheard one of the men one day urging him to sing a negro song. "Si" says, "no," "we were all good people at my home & I can't sing like that cause its wicked." He struck up some little Methodist hymn, of which he knows enough to stock half a dozen camp meetings. One of the men let him have an old spelling book & without any help he has learned to read in words of three and four letters. For a time after coming on board he was very homesick & wanted to go back. He wanted to see his mother, he said, & his "*girl.*"† Those who think such people have no feeling should hear how affectionately he spoke of his mother & his girl. Capt. J. told him he would send him back the first opportunity but his master would probably give him a flogging. Yes, "Si" said he would, but he would take that for the sake of seeing his mother. His mother however sent him word by some of the other slaves who came off one night not to return as his master would shoot him, besides his girl had made a practical declaration of independence. So, "Siah Carter," as I have christened him on my books, willing[ly] agreed to serve till the close of the war. He has been shipped & now draws his ration & ten dollars per month.

Besides him we have a light free mullato, a deserter from the rebels who had been taken from Norfolk by them when they left that place & carried to

---

* Siah Carter, who is first mentioned in the letter of May 12, 1862.
† He married his "girl" at war's end. See Biographical Notes.

Richmond. He was at Fort Darling when we had the fight there. He says word was passed in the batteries not to fire at the *Monitor* as it would only be a waste of ammunition. He managed to get away from the enemy during one of the skirmishes opposite this place, hiding himself in the swamps & living on berries for four days before he could get to us.

On the twelfth I left here for Old Point on one of the Government boats, the *Mount Washington*, & reached there about dark having a very pleasant trip down, being the only one on board beside her officers & crew. It being too late to get to Norfolk that night I quartered upon my friend Kimberly once more.

I found a good deal of confusion & excitement about the place consequent upon the arrival of large quantities of heavy stores from McClelland's camp up the river, the knowledge of some important movement taking place & the ignorance as to what that movement was or what it portended. Many would have it that our army was seized with a panic & was leaving in a fright, destroying camp equipage & stores — in fact a great skedaddle. I was surrounded by a crowd of news mongers, letter writers & idlers as soon as I reached the dock & it was found that I was a naval officer from up the river.

The next morning [August 13] I took the boat for Norfolk, went aboard of the *Minnesota* (the Flag ship) [and] delivered my despatches to the Commodore—beg pardon, Rear Admiral, I should have said as that is his title now.* Staid to dinner, not with the Admiral however that would have been an honor to[o] great for common man. I am not positive however that the Great being aforesaid lives by eating but rather think it is by nursing his dignity. I was invited to dinner in the Ward Room with some of the Lieutenants, the Fleet Paymaster, Surgeon, Chaplain & others, all a lot of old fogies who have been in the service till they are grey. They made a very pleasant company however.

The afternoon, having nothing to occupy my time, I devoted to a stroll about the place. I went to the Atlantic Hotel, the largest one in the place & kept moreover by a rabid secessionist, & registered my name, "U.S.N., U.S. Steamer *Monitor*" & asked for a room. The clerk looked at the book & then at me & then at the book & finaly wanted to know where the *Monitor* was. "Up the river, can you give me a room?" & a boy was sent with me up stairs to shew me the desired spot. As I came down a group of idlers who had gathered about the office glared at me as though I had been an ague & so it was with those I met in the streets, my uniform of course telling them my *trade* & *occupation*.

---

* Goldsborough's promotion helped to assuage his bruised and oversized ego. Stung by the appointment of Charles Wilkes to the independent command of the James River Flotilla, he had asked to be relieved of command of the North Atlantic Blockading Squadron the month before. When his replacement, Acting Rear Admiral Samuel Phillips Lee, arrived in September, Goldsborough headed to Washington where he spent the remainder of the war behind a desk.

Civil War Years: USS *Monitor* (1862)

In my walk through the business streets I found the greater part of the stores closed. An occasional grocery had the shutters down & doors open waiting for a customer, others merely had a door open leading to almost vacant shelves within. Everything had a silent deserted appearance as if it was a perpetual Sunday or the entrance to a grave yard & to carry out the latter idea many of the females I met were dressed in black. Most of the men were old, it was but seldom I met a young one & I was told what few there were in the place were from the north. Blacks of both sexes & all ages & sizes & shades of color abounded, having apparently nothing to do but sit under the fences, sun themselves & chatter. They shewed more civility when meeting me than most of the whites.

The buildings in the business portion of the place had an old & dingy look, nothing showy or attractive in their appearance. So also in the suburbs the dwellings had an old solid substantial look as if built for real comfort & convenience without any regard to architectural taste or display. No nice elegant airy cottages so often to be seen in our northern villages & which one would expect to meet with in this more southern clime. If any attempt at style it was that of years gone by. They were too frequently interspersed with the small dilapidated huts & hovels of the poor whites & free blacks which often formed an exceedingly disagreeable feature to what would otherwise have been a fine location.

But the trees & shrubbery were beautiful, though but little apparent care was manifested in their disposition or cultivation. Large magnificent magnolias with their wax like buds & blossoms raised their heads in every yard & beautiful Atheas covered with blossoms in all their variety of color were abundant, not in their dwarf bushy form as with us, but large beautiful shrubs. Another fine large shrub having the same general appearance as our lilachs & covered with a mass of beautiful pink blossoms was abundant. Clusters of the Yucca were plentiful though they as well as most of the roses were mostly out of blossom. Other vines & shrubs & trees with whose names & natures I was not familiar were plentiful. What a beautiful spot care & taste & cultivation could make in such a place where one would not have to contend with the rigors of our northern climate.

No direct insult was offered me as I strolled through the streets by the older persons, but ladies—females—would draw up their skirts & keep on the opposite side of the walk, while the men would look intently in an opposite direction, their intense hatred of my northern uniform being sufficiently manifested in their sullen surly look & apparent indifference to my presence. They felt I suppose as a conquered people in the presence of their conquerors & I confess to passing among them with a feeling of exultant pride. The children however were more demonstrative in their feelings, little girls leaving their play as I passed them to spit at me, boys cheering for Jeff Davis & shouting in their plays that "one Southerner was as good as half a dozen Lincoln men." The women too in the houses would strike up a secession song as I passed. Gen. Vilie* holds the reins too loosely over this nest of secessionists & much fault is found with him in consequence by the few Union folks in the place. This is a sample of the strong Union feeling that was to shew itself as soon as our folks obtained possession. The secession inhabitants are firmly of the belief that their forces will yet take possession of and hold the place.

The company at the supper table consisted of half a dozen of our army & navy officers, including Col. Wardrop† formerly of the Coast Guards, now of the N.Y. 99th. I noticed the coffee when brought on had a very peculiar taste & was told on enquiring of the waiter that it was made of rye (regular secession). It was all that they could get he said.

The next morning [August 14] I was called at half past four for the purpose of buying a lot of fruit in the market in time to take with me on the Old Point boat & up the river. The fruit & vegetables was brought in from the surrounding country in little one horse carts by the blacks & "poor white trash," the former being the most intelligent of the two. I bought some very nice peaches at four dollars per bush[el]. Nutmegs & watermelons were quite plenty, as were tomatoes, apples & most kinds of vegetables, but the manner of purchasing was exceedingly vexatious, especially when one's time was limited, as but a small lot of any one thing could be had of any one person before his limited stock would be exhausted. So I passed along buying half a dozen melons from one, a dozen cucumbers of another, half a bushel of apples here & a little lot of tomatoes there. No pains seemed to be taken to cultivate choice varieties, consequently everything was of the most common sorts. No one knew when I bought of them where a box or barrel could be obtained. Some could hardly comprehend what they were, or why I should want to pack my purchases. They wanted a good price for everything, but I had supplied myself the previous day with city shinplasters & Southern money (no Confederate notes, as they are forbidden to be used as a currency) at a discount of thirty five per cent which I used in making my purchases, at par, & in this manner reduced their extravagant prices somewhat.

What with the time spent in rummaging through the market & looking up boxes & barrels & hunting a dray, I barely had time to get to the boat as it shoved off & had to fall back on my Old Point friends for a breakfast after reaching there.

[No signature]

---

* Egbert L. Viele, the military governor of Norfolk.
† David W. Wardrop.

Civil War Years: USS *Monitor* (1862)

No. 32—

Monitor
James River
Aug. 19th, 1862

Dear Anna,

My last letter (No. 31) containing nearly three sheets was brought to rather an abrupt termination upon finding that I had an opportunity of sending it down to Old Point notwithstanding the embargo upon mail bags by superior powers. Why this injunction upon the mails I cannot conceive [since] every rebel paper is filled with this last move of our army & conjectures as to the future. All that we know here is that the entire army is gone & can only surmise where & for what purpose. Everything about us wears a most deserted appearance, nothing moving on the shore & only a gun boat now & then creeping up the river throwing an occasional shell into the trees & bushes which skirt its banks where a rebel may be supposed to be lurking. From their lookouts at a distance, which the rebels no doubt have, they can see all these things as well as ourselves & are as abundantly able to draw conclusions.

Yesterday our "most noble Captain" bade us adieu & left for the east where he is ordered to superintend the building of "iron clads."[*] I can assure you we parted from him without many regrets. He is a person of a good deal of scientific attainment, but brutal, selfish & ambitious. Commander Stevens, who takes his place, has the appearance of a quiet modest man. So far I like him, but I find that first impressions are not always to be trusted. He has the reputation of taking a glass too much occasionally, the curse of the navy.

My last [letter] left me at Old Point, just arrived from Norfolk. I left about noon the same day in one of the gun boats & got *home* about dark without any mishap.

Yesterday [August 18] a flag of truce went down having on board the officers captured from the *Wachusett* last spring, also Col. Corcoran & a whole boat load of others who greeted the "bully little *Monitor*" with the most vociferous cheers as they passed.[†]

Wednesday, 20th—A boat came up last night bringing the accumulated mails for the last five days, among the rest your No. 12. I went down to my State room after reading it to write a few lines in reply but the mosquitoes drove me off.

The weather since my return from Old Point has been cool & comfortable, so cool a portion of the time that even with our flannel clothing we were glad to get into the sun. I find it very comfortable sleeping below now, my bar protecting me from mosquitoes.

---

[*] Suffering from chronic rheumatism, Jeffers had requested a transfer to dry land and spent the rest of the war on ordnance duty at the Philadelphia and Washington Navy Yards.
[†] Corcoran was exchanged on August 15 after being imprisoned for more than a year.

James River (May to August 1862)

I got a *N.Y. Herald* to day containing a list of the killed & wounded at the battle of Cedar Mountain & find among the list of wounded Lieut. Dutton of the Conn. 5th. This must be Melzar. Have you heard from home? If so write me for I feel very very anxious to know something definite.

Mr. Newton, our Senior Engineer, was detached to day & ordered to New York to superintend the building of iron clad vessels. He was a good officer, a pleasant companion & all felt sorry to have him leave.

We are all looking anxiously for the time when we shall be ordered to Washington for repairs as all are expecting to get leave for a short time. If we are kept here till the new Monitors are done it will be three or four weeks before we can get away.

When is Henry going to leave for New Haven? I fear this news of Melzar's injury will interfere with your Mother's trip to lake George, though I cannot but hope it is nothing serious as the merest scratch is very frequently put down as wounded.

Illinois I see is doing nobly in the way of raising troops. I am agreeably disappointed, as just at this season of the year when farmers are busy with their harvests. I supposed it would be very difficult to enlist men.

What has become of Ham Brown? Did he succeed in getting the place he wanted & how has John made out on the gun boats?* I wish he was within reach of the *Monitor* as I could give him a place that would probably be better than any he would get on any of the river gun boats & at probably better pay, $30.00 per month & a ration. I would like to help John if in my power.

Thursday morning early [August 21] —Some friendly hand has just been thrust through my deck light & let fall a shower of letters & papers. To make no mention of official documents from the Department, I had one from Sarah (from Litchfield), two from yourself dated *May 19th* & *30th*. Enclosed in them was one from Almon, one from Henry & one from dear little Eddy. Though old they were read with a good deal of interest I assure you. I knew there was a break in your letters from some things which remained unexplained. Eddy's letter had a picture of the *Monitor* & *Merrimac*. I shall write to him in my next. Where you[r] letters have been wandering I don't know. Very likely they have made a trip down to New Orleans or Roanoke island or they may have laid in some post office for unpaid postage as there was marked "Due 3 cents" on each — this probably was the cause of the delay. Be particular & prepay all postage & don't forget to number your letters as I know then when any are missing. So far I get them with great regularity four days after they are mailed.

From some indications I think we are going to try the Fort Darling batteries again. Pilot houses are being protected with iron plates, sand bags are being filled as additional protection around the guns, heavy chain cables being hung on the sides to defend the boilers. I should not wonder if our new

---

* Keeler's brother-in-law's younger brothers Hamilton and John Brown.

commodore [Wilkes] meant to see what he could do before he leaves the river & it may be that we are to attack on this side while the land forces attack on the opposite one. These are all surmises. I know nothing.

I am scratching this off in a hurry as I hope to be able to smuggle it down the river this evening. I have written to Sarah & hope to be able to send that too. Remember me with love to all,

William

[Marginalia] In speaking of protection to vessels I mean others not our own as we require no additional defense.

No. 33—

Monitor
James River
Sunday morning
Aug. 24th, 1862

My Dear Wife,

I have just received yours of the 15th (No. 13) with the sad news (if true) of Melzar's death. I had previously sent you a copy of the *New York Herald* where he was put down as among the wounded. I think we have good grounds to *hope* that there may be some mistake as these lists are made out in the hurry, confusion & excitement always following a severe battle & must necessarily very often be incorrect. Let us hope for the best till we know the worst. Should it prove to be true that Melzar has realy given his life for his country it is needless for me to say, as closely related as we are, how sincerely I sympathise with you. "Brave, noble brother" truly, he has died a brave & noble death, better so than to have saved his life at the expense of his reputation for courage & manliness. How your Mother will feel the blow. It will completely paralise her. He was her darling & she will feel the loss proportionately. Your Father I think will view it in a different light. His calm, cool powers of reason & judgement will enable him while he mourns his loss to regard with feelings of pride the sacrifice he made for his country's liberties.

How many homes are already desolate & how many more will be made so before this war is brought to an end. The end now seems as far if not farther off than ever. How many mourners there will be all over the land. How few families there will be where there will be no vacancy, no one to mourn.

With this I send you a *New York Herald* (please preserve it) containing a letter from Sec'y Seward which speaks my sentiments more to the point or in much better language than I can do myself, in regard to allowing politics to interfere with the conduct of the war.* For this crusade against McClelland is

---

* The letter by Lincoln's Secretary of State was in response to a Pennsylvania Democrat's demand that the Administration "declare hostility to the policy and measures of all who

nothing more than a political move of some who fear his popularity in a political way. If those who have stooped so low and have become so barren of argument as to use Wilkes as authority, knew that all his abuse of McClelland arose from the fact that McC. refused him a pass up the peninsular at a time when all civilians without exception were excluded from the lines, they could see upon how small a base their borrowed arguments rest. When Gen. McC.'s enemies are reduced to such extremities their arguments are hardly worth refuting.

I rec'd a long letter from Birdsey the other day. He had just returned from Minnesota where he had been on a visit with his wife. They went to Rockford & regretted they had not time to go to LaSalle. He mentioned having received a paper from you & wanted to know if I thought it would be a sufficient pretext for writing you.

From your accounts our little place will be nearly depopulated of young men. I wish the Masons were compelled to go. I suppose as usual with them, they stand back ready to clap their hands & shout s'tuboy to those who may feel willing to peril themselves in defence of their country, but are careful to keep out of harm's way themselves.

I have felt sometimes as if I did not care if I died in poverty, I have fought for my country & can leave my children an honourable name. It makes but little difference in what station, whether as General or private, so long as one serves faithfully & to the best of his capacity.

Let me know if John Brown succeeds in getting a place on one of the gun boats. It may be in my power to help him by & by if he should fail & I should be glad to do so.

I hope Henry will still be able to go to New Haven. It will be a greater disappointment to me than to him if your father should change his plans, for I so want him in a good school.

What our next move up the river here will be I do not know. As I have previously written you there are some indications of another attempt on Fort Darling by the gun boats. If it should be made it will result in our defeat & a useless loss of men & expenditure of time & ammunition.

I am glad to hear you speak so well of Lucius. I know he was always a favourite of yours. Mr. Collins I think will make a good officer & I am glad

---

seek to prostitute the country to the purposes of abolitionism." The sentiments that Keeler so liked are expressed in the final paragraph: "I am occupied here either in mediating between differing parties and jealous sects, or else in watching and counteracting the intrigues of traitors in Europe. But I sometimes think that if, instead of being charged with these duties, I were at liberty, as you seem to be, to serve the country in my own way, I could make an appeal to democrats and republicans, abolitionists and slaveholders in behalf of our distracted country that would bring the whole people at once under arms, and send treason reeling back into the den of darkness from whence it sprung. I do not know how this would be, but I do know that if I were in your place, I should try." (*New York Herald*, New York, NY, August 22, 1862, p. 8).

to hear he has succeeded in raising a company.* I only wish our six hundred thousand men were now in the field well drilled & armed. The rebels will try & make their stroke if possible before these new men are brought into the field.

Tell Dave to hold on to McClelland. I firmly believe he will maintain his reputation as a military leader. I am glad that both him & Campbell coincide with me in my views of these things.

The weather for the last few days has been deliciously cool & comfortable, a luxury we can appreciate I assure you. I hope you have received the box before this. The photographs I would like to have kept. When I go to New York I suppose they will be for sale & will get some for our friends if they wish them. Will send one to Almon as you wished. My Appointment & Orders I would like to have you keep carefully as they may be of importance to me & I may find it necessary to send for them.

You must have had a fine garden this summer. I would like very much to have seen it. I still hope to see the last end of it & eat some grapes with you. From Sarah's letter she seems to be enjoying her visit highly. I am glad she had the opportunity.

Monday, 25th—The weather continues cool & comfortable. In fact so cool as to remind us strongly of fall. How I hope to see you all before winter. It cannot be that we shall remain up here much longer. We may make an attempt on fort Darling, then lie two or three weeks around Newport News & then for Washington. Some time ago when the Washington folks thought we were coming there great preparations were made to receive us. Wonder if they will do so now.

William

[Marginalia] Tell Eddy that when I come home I will wear my cap so that he can "*sawn*" it. My love to you all. New Haven & LaSalle papers just rec'd.

---

* Keeler's William Collins friend had resigned as chaplain of the 10th Illinois Infantry and returned to La Salle where he raised a company of soldiers, which formed part of the 104th Illinois Infantry.

Off Newport News (August to October 1862)

How much pleasanter we find it here with the breeze of old ocean sweeping over us, than in the heated furnace like air of James River I need not describe. You may well imagine the contrast between the two places & our joy at being released from our imprisonment amid the turbid waters of that stream, whose banks though romantic & beautiful served but to conceal the rifles of a foe whose unexpected & deadly fire might sweep our decks at any moment from the shrubbery which fringes its borders. (1 September 1862)

With the withdrawal of the Army of the Potomac from the Virginia Peninsula the James River Flotilla was no longer needed. In late August it was disbanded and the *Monitor* and the *Galena* sent back down the river to Hampton Roads to blockade the mouth of the James River against the egress of the rebel ironclad CSS *Richmond*.

Pleased with this change of scenery, Keeler and his fellow officers feasted on oysters, crabs, fresh fruit and vegetables, and spent their leisure time fishing and sailing. Keeler was also getting to know their new captain, Thomas Stevens, and found him to be "good company & a plain pleasant sociable man." However, Stevens' time on the *Monitor* was short lived, for he ran afoul of the new regulation banning alcohol on U.S. Navy vessels except for medicinal purposes, and was relieved of command in mid-September as a result of a drinking incident on board the *Monitor*. Keeler, the teetotaler who forever railed against the evils of alcohol, never spoke badly of Stevens, whom he knew had a reputation for drinking, and was sad to see him go.

Stevens' replacement was 41-year-old bachelor Commander John Bankhead, a South Carolinian by birth who had remained loyal to the Union. Unlike the sociable Stevens, Bankhead was "still & quiet, very gentlemanly, but seems cool & distant." Over the course of the next four months, Keeler's respect and admiration for Bankhead grew. The feeling was mutual, for when Bankhead was given command of the USS *Florida* in early 1863, he requested that Keeler serve as his paymaster.

While they lay idle at Hampton Roads waiting impatiently for word they would be sent north to the Washington Navy Yard for much needed repairs, the war in the East had heated up to another fever pitch. By mid-August the center of action had moved to northern Virginia. Following Pope's crushing defeat at the Second Battle of Bull Run in late August, Lincoln merged Pope's demoralized army into the Army of the Potomac, sent Pope out West to fight the Sioux and put McClellan in charge of the combined army. In early September Lee crossed the Potomac River into Maryland, and on September 17 fought McClellan to a standstill at the Battle of Antietam, the bloodiest single day of the Civil War. The battle ended Lee's invasion of Maryland and gave Lincoln the opportunity to announce the preliminary Emancipation Proclamation freeing all slaves in States in rebellion as of January 1, 1863. McClellan, however, failed to destroy Lee's battered army before it crossed back over the Potomac, and for this was permanently relieved of field command.

On September 30 the *Monitor* was finally ordered to the Washington Navy Yard for repairs. Unable to travel under her own steam, she had to be towed. Upon their arrival at the yard on October 3, visitors started flocking in droves to see the famous ironclad. The following day the crowds had grown so large that the Marine guards opened the gates of the yard and let the people pour in. Souvenir hunters carried away every small removable item they could find on the *Monitor*, which included door knobs, the ornamental plates around key holes, and the keys themselves. On October 5 the vessel was turned over to the superintendent of the yard, and the officers and crew of the *Monitor* were moved to the USS *King Philip*. As the person responsible for arranging the funds to pay off the officers and crew, Keeler was one of the last to leave. On October 10 his four-week leave was granted, and he caught the train back home to La Salle and his loved ones.

Letters of special note: September 3 (life in Norfolk at the start of the war); September 6 (a visit to Captain Smith's house); September 22 (news of the Emancipation Proclamation); October 6 (at the Washington Navy Yard; lions of the day).

No. 34—

Monitor
James River
Aug. 27/62

Dear Anna,

The flag ship has just signaled, "get under way & follow" & as she is proceeding up stream our destination as we *suppose* is Fort Darling. All that we *know* however is that we are to get under way & follow the flag ship in obedience to orders. These are usually given without explanation so that all that is left us is blind obedience. Should we make the attempt up the river it will be unsuccessful. The only result will be a waste of time & ammunition & probable loss of life. I have reason to think we will not be able to get as far up the river as we did in our attack on Fort Darling as we have reason to think that strong batteries & obstructions have been erected & placed in the river some distance this side of Fort Darling.

Evening. I had taken my pen & got thus far when I heard the order given to "let go the anchor" & going on deck found the whole fleet (some dozen vessels) at anchor at the mouth of the Appomatox & off City Point. "What's up now?" is in every one's mouth. "Are we going on another expedition up the Appomatox?" "Well what is to be will be" & with that we must be content. All of us are satisfied with our former trip up this narrow crooked stream & have no desire to try it again.

OFF NEWPORT NEWS (AUGUST TO OCTOBER 1862)

Thursday Morning 28th—The song of the "old man that marched up the hill & then marched down again" has been fully exemplified in our case. Just after daylight this morning the fleet was signaled to "get under way & follow." This time however it was down stream instead of up. So down we all went to our old anchorage off the deserted camp [at Harrison's Landing] leaving behind a schooner loaded with ammunition & a small tug. We had no sooner let go our anchor than firing was heard from the tug left behind & the signal was made for the *Monitor* to go up the river to her assistance. So we up anchor once more & started up stream [&] found the tug. Imagined she saw some men ashore in a small piece of woods & was letting drive at them. We couldn't stretch our imaginations quite as far, so concluded to try something more real & fired half a dozen shell into Dr. Epps' house, somewhat to the disturbance of wood work & masonry. We convoyed our schooner load of ammunition down to the fleet & resumed our anchorage, wondering what the next move will be.

Friday 29th—Signal this morning "get under way & follow, the *Monitor* in the rear." This time we followed in a more desirable direction — down the river. We had a pleasant sail down passing the different familiar localities, the batteries from which we had been fired at as we came up just three months & eighteen days ago, now vacant & silent, old fort Powhattan of revolutionary fame, Jamestown Church in which Pocahontas was married, & the various plantations scattered along on the banks, now apparently deserted, not even a contraband to be seen.

We came to anchor for the night off Day's Point. The earthworks still remain overgrown with weeds & grass but the guns are employed in a nobler cause.

Saturday 30th—We were under way at daylight this morning & taking advantage of a good strong tide came to anchor off Newport News just as we were through breakfast — 9 o'clock. We are anticipating a pleasant time, having been ordered down by the Department to recruit the health of the crew & give us all the benefit of the fresh sea air, something we need as many of the men begin to feel the malaria of the river.

We find that our James river fleet [Flotilla] is to be dispersed. Some going up the Potomac, some down the coast, while we are to remain here for the present, how long I don't know, probably till some of the new Monitors are completed. We are to blockade James river against the egress of the new *Merrimac*. We lie but a few rods from the sunken *Cumberland*, a sad reminder of the old one. Once more we come under Rear Admiral Goldsborough's regime but I don't think it will add much to our anticipated enjoyments.

Capt. Stevens says that he desires to do everything in his power to add to our comfort & pleasure. So far we find him a very different man from Capt. Jeffers. I think we shall find it much pleasanter with him than with Capt. J.

This afternoon we took our first cutter, fitted it up with sails & spent the remainder of the day sailing about the harbour with a fine stiff breeze. I wish you, Henry, could have been with us. You would have enjoyed it as much as any of us. We mean to have many a good sail in it between here & Norfolk, about 12 miles.

Visitors have already commenced their calls — the boat has been full all the afternoon. Among others I found a Mr. Sturdevant from Bridgeport. Ladies formed a good proportion of our callers.

The steam has been blown out of our boilers & the fire allowed to go out, the first time since the 21st of last Feb'y.

The *Ironsides* lies in the harbour & I hope to have an opportunity to go on board of her to morrow. She carries a tremendous battery. Woe to anything that receives one of her broadsides.*

I fear you will find this letter hardly worth the reading for I feel as stupid as can well be conceived. A sty on my eye for the last day or two has not added much to my comfort & take mosquitoes & heat & they do not help to make an interesting epistle.

Your *Independent* has never reached me. I am sorry as I had considerable curiosity to see the article you mentioned.

I hear nothing more of Melzar since you wrote me contradicting the report of his death. I hope to have my anxiety relieved soon.

I should have a letter from you to morrow & hope not to be disappointed. Remember me to all our friends. Love to Father & Mother & lots of kisses to yourself & the children.

William

U.S.S. *Monitor*
Off Newport News
Sunday, Aug. 31st, 1862

Dear Anna,

I went down to Old Point to day & there found your letter of *no date*, No. 14. I felt sad upon opening it to find our worst fears more than realised in regard to Melzar. I say "more than realised" as I hoped even if the worst should prove true that your Father would be able to recover his body which it seems by your letter he has not been able to do.† I have been thinking the matter over to day & have pretty much come to the conclusion, in case I get leave of absence in the course of the next few weeks, to go to the battle field & see if I cannot succeed in finding his body. I shall write to night to your Father & Mother & if they desire it, will make the effort. I take it for granted

---

* The USS *New Ironsides* was one of the three ironclads selected by the Ironclad Board in 1861. She was sent to Hampton Roads to help the *Monitor* and *Galena* guard against the egress of the ironclad ram CSS *Richmond*.

† Henry Dutton had travelled to Culpeper, Virginia to recover his son's remains, but was unsuccessful. Melzar's body was never found and lies in an unmarked grave on or near the Cedar Mountain battlefield.

OFF NEWPORT NEWS (AUGUST TO OCTOBER 1862)

that you will approve it although by so doing I may miss seeing any of you. As an officer I should have facilities for prosecuting my search which a civilian would not have, even one occupying the position of your Father. When you hear from home please let me know. I have written to Geo.* but have as yet had no reply. I write this hasty note in addition to my letter to send off early to[morrow] morning. Will try & write you more at length in a day or two. With much love

William

[Marginalia] I send by this mail two papers to you & one to Eddy. Rec'd a letter from Helen [Plant] yesterday. Your Litchfield paper rec'd. I return the piece as you desire that it may not be lost.

No. 35—

U.S.S. Monitor
Off Newport News
Sept. 1st, 1862

Dear Anna,

I do not know as I can pass the evening more pleasantly & profitably than in writing to the loved ones at home. Happy am I to have them <u>all</u> to write to & to be in good writing condition myself. I have just finished a half sheet to Dave & a diminutive scratch to Fan to assure her that I am still in fighting & writing trim & that she had not entirely passed from my remembrance. Much as I desire I cannot undertake to write to all my friends individually & so write to them collectively through you. In the first place I glean up all the news to fill my frequent sheet to you. Then my duties take a portion of my time, notwithstanding friend Hough [who] says I "have nothing to do but pace the quarter deck" (which by the way is a thing we don't possess, though we do a large amount of travelling over iron plates). Then I have other correspondents away from home, including pretty cousins, who must need be attended to. I have an unanswered letter from Birdsey, one from Helen & one I must write to your parents (which I have not yet done) to say nothing of official correspondence which is no small item.

Tell friend Hough this, if he is still dissatisfied he can send me the heads of a discourse & I will try & fill them out, otherwise I should not know what to write him. My legal knowledge he well knows is limited, I can't conscenciously abuse McClelland, don't feel competent to criticise the abilities of our Generals & the proper mode of conducting the war, no chance for a discussion on the slavery question for we agree there. Should like to hang Jeff Davis, so would he. Should advise him to shoulder arms & enlist under Parson Collins, which advice he wouldn't follow nor pay me for. Might open on him

---

* Keeler's brother-in-law in New Haven.

with iron clad & 11 inch guns, probably to his great disgust & want of appreciation. So what am I to do?

How much pleasanter we find it here with the breeze of old ocean sweeping over us, than in the heated furnace like air of James River I need not describe. You may well imagine the contrast between the two places & our joy at being released from our imprisonment amid the turbid waters of that stream, whose banks though romantic & beautiful served but to conceal the rifles of a foe whose unexpected & deadly fire might sweep our decks at any moment from the shrubbery which fringes its borders. Though much the most dangerous kind of warfare we could gain no credit, no honor, but great risks. For the last three months I have not tread the deck without thinking of what might be in the bushes by our side & night after night we have slept when a discharge or two of canister would have swept us off the deck.

We hear at one time that we are to go to Washington in a few days, then again, it will be six or eight weeks before the new Monitors are done & that we cannot leave till then. So we are left just as much in the dark as ever. Time & patience will bring it all about.

I see by the late papers that McClelland has command of the army of Virginia, just as you wrote me you thought he would.* Strong proof of the unshaken confidence of the Administration in him, notwithstanding the howls of the *N.Y. Independent* & *Chicago Tribune* echoed by unscrupulous political demagogues all over the country. I would like to have my way with these mischief making curses (for they are a curse to their country & the cause). They should have an opportunity of manifesting their professed patriotism by building entrenchments for our soldiers. The boasted superior skill & knowledge of these Sir Oracles could not find a better place for display than in the trenches which they might have the animal strength to erect, but not the courage to defend. I loose all patience when I think of them & see the rule or ruin policy which they are pursuing. What do these persons care for the country, our government or our institutions? Just nothing, only so far as they tend to their own political advancement. I might have thanked heaven if I had seen daylight as a negro slave, but as a politician, never. But I must quit [discussing this] or I shall never write a *letter*.

As to sending Henry to New Haven, you must use your own judgement as to how & when. Probably some of the merchants will soon be going east after their fall goods. I shall hope to see him either there or at home. I cannot form any idea when I shall be in New Haven. I think Henry would be some comfort to your parents if he was there, though it would not be so pleasant for him. I am very glad you had his teeth attended to. It was something that

---

* Three days after Pope's defeat at the Second Battle of Bull Run on August 30, Lincoln merged the Army of Virginia with the Army of the Potomac and placed McClellan in command.

Off Newport News (August to October 1862)

had entirely escaped my memory or I should have mentioned it some time ago.

I wish you would write me what you think about my endeavouring to recover Melzar's body in case your parents desire me to make the attempt. I shall write them offering to do so if they wish. It would be a great consolation to them if they could visit his grave. It is possible that I might be able to do that & make a visit home too.

You say "Sarah will be disappointed in not getting a letter from me." Why so? I wrote her at Litchfield & if she remained there she should have rec'd it.

I am glad the garden looks so nicely & you have the promise of so many grapes. I hope I shall have a taste of them.

I will try & send you a [New York] *Herald* frequently as I receive one regularly every day from the office, *gratis*, & will send them on to you when there is anything of interest. For the next few days they will probably be full of news from our army of Virginia, & I hope the news will cheer us up.

My love to all, not forgetting yourself & the children.

William

No. 36—

U.S.S. *Monitor*
Off Newport News
Sept. 3rd, 1862

Dear Anna,

I sent you No. 35 by to day's mail & cannot think of anything very interesting with which to fill this sheet unless I give you my journal for Sunday, or what is Sunday at home. Here we have none. This you must bear in mind or I fear you will think I sometimes desecrate the day. The manner in which the day is regarded is perhaps best exemplified by a large placard posted on the door of Adams & Co.'s Express office — "This office is closed on Sunday. Remember the Sabbath day. Six days shalt thou labour & do all thy work, the Seventh belongs to the Clerks."

I had my choice of remaining on board through the day & being overslaughed with company or going down to Old Point & visiting the *Ironsides*, & chose the latter. Four of us started a little after daylight in our sail boat, distance about ten miles, but after beating about for an hour with a light head wind & tide against us we gave it up & hailed a steamboat that was passing to be taken on board. So sending the boat back by one of the sailors we made the rest of the trip by steam, much the most sure. Reached Old Point & got some breakfast from friend Kimberly & found that the *Ironsides* was momentarily expected to sail. Upon application to the Capt. of the Port (Capt. Millward) he furnished us with a small tug or steamer by means of which we reached her in time to make a hasty inspection of this new huge fighting machine. I will not attempt a description for it would be impossible for me to convey to you any adequate idea of her appearance, outside or in. She resembles a huge floating fort. Her battery consists of fourteen such guns as ours, two, two hundred pounder rifled Parrotts & two, one hundred pounder rifled Parrotts, the heaviest battery afloat in the world. Notwithstanding this, Capt. Stevens says he believes the *Monitor* could whip her. At any rate if she was in possession of the rebels he would not be at all afraid to try the experiment, as she has her vulnerable points.

We left her after a hasty look just as she was getting under way & on getting ashore came across an acquaintance, a Mr. Davids, the superintendant of the Government shops here & went home to dinner with him & made the acquaintance of his wife, quite a pleasant intelligent lady.[*] They formerly lived at Norfolk & her account of things there at the time of the breaking out of the rebellion was very interesting. She is a southern woman & at the commencement of the war was inclined to favour the south although her husband was from the first a strong Union man. All her friends & connexions were with the south & at first it seemed hard to sunder all the ties & attachments that held them together. But she said she would go with her husband although against her inclinations. They were the last ones that left Norfolk except under flags of truce. Her account of the various subterfuges resorted to to get away her library, sewing machine, piano & other articles of furniture was amusing, though they were obliged to leave much behind which was pretty much destroyed by the rebel troops while they held possession of the place. After Norfolk was again occupied by our troops she went up to visit her former friends & acquaintances with many of whom she had been on the most intimate terms, or as she said they seemed like sisters. Knowing that they had been cut off a long time from sources of supply, she carried up a box filled with needles, thread, buttons, tape & such things, supposing they would appreciate her kindness in supplying them with articles she knew they must be out of & need badly. She met some of them in the street but they passed by without recognising on the opposite side of the walk, gathering up their skirts as if afraid of being contaminated. The wife of Henry A. Wise[†] was one of her former intimates & called on her. From Mrs. Davids' account of the call they must have had quite a spicy debate of the times. Mrs. Wise declaring that they could never be conquered, & if they were they would never remain so. Mrs. Davids replied that if she could have her way they would be conquered & would remain so if she had to exterminate ever[y] man, woman & child in the southern states. I judge from her conversation that her southern feelings had pretty much faded out.

---

[*] New York born Garret B. Davids (1823-1885) managed the machine shops at Old Point Comfort and later was inspector of ironclads at Fort Monroe. Prior to the start of the war, he was a machinist at the Gosport Navy Yard. His wife Mary was a native of Washington, DC.
[†] Former Governor of Virginia.

OFF NEWPORT NEWS (AUGUST TO OCTOBER 1862)

We got back to the ship without accident just in time for supper. Coming up in the steamboat I had for a fellow passenger Mr. H. L. Sturdevant from Bridgeport whom I believe I have mentioned before. He gave me many items of Bridgeport news, among the rest that Henry Bishop* had become a regular bloated sot. Mr. S. had come on here after his wife who had come here as nurse & had been taken sick.

In the evening we had a melancholy exhibition of the effects of whiskey. Our Ward Room Steward† had been allowed liberty ashore & of course must come back drunk. His first act after getting aboard was to seize an axe and try to split my boy's head open. The usual punishment in such cases was resorted to, he was put in double irons, his hands being confined behind him. In this condition he managed to get to the side & jumped overboard, being so heavily ironed of course there was no chance for him & he never rose. His family I believe are in California, but I doubt if he is much loss to them.

I enclose a couple of newspaper articles that you may see how little confidence is to be put in their reporters. All that gave rise to these *terrific* articles was the few shells we threw through Epps' house of which I have before written you — no burning or other destruction was attempted, the place has been deserted for a long time & was partially destroyed the time we went up the Appomatox.

Our news from the army is not very encouraging, but we must hope for better things, "the darkest hour is just before day."

Started off in good season this morning & before breakfast we had caught 4 doz. crabs close by the wreck of the *Congress*, getting back to breakfast. 'Twas fine fine fun & better eating. Wouldn't you like to have been along Hen? I often wish for you. But I must close with love & kisses to you all.

William

No. 37—

U.S. Steamer Monitor
Off Newport News
Sept. 6th, 1862

Saturday night Dear Anna & the old toast of "Sweethearts & wives" comes strongly to mind as my thoughts wander homeward. I have just been wondering what I should find you all about if I could just open the door & walk in upon you. Don't you wish I would do it? I wish I could spend the evening with you, wouldn't we have a chat. With us the evening is superlatively beautiful, if such can be. A bright full moon beaming down upon the

---

* Henry R. Bishop (1839-1895), another Bridgeport resident, who at a young age inherited a large fortune from his father. In 1860 he married Margaret Mallory, the daughter of the Confederate Secretary of the Navy, Stephen R. Mallory, who was then a U.S. senator from Florida.

† Lawrence Murray.

waters ruffled with one of the finest breezes of old ocean. We have just done supper & most of the officers have just started off for a moonlight sail, singing the "Star Spangled Banner" & shouting for the Paymaster to "come along" but I shall forego the pleasure to converse with the loved ones at home.

The afternoon I spent with Capt. Stevens & our M.D. fishing, though with rather poor success. Had our supper depended upon our luck I fear we should have gone to bed hungry, but our caterer during our absence used a silver hook to a very good purpose. We are enjoying sea food, oysters, crabs & the finest fish in great abundance. I only wish you could have a taste now & then.

Had a very pleasant time with Capt. Stevens. He is good company & a plain pleasant sociable man. Capt. Jeffers, although not ranking as high as Capt. S., would never have outraged his dignity or trespassed upon his indolence so far as to have gone a fishing with his Surgeon or Paymaster. Capt. S. is very fond of company & very frequently asks one of the officers in to dine with him. He was speaking one day of being on the Coast Survey & I enquired if he was acquainted with John Rockwell. "Oh yes," he said, "very well, & a very fine young man he was too." Capt. S. commanded the vessel to which Mr. R. was attached.

Yesterday morning Capt. Craft[s]*, of one of the merchant vessels lying in the harbour, came alongside with his boat & invited me to go & get some peaches with [him]. I provided myself with a basket & man to carry it. We went up the river about five or six miles & landed at a place owned by J. Pembroke Jones†, Capt. of the rebel ram *Savannah*. It was a beautiful location, but his house, a fine brick one, had been burned by our troops & nothing now remains but the walls, fire cracked & partly fallen. We went to his peach orchard & helped ourselves, no one to demur or assent. It was natural fruit & of course small & not of superior flavour, but *much better* than none at all. The trees grew pretty much as they choose, receiving but little care from man. The whole place was overgrown with course rank weeds, fences broken down, farm implements scattered about & destroyed, well partially filled with a promiscuous collection of rubbish on the top of which lay the skeleton of a dead porker, out buildings were broken down, overturned & partly burned. In fact the destruction was as complete as possible, a good picture of civil war.

---

* Samuel P. Crafts*. He later served on the *Florida* with Keeler.

† John Pembroke Jones (1825-1910), flag officer on the *Virginia* in April 1862. His house (Pembroke farm), which had been in his family for generations and where Jones was born, was located about a mile west of St. John's Episcopal Church in Hampton. Following the Confederate evacuation of Norfolk in May 1862, Jones was sent to the Savannah Squadron. In September 1862, the rebel ram CSS *Savannah* was still under construction in Savannah, GA.

OFF NEWPORT NEWS (AUGUST TO OCTOBER 1862)

Many other places along the bank have been laid waste in the same way by the N.Y. 7th regiment (not the 7th N.Y. city but a German regiment). They burned every house as they passed along which they found unoccupied & whose owners were supposed to be secesh. The numerous tall monumental like chimneys & heaps of blackened rubbish were plainly visible at frequent intervals as we skirted along the bank marking the spot of once pleasant happy homes. It seems a sad necessity that requires such destruction, but after seeing what I have I believe it is necessary to convince them that we are realy in earnest & make them feel the iron hand of war. It is about the only way you can reach the purse proud, slave driving aristocrats of the South & make the[m] feel the reality of the war they have brought upon the country.

We left the men to gather the fruit & continued our way on foot up along the bank of the river to a place occupied by Capt. Smith, an old retired sea captain & an acquaintance of Capt. Craft. He has a beautiful place built upon the bank & overlooking the river surrounded with fine trees & shrubbery.* The Capt. was at home & gave us a cordial welcome, inviting us in to the inevitable *whiskey* & sigars. His wife however did better than that for finding that we could not stay to dinner gave us a lunch of peaches & milk & good fresh bread & butter. Every [Ever] since our army landed on the Peninsular they have been very peculiarly situated, placed as it were between two fires, visited by both parties, first one, then the other. Some of our officers to breakfast & the rebels to dinner, & a number of times she said she had not got her breakfast table cleared off for our officers before she would be called on by the rebels & she was always in fear of a collision in her house, though fortunately it never took place. It was known to the officers of each side that the place was a resort for both, so that at dinner rebel Capt. Smith would leave his respects to Union Capt. Jones, should be happy to meet him &c, & vice versa. At the time of our fight with the *Merrimac*, Magruder was at her house with 17000 troops waiting to pour into Fortress Munroe when the *Merrimac* should have cleared the harbour. She showed me an album belonging to a Miss Talley†, a somewhat celebrated Southern poetess, which among other curiosities had Magruder's autograph written during the fight between the two vessels. The Capt. & his wife when we left gave us a cordial

---

* English sea-captain Nelson Smith (1814-1883) purchased the two-story house in the 1850s and named it Cedar Grove. One of the few remaining pre-Civil War houses in the area still standing, it nearly did not survive the war. When Confederate Major General John Magruder burned the nearby town of Hampton in August 1861, a friend of Smith's asked the general to spare the house. When the Union army later tried to burn the house, his New York born wife Margaret (1815-1897) refused to leave, saving it once more from destruction. Smith's wife, who had a reputation for courage and determination, was well known for helping the sick, reputedly enduring seven-day carriage rides to Richmond to get medical supplies during the war.

† Susan Archer Talley, whose volume of poems was published in 1859. During the Civil War she was accused of being a rebel spy and was imprisoned at Fort McHenry in Baltimore.

invitation to call whenever we could. Capt. Craft, who took me up, is well acquainted with your Father, lived near him in New Haven.

I got back in time for supper & after it started off on another excursion, not so pleasant or agreeable. The body of our Steward had been picked up during the day & one of the engineers & myself volunteered to take it ashore for burial. 'Twas just such a night as this. We took a boat's crew & buried him by moonlight among the hundreds of Union soldiers whose graves are thickly strewn along the sandy shore.

The mail is just in bringing me a couple of papers but no letters much to my disappointment. I return some pieces cut from the papers which I thought you might like to preserve.

I have written to your parents offering to make an effort to recover Melzar's body if possible but have not rec'd a reply as yet.

With much love to yourself, the children & all friends.

William

No. 38—

U.S.S. Monitor
Off Newport News
Sept. 8th, 1862

Dear Anna,

Yours of Sept. 2nd No. 15 reached me last evening & was as welcome as yours always are. I set down immediately & attempted to commence a reply but my wits, if I had any, left me as the mosquitoes commenced an attack, first on the right flank, then on the left, then a vigorous assault on the rear quickly followed by a combined movement on my front. I was finally compelled to beat a retreat & leave them in quiet possession of the field. Their victory was not a bloodless one as the numerous bodies scattered over my desk lid attested. They accumulated in our state rooms while up the river & all the persuasive force of towels flourished fiercely, suffocating smudges & hard words & threats have not induced them to withdraw from our society. For size & strength & pertinacity & fierceness they are immensely superior to any of the breed I have ever seen. The audacity with which they present their bills is realy refreshing & is only equaled by the length & strength of the same.

The letter from Mary you enclosed I was very glad to read & to see that notwithstanding her trials*, she is, or tries to be somewhat cheerful. There was another sheet you sent me covered with hieroglyphics or written in one of the lost languages which I have not been able to decipher or translate, though I spent last evening over it till the "ten o'clock sir" from the Master

---

* Based on the comments in the letter of September 12, 1864, Keeler's brother-in-law Henry Graves was an alcoholic.

at Arms told the hour for retiring. I was up by day break this morning to continue my study of the mysterious characters & have followed it up with the most persevering pertinacity through the day & have finally assumed the alpha & omega to be "dear sister" & "Hattie" or something very similar. It occured to me while turning the sheet over in my hands & pouring over it with my brains that it was possible that Sister Hat had had a hand in it in some way. If she is the inventor of this truly original style of chirography, please congratulate her for me for she must have made a discovery which Layard* spent a life time amid the ruins of Ninevah in a vain endeavour to find out. As an illegible amuensis [amanuensis] to her legal husband she must be invaluable.

Your excuse for the want of your usual pro[m]ptitude in writing is good & sufficient. I always feel sure you will write when you can & have a good reason for it when you do not.

I am very glad that Henry had so good an opportunity to go east. Did Mr. Gridley go on to New Haven or was Henry to go on from New York alone? I have been expecting to hear from him of his safe arrival & hope to do so in the course of a day or two. It will be lonesome for him for a time till he gets a little acquainted. I can appreciate your feelings at parting with him especially at this time. 'Tis indeed "a step from boyhood towards manhood" & I only hope in the right direction.

You shall not be disappointed in your visit east. When I leave Uncle Sam's employ for good you shall come east to go home with me.

I have written Dave in regard to John telling him that I thought I could give him a place or get him one. For some reasons I would rather get him a place on some of the other gun boats than give him one on the *Monitor*, as I think it would be much pleasanter. On them he would be more by himself & not be brought in such close contact with the sailors as on board of us where we have so little room to eat, drink & sleep. Here he would have to swing his hammock with the sailors & eat on the same deck with them, though he would mess with some of the other petty officers. On board a larger vessel with more men his pay would be more & then the idea of having a person under me as a subordinate whom I have considered an equal at home is repugnant. However if John thinks the place will suit him he shall have it as soon as I can dispose of my present steward, if I can do no better for him.

No wonder our lists of killed & wounded count up so fearfully when such men as A. B. Moore† are chosen to lead troops into battle. Why will they persist in selecting ignorant politicians to fill such positions when one false move on the battle field may cost hundreds of brave men their lives & deprive the country of their services. The history of the war is full of instances where hundreds of valuable lives have been sacrificed through the ignorance of

---

* British archaeologist Austen H. Layard.
† La Salle County politician Absolom B. Moore*, colonel of the 104th Illinois Infantry.

incompetent officers. 'Tis horrible to think of the idea of placing the lives of a thousand men at the disposal of such a person. It cannot be said that we have no suitable persons to entrust with such a command. Our armies are full of them. Good tried men, true as steel, who have proved themselves equal to any emergency on many a hard fought battle field. Take them from the ranks, they are worthy of it. We must not expect to succeed so long as our armies are officered in this way. Such officers may satisfy raw recruits but not old soldiers. They appreciate the value of competent men to lead them into battle. I know how these latter feel for I have heard them talk.

I have read Mr. Campbell's* address & like it for no other reason than that he supports the President. The currency question I don't know anything about, therefore can't criticise it.

Thursday, 11th—I have neglected finishing your letter till now, having since I left off been out of the vessel on business most of the time except evenings & then the mosquitoes are so exceedingly annoying that I find it impossible to write.

Another change this morning. Capt. Stevens has been relieved of his command & Commander Bankhead takes his place.† Capt. S. has been ordered to the command of the *Sebago* at Port Royal. We parted with him with regret for he had won the respect & esteem of us all. We could better appreciate his many good qualities after having endured so much from our former brute of a Captain. The short time that he has been on board has made our vessel seem like another place. His treatment of his officers & men has been so kind & pleasant.

I enclose you two letters just rec'd from New Haven thinking you would wish to see them. I feel very much relieved to hear that Henry has reached there safely. I send you papers almost every day. My kind love to yourself & the children.

W.

No. 39—

Monitor
Off Newport News
Sunday, Sept. 14th, 1862

Dear Anna,

Your No. 16 containing the boys' photographs reached me last night. The pictures as you say do not stand very high as works of art, but I think them quite good likenesses & as such prize them highly. I wish I had yours & baby's

---

* The La Salle politician.
† Stevens was relieved of command for being too inebriated to entertain visitors, one of whom was the captain of the USS *New Ironsides*, a strong opponent of drinking in the Navy. Replacing him was John P. Bankhead*.

Off Newport News (August to October 1862)

to put with them. Should I go to New Haven I mean to have Hen's taken again.

I got a letter from Henry last Friday telling me of his safe arrival [in New Haven] & giving me some account of his journey, which I judge must have been quite pleasant, especially the trip down the river which he seemed to enjoy very much. I answered him immediately as I thought he might be a little home sick & a letter would do him good. Besides I want to encourage him to write often as a means of improvement. You must miss him very much, not only his noise but his services — his head, hands & feet as well as his tongue. I only hope he will not take it into his head to teaze Hattie's children when he gets a little better acquainted.

The first Confederate shin plaster I get hold of I will send you to pay off your indebtedness to Hough.

You ask me how I came to get the [*New York*] *Herald* gratis? I met one of its correspondents one day when I came down from James river & finding I was from up the river & from the *Monitor* he handed me his card & wanted to know if I couldn't give him some news for some items for the paper. I told him all I knew that I dared to, he took my address & I have rec'd the paper ever since. I think it a good paper for news but I don't subscribe to all its sentiments, neither do I to any of the other papers that I read. We have established a newspaper fund on board, each one of the mess paying in a certain sum, & take two Baltimore, two Philadelphia & three New York papers, so that now we keep pretty well posted in what is going on about us. But for a long time while we were up the river we were without papers except a stray one we now & then got hold of. It is a great deprivation I assure you. Only those who have experienced it can fully appreciate it. I hope I shall get the paper containing the piece of your Father's as I would like very much to see it.*

Politics *rage* so at home (if you can call it by that name) that I shall hardly dare to shew myself there lest I be eaten up by one party or the other. But if I come they must all understand it is to see my friends, not to talk politics. As to politics I don't know anything about them, except so far as they relate to assisting the administration to bring the war to a speedy & triumphant close. *Every other* consideration should be laid aside till that is accomplished. Of one thing I am fully & firmly satisfied, that the axe is laid at the root of slavery & its downfall is certain. It may not be as speedy as some would desire but it is none the less sure. I enclose a scrap cut from some of the papers which reiterate what I wrote you some time ago, opinions which are daily being strengthened. I earnestly wish that *all* others could see it in the same light & feel that whatever aided to crush the rebellion aided also to extinguish slavery. I hope this war of words may not be the means of breaking up our pleasant social circle. These are gloomy looking times for our country but I

---

* See letter of September 17, 1862.

feel convinced that right & justice will yet prevail & that McClelland if left untrameled by demagogues & politicians will fully come up to the expectations of his friends in the defeat of his enemies both *north* & south.

The piece you sent me about Capt. Worden is ridiculously untrue unless he is changed to a very different man from what he was when I knew him.

We were discussing the probabilities of the next Presidency at the breakfast table this morning when Capt. Bankhead (who by the way is a cousin of Magruder's*) said, "McClelland will never be President, he is to[o] high minded [and] honorable a man to mix up with the dirty, dishonest politicians of the Capital."

By my last letter to you enclosing one from your father you will see what he thinks of recovering Melzar's remains.† I fear the chance is but a small one, especially as the enemy holds possession of the ground. Still I might go under a flag of truce if I could be provided with one, but that would be doubtful. I would not give the matter up without a more extensive search.

The daily expectation of seeing the *Merrimac* [*Richmond*] down from Richmond keeps us pretty closely confined. Our hopes of being allowed to run around some, to Norfolk, Craney island & other places are disappointed, though we are allowed to take our boats & go sailing, fishing &c as much as we please.

We are feasting on the finest fish, crabs, oysters &c in the greatest abundance, catching them [our]selves adds to their flavour. A few rods from where we lie a small boat can be loaded with oysters in an hour. The bottom of the river is covered with them & in a very short time, from the side of the ship, we can catch crabs or fish enough for a meal. We have the very finest of sweet potatoes, dry, sweet & mealy, in abundance, cheaper than the common ones. Watermelons grow very large but no better flavoured than with us. Fruit in this region must succeed finely if properly managed. We went after peaches again to day but found the trees had been stripped, nothing but some hard green ones left.

We lie right between the sunken *Cumberland* & the wreck of the *Congress* in the neighborhood of our memorable fight, but a stone's through [throw] from the shore. The numerous large barracks are filled with sick & wounded to the number of about 2000. I went through them with Mr. Meech‡, the Chaplain, & saw many a pitiable sight. The buildings are clean, well ventilated & the patients have good care, but it is not *home*.

Monday evening [September 15]—We hear good news from our army, that Burnside has defeated the rebels & is driving them towards McClelland who is between them & the Potomac which stream has risen so they cannot

---

* Confederate Major General John Magruder.
† Since Keeler never mentioned this again, he must never have made the attempt.
‡ William W. Meech (1825-1902), chaplain of the Union hospital at Newport News.

Off Newport News (August to October 1862)

cross.* We all hope it may prove true. Capt. B. who is a S. Carolinian by birth, said he hoped we would take no prisoners. "How so sir, why not?" "The bayonet," he replied, "we want no paroled prisoners to fight over again. I wouldn't let one of them cross the Potomac alive."

If you don't hear from me as frequently as you would like, attribute it to the dearth of news & quantity of mosquitoes, more particularly the latter. Love to yourself. Kisses to the children.

William

[Marginalia] If the news is true it may make great changes for us.† I don't know what to say about that tormented range. If I was sure of coming home I should say try & get along till I come, but if I can't come get a stove. I hope the thing will be mended soon. Have rec'd the LaSalle paper from Fan. Your Father speaks my sentiments exactly.‡

All quiet on board the *Monitor* up to this date, Tuesday morning [September 16]. No fight nor any prospect of any whatever the papers may say to the contrary. If you see any sensation articles in them it has all been caused by our testing some hand grenades on board.

No. 40—

U.S.S. Monitor
Off Newport News
Wednesday, Sept. 17th, 1862

Dear Anna,

Yours of the 11th (No. 17) I found lying on my desk on my return just now from a visit to one of the gun boats. As I have a little spare time before supper & lamp light & the mosquitoes are in a partially quiescent state I will commence a reply. There is but little use in attempting to write with a light in my room for the mosquitos would drive me from it.

No wonder you are "awful mad" at the abuse of your Father.§ It would be enough to raise the indignation of any one to see such a person abused. I

---

* The Battle of South Mountain. On September 14 Burnside defeated the Confederate forces guarding the gaps across the mountains to the east of Lee's army which had crossed the Potomac River into Maryland ten days earlier.
† The news of Burnside's victory, perhaps.
‡ Keeler is perhaps referring to the sentiments expressed by his father-in-law in his letter to the *New Haven Palladium* (see next letter).
§ The "abuse" Henry Dutton suffered was for a letter he wrote to the *New Haven Palladium* (August 29, 1862) in support of Lincoln's enigmatic response to Horace Greeley, the editor of the arch-Republican *New York Tribune*, in which Lincoln stated that his paramount objective was to save the Union, not to save or destroy slavery. In his letter Dutton stated that "our only direct object should be to crush the rebellion. . . . If the result of blows thus given should be the destruction of social or moral evils [i.e., slavery], we should have cause to rejoice. Neither the President nor Congress can emancipate slaves. . . . They cannot unmake a slave, because they never made one. They can free slaves by confiscation, but

console myself with the reflection that he is so far above the abuse of the puny fools, that their idiotic drivelings affect him as the waves do some old time worn rock which has withstood their surges undisturbed for centuries. I will not attempt to defend him. He does not need it & I suppose cares less about the snarling curs at his heels than we do. I am perfectly willing that his memory should go down to posterity with that of his self constituted judges & let posterity decide who was the true patriot, who *acted* for the good of his country, yes & who was the *real* benefactor of the slave. In these times it is deeds that tell, not empty words & windy meaningless speeches. A person that sets himself up to judge others, especially those above him, must make it apparent that he is competent to the task or his impotent efforts will soon sink him to a still lower level. I am just as confidant that your Father is right, & that events not far in the future will prove him to be so, as I am that tomorrow's sun will rise. Who are the true patriots? Those who give themselves, their friends & children to the country without a murmur or complaint, or those empty narrow minds who by their comfortable fire sides indulge in invection & abuse because their own narrow minded & selfish aims are not carried out. I claim to be as strong & as good an abolitionist as can be found in the country & I candidly think that every effort made to crush this rebellion, caused by slavery, is a blow for freedom. If abolitionism consists in abuse of the patriots, the working men of these trying times, then I must confess that I have been deluded & I wash my hands of it. The only fault I find with your Father is in placing Pres't Lincoln & Greeley in the same category — Niagara falls & a pewter squirt.

Nothing has occured since I last wrote you to give us any idea of when we are going to Washington, or whether we are going at all or not, though we have had the promise. It may be that the recent successes of our army may be the means of sending us up the river again to Fort Darling. I would like very much to walk the streets of the rebel capital as one of its conquerors.

We hear one day that the *Merrimac* [*Richmond*] is in the river in the neighborhood of City Point. The next day contradicts it & then we hear by some "perfectly reliable" person that she will not be completed for some weeks. Then the "very intelligent" individual follows him with the information that she is a failure & will never be of service. We think we know pretty well what she is from plans found in the *Teazer*. When she does come, if at all, we do not mean to be taken unawares for a most vigilant lookout is maintained day & night & we live in a constant state of preparation. In fact we are living our old life of watching the *Merrimac* [*Virginia*] over again. Ten minutes warning at any time will place us in readiness for whatever may turn up. We are allowed to go about on the water wherever we please, if not too far from the

---

this power should be used not to benefit the slave, but only to crush the rebellion." Although he hated slavery and would rejoice in its demise, Dutton believed that the Constitution forbade the federal government from waging a war for the purpose of destroying slavery.

vessel, but have but few liberties ashore. Capt. B. sent to the Flag ship a few days ago for permission for one of our officers to go to Norfolk. The reply was "allow no one to leave the vessel whose absence would impair its fighting effectiveness."

The 139th New York regiment has just come down here to go into camp & of course visitors are plenty. They are new recruits & have not the "old soldier" look that the troops around Harrison's Landing had.

In my last I added a postscript telling you not to believe any newspaper reports of a fight here. We were trying some hand grenades on our deck which burst with a loud report. The smoke & noise was seen & heard from the shore just as some one was leaving for Old Point. They carried terrible reports of the *Merrimac* [*Richmond*] coming down the river, the *Monitor* firing signal guns &c. The Baltimore boat just on the point of leaving the dock carried the news with her I presume for a flaming article. How little it takes to make a big story.

Friday, Sept. 19th—We are all feeling so jubilant over the news.* I hope what is to come will subtract nothing from it. How about McClellan now, will his enemies give him credit for what he has accomplished?† If they do the[y] are possessed of more honor & generosity than I credit them with.

It may not be generally know[n] that McC. could have taken the position of Commander [General] in Chief that Halleck now holds. Such is the fact however. Pres. Lincoln when he was up the river at Harrison's Landing urged it upon him. He declined & it was upon his solicitation that Halleck rec'd the appointment. This does not look as if the Administration had lost confidence in him. All these things will come out in time & the future will do him justice, if the present refuses it.

What great changes a few hours are producing in our country's history. They are pages written in blood and record the cost of freedom.

I see by the paper also that Charleston has been attacked. This is I think incorrect as we have nothing but wooden gun boats there which would not prove very effective. My opinion is that no effort will be made there till a number of our iron clads are completed when this nursery of treason will be extinguished. I hope the *Monitor* will play a part.

Just done dinner. Bill of fare, oyster soup, fried oysters, boiled & fried crabs, broiled trout, roast beef & broiled chicken. In the way of fruit, grapes, peaches, pears, fresh figs & apples. Not so bad is it? It goes to make up our scanty fare while up the river.

---

* The Union victory at the Battle of Antietam on September 17.
† McClellan's days, however, were numbered, for after his victory at Antietam he allowed Lee's army to cross back over the Potomac unscathed. This was the final straw for Lincoln, who on November 7, 1862 relieved McClellan of field command for good.

Civil War Years: USS *Monitor* (1862)

I return the piece of poetry you sent me. I like the sentiment better than the poetry. Tell Father that McClelland is not a goblin or a demon. I hope he will discover some good quality in him yet.

Love to all. Lots of kisses to yourself & the little ones.

William

No. 41—

U.S.S. Monitor
Off Newport News
Sunday, Sept. 21st, 1862

Dear Anna,

Here I commence my letter without the remotest idea of what I am going to fill it with. Ourselves & everything about us have settled down into the steady sober round of monotonous every day life leaving but little to be said under that head but what I have already told you.

This has been a sort of a cloudy rainy disagreeable day, close warm & muggy. Our army visitors are glad to remain in their quarters, I suppose, as but few of them have been on board to day.

Yesterday I spent at Old Point very pleasantly. Went on board of the *Sonoma* & passed a portion of the forenoon & took dinner with our former commander Capt. Stevens. I found quite a number of army & navy acquaintances on shore whom I was very glad to meet. I also made the acquaintance of two or three Baltimore folks, wea[l]thy people, who pressed me very strongly to call on them if I ever passed through Baltimore, which I intend to if I can as I found them very pleasant people.

The *Monitor* is an open Sesame wherever I go. I only regret that we were so unfortunate in our commander through the past season. With a good officer such as Capt. Stevens the *Monitor* would have maintained & added to the reputation she made under Capt. Worden instead of spending the whole season in a state of torpid inactivity. Such a Commodore as was at the head of the fleet & such as officer in command of the vessel would ruin the reputation the finest ship could make under the best & bravest officers. What our present captain [Bankhead] will make it is hard to say. He is still & quiet, very gentlemanly, but seems cool & distant. None of that genial warmth of character that attatched us all so strongly to Capt. Stevens. I believe him to be a brave man, but when he is tried we will know him better. He was saying the other day that with the reputation the *Monitor* has made, a person, if he lost her, had better loose his life with her. We find it immeasurably more pleasant with him on board than we did with Jeffers. I shall always regard that man as a small, narrow, contracted, selfish, brutal piece of humanity & I sincerely believe to day that his entire sympathies are with the South. Nothing but selfish motives keep him where he is. The dollars & cents control him.

Off Newport News (August to October 1862)

The value of time & the immense importance of quick decided movements in our operations were never more fully manifested than in many of the movements of our navy in the river here the past summer & never were decided, resolute, energetic men more needed to direct & carry out the important work which should & could have been done by our vessels while we have been in the river. With the proper men the most important results could have been secured to the country, but instead of this our James river fleet [Flotilla] was placed under the control of imbeciles & old fogies whose do nothing policy has kept the whole fleet inactive & useless the entire season. By reference to some of my old letters you will find that our whole progress when we first went up the river was marked by a sluggishness of action almost criminal. Dawdling along up the stream, stopping here & there to conciliate half a dozen poor harmless darkies whose good or ill will could not affect us, allowing flags of truce to go by us up the stream & carry the news of our approach, anchoring off City Point & wasting the precious moments in glorifying the Star Spangled banner to the small remnant of poor white trash remaining in the place, carelessly running aground every few miles of our progress up the river & all this while the stream was bearing down to us indisputable evidences of an attempt to obstruct the river & dispute its passage. So it has proved we know now to a certainty that twenty four hours before we attacked Fort Darling not a gun was in position, not a plan was laid for its defence, the obstructions were very incomplete. The *Monitor* alone could have steamed up to the city [Richmond] & had it at the mercy of her guns. Never was a place in a greater panic than the rebel capitol after they learned of our approach till they knew we were driven back. Just so too after driving back the *Merrimac* — for a month while she was in dock repairing, we could have gone up to Norfolk at any time without interruption except from the batteries ashore which we could have passed without difficulty.

What a pity we could not have had a *man* here suited to the exigencies of the times. How much the *Monitor* might have accomplished had a proper person "held the wheel" we can only surmise. We know what she did do & we judge from that what she could have done had the opportunities that presented themselves been followed up. We imagine Norfolk taken a few days after the fight with the *Merrimac*, that great naval bugbear captured, the James river blockade opened & the transports with McClelland's army landing his forces at City Point as his base of operations on Richmond, as was his original intentions. It is vain to regret the past but I cannot often help thinking what great changes all this might have brought about & how different might be the present situation of affairs.

We are collecting a large body of troops at Suffolk, mostly new levies. Some 15,000 being there now & more daily arriving. What they are for I do not know, but there are rumors of large bodies of rebels in that part of the country apparently threatening Norfolk. From Suffolk they are in rail road communication with Petersburg & Richmond & I have sometimes thought it was the intention to advance on Petersburg & be ready to cut off the retreat of the rebels south when McC. drives them out of Richmond, or attack it on the south while McC. tries it on the north. A few weeks now will tell.

Remember me to all our friends. I hope something will happen that will help me to make my next sheet more interesting. Lots of love & kisses to yourself & the children.

William

No. 42—

U.S.S. Monitor
Off Newport News
Sept. 22nd, 1862

Dear Anna,

Like Micawber* I have been waiting since my last "for something to turn up" out of which I could manufacture a letter. But "nary" turn do I find after patiently waiting & vigilantly watching. Not a ripple disturbs the smooth current of our daily life from which could be extracted even with the high pressure power of a newspaper reporter the material for a single item. We go fishing, crabbing, oystering, sailing, rowing & visiting among our camp friends but these are getting to be stale & uninteresting & we are all beginning to long for a change.

I have lost my Bill [William Scott]. Not a pecuniary loss of a "green back" bearing the likeness of "Old Abe" but my wooley headed, good natured, factotum. Lost by promotion to our old Steward's place [Lawrence Murray]. To be sure the bread is sometimes rather heavy, the sweet potatoes underdone & the beef nearly raw, but these minor things we put into the scale of our great sacrifice to our country's cause & hope for *better things* to come.

Robert fills, or rather is supposed to fill, his place.† Now Robert is a real genuine contraband & a capture of mine at Old Point. I was down there one day while mourning the loss of Billy & seeing this chap asked where he lived.

"No where now massa."

"Well where's your Master?"

"Dunno massa, spec he's dun gone wid de sogers to fight."

"Well where did he live?"

"Yorktown sir."

"How come you down here?"

"Massa he go off & leff us all den I come down here."

"What did you used to do?"

"Wait on massa's table sir."

---

* The eternal optimist in Dickens' *David Copperfield* whose guiding principle was that "something will turn up."
† Robert Cook. The 18-year-old escaped slave enlisted at Hampton Roads on September 8, 1862 as a first-class boy. He drowned when the *Monitor* sank off Cape Hatteras.

Off Newport News (August to October 1862)

I found he was just the individual I wanted & telling him to follow me have given him a home on the *Monitor* where he will be paid for his labour by Uncle Sam as a free man. He is a bright smart fellow & appears well pleased with the change in his condition. What nonsense to say such fellows can't take care of themselves.

Wednesday, 24th—Something has turned up at last. The very greatest event which any combination of circumstances could possibly have turned up in our Country's revolving wheel of fortune — the President's proclamation freeing all slaves in rebelious states after the first of Jan'y. Now isn't this enough to satisfy the most radical abolitionist — if not, what more could they ask. I am not at all surprised. I knew it must come but did not expect it quite so soon. I felt satisfied from the nature of events that it must come about & have so expressed myself to you, adding that I felt satisfied to wait patiently the time.

Congratulate friend Hough. I suppose now the President must be one after his own heart & McClelland a model general. Tell him if long waiting has not soured his usually mild, peaceable & genial disposition to throw up his hat & cheer. But if from long suspense & continued waiting his philanthropy is at all disposed to curdle I would advise homeopathic doses of the *N.Y. Herald*. His system has been so reduced by the malpractice of Dr. Greely that extremely light doses of my prescription should at first be tried with great caution.*

Sept. 27th—Yours of the 18th (No. 18) reached me day before yesterday & found me sick on my back with a slight fever. The curative effects of your letter have placed me on my feet again though rather weak. But I hope to be very soon as good as new. Don't magnify it into anything serious. The attack has not been enough so as to make it necessary for me to use any medicine, the M.D. telling me that with my constitution nature would do more for me than medicine.

At the time your letter reached me I was beginning to worry (I was just in the frame of mind for it) for fear that something was the matter at home as it was eleven days since your last one was received & I knew you would not neglect writing unless for some good reason. I am realy sorry that baby is worrisome, but the poor little thing must suffer with her mouth. Don't neglect getting medical advice when it is needed. I am inclined to think that her system is out of order & requires building up & strengthening by a proper use of tonics. I think you had better see either Dr. Brown or Bry about her.

What do you think has annoyed me excessively for the last three or four days? You know when one is slightly feverish a trifle serves to annoy them & when once in the mind it is exceedingly difficult to get it out. It was that I

---

* Keeler was recommending that his Republican friend take a mild dose of the *New York Herald*, a Democratic paper which was highly supportive of McClellan, in contrast to Horace Greeley's arch-Republican *New York Tribune*, which wasn't.

was going to be sick & should have to send for you & you would be obliged to come on *without your teeth*. I believe it kept me awake one whole night.

There is still a talk about our going to Washington. The *Ironsides* which is hourly expected here we hope will relieve us.* A board of survey has condemned our engines & boilers, stating that in our present state we were "in a very precarious condition." I hope their report will effect our release for a time. It would do me good I know, especially if I could get home, though outside of my own family I should not anticipate much pleasure while there is so much political animosity. If I do go home it will be with a firm resolve to have nothing to do with politics the few days I shall be able to stay.

Ever since I have lived in LaSalle, Ottawa has contrived to monopolise all the offices of any account & Mr. Hough has been one of its bitterist opposers on that very ground. Not being there I am not able to judge, but from here I cannot see the consistency of his course especially when he opposes one of our own townsmen, a man whom we all know to be good & true & who has declared his resolve to support the Administration. I am truly surprised that Father should be among his opposers. I know nothing of Cook, pro or con, except that he has always been an Ottawa politician.† Mr. Campbell I do know & as long as he would give his support to the Administration it would be enough for me, every other consideration would be a minor one & laid aside.

I still hope to eat some of our grapes with you. Am glad that they have done so nicely. We have very nice fruit sent us three times a week from Baltimore. Now don't neglect getting some medical advice for baby. I hope to hear that she is better soon. How I want to see the children. Did you think I would be absent so long when I left? I didn't. My best love to yourself & kisses to the children. Remember me to all our friends, personal & *political*. Tell Dave I have not forgotten John. Wish I had him here now.

William

No. 43—

U.S.S. *Monitor*
Sept. 30th, 1862

Dear Anna,

I have but a moment to spare. We have just rec'd orders to go to Washington for repairs & are now on our way there, between Newport News & Old Point & I want to get this in the mail at Old Point as it will reach you sooner. How long we shall be there & whether I can leave to see any of you I cannot tell but hope to be able to. Will write you again as soon as we get to Washington. Am sound again, well but not quite as strong as ever. Rec'd your

---

* The *New Ironsides* had been sent back to Philadelphia for repairs in late August and returned to Hampton Roads on September 23.
† Burton C. Cook, a lawyer in Ottawa, IL and a Republican politician.

Off Newport News (August to October 1862)

No. 19 enclosing one from Henry yesterday & by the same mail rec'd one from him. He is homesick, poor fellow & I don't wonder — a year will be a long time. *Was very glad to hear* that baby was better. Hope she will continue to gain. With much love to yourself & all friends.

William

No. 44—

U.S.S. Monitor
Potomac River
Oct. 1st, 1862

Dear Anna,

We left Old Point yesterday about noon bidding good bye to all its memorable (to us) surroundings, for we don't know how long. I wrote you a hasty note just to let you know that we had departed & our destination.

We steamed slowly along up the Chesapeak in tow of a small tug crippled like ourselves & at daylight this morning entered the Potomac.[*] The river through the day has been quite wide & we have kept at such a distance from either bank that nothing was visible on them.

The weather has been beautiful, the water smooth, & a cool delicious breeze. Smooth as it was in the Chesapeak last night it would manage to wash up on our decks occasionally making it necessary to close our deck lights which turned us all out below about midnight, the air was so close & stifling.

We came to anchor at dark, the pilot not thinking it safe to run through the night. Of course we are all impatient to get to Washington & do not like the delay but the safety of the vessel is the first thing to be considered.

Thursday, Oct. 2nd—Our anchor was up & we were under way as soon as it was light enough to see this morning. The river, the fore part of the day, presented very much the same appearance it did yesterday. In the afternoon it grew narrower & the banks were more plainly to be seen. They were for the most part a succession of smooth undulating knolls looking as if they had been covered with crops. The northern shore was by far the most promising in appearance — but though the banks had the appearance of being more generally cultivated they lacked the fine buildings & tasty lawns that adorn the banks of the James.

Although the most beautiful & romantic sites abounded, few or none of them were improved. The buildings, all that could be seen, were miserable, tumble down shanties & numerous large fishing houses or sheds for curing fish. The aristocratic mansions, if any there were, were placed back from the river & were not visible.

---

[*] The *Monitor*'s hull was so encrusted with marine life that she had to be towed.

Civil War Years: USS *Monitor* (1862)

About the middle of the afternoon we passed Cockpit Point, Aquia Creek & other places whose names were so familiar about a year ago.* Now the batteries are destroyed & deserted. But few persons were to be seen in our slow progress up the s[t]ream, the houses for the most part appeared to be deserted & everything had a dreary desolate look.

Just at sunset we passed the place of all others, Mt. Vernon.† I was however disappointed in its appearance as from what I had heard I expected to find a fine smooth grassy lawn sloping down to the water's edge, crowned at the top by the old mansion. Such however is not the case or at least such is not the view you get of it from the river. As you approach it & Mt. Vernon is pointed out to you, you see a chimney or two & a few patches of white through the thick forest like trees with which the rough projecting point of land on which it stands is covered. As you get opposite you see a little more of the building & now & then a small portion of the sloping lawn on which it stands. Still not enough is in view to give you any idea of its general form or appearance. The best view is just after you have passed it. You can then see through an opening in the trees a portion of the piazza & lawn in front. The trees about it are so thick it gives it the appearance of being in the midst of a dense rough forest & is not at all pleasing. Should I have an opportunity I mean to make a visit there.

We are at anchor now (10 o'clock) for the night about ten miles below the City which we hope to see in good season to morrow morning. Till you are differently directed send my letters to "*Washington Navy Yard.*" My next letter will be from that city & I hope will tell you that I am coming home.

Good night. Much love & many kisses. Fat[ten] baby up before I get home. I shall almost dread to see the poor little *lean* thing.

Friday morning [October 3], 9 o'clock—We are just drawing up to the navy yard dock, everything is confusion & excitement. The Capitol, White House, Treasury, Patent Office, Monument, Arlington Heights &c are all in sight. The hill tops in all directions are crowded with fortifications & their sloping sides covered with the canvass cities of our soldiers.

You shall hear from me again soon. Just now there is a call for the Paymaster so good bye for the present.

William

---

* Batteries along the Potomac River that the Confederates had abandoned seven months earlier.
† George Washington's home.

OFF NEWPORT NEWS (AUGUST TO OCTOBER 1862)

> U.S. Steamer *King Philip*
> Washington Navy Yard
> Oct. 6th, 1862

Dear Anna,

The last time I wrote you I thought I should be the bearer of the next letter myself but so far have been disappointed from the vexatious delays in getting funds from the Department to pay of[f] our Officers & men, as I cannot leave until that is done. I have made out an application for four weeks' leave of absence which I have every reason to think will be granted but it takes a long time to get any such thing through the red tape of the Department.* Capt. Bankhead has left on three weeks' leave. Before he went he made such arrangements with the Dept. as he thought would procure me leave for what is considered a very unusual length of time.

I did not wish to raise any expectations that will not be realised, but I think you may look for me in about a week after you get this. I shall stop 24 hours in New York, about the same length of time in New Haven & a few hours in Utica & then for home direct. Our vessel will be detained here for 8 or 10 weeks. I shall want for John Brown to return with me, that is if he desires the place.

We have all been sent from the *Monitor* to this vessel which is anchored in the river just off the Navy Yard. She is like the North River Steamers, fine accommodations, large cabins, one of which we use for a ward room, others for talking, reading, writing, lounging &c. The state rooms are large, comfortable & airy — & *inhabited* — but the change from our cramped quarters on the *Monitor* is most agreeable.

Everything was tumbled out of the *Monitor* in the greatest haste, no time to pack anything. I *shoveled* my effects into one or two old flour barrels & dumped them onto my state room floor on this boat, a huge pile of clean shirts & dirty ones, candles, ink stands, boots, breeches, papers, tooth brushes, iron safe & *crockery* &c &c. It looks as if it would take no small time to sort over the pile & find what there is there. If I get my leave granted there won't be much sorting, I shall just put a shirt & a collar in my carpet bag & leave, locking my state room door to wait my return.

The *Monitor* & her officers are the lions of the day. We got here Friday morning & the news soon spread drawing crowds, all that could pass the guards at the entrance. On Saturday the Yard was thrown open & they rushed in by thousands & thousands, whole regiments of soldiers were marched from their camps by their officers to see the sight.

Our decks were covered & our ward room filled with ladies & on going into my state room I found a party of the "dear delightful creatures" making their toilet before my glass, using my combs & brushes. We couldn't go to

---

* Keeler's four-week leave was granted on October 10.

any part of the vessel without coming in contact with petticoats. There appeared to be a general turn out of the sex in the city. There was women with children & women without children, & women — hem — expecting. An extensive display of lower extremities was made going up & down our steep ladders.

The docks were lined with carriages — & it was in fact a perfect jam — no caravan or circus ever collected such a crowd, not only in numbers but respectability. I made a large number of what would no doubt be very pleasant acquaintances if I had the time & disposition to follow them up — as all that I shewed over the vessel gave me their address with an invitation to call. It was the intention to give us a public reception but we came upon them unawares & gave them no time. About dinner time the crowd was so great that we were obliged to station a guard of marines on the dock to keep the people off till the boys could set the table & we could eat.

Yesterday the vessel was turned over to the mechanics of the Yard, so that now we have nothing to do with her. To day at different times I shewed Mr. Lincoln's private Sec'y[*] & Mr. Hatch (one of our Ill. state officials)[†] over her, then one of Gen. McClellan's aids, who gave me a pass to go *any where within the lines* of Gen. McC.'s division, then Gov. Andrews[‡]. Gen. Banks was also on board. In fact there has been no end to company.

You will probably expect me to give you some little description of Washington & will no doubt be surprised to hear that I have not been outside the Yard gates. Such is the fact. I am straining every nerve & using all my time to get through with my business here so as to start for home. When I return I intend to do the city. To morrow I shall be obliged to visit the Department on business when I shall probably have an opportunity to see some of the lions[§].

Your No. 20 reached me to day. I was realy glad to hear of baby's recovery & hope to witness it before long. I count the hours I assure [you] till I can find myself homeward bound & I most sincerely hope nothing will arise to disappoint me. You may imagine me bringing the next letter. Till then good by with my best kiss[es] for yourself & the children.

William

---

[*] John G. Nicolay probably.
[†] Ozias M. Hatch, Illinois secretary of state.
[‡] John A. Andrew, governor of Massachusetts.
[§] To do some sightseeing.

Cape Hatteras (November to December 1862)

> *The telegraph has probably informed you before this of the loss of the* Monitor *& also of my safety. My escape was a very narrow one. My personal effects at this time may be summed up thus — 1 pr. pants, 1 do. stockings, 1 shirt. In fact I lost everything but the few clothes I kept on, most of them having been thrown off for a swim. I have been through a night of horrors that would have appalled the stoutest heart.* (4 January 1863)

When Keeler returned to the Washington Navy Yard after his four-week furlough, he found everything in disarray on board the *Monitor*. Workmen were madly putting the finishing touches on the alterations. Fresh white paint covered the once dark woodwork in the officers' quarters. Tools, lumber and machinery lay scattered about. The engine had been completely overhauled and was working like new. To help ensure that water did not enter the vessel from heavy seas, a 30-foot tall telescopic smoke pipe had been installed over the low smokestack boxes. To make the vessel more livable, the berth deck had been widened and a large blower had been installed to improve ventilation.

In addition to the changes in the vessel, there were also changes in personnel. Keeler's friend Acting Volunteer Lieutenant William Flye, who joined the *Monitor* immediately after the fight with the *Virginia*, had been detached and given a separate command. The two would remain in touch for the remainder of the war. Acting Assistant Surgeon Daniel Logue had resigned and was replaced by 24-year-old Grenville Weeks. Like his predecessor, Weeks would also share with Keeler his correspondence with his "lady love" back home. Two new officers who would not survive the *Monitor*'s final voyage were Third Assistant Engineer Samuel Lewis and New Haven resident Acting Ensign Norman Atwater.

On November 8, with the repairs completed, the *Monitor* left for Hampton Roads. While stationed at their old anchorage off Newport News on the lookout for the CSS *Richmond*, the first of Ericsson's new monitors, the USS *Passaic*, arrived. They waited anxiously for another of those monitors, the USS *Montauk*, commanded by their esteemed first captain John Worden, which arrived only after they departed. The *Monitor* and the new monitors were to be towed south for an attack on Charleston, South Carolina. On their way down the *Monitor*, *Passaic* and *Montauk* were also to shell out the forts guarding the mouth of the Cape Fear River, the entrance to the Confederacy's vital port city of Wilmington, but that attack never materialized.

On December 29 the *Monitor* left Hampton Roads in tow of the USS *Rhode Island*. Although the day began clear and pleasant, by the time they reached Cape Hatteras two days later, a ferocious gale was blowing. Huge waves rolled over the deck, crashing against the pilot house and turret. As the *Monitor* plowed headfirst into the storm, the bottom of the hull smashed with unrelenting force against the waves. The pumps were no longer capable of dealing with the amount of water pouring in between the upper deck and lower hull which had begun to separate. By 9 pm the water was a foot deep in the engine room. By 10 pm the water had reached the furnaces and extinguished the fires, sealing the *Monitor*'s fate.

Bankhead signaled to the *Rhode Island* that they were sinking. Minutes passed before the *Rhode Island* finally responded. Fearing that the two tethered ships would collide, Bankhead ordered the hawser connecting them cut, and asked for volunteers. The first two men who tried were swept into the sea and drowned. After nearly being washed away as he was hacking away at the five-inch diameter hawser, the third volunteer, Acting Master Louis Stodder, managed to cut it and returned safely to the top of the turret, where all who were not operating the vessel had sought refuge.

By then the *Rhode Island* was close enough to launch lifeboats to rescue the *Monitor*'s crew. Bankhead and several other officers went below to bring out those still left in the ship's interior. Several men who were either too sick or too afraid refused to leave their bunks and were left to their fate. Keeler also went below to retrieve his account books. Descending the turret ladder, he made his way to his stateroom which was waist-deep in water. After groping around in the pitch black he collected his books and papers only to realize that to carry them back across the wave-washed deck would be suicidal. By the time he returned empty-handed to the turret, the first rescue boat had reached the *Monitor*. Ordered to lead the first group of men to the lifeboat, Keeler was swept into the sea by a wave that carried him a dozen yards from the vessel, but was saved from certain death by another wave that swept him back to safety. Bankhead remained on board the *Monitor* until the end, pleading in vain with the few men who still remained on top of the turret too afraid to risk the trip across the open deck.

At 1 am on December 31 the *Monitor* slipped below the waves. Four officers and twelve crew members were lost, some swept into the sea during the rescue, the rest going down with the ship.

Letters of special note: November 17 (change in personnel; description of the alterations to the *Monitor*); December 20 (thoughts on Burnside's defeat at Fredericksburg); December 25 (Christmas dinner on board the *Monitor*); January 4 (short note stating that the *Monitor* was lost and that he was safe); January 6 (account of the *Monitor*'s final voyage).

No. 45—

Monitor, Newport News,
Nov. 11th, 1862

Dear Anna,

I wrote you a hasty note from the Washington Navy Yard just as we were about leaving to tell you of my safe arrival & probable destination.

Cape Hatteras (November to December 1862)

It was well I left home as I did, as with the time I was delayed at Harrisburg and Baltimore I did not reach Washington till late Thursday evening. I went immediately to the Navy Yard having found on board the train from Baltimore, Mr. Stodder, one of our officers, whose company served to dispel the gloom of a cheerless ride with a company of rough soldiers who crowded the cars to the exclusion of every one else. As far as Harrisburg the trains were filled with ladies & gentlemen & there was no trouble in finding plenty of pleasant agreeable companions, but after leaving Harrisburg they began to diminish till from Baltimore nothing was to be seen but uniforms, many of them though covering up agreeable intelligent men.

We went to the Yard through a raw chilly wind & air that threatened a storm. After shouting for a time we succeeded in getting a boat from the *King Philip* & got on board [the *Monitor*] to find everything as dismal & cheerless as can well be imagined — no lights, no fire, no supper, no nothing but a cold stove, unfilled lamps & an empty pantry. Some of our cooks, stewards, & boys were still absent, no provisions on board & those of the mess who were here living at some of the eating houses. We roused out the boys, got a fire started, hunted up two or three old candle ends, struck a light, improvised a candle stick out of an inkstand & in a little while things began to look more cheerful & feel more comfortable, though had it not been for a plate of oysters on our way to the Yard we should have gone supperless to bed.

Upon going to "lay me down to sleep" I found some evil disposed person not having the fear of the Paymaster had appropriated my matrass, leaving a wooden gridiron for anyone desiring to experience a *cold* broil on the naked slats through the coming night. I found Mr. Greene was not expected back, so laying off coat & boots I rolled myself up in his blankets & woke the next morning to a shivering sense of a cold room, a cheerless aspect within and a furious snow storm without. I furnished my boy with half a dollar & he brought me back a tolerable breakfast from some of the eating houses outside the Yard.

I found the authorities had rec'd a dispatch from Old Point that the *Merrimac* [*Richmond*] was on her way down the river (which any school boy after a moment's reflection might have known was false). However the Merrimac fever was raging & nothing would allay it but to start off the *Monitor*.

Everything was in confusion on board, workmen were still busy, tools, boards, timbers & pieces of machinery were scattered about in every part & fresh painted wood & iron work greeted you in every door & passage way. Snow & slush covered the vessel outside, as well as the paint did inside, & carpeted every walk & street through the Yard & continued to "fall fast & furious," still it mattered not with the powers that be. I had my stores & provisions to get on board, snow & slush to the contrary notwithstanding. I gathered up what I had left on board the *King Philip* & stored in the ware houses in the Yard, made out my papers for what more I wanted & which by the way I got signed without paying a darkey half a dollar or waiting a day in the Commodore's ante room. That Functionary having the fear of the *Merrimac* or the Department before his eyes seemed disposed to lay aside some of his dignity, dispense with the usual amount of red tape & formality & condescend to hasten our departure.

I had a splendid time getting my stores on board tramping about in the snow & slush — just such a time as we had in starting from Brooklyn last winter. However everything was tumbled aboard after a fashion before night & not having time to get my personal effects from the *King Philip* I returned to that delectable vessel to pass the night & had the felicity of eating a cold supper in a colder room. My *traps* were aboard the *Monitor* in good season the next morning. Our steam heaters were going & we had a tolerable breakfast in a comfortable room.

At noon we were under way down the Potomac. The weather had cleared off but it was raw & chilly & I was glad to keep below, going on deck occasionally to see the banks of the river dotted with large patches of yesterday's snow.

We reached Hampton Roads on Monday noon [November 10] (the day my leave expired) & run up to our old moorings off Newport News. Many changes have been made in the vessel of which I will speak in my next.

Thursday 13th—Your note of the 5th enclosing one from Hen & your Mother reached me to day by way of Washington. I was very glad to hear you were all well. Hen appears more contented. I am glad of it.

I have been very busy since my return & shall be for some time yet. Work has accumulated during my absence, still I shall find time to write to you, but not as often as by & by when I get some of my work off my hands.

Kreosote has declined in price, there being no demand. My leg is mending slowly, I continue Dr. Bry's prescription.*

My love to you all & a kiss to those who will take it.

William

[Marginalia] The weather since our arrival here has been delightful. Five regiments were marched through the snow & slush in the streets in Richmond barefooted & bareheaded, the day it snowed so — I have just seen a Richmond paper commenting severely upon it. Gen. Corcoran's troops are forming a camp of instruction here, so we shall have plenty of company.† I was politely offered a horse by one of his staff yesterday for a ride but didn't accept. I sent Tibbie a paper & have started the [*New York*] *Herald*s to you once more. This is the 16th letter I have written to day, not all as long as this.

---

* Keeler must have hurt his leg while he was back home in La Salle.
† After his return from captivity Corcoran returned to New York City where he raised a brigade of his fellow countrymen. His Irish Legion started arriving in Virginia in November and were based near Suffolk.

Cape Hatteras (November to December 1862)

No. 46—

U.S. Steamer *Monitor*
Off Newport News
Nov. 17th, 1862

Dear Anna,

I have just been reading your No. 22 enclosing one from Henry, with what degree of pleasure you may imagine, separated as we are by so many miles. My brief but pleasant visit home seems now when I think of it like a pleasant dream. As I sit here in my close confined quarters, 'mid the old surroundings & among my former associates I can at times hardly persuade myself but what my visit was one of fancy. I feel just like having a chat with you to night. What say you?

You ask "what changes have been made in the vessel & its inmates while at Washington?" Well in the first place Mr. Flye has been detached & given a separate command.* Mr. White† has also been detached & ordered to one of the new Monitors. Dr. Logue has resigned. These are all that have left us. A Dr. Meckley‡ who was a regimental surgeon in the army during its march up the peninsular & accompanied it in the retreat from before Richmond, was at the battle of Antietam but got tired of army life & for a change entered the Navy, was ordered to us when we left Washington. He accompanied us down here & on our arrival found orders detaching him & ordering him to Philadelphia for examination for the regular service. We all felt sorry to have him leave. We had just got acquainted & found him a pleasant sociable companion. To fill the vacancy a Dr. Weeks§ was ordered to us. He is quite a young man & I think withall a little self conceited, but that will wear off in time as he finds his level & he will make a companionable inhabitant of our iron craft. Then in the place of Mr. White we have a Mr. Lewis** from Baltimore, a mere boy, nearly a cypher in our little society. Mr. Frederickson, one of our Master's Mates, has been promoted to Ensign, which brings him into our Ward room. Another Ensign has also been added, a Mr. Atwater†† (from New Haven of course as the name indicates). He lives near your Father's & says he knows him well. These are all the changes in our little community.

---

* Keeler's friend and former mess mate had been given command of the gunboat USS *Underwriter*.
† Acting Third Assistant Engineer George H. White had been transferred to the ironclad USS *Nantucket*.
‡ Thomas H. Meckly (1840-1890). The son of a doctor from Milton, PA, he graduated from Pennsylvania College Medical Department in 1861.
§ Grenville M. Weeks*.
** Samuel A. Lewis (1842-1862). From Chester County, PA, the third assistant engineer drowned when the *Monitor* sank off Cape Hatteras.
†† Norman K. Atwater*.

Civil War Years: USS *Monitor* (1862)

Our vessel has undergone a variety of changes. A large telescopic smoke pipe capable of being run up some thirty feet, takes the place of the two low square box like things you see in the photograph. The fresh air funnels have been replaced by two much higher.

Our old boats were all left behind & we were furnished with others better adapted to our wants & large iron cranes & davits to raise them out of the water & carry them on, instead of draging them up to our decks to be in the way, or draging them in the water after us.

The ragged shot marks in our sides have been covered with iron patches & the places marked "Merrimac," "Merrimac's Prow," "Minnesota," "Fort Darling" to indicate the source from whence the blow was received. New awnings have been furnished us, ventilators for our deck lights & many other little conveniences which would have added greatly to our comfort last summer could we have had them then.

Our guns have had engraved in large letters, on one of them

Monitor & Merrimac
Worden

on the other

Monitor & Merrimac
Ericsson

Below, the Berth deck has been raised so that we can barely stand erect under the deck above & the store rooms on each side (see *Harper's Pictorial*) thrown back some four feet. This arrangement makes the berth deck considerable wider but not as high. The width however is what we want.

Below this deck I have two good store rooms for provisions & there is also a shell room. A large blower, driven by an engine attached, is placed partly above & partly below this deck, which draws the air down through the pilot house & through the deck lights (when open) in the Ward room & our State rooms & forces it into the engine room to aid the draft of the furnaces.

Three or four nice blackwalnut steps lead down from the berth deck to the Ward room. This room & our state rooms have been newly painted white & a new oil cloth put on the floors. With our bright lamps burning at night our Ward room looks as bright & cheerful as could be desired. When cool, steam is turned on the radiators & a very comfortable temperature maintained.

Last summer's roasts exists now only in memory, but they have a place there I assure you. We have a warm recollection of them. I doubt whether with our present appliances the vessel would be endurable in such an atmosphere as we lived in last summer. Now it is very comfortable.

As to our living, about which you enquire, I doubt if you could find better at few hotels on shore. Mr. Stodder is Caterer. He bought in Baltimore just before we left Washington a bill of provisions for our Mess amounting to over $700.00 intending it for two months. We have a new Cook & Steward who havn't fairly got the hang of the school house yet, but we set a good table with a prospect of its improving.

We breakfast at 8, lunch at 12 & *dine* at 5. Our breakfast is usually fried oysters, beefsteak, fish balls, mutton chops, with an abundance of vegetables, *sweet* & common potatoes &c. For lunch we usually have oysters raw, cold tongue, lobster (in cans), cold roast or corned beef, sometimes cold boiled ham, sardines, crackers, cheese, &c &c. Dinner is *the* meal — Soups, Stew'd Oysters, boiled Salmon, Roast beef, Mutton, or Turkey, boiled ham, & so on through a whole hotel bill of fare with all the sauces, condiments & fancy pickles. But our attempts at pies, puddings &c makes me wish for home made. We are well supplied with apples, nuts, raisins & figs &c. Don't imagine we are going to starve.

[Marginalia] No room. Tell Dave it will be his turn to laugh yet, I will predict that. How are his eyes now? If a better defence of Gen. McC. is wanted than what Prince de Joinville is making I don't know where you will find it.* Save all the papers that has it in. My best love

William

No. 47—

U.S. Steamer *Monitor*
Off Newport News, Va.
Nov. 25th, 1862

Dear Anna,

I have just returned from Old Point & Norfolk. Have taken a look around to see if everything had gone straight during my absence, have straightened matters out where they needed it, have replied to half a dozen letters (business, no young ladies in the [this] case) & now have laid accounts, books & papers aside & propose to chat awhile with you.

I went down to Old Point yesterday morning on business & not finding the person I was in search of concluded to take a trip up to Norfolk with my friend Kimberly whom I found just going on board the boat which was just shoving off. On reaching Norfolk I found the regulations more strict than they were last summer as each one had to pass a line of guards on going ashore who required a pass from every one without distinction. I had no time to supply myself with one before leaving Old Point but one of my naval acquaintances who happened along made good the deficiency with one of his *old* ones which I found answered every purpose as I handed it to the guard with my thumb covering the date, "all right" & I passed on. I went to the

---

* In October 1862 François d'Orléans (Prince de Joinville) published a long article in a French journal discussing the Peninsula Campaign in which he praised McClellan's organizational and leadership skills. Abridged translations of the article appeared in newspapers across the North.

Civil War Years: USS *Monitor* (1862)

Provost Marshal at Norfolk with whom I was acquainted & got a pass to return & was never required to shew it, so easy it is to get back & forth between important points through careless guards. I enclose the paper to you.

Norfolk, if anything, looks more dismal & gloomy than it did last summer. I went into the store of an acquaintance from New York & saw a large placard conspicuously placed, "no goods sold to citizens except by a special permit of the Provost Marshal." Just think of living in a place where you were obliged to procure a pass to leave or return & a permit to buy a spool of cotton, a pound of starch or a yard of cotton cloth, pleasant ain't it? But very few goods are allowed to be taken there for sale & those only by undoubted Union men.

Ladies going into Kimberly's store would shew their permit to purchase "a few articles indispensably necessary for domestic purposes." Many of them were richly dressed, but the late[st] fashions evidently had not reached there for their garments were "All of the olden style" & it was very apparent that they eschewed hoops, probably as a diabolical invention of the enemy. It must have been mortifying to their pride and intensely aggravating to their disloyal sympathies to be compelled to apply to Union officers for permission to purchase Union goods of Union men or to apply to the same source for liberty to leave the city & when obtained to pass through loyal swords & bayonets producing at their order the pass of a military governor. Such is Norfolk now & such she will remain till her citizens will use common sense enough to return to their allegiance.

On my return to Old Point I found your No. 23 waiting my arrival. Tell Eddie that I got his picture & thought it was very pretty. He must send me another some time.

How little there is in the papers now. Burnside is moving quietly & I hope surely. It is thought here that his attack on Fredericksburg is but a feint. We shall soon see what it means.* I should not be surprised if we had to go up James river again.

The critics are still pitching into McClellan. Depriving him of his command is not enough, they would follow him into private life. If they would be satisfied with expressing their dissatisfaction with his military movements I would not care, of course they have a right to their opinions, but their disapprobation of him as a leader has degenerated to a personal enmity as if he had robbed their hen roost or stoned their dog. They have brooded over their paltry petty dislike & nursed it till it has become a malignant hatred as unjust & ungenerous as it is harmless to their object. Blinded by prejudice & this almost fiendish hatred, with a mountain of imaginary wrongs pressing upon their *disloyal* shoulders, they have pursued him regardless of our country's welfare or their own reputations. Ignorant of the first principles of

---

* Ambrose Burnside, who had assumed command of the Army of the Potomac following McClellan's dismissal, was poised to cross the Rappahannock River to Fredericksburg whence he would move on Richmond.

miltary tactics these egotistical ninnies have arrogated themselves to be oracles of everything pertaining to the art of war. They criticise the movements of our immense armies, the operations of a campai[g]n & the ability of the Generals with all the freedom & effrontry of another Napolean. They would almost convince you that they could have done all this with the ease & facility of the "presto change" of a Majician. It is just such persons as these that on a certain occasion cried "away with Him" when reason & right & justice were lost in prejudice, ignorance & bigotry. The world hasn't changed much after all. Their small, narrow contracted minds seem incapable of containing a generous, noble idea. How true it is that "fools rush in where angels fear to tread."[*]

How revolting it appears to see some members of a family by the side of a comfortable fire at home abusing the leaders of our armies as traitors & villains & putting every obstacle in the way of their success, while others of the same family have given up all the comforts of that home & are risking their lives in defence of their country, fighting perhaps under the same general so villified in their own home. This may be loyal & patriotic but "I can't see it."

As I have repeatedly said I have no personal feeling in the matter. Give me the man who will press the war with the greatest energy & ability till the last vestige of disloyalty is swept from existence. I care not who it is so [long as] he but bring about an early & honourable termination to this unnatural strife. From what I have seen & heard I am fully & firmly satisfied that Gen. McClellan is the most able & accomplished military leader yet brought before the public. True there are some things, some of his movements, I don't fully comprehend—such as his apparent neglect to follow up the enemy after the battle of Antietam, but I have confidence in him to believe that his reasons for all such things that are not now understood by the public are good & sufficient & will some day see the light. Burnside is but following out his plans & I only hope he will do it as completely & successfully as McClellan himself would do it. The graceful unassuming dignity with which he retired from his command adds new lustre to his name. I suppose he has the material in his own hands to open a new page of the country's history, for I am told that he has preserved every document, official & unofficial, every order or dispatch that he has ever received & is fully able to completely justify himself at any time when so disposed. But like a true patriot he prefers to suffer in silence rather than bring his personal matters before the public to add another wave to the angry elements that now agitate the public mind. The future will do him full justice if the present will not.

But I am occupying too much time & space with this matter & will dismiss it simply saying that we will yet see the time before this war is over when all the patriots will be glad & anxious to see him resume his former position.

---

[*] Alexander Pope's poem *An Essay on Criticism* (1711).

Civil War Years: USS *Monitor* (1862)

Thursday, 27th—Thanksgiving — My letter has been waiting till now to have the page filled. We have had a most delightful day—perfectly clear & still—not a cloud visible—a bright warm sun shining—the water quiet & smooth as a mirror—just warm enough to be comfortable in our winter clothing.

How many times I have thought of you all to day & wished you were enjoying our fine weather. We have just finished our dinner (1/2 past 6). Of course we had everything good that was to be procured, only one relish was wanting — *home*.

I had a letter from Henry yesterday, the first since my return. Nothing in it of consequence. No news here of consequence. We are looking for the *Passaic* (another of the Monitors) here every day. A storm is gathering here to burst somewhere on the coast, but none of us are able yet to point out the spot. You will have some stirring news before long I think.

Remember me to all friends with many kind kisses especially to those at home & our little circle.

William

No. 48—

U.S. Steamer Monitor
Off Newport News, Va.
Dec. 2nd, 1862

Dear Anna,

I have just dispatched a long letter to Henry in reply to one rec'd from him a day or two ago, the first I have had from him since my return. I told him I would allow him fifty cents a month pocket money if he would send me a correct cash account every fortnight. I did it partly to have him keep an account of his expenses, to learn him to keep a cash a/c & then I shall be sure to hear from him every fortnight. It was realy gratifying to have your Mother & Hattie speak so well of him. I am sure he deserves it. I am sorry your Mother persists in making him wear undershirts, so much against his will. He never seemed to feel the cold. I think however one requires under clothing more in the damp air of the sea coast than in our dry bracing atmosphere.

Just four weeks to day since I left home. How quick they have passed to me. I have had plenty to keep me busy since my return. The changes among the officers require long transfer accounts, then my last last quarter's returns had to be made out, requisitions made out for a fresh supply of stores, the invoices to be examined & copied, then some dozen of our men deserted which made it necessary to fill their places with others. Of course the accounts of the old ones had to be closed & new ones opened, with the new comers all together involving a large amount of writing which is not all

Cape Hatteras (November to December 1862)

finished yet, though I must confess that I don't work very hard or many hours in a day — that's not the way when you work for Uncle Sam.

Your No. 24 reached me the same day I rec'd Hen's & was as welcome as letters from home always are. I think from what you say that you have not had as pleasant weather as we have been favoured with here. With the exception of one partly rainy day the weather has been delightful though rather cool, but no freezing weather except one or two nights when I saw a little ice in the morning. We don't know much about the cold when once in the bowels of our iron box. What it would be in severe cold weather we don't know, but I hardly think it would ever be uncomfortably cold with our steam heaters in operation. We are now putting up two more in the Capt.'s rooms.

Everything goes along quietly & smoothly on board — very different from what it was under our former Captain. My *next door* neighbor, the M.D., has a "Mary" to whom he is always writing letters & the replies are about as frequent & I am favoured (sometimes bored) with the soft things on both sides. It seems that "Mary" is living in New York with some jealous uncle & aunt upon whom she is partly dependent for a home & her "lovyer"* has incurred their sublime wrath by directing "Mary's" letters to the care of another person for fear that some of her over curious friends might open them. Quite a spicy correspondence has been opened, pro & con, of which I have had the full benefit, though I cannot help but wish sometimes that pretty Mary's curious uncles & jealous aunts when on their pilgrimage to Chinese Tartary when I am interrupted in the middle of a long column of figures to listen to their epistolary quarrels.

Last Sunday [November 30] was a beautiful still clear day. I took advantage of it to go ashore for a walk, the first time I have been on shore *here* since our return. I formed the acquaintance of the Col., Lieut. Col. & Maj. of the 26th Maine regiment & we strolled out a mile or two to where Gen. Corcoran was exercising his troops, about 6,000, in brigade drill.† I should think in getting up his troops he had been out in the by ways & ditches and compelled them to come in. Halt, lame, hump backs, decrepid old men, boys, everything in fact "who would a sogering go" that would count *one* in the ranks. Many of them will have to be sent back as unfit for duty. The remainder are a set of wild irishmen from the vilest holes of New York city, but one remove from the brute creation. Moraly and physically they are not to be compared to two Maine regiments in camp here.

---

* An obsolete form of the word lover.
† Corcoran's Irish Legion served in eastern Virginia under General John Dix and saw action in the Suffolk area in 1863. Corcoran's time as its commanding officer, however, was short lived. In December 1863 he invited his friend and fellow countryman Brigadier General Thomas Meagher to spend Christmas with him. On their ride to the Fairfax railway station, where Meagher was to pick up his wife, Corcoran fell from his horse, went into convulsions, and died several hours later.

Civil War Years: USS *Monitor* (1862)

Near where they were drilling was a three story brick house or rather what had been one. The interior had been completely gutted from the ground to the roof, no floors or partitions, even the lath & plaster had been torn from the walls, through which loop holes had been punched for musketry. All around the building, enclosing a space about as large as our garden, a heavy earthwork had been thrown up, leaving a trench on the outside at least twenty feet deep. Cannon had been mounted in the corners of the enclosure. But the place is now vacant.

One of the new Monitors, the *Passaic* reached here Sunday but was obliged to proceed immediately to Washington to repair some defect in her boilers. The *Ironsides* & *Galena* are still here & a number of wooden gun boats. The *Passaic* is said to be much more roomy & comfortable inside than our vessel.

Our old friends on shore here had all left when we returned from Washington & the long barracks which formerly contained two thousand sick were filled with a conglomeration of filth & contrabands. Corcoran's troops are all living in tents.

Remember me to all friends. With love to yourself & kisses to the children

William

[Marginalia] Is any one getting impatient to see Burnside moove?* I *paws* for a reply. Heavy firing heard to day in the direction of Suffolk. I send some change. Tell Dave I have rec'd his letter, many thanks.

No. 49—

U.S. Steamer *Monitor*
Off Newport News, Va.
Dec. 3rd, 1862

Dear Anna,

I scratched off a letter to you last night in a most hurried manner, in so much haste in fact that I hardly knew what I wrote & have since been trying to call to mind what I filled it with. I fear it won't prove very interesting, for I wrote more from a sense of duty than from inclination. I had been puzzling over long colums of figures all day long till I could hardly see or think of any thing else than the numerals.

After finishing a letter to Henry it seemed so long since I had written home that it was my *duty* to [do] so at once. How successfully you can tell better than I.

I think from what you say that Graham must have been a good man in the garden. If so I am very glad I got him. It would be a good plan to engage him for the spring as even if I should be at home I should need some

---

* Burnside was on the north side of the Rappahannock across from Fredericksburg waiting for the arrival of the pontoon bridges he needed to cross the river.

assistance. It looks now as if it was very doubtful if I should be home by that time for the end of the war seems as far in the future as ever.

Banks' expedition is to leave here to morrow morning.* What its destination is none of us knows, the secret has been well kept. No one here however supposes that it is going to Texas as has been stated in the papers. The opinion here is that it is bound for some portion of the coast, probably Charleston. But why some of the iron clads are not made to form a portion of the force I can't comprehend. The two Maine regiments that I mentioned in my yesterday's letter form a portion of his force.

You speak of butter at 20 cents, here it is 50. I wish I could send you a lot of our splendid oysters. It would be next to going myself. I know you would agree with me that they are delicious. I never tire of them, eating them always once a day & frequently three times, besides frequently having one of the boys open some for me through the day to take down from the shell. Then we have a new way of cooking them in the shell, steaming, which I think is, next to raw, the perfection of oysters.

By the way I stand corrected in my spelling "Peninsula," more from habit than ignorance however.†

I think I mentioned the rec't of Dave's letter in mine of yesterday, I am realy glad to hear that his eyes are improving. I only hope the improvement will be continuous & lasting. I wish you would ask him to send me his *LaSalle Press* occasionally. I was going to write an article for it but cannot find enough that would interest the public to make a letter.

What is the occasion of Moore's dislike to Collins?‡ I can't understand it. I thought Mr. C. helped elect Moore. Jenkins I fear will find it hard work to fill his regiment.§ Is Carter still with him?** I am not surprised at what you tell me about Coates as I knew his former habits & that it would be hard for him to break off.

Has one of the copies of the *Sci. American* been discontinued? If not, let me know. You are mistaken about Atwater being a brother of E. Olmstead's husband, he never had a brother.

"I had no idea I had so much to say when I commenced to night" (I quote from you). I thought I would write a page each evening till completed, but I

---

* Having been beaten twice by Stonewall Jackson, Banks was sent to New Orleans where he would hopefully do less damage, and was put in charge of the Department of the Gulf and tasked with the administration of Louisiana and gaining control of the lower Mississippi River.
† Keeler had been spelling it "Peninsular", i.e. with an "r" at the end.
‡ Keeler's friend served in Absolom Moore's regiment, the 104th Illinois Infantry.
§ David P. Jenkins, a lawyer from La Salle and major of the 1st Illinois Cavalry during the first year of the war. In the summer of 1862 Illinois Governor Richard Yates permitted him to raise a regiment of cavalry, but volunteers were hard to come by since the state had already filled its quota for that year. It was not until February 1863 that the new regiment, the 14th Illinois Cavalry, with Jenkins as lieutenant-colonel, was mustered into service.
** This suggests that Keeler's friend Samuel B. Carter served in the 1st Illinois Cavalry.

find my pen *like a woman's tongue* don't know when to leave off. No personalities intended.

To day has been quite unpleasant, drizzling incessantly. It now looks like clearing off with a cold north west wind.

But I shall leave the remainder of my sheet for tomorrow night. So good night.

Thursday, Dec. 4th—Burnsides' [Banks'] troops left here this morning in twenty transports. Their destination remains unknown. Forty thousand are on their way from Washington to Aquia creek to reinforce Burnside. Corcoran is daily looking for two thousand from New York to join him here.

This has been a clear still day but quite cool. One of our boats went out a little while this afternoon & returned with six barrels of oysters. I wish I could send you two or three barrels of them.

Don't forget *that group* that I was to have a photograph of the first opportunity. I should prize it highly if I could get it.

I wish I could look in upon you all this evening. I can imagine you around the table reading & sewing but I should prefer the reality to imagination.

How do you like the President's Message? I have only had time to glance over it hastily. Isn't the last paragraph fine?[*] I don't think the Message is calculated to suit the ultras on either side. I think it a good practical common sense thing & I think it will be generally liked.

How do the children manage to pass the time? I suppose the unpleasant weather keeps them in doors most of the time. I am glad that Eddie liked his paints so well. It was a good investment of a quarter. I must try & write to him & baby.

I send you a [New York] *Herald* every day. Hope it is received. All the papers are barren of news now-a-days.

We are hoping to see Capt. Worden here in a few days in another of the Monitors.[†] I know of none of my naval acquaintances I should be more glad to meet.

---

[*] Lincoln delivered his Second Annual Message on December 1, 1862. In the last paragraph which Keeler so liked, Lincoln tied the survival of the nation to freedom for the slaves: "Fellow-citizens, we can not escape history. We of this Congress and this Administration will be remembered in spite of ourselves. No personal significance or insignificance can spare one or another of us. The fiery trial through which we pass will light us down in honor or dishonor to the latest generation. We say we are for the Union. The world will not forget that we say this. We know how to save the Union. The world knows we do know how to save it. We, even we here, hold the power and bear the responsibility. In giving freedom to the slave we assure freedom to the free—honorable alike in what we give and what we preserve. We shall nobly save or meanly lose the last best hope of earth. Other means may succeed; this could not fail. The way is plain, peaceful, generous, just—a way which if followed the world will forever applaud and God must forever bless."

[†] Worden had partially recovered from the wounds he received in the fight with the *Virginia* and was in command of the USS *Montauk*. Keeler did not have the chance to meet him at this time since the *Monitor* left Hampton Roads before the *Montauk* arrived.

Cape Hatteras (November to December 1862)

Remember me to all our friends especially to our circle & don't let them forget that photograph.

Love to Father & Mother & kisses to yourself & the children.

William

No. 50—

U.S. Steamer *Monitor*
Off Newport News, Va.
Dec. 6th, 1862

Dear Anna,

Yesterday was an unpleasant disagreeable day & to day has added another to what I fear will be a long list if we are to lie here all winter. Yesterday it rained & drizzled & drizzled & rained without cessation all day long. Last night it cleared off with a cold northerly wind & has been blowing almost a gale through the day, raising a sea which has been washing over our decks ever since last night.

I have spent the day in my little *snuggery* reading & writing by the aid of the few rays of light which straggled down from a bright unclouded sun through the little circular opening over my head, closed by the thick plate of glass & covered by some six (or eight) inches of water. I went to sleep last night to the swash, swash of the waves as they rolled over my head & the same monotonous sound still continues & will be my lullaby to night.

Nothing would strike a stranger with more surprise after walking our cheerless wave washed, iron deck than to go below & see our bright, cheerful, well lighted, cosy Ward Room with the officers grouped around the table reading, writing or talking. The dash of the waves as they roll over our heads is the only audible sound that reaches us from the outer world. One would hardly suppose from the quiet stillness that pervades our submarine abode that a gale was raging around us.

Our life I assure you is getting to be monotonous enough, even a trip up James river would be acceptable.

Have you read the correspondence between Gens. McClellan & Halleck? They have solved what has heretofore been a problem to me, the reason of McClellan leaving Harrison's landing last summer instead of crossing the river to City Point & advancing to Petersburg & from there to Richmond.[*] Certain indications at one time led me to think that was his plan as it certainly appeared feasible. These letters clear up the mystery. Read McClellan's letter

---

[*] The correspondence between McClellan and Halleck, which was dated August 4 and 6, 1862, was included in Halleck's annual report to Secretary of War Edwin Stanton. In it Halleck makes clear why he refused to send the thousands more troops that McClellan had requested and why he ordered him to withdraw to Aquia Creek.

to Halleck & his letter to Fitz John Porter in the paper I send you to day.*
Does it seem possible that any candid person could accuse him of disloyalty?
I tell you such sentiments as we find in those letters never came from any but
a true, noble, loyal heart. Very evidently they were never intended for the
public. In them, he, himself is nothing, it is all his country. His enemies of
course will see nothing in them. No evidence of loyalty. Nothing that speaks
of a noble self sacrificing spirit. They will believe nothing except what suits
their own prejudiced, prematurely formed opinions—"neither will they be
persuaded though one rose from the dead." When Gabriel is proved disloyal
to the Almighty then we may look for a traitor in McClellan. The more I read
& hear of him the more I find to admire in him.

Sunday, 7th—When I went on deck this morning just after breakfast I
found it covered with ice from the water left by the seas which were rolling
over us all night long. The day has been bright & clear but the strong north
westerly wind still prevails, cold & cheerless & sweeping the green waves in
torrents of foam across the deck. The uninviting aspect of things *above* water
has kept us all *below*, where we have contented ourselves & passed the time
as each one has seen fit, some reading, some writing, some talking & all
wishing for the mail. It came with its usual regularity, about 11 o'clock, & an
anxious group gathered around the Ward Room table as the matter was
distributed. Nothing from home however for me but two LaSalle papers &
they have been read & reread—patent medicines, sheriff's sales, funny
stories, dry editorials & "*special notices*" till I could almost repeat them by heart.
As a last resort I got out what few old letters of yours I have & made a careful
search hoping that I might come across something that had escaped me on
the first perusal. I was eminently successful. In one of the many little nooks
& corners which you always contrive to fill, you say. "I am *all right*." To what
do you allude? I never suspected you of being anything wrong. Pray explain.

I enclose you a letter I rec'd a few days ago from Mr. Flye, some portions
of which you may find interesting. He is a very pleasant easy writer & a well
educated person. He was formerly a Prof. of Mathematics in the navy. I also
enclose a photograph of Acting Master Stodder, one of our officers. Don't
forget that photographic group that I am to have.

---

* In McClellan's August 4 letter to Halleck he urged the General in Chief to rescind the order to withdraw and laid out his reasons for remaining on the Peninsula. He closed by stating that he was "strong in the consciousness that I have ever been and still am actuated solely by love of my country, knowing that no ambitious or selfish motives have influenced me from the commencement of this war." McClellan's letter of September 1, 1862 to Fitz John Porter was also published in numerous papers (e.g., *The World*, New York, NY, December 5, 1862): "I ask of you for my sake and that of the country, and the old Army of the Potomac, that you and all my friends will lend the fullest and most cordial co-operation to General Pope in all the operations now going on. The destinies of our country, the honor of our army, are at stake . . . I am in charge of the defenses of Washington, and am doing all I can to render your retreat safe, should that become necessary."

Cape Hatteras (November to December 1862)

Monday, 8th—Your "No. 25" reached me to day, as you may well suppose it was a welcome visitant. How I wish I could have made one of your number on Thanksgiving. I knew I was not forgotten. I think our parlour must be quite a cosy looking room when filled with company, now that the curtains are up. I was right glad to hear from Hen & that he seems to feel more contented. He appears to feel quite interested in his studies.

We hear no news from Banks yet. Of course the destination of the expedition is discussed in our Ward Room. We all incline to the opinion that it is bound up the Albermarle Sound & Roanoke river to Weldon where they will intercept the rebels' principal railroad communication with the South & then "forward to Richmond." It certainly appears very feasible at any rate, but it is only a surmise with us. We shall hear from it soon.

When our little social circle meets remember me to them all. I send lots of love, help yourself, distribute the remainder if you have any left.

William

[Marginalia] I will act upon your hint of skates for Hen & will send him some money to get them. It has been still & clear to day but cold. Stodder & myself are going to Norfolk to morrow morning, just for a change of air. We run around now where we please. If I return in time to morrow night I shall commence another letter home. A kiss to yourself & the children.

William

No. 51—

U.S. Steamer *Monitor*
Off Newport News, Va.
Dec. 9th, 1862

Dear Anna,

I have just ret'd from a trip to Norfolk. Have had my supper (or dinner as we call it on board) & have seated myself at my desk to perform the promise I made in the letter I mailed to you this morning, "to begin a letter to you to night."

It has been a beautiful day, clear, still & warm—just such a day as one would have selected for the trip. We leave here at 8 in the morning, get to Old Point about 10, leave there at 11 & reach Norfolk about 12. On the return we leave Norfolk at 2, reach Old Point about 3, leave there at 4 & get *home* just in time for supper, 5 P.M. So you see that the trip although a short one consumes the day. I had Stodder for company from here & one of the Kimberlys joined us at Old Point.

Norfolk appears very much as it did when I have been there before, though an unusual number of ladies appeared to be taking advantage of the beautiful weather for a street promenade. I took dinner at Mr. Kimberly's & met a gentleman there who has resided in the place for a number of years.

Civil War Years: USS *Monitor* (1862)

He is a strong Union man but managed, with his family, to remain on his place, which is three or four miles out of the city. He confirmed what I have heard before, that on the return of the *Merrimac* after the fight, the whole inhabitants were completely panic stricken & made instant preparations to abandon the place expecting us to follow her right up. Had we been allowed to have done so we should not only have taken the place, but the *Merrimac* would have been surrendered to us. For some days the population appeared paralized, expecting every moment to see the *Monitor* turning Sewall's Point on her way up to the city. Finding that we did not venture, they took fresh courage & commenced to repair their vessel for fresh operations.

Only see what we lost by the imbecility & the want of courage & decision on the part of those who controlled our movements. It is an opportunity which will never occur again. It vexes me whenever I think of it. Everything we could wish for just within our grasp, honor, fame, notoriety, whatever the love of country or the desire to do a patriotic deed might prompt, to say nothing of the large amount of prize money involved. That all this just within our grasp should be lost & not by any fault of our own is vexatious, don't you think so.

Any time within a month after the return of the *Merrimac* we might have gone up there & taken possession of her as she lay defenceless in the dock. Of all this Mr. Paterson (the person of whom I have been speaking)[*] & other good Union men kept Gen. Wool & Com're Goldsborough informed & repeatedly sent down urging them to send up forces to take possession of the place, offering upon a preconcerted signal to take possession of the ferry boats that run between Norfolk and Portsmouth thus cutting off all communication between the two places. Their intreat[i]es were all disregarded, for what reason of course we do not know, but I only hope that the history of the whole matter will some day see the light.

Wednesday evening [December 9] — I have just finished a full sheet to Hen & a good long note to Mary Graves[†] in reply to some [letters] received from them to day. Mary wrote me asking me to let Hen go up there & spend the Christmas holidays, when he will have a vacation. It was enclosed in Hen's in which he stated the request & wound up with "please say no." So I wrote Mary that I thought it would be better & pleasanter for all of them to have him defer his visit till sometime next summer. He would enjoy a visit there at this season of the year but very little as in all probability he would be shut up in the house all the time. In the summer he could ramble about with the girls, run, "*holler*" & kick up his heels to his heart's content. Don't you agree with me? I sent him three dollars to buy a pair of skates or whatever he wanted most & two dollars to get some things for the children if his Grandmother should send a bundle as she usually does.

---

[*] Possibly Edward Patterson, a 45-year-old French-born shoemaker in Norfolk.
[†] Keeler's sister-in-law in Litchfield, CT.

Cape Hatteras (November to December 1862)

I wish I could tell you all I know about army & navy movements—but it is news I would not dare to trust to the mail, & government gags us with its mandate forbidding us to give "any information to any person whatever." You may be prepared to hear exciting news in from ten to fourteen days. I think the *Monitor* will have a hand in.

Our turret machinery is very much out of order. In the disgraceful haste with which we were sent away from the Washington Navy Yard they neglected even to examine it. We have workmen on board repairing it temporarily. It is the center of life, the heart of our craft & it would be unfortunate to have it give way in the midst of a fight.

Myself & *Sword* goes down to Old Point to morrow morning on a visit to the Admiral*. *We* have a steam tug for *our* sole & special use. Wouldn't you like to be along?

What news to day's paper brings us. *Actg. Brig. Gen. Moore* & his whole brigade taken prisoners.† I only hope he will remain a prisoner till the conclusion of the war. What folly to give such men a command. Have you read what the Prince Dejoinville says on the subject? It is true, every word.

Capt. Bankhead has just shewn me a communication from the Department containing extracts from letters from our Consuls at the different English ports, giving long lists of vessels preparing to run the blockade, a description of them & of their cargoes. Their plan is to make a dash at some of the southern ports together, a few they expect to run in, the rest will be taken. The vessels are of the finest class for speed & light draught & have very valuable cargoes. Some of them are made of thin *steel* plates. How I wish I was in a good blockader—*don't you*? But 'tis ten o'clock so a kiss & good night.

William

[Marginalia] Some stamps for the children, as I think they should find something interesting in my letters as well as the older ones.

No. 52—

U.S. Steamer *Monitor*
Off Newport News, Va.
Dec. 13th, 1862

Dear Anna,

Your No. 27 was timed just right to reach me to day (Saturday) making, as you say, "the week to end well with me." I don't plead guilty of your charge

---

* Samuel Phillips Lee, the new commander of the North Atlantic Blockading Squadron.
† The Battle of Hartsville, TN on December 7, 1862. The La Salle County politician had been placed in command of a brigade that was protecting a crossing of the Cumberland River in Tennessee. They were taken by surprise at their camp early in the morning by a much smaller force under Confederate General John Hunt Morgan. More than 2,000 men were killed, wounded or captured. Moore was one of those who was captured.

of "growing indolent" by any means, for if I remember aright I have sent off to you three letters within a week & here is the commencement of the fourth. As to my deeming it "prosaic work" writing to the auld wife and children, that is a mere matter of opinion of yours to which I do not attach much weight especially as it is not warranted by facts. The M.D.'s love letters are a regular bore as such things *always are*!?, well perhaps you don't agree with me. I may be wrong but you must attribute it to my *youth* & inexperience or I think I will insist that you are in error & attribute it to your "shallow patedness."* Ha, ha, well that's a good joke, "two shallow pated women" for a wife & mother, but isn't it strange I should have lived with them so long without knowing it & left it to be discovered by a stranger. I don't think however the joke would have ended with his strange discovery if I had been at home. I can't exactly see where the laugh comes in.

Capt. Worden, I see by to day's paper, is to receive the thanks of Congress upon the recommendation of the President which will promote him one grade making him a Captain. There are only two higher grades, Commodore & Admiral. He is now a Commander, the same grade as Capt. Bankhead. Never was promotion more deservedly bestowed. His honors will be well worn & his former reputation sustained I know.

I also have a copy of Prince de Joinville's work, I presume the same as Dave's. I was going to read it and send it home.

I was much amused at the puff of Laning in the St. Louis paper.† It sounds so much like him. If he did not write it he procured its insertion with his assurance it would be no difficult matter. I think I will get around some of the newspaper reporters or editors & get a puff too, for an improvement I have been the means of having made in our vessel. I suggested to Capt. B. one day as I was walking the deck with him the advantage of having an iron breastwork built on the top of our turret of sufficient height & strength to protect those behind it from sharp shooters. He made no reply at the time but a day or two afterward as we were walking the deck together, says he, "Purser (that is the name he always gives me) that is a very good idea of yours. I wish you would go & see the Admiral [Lee] about it, if we can have it done & if the iron can be had at Old Point." The result is we are having a breast work made of boiler iron on the top of the turret which will add that much to its height & be musket proof. It will be pierced with loop holes for our rifles so that we can try our skill as sharpshooters when an opportunity offers. We shall have it up in a day or two.

The weather here is delightful, so warm that numbers of the soldiers were in bathing to day, while in the *N.Y. Herald* just rec'd I read that "the upper fords of the Rappahanock are frozen over so that troops can cross."

---

* Superficial intellectual ability.
† Keeler's friend James Laning had evidently written a self-promoting advertisement about the construction of gunboats he was supervising in St. Louis.

Cape Hatteras (November to December 1862)

Sunday, 14th—Have been down to Old Point & spent the day, glad to see some new faces. What glorious news we are getting from Burnside.* I hope he will follow up his success & "drive the enemy to the wall." You say you want to hear from Banks. All that has been *heard* here is that his fleet was seen passing Wilmington on its way south. Don't be surprised or concerned to see among the telegraphic items in about a week that "the *Monitor* has left Hampton Roads bound down the coast." We are preparing for it & if nothing unforseen happens will leave in about a week. Nothing is know of it publicly & till the telegraph makes it known it would be as well not to mention it except to a few of our friends.

I occasionally stumble upon some of my Harrison's Landing acquaintances. To day I came across Col. Van Wyck, much to my satisfaction. I had a long chat with him of the scenes of last summer.†

Do you hear anything of "Absolom" [Moore]? His military career was brought to a sudden halt & about as inglorious as it was short. If the [*La Salle*] *Press* has anything to say about it please send it to me.

I saw to day at Old Point a steamboat load of Sesesh prisoners just from Fredericksburgh. They were a sorry looking set I assure you, dirty, ragged, dejected & forlorn. They looked as if they "didn't care whether school kept or not." Upon my remarking that they all seemed tolerably well shod notwithstanding what we had read in the papers. "Yes," said the officer with whom I was talking, "our boys gave them shoes after capturing them, they were all nearly barefooted till then." They will be paroled, sent up James river & set at liberty, probably to go right into the ranks again, for the rebel officers have but little regard for the parole.

I fear your anticipated festival will be a failure especially as some of the working ones seemed to have retired to *private* life. I received the *Press* from you to day. Send it as frequently as you can when it contains anything interesting. I want to impress it upon your memory that I have the promise of the photograph of a group of certain ladies & I don't want you should let them forget it. Please remind them of it occasionally as I shall you.

What does Bennett do with his wife, leave her at home, or take her on the gun boats with him?‡ Much obliged for the sesesh letters. When I find that "writing to the auld wife becomes prosaic" I will avail myself of your permission & copy them for your edification. I suppose the children will look for their stamps, so I enclose each of them one & a kiss which please deliver. Remember me to Father, Mother, Dave & all. With much love & kisses.

William

---

* First reports of the Battle of Fredericksburg.
† See letter of July 25, 1862.
‡ Keeler's friend from La Salle, William C. Bennett*, was an acting ensign in the Mississippi Squadron. He later served on the ironclad USS *Choctaw* which was being built in St. Louis. The 26-year-old had recently married for a second time.

[Marginalia] Continue to write & direct as heretofore. Your letters will all reach me from this point.

No. 53—

U.S. Steamer *Monitor*
Off Newport News, Va.
Dec. 16th, 1862

Dear Anna,

We have passed a very disagreeable day, it raining hard all the forenoon, clearing off about noon & blowing hard & cold from the north west & to add to the general gloom of the weather came the news, just as we were sitting down to the dinner table, of the retreat of Burnside across the Rappahanock after having lost thousands of valuable lives & without having brought about any useful result.* Although hoping for continued victories for our troops, we were not altogther surprised at the discouraging intelligence, for Capt. Bankhead, whose judgement in military matters is of the very best, has from the outset been prophesying reverses if Burnside crossed the river. Events have proved the soundness of his judgement.

Gen. Dix & Staff were on board yesterday. He said, speaking of our movements on the Rapahannock, that "it (refering to Fredericksburg) is not the way to approach Richmond, any military man could or should see that." That "Burnside was opposed to the movement." I think his opinion should have some weight.

Capt. B.'s father was a Brigadier General under [General Winfield] Scott in Mexico & Capt. B. was chief of his staff so that he has had a good military as well as naval training. He is "down" on the politicians who he claims are attempting to control the movements of our armies, he denounces them most bitterly, attributing to them most of our reverses. He is well acquainted with most of our prominent military characters — McClellan, Burnside, McDowell, Halleck & Pope he has known from his boyhood. Burnside, he says, will make a good officer but is not the man to handle our large armies that McClellan is. He has not the quick comprehension of intricate combination of movements & plans that McClellan has. Capt. B. says that in his estimation McC. is the most accomplished General in the country, that if the politicians could only be locked up in the State prisons & Gen. McC. be given the command of the army as it is, in three months he would end the rebellion. Capt. B. says that the charge of drunkeness brought against McDowell is ab[s]urd, as there is not a more abstemious man in the army, not even using tea or coffee.

---

* On December 13 Burnside launched multiple frontal attacks against Lee's entrenched line on Marye's Heights overlooking Fredericksburg. It was a fearful slaughter, with the 13,000 Union casualties nearly three times those of the Confederates.

Cape Hatteras (November to December 1862)

Gen. Dix & Staff made quite a display. They came up on a boat from Old Point to review Corcoran's brigade & spent an hour or more on the *Monitor*. He [Dix] is a fine looking man & as a soldier appears much better than Gen. Wool. Speaking of cavalry raids he said that all that our troops did was not made public. A short time ago he said that one of our cavalry officers (Gen. Naglee) took 3 or 4 regiments of cavalry, went up the Rapahannock, crossed over to *Hanover courthouse*, went on beyond Richmond & returning, passed just in the rear of the rebel army at Fredericksburg, getting back without losing a man & bringing quite a number of horses, cattle & a few prisoners. They found no troops in the country through which they passed shewing that the rebels had collected all their forces at Fredericksburg. I fear the news we have just heard will change our plans should it prove true.

Wednesday, 17th—To day's mail brought me yours of the 11th enclosing one from Hen. It also brought another directly from him containing a few lines thanking me for the money I sent him for some skates, also telling me how glad he was that I wrote Aunt Mary [Graves] that he had better put off his visit till warm weather as he didn't want to go up there a bit in the winter.

What will become of Absolom? The best things the rebels can do for us is to keep him till the war is over as there his cowardice can inflict no further injury on us, but to help their own cause they would turn him loose, sans ceremony.* Do you think I would go back to Ottawa again standing in his shoes – never – I'd go to Salt Lake or some other barbarous portion of the globe where vagabonds most do congregate & establish an asylum for sneaks & cowards. Pleasant, decidedly, on his return to face the public, his friends & family. Better have deposited himself in the "last ditch." I am not at all disappointed in him, I am only sorry that true brave men have been made to share his fate. What an excitement it must make in LaSalle county where his regiment was raised. Send me the [*La Salle*] *Press* with its comments when it comes out. What a name to hand down to posterity.

How I should like to be with you at Christmas. What are you going to do to amuse the children? Will any of "our folks" have a Christmas tree? You must imagine me with you, as I shall be in spirit with a Merry Christmas for all.

I am sorry that the group are not *photographable*. Can Mrs. Rockwell *delay* operations a little while to gratify me? If I can't get it I must summon what patience I possess to my aid.

A number of large steamers have just come up (8 P.M.) to take off the troops here numbering some 12,000. This is an unexpected move. We cannot tell what it means, nor can we surmise where they are going.

How cheerfully Hen writes. He seems to be getting quite contented & I think will soon begin to enjoy life in New Haven. I am making up a package

---

* Absolom Moore was being held at Libby Prison and was exchanged several months later.

to send him with pieces of the *Monitor, Merrimac, Congress* & *Cumberland* &c for himself & Alex McAlister*.

What kind of weather are you having? It has seemed but little like winter here yet. Once in a while a raw chilly north westerly wind, but no real cold freezing weather.

Ask Dave if he wants to come to Baltimore & buy out Kimberly's soap factory. I expect it is a large concern. They have made money out of it. It is for sale.

In case you don't hear from me again before Christmas, I wish you all a Merry Christmas. I send the children their *stamps* with a kiss. With much love

William

No. 54—

U.S. Steamer *Monitor*
Off Newport News, Va.
Dec. 20th, 1862

Dear Anna,

Saturday night as well as yours & Sarah's letters which reached me to day remind me of the toast of this evening, "Sweethearts & wives."

I was just wondering how many *sheets* of paper I had written over since leaving home. Here is *letter* No. 54 since I began to number them. Yours I see is No. 28. Hadn't I better hold on a while till you catch up? Or would you rather get an occasional letter if there is not much in it? Mine of late could hardly have been worth the postage.

"All has been quiet along the line." No news of any kind. Nothing from which to manufacture a letter. The same dull monotonous round day after day. We are all anxiously longing for a "change of base" & I shall be glad if for no other reason that I shall hope to find new material for my despatches home.

It seems our worst fears are realised in regard to the late movement of Burnside. What the feeling is among civilians of course I can't say as I see none, but among the military there is a deep feeling of indignation that Burnside should be forced against his judgement to place himself in a position & fight a battle knowing that it would result disasterously. Burnside is blamed to a certain extent for consenting to make the move in the first place, but the great responsibility is laid where I think it should rest — on the Administration. There seemed to have been no regular plan, no concert of action, else where was Siegel & his troops† & one or two of our other Army Corps who could in all have brought 60,000 troops on the enemy's flank. If acting in concert & by a pre-arranged plan these forces should have attacked the

---

* Keeler's friend in New Haven.
† Franz Sigel's two corps remained in reserve and did not see action at Fredericksburg.

enemy in the rear or on the flank while Burnside held them in front. This, every military man here though[t] was the programme & was utterly astonished to learn that Burnside had thrown his whole force fair against the enemy's front after allowing them days & weeks of preparation. No one here will believe such a movement was advised or desired by him. He is blamed only for being forced into it.

What will be our next move it is impossible to say. I hear the subject much discussed & every one agrees upon one thing — that Richmond if taken at all must be approached by the way of James river according to McClellan's original plan. It cannot be that our army will go into winter quarters where they are. That would be suicidal for the administration. I see that indignation meetings are already called in New York by prominent influential persons. Where is this going to bring us, when is it to end?

There is a very uncertain future before us not pleasing to contemplate.* On one side we have our country distracted by civil war, its councils divided by political factions, each striving to use the blood and treasure freely offered by a patriotic public to advance its own selfish ends & purposes. On the other we have the country divided into petty provinces, a north, south, east & west, a district of slavery & a country of freedom, an agricultural district & a manufacturing one, the interests of each one in direct antagonism to its neighbor, laying the foundations for future & unending wars & disturbances.

Then again we have the people sick, tired & disgusted at the manifest imbecility & want of energy of the administration & the utter heartlessness & selfishness manifested by the political jugglers whose motto is "rule or ruin," rising in their might & freeing themselves from these clogs upon their patriotism & loyalty & a military dictator takes the reins & his word is made the law of the land. This is by no means a pleasing aspect of the future, still it is one that will come up in thinking of the future & it will come in reality too if the treasure & blood of the country is to be squandered & sacrificed to gratify the petty animosities & jealousies of political factions. I consider the present a very critical period of our existence. A crisis has arrived which must produce a change of some sort. What it will be the future will disclose.

The events of the last few days I fear has wrought a change in the plans laid out for us. It looks now as if our present inactive life was to continue for an indefinite period.

Sunday 21st—I rec'd a *Chicago Tribune* from you to day, it was like meeting an old acquaintance, but either that or myself have changed very much since our last acquaintance.

I have sent to Birdsey for the book you mentioned. If you do not see a copy of it I will send you mine when I have read it. I must make one request

---

* The Union defeat at Fredericksburg ushered in the darkest days in Washington since the start of the war. Rumors abounded that Lincoln's cabinet (even Lincoln himself) would be forced to resign or that McClellan would be recalled to lead a military government.

& that is in writing to write *proper* names more distinctly. I can make out all your letters without trouble with the exception I mention but I frequently get stuck there.

We have just received intelligence (reliable of course!!) that the new *Merrimac* [*Richmond*] is out in the river against Fort Darling but from defective engines she is exceedingly slow. The rebels also have a floating battery off there. We do not anticipate a visit from her as it is no part of their policy to send her down the river which would only result in her destruction. They know by keeping her up the river that she neutralises three or four of our heavy iron clads which are kept blockading the mouth to prevent her exit. If the weather of the past 3 or 4 days continues much longer, Jack Frost will establish a more effective blockade than all our iron clads.

We are daily looking for 3 or 4 new Monitors — the *Passaic*, *Montauk* (Capt. Worden) & one or two more. It can't be that they will keep the whole of us here inactive. We shall soon know, unless like the *Passaic* they all get here disabled & have to return for repairs.

Remember me to all with a Merry Christmas.

William

[Marginalia] I wish you would preserve the letters of the Sec'y of State of N.Y. & Capt. Worden in Friday's *Herald*.

No. 55—

U.S. Steamer *Monitor*
Off Newport News, Va.
Dec. 23rd, 1862

My Anna,

It is nearly ten o'clock but I cannot resist the impulse to scribble a few lines to you before the Master at Arms comes 'round with his "Four bells (10 o'clock) Gentlemen." At 8 o'clock all lights & fires on board the ship are put out except those of the Ward Room officers & the Captain. At 10 the officers' lights must be extinguished, the Capt. of course burning his as long as he chooses.

This has been a most lovely day, of which I have taken advantage this P.M. to take a long stroll ashore, returning in time for dinner rather tired. With such a life of inactivity as we are leading I find it takes but little exercise to tire me out. I think using a spade in the garden now would be *somewhat* fatiguing especially if I was to keep it up all day.

Gen. Corcoran's forces did not leave here as I wrote you a few days ago, it was the Maine & Penn. Regiments which were in camp here. Gen. C. & his wife were on board this afternoon while I was absent so I did not see them. In reply to my enquiry as to "what kind of a looking woman she was," Capt. Bankhead said that "she was a good healthy substantial looking irish woman with a leg from the knee down nearly the size of a barrel & about as symmetrical." (No one goes up & down our ladders without a display of ancles &c.) The Capt. did not seem to be very much smitten with the graces of either her mind or person.

His [Corcoran's] troops were out on regimental drill. They improve, but slowly enough. They are preparing to go into winter quarters, which looks like spending the winter here. They are at present encamped in tents which are pitched on level land with all the regularity of a well laid out city. The streets which intersect each other at right angles are swept scrupulously clean, the tents are surrounded with screens made of the branches of the live oak & pine, the sides of the streets are also lined with them & over some of the narrower ones there are arches formed of the same material, from the center of which is suspended a wreath, a cross or the number of the company occupying the street, formed of evergreens. A good deal of taste is used in this or[na]mentation & the effect is very fine as you pass along the long street & catch glimpses of the white tents through the evergreen arches & screens, each with its stack of polished muskets standing before the entrance, glittering in the sun shine. The soldiers in their uniforms lounging about or crossing the streets on a visit to some neighbor. It looks more like some holiday festival than the preparation for war. On such a day as this it looks very fine but in cold wet stormy weather give me the bowels of the *Monitor* for a residence.

Wednesday evening, 24th—Following the call of the Master at Arms at my room with his "six bells" &c last evening came Mr. Campbell with a big mince pie & a pitcher of cider, so instead of obeying the hint just rec'd we hung our blankets over the sky lights & other openings making the officer of the watch believe the report made to him by the Master at Arms of "lights all out sir." Campbell had just rec'd a large box from home filled with a variety of cakes, candies, some very fine mince pies & six gallon cans, filled with mince meat. He is one of that sort who will never eat such things by himself so, as I said, he brought one of his pies, some real nice crullers & a pitcher of cider in to my room & himself, the M.D. & myself had a time till 12 o'clock.*

A number of our officers living in New York, Brooklyn, Phila., Baltimore & other places not too far off have had boxes of "good things" sent them to keep Christmas with. I often wish "my folks" were nearer where I could get my box from them, not that I would wish it for the sake of merely gratifying my appetite but I could make some return to those who always give me a portion of theirs.

"Well, Purser," said Capt. Bankhead as one of the boxes was being unpacked in the Ward Room & the contents laid on the table, "I think you & me will have to depend on the rest for our good things. I have neither

---

* Four days later Chief Engineer Albert Campbell was hospitalized after injuring his leg while inspecting a pump, and thus missed the *Monitor*'s final fatal voyage.

Mother, wife or sister to send me such things but I hope some of my New York friends will send me some good wine & cigars."

The *Ironsides* yesterday rec'd over 50 Boxes of various sizes by Express for her officers & crew, most of them probably from their friends at home & filled with Christmas gifts.

Well here we are in Hampton Roads once more just where we lay so long watching the *Merrimac*, so far on our way to new scenes & fresh operations. I wish I could tell you more but I cannot & would not dare to say as much as I have, but before you read this I suppose the telegraph will have made it public that "the *Monitor* has gone to sea." All hands were mustered to day & an order from the Department read forbidding in the most positive manner any person in the military or naval service communicating any news respecting the army or navy either to the papers or to individuals. So we must perforce bow to the mandate though we may condemn it. Capt. B. said after we were through dinner to night, "Gentlemen, you all see the vessel is preparing for sea but I trust in any letters you may write you will make no mention of it, I ask it as your duty to Government & a favour to myself."

Here it is 10 o'clock again. So good night. A line or two more in the morning.

[Thursday, 25th] A Merry Christmas to you all there this morning, my friends. I wish I was where I could tell you so instead of having to write it. I shall think of you often to day. All is hurry on board preparing for sea, though it may be a day or two before we leave. Good bye. With much love.

[No signature]

No. 56—

U.S. Steamer *Monitor*
Hampton Roads, Va.
Dec. 25th, 1862

My Dear Wife,

How I wish I could drop in & have a chat with you all to night but as I can't I must do the next best thing—make my pen the medium. I write you on this occasion with a full & overflowing ------- stomach, the receptacle of no less than three Christmas dinners. I went ashore in the forenoon & meeting Mr. Davids* received a very urgent invitation to dinner at 12 which I accepted & sat down to a table well loaded with a variety of good things. After getting through with him I was met by Kimberly who *demanded* my company at dinner at 2. There was no use of apologising or saying no to him, as he wouldn't hear to any thing of the sort, so I surrendered unconditionally & pitched into roast turkey, mince pies, &c &c &c with all the zest my appetite would allow & I left him with a bottle of nice blackberry wine of his

---

* Manager of the machine shops at Old Point Comfort.

wife's make, a box of cigars & a huge frosted cake which he compelled me to take with me *as I didn't eat any dinner.*

Well I returned on board at 5 just as the Ward Room Mess was sitting down to dinner. Of course while paying my proportion of the expenses of our table it would be folly to allow my proportion of the food to remain uneaten, I concluded to make the attempt, go through the motions at any rate. So the attempt was commenced at *5* & concluded at *8*. As you will imagine the whole three hours were not occupied entirely with eating, considerable talking was done & some vast enterprises were plan[n]ed if not executed. The rebels on the Rappahannock were annihilated, Richmond taken, Charleston blotted out, the Old *Merrimac* fought over again, our military leaders hauled over the coals, "Little Mac" placed in command, the sesech thrashed thoroughly all over the country, a peace conquered, we "iron clads" reigning over the conquered provinces which were divided among us, Johnny Bull taken across our knees & most thoroughly & convincingly spanked with our 15 inch guns, ditto the French if they were found at all saucy. In fact we arrived at the conclusion that the Star Spangled Banner next to us "iron clads" is about the "biggest thing" to be found just now outside of Barnum's Museum.

I cannot give you our bill of fare without using the remainder of my sheet, which I could not afford to do as room is valuable when I have so much of importance? to say. A very brief synopsis will have to do—Soups, Fish, Oysters of course "in every style," Turkey & other poultry & Meats enough to start a Chatham Street eating house. For dessert Oranges, Pineapples, Apples, Figs, Ra[i]sins, five different kinds of nuts, Peaches, Strawberries, Raspberries, Plums, Cherries, Quinces &c &c in cans, Mince & apple pies & cakes without end, Cider, Blackberry & Currant wine. These were not all the products of our own larder but in part the contents of the various boxes received by members of the Mess from friends at home.

The table after it was cleared off & set with the desert looked beautifully. Though no female hands arranged it, still their taste was displayed in the beautiful cakes that ornamented it, not the least conspicuous was a large dish filled with fried cakes. The evening passed very pleasantly & every one "turned in" at 10 in good humour with himself & mankind in general. I felt well satisfied with my day's *work* but my stomach complained a good deal at the work imposed upon it.

Besides the dinners eaten I had invitations to three others — on board the *Brandywine*, on the *Colorado* & in the Fortress which pressure of business compelled me to decline. The Paymaster of the *Colorado* whose acquaintance I have formed is a son of Dr. Williams of Brookfield, Conn.[*] He appears to be a very fine man.

---

[*] William H. H. Williams. The 23-year-old bank teller from Bridgeport, CT enlisted in September 1861. He served on the gunboat USS *Sagamore* in the East Gulf Blockading

Civil War Years: USS *Monitor* (1862)

The day has been a very pleasant one, clear, warm & still & appears to have been kept, as far as could be in this military region, as a holiday. The men of war especially seemed willing to allow their men a little more license than usual, as in the afternoon the place was crowded with them. Though the most stringent regulations exist prohibiting liquor being brought here, still the sailors manage to find it & of course get drunk.

Four English men of war are lying in the Roads whose crews had liberty ashore mingling freely with our men on the best of terms till the parties got too much whisky when a fight would have to decide who was the best man of the two. When I left the beach at evening, there seemed to be a sort of general mess, black eyes, bloody noses, & battered faces seeming to predominate. The soldiers running here & there & the guards busy carrying drunken fighting sailors off to the lock up in the Fortress.

To add to the excitement a heavy & almost continuous firing has been kept up by the Fortress & vessels for some six hours or more. The *Ariadne* (one of the Englishmen) & the *Colorado* were at target practice with their heavy guns. Then the *Melpomene* (another Englishman) came in firing the customary salutes to the flag & admiral which were returned by the Fortress & our vessels. Then came a Frenchman with a similar interchange of compliments. The powder smoke hung like a thick fog over the water & was so dense that at one time it was impossible to see vessels lying a few yards distant from the shore.

Saturday, the 27th—I have kept these few lines hoping to be able to send you some news but there is none of consequence. The *Passaic* is in & lies close by us, the two looking as much alike as possible.

A heavy storm is just coming on which when over is usually followed by several days of calm fine weather. We shall hold on here till the storm is over & take advantage of the calm that follows for our *trip down the coast*.

I hope to have *news* soon to send you. Write me frequently & direct as you always have done. Love to you all.

William

[Marginalia] We feel anxious to hear from the *Montauk*, Capt. Worden, who left New York last Tuesday.

Squadron before being transferred to the USS *Colorado* in December 1862. He met Keeler on his way down to join the blockade off Mobile, AL.

Cape Hatteras (November to December 1862)

No. 57—

U.S. Steamer *Monitor*
Hampton Roads,
Dec. 28th, 1862

Dear Anna,

    I sent letter No. 56 off to you this morning thinking that in all probability it would be the last from Hampton Roads for the present at least. Here we lie weather bound, a strong easterly wind with a heavy sea prevaling outside, rendering unsafe for us to venture. Yours of the 21st No. 29 intended to reach me on Christmas for some unaccountable reason was not received till to day. It was none the less welcome however for being a little late. I was glad enough to hear from you once more before leaving here as I don't know when I shall hear from you after we get away. I wish I could whisper in your ear our destination & plans. I do not hesitate to write it to you "privately" for fear it may leak out, but there is the bare possibility that it (my letter) may miss you & fall into other hands & our plans which government so rigidly guards & justly so be thwarted. You will have to nurse your curiosity & patience for a little while, when we hope again to make "the little *Monitor*" a household word. I am glad now that I wasn't detached & ordered to some other vessel as I desired to be. I wouldn't exchange our "iron box" for any vessel in the navy with our present prospects.

    How I wish I could sit by your side to night & tell you all I know about our plans & purposes but it will perhaps be better to wait & describe them to you in detail after their accomplishment. I also got the [*La Salle*] *Press* with Steven's letter. How awkwardly he writes, I don't see as he does much better than I do & I don't think Coat[e]s has improved much in his style with his advancement.

    Tell Eddie his pictures were real pretty & I was very glad to get them. He must send me some more some time & write me a letter too. Sarah's letter reached me safely & a reply was mailed forthwith. By the way when some of you are writing to Utica say to Helen [Plant] that I wrote her (in reply to hers containing her Mother's photograph), just after we reached here. I have not heard if she received it. I feel quite curious to know how your Christmas Festival succeeded. I hope you will tell me about it when you write again.

    The Commander of the gun boat *Cairo* lately blown up on the Yazoo river by a torpedo was the Commander of the *Monitor* for three or four days after Capt. Worden was hurt till Capt. Jeffers came on board.[*] He was on the *Cumberland* when she went down & sunk with her having a very narrow escape. He has lived a good while for a young man.

    I have just been on deck listening to some very fine music from our English neighbor, the *Ariadne*. She carries a fine brass band. Every morning

---

[*] Thomas Selfridge.

Civil War Years: USS *Monitor* (1862)

St. George's cross is hoisted to the tune of "God Save the Queen" as I suppose they call it, we call it "America." After they are done saving the Queen they compliment us Yankees with the "Star Spangled Banner," "Hail Columbia" &c &c which being well played are duly appreciated.

I see by the *Press* that a Photographic *gallery* has been opened in Peru*. Why can't you make up a party & go down there?

By the way you don't mention Mr. Flye's picture. Was it rec'd? I will send you my friend Kimberly's of which I have a promise as soon as I get it. He made me a visit on board to day with his daughter & niece (14 & 16 years old). I havn't had any visitors whom I have shewed around with any greater satisfaction. He has shewn me a great many kindnesses since we have been here. His house has always been open to me & it is very seldom he will take pay for any little thing I want from the store.

We hear no news from the Army on the Rappahannock. For ought we know they are going into winter quarters. I hope you will receive the [*New York*] *Herald* I sent you a day or two since contain[in]g the account of the battles before Richmond written by a rebel officer. You will see that they appreciate McClellan if we do not.

You ask me if "I intend to renew the other papers." I have often thought the Bridgeport paper might as well be stopped as we have so little to interest us there now. Do just as you please about. Should you wish it discontinued you had better write to Henry to get your Father or Geo.† sometime when they are over there to stop it & pay the bill. You can send Henry the money when you are sending for other purposes.

I hope you have met with success in your Festival enterprise notwithstanding the seceders. The President should issue his proclamation commanding them to return to the bosom of the Union.

You must remember me with much respect to all our friends, especially Mr. & Mrs. Rockwell & Mr. & Mrs. Hough, Mr. Campbell &c. Tell Mr. Campbell to hold fast to McClellan. I confidently believe he will yet be the one to lead our armies to victory.

I think you have made a good use of the stamps I have sent the children—books last longer than candy. I think I forgot to put any stamps in my letter for them this morning but send some now. Tell Tib that Papa's "fiskers" flourish finely, they are getting to be ornamental.

I shall probably not have an opportunity to write you again from this place, but you will not be long without a letter from me & I hope to be able to make it interesting. I do not think material will be wanting from present prospects.

Tell Dave I have not forgotten the promise I made Ham to try & find a place for him down here. But since my return here I have been brought so

---

* A town near La Salle.
† Keeler's brother-in-law in New Haven.

little in contact with our army officers that I have had no opportunity. I shall leave these few lines for tomorrow. Good night.

Monday morning [December 29]—We are preparing to leave. Good bye to all.

William

Fortress Munroe
Sunday [Jan. 4, 1863]

My Dear Wife,

The telegraph has probably informed you before this of the loss of the *Monitor* & also of my safety. My escape was a very narrow one. My personal effects at this time may be summed up thus — 1 pr. pants, 1 do. stockings, 1 shirt. In fact I lost everything but the few clothes I kept on, most of them having been thrown off for a swim. I have been through a night of horrors that would have appalled the stoutest heart. The first moment's leisure I can get I will send you full details. In the mean time rest assured I am safe, though bruised & sore, but not seriously hurt. I am waiting here to know where the Department are going to order us & what they are going to do. I am in friend Kimberly's kind keeping & want for nothing. I went to the P.O. as soon as landing & found your letter wishing me a happy New Year & you may rest assured that it could not have come at a more acceptable time. This morning I rec'd one from Helen Plant. You shall hear from me in a day or two. Till then good bye. Love to all,

William

(No. 1)

Washington, D.C.
Jan'y 6th, 1863

Dear Anna,

Another chapter has been added to my eventful life. The *Monitor* is no more. What the fire of the enemy failed to do, the elements have accomplished.

We left Hampton Roads Monday afternoon (Dec. 29th) at 2 o'clock in tow of the side wheel gun boat *Rhode Island*. We were attached to her by means of two large hawsers, one 11 inches, the other 15 inches in circumference and from 250 to 300 feet in length. Everything passed quietly & pleasantly that afternoon & evening. A smooth sea & clear skies seemed to promise a successful termination of our trip & an opportunity of once more trying our metal against rebel works & making the "Little *Monitor*" once again a household word.

Tuesday morning cloud banks were seen rising in the south & west & they gradually increased till the sun was obscured by their cold grey mantle. The wind which in the morning was quite light continued to increase till the middle of the afternoon when it blew quite heavy, the sea rolling with violence across our deck rendering it impossible to remain on it without danger of being swept off. We amused ourselves for an hour or more watching two or three large sharks who glided quietly along by our sides observing us apparently with a curious eye as if in anticipation of a feast. We made no water of consequence. A little trickled down about the pilot house & some began to find its way under the turret rendering it wet & cheerless below.

At 5 o'clock P.M. we sat down to dinner, every one cheerful & happy & though the sea was rolling & foaming over our heads the laugh & jest passed freely 'round. All rejoicing that at last our monotonous inactive life had ended & the "gallant little *Monitor*" would soon add fresh laurels to her name.

It was dark when I returned to the top of the turret. We were now off Hatteras, the Cape Horn of our Atlantic coast. The wind was blowing violently. The heavy seas rolled over our bows dashing against the pilot house & surging aft would strike the solid turret with a force to make it tremble, sending off on either side a boiling foaming torrent of water.

Word came from the engine room that we were making water, more than the ordinary pumps (which had been kept working) would throw out. It sounded ominously. Orders were given to start the Worthington pump, which for a time kept the water down, but again the report, "The water is gaining on us, sir." As a last resort the large centrifugal pump, of a capacity of three thousand gallons per minute, was started & once more the water diminished, but it was of short duration. The opening through which the water was rushing was rapidly enlarged by the constant beating of the sea, which was now at times rolling over the top of the turret. Again came the report that the water was gaining & had risen above the engine room floor. It was the death knell of the *Monitor*. The storm continued to increase in fury.

In order to understand our situation & contrast it with our passage from New York to Hampton Roads last spring, it will be necessary to bear in mind that in the latter case "the sea was on our beam" as sailors term it, that is, the waves would come up on our side, rolling on to us on one side & off on the other. Now we were going "head on," or in other words were crossing them at right angles. As we were unable to carry our boats at sea, they had been sent on board the *Rhode Island* & nothing whatever remained to support us in the water were we obliged to trust ourselves to that treacherous element.

But our brave little craft struggled long & well. Now her bow would rise on a huge billow & before she could sink into the intervening hollow, the succeeding wave would strike her under her heavy armour with a report like thunder & a violence that threatened to tear apart the thin sheet iron bottom & the heavy armour which it supported. Then she would slide down a watery mountain into the hollow beyond & plunging her bow into the black rolling billow would go down, down, down, under the surging wave till naught could be seen but the top of the black "cheese box" isolated in a sea of hissing

Cape Hatteras (November to December 1862)

seething foam, extending as far as we could see around us. Then as she rose slowly & sullenly under the accumulated weight of waters, the foam pouring in broad sheets off the iron deck, a wave would roll over the bow & strike the pilot house with a force that would send the water in torrents on to the top of the turret where our little company were gathered. From behind the iron breastwork which surmounted the top of the turret, a circle of anxious faces were gazing over the expanse of angry waters & awaiting with anxiety the report from the pumps. It came as I have stated.

About this time too it was found our smaller hawser had parted, a disaster which no human agency could remedy, as well might one stand under Niagara, as to attempt to breast the waves which were rolling over our decks. It was with the greatest reluctance that our Captain now gave the order to make the signal for assistance. Every pump was at work & gangs of men had been organised to bail, more however with the design of keeping them employed & preventing a panic, than with the hope of any good result. The water was already a foot deep on the engine room floor & was fast deepening in the ward room. From its rapid influx it was very evident that but a short time would elapse before it would reach the fires & then the iron heart of the *Monitor* would cease to beat. Every expedient which human ingenuity or skill could suggest had been tried in vain & all that remained was to save the lives of those on board.

At the order our signal flashed upon the darkness, lighting up the tumultuous sea for miles around. Our consort stopped & attempted to come alongside, but with the two vessels connected with the hawser it was found impossible. At the call for a volunteer to go forward & cut it (a task involving almost certain destruction), one of our officers seized a hatchet & going cautiously forward holding on the life line, which was stretched around the deck, with a few blows severed the connection while the waves were rolling high over his head & returned in safety to the turret.[*]

We hailed our consort as soon as sufficiently near, "Send your boats immediately, we are sinking." A hoarse unintelligible reply was all that we could get amid the roar of the elements. Again & again it was repeated & signal after signal flashed out amid the storm as we saw no sign of boats, & the same unintelligible response induced us to believe that they understood neither our signal or our hail. Words cannot depict the agony of those moments as our little company gathered on the top of the turret, stood with a mass of sinking iron beneath them, gazing through the dim light, over the raging waters with an anxiety amounting almost to agony for some evidence of succor from the only source to which we could look for relief. Seconds lengthened into hours & minutes into years.

About this time the report was brought from the engine room that the water had reached the furnaces & the fires were being extinguished. Our

---

[*] The volunteer was Louis Stodder.

Civil War Years: USS *Monitor* (1862)

Commander's orders were given calmly & cooly & met with a ready & cheerful response from officers & men. No one faltered in obedience, but a ready aye, aye sir, met every order. Some however obeyed mechanically, while others worked cooly & resolutely as if realising that our safety depended upon the prompt & ready execution of every order.

After an hour that seemed an eternity to us, boats were seen approaching. What a load was taken from our anxious hearts. With what interest we watched as they toiled & struggled slowly over the heavy seas, now hidden from our sight in a watery hollow, then balanced on the foaming crest of a mountain wave.

Hoping to be able to get off in one of the approaching boats & to take with me the books & accounts of the vessel, I started for my state room to gather them up. I passed down the turret ladder, felt my way around the guns & making a misstep fell from the top of the berthdeck ladder to the deck below. A dim lantern swinging to & fro with the motion of the vessel just served to make the nearest objects visible in the thick darkness, rendered more dense if possible by the steam, heat & gas which was finding its way in from the half extinguished fires of the engine room. I passed across this deck, down into the ward room, where I found the water nearly to my waist & swashing from side to side with the roll of the ship, & groped my way through the narrow crooked passage into my state room. It was a darkness that could be felt. The hot, stifling, murky atmosphere pervaded every corner. After groping about for a little time, I collected what books & papers I deemed it important to save, but found they made so large & unmanageable a mass that the attempt to save them would be utterly useless & would only endanger my life, as my whole physical energies would be required to get me safely over the wave washed deck & into the boats. I took down my watch, which was hanging on a nail near by &, putting it in my pocket, took out my safe keys with the intention of saving the Government "green backs." The safe was entirely submerged. In the thick darkness, below the water & from the peculiar form of the lock I was unable to insert the key. I desisted from the attempt & started to return.

My feelings at this time it is impossible to describe, when I reflected that I was nearly at the fartherest extremity of the vessel from its only outlet & this outlet liable to be completely obstructed at any moment by a rush of panic stricken men, & the vessel itself momentarily expected to give the final plunge. Everything was enveloped in a thick murky darkness, the waves dashing violently across the deck over my head, my retreat to be made through the narrow crooked passage leading to my room, through the ward room where the chairs & tables were surging violently from side to side, threatening severe bruises if not broken limbs, then up a ladder to the berth deck, across that & up another ladder into the turret, around the guns & over gun tackle, shot, sponges & rammers which had broken loose from their fastenings, & up the last ladder to the top of the turret.

Cape Hatteras (November to December 1862)

I reached the goal & found our consort close alongside, so near in fact that I expected every instant to see her thrown against our iron side & both vessels go down together. Her launch was under her quarter & was crashing & grinding most fearfully between the two vessels. Its crew had leaped upon our deck to escape being crushed with the boat & for a time it seemed as if we had but received an addition to our imperilled number. Ropes were thrown from over her bulwarks, which towered far above us but none of the crew seemed to have the courage & resolution to make the perilous passage of the deck & seize them. Fortunately she remained but a short time in this position. She forged slowly ahead, clear of our iron mass, leaving her launch tossing & pitching against our side with a violence that threatened its instant demolition. It was necessary that she should receive her living freight without delay & leave the dangerous spot, but the embarkation was an undertaking of the most perilous nature as sea after sea was sweeping the deck with resistless violence. Already two or three of our number had been swept off & those who remained seemed to hang back fearing to make the effort. It was a scene well calculated to appall the boldest heart. Mountains of water were rushing across our decks & foaming along our sides. The small boats were pitching & tossing about on them or crashing against our sides, mere playthings on the billows. The howling of the tempest, the roar & dash of waters, the hoarse orders through the speaking trumpets of the officers, the response of the men, the shouts of encouragement & words of caution, "the bubbling cry of some strong swimmer in his agony,"* & the whole scene lit up by the ghastly glare of the blue lights burning on our consort, formed a panorama of horror which time can never efface from my memory.

Upon the order from Capt. B. to "lead the men to the boats," I divested myself of the greater portion of my clothing to afford me greater facilities for swimming in case of necessity & attempted to descend the ladder leading down the outside of the turret but found it full of men hesitating but desiring to make the perilous passage of the deck. I found a rope hanging from one of the awning staunchons over my head & slid down it to the deck. A huge wave passed over me, tearing me from my footing & bearing me along with it, rolling, tumbling & tossing like the merest speck. My feeble powers of swimming were of no avail in this whirlpool of foaming waters. I distinctly remember at this time making a hasty review of natural history, piscatorially considered, especially where it related more immediately to the specimens who had favoured us with their company during the forepart of the day & I attempted a mathematical calculation as to the number of rations that 150 pounds of humanity would make them. I however had but little time for thought or reflection as I was borne helpless along with the moving mass of water. I was carried as near as I could judge ten or twelve yards from the vessel when I came to the surface & the backset of the wave threw me against

---

* Lord Byron's *Don Juan* (Canto II, 1819).

the vessel's side near one of the iron staunchons which supported the life line. This I grasped with all the energy of desperation & drawing myself on deck worked my way along the life line & was hauled into the boat into which the men were jumping one by one as they could venture across the deck.

We were soon loaded and shoved off but our dangers were not yet over. We were in a leaky overloaded boat, through whose crushed sides the water was rushing in streams & had nearly half a mile to row over the storm tossed sea before we could reach the *Rhode Island*. This, after a hard long struggle, was accomplished & we found ourselves under the weather quarter of our consort in imminent danger of being swamped as she sunk in the hollow of the sea. The ends of ropes were thrown to us from the high bulwarks over our heads, which the more active of our number seized & climbed up. Others grasped them firmly & were thus drawn over the side. In my exhausted state & with my crippled hand I could do neither of these, but watching my opportunity till I saw a loop, or what a sailor would call a bight of a rope, let down, I passed it under my arms & was drawn on board the *Rhode Island* to receive the congratulations & hospitalites of her officers, & I assure you they were not deficient in either.

Other boats soon came alongside bringing the remainder of our officers & crew & a little before one o'clock on the morning of the 31st the *Monitor* disappeared beneath the surface. On mustering the officers & crew, four officers & twelve of the crew were missing. Those who escaped did so without receiving any serious injury with the exception of our surgeon, whose fingers on one hand were so badly mashed by being caught between the boats as to render partial amputation necessary.

One of the *Rhode Island*'s boats was still absent & we spent the remainder of the night & the next day in search of it, when we proceeded to Wilmington where the vessel was ordered. From there we were ordered to Beaufort & thence to Hampton Roads where we received every kindness & hospitality that friendship & our destitute condition could suggest.

During all the time we were standing on the sinking ship, & while whirling over & over in the water, I am not aware that the idea occurred to me that I might be lost. Although I fully realised the danger, I looked forward with just as much confidence to being saved as if it were a fact already established. When we left Hampton Roads we felt convinced that if we should encounter a severe gale we should go to the bottom & had it not been for shewing a want of confidence in our vessel & a tendency to create a panic among the men, all the officers would have transfered their effects to the *Rhode Island*. As it was we got on board of her perfectly destitute & had it not been for the kindness & generosity of her officers we should have fared poorly indeed. I still hope to visit Charleston in an iron clad.

Yours truly,
W. F. Keeler

Cape Hatteras (November to December 1862)

[This note was appended to the bottom of the previous letter]

New Haven
Jan'y 14th, 1863

Friend Webster*,

The accompanying sheets were intended for my wife, but find she is on her way here to join me, so place them at your disposal if you see fit to publish them. Had I intended them for print they would have been more carefully written, so when you see a gross error (as no doubt you will, many) please correct & when through with the Ms. [manuscript] please return to Mr. Brown† as I desire to preserve it.

Yours truly,
W. F. Keeler

USS *Florida* (1863-1865)

> *In the dusk of evening and early dark the blockade is run by steamers (perhaps not showing black smoke), who thus get a safe and long run off the coast. At morning twilight and at night, guided by shore signals, the runners get in under the batteries. When a runner is seen coming out, it is desirable not to make the signal until his retreat can be cut off by getting between him and the bar or coast. It is best to capture or destroy runners when discovered, but not to throw away the chance of doing one or the other by prematurely alarming them and causing their retreat over the bar, or under the batteries, to escape under more favorable circumstances.* (Part of Acting Rear-Admiral Samuel Phillips Lee's detailed instructions to the commanding officers of the blockading vessels off Wilmington, 16 December 1863)‡

Four days after the *Monitor* was lost, Navy Secretary Gideon Welles granted the officers and crew who had served on her from the date of muster to the sinking, two-weeks' leave of absence, along with a portion of the pay due to them. As paymaster, Keeler had to remain at the Washington Navy Yard to reconstruct the crew's pay accounts which had gone down with the vessel. Unable to return home, he was joined by Anna who made the long trip east, leaving their two youngest children Eddie and Tibbie at home in La Salle with his parents. Keeler divided his time between Washington and New Haven where their 15-year old son Henry had been living and studying for the past few months.

---

* Edward C. Webster, editor of the *La Salle Press*.
† Keeler's brother-in-law in La Salle.
‡ ORN, I:9, pp. 355-56.

Civil War Years: USS *Florida* (1863-1865)

In early January Keeler was ordered to the USS *Florida*, which was being re-fitted at the New York Navy Yard. Command of the vessel had been given to John Bankhead, who had requested that Keeler serve again as his paymaster. Those orders were revoked on January 10 so that Keeler could complete his work on the *Monitor*'s pay accounts. On February 7, with that work completed, he was ordered to New York to report to Rear Admiral Hiram Paulding for duty on board the *Florida*.

The *Florida* was a wooden side-wheel steamer, 214 feet long and 35 feet abeam, with a top speed of 13 knots. She was built on the East River in New York in 1850 for the New York & Savannah Steam Navigation Company as a passenger liner, making regular trips between those two cities before being purchased by the U.S. Navy in August 1861. Fitted out as a warship in New York, she was commissioned USS *Florida* in October 1861 and served in the South Atlantic Blockading Squadron for one year. In November 1862 the *Florida* returned to New York for major repairs and an upgrade in her armament. Her new compliment of guns consisted of a 100-pounder Parrot rifle at midship on the main deck, a 50-pounder Dahlgren rifle at the bow, four IX-inch Dahlgren smoothbores (two on the main deck aft of the Parrot rifle and two on the quarter deck) and one 12-pounder rifle.

On March 7, 1863 the *Florida* was re-commissioned and ordered to the North Atlantic Blockading Squadron in which she would serve for the remainder of the war. For much of the time, the vessel was stationed off the coast of North Carolina, blockading the port city of Wilmington, located 20 miles upstream from the mouth of the Cape Fear River. By March 1863 the city had become the Confederacy's most important link to the outside world, where armaments, clothing and supplies from abroad came in, and cotton, tobacco and naval stores such as turpentine and rosin went out. Compared to the other major Confederate ports still open (Mobile, Charleston and Galveston), Wilmington was much closer to the Army of Northern Virginia. Good rail connections between Wilmington and Richmond enabled that army to be supplied.

Goods for Wilmington were loaded onto regular merchant ships in European ports and shipped to either Nassau in the Bahamas or Bermuda where they were transferred onto the much faster blockade runners, most of which were sleek iron-hulled steamers built in ship yards in northern England and Scotland. The distance from Nassau to Wilmington was 570 miles, a trip that took about 50 hours. From Bermuda, a distance of 674 miles, the trip could be made in about 60 hours. Once the blockade runners were within view of the coast, men on shore guided them in by pre-arranged signal flags during day and signal lights at night. Moonless nights were the preferred times to run in (or out). Once they had slipped past the blockading fleet and were under the protection of the Confederate guns, the blockade runners were effectively safe. To compel the blockaders to remain even further from shore,

CIVIL WAR YEARS: USS *FLORIDA* (1863-1865)

the rebels also employed mobile batteries of rifled Whitworth guns which could fire shells up to five miles.

Entrance to the Cape Fear River was by two navigable channels: Western Bar channel (or South Inlet as Keeler called it) and New Inlet. Between those two channels lay Smith's Island which protruded about 10 miles into the Atlantic. Stretching a further 15 miles out into the ocean from Smith's Island was the Frying Pan Shoals, which could not be crossed by any but the shallowest draft vessels. The presence of the shoals meant that the blockading squadron had to be broken into two groups. The group of vessels on the south side of the shoals watched the 30-mile length of coastline from Western Bar channel to the South Carolina border, while the group on the north side watched the much longer (100-mile) stretch from New Inlet and Beaufort. Due to the greater distance covered on the north side, as well as the presence of the long narrow sounds running parallel to the barrier islands that provided safe passage for blockade runners, the blockaders on that side had a far more difficult task than those on the south side.

Four forts protected Wilmington, the two largest and most important being Fort Caswell, a masonry structure built in the 1830s which guarded Western Bar channel, and Fort Fisher, an earthwork fort that did not exist before the war, which guarded New Inlet. Of the two, Fort Fisher was by far the most important. Bristling with over 40 heavy guns by the end of the war, it had grown in size from a single battery in 1861 into the largest earthwork fort in the Confederacy, stretching more than a mile in length. Capturing Fort Fisher was the key to capturing Wilmington.

It was during the tenure of Acting Rear Admiral Samuel Phillips Lee that the Wilmington blockade became the most advanced. Lee had taken over command of the North Atlantic Blockading Squadron from Louis Goldsborough in the fall of 1862. Efficient, meticulous and details-oriented, Lee was known throughout the Navy as "Old Triplicate." He developed the most complex system of blockade of any of the squadrons. His system comprised three tiers of vessels. In the first tier, which consisted of small shallow-draft gun boats and tugs, the vessels were positioned as close to shore as possible at night. They acted as pickets, warning the second tier of larger and faster vessels located further from shore of the presence of blockade runners. The third tier comprised the fastest vessels, which cruised as far east as Nassau in search of blockade runners they could pick off. Being a moderately fast vessel, the *Florida* served on both the second and third tiers.

Despite Lee's efforts, the Wilmington blockade was never completely effective owing to the continually increasing improvements in blockade runner design and an insufficient number of vessels needed to guard the miles of coastline. When Wilmington finally fell in January 1865, Lee was no longer in command of the squadron. Believing that he was not up to the task of taking Fort Fisher, Navy Secretary Gideon Welles had replaced him with Rear Admiral David Porter in October 1864.

Civil War Years: USS *Florida* (1863-1865)

Off Wilmington (March to September 1863)

The officers stood grouped about the deck with glasses to their eyes watching the chase & speculating as to the probability of our catching her. A thousand surmises & opinions were passing around as to her speed, character, cargo &c &c, & when our first shot tore howling through the air & we saw by the splash of the falling missile that we had her in range we knew that she was ours & there was a lot of light, happy hearts on board. (12 June 1863)

When Keeler arrived at the New York Navy Yard on February 10, 1863 he was surprised to learn that three of his fellow officers from the *Monitor* would also be serving with him on the *Florida*. Lieutenant Samuel Dana Greene, who pulled Bankhead from the frigid waters off Cape Hatteras, served again as executive officer. Peter Williams, who steered the *Monitor* in the fight with the *Virginia* and was praised by Bankhead for his actions during the sinking of the *Monitor*, was an acting ensign. Like Keeler, both men were assigned at Bankhead's request. Grenville Weeks, whose fingers were crushed during the rescue operation, served again as acting assistant surgeon, but at his own request. The four other wardroom officers were transferred from other vessels. Acting Ensign Samuel Crafts, an inventor's son from Woodbury, Connecticut, eschewed a college education for a life at sea. It was when he was captain of a merchant ship that he first met Keeler when they went on a hunt for peaches at Newport News in the summer of 1862. He enlisted and received his appointment in December 1862. Acting Ensign Robert Wagstaff, son of a Great Lakes steamer captain, began his career as a salt water sailor at the age of seven. He was appointed acting master's mate in December 1861 and served on one of the mortar schooners in the attack on the forts guarding New Orleans in April 1862. Acting Chief Engineer John Ziegler, son of a Philadelphia shoemaker, enlisted in February 1862 and had been serving on the *Florida* since that time. Acting Master John McGowan, the youngest of the officers at only 19 years of age, was a sea captain's son. He was appointed an acting master's mate in March 1862 and commanded a gunboat on the Potomac and Rappahannock Rivers before joining the *Florida*.

On March 9 the *Florida* steamed out of the New York Navy Yard bound for Beaufort, South Carolina towing one of Ericsson's new monitors for the upcoming ironclad attack on Charleston. After delivering the monitor they returned to Hampton Roads where they were ordered to the Wilmington blockade. They spent their first three months on the north side of the Frying Pan Shoals, guarding the New Inlet entrance to Cape Fear River. In June they were ordered to the south side of the shoals. There they made their first capture, the iron-hulled British-built screw steamer *Calypso* which was making its seventh trip through the blockade, running in from Nassau with cases of wines and liquors, barrels of fruit, butter and cheese, stores for fine living, as well as armor plating for ironclads. They followed this soon after with their second capture, the schooner *Hattie*, which had run out from Wilmington with a load of cotton, turpentine and rosin. It was these adrenalin-filled rushes of the chase and the allure of prize money from a capture that kept the men going and lessened the day-to-day monotony of the blockade.

In early August Bankhead was forced to leave due to illness. Command of the *Florida* passed temporarily to Lieutenant Commander James Parker pending the arrival of Lieutenant Commander Walter Queen. According to Keeler, Queen was an ineffective and timid commander, who was greatly disliked by all on board. A welcome arrival was 24-year old Acting Assistant Surgeon Hiram James, who replaced the incompetent Grenville Weeks in August after he was forced to leave. Not long out of medical school in Philadelphia, James served three months on the USS *Kensington* before joining the *Florida*. Suffering from constant and debilitating sea sickness, he was sent home on sick leave in early January 1864.

Letters of special note: March 8 (description of his stateroom); March 28 (drills and daily routine); April 11 (inspection of the crew's clothing and the "lucky bag"); April 18 (nighttime on the blockade); May 9 (visits to Beaufort, Morehead City and Fort Macon; the joys of beachcombing); June 12 (capture of the *Calypso*); June 30 (a visit to New Bern; encounters with friends Flye and Beecher); July 20 (description of crew members and fellow officers); August 1 (an encounter with a poor-white farmer); August 9 (Captain Bankhead's departure; nighttime on the blockade).

No. 1—New Series

                                          U.S. Steamer *Florida*
                                          New York Navy Yard
                                          March 8th, 1863

Dear Anna,

I wanted very much to go up & see you once more after bidding you good bye in the carriage, but found with all my duties that it was impossible. In a few minutes after you left, the ship was hauled out into the stream & an anchor let go.

Mrs. Crafts* left just before the gang plank was taken down. She appeared to feel bad enough. I felt sorry for her, though I could not see that she was any worse off than some others I know of.

We lay at anchor all day, with a thousand things to see to, all requiring my immediate attention—it seemed but little like Sunday. It was a busy day & I was not sorry to see it come to an end. Learning something by my first night's experience on the *Monitor*, I carefully avoided linen sheets & rolled myself upon two pair of heavy warm blankets & slept soundly till morning.

---

* The wife of Acting Ensign Samuel P. Crafts.

Civil War Years: USS *Florida* (1863-1865)

I was awakened about midnight by a messenger bringing on board a dispatch from Washington ordering us to proceed to sea "immediately," to wait for nothing. Capt. B. [Bankhead] was not on board & one of the officers was sent to New York for him in the midst of a terrible storm of rain, snow & sleet. I heard the order given him to go for Capt. B. & listened to the storm beating on the deck over my head and, thanking my stars that I was not a watch officer, I rolled over in my berth to sleep again.

Monday, March 9th—The Captain came on board about three o'clock in the morning in the midst of a pouring rain, but the pilot declaring it was useless to attempt to move amid the fog & darkness we lay till morning. The sun rose bright & clear & all on board were active early. Everything was bustle & stir preparing to leave. Boats were sent ashore for the "last things" & among them I managed to secure a nice crimson plush chushion [cushion] for the lounge in my state room.

On attempting to get up our anchor we found it entangled in the *Sabine*'s moorings so that we were obliged to slip our chain & let it go. We moved down to the Battery* & came to anchor again. Towards noon the *Nantucket*† steamed down to us and made fast with a big 15-inch hawser and we started once more about the middle of the afternoon with her in tow.

Weather clear but cool.

I got my room put to rights & made matters look a little more comfortable than when you saw it—my clothes stowed away in my drawers, the contents of various boxes & bundles disposed of, a carpet down on top of the oil cloth, cushion on the lounge &c &c. I wish you could see it as it is now with a bright sun shining in the air port.

At dark we were out of sight of Sandy Hook & our pilot left us, taking with him a number of letters—one for yourself among the others. This is the anniversary of our fight with the *Merrimac*. A year has brought about some changes.

Tuesday, 10th—This has been a rough stormy day—rain, hail, snow & blow. But though so cheerless without it has been comfortable & pleasant within. We don't look up now to see the sea rolling over our heads. Our decks are dry, with plenty of room to move about.

The *Nantucket* has been surging and splashing through the water behind us with the seas constantly rolling over her. I congratulated myself every time I looked that way that I was not one of her inmates. Towards night the weather was so bad & looked so threatening that she signaled us to put into the [Delaware] Breakwater, which we did & lay there all night among a mass of schooners which like ourself had put in there for shelter. The night was very dark & stormy. The *Nantucket* must have felt much safer than out at sea.

---

* The park at the southern tip of Manhattan Island.
† The monitor they were towing to Beaufort, SC for the ironclad attack on Charleston.

Off Wilmington (March to September 1863)

Wednesday, 11th—The morning was cold & stormy, a mixture of snow & rain covering our decks. The whole forenoon was spent in clearing our chains & hawser from a schooner with which we got tangled up during the night. About noon the weather cleared up & we started off once more. The afternoon was clear but cool. The men were called to quarters & exercised at the guns for the first time since we left.

Thursday, 12th—The weather has been clear and pleasant during the forenoon but quite cool—in the afternoon occasional snow squalls. At sunrise we were off the entrance to Hampton Roads & at noon off Hatteras, not far from where the *Monitor* went down. The wind is light and water tolerably smooth, an occasional sea breaks over the deck of the iron clad astern. So far she has had very favourable weather.

Friday, 13th—About breakfast time this morning we were off Cape Lookout. The weather has been clear & pleasant but cool. Overcoats are still comfortable on deck and we find a fire agreeable in our Ward Room.

Saturday, 14th—This has been a clear pleasant spring like day—a soft mild air & water smooth as a mill pond. At noon we were of[f] the famous city of Charleston. Fort Sumpter was plainly visible & with a glass I could distinguish its embrasures & rebel flag waving us defiance. They were at target practice in some of the shore batteries & from the sound of the guns I should think they had some pretty heavy pieces. The shores both above & below the entrance to the harbour appeared in the distance like long low stretches of white sand beach with a skirting of scrubby underbrush. The *Ironsides* with quite a fleet of gun boats were off the entrance. They were enough in number to guard it pretty effectually. We ran in among them & remained for about an hour.

I was the only one who brought any [news]papers & those were only the ones I brought from Uncle B[rush]'s. How eagerly they were sought for & how gladly received, those only can imagine who have been days & weeks without their daily paper, shut out from the world about them. As we got under way once more, a large boat having the appearance of one of our western river steamers came down from the city (whose spires could be plainly seen in the distance) & steamed slowly around the fort as if to see what new accessions the fleet had had.

Sunday, 15th—We came to anchor last night off the entrance of Port Royal harbour, not caring to run the risk of entering in the night time.* "Up anchor" at day light & ran in, passing Hilton Head on our left. But little of it was visible through a thick hazy atmosphere but long lines of barracks & sheds & scattered negro quarters. In the foreground was the usual long white

---

* Captured by a naval force commanded by Samuel F. Du Pont in November 1861, Port Royal was the most important Union naval base south of Hampton Roads. When the *Florida* arrived at Port Royal, Du Pont was on board the USS *Wabash* preparing his ill-fated ironclad attack on Charleston.

Civil War Years: USS *Florida* (1863-1865)

sand beach. We passed on & up toward Beaufort & anchored near the flag ship (the *Wabash*) about 15 miles from the city. What with store ships, transports, supply vessels, schooners & gun boats, a large fleet is here, including (with the one we brought down) seven Monitors. Great preparation is being made for an attack on Charleston which will not be long delayed.

You will probably remember that I told you that the great danger I feared for the Monitors was from sunken torpedoes. So it has proved. The *Montauk* (Capt. Worden) had a hole blown through her bottom a few days since by one & was only saved from sinking by running her ashore where she was repaired & is now as good as ever.[*] In the attack on Charleston they will shove a raft in front of them, so constructed as to catch & explode the torpedoes before the vessel gets near enough to be injured by them. The *Passaic* in a fight with some of the batteries here received a shell on her deck from a mortar which went nearly through, so I am told.

This has been a beautiful warm day, the sun shining so warm as to make us seek the shade. No boat has been ashore, so I have had no opportunity to see how it looks there.

Monday, 16th—Another beautiful day, so warm as to make thinner clothing comfortable. We left Port Royal on our way to Hampton Roads about 4 o'clock P.M., taking a large mail from the fleet at Port Royal. We made the quickest trip down from New York with our iron clad that has yet been made.

I find our vessel very pleasant, roomy & comfortable, even more so than I had expected. I can appreciate these things more after being "cabined, cribbed, confined"[†] on board the *Monitor* for nearly a year. I wish you could see us now that everything is put to rights. It looks very different from what it did that stormy cheerless Sunday you took such a hasty look around. My state room is a real cosy spot. A nice piece of brussel's carpet covers the oil cloth in front of my berth & [a] handsome crimson cushion covers the lounge on the opposite side. An easy camp stool occupies the end opposite the door near my desk & your pin cushion ornaments the space over the wash bowl by the side of my glass. My bed is nicely made & my clothes hung up or neatly stowed away in the drawers.

A handsome solar lamp burns brightly in the Ward Room over our table & I am writing (9 P.M.) at my secretary by the light of our usual navy candle. Some of our officers are gossiping around the table, others are on deck having a smoke or enjoying the fresh sea air. We are bounding along at a spanking rate, with a full head of steam & every sail set on our way to Hamp-

---

[*] Worden was in command of the USS *Montauk*, one of Ericsson's new monitors. On February 28 in a trial run for the upcoming attack on Charleston, the *Montauk* struck a torpedo in the Ogeechee River in Georgia, but suffered only minor damage.
[†] William Shakespeare's *Macbeth*.

ton Roads to bring down another iron clad, when we expect the ball will open at Charleston.

We count eight officers in our Ward Room (with six servants), so far a very pleasant circle. They are (in order of rank) Lieut. Greene, Master McGowan*, myself, Surgeon Weeks, Chief Engineer Zeigler†, Ensigns Crafts, Williams & Wagstaff‡. Mr. Crafts I find to be a very pleasant companion & am very glad he came out with us.

I have had my hands full ever since we left endeavouring to bring something like order & system out of the chaotic confusion which seemed to reign in my department as well as all others & it was not till to day that I could tell correctly the number [of men] on board. We count 184 souls, the supplying of which with their regular allowance of provisions, clothing, money and a variety of small articles, besides keeping the accounts of each one, falls on me.

I find I shall not have as much idle time as when on the *Monitor* & I am right glad of it for time will not hang as heavy on my hands, besides I am so much more pleasantly situated. Besides my state room with its little desk, I have my secretary in the Ward Room as you will recollect & a large office about three times as large as my state room with every convenience for writing. We have a capital Cook§ & Steward** & though our provisions are not as choice & expensive as on board the *Monitor* they are incomparably better cooked. But here is the 10 o'clock call so good night.

Tuesday, 17th—Our pleasant weather continues. Instead of following the coast as when we went down we are making a straight course for Cape Henry, at the entrance of the Chesapeake. In the evening, very strangely & unexpectedly to us all, we found ourselves going on to the Frying Pan Shoals. Our course was quickly altered & after running east till nearly midnight we once more turned to the north.

Wednesday, 18th—We have had another pleasant day, but now (evening) the wind is blowing heavy from the north west & the weather looks threatening. The vessel rolls & pitches & the timbers groan & creak to a degree we never experienced on the *Monitor*. We had some trouble to keep our dishes on the table at supper as we neglected to put on the rack. With a good vessel we do not heed the storm.

---

* John McGowan, Jr*.
† John Q. A. Ziegler*.
‡ Robert M. Wagstaff*.
§ Bishop A. Tyler, a 28-year old African American. Born in Washington, DC, he enlisted in New York for a one-year term as a landsman in March 1863. In April 1864 he enlisted as a private in the 31st U.S. Colored Infantry and served as cook for Company F. His regiment joined the Army of the Potomac and took part in the Siege of Petersburg. He was mustered out in November 1865.
** Keeler's 22-year-old steward David R. Ellis*. He served on the *Monitor* first as a coal heaver and later as Keeler's steward. He served on the *Florida* at Keeler's request.

CIVIL WAR YEARS: USS *FLORIDA* (1863-1865)

We had quite an exciting time for a little while to day. About the middle of the forenoon we sighted a large bark which although shewing the Stars & Stripes appeared anxious to get away from us. We gave chase & overtook & compelled her to heave to. We boarded her & found she was bound from the West Indies to Baltimore.

As we left her a large propeller* was discovered bearing down on us. We soon made her out to be an armed vessel & the long roll called all hands to quarters. Magazines were opened & guns shotted & kept trained on the stranger as she approached us. She wore the American colours, [but] so did the *Alabama* when she approached the *Hatteras* & we were not going to be caught napping.† Speculation was rife among us as to what she might prove— the *Alabama*? *Florida*? (our Secesh namesake).‡ Some new pirate just started out by our *neutral*? English neighbour? Or one of our own armed vessels? It was quite exciting for a short time. She however replied to our private signal & proved to be the gun boat *Sacramento*.

The bark to which we first gave chase we hoped would prove a prize & some had even began to estimate their share of prize money§, but as the sequel proved their chickens were counted a little to[o] soon.

I hope you will be able to read my writing. It looks as if the boat was on a spree or I was. I am inclined to think the boat is a little unsteady. However I presume I shall sleep as soundly & composedly to night as yourself.

To morrow morning I hope will find us in Hampton Roads. I have been very busy all day supertending the arrangement of my store rooms & serving out clothing &c to the men & go to bed pretty well tired out. Just imagine a kiss & good night. If I don't find some letters from you at Hampton Roads I'll take the kiss back.** I suppose you are home by this time & only hope you have had a safe & pleasant trip & found all well there. How glad the children must have been to see you.

---

* A screw (propeller-driven) steamer, as opposed to a side-wheel steamer like the *Florida*.
† Built in England in 1862, the sloop-of-war CSS *Alabama* sank or captured dozens of American merchant vessels before being sunk in battle off the coast of France in June 1864. In January 1863 she was cruising off the coast of Galveston, TX when she encountered the gunboat USS *Hatteras*. When the *Hatteras* approached within hailing distance the *Alabama* struck her colors, raised the Stars and Bars and raked the *Hatteras* with heavy gun fire. The *Hatteras* sank within an hour.
‡ The CSS *Florida* was another British-built sloop-of-war.
§ After the government took its 50% share for a navy pension fund, the prize money was divided among the officers and crew of the vessels involved in the capture, with the amount that each man received being proportional to his salary. In order for a vessel to share in the prize money, it had to be within signal distance of the capturing vessel. Acting Rear Admiral Samuel P. Lee received over $110,000 in prize money (roughly $2 million today) over the course of the war, the highest amount paid to a single person.
** Keeler marked an asterisk here, pointing to the following text in the margin: "As I rec'd the letter you may consider the kiss yours."

OFF WILMINGTON (MARCH TO SEPTEMBER 1863)

Thursday, 19th—We were off the entrance to Hampton Roads about midnight last night & stood off & on till daylight when we ran in & up to the familiar localities of Newport News. One of our officers was started back to Old Point for the mail & returned bringing with him yours of the 10th. Though of a somewhat ancient date it was none the less acceptable.

I was very glad to hear from Henry & shall try & write him a few lines to night.* The list of our officers should have been in Tuesday's [*New York*] *Herald*, as it was sent from the Navy Yard Monday morning. I am very glad you went to Birdsey's & to see Lucy. I would liked to have called at the latter place with you. I am sorry I could not see Tibbie's picture. Don't fail to send me a copy if you can get some taken—I should think very much of it, but would like much better to see the original. I suppose you have found before this that I did not forget to send a line by the pilot to "Yours truly."

You will find this a dull letter I fear, for in the first place I have had a great deal on my mind & hands and have had but little time for letter writing & I have found but little to make a letter interesting. However I send it such as it is & will try & do better next time.

This has been a most dismal stormy day—hail, sleet & snow with a strong wind. To night it is extremely dark & the storm continues. To morrow I have business at Old Point & leave early in the morning.

Remember me to all the family with much love & to all our friends especially "our circle." With a kiss good bye.

"Yours truly"
William

No. 2—

U.S. Steamer *Florida*
Off Wilmington,
March 28th, 1863

Here we are Dear Anna, on "our Station," and here we are like to be for I don't know how long. It may be till the war is over or till Wilmington is in our possession, an occurrence which I hope is not far in the future.

It is to be one dull monotonous round, day after day, week after week, yes & month after month, for we expect to count the time here by months. No papers, no letters, no news, "*no nothing.*" We are completely shut out from everything & everybody (except ourselves). You may be rejoicing over victories won or sorrowing over defeats no tidings of which have reached us. New York may have been shelled by the iron clads of the enemy or Toombs may at this moment be calling the roll of his slaves on the crest of Bunker Hill†, but our indignation is not excited thereat. What is it to us whether

---

* His son was still attending school in New Haven and living with Anna's parents.
† Keeler is referring to the inflammatory speech made by the former U.S. Senator from Georgia Robert A. Toombs in 1855 in which he reputedly stated that he would live to see

Civil War Years: USS *Florida* (1863-1865)

stocks rise or fall, or gold is at a premium or discount? Our exchequer is not affected. The latest fashions, the last great murder or railroad accident we regard with the same stoical indifference. We are most effectually secluded, shut out from the world, hardly having communication with our own vessels except by means of signals.

We see nothing. To sea ward there is nothing but the same wild watery waste very rarely now dotted by the solitary sail of the coaster. In the opposite direction the extended line of white sandy beach stretches far away up & down the coast with its dark back ground of underbrush broken at intervals with batteries of unknown strength & undefined proportions, their rebel flags waving us defiance, while guns of prodigious range bid us stand off.

Up & down the coast just withing [within] sight are others of the fleet going through the same dull routine of duty as ourselves. At night after dark we run in as close to the batteries at the mouth of the [Cape Fear] river as we dare, to intercept the blockade runners if there should be any. Every opening in our vessel through which a ray of light may escape is carefully closed. Every sound which would betray our presence in the close vicinity of the batteries is hushed. The most vigilant watch is kept up. Every one has his station assigned & must be there at a moment's notice. Thus the night is passed till just before daylight when our anchor is raised & we stand off beyond the reach of the batteries & our anchor is let go again. Then comes quarters & drill & exercise.

Let me give you the programme of one day, promising that all other days have the same unvarying round. The first sound that greets my ear in the morning is the harsh grating of the "holystone,"* accompanied with the swash, swash of water directly over my head as the men are washing & cleaning the deck. What time they "turn out" ('twould not be nautical to say get up) & breakfast I don't know—never had the curiosity to enquire. I attempted to investigate the holystoning operation one morning when I happened to feel more than usually inquisitive, which investigation was performed at the expense of a pair of slippers, wet feet, ruffled temper & an utter & entire disgust with all outward things visible.

But to return. My boy calls me at 1/2 past seven. Breakfast is on the table punctually at 8. (Mr. Crafts is Caterer.) The drum beats to quarters at nine. As you & myself are non combatents & have no place at quarters we will take our place on the hurricane deck, which is the highest one of all, one you did not go on when you visited the vessel. Lieut. Greene, trumpet in hand, is the only other occupant. It is the only place where we can stand as spectators & be out of the way. Walk to the edge of the deck & look forward to the to'gallant fo'castle, which is what you would call the bow of the vessel, where

---

the day when he would call the roll of his slaves under the shade of the Bunker Hill Monument in Charlestown, MA.

* A piece of soft sandstone used for scrubbing the deck.

Off Wilmington (March to September 1863)

I shewed you the small Parrott rifle. The covering is taken off & the gun's crew are drawn up on each side at quarters in charge of Ensign William[s], an "old Monitor."

Just below us on the main deck is Mr. Crafts in charge of the big 100 lb. rifle with its crew. The men are hurrying, each one to his proper station, most of them as you see armed with cutlasses & revolvers. Those who are not have muskets, boarding pikes, rifles or battle axes where they can be caught up at the word of command.

Listen, Mr. C. is calling the roll of his crew to see that all are there & that each one knows his station & the duties of that station.

"No. 1?"

"1st Captain & 2nd boarder."

"No. 2?"

"1st Sponger & 2nd boarder."

"No. 3?"

"2nd Loader & 1st boarder."

"No. 4?"

"1st train leverman & fireman."

"No. 5?"

"1st Compresserman & pikeman."

&c &c and so it is around each gun on board. Just aft of the large rifle are two nine inch guns (one on each side) in charge of two "long lanky" Master's Mates, each gun of course surrounded by its crew.

Now walk aft & look down on the quarter deck. Here are two more 9 inch guns (one of them directly over my state room). On the port side of the deck the marine guard are drawn up with their white belts & bright muskets, while right aft on the small platform is the howitzer.

Capt. B. is sitting on the starboard side on the end of the platform quietly smoking his cigar, apparently an unconcerned spectator of what is going on around him. I say apparently unconcerned, for let some unlucky dog neglect some portion of his duties & he finds to his cost that sharp eyes are on him.[*]

Now the roll is called & every one is at his station or accounted for. Mr. Greene gives the order through the trumpet, "cast loose the batteries & provide." Instantly all is activity. Shot & shell are being passed up through openings in the deck, powder boys are hurr[y]ing back & forth with their powder boxes, the guns go through the varied evolutions of an imaginary battle, the quick orders of the officers in charge mingle in confusion as they reach our ears, "run out"—"man the starboard battery"—"serve vent &

---

[*] Bankhead's stern demeanor belied a warm and personable character, as described by his 19-year old clerk Charles Post: "[He] is a splendid fellow and charming companion, though he never forgets that he is captain. We dine alone in the cabin every day, and chat together like old friends, but when on deck all this intimacy ceases at once." (*A Diary on the Blockade in 1863* by Charles A. Post, U.S. Naval Institute Proceedings, Vol. 44, Number 10 (October), 1918, p. 2337).

Civil War Years: USS *Florida* (1863-1865)

sponge"—"fire"—"elevate 1700 yards"—"three points abaft the beam." These are interspersed with the "order arms," "charge bayonet" &c &c of the marine guard.

Now comes the harsh startling sound of the rattle* & the order, "boarders away on the starboard bow," & a portion of each gun's crew hasten to the spot indicated, drawing cutlasses & revolvers as they go with which they slaughter many an imaginary foe. "Pikemen support boarders," & and another portion hurry after the first with pikes, muskets & bayonets. Then the rattle again & "repel boarders on the port bow" & away go pikes, muskets & cutlasses to another portion of the vessel. Now the rapid tolling of the bell & the cry of "fire near the forward magazine" starts still another portion of the crew in frantic haste with buckets & hose & blankets to extinguish an imaginary fire with an imaginary stream of water.

Everything to a stranger to the scene is in the utmost confusion, but to the initiated it is a piece of beautiful mechanism in which each man forms a part of the whole, each part performing its function. We have not yet arrived at such a perfection of drill that our machine works with clock work regularity & nicety, but we hope that time & hard drilling will improve us some.

This exercise is kept up for an hour when the drum beats the retreat. Guns are "run in & secure" [and] the men around each gun are drawn up in line & inspected by the officers to see that they are properly dressed & are neat & clean in their persons. Then comes drill at small arms for an hour, then the cleaning of brass & bright work about the guns & in various parts of the ship.

The men have their dinner at 12 for which an hour is allowed. At 1, small arm[s] drill again till 2, then various work about the ship, in the rigging, the holds, the boats &c, till 4 when the men go to supper till 5. Then the long roll calls all to quarters again & exercise at the big guns till six, after which each man has the time till 8 at his own disposal. Then all lights, except the officers, are put out & all except the watch must be in their hammocks.

Our Ward Room Mess have dinner at 2, supper at half past six, lights out at 10. All the Ward Room officers except the M.D. & myself are "watch officers," that is, they are concerned in the management & navigation of the vessel & have their watch to stand day & night, four hours at a time & their ignorance or carelessness occasionally brings them in contact with the superior powers when they sometimes get severely reprimanded.

The M.D. has his sick ones to see to. He also has his trials, as he will sometimes be imposed upon by some one having a severe fit of laziness & put him on the "sick list" which frees him from all work or duty while on the list. Then the Dr. "gets a raking down" for putting a man on "the list" without sufficient cause.

With the Paymaster "everything is serene." I make it a point to see that every duty devolving upon me is done thoroughly & at the proper time & I

---

* The wooden rattle used for calling the crew to their battle stations or during an emergency.

have now been in the service a sufficient length of time to know what my duties are & how to perform them. Besides I am responsible to no one on board for the correctness of my accounts. So long as the ship is properly provisioned, a supply of money kept on hand & the men are fed & clothed my duty with those on board is performed.

When we first got out Mr. Greene tried to put off some of his work on me. I had formerly done it on the *Monitor* as I had plenty of time & supposed it belonged to me but I found by enquiring when I was in Washington that it did not. I told him that all work devolving upon me I meant should be done fully & faithfully, but that I had enough of my own to do without doing for others unless I did it as an accommodation. We had some words & I finally told him that I should refer the matter to the Department through Capt. B. He found that he was wrong & that I was right & intended to adhere to what I said. So he gave it up & has been as pleasant as you please ever since.

No interference is attempted with my duties. I go along as I please without consulting anyone—only I make sure I am going right.

I see Capt. B. but seldom except as I see him on deck or on business in his cabin. Last Sunday he invited Mr. Greene & myself to dinner—roast turkey &c. I spent some three hours with him very pleasantly.

The watch officers sometimes carelessly neglect their duties when they are pretty sure to get a reprimand, sometimes a severe one. He [Bankhead] is a thorough seaman himself & knows when an officer does his duty. He uniformly treats me with the greatest kindness & courtesy. I have never had a harsh word from him.

Of course, I was gratified to have an invitation to dine with him, though for some reasons I was sorry, as it tends to create a feeling of envy & jealosy among the other officers. I only hope he will ask them in turn, but I am inclined to think he is one of that kind who have their likes & dislikes & does not hesitate to shew them.

Sundays pass very much as other days except there is no work done, or rather the men are not exercised at the guns. At 9 A.M. the men are mustered by divisions & inspected by their division officer. At 10 they muster again, dressed in their best, & are closely inspected by Capt. B., after which the articles of war are read to officers & crew who stand with uncovered heads. It sounds very much like the Episcopal Service—the same thing repeated day after day—& I presume is about as useful to the men. After the reading is completed the Capt. in company with the Lieut. visits every part of the vessel. All this performance occupies an hour or so after which the day is spent by the men in reading, sewing &c. The officers, if any other vessel is near enough for the purpose & they feel inclined, take a boat & visit.

April 7th—Here it is a month since we parted & all that I have heard from you in that time is the letter you sent me from Brooklyn. Not but what you have written me, for I do not doubt that, but since we left Hampton Roads on the 23rd of last month not a letter or paper have we seen, no mail has reached us, none has left us. As far as any knowledge of what is going on in the world is concerned we are completely shut out from it. But when a mail does come won't it be a big one—the accumulations of a month. Look out if I don't get some letters then. Don't stop writing because I don't get your letters regularly—they will all come around in time & will be all the more welcome.

Now then will be a good opportunity to make good the balance in our letter account which I believe is up to this time largely in my favour, in number I mean, not matter. I am completely run out of material. Nothing whatever to write about. The same thing day after day & week after week. No change, no incidents, nothing from which I can manufacture a line even. I might to be sure copy our log from day to day, giving you the force and direction of the wind, thermometer, barometer &c &c, but I fear you would find it too insipid to endure.

A few mornings since, we lost an anchor as we were getting under way just before daylight but marked the spot with a buoy, leaving a boat with it[s] crew by the buoy. Along in the middle of the forenoon we stood in to pick up the boat & to try & get our anchor. I was standing on deck watching operations when an old familiar sound, a whirr, just over my head greeted my ears. I looked towards the shore where a small white cloud & the report of the gun as it came rolling up told the story. The ball as I say passed just over us & fell in the water about half a mile beyond & we lay at least four miles from the battery. It was good shooting for such a distance. The next shot struck in the water right abeam of us & I expected it would richochet & strike us but it did not. We lay & took five shot in this way, each one coming closer, when thinking "discretion the better part of valour" we moved off. With our guns we could not reach them.

Wednesday morning, 8th—The mail boat is coming as we hope. I don't know as I shall have a chance to send this but mean to have it ready. So good bye with love & kisses to you all.

William

Thursday evening April 9th—Well the mail boat arrived yesterday morning but brought nothing whatever for the *Florida*. We got one or two *N.Y. Herald*s of the 4th which afforded us the only glimpse we have had of the outer world since our arrival here. We had no opportunity to communicate with her, [for] as we neared her we were signaled by the flag ship "a sail in sight give chase." We gave chase for two hours & found it to be the U.S. Brig of war *Perry* on blockade duty like ourselves, so returned to find the mail boat gone, giving us no opportunity of sending letters home.

This morning we had a mail from Port Royal, all the officers getting from four to twelve letters from home but myself. As for me I got nothing but a handful of official letters which have kept me busy all day. You may imagine how anxiously I watched letter after letter as they were taken from the bag,

Off Wilmington (March to September 1863)

hoping that the next one would be mine. The only consolation I had was hearing from you through Mr. Crafts' *4 or 5 letters from his wife* who mentioned your having taken tea with her. It must be that you have written but it has failed to reach me. You can't imagine how anxious I am to hear if you have arrived safely home & hear how all are there. Do write me and let me know all that is going on, no matter how trivial. You must do the letter writing now, I have nothing to write about.

As for myself I am well & hearty, weighed just before we left Hampton Roads 155 lbs. Our vessel is a fine comfortable one. Our mess quite as pleasant as I expected, & if I could only hear from home occasionally I should enjoy myself right well.

The weather since we have been here till within the last few days has been stormy & unpleasant, either blowing furiously or raining. However here we don't have to go on deck to get out of each other's way [since] our Ward room is comfortable & roomy—only eight of us to use it.

We have just had word that there will be an opportunity of sending letters to morrow morning, so I shall get this ready once more, hoping that this time nothing will prevent its going.

For the last few days we have had mild pleasant spring like weather, still we keep on winter clothing. If we are obliged to remain here through the summer we shall not find the heat excessive, as we shall have the cool sea breezes & I hope we are so far from shore that we shall be free from mosquitos.

We hear that our iron clads have commenced operations at Charleston.* If that is so & they are successful we shall look for them up here very shortly & if successful here also, it will relieve us from blockade duty.

Have you heard anything from Harry Joy? I suppose they will be looking for him home very soon. Now do write [and] let me know how you got home, how you all are, what you are doing &c. Get Graham to take care of the garden this spring, the grape vines especially. You had better engage him before hand & keep him to fix up everything you want.

Good bye once more. Kiss the children. Don't let them forget Papa. With much love,

William

[Marginalia] What do the folks think of my photographs? I send money for the children.

---

* The attack took place on April 7. Beset with problems from the start, the nine ironclads had difficulty approaching Forts Moultrie and Sumter due to the strong current. The lead vessel, the USS *Weehawken*, which was pushing an explosive-filled raft for detonating torpedoes, was steering so badly that the raft had to be cut off. The deep-draft USS *New Ironsides* was too far away from the two forts for her shots to have any effect. The remaining ironclads, including Worden's USS *Montauk*, approached within a thousand yards or less of the forts and took enormous punishment. Having done almost no damage to the forts, Du Pont called off the attack after only two hours.

Civil War Years: USS *Florida* (1863-1865)

No. 3—

U.S. Steamer *Florida*
Off Wilmington, N.C.
April 11th, 1863

Dear Anna,

    I commence my letter this time from a sense of duty—nothing else—for what I am going to fill it with I cannot even imagine—never saw it such hard work to write letters before. Heretofore I could always find something, however little or trifling, that was in a measure interesting—now there is nothing. I sent you off No. 2 yesterday & hope it will reach you safely. You might as well imagine it stereotyped & call it No. 3 as I think it would prove quite as interesting as this will unless something should "turn up" before this is brought to a conclusion, a thing not very likely to happen. It seems like a waste of ink & paper & I was going to say time, but we have plenty of that on the blockade & are only too glad to devise some way of passing it off. When I tell you I have just finished reading the *Count of Monte Christo* you will not doubt what I have just said. I do not doubt but that you will all be glad to hear that I am well &c, but that won't fill my sheet.

    This morning was ushered in by the arrival of another mail—*nothing for me*. Well it's of no use to complain, as that won't hasten the mails, but it [is] awful hard waiting. *It's over a month since I've heard from anybody.* I feel sometimes as if I should get desperate & hire a desert island & play Robinson Crusoe, though I shouldn't fool away my time with a cat & goat as that old fogy did. My first effort would be to start a Post Office & establish a telegraph. Then I would have lots of little news-boys scattered all over the island to sell me the morning papers as I took my solitary rambles. All the leisure time would be occupied in reading the letters of my numerous correspondents. If I have any friends left I would like to see a proof of their friendship in the form of a letter.

    We have had some sickness on board, mostly typhoid fever. We sent six to the hospital at Norfolk & one of our marines is just getting up from what we all thought was his death bed—wasted away to a mere shadow, still in a fair way to recover now.

    We amuse ourselves occasionally by watching a huge sand pile which the rebels are making on the beach probably for the purpose of mounting guns to defend the entrance to the river.* A track leads up to the top, up which the cars of sand are drawn by a stationary engine. The labourers at times look like a swarm of bees covering the white sand heap. Occasionally they have target practice. We can see the smoke of the guns, hear the report & trace the shot as it richochetts over the water. In case our attack on Charleston should prove

---

* This was to become the Mound Battery, a 60-foot high man-made hill on the south end of the sea face of Fort Fisher on which artillery was placed, as well as a beacon light to guide blockade runners in at night.

unsuccessfull we expect to be made acquainted of the fact by a salute from their guns.

It would amuse you to see our decks to day. As one of the preparations for the warm weather we expect soon to experience, the men must be provided with straw hats. These are made on board by themselves from a species of grass or rather palm leaf, several bales of which I provided myself with before leaving New York, which my steward has served out to them to day, & our man of war has been converted into a straw hat manufactory. Nearly each one of our hundred & fifty men seated around our various parts of the deck, singly or in groups, each one busy in plaiting or sewing "sennite braid."*

Saturdays the men have for making or mending their clothing. In the morning each one brings up his *trunk* (which is a canvass bag). The contents are taken out & inspected by an officer, who condemns that which he deems unfit for further wear & it is thrown overboard. Articles requiring mending he directs the owner to put in repair. Most of the sailors do not require to be told all this, but there are always some lazy shiftless ones who require watching & have to be treated more like children than men in many things. Each man must have everything belonging to him marked. Anything found in his bag not having his name on it is considered as stolen property & is put into the "lucky bag." Into this receptacle also is put any article of clothing found about the decks whether it has the owner's name on or not. At stated times the contents of the bag are taken out & exposed for sale at auction. Articles claimed are given to their owners if they can give a reasonable excuse for their being in the bag. If they cannot they are sometimes allowed to take the article but take a punishment with it, at other times not daring to claim it for fear of the punishment they allow it to be sold. This learns men to be careful of their clothing, not to leave it carelessly about the deck.

The weather is daily growing warmer & more pleasant. We have taken down the stove in our Ward Room, which with a bright sun shining down our skylights looks as pleasant & cheerful [as] can be. We shall soon begin to think of getting up awnings, then thin clothing.

I suppose you will soon be making garden. How I wish I could be with you, if no more than just to take a look. Have Graham to fix everything up right, then have him at intervals through the summer whenever he is wanted. Have the grape vines well taken care of & you should have a good lot of fruit next fall *when I come* home. You see I am a little selfish about it. I would also have the suckers kept away from the currant & gooseberries & the raspberries thin[n]ed out & fastened up. Plant such vegetables as you may think you will need. I fear that I shall not get many fresh vegetables this summer. I hope the children will keep well.

---

* Straw braid used for making hats.

Civil War Years: USS *Florida* (1863-1865)

Wednesday April 15—A vessel with mail arrived yesterday. As usual everything went on board the flag ship where it was kept till to day when they graciously condescended to signalise for us to come & get our mail. Hearing from home as seldom as we do here it is excessively provoking to have our letters unnecessarily detained for twenty four hours after their arrival. However the same negligence & imbecility which characterises this squadron in these small matters extends through all its larger & more important ones. The same fault exists as heretofore when we were in James river—putting old worn out fogies, surrounded with red tape, in positions requiring young energetic men, free to act in an emergency as they may deem the good of the country requires. Well it is my privilege to grumble & having got off the above feel better.

I had got so that I regarded the arrival of the mail with perfect indifference. Having heard from no one in so long a time I had given up expecting any more letters when I was most delightfully disappointed by the arrival of two—a joint one from Mother & Sarah & another from Hen.

Tell Sarah that my gratitude to her is unbounded. I could think of no terms which were expressive enough to convey my thanks & the pleasure I experienced on the rec't of hers, so I looked *Webster* Unabridged through & failed to find it there. Tell her t'was bully & she's a trump—if that's not in *Webster* it's in Beecher[?] which perhaps is still higher authority.

Your not having arrived home I suppose explains your silence, but I presume you have got there before this & now if I don't get a letter, & a lengthy one at that, look out. But I won't make any threats yet. I will wait a while longer first.

I am very glad Mother opened my letter, as I should have directed it to her had I supposed you had not reached home. Tell Mother that I am rejoiced that she got along so well & gave you an opportunity to lengthen out your visit, which I was glad enough to hear you had done. You must have had a fine time visiting our friends at New Haven, New York & Utica. I shall expect to hear all about it.

Hen writes me that you left New Haven the 25th of March. I suppose he felt as if the last link was broken. He writes me in very good spirits. I wrote him a short letter. Did he get it before you left?

From what Mrs. Crafts writes her husband, I infer that you have written one or two letters which I have not rec'd. I suppose they will come 'round in time. They will be welcome when they do.

Sarah gives me some very interesting items of news. Among others that Dave was on the eve of selling his house. Is he going to leave LaSalle & when?

I hav'nt rec'd Tibbie's picture yet. You don't know how I should prize it. Did you have any copies made in New York?

Sarah says that "a good many desire to know if I occupy the same position on the *Florida* as on the *Monitor*." Tell her she can tell *my friends* that I have a higher one & am entitled to indulge in the expensive luxury of *two* gold bands

Off Wilmington (March to September 1863)

on my sleeves, instead of one. This I was not aware of till Capt. B. informed me a few days since. He told me that ordering me to this vessel placed me in a position not given to any other volunteer Paymaster in the navy. Unfortunately the pay is not increased in proportion. Sarah can tell this to my friends. Those who ask from curiosity had better apply to the Sec'y of the Navy for particulars.

A large steamer ran the blockade night before last, out. She did not make her exit however by the channel which we are watching. We had been watching her for three or four days as she lay at the mouth of the river waiting for a chance. The next morning she was nowhere to be seen, having slipped between two of our vessels in the darkness & got clear.

Last night another large one ran in & we had the mortification of seeing her at daylight this morning lying under the guns of the batteries at the mouth of the river, unloading into lighters. But this was not all. In going in she passed close by us. I say close by—we do not know how close as we did not see her but could hear her for some time distinctly before we could make up our minds what it was & give chase & when we did get under way it was in pursuit of a sound, uncertain from what direction it came.

We begin to appreciate the difficulties of keeping up a thorough blockade. Let no one condemn the occasional running in or out of a vessel till they have experienced some of the difficulties of preventing it. You may imagine one of our vessels at Peru, one at La Salle, another at Rockwell & another at Utica*—scattered along from two to four miles apart. What is there to prevent a vessel from running between them in the darkness when it is impossible to see more than three or four hundred feet from the ship. They make but little noise as they approach, & that little it is difficult to distinguish from the beating of the surf on the beach. They come upon us & flit by like a phantom. If they happen to come directly upon one of us it is all up with them. But the chances are greatly in their favour that they slip by. To make the blockade effective it would require all the vessels in our navy. They would have to be strung along but a few hundred feet apart over a long extent of coast.

Besides all this the red tape of the Department has its rammifications on ship board & I assure you it does not help to promote efficiency. The watch officer having charge of the deck has no power to act whatever he may see or hear. He must first report to the Captain, then wait for orders from him. The Capt. comes on deck, looks around, satisfies himself as to the correctness of the officer's report & makes up his mind what to do. All this takes time—& when a fast steamer is gliding by us, precious time that cannot be recalled or made up for.

---

* Peru, Rockwell and Utica were towns within a five-mile radius of La Salle.

Civil War Years: USS *Florida* (1863-1865)

We boarded the *Massachusetts* to day on her way from Charleston to Phila[delphia].* She didn't bring very good or gratifying intelligence from Charleston. The *Keokuck*, which you was on board of, was sunk. Some of her officers whom I saw said that there never was such a storm of iron known as showered around her. Shot, shell, steel headed bolts, bars & pieces of iron were literally rained upon them by over 300 guns. You will probably learn all the particulars through the papers before this reaches you.†

My kind regards to all, especially to Mother & Sarah for their welcome letter. A kiss & lots of love to yourself & the children.

William

To give you an idea of our position here I send on the opposite side a rough plan of the shore, position of the vessels, &c.‡ The vessels lie from three to six miles from the shore & about the same distance from each other. I give the names of the vessels on the "South Side" but do not know their positions. Fort Caswell, in possession of the rebels, defends the entrance on the South Side, while Fort Fisher & the sand batteries defend the entrance on the side where we are. I have marked in red ink the place the blockade steamer was run ashore (mentioned in No. 4), also her course (shown by the dotted line) before we run her ashore & after the rebels got her off & run her in. There are probably other batteries than those I have given in the plan, but these are all those with which we have as yet formed an acquaintance.

There is no communication between the North & South Sides except around the "Frying Pan Shoals" which is some distance.§ On the Shoals the water is quite shallow.

Vessels are also run into "Masonborough inlet" & their cargoes carted across the country to Wilmington.** We can see every day steamboats running up & down the river to & from Wilmington. How it is on other parts of the coast I do not know, but there are goods enough run in here to supply the whole southern confederacy. The Secesh boast that Wilmington never before had so much trade, & I am inclined to believe them. Much more might be done to prevent them from running out & in than what is now accomplished.

There is a rumour that Creek [Smith's] island is to be occupied by Gen. Foster's forces.†† I cannot vouch for its correctness. I hope it is so. It will be

---

* The USS *Massachusetts* was the supply ship for both the North and South Atlantic Blockading Squadrons.
† The ironclad attack on the forts guarding Charleston Harbor failed (see footnote at end of March 28, 1863 letter). The USS *Keokuk* was so badly damaged that she sank the next day.
‡ See Sketch No. 7 at the beginning of the book. The last 2 pages of this letter starting with this sentence and including the map were bound out of sequence in Keeler's letter book.
§ The distance around the shoals between South and New Inlets was roughly 30 miles, making for a travel time between those two points of roughly four to six hours.
** Masonboro Inlet was located about 20 miles north of New Inlet.
†† The rumor was correct. The plan was for a joint land-sea operation to capture the island at the mouth of Cape Fear River, with John Foster leading the land attack. By closing both

one step towards Wilmington which should be in our possession, or at least we should hold the mouth of the river, for I have no doubt but what it is the main inlet through which the rebels get their supplies. I don't expect our fleet to accomplish impossibilities, but we are doing nothing that is what I complain of. How anxiously we are all looking for a change. It cannot be for the worse & it may be for the better. After a few weeks stay here it is no mystery how the rebel armies are so well fed & clothed.

[No signature]

No. 4—

U.S. Steamer Florida
Off Wilmington, N.C.
April 18th, 1863

Dear Anna,

The *Iroquois* left here to day for Beaufort taking the mail, in which was No. 3. She had hardly got out of sight before "Sail ho" from the mast head brought us all on deck. Our anchor was soon up & we were after the stranger whatever she might be, friend or enemy. She proved to be the *Mount Vernon* from Beaufort with a mail for the Squadron.

Among the package of letters I recognised your familiar hand & I need not say after hearing nothing from you since the 10th of March how eagerly & anxiously it was opened & read. The same mail also brought me one from Mr. Flye dated the *30th Dec. last* which I will send to you as you will find some things in it that may interest you.

The letters you mention having sent me from New Haven & Utica have not been received. I shall write to the Lyceum & ascertain the cause of their detention. I am sorry I had you direct them there. It is considered the "circumlocution office" by our Naval officers who never have a letter go through it if they can avoid it. I began to feel very anxious about you, fearing something might have happened to you on your way home. Your truly welcome letter has removed a load from my mind I assure you.

Aside from the weather you must have had a pleasant time returning. I suppose when I receive your Utica letter it will tell me something of the news from there & also explain some things which I don't now understand. Sarah speaks of Henry Plant* being sick & you speak of him at home. Has he been wounded or sick or is he home on furlough?

---

channels of the river, blockade runners would be prevented from reaching or leaving Wilmington. However, the operation was abandoned in early May when the troops requested by Foster could not be detached due to all of the fighting that was going on in the eastern and western theatres.

* A relative from Utica, NY perhaps.

Civil War Years: USS *Florida* (1863-1865)

I was glad you went to Hudson. Why didn't you stay longer? I suppose you felt as you got nearer home, the sooner you wanted to get there. How fortunate your meeting with Tom*. It must have been very pleasant having to stay over night in Chicago. How I should liked to have witnessed the meeting between yourself & the children, or better still, to have made one of the party myself.

I am sorry to hear of Father's cold. I fear it will interfere with his projected trip east, which I suppose will not suit Sarah very well.

Tuesday 21st—This has been a bright spot in our blockade life, made so by the arrival of the *Penobscot* from Port Royal with a mail. I received by it your two missing letters (one from New Haven, the other from Utica). Though long delayed they were none the less welcome. I have read & reread them, searched every nook & corner for some stray paragraph which I thought might have escaped the previous perusals, examined and compared dates, followed you on your homework journey, at times anxious & at times laughing—I think you may safely be trusted alone.

I had to laugh at your piloting Aunt Mary over the [Brooklyn] ferry & through the market. I should like to have seen her face when Uncle B. invited her there with her *husband*. I can imagine the blushes. How very kind Aunt & Uncle B. were to us. I have always found them just so—it is always pleasant there.

I don't wonder Hen felt bad at you leaving—poor fellow it must have been lonesome enough for him for a time. When is he going to Litchfield, not before warm pleasant [weather] I hope? I take it for granted that they do sometimes have such weather there. I wish I could get somewheres where I could keep him to a good school & then Eddie will soon be coming along. I think Hen begins to appreciate the advantages of an education & if so will make the most of his time.

Can't say that I admire Tib's picture—looks as if she had the belly ache & it had struck out. I have placed it among my collection & try & think it looks like her. Sade [Sarah] forgot one thing—to cover her face with a shawl. Then it would have been complete, the likeness striking. However I will give Sade credit for good intentions & for that & her welcome letter (which by the way I think some of answering one of these days) she may consider herself entitled to my most profound thanks.

But do for gracious sake have a *good* picture taken of her & Eddie, together if possible, if not singly. If the artist can't take them on paper, perhaps he can on iron, tin, zinc or brass. Anything so that you get a good picture, one to keep. You must have quite a number to go into your album—how pleasant to sit down with your friends occasionally so long as you can't visit them in person.

---

* Thomas Lord, a friend from Chicago whom the Keelers knew in Bridgeport.

OFF WILMINGTON (MARCH TO SEPTEMBER 1863)

You hav'nt told me anything about your visit to Hudson yet. I want to hear all about that.

I meant to have told you to send one of my photographs to Cousin Mary [Joy]. Did you give her one? How I wish I had been there with you.

I see that Conn. has gone Republican or anti-copperhead.* How is the feeling in LaSalle? I think with Cannon† for mayor LaSalle has reached the bottom. Tis impossible she should go lower. I hope that better things are in store for her. What do Dave & Hough say to the change?

Thursday April 23rd—Well something has turned up at last. On going on deck yesterday morning I saw a schooner [*St. George*] anchored close by one of our blockaders (the *Mount Vernon*) which proved to be a prize she picked up during the night trying to run in with a load of salt. Now don't launch out into any extravagancies on the strength of the prize money as I sold my share to our Dr. for $1.00, which will be just one hundred cents more than he will ever get for it, as the costs & expenses of sale will more than eat her up.

We lay quietly at anchor through the day till just in the edge of the evening we heard the signal of alarm (3 guns) from the *Perry* which lay 6 or 7 miles above us near the shore. Of course our anchor came up on the double quick & we were off for our consort. Darkness came on before we could reach her, but we knew from her guns & from the secesh signal lights on the shore, which we kept running within a mile of, that blockade runners were on hand. The lights from the shore were made to guide them in, in the darkness.

By this time it was quite dark. Bonfires were burning at intervals for a long distance up & down the beach. Various coloured lights flashed out every little while. From numerous different points, near the shore & farther inland, huge clouds of dense black smoke & half smothered flame were rising from the turpentine kilns, hundreds of which are in full blast all over the country & unquestionably making money at the present high prices of their products, which they ship abroad with nearly as much ease & safety as they would from one of our New England ports.‡

Well we poked around in the darkness for some time without hearing or seeing anything but the lights. I have already mentioned when we anchored & at 10 I turned in & slept till the deafening report of the 9 in. gun directly

---

* Republican Governor William A. Buckingham narrowly defeated Thomas H. Seymour. Buckingham was a strong supporter of Lincoln and the Union war effort. Seymour was an avowed Peace Democrat (Copperhead), who had opposed the war from the start and wanted peace with the South.
† Nelson C. Cannon was a lawyer, one-term mayor of La Salle, and chairman of the Democratic Central Committee in La Salle County in 1863. Based on Keeler's comment, he was a Copperhead.
‡ The collection and distillation of turpentine was coastal North Carolina's leading industry in the years leading up to the Civil War. Turpentine was collected from the longleaf pine and distilled into spirits of turpentine which was used as a solvent for rubber. The by-product of the distillation process was rosin which was used in the making of soap.

over my head followed in a moment or two by the rush of a rocket *slightly disturbed* my *quiet slumbers* & led me to suspect that something was in the process of "turning up." Of course I wasn't long in getting on deck to investigate the matter.

A dense thick fog enveloped us on every side rendering objects invisible but a few feet from the vessel. Our sides were lined with anxious faces peering into the surrounding darkness in search of the object of our alarm. This as the officer of the deck stated was a large steamer which stole noiselessly out of the fog & glided by us as quickly & quietly as a shadow. Before he could train the gun on it, it had disappeared in the fog.

Of course, all was bustle & activity on board. Our anchor was slipped, signal guns fired to alarm the vessels below & we backed & filled here & there at the risk every moment of going ashore, but nothing could we see nor did the least sound indicate the object of our search. I finally got disgusted with things turning up in such shape & went back to my room & laid down on the lounge.

It seemed as if I had but just got into a doze when the whirrrr of the rattle calling all hands to quarters started me on deck once more. It was barely light. The fog still hung round us but not as dense as through the night & joy! there was the steamer close in shore but four or five miles from us. What a crowd of laughing smiling faces we carried. A grin of unalloyed satisfaction lit up every countenance at the prospect of so fine a prize. The men worked the guns with an ease & readiness never displayed in the daily drill.

As we neared her we discovered her to be ashore—hurrah! The probability is now a certainty—"She's ours [for] sure." "If we can't take her we'll smash her." "What will you give for my share of prize money?" "Don't sell now she's a rouser & will pay big." "I'll volunteer to go in the boats & cut her out." This was the talk as one after another took a look at her through the glass, giving expression to their feelings in a variety of ways. I assure you we carried a load of light hearts.

Crowds began to collect around her on the beach. Teams were rapidly driven down & horses were galloping back & forth. They very evidently meant to loose no time & had already began to discharge the cargo.

By this time the other vessels had come up & we had all opened fire, Mr. Crafts opening the ball with his one hundred pound rifle. After a short time they began to return our fire from *two light field* pieces placed behind some mounds of earth, one about half a mile above the vessel, the other the same distance below, their balls falling nearly a mile short of us.

Of course all was excitement with us as shot after shot was fired from the different vessels in rapid succession & we watched their progress & marked the result—"a splendid line shot," "that fell short," "too much to the right," "splendid, see them skedadle," "there goes the battery, that's for the *Florida*, but a little more elevation if you want to reach us old fellow," "secesh powder's too weak," "there goes Crafts' rifle, just missed them, too bad,"

Off Wilmington (March to September 1863)

"there goes the *Daylight*'s broadside, how they howl," "signals from the flag ship." This last from the Quartermaster put a damper on our morning's entertainment, for being interpreted it read "cease firing, commanding officers repaired on board [the flagship]."*

Of course, a council of war must be held before the steamer can be destroyed or the rebels stopped from discharging her cargo. For our firing instead of stopping them seemed to make them redouble their efforts. Now & then a close shot would scatter them for a few moments, but they were soon at work again. While the grand pow wow was being held on the flag ship they were working on shore. It was precious time to them & they made good use of it. We were the nearest in & watching them closely became convinced that they were endeavouring to get her off. We ran up to the flag ship & reported the fact & were answered, "aye, aye, pipe all hands to breakfast."

After the talk was over & everything well enveloped in red tape Capt. B. returned on board. All hands were called to quarters & everything made ready in man of war style & according to the rules & regulations of the Navy & the requirements of "grandma Gideon"† just as "*our prize*" was seen to start off for the batteries at the mouth of the river running close in to the beach & paralell with it. She had 5 or six miles to go to reach the goal & was rapidly accomplishing the distance when it seemed to occur to our sapient flag officer that it would be best to stop her if possible & opened on her with his guns, followed by all the vessels, five in number mounting about thirty guns, which was returned by the two little field pieces I have spoken of before.

Now the race became exciting. The steamer glided swiftly & quietly along close in shore, all the gun boats abreast of her but taking good care to keep out of reach of the two field pieces I have mentioned. Our shells were bursting over & on all sides of her, still she kept steadily along, the *English* flag flying from her stern. Some of our shot may have hit her. If they did it produced no visible effect. The chase was kept up in this way till our vessels came nearly in range of the batteries at the mouth of the river when we all hauled off.

Under the guns of these batteries was lying another & a much larger steamer which had also succeeded in getting in during the night & one large one which had come down the river during the day was not to be seen, probably having run out, & this is what is called an "effective blockade."

Our vexation & mortification at this most terribly mismanaged piece of business I leave for you to imagine, if you can. My pen & powers of description fail me entirely. It makes one's blood boil with indignation to think of it & he is ready to blush to own his citizenship. No excuse can be offered,

---

* The commanding officers met on the USS *State of Georgia*, which was commanded by James Armstrong, the senior officer at New Inlet.
† Secretary of the Navy Gideon Welles.

nothing to palliate this most gross & criminal neglect of duty (to call it by its mildest term).

I understand that the senior officer present, & who of course has command, in his report tries to gloss the matter over & tells of "masked batteries opening upon us with large rifled guns," all of which is sheer falsehood & the fabrication of a pusilanimous coward.* Capt. B. says his orders were to destroy the steamer if he could *without endangering his own vessel*. Comment on such things is unnecessary.

I only wish that those who furnish the "sinews of war" could have been spectators of the scene. Like some others, I was verdant enough when I entered the service, to do so partly from patriotic motives, but after witnessing such scenes as I have described is it any wonder that one's ardour begins to cool down & he talks of policy & thinks somewhat of interest & expediency. No redress is left us. We cannot complain nor make such things public. In writing what I have, I have broken one of the most positive orders of the service, made for the express purpose of keeping such things as these still.

I am free to say that I admired the man, rebel though he was, who commanded the steamer & could cooly work her off the shore & run her in with the shells of our fleet exploding on all sides of him threatening him momentarily with destruction.

An "effective blockade" is a perfect farce & the sooner it is proclaimed so to the public the better. I believe there is scarcely a night passes but what there are vessels of some kind run out or in. There is just risk enough about it to give it a zest with those who are fond of adventure—the chances are largely in favour of their going clear.

I have heretofore thought that the lists of vessels running the blockade that we see published in the southern papers was very greatly exaggerated but I am satisfied now that the truth is not all told. Here is the heading from a Richmond paper *to be* published—"The blockade at Wilmington raised." "The whole Federal fleet driven off with two light field pieces." "Our vessels entering without obstruction." All this may sound to the uninitiated as a base fabrication & a fine specimen of southern lying, but it is not far from the truth nevertheless.

Tell Dave I am getting ready to come home & go in for a "Western Republic," for I believe it will come to that yet. As for patriotism & love of country that's a thing of the past. If found at all now it is only in the vulgar minds of the privates of the army & navy & it may possibly be found to a small extent in the minds of a few of the green volunteer officers, however they will soon get over that if properly disciplined.

---

* In his report to Admiral Lee (ORN, I:8, pp. 820-21), Armstrong stated that the beached steamer was protected by two batteries of Whitworth guns, which is what Keeler claimed was "sheer falsehood." Bankhead's report (ORN, I:8, pp. 821-22) only mentions "two small batteries."

OFF WILMINGTON (MARCH TO SEPTEMBER 1863)

You may congratulate yourself that your *better half* is on a splendid sea boat, with the best of accommodations, living first rate, taking his ease & enjoying himself on a good salary at the expense of his beloved country & all this in perfect safety to life & limb, where if I was at home I might be drafted & have to fight. Think of it. How horrible. How rejoiced you should be that I am here out of the way of all harm. This playing war—great fights & nobody hurt, I am getting most heartily sick of. We had better go to work in earnest if we intend to accomplish anything. If not, why the sooner we give it up to the better for all parties concerned.

I suppose you will say while reading this, "Will's out of sorts somewhat." I am & I think I have good reason to be & moreover I am not alone. I believe every expletive in the english language has been expended at the expense of the cowardly traitor whom circumstances had placed in command of the fleet at the time of this occurrence. The more I see of the navy the more I am convinced that a greater amount of imbecility, ignorance, self conceit, stupidity, drunkenness & useless rubbish does not exist in any organisation in the world. When I say "navy" I mean that self laudation society, the *regular service*. The very life & soul of the Navy in this war, when the truth is told, if it ever is, will be found to have been the volunteer officers whose well earned laurels have in most cases been appropriated by the "*nobility*" of the service. It is a dense mass of weeds & briers & poisonous loathsome plants with now & then a flower or useful shrub forcing its way through. It needs a strong hand put in to give it a thorough weeding & until this is done the country need not expect much from it.

This letter must be my safety valve to blow of[f] my surplus indignation, otherwise I believe I should burst. So you have the full benefit of it, though I fear you will not find it very interesting.

It is a hard matter to find anything very interesting with us, for our life is one dull monotonous round. It is seldom we have an incident as I have related to give us food for letters & when we get it why [not] make the most of it. If we accomplished nothing we had the excitement of the chase & the roar of cannon & howl of bursting shell made one's blood run a little quicker.

I have been much amused the last few days in reading a new work of fiction just issued by the Navy Department styled the *Report of the Sec'y of the Navy for 1862*. Judging from what I have seen myself of what is related in it, I will venture to say that there is not a work published in the English language of the same size which contains a greater amount of falsehood & exageration. If it is from such material as this that History is to be made how little will posterity know of the reality of the "*Great Rebellion*."

Monday morning April 27th—An unexpected [chance] has just presented itself for sending our mail so I must close my unfinished letter with love & good wishes to all.

William

Civil War Years: USS *Florida* (1863-1865)

I don't send Mr. Flye's letter, as you will have reading enough for this time & I have not answered it yet.

No. 5—

U.S. Steamer *Florida*
Beaufort, N.C.
May 8th, 1863

Dear Anna,

You will be somewhat surprised to see me dating from this place & not "off Wilmington." We left the blockade last Saturday morning [May 2] & came up here after coal & stores & will probably return next Sunday or Monday. Since I have been here I have visited Fort Macon (taken from the rebels by Burnside)*, Beaufort and Morehead city & have Capt. B.'s permission to go to Newbern, a distance of 35 miles by rail road, before we leave, but I fear my duties will prevent [it]. Should I do so I will try & hunt Chapin† up, who you said was in one of the hospitals there.

I rec'd your No. 3 last Tuesday containing one from Aunt Brush, one from Henry & a boquet from *our* garden. I send you one in return, a rose from one of the gardens in Beaufort, very similar to our purple Boursault but I think a deeper richer color, also the blossom of a shrubby weed which grows in great abundance around the place. I also enclose Mr. Flye's letter, as my own will be short, in fact a mere note to let you know where I am & that I am well.

Most of my leisure time has been spent running about. The result of my rambles I am going to send you as soon as we get back on the blockade & everything gets settled down in the usual routine. I have also gathered quite a quantity of shells, sponges, corals, &c which I wish I could send to the children. I should have been better pleased to have had their help in gathering them & would [not?] have objected to your company.

If I told you Beaufort, S.C., I was wrong, as it is N.C. There is a Beaufort in that state near Port Royal but you want to direct to N.C. It don't make so much difference if you only give the name of the ship, squadron, and where we lie, plainly, letters will be pretty sure to reach me.

I have written to Henry since I have been here. I suppose he is at Litchfield now.‡ I hope he will enjoy his visit, but I fear it is most too early.

---

* Located on the Outer Banks which shield the city of Beaufort from the Atlantic Ocean, Fort Macon was captured by Burnside's troops on April 26, 1862 after a one-month siege.
† William E. Chapin*, Keeler's friend from La Salle. He enlisted as a private in a New York artillery regiment in 1862, but fell sick soon after arriving in North Carolina. Sent to the Beaufort General Hospital to recover, he proved to be an excellent nurse and remained at the hospital as an orderly and also managed the hospital garden located on the edge of town.
‡ Litchfield, CT was where Keeler's sister-in-law Mary Graves and her family lived.

OFF WILMINGTON (MARCH TO SEPTEMBER 1863)

We are living on *blue fish*, which you know is my favourite (but are not confined to them as there are many varieties), clams, oysters, turtle, fresh eggs, &c &c, which is an agreeable change after being so long without these things. Sea food is abundant & cheap, eggs 25c per doz., chickens 75c per pair, milk *15c per bottle.*

Don't consider this a letter. It is not intended for such, but merely to let you know that I have not forgotten you all. You shall hear from me at length soon. I am very busy now taking in provisions but expect to get through to day. Remember me to all. Assure Dave of my sympathies with him in his affliction. I hope to hear from you again before we leave. Good bye. Love and kisses to yourself & the children.

William

No. 6—

U.S. Steamer Florida
Beaufort, N.C.
May 9th, 1863

Dear Anna,

We left our station on the blockade and ran up to this place for coal & provisions last Saturday May 2nd. We left about daylight in the morning, reaching here at 3 o'clock P.M. & anchored just off Fort Macon, over which the Stars & Stripes were waving. It was too late to go ashore that afternoon but the next morning (Sunday) after muster a number of the officers, myself included, took one of the boats for Beaufort, a distance of three or four miles. From the vessel the appearance of the place was not at all preprocessing & a nearer approach only served to confirm the opinion first formed. In front of the place lies low swampy flats covered with coarse rushes & left bare with every receding tide. The approach from our vessel, in the usual anchorage, was through a narrow devious channel lined on both sides with the coarse rushes just spoken of.

We landed at a low dock on which was the usual number of lazy contrabands, lounging soldiers & idlers curious to see the last arrival. The sky was clear, the sun shining too hot for comfort. Nevertheless I started in company with our Chief Engineer Ziegler to "do the place." The place is essentially Southern in every particular. Chimneys built on the outside of the houses, most of which have never formed the acquaintance of a paint brush. Some of them were surrounded with cool comfortable looking verandahs displaying however no architectural taste or evidence of wealth or refinement. The fences were rough sticks split out of the pines, in many cases secured by driving them into the ground & now & then one boasted of a coat of whitewash.

With the exception of the main street running through the place the buildings seem sprinkled down pretty much as the caprice or fancy of the squatter dictated or swamp holes would admit. Sidewalks I believe are not a southern institution or, if they are, they have not yet been adopted by this place or have been discarded by the inhabitants as a barbarism of the nineteenth century. Where there are no swamp holes there is sand & where there is no sand there are swamp holes, so that the pleasure seeking pedestrian has his choice of dry yielding sand to his ancles (or deeper) or moist swamp mud to (to me) unknown depth. As hot weather comes on these holes will make most admirable nurseries for mosquitoes, while the sand will perform the same office for the fleas & sand flies. I am firmly impressed with the belief that, for any one given to the study of insect life, this place affords facilities surpassed by no other, especially of the genus *pulex* & *culex*.[*]

One of the first calls we made was at the hospital, a large rambling tumble down looking building erected for a hotel for those desirous of experiencing the beauties of nature as developed here.[†] No doubt a close examination here would have added the genus *cimax*[‡] to the former entomological varieties. The invalids at the hospital were being paid off & all seeming busy our stop there was a brief one.

The almost forgotten sound of the "church going bell" next attracted our attention, not from the "solemn sweetness" of its tones but from its marvelous resemblance to the jingle of that attachment to a yankee locomotive with steam up & "all aboard." So in that direction we bent our steps. We found a building about half the size of that occupied by "The First Congregational Society of the City of LaSalle" (I believe I have the name right), but with a belfrey or steeple or some other architectural appendage containing the bell, of double the dimentions of its northern prototype. But the congregation, a collection of the intelligent & reliable contrabands of Beaufort, who can do them justice. *Leslie's Magazine of Fashion* evidently has a very limited circulation among them. Such a variety of costumes, of fashion, style, color, it was never my lot to witness before. Dresses from the costumer of Noah's first theater & from that up to Christie's minstrels of the present age, the odds & ends of some Chatham Street[§] clothing shop, the last gleanings from a shoddy contractor, the pickings of some deserted camp or battle field & the cast off butternuts of secesh, all lent their aid to produce a varied effect & I assure you with a most triumphant result. We stopped a moment at the door to hear them sing, but having no ear for music (as you know) & not an artistic taste for *color* I concluded to pass on, & did so till tired with wading through the sand I was glad to rest myself on the verandah of one of the hotels, kept by a newly arrived yankee & filled with our soldiers & officers who have a

---

[*] Fleas and mosquitoes.
[†] Hammond General Hospital, formerly the Atlantic House Hotel, was located on the Beaufort waterfront between Marsh and Pollock Streets. It was turned into a hospital when Union troops captured the city in March 1862.
[‡] Bed bugs.
[§] A street in New York City with numerous used clothing stores and pawn shops.

small force in & around the place, the larger portion of our troops having gone to Newbern.

I could not help making a comparison as I walked about the place between it & one of our northern villages. Here everything wore a dull dreary desolate look. No one in the streets except our soldiers & contrabands & the few secesh we met appeared to be wandering about without aim or purpose. Most of the families living in the place when taken by our forces remain there, shutting themselves up in their houses & going out only when compelled to, spending the time in "snuff dipping," a habit to which I am told they are much addicted. The few I did meet in the streets looked thin, sallow & forlorn.

The most pleasing sight was the roses, growing in huge tangled masses with which taste, cultivation or the pruning knife had nothing to do. Wherever the soil would allow one to take root it grew with a luxuriance I never saw before. But one variety was in blossom—very similar to our purple Boursault, but I think of a deeper richer color. I sent you one in No. 5 from Beaufort.

Notwithstanding the sand, mud & the desolate appearance of the place it realy seemed good after having been shut up on ship board for seven weeks to tread once more on terra firma, to hear the birds sing, roosters crow, pigs squeal & children cry, contrabands though they were. Then there was the green grass (when the sand would let it grow) & trees & flowers & some faint attempts at gardening made by drawing the sand up in ridges to elevate the _peas_*, cabbage & onions, which graced their tops, above the water. As to getting anything of this kind to eat it was out of the question when so many of our troops are about, they devour every green thing like so many locusts.

In the course of my ramble I came across the place—I was going to say grave yard, I wish I could—where our soldiers are buried, a spot just in the outskirts of [the] place where the scrubby underbrush had been cleared away to get at the loose white sand. A few sandy hillocks partially trampled down by cattle was all that marked their last resting place. A rough pine slab smoothed on one corner with their name, state, regiment & company marked in pencil was all that indicated who slept beneath. A few rains will soon efface all this & the combined efforts of secesh cattle & winds will level the little sand heaps & all trace is gone forever. Surely our soldiers deserve better than this.

It was a long day. I loafed away at the hotel till our sundown boat came off for us & glad was I to return on board to clean comfortable rooms, a plank to walk on & something to eat. I can't say that my first impressions of No. Carolina are very favourable. A few northern families are living in the place whom business connected with the army or navy have recently brought

---

* Keeler has triple underlined the word "peas" and drawn a small hand with a finger pointing to it. Clearly, a not-so-subtle hint to Anna on how to grow (or not to grow) peas.

Civil War Years: USS *Florida* (1863-1865)

there. What the secesh families do for a living, or in fact what they have ever done, is a mystery.

As soon as one of our vessels come in, numbers of small boats put off to her for clothes to wash & to sell to the sailors cakes, pies, apples etc. With the rest of the Ward Room officers I let my clothes go to a young lad who upon being questioned was decidedly neutral in war matters—father dead, mother poor, but could "wash right smart." The latter reccomendation decided us & we let him have our two months' washing, which in due time was returned washed "right smart," but the use of the flat iron must have been among the lost arts & starch, a chemical compound to them, unknown. One of my pillow cases into which my clothes were *jam[m]ed* when they were returned might have undergone the washing process, but if so it had imbibed a quantity of No. Carolina filth no way conducive to pleasant dreams when one is partial to clean bedding.

The next day (Monday 4th) I was ordered up to Morehead City to hold a survey on some damaged government stores. Capt. Carr[*] of the U.S. Storeship [*William*] *Badger* came for me in the morning in his sail boat with Paymaster Whittemore[†]. We had a fine sail up to the place, a distance of some of six miles. There is a large rail road dock & warehouse at which we landed. The place itself is some two miles back. Vessels of good size can lie alongside the dock & receive or discharge their cargoes, which gives this embryo city a decided advantage over Beaufort to which it is a rival. The Rail Road runs from here to Newbern, a distance of twenty five or thirty miles. The whole line as well as the cars & buildings are in possession of & used by our troops. The large depot was filled with government stores of various kinds around which sentrys paced their rounds.

I dispatched my business as soon as possible & started with a number of others through the sand to explore Morehead City. We managed to avoid wading through the sand by jumping from one rail road tie to another, which manner of locomotion we found to be quite conducive to a healthy perspiration after half an hour's trial in a hot sun. Morehead City consists of fifteen or twenty houses strung along on each side of a rail road track, the buildings being newer, somewhat larger & more aristocratic looking than Beaufort. Besides these there is the usual accompaniment of negro huts & hovels & fishing shanties. Its soil is decidedly sandy, principle production sand to which hot weather under favourable circumstances would add sand flies, fleas & mosquitoes. The face of the country is a sandy plain *agreeably* diversified

---

[*] Henry P. Carr (1821-1863). A sea captain before the war, the native of Warren, RI was appointed acting master in June 1861. He died from a miasmatic fever at the Hammond General Hospital on Christmas Day, 1863.
[†] William M. Whittemore. Appointed acting assistant paymaster in August 1862, the New York native was dismissed in February 1864.

Off Wilmington (March to September 1863)

with low sandy hillocks, into which an audacious gum tree & a few scrubby cedars have now & then dared to root.

The inhabitants are mostly temporarily union soldiers, permanently secesh, another class termed contrabands are in a sort of transition state. The mechanic arts are evidently at a low ebb judging from three or four primitive looking wind mills which we passed on our way, looking like a small stable on stilts endeavouring to fly. It may be that they are the mills of the gods which are said to grind slow, which they most assuredly will do whenever old Boreas takes the sulks & ceases to bluster. However any illusions of this kind were speedily dispelled when I read over the door of one of them, "*mel* (meal) is cash." The better class of buildings here as at Beaufort are occupied by our soldiers as quarters, offices etc. We loafed about the place for an hour or two. When the train from Newbern came along, we jumped on & rode down to the depot where our boat was waiting & was back to the ship in time for supper.

We are supplied here with an abundance of the finest fish (among which is my favourite blue fish), hard clams, oysters & scallops. The two latter are not as good, it being most too late in the season, but fish & clams can be had in most any quantity for a mere song, so that we have fish & clams for breakfast, clams & fish for dinner & both or either for supper. Poultry & eggs are tolerably plenty at reasonable prices. Milk 15 cents per *bottle*—whether it partakes of the sandy nature of the soil I have not ascertained.

Wednesday morning, the 6th I went ashore to take a stroll on the beach & visit Fort Macon, taking the M.D. as a companion, not because I had any preference for his society but he was the only available candidate, the others having some duty to detain them. Fort Macon is built on the extremity of a narrow sand spit which stretches along between Beaufort harbour & the open sea. None of its guns are in embrasures but are mounted en barbette & does not look as if it could withstand a very heavy assault. Its masonry has many patched up scars made by Burnside's shot & shell during his seven days' siege. The rebels cooped up in its narrow limits must have made a good fight, as when they surrendered the works all but three of the guns had been dismounted. A number of our soldiers were in confinement there for some misdemeanor, a twenty four pound shot chained to the ancle of each one—with so strong attachments to the place it must be very difficult for them to leave.

A short stop at the fort & we crossed over the narrow strip of sand & stood upon the smooth sea beach with the waves of old ocean rolling up to our feet. I have seen many fine beaches in different parts of the world where I have been but never have I seen one equaling this. It is as smooth & level as any floor, with a gentle slope towards the sea, not a stone, pebble or shell disturbs the uninterrupted level which stretches miles away, skirting along the water & which the receeding tide had left bare to a width of some two or three hundred feet, a plane of the cleanest, finest, whitest sand & so firmly packed by the action of the water that our boot heels made no impression as we passed along.

Upon leaving the water & crossing the beach we came to a strip of loose dry sand probably reached by the waves during the violent gales sometimes experienced here. Beyond this were loose piles & hillocks & small mountains of sand with smooth rounded tops & sides as blown up by the wind, like huge drifts of discoloured snow. At rare intervals a little tuft of coarse grass had found something to nourish it into life & was waving its green blades over a scene of dreary sterile desolation. A few moments among these hills & ridges of sand would convey to one the reality of the descriptions we sometimes read of the great African desert or the one on our own continent.

On the intermediate strip of loose sand we found quite a variety of shells in large quantities, some sponges & corals of which I gathered enough to fill my pockets & handkerchief. I often wished, as I strolled along among the vast multitude of shells unable to decide which was the finest & best & wishing that I could take the whole, that you & the children were with me. How you would have enjoyed it. I imagined the children filling their aprons & then dropping them to pick up some still finer & handsomer. How they would run & shout & roll on the smooth sandy beach. No heaps of dirt or unsightly sticks of timber, or long winnows of decaying sea weed thrown up by surf, no rocks or stones. Never was a floor washed or scrubbed cleaner or nicer than that smooth sandy levels. And then the waves of old ocean came rolling in, their force & violence checked by the long stretch of shoals over which they passed, breaking in foam at our feet with hardly sufficient force to disturb the few loose grains of sand that were rolling back with the receeding wave & the cool refreshing sea breeze as it came rushing over the curling tops of the waves bringing old Neptune's choicest perfumes (not that I have felt the want of any lately). But the whole combined made me feel as if I wanted to run & shout & holler & be a boy again.

Everything seemed so pure & clean. The sky, the air, the water breaking in the purest ripples at our feet & the long stretch of clean white sand, all seemed so different from what we see in the vicinity of some large city where sewers mingle their contents with the waters & poison the air with their effluvia. Here there was nothing to indicate the presence of man except the "Star Spangled Banner" just visible over the sandy hillocks, floating over the walls of Fort Macon.

Away up the beach at the turning point of our ramble was the spot where Gen. Burnside placed his guns when he drove the rebels from Fort Macon. Almost every vestige of his works (if he threw up any) have already disappeared, covered by the loose drifting sand. The burned remains of a shanty & a few old empty barrels lying on the beach are all there is to indicate that man has ever been there. In all probability but little labour was expended in throwing up works, as the natural mounds & ridges of sand formed defenses of the best kind. Behind these his guns were placed & his troops sheltered.

Off Wilmington (March to September 1863)

Scattered along on the beach were numbers of shot & loaded shell & fragments of exploded ones thrown from the fort at our forces. In wading through the loose sand we would frequently kick up pieces of shell or stumble over heavy shot.

Going back to the vessel we struck across the point, passing over a low marshy piece of ground alive with fiddler crabs (mother can tell you what they are if she has ever been to Branford [Connecticut]), whole armies of which scuffled off to their holes with their large claw raised in front for protection. I returned on board completely used up with my six or seven miles tramp.

With so little exercise as I get on ship board it takes but little to tire me out and besides my legs have a heavier load to carry than formerly if the scales at Beaufort are to be relied on, they making me weigh *159!!!* Just think of it. Supposing some of our western cities as a punishment for this offense should visit me with aldermanic—yes honors! I should at least have the consolation of knowing that my *growing* experience at sea had not been entirely thrown away.

In the evening in attempting to get clear from a schooner from which we had been coaling we got aground & half the night was passed in an unsuccessful attempt to get the vessel off. The next morning with a high tide and a tug sent to our assistance we were again afloat. Our coal was now all in (some 300 tons of Anthracite) & my stores were to come in next, so of course there was no more play for me. This day (Thursday 7th) I had intended to go to Newbern, but the probability of being able to get in my stores & a rainy day deterred me. The next day it rained too so I had my usual luck of getting in stores in a storm. Everything was ready by Saturday morning [May 9] & we left at 10 o'clock, our pilot bringing on board with him a small basket of <u>peas</u>, lettuce, radishes & new potatoes which you may rest assured were relished. We reached our station [on the blockade] & took up our moorings at six in the evening, bringing the mail for the squadron, & now here we are & here ends my story.

But I must fill my sheet with a record of humiliating & disgraceful facts. I only wish such things could be published to the country to force upon government more active energetic measures. On the night of the 13th *three large steamers ran in*. On the night of the 14th a schooner ran out. On the night of the 16th a large steamer & a schooner ran out. On the night of the 18th a large steamer & schooner ran in & on the night of the 22nd a large steamer came in & *anchored among the fleet* till early daylight when she got under way, chased by the *Penobscot* who followed her close under the batteries whose guns were opened upon her (the *Penobscot*), only one shot however striking her. That struck an awning staunchion and, glancing, passed through the deck into the sick bay where the surgeon happened to be. A large splinter from the deck struck him on the head breaking it into fragments so he lived but a few moments. One or two others were also injured more or less.

Civil War Years: USS *Florida* (1863-1865)

These are what we see & know & it is but fair to presume that others run out & in of which we know nothing. You will naturally suppose that we make some effort to prevent these vessels from running out & in & that some attempt is made to capture or destroy them. Such however is not the case & with the exception of the instance related above & the one mentioned in one of my former letters I know of no interruption offered to their free intercourse back & forth. We lie at our anchor during the night, frequently in the same position we have occupied through the day, sometimes running a little closer in shore & out again at daylight. During the day, if a strange sail is descried, some of the fleet, usually ourselves, start off after it. We kill time the best we can—reading, writing, dominoes & fishing & we have been catching an abundance of the finest fish, till now they have become almost a drug. We have no desire to spend our time in this manner. We would much rather be doing something, usefully employed & we could be with the right kind of a commanding officer here. There is enough to do & there are those here who are anxious to do it.

With the first light of morning all eyes are turned to New Inlet to see how many vessels ran the blockade during the darkness. They usually run in under the guns of Fort Fisher where they lie till the middle of the forenoon when they proceed leisurely up the river carrying the English & rebel flags. The strip of land intervening between the coast & Cape Fear river is level & clear of timber & with the aid of a glass we can distinctly see them as they pass up to Wilmington. It cannot be said that they come upon us unawares, for the same lights displayed by the rebels to guide their vessels in also give us warning of their coming, so that we all know when a vessel is expected. They find some way of telegraphing their arrival to their friends on shore by whom lights are displayed to guide them in. They probably make the coast some 15 or 20 miles above the fleet (the northern one of which is the *Perry*) & communicate to the rebels who are stretched for miles along the shore where they will attempt to run in. This is immediately sent to New Inlet by a telegraph line which is stretched along the coast & on the appointed night fires are lighted & lights are shewn in a peculiar manner telling them of the position of each of our vessels & the course they must steer to avoid them. Since I have been here one poor miserable little schooner loaded with salt has blundered into our clutches—the sum total of the labours of a large & powerful fleet for three months.

What a howl there would be through the country could all these things be seen by the public as we who are the actors see them. It is very evident to me that something must be done soon by the fleet here to redeem its credit for it is impossible to keep these things still much longer—murder will out & the people will talk & they will want to know why these things are & who is to blame. I see in a late number of the *Scientific American* a letter from some one on board the fleet here, with a prodigious quantity of blanks, letting out some things but the half was not told. An order from the Department places a seal upon our lips which it is at the risk of one's life or liberty to break & behind this order it shields itself & the imbeciles acting under its direction.

Saturday May 23rd—No. 5 from you reached me yesterday & I need not say how welcome it was & how glad I was to hear from home once more. Your letters reach me with regularity, though they are some time about it. Don't fail to write as often as possible. Let me know all that is going on. I prefer our local news to war matters through the *Chicago Tribune*, as these things reach us through the N.Y. papers before I can get them from you. I enclose a photograph of one of your acquaintances with his regards. It has been a long time since I have had a chance to write you but the length of this letter must make up for that. Another vessel leaves here in about a week & I will write you again then. Till then good bye with love & kisses

William

No. 7—

U.S. Steamer *Florida*
Off Wilmington, N.C.
May 24th, 1863

Dear Anna,

The *Penobscot* which left here yesterday for Beaufort took with her No. 6 which I hope will in due time reach home & find you all well. This I suppose will go by the *Massachusetts* on her return trip & will reach you via Philadelphia. This latter vessel is running for the express purpose of supplying the blockading vessels with fresh provisions & ice—no private speculation—vessel & stores belong to government. She gets here on her downward trip once every three weeks & is gone about nine days when she stops on her return for mails &c. We find it very convenient sending mail home, though most of our letters reach us via Beaufort when some one of our vessels is going for coal & stores, usually once a week or ten days, on their return bringing the mails for the squadron.

From the *Massachusetts* we get the latest papers, express matter &c as well some letters, so you can imagine how eagerly we look for her about the time she becomes due. To feed my *family* I usually get from her half a ton of beef & 12 or 15 barrels of potatoes. The ice she brings is as acceptable as warm weather can make it.

Since our return from Beaufort we have been catching such an abundance of fish that the fresh meat has gone a begging & a good portion of the last lot had to be thrown overboard. We expect to go to Beaufort again in July. Till that time we are a fixture here.

Did I mention in my last that your No. 5 had reached me? It is useless for me to say with how much pleasure every letter is received & read—you can imagine that. Those messengers from home are always welcome. I only hope they may never be the bearers of unwelcome news.

Civil War Years: USS *Florida* (1863-1865)

So Dave thinks Hooker* a jackass. Tell him I agree with him. But it amuses me to see how anxious the war Department is to cover up his sins of omission and commission as far as they can by telling what he would have done—if—aye there's the rub—that if—if he had not assailed McClellan quite so fiercely I should have thought more of him & I think the public would have felt more charity for him.

I am glad to hear of Bennett's promotion.† If he was Ensign before he must be a Master now, that being the next higher rank. There is first, Master's Mate, then Ensign, Master, Lieutenant Commander, Commander, Captain, Commodore & lastly Admiral. These are termed "line officers." Paymasters, Surgeons & Engineers are "staff officers" & rank with line officers according to the time they have been in the service, the position assigned them by the Department &c. My position here entitles me to rank with Lieut. Comdr.

You ask me if "we kept Fast day on ship board." Your question was the first intimation that there had been or was to be such an eventful day. Every day is fast day with us—that is fast at anchor, which any one will admit after trying it a few months is the most tedious fast that can be imposed upon them.

What a dismal snow storm you have had. I don't wonder at your exclamation of "horrors." I hope all the fruit is not killed. It is like undergoing martyrdom every spring to see fruit blossoming out so finely & then nipped by a frost just as you are anticipating so much pleasure in watching it grow & ripen.

I received a New Haven paper from Henry a few days since, so I suppose that he has returned from Litchfield. I hope he has made a pleasant visit, though I fear it was most too early in the season.

I think our neighbor O'Brien's garden, the arbour part at any rate, will be a curiosity. I suppose he is initiating some of the old country ways. I think of the two I should prefer just now to see the garden across the way & have a chat with the gardeners. Our roses must be beautiful. You have no idea how much I want to see them & smell their fragrance & the lilachs, & have a taste of some good fresh vegetables. Can't you send me some?

It must seem lonesome enough to you in the garden with Hen & myself both gone. Does he say anything in his letter about coming home this summer? What do you propose doing with him, for I presume he will expect to return when his year is up? His improvement appears so great I would like very much to have him stay. I shall leave it to you to do as you think best. If Father & Sarah get as far as New York I hope they will go & see him or if not have him go & see them. It would be next to seeing you or myself.

---

* Major General Joseph Hooker.
† Keeler was mistaken. His friend from La Salle was still an ensign in the Mississippi Squadron.

Off Wilmington (March to September 1863)

Tell Mother that she has my sympathies in her feline trials & hope she will succeed in raising her brood [of chickens] so that I can have a good potpie when I return *next fall*.

My hopes of prize money, as things are managed here, is diminishing daily, but if I only get back safe myself I will not grumble.

We are expecting another mail down every day. I hope it will bring a letter from home. Send me a paper occasionally—I think it will reach me.

When you write tell me where Wm. Chapin is, in what Hospital in Newbern & in what capacity, if you can find out, as when we go to Beaufort again I intend to go to Newbern & will try & find him.

Thursday evening May 28th — Here my letter is yet. The *Massachusetts* got here on her way back one day sooner than we expected her, so my letter was unfinished & of course not sent. The *Penobscot* did not leave as we supposed she did, so the *Mass.* took the letter I expected to send her.

In future we are going to have our mail sent via Nassau & from there here by the blockade runners if we can make satisfactory arrangements, they having established a daily line. We can get our mail much sooner & oftner that way than any other, if their vessels will only stop & send it aboard as they pass through the fleet. On the night of the 23rd two steamers ran out, on the night of the 25th one ran in & last night another. What a record.

The past two or three days it has been very stormy, raining & blowing furiously, the vessel rolling & pitching at her anchors in a manner which would be anything but pleasant if we hadn't our sea legs on. However the weather is something I feel but little interest in as I am not obliged to be at all exposed, so I feel at liberty to laugh at Mr. Crafts & the other unfortunates as they come down soaked through after a four hours' watch on deck.

Ten days to day since we have had a paper or letter & it will probably be from five to seven more before any will reach us. What an age in this mighty rush of events. What may not have taken place in that time. Do you wonder that we sometimes get impatient.

Remember me to all, not forgetting "our circle" individually & collectively. With much love

William

No. 8—

U.S. Steamer *Florida*
Off Wilmington, N.C.
June 3rd, 1863

Dear Anna,

A long long time has passed since we have heard from the outer world & our patience was upon the point of descending from its monumental elevation for the purpose of remonstrating with "Gideon" for the long tedious delay when "sail ho" from a more lofty position than the one ascribed to that cardinal virtue caused remonstrances to be forgotten, grumbling to cease & patience to resume its smiling occupation. The stranger on coming up proved to be the *Mount Vernon* from Beaufort with mails for the squadron.

You folks who live right next door to a post office & can run in forty times a day if you choose for letters & have the pleasure of seeing others get them if you don't experience the gratification yourself. You don't know how to feel for us who have to trust to a migrating concern very uncertain in its hours, irregular in its habits & unequal in the distribution of its favours. This time however, to its credit be it said we were not forgotten, as a large mail for the *Florida* bore witness. My share of the spoils being two letters from yourself (Nos. 6 & 7), enclosing two from Henry & five papers from him, a letter from Birdsey, besides 12 or 15 official letters from the Department & other sources. I barely had time to open yours to learn the numbers & scratch them down on a slip of paper before our letter bag closed. I sent by it No. 7.

I knew you would complain of the length of my letter [No. 5] from Beaufort or rather the want of it, but I wrote all I had time to at that time. It was that or nothing for you & I supposed you would prefer a few lines to none at all. Besides I am inclined to think that my next letter made ample amends for all short comings of the previous one. Moreover you will please allow me to remind you in the most gentle & loving manner my dear connubial companion that in the number of sheets used, ink expended, *brilliant ideas* effervescing like a glass of soda water, sparkling & refreshing, able criticisms on the conduct of the war &c &c, all these far outnumber anything received from you as the profile of the Father of his country so frequently used can testify.* Now it ill becomes the weaker vessel & the recipient of so many distinguished favours to assume a fault finding character at this late date—it shews a very ungenerous disposition. However I will condescendingly overlook these evidences of woman's weakness in consideration of ample apologies for the past & promises for the future which I think I hear you pledging in the form of numerous home missives to the absent one.

I laughed heartily at your description of Eddie borrowing three cents to get my letter. The little fellow certainly deserves credit for his financial ability displayed so young. I can imagine how proudly he trotted home with it.

Let me congratulate you upon being through with that unenviable task & trial of housekeeping—house cleaning. A letter from you at such a time & written under such circumstances I can & do appreciate & value all of the more. I am glad you had Graham to assist you.

The pressed flowers from the children remind me so much of home & themselves. I could almost see the little things trot[t]ing around the flower beds gathering something to send to papa. I am glad Eddy was so well pleased with his visit on the prairie. I suppose he don't often get a chance to get so far from home.

---

* Keeler is referring to the 3-cent stamp that was used for letters weighing less than 0.5 oz.

Off Wilmington (March to September 1863)

I believe our garden always does its best when I am absent. I almost envy you your pleasure in watching lilachs, snow balls, peonies, roses &c as they blossom. They must look beautiful from your account. I am sorry the strawberries were so badly winter killed. I fear the covering was so thick it smothered them.

Tell Dave that I do not consent to his being called a Copperhead at all for I don't believe that he is. I think he feels a good deal as I do, for though I may condemn the Administration in many of its measures or its want of them, I feel it to be my duty to support it, for in so doing I support my country & further its int[e]rests, but in opposing & thwarting the Administration I only injure the cause for which we are all fighting. A person cannot be an active opponent of the Administration & a loyal citizen, nor is there any neutral ground—"he must either serve God or Mammon." That is the view I take of it.

Let us decide this great question first, then we will have time to decide who was the greatest general, who the most available candidate for the next presidency, the expediency of the President's proclamation & all the rest of the side issues. Active opposition to the Administration cannot do any good & may do much harm.

A military dictator would be my choice, *if he was the right sort of a person.* One that would crush the cowardly heart of such cursed traitors as Vallandigham[*] & follow it up on such as [those who] chose to condemn the act.

I presume you will think it queer that in one letter I can condemn the administration & in the next support it, but I would make this distinction, that while I may condemn the measures of the administration, I look upon it as my duty to lend my aid in carrying them into execution, the Administration being de facto the government of the country which we are all striving to uphold. We do not recognise politics in the matter at all. I think Dave will agree with me.

But to change the subject. Have you just discovered that Mrs. Thompson is so excessively disagreeable? I never thought her anything else. Her conformation may be feminine, numerous childish evidences prove that, otherwise I should doubt the sex & call her neither masculine or feminine but neuter. If she heads a loyal league, have nothing to do with it. I don't believe you[r] loyalty will be doubted in consequence. But how is it that Mrs. Larkin is one of her opponents? I thought that she was the Dr.'s aid decamp.[†]

---

[*] Clement L. Vallandigham, member of the U.S. House of Representatives from Ohio and the leader of the Peace Democrats. On May 5, 1863 he was arrested for disloyalty and sentenced to prison for the remainder of the war. Not wanting to make a martyr of him, Lincoln commuted his sentence to banishment to the Confederacy where he remained until June 17, 1863 when he boarded a blockade runner in Wilmington and headed to Canada.

[†] Lyman B. Larkin, a Massachusetts-born physician who lived in La Salle from 1857 to 1864 with his third wife Harriet. His 20-year old son John from his first marriage was killed at the Battle of Antietam in 1862.

Civil War Years: USS *Florida* (1863-1865)

I am glad that something is being done with the side walks. They certainly needed it, though I was in hopes that they would be repaired with a more durable material than wood.

I must try & write to Henry, though he owes me one or two letters. I think his letters shew a marked improvement. Send me his letters when you can.

Remember me with much love to all friends. With much love & many kisses to yourself & the children.

Affectionately,
William

Sunday morning June 7th—A fine pleasant morning, cool & comfortable. We are just on our way back to our anchorage after having spoken the steamer *Pilot Bay* from Port Royal for Hampton Roads. It seems strange to meet these little river boats so far out here to sea. Before the war one would hardly have dared to trust himself in one of them on this sound. Now they are transformed into sea going vessels. A few days since we spoke, the *South America* from New York to New Orleans, an old boat in which I used to go up & down the North river when a boy.* In those days she was considered something extra. Now she is as insignificant as she is old, compared with the floating p[a]laces of the Hudson river.

To morrow morning we leave for the "South Side" to assist in the blockade of "South inlet."† By reference to the little map I sent you‡, you will see our locality. I do not like the change, as our mail facilities will not be as good as where we are, the communication from the South Side with Beaufort being less frequent.

You can continue to direct to me as you have done. Your letters reach me with a good deal of regularity in from ten to fifteen days after they are mailed. Yesterday one of the New York ferry boats, fitted up as a gun boat, arrived here bringing mail matter for the *Monitor*'s officers *mailed in Dec. last. That letter* of yours wasn't among them.

Henry's papers that I have mentioned in another part of the letter gave us the first intimation we had of the capture of Vicksburgh.§ Their arrival was opportune I assure you & they were eagerly sought for by all on board.

I suppose you will get a letter from Birdsey, as he told me in his that he was going to write you. Business he says is good in New York & the public mind has settled down into a determination to support the Administration to the end should the war continue for twenty years to come.

---

* The North River is the name given to the stretch of the Hudson River from the tip of Manhattan Island northward for ten or so miles.
† Western Bar Channel.
‡ He is referring to the hand drawn map in his letter of April 11, 1863 (Sketch No. 7 at the beginning of the book).
§ False news. The Confederate stronghold on the Mississippi did not fall until July 4, 1863.

Off Wilmington (March to September 1863)

I am a rejoiced to hear we are doing so well in the west. They have one advantage not possessed by the eastern troops—they are further removed from the Capital & its political leaders & generals & are less embarassed & hampered by their intrigues & jealousies.

Our pecuniary prospects in the way of prizes does not brighten very much. The apathy & indifference manifested here is disheartening. Boats are continually running out & in without any serious attempt further than our mere presence here to prevent them. I hope we will find it different on the other side. There is but little encouragement to take prizes as a large portion of their value is eaten up in costs of sale, condemnation &c, leaving but little anything to divide among the captors.

It is possible that we may go to New York in the fall for a new crew, as the time of most of our men expires then. It may be that men will be sent out here to us.

I hope Father & Sarah will enjoy their trip & meet with no mishaps. When do they expect to return? They had ought to go to New Haven & from there to Branford. I think they would be pleased with their visit. Let me know when you hear from them. Good bye.

William

No. 9—

U.S. Steamer Florida
Off Wilmington
June 12th, 1863

Dear Anna,

"Veni, vidi, vici." & here it is, just astern, the rebel steamer *Calypso*, a prize to the *Florida*, "& this is how it happened."

On the 8th inst. we were ordered to the "South Side" to watch South Inlet, where we are now. It is very different on this side from what it was on the other, there being nothing to do through the day. The vessels lie in a "huddle," the officers visiting from one to another to pass away time the best way they can.

Tired of this way of killing time we started off yesterday morning on a fishing excursion, catching a large shark just before starting which we cut up for bait. We had splendid luck catching hundreds of the finest blackfish till 3 o'clock P.M. when tired of the sport we were just getting up our anchor to return to the fleet when "sail ho" from the look out would have startled us all into activity had it not been so many times repeated & we been so often fooled in chase of one of our own vessels that it attracted scarcely any attention save from the officer of the deck who went through the usual formality of sending the orderly to the Capt. to report the sail & the Capt. making the usual reply of "signal to the flag ship, 'a strange sail in sight'," to which we received the customary reply, "give chase," which as by this time our anchor was up we did & soon made her out to be a steamer & shortly after the black smoke issuing from her pipe gave suspicious indications of her character.*

We signaled the flag ship "the strange sail is an enemy" & soon flag ship & enemy were lost to view in a terrible rain & thunder squall which continued for half an hour or more. However our compass gave us our course & we kept steadily on despite the storm.

When it lighted up we could see the chase†, on which we had apparently gained. Still she was the merest speck on the far off horizon & over her hovered the little black tell tale cloud, but our consorts were no where to be seen. In this way we chased her through three or four successive squalls which while they lasted hid her from our view & then as it lighted up we could see her far ahead. At times it would seem as if we gained on her & then it would appear as if the distance between us had increased.

It continued in this way from 3 o'clock P.M. till about half past six & it began to be doubtful if we shouldn't loose her in the approaching darkness when we found that we were rapidly overhauling her & were soon near enough (about 4 miles) to give her a shot from the rifle on our forecastle.

We saw that she had stopped & was lying broadside to us, no colors up. Our first shot fell some distance astern, the next a little ahead, the third however came but a few feet from her, so close in fact as to splash the water over the decks & cause a white flag to be run up.

As you may well suppose the chase was an exciting one. Whether she was armed & ready for a fight or an unarmed blockade runner we did not know, but every nerve was strained to increase our speed to bring us up with her. Oil, grease & pitch was freely used in our furnaces & it was difficult to say from whose pipe issued the blackest smoke. Every sail that would draw was set & every exertion made to bring our vessel up to her highest possible speed & keep her there.

The officers stood grouped about the deck with glasses to their eyes watching the chase & speculating as to the probability of our catching her. A thousand surmises & opinions were passing around as to her speed, character, cargo &c &c, & when our first shot tore howling through the air & we saw by the splash of the falling missile that we had her in range we knew that she was ours & there was a lot of light, happy hearts on board. Every one felt as if he wanted to shake hands with everybody else.

As we rapidly came up with her we saw that she had lowered a boat which a nearer approach shewed to contain women & also that those on the steamer were throwing overboard papers, packages, boxes &c, quantities of which were floating about on the water. One of our guns had been loaded with

---

* The black smoke resulted from the use of bituminous coal which burned very dirty. Consequently, the term "black smoke" was used for a blockade runner.
† i.e., the blockade runner.

canister & as we ranged along close under their stern, Capt. B. hailed them, "If I see anything more thrown overboard from you I will sweep your decks with cannister."

"We are throwing nothing overboard, sir."

"You lie. The water is covered. Now, the next thing that goes over I fire into you."

In the meantime two of our boats had been lowered, one in command of Mr. Crafts, to pick up the papers &c from the water, the other in command of Mr. Greene to board our prize. On getting on board he hailed us "She is sinking."

Capt. B. replied, "If she went down, her crew should go down in her."

Mr. Greene had with him our Chief Engineer Mr. Ziegler who went immediately to the engine room & found the water over the floor & accused a person who stood near & whom he took to be one of her engineers of having scuttled her. "Yes," he said, "we have cut all the pipes & she is bound to go down." He refused to go down & shew where the leaks were till *persuaded* by a revolver & even then he was dragged down into the fire room by force & compelled to shew the principal leaks.

The safety valves of the boilers were also found to be tied down, heavy fires in & a head of steam on that threatened every moment to burst them. For a short time it was a question whether the boat wouldn't sink or blow up with those of our folks on board as well as her own crew & it was only by almost superhuman exertions that she was saved. The safety valves were raised, shot plugs driven into the leaks & then our folks had time to look about.

Her crew had broken into the cabin, got at the liquor & of course were crazy drunk & playing smash with everything. While all this was taking place the boat containing the women had been ordered alongside of us. In it was four females, two or three men, besides a couple of the crew to row, & a more forlorn bedraggled set I never saw. The boat was half full of water & into it had been thrown band boxes (*a fitting fate*), trunks & bundles. Some were smashed, some dissolved, & all were floating about in a very promiscuous manner in the bottom of the boat. Bonnets of the latest style were mixed up with sailors' pea jackets, hoop skirts, broken oars & parasols, smashed trunks, soaked bundles & carpet bags & submerged feet & ancles in the half filled boat.

I was deputised by Capt. B. to receive the females & conduct them to his cabin. You can imagine their appearance & condition on our quarter deck coming from their boat in which they had been seated to their waists in water. With a *very vivid imagination* one might have taken them for the last of the mermaids covered with the dilapidated fragments of the latest fashions. However in obedience to orders I took them into the cabin. One of them in her terror seizing me so tightly by the arm that I began to question if she didn't mean to "hold fast all she had got." I quieted their fears by assuring them that they should not be harmed &c & made them as comfortable as circumstances would admit.

The party was an elderly lady & her three daughters. She had been living near New York but had recently lost her husband who left but little to support them & was on her way to Charleston to take up her residence with a wealthy daughter living there. She had gone to Nassau & had engaged passage in this vessel, hoping to get to her destination.

The Captain of the steamer, after scuttling his vessel, had put them into the boat with the few things they could hastily pick up & in launching the boat had nearly capsized it, half filling it with water & thoroughly wetting its occupants. The men accompanying them were in no better condition. All in the boat appeared as if they expected us to swallow them alive.

As soon as the leaks of the prize had been temporarily stopped to prevent any fear of her immediate sinking, all her officers, passengers & crew were transfered to the *Florida*, numbering, with the ladies, fifty souls. None of them were allowed to bring an article with them, precious little ceremony was used in hurrying them into the boats. If one hesitated an instant, a cutlass or revolver hurried him up. Though rejoiced at having taken a prize, we did not like the way in which she was given up after raising the white flag—in a sinking condition, her boilers momentarily expected to explode & withall on fire, for a fire broke out in the course of the night in a bale of cotton waste, which had been fired & had smouldered till then & was with difficulty got under [control].

The Capt. took charge of the ladies. Most of the passengers & officers we took in the ward room & made as comfortable as possible. The rest were turned out on the berth deck among our own crew. They were a ha[r]d looking set of wretches, in wet dirty clothes begrimed with coal dust & smoke. The passengers did not present a much better appearance. The next day we brought their trunks from the prize which enabled them [to] look a little more respectable & after getting a little acquainted with them found them quite companionable.

The Dr. (Kinnifick)*, my room mate whose likeness I sent you, was a real wit & kept us all laughing while he remained on board. When he left I sent by him to engage a good room in the best hotel in Charleston, should it be my fortune to go there. I have no doubt but what I should find a friend in him.

Besides the women there were five other passengers, most of whom claimed to have been aboard for their health. For one of them I felt a good deal of sympathy. He was a young man, married about two years ago & went

---

* John Kenifick (1826-1866), a druggist in Charleston. In June 1861 he enlisted as a private in the 1st South Carolina Infantry and was wounded at the Second Battle of Bull Run on August 29, 1862. He returned home to Charleston disabled and remained there for the rest of the war.

to Europe for his health soon after, leaving his wife in Wilmington. He was now on his way after her to take her to Europe with him. He cared nothing for either North or South he said. He knew he had but a short time to live & wanted to spend the rest of his days in quiet with his wife on the banks of the Rhine where the climate suited him. All but him took their capture quite philosophically & evidently tried to make the best of a bad bargain. The tears would come in his eyes whenever wife or home was mentioned.*

One of them we had captured before in the schooner *St. George* of whose capture I wrote you at the time. Her Capt., Black,† was disposed to be a little surly at first but soon got over it & acknowledged that if he was to be taken again he hoped it would be the *Florida*. Of course we all coincided.

The next day their baggage was all brought on board & searched before being given to them. All articles of their own wearing apparel they were allowed to keep. All else, presents & purchases for friends and private ventures in an almost endless variety was retained by us as were all letters & papers. By the time the search was over our quarter deck had goods in quantity & variety—enough to stock a country store—from children's toys up to ladies' silk dresses. Ladies' & children's shoes seemed to be the leading articles. If I had known your size I could have got enough to have lasted you the rest of your life. I sent Hen for you three nice handkerchiefs as a trophy which I hope will reach you. Hen can send you the Hdkfs by mail, one at a time. He must be careful & *fully* prepay the postage or by the new law they will go to the dead letter office. Other things which I have I will send home the first opportunity.

Our clothes lines the next morning presented a singular appearance for a man of war, covered with ladies' dresses, skirts, petticoats, & *other articles* of dress whose names and uses I have forgotten, it is so long since I have seen a female. The fair? owners I imagine were obliged to lie in bed till their baggage came on board, Capt. B.'s steward hanging out their soaked garments of the previous day. Their trunks, 4 or 5 large ones, were examined with the rest (ain't it fun to see the women's trunks overhauled?!!). Though there was a good deal in them that we might & perhaps should have taken, Capt. B. allowed all to pass, much to their joy, but it was laughable to see the variety taken from some of the men's trunks.

The next morning I went on board the prize & such a scene of confusion & destruction it would be difficult to imagine. Cases of wines & liquors had been stored in the cabin, also barrels of fruit, butter, cheese, lard & a great

---

* The young man may have been John C. Bauman, who is listed in the prisoner-of-war records as being a citizen of Wilmington. He was suspected of being an agent of the Confederate government (ORN, I:9, p. 74).
† Described as "a desperate blockade runner" and "a most daring man" (*The New York Times*, New York, NY, June 21, 1863, p. 5), William Black, the captain of the *Calypso*, also commanded the blockade runner *Stonewall Jackson* which was run ashore and destroyed two months earlier while trying to run the blockade at Charleston.

variety of stores intended for good living. These had been broken open & their contents formed a strange compound on the handsome carpet of the cabin floor. Mackeral, banannas, butter, limes, sugar, codfish, coffee, oil, pieces of silk & other dress goods, cheese, pineapples, pickles, tea, boots & shoes, parasols, linen handkerchiefs were all mixed up & trod together, the whole well moistened with hundreds of bottles of wines, liquor & ale, the broken glass of which entered largely into the compound. The Cabin floor was covered ankle deep with this mixture which our men when I went on board were shoveling out. Trunk[s] & chests had been broken open & their contents when not stolen had been scattered about in the dirt. We replenished our Ward Room stores from what was left, among other things getting quantities of banannas, pine apples, limes, some apples and preserves.

Both officers & men have refused to tell us of what the cargo was composed but give us to understand that it is valuable. We have good reason to believe that one hundred thousand dollars in specie was thrown overboard before we reached them. Some large iron plates which they had on deck were also thrown over. From what we can see of the cargo we think it is composed mostly of choice wines & liquors, coffee & a general assortment of groceries.

The vessel was purchased a short time since for $125,000.00. One half of the nett proceeds will go to the government, the other half will be divided among the officers & crew of our vessel in proportion to their pay. No other vessels of the fleet will share with us, they not being in sight when the capture was made, thanks to the squall in which they lost sight of us, when they returned. They feel sore over it, I assure you.

The prize was nearly if not quite a match for us in speed. We should have lost her in the darkness of the coming night had not their shaft broken which enabled us to come up with them so rapidly. They were agreeably disappointed to find themselves so well treated on board of us, as they all expected to be put in irons. We have to keep a strict watch over them and all of us sleep with our arms handy, for some of them are desperate fellows & would hesitate at nothing if they could get back their vessel. No arms or ammunition were found on board, no papers or flag except a large confederate one under which the Capt. frankly acknowledged he sailed. This will save us the time & expenses of a long suit for her condemnation.

Sunday, 14th—Mrs. Gray & her daughters & their baggage were sent ashore to Fort Caswell to day under a flag of truce. They appeared glad to get off, expressing their appreciation of our kindness to them as they left. The Gunboat *Victoria* took them from us, being of lighter draught, & stood in towards the fort with the white flag flying, Capt. Bankhead being on board. They run in as near as was prudent when they took a small boat & were met by another from the fort who received the ladies, but could or would give us no news except that they had heard that we had lost 30,000 men in the attack on Vicksburg, which they affected not to believe. Our Wilmington prisoner had permission to send an open letter to his wife. It seemed hard to be almost

Off Wilmington (March to September 1863)

within sight of home & not be allowed to go there after being absent so long. I expect they will carry the first news of the capture of the *Calypso* with them.

Wednesday, 17th—The *Massachusetts* came along this morning on her upward trip & all our prisoners were transfered to her. Those who had lived in the Ward Room with us left with regret, feeling that they would not be as well treated wherever they might go. Dr. Kinnifick assured me he would not forget my room in Charleston. He bowed to Capt. B. just as the small boat was shoving off & shouted that he was obliged to him for the quickest trip he had ever made from Florida to Mass. (the names of the vessels.)

We all had good sense enough on both sides to avoid all disagreeable topics of conversation & for the few days rather enjoyed the interruption to the monotony which their society gave us. They made an effort to be agreeable which under the circumstances which forced them upon us must have cost some of them no small effort, as some of them were large loosers by the loss of their vessel. However we were glad to get rid of them, as every one on board a man of war beyond her regular complement is out of place & in every body's way.

I accompanied them on board the *Mass.* & introduced them to her officers where I left them, carrying back with me their best wishes. One of them gave me the 1862 volume of *Harper's Weekly* which I have sent to Hen for safe keeping. All of them had more or less money in specie, mostly American quarters. Capt. Black told me that a great deal of money had been made in Charleston in running the blockade. It is done by a sort of joint stock companies. Persons unite & send an agent to England to purchase a suitable vessel, buy the cargo, employing a Captain to take charge of her, they dividing the profits, which are large. But few goods are taken on freight, the owners prefering to load their own vessels.

We were unable for want of time & facilities for doing work to repair her machinery here so the *Mass.* took her in tow for Philadelphia where the vessel & cargo will probably be disposed of. Mr. Crafts went in her as prize master. He will go to New Haven before he returns & has promised to call & see Henry & your folks & give them all this news.

I commenced this letter before he [Crafts] left but was unable to finish it, so wrote a hasty note (No. 10) & sent by him also a letter to Hen. I also sent you a package of those papers. The *Southern Illustrated News* is a curiosity, the fine arts evidently have not yet arrived to a very great degree of perfection there. No. 8 from you reached me the 10th & I believe has not yet been acknowledged. I long to hear once more from home. The *Chocura* is daily expected down with a mail for us when we are going up to Beaufort for supplies.

Sunday, 21st—Your letter of the 3rd (No. 9) reached me yesterday as did also one from Hen directed to me on the "*Monitor*, Hampton Roads"—careless little scamp & then he wonders why his letters don't reach me. Fortunately the P.M. [Post Master] at Old Point knew me or I never should

Civil War Years: USS *Florida* (1863-1865)

have got his letter. I was right glad to hear that you were all well at home & that things went on so smoothly. I am glad too that Father & Sarah are making so pleasant a visit east.

"*Bully.*" We have just captured the Secesh schooner *Hattie* loaded with 500 bbs turpentine, 100 bbs rosin & 50 bales cotton. A good Sunday's work. Vessel & cargo worth not far from $75,000. We left "South inlet" about dark last evening for Beaufort & overhauled this fellow a little after daylight this morning, he having run out last night *through the fleet at* "*New inlet.*" As no other vessels were in sight we share this vessel alone also. If we keep on at this rate I shall have some prize money soon.

The *Banshee*, one of the fastest blockade runners that the Secesh had, took fire at the dock at Wilmington a few nights ago & burned up. So they go. They are thinning out fast. Two sunk by our gun boats off Charleston a few days ago, the *Calypso* taken by us & the *Banshee* burned. At this rate they will have but few left in a short time. Still they will be bought in England as long as running the blockade can be made to pay.

We feel quite elated at this last capture just after it had slipped through the whole blockade fleet of "New Inlet" & so rich a prize too. How sore they will feel when they hear of it. Some of them have been down here over eighteen months & have not made a capture for the want of judgement & energy on the part of the commanding officer. They will lie at anchor day after day without attempting to give chase to strange sails that are often reported. Not so Capt. Bankhead. No sooner is a sail reported than up comes our anchor (if it is down, for we lie a good deal of the time floating around, not coming to anchor) & off we go flying the signal, "a strange sail in sight," not waiting for orders to give chase. If Capt. B. had the control of matters on the blockade things would be hurried up some I assure [you]. There would be less writing done & but little regard paid to red tape, but the blockade would be far more effective. He is untiring, up day & night. When he does sleep, it is usually during the day & in his clothes. No one knows when he will be on deck during the night & woe betide the one found wanting when he does come.

Tuesday morning, 23rd—We have been lying outside of Beaufort harbour since Sunday evening waiting for a heavy gale to abate that we might go in. We are now under way & in a little while shall be at anchor under Fort Macon. I have just had four days' leave from Capt. B. to go to Newbern & shall leave to morrow morning if nothing happens.

Good bye with much love,

W.

Off Wilmington (March to September 1863)

No. 10—

U.S. Steamer *Florida*
Off Wilmington, N.C.
June 15th, 1863

Dear Anna,

"We have been & gone & didn't." Something has turned up—we have not waited so long & so patiently in vain. But to descend to plain english & common sense, last Thursday, the 11th inst. we captured the rebel steamer *Calypso* with we think a valuable cargo. What it is or what it will pay us I cannot tell you but I hope to make up my *Monitor* loss by it. We have reason to think that *100,000 dollars* in specie was thrown overboard during the chase. Mr. Crafts goes home in her as prize master, will visit New Haven & see Henry there.

Since the capture we have had 50 prisoners on board taken from her. To day we sent 4 of them (ladies) under a flag of truce to fort Caswell from whence they go to Charleston. The rest are still on board & are to be sent north the first opportunity. The officers, 8 or 10 in number, are living in the Ward Room with us, & now while I am writing are seated around the table just behind me enjoying a game of dominoes with as much zest as if no such thing as prisoners ever entered their mind. You can imagine under how favourable circumstances I write with all of them laughing & talking behind me. They are a jolly set I assure you. One of them [Dr. Kenifick], who occupies the lounge in my room, I send you [his photograph]. He is just as jolly & witty as he looks & keeps the whole Ward Room in a roar of laughter continually. He is one of the Aldermen of Charleston & of course a regular live rebel, [but] war topics are but seldom touched on.

I commenced a letter to you just after the capture giving a full account of it but there was so much noise & confusion about me I found it impossible to go on with it while our prisoners remained on board, so gave it up & scratch you this hasty note to tell you of my good fortune & assure you of a full & detailed account of it soon. This will reach you before No. 9 which will be the no. of the one containing the account of the capture.

I have been so busy making out prize lists, claims, prisoners lists &c that I have hardly had time to think. We captured her by ourselves so that we divide with no other vessels. The few hours of the chase was the most exciting period of time I have ever pass[ed] through. I send a book to Hen by Mr. C. taken out of her & 3 handkerchiefs for you which I hope he will find means of sending to you. Fearing you may be short of funds I enclose you a *small sum* which you can use on your trip south. My best love to all, not forgetting yourself & the children.

William

[Marginalia] We go to Beaufort in a day or two.

Civil War Years: USS *Florida* (1863-1865)

No. 12*—

U.S. Steamer *Florida*
At Sea
June 30th, 1863

Dear Anna,

We have just left Beaufort on our way down to resume our station on the blockade. I wrote you just as we got in acquainting you with our good luck in the capture of another prize, a schooner with a valuable cargo & I wrote you a short hasty note before leaving to tell you of my whereabouts & promising you an account of my visit to Newbern which promise I will now proceed to fulfill.

On the Wednesday evening [June 24] after our arrival at Beaufort Capt. B. gave me an invitation to accompany him to Newbern the next morning. So early on the succeeding day I took a seat beside him in his gig† for Morehead City, from which place the cars leave for Newbern, a distance of 40 miles. On our arrival there we found that owing to unexpected demands for transportation for troops (many regiments of which are being hurried north‡) no cars had left that morning & probably would not through the day. So naught was left us but to return, the Quartermaster promising to send his tug after us in case a train should leave.

The next morning early the tug was alongside for us & we were soon in the cars & on our way for Newbern. One passenger car, a rough thing with an uncushioned seat on each side running the whole length, was nearly filled with Army & Navy officers & a few civilians. The latter are not allowed to pass over the road unless their loyalty is undoubted. As it is one of the U.S. Military Rail Roads, all government employees pass over it free, all Army officers & soldiers being required to shew a pass from the proper authorities. The uniform of the Navy seems to be a sufficient pass for all its officers.

A freight car was filled with the natives of the country (intelligent contrabands) on their travels. The remainder of the train, a number of open freight cars, were loaded with shot & shell of various sizes, perched on top of which were numbers of soldiers apparently on their way to join their regiments stationed at different points along the road.

The country for the first few miles was the white beach sand, spoken of in some of my previous letters, thinly covered with a coarse sparse growth of stunted grass &, at intervals, dwarf scraggy pines looking prematurely old as if their life had been passed in an unceasing effort to extract a scant supply of nourishment from the impoverished soil. That soon gave way to a

---

* Letter No. 11 is missing from the collection.
† A light narrow boat used as the captain's taxi.
‡ Troops were being sent north to counter the threat of Lee's invasion of Pennsylvania in the lead-up to the Battle of Gettysburg.

yellowish loam covered with a thick, second growth of tall pines shooting up from midst dense thickets of underbrush.

In some places many acres of the underbrush had been cleared off for the convenience of the turpentine gatherers & the pines had been stripped of their bark a portion of their circumference & to a height of nine or ten feet from the ground to allow the sap to flow. The trees looked fine & healthy as if such rough treatment was not injurious, but I was told that it would kill them in a few years. The miserable hovels of the turpentine gatherers stood in the edge of the clearing, sometimes surrounded by a small, half neglected garden patch, all bearing the most unmistakeable evidence of the want of free labour directed by the brains & energy of the north.

Then we passed through large tracts of larger pines & fine oaks in grove like order & beauty free from under brush but covered with an abundance of whortleberry bushes. These were succeeded by dark gloomy cypress swamps through whose dense foliage the sun but rarely penetrated to the stagnant water beneath. Then we were whirled along through miles of dead pines, whose sentinel like trunks stood up without a leaf of verdure to relieve the drear monotony.

Close by the track & where the ground had been disturbed to kill the brush, blackberries had sprung up in abundance & were black with fruit, no one to gather it but the birds. We made occasional stops for wood & water, but not as at the north, at pleasant thriving villages with their hotels, omnibusses & the stir & bustle of business, but at solitary water tanks in the midst of pine forests, now however peopled by our soldiers whose white tents shone out from the dark evergreens. The block-houses & earth works thrown up around the water stations for their defense shewed that our troops were not idle & could handle either axe or shovel. A large portion of the country we passed through looked as if with proper care & cultivation it might be profitably farmed.

On getting out of the cars at Newbern about the first person we met was my old friend Flye of *Monitor* memory now in command of the gunboat *Underwriter*, formerly commanded by Capt. *Jeffers*. He was expecting us, having delayed the departure of his vessel a day that he might see us. His greeting was as warm as one could wish. Gen. Foster had sent one of his aids to bring us to his head quarters, he being an old acquaintance of Capt. B's. I would have much prefered going off with friend Flye but could find no excuse for a retreat as Capt. B. had asked my company.

So with Capt. B. we both accompanied the Aid to the General's head quarters which was in a beautiful house formerly the residence of one of the wealthy rebels of the place who was obliged to leave when we took possession of Newbern, leaving the house & everything in it as though the family had merely gone out for a call at a neighbor's.* The most expensive furniture, nice carpets, fine paintings & engravings, books & ornaments of the center table & mantle & all the paraphranalia of house keeping bore abundant evidence of the wealth & taste of the former owners and occupants. This was not a solitary case. I made many calls with Mr. Flye on northern men connected in various ways with the army, who were comfortably domiciled with their families in *"ready made" homes,* such as I have described. As may be supposed the tenants did not consider themselves responsible to any landlord & houses and furniture did not have the most careful usage in all cases.

Upon our arrival at head quarters I found that a big dinner party was on the tapis at which Generals Heckman & Spinola† & their staffs were to be present & a "good time" was expected. As I did not consider a champain supper a very "good time" I made an apology to Gen. F. [Foster] & Capt. B. on the ground that I had business with Mr. Flye & wished very much to see him, & so got off.

Gen. Foster's staff furnished Mr. Flye & myself with horses & some of them offered to accompany us but we declined their company as I saw they desired to be at the supper & with Mr. Flye for a guide I rode through the place & out to the battle ground which still bears abundant marks of the fray.

Newbern is a beautiful place, the prettiest by far of any of the southern cities which I have yet seen, reminding me a good deal of New Haven. The place is perfectly embowered in trees & shrubbery, not the tall arching elms of the former city but lower trees with wide spreading heads & thicker, denser foliage in which are mingled many elms of smaller growth. There is the same sandy soil of New Haven, but the streets are not as wide nor are the side walks paved, the nature of the soil rendering it unnecessary.

There is not as much taste displayed in architectural elegance of the buildings, but more regard to comfort. Their wide roomy halls, large open doors & windows & spacious verandahs covered with vines & shaded with shrubbery gave them a cool comfortable air of luxurious comfort. But there was one invariable drawback—the negro quarters in the rear bearing about the same relation to the dwelling as our stables do with us, though in most cases not as much pains was taken to place them in the back ground to give them as little prominence as possible. Not as much care seemed to be bestowed on the cultivation of flowers but more on shrubbery & trees, probably for their shade. I saw the Althea with a body a foot through & full of blossoms.

---

* The two-story red brick house (still standing and now called the Jones-Jarvis House) was built in the early 1800s. The wealthy rebel who was living there at the time of the Battle of New Bern in March 1862 was Alonzo T. Jerkins, a banker, merchant, politician and in 1860 an owner of 24 slaves.
† Charles A. Heckman and Francis B. Spinola.

OFF WILMINGTON (MARCH TO SEPTEMBER 1863)

There were some fine churches, stores & public buildings. Many of the stores were open & business appeared to be good but it is done solely by loyal persons or those professing to be. A large fine building which a showy sign indicated as the "Bank of North Carolina" I found occupied by the Quartermaster. The passers by in the streets were mostly officers & soldiers mixed with civilians & a few ladies. The inevitable contraband of course should not be left out as they seemed to form one half the population.

After riding through the place, visiting the battle ground & riding along our line of defences, stretching along just back of the city from the Trent to the Neuse rivers, we went out to the contraband camp, or the camp of the "1st No. Carolina colored volunteers," *Acting Brigadier General James Beecher.** He received us very cordially & invited us into his tent where we sat a long time talking over old times. We went out with him to see his regiment in battalion drill & on dress parade. He is proud of them & well he may be for a finer & more soldierly appearing body of men I have not seen since the war commenced. They stood straight & erect with a bearing quite as proud & dignified as any of our white troops, their average height being considerably more.

I never was more agreeably disappointed than in witnessing their drill—none of the negro carelessness and levity we usually attribute to them. They went at it with a will, every energy concentrated upon the work before them. You could see by the way they watched the commanding officer that their whole soul was in it & they have proved apt scholars, for six weeks ago [when] Col. Beecher said he came there to start the thing he had not a man.† Now he has one regiment & a part of another who will equal any body of troops in any place for the length of time they have been drilling. They are daily coming in from different portions of the state & he thinks he will soon have three or four regiments which after proper training he will bring up against the same number of rebels without any fear of the result.

---

* Following the capture of New Bern by Federal forces in March 1862, William H. Singleton (1835-1938) recruited a regiment of escaped fellow slaves. It wasn't until late May 1863 when Keeler's friend Jim Beecher took command of the regiment that it was accepted into the federal service. Later renamed the 35th U.S. Colored Troops, they served in South Carolina, Florida and Georgia. They first saw action in February 1864 at the Battle of Olustee where they covered the retreat of the army and suffered huge casualties (230 men and 10 officers). Beecher, who was on furlough at that time, missed the battle. Singleton, who was sergeant of Company G, was wounded in the battle. Their bravery prompted Lincoln to pronounce two months later that "there have been men who have proposed to me to return to slavery the black warriors of Port Hudson & Olustee to their masters to conciliate the South. I should be damned in time & eternity for doing so." (*The Collected Works of Abraham Lincoln*, Vol. 7, 1953, p. 507).

† This contrasts with Singleton's recollections in which he stated that he recruited the troops before Beecher's arrival. (*Recollections of My Slavery Days*, William H. Singleton, Peekskill, NY, 1922).

Civil War Years: USS *Florida* (1863-1865)

He said, "I believe there are nearly as great transformations takes place in the river here as ever there did in the Jordan." Says he, "they (the contrabands) come in daily in squads of from 30 to a hundred, ragged, dirty, crooked up with hard work & ill usage. I give them soap & cloth[e]s & send them down to the river in charge of a Sergeant & they come back clean, straightened up, dressed in uniform & acting & evidently feeling like men."

I will venture to say that let the greatest negro hater see these troops without knowing that they were black & he would say that they were the finest body of troops he had ever seen. All are coal black, no mulattoes among them which I thought somewhat remarkable as there were plenty of them about the place. They are anxious to get to work & I am satisfied that when they do they will prove a most formidable foe.

The Col. says he has them from every part of the state. There is not a road, path, or hiding place in it but what he can find some one among his troops who is familiar with it, the best of spies & guides he carries with him & besides they are acclimated, so that no large percentage of his forces will be shut up useless in a hospital. There is a firmness & determination in their looks & the way in which they handle a musket that I like. It looks like fight & Port Hudson has proved that they will do so.[*]

I never [would] have believed that a common plantation negro could be brought to face a white man. I supposed that everything in the shape of spirit & self respect had been crushed out of them generations back, but am glad to find myself mistaken. Col. B. told me that out of his regiment he "could pick one company of as big "dare devils" as could be found on the face of the globe," "no risk too great for them to run, no danger they would hesitate to face," "all they asked was to be allowed to *pitch in* & applications were daily made by small parties to be allowed to go out scouting." He found it difficult to hold them back.

I shall be mistaken if these troops do not make themselves a name. Some object to using them, I think most foolishly, for as long as they will make good reliable troops, why not employ them? This war is to benefit them as well as ourselves & they certainly offer no choicer food for rebel balls than our friends & connections. This has been a bone of contention in our Ward

---

[*] On May 27, 1863 the 1st Louisiana Native Guard, a regiment made up of free blacks from New Orleans, was ordered to make a near-suicidal attack on a heavily defended redoubt at Port Hudson on the Mississippi River. Leading the attack was Captain André Cailloux of Company E, a cigar maker from New Orleans who was born a slave but was manumitted when he was 21. Despite coming under heavy fire, they advanced fearlessly until heavy losses forced their retreat. Although the Union troops were allowed to recover the remains of their white comrades, Confederate sharpshooters prevented them from collecting the bodies of the black soldiers, which included Cailloux's, which remained on the field for 47 days until Port Hudson finally surrendered.

Off Wilmington (March to September 1863)

Room but all now vote for negro regiments except one [who] owns or did own a plantation & slaves near Richmond & he says nothing.*

I want you should tell Mr. Hough what I have said [about the negro regiments] as I know he will feel interested in it. I was going to make it the subject of a special letter to him but concluded he would think more of it going through you & then I fear he would not prove as good a correspondent as yourself. I am glad I saw for myself & not through some one else's eyes.

But to return. After parade we went with Col. B. back to his quarters & staid to tea & after bidding him good night I went with Mr. or rather Capt. Flye (by courtesy) on board his vessel the *Underwriter* where we passed the evening reviewing Ja[me]s river, the *Monitor* & old times generally. I remained on board through the night & after breakfast we went ashore to Col. Beecher's head quarters to bid him good bye.

Had a stroll through Newbern till time for the cars to leave when I got aboard & after waiting two hours & a half for Gen. Spinola we were of[f] for Morehead City. I had an opportunity to see a considerable [amount] of Gen. S. on our way back & was not at all favorably impressed by what I saw & heard from him. I can sum it all up as to his qualifications, competency, &c by saying that he is one of the political generals by whom I fear our country is to be disgraced.†

When about half way back it commenced raining heavily & the leaky covering of our uncomfortable car failing to keep out the water we all sought refuge in a freight car already filled with reliable contrabands & it must have been a somewhat amusing sight when we arrived at Morehead to watch the car disgorge in a very promiscuous manner, heavy wenches with *light* babies, Brigadier Generals with big spurs, Colonels in long boots, little contrabands in rags, "yaller gals" in their run away mistresses' wardrobe, a Major's sick wife on a lounge, a drunken soldier cursing things generally & a lot of officers in soaked uniform [cursing] the rain particularly. I don't believe a greater variety ever travelled before in one car.

Arriving at Morehead I found no boat could be had for the vessel so I got on board of a little dirty stern wheel steamer for Beaufort where I hoped to find one of our boats but they had all left before I reached there. So nothing was left me but to remain there all night. The miserable filthy hotel was "all full, but one bed." To that I was shewn a narrow matrass on a knock-kneed cot with sheets of a dubious white in a small room containing eleven others of the same sort, each containing a panting, perspiring occupant, doors & windows closed, no air, thermometer well up towards the top. How the

---

* Keeler is referring to Quartermaster Corbin Washington (1826-1871) who was a great grandnephew of President George Washington. A mariner at age 19, he enlisted in the U.S. Navy in October 1860. First appearing on the *Florida*'s muster rolls in March 1863, he was discharged in October 1863 at the expiration of his three-year term. His first cousin Lewis Washington was one of John Brown's hostages at Harpers Ferry in October 1859.
† Spinola was a Democrat and a three-time alderman of Brooklyn.

occupants of that room survived the night, if survived it they did, has been a mystery to me.

A short survey of the premises satisfied me that it would be conducive to my health to change my base of operations for the night, so I persuaded the landlord to give me a matrass on the upper floor of his two story verandah. To procure the necessary sleeping conveniences I was obliged to roust out a small legion of youthful ethiopians who had gone to roost on the spare bedding of the hotel without any regard to the monopoly they established against all late arrivals. After some effort I succeeded in securing from them an equitable division of their "downy couch" & I passed the night dodging the rain drops as they trickled down over my head & listening to the nasal music of the highly perfumed descendants of Ham who flanked me in large numbers on the right & left. The rain drops beating time on various parts of my body to the music of the perfumed performers allowed me but little sleep & I was no ways sorry when morning came bringing with it the *Florida*'s market boat.

I breakfasted on board & then taking one of our messenger boys for a companion (a bright intelligent little fellow) I started for a stroll on the beautiful beach of which I have already given you a description. I added to my collection of shells & enjoyed a bath in the splendid surf, though unfortunately the sun to shew his spite must take a look out from behind a friendly cloud which I thought had obscured his face for a time & the consequence was that the next day my back and shoulders presented a sort of parboiled appearance producing a sensation not at all pleasant or agreeable. With this experience in separating the cuticle from "the human form divine" I am at no loss to account for the wriggling of an eel as he is made to undergo the process.

Wednesday, the 1st of July—Our coal & stores were all in & we started for our station on the blockade. We arrived the next day and shortly after the *Massachusetts* came in bringing Mr. Craft who had left our prize, the *Calypso*, safe in Philadelphia. He had spent an evening at your house [in New Haven] with your Father, Mother & Hen. They were very much pleased to see him & hear his account of the capture & how things went on board & the news generally. Your Mother sent me a few lines by him enclosing [a photograph of] "the old folks at home" as she said— your Father and Mother on one card—good likenesses— you should have one.

The rebels from what we hear are stirring up the Pensylvania dutchmen*—they should have some negro regiments from the South to protect them. These are exciting times & makes one want a daily paper. Our wants of this kind are supplied about twice a month, the intervals we spend in anticipating what will come next. I expect our next will contain the intelligence that

---

* Five days earlier, the Army of Northern Virginia crossed the Potomac River into Maryland and thence into Pennsylvania, followed closely by the Army of the Potomac.

Off Wilmington (March to September 1863)

"Washington is safe," "all quiet on the Potomac," "affairs at Vicksburg unchanged," the "blockade growing more stringent," which means that more vessels than ever are running in. The capture of the *Fingal* [CSS *Atlanta*] by the *Weehawken* was a fine thing & is highly spoken of by naval men.*

The rebels on shore here seemed to evince more patriotism than ourselves on the 4th, for while we remained silent through the day they fired salutes morning, noon & evening. Capt. B. was quite sick with the dysentery which probably accounted for our silence.

July 8th—The attack on Charleston was to be renewed to day if nothing occurred to prevent. I hope this time it will be a success. I am told that we have sixty heavy guns in position commanding Morris island, which I hope will be able to give the iron clads some assistance.†

Capt. B. is quite low with the dysentery. Otherwise all on board are in good health. As for myself I never was better—haven't an ache or pain & if I could only make a visit home once a week should feel contented. We have one of the most, if not the most, roomy and comfortable vessel in the service & I am not at all anxious to make a change. But I must close with lots of love to all, yourself & the children particularly.

William

[Marginalia] I send some flowers from the battle field at Newbern. One was a beautiful flower clearly resembling the "passion flower."

No. 13—

U.S. Steamer Florida
Off Wilmington, N.C.
July 12th, 1863

Dear Anna,

I have just sent off No. 12 by the *Victoria* which has left for Beaufort for supplies. Our firing to day has been quite an agreeable break upon the monotony. We have been compelled by the illness of Capt. B. to take the part of silent spectators. It seems a rebel steamer [*Kate*] was run ashore on the other side of the island [Smith's] last night by our vessels there & they have been trying to destroy her to day with their shells, their fire being replied to by the rebel batteries within range. The sand heaps & trees on the island conceal the vessels from our view but the smoke of their guns is distinctly seen, every now & then a shell exploding high above the trees. Some field pieces were

---

* On June 17, 1863 the ex-blockade runner *Fingal*, which had been converted into an ironclad and renamed the CSS *Atlanta*, ran aground and was shelled and captured by the monitor USS *Weehawken* as she was attempting to break the blockade at Wassaw Sound near Savannah, GA.
† The attack on Fort Wagner on Morris Island, which guarded the entrance to Charleston Harbor, commenced on July 10 with 2,000 troops advancing on the fort while the ironclads shelled it. The advance halted on July 11 when it came within range of the fort's artillery.

sent from Fort Caswell to assist in driving off our vessels when we, on this side, opened fire on them & compelled them to stop.

I happened to be looking at one of the guns, which was plainly seen with the aid of a good glass about four miles off, when a two hundred pound shell from the *Sacramento* burst just over & in front of it. The rebs left without ceremony, leaving one of their number stretched out by the side of the gun on the sand.

Evening—The gun remains deserted on the beach, not another shot was fired from it & no one has been near it since it was deserted.

I have just finished *two sheets full* to Henry, in one sheet telling him I thought he had better stay in New Haven another year—giving him my reasons & trying to make him feel the disappointment as little as possible. The other sheet I filled with *news* that he might have some to give when asked.

Monday morning [July 13]—Just as I expected, after expending a thousand dollars worth of ammunition on the steamer yesterday she succeeded in getting off & is now quietly on her way to Wilmington.

A few nights ago *three steamers ran in at one time*. The peculiar shape of the inlet on this side enables us to stop it effectually so that nothing goes in or out here. The north side is where the leakage is. The Admiral [Lee] wrote down here a short time since stating that "from the best information he could get *thirty five vessels on an average ran the blockade here every month*"—just think of that. Wilmington is said to be glutted with most kinds of goods & no wonder with a vessel running out or in every day.

A terrible disease is prevailing in the fleet here. Commanding officers seem to be most severely attacked with it though no one as yet has been lost. It is termed "ram fever" & is supposed to be brought on by occasional sights at a rebel iron clad passing up & down the river between Fort Caswell & Wilmington.* The premonitory symptoms appear to be a disposition to gaze long & anxiously in the direction of the Fort, the frequent mistaking of little river steamers & tugs for rebel iron clads & rams, sometimes even taking a small brown building on the beach with an escape pipe puffing out jets of steam for the dreaded rebel ram—the windows being the ports & the roof her sloping sides—then sketching out on paper "the ram" as they saw it, an infernal machine covered & filled with torpedoes, prows, rams, saws, & every other sort of diabolical contrivance for blowing up, running down, sinking, smashing & otherwise destroying us yankees. The frequent enquiry on the appearance of a cloud of smoke shorewards, "do you see the ram?" As the disease is developed, an inclination is shewn by the sufferer to keep his vessel well out to seaward, she being faster, stronger & having a heavier battery is best adapted to carry "the astounding & unexpected intelligence of the appearance of a rebel ram" to G. Welles, Esqr.

---

* The rebels were building two ironclad rams in Wilmington, of which only one, the CSS *Raleigh*, would become operational. See letter of May 15, 1864 for more on the *Raleigh*.

OFF WILMINGTON (MARCH TO SEPTEMBER 1863)

The power of those 15 inch guns you saw in the Navy Yard was pretty effectively shewn in the capture of the *Atlanta*.* It was well for us that she was taken, for her plans, as we have since discovered, were to clean out our fleet off Savannah, then up to Port Royal where a similar operation was to be performed, then to Charleston where she was to be joined by the rebel iron clads in that place & our fleet there was to be obliterated, after which a similar performance was to take place off Wilmington & the rebel rams & iron clads here would be added to their strength. They were then to proceed up the coast, gobbling up Fortress Monroe, Philadelphia, New York, Boston & all the rest of the small seaport towns & put an extinguisher on the whole yankee navy. What a narrow escape the country has had. Happy are they who live on the prairies far from rebel rams & beyond the reach of the severe fevers engendered by them.

We all feel anxious to hear from Charleston, though we do not anticipate any immediate result, the design being to advance by regular approaches on Morris island.

Saturday, 18th—We have had a fine time fishing to day, having caught I should think a thousand fine blackfish—I wish I could send you a mess in exchange for something green out of the garden. I do miss the garden so much—no berries, fruit, vegetables or anything of the sort. Except when the *Massachusetts* comes down with fresh beef (which lasts about two or three days) we live mostly on can'd meats, fruits &c & I get tired of them & long for something right out of the garden.

The weather for the past week or two has been very warm & sultry, a continuous south wind from off the Gulf Stream has not added much to our comfort. Heavy storms have been frequent with thunder & lightning. We were struck last night, the fluid running down our mast on the copper conductor & into the water. The officer of the deck, who was standing near the mast, was knocked down & stunned for an instant. The knowledge that some 15 tons of powder was just under my state room did not make me rest any easier while the storm continued.

Sunday, 19th—The *James Adger* has just come in, having been added to our fleet here. She brings New York papers of the 14th with the details from Vicksburgh, the capture of Port Hudson, our successes at Charleston, the retreat of Lee across the Potomac with heavy losses†, Rosecrant's successes‡, which is all as good as we could reasonably expect but it is offset by the news

---

* See footnote on the capture of the CSS *Atlanta* in the June 30, 1863 letter.
† Following his defeat at Gettysburg, Lee retreated south through Maryland and crossed the Potomac River to safety in Virginia on the night of July 13, losing 5,000 men in the process.
‡ On July 3 William Rosecrans, commander of the Army of the Cumberland, drove Confederate general Braxton Bragg's Army of Tennessee out of central Tennessee.

of the riots in New York*. I only wish we had our guns trained on the streets there when they were filled with the rioters. I would like to have pulled the lock string.

Remember me to all friends. With love & kisses to yourself & the children.

William

[Marginalia] Monday morning 20th—This [letter] goes up by the *Violet*—leaves us all well. Nothing from you since the date of this. We expect the *Victoria* back to morrow when I hope for a letter.

No. 14—

U.S. Steamer *Florida*
Off Wilmington, N.C.
July 20th, 1863

Dear Anna,

The *Violet* left here for Beaufort to day. I sent by her No. 13 & now am taxing my brains for matter to fill this sheet. I think my letters must be getting a good deal like our life down here—rather monotonous and somewhat dull. Still I suppose as long as they tell you that I am well, it is better than total silence or no letter at all. After all, time somehow passes quickly—it is now over four months since we left New York.

The summer is half gone & we are beginning to look forward to a return to the north in the course of two or three months. When we get there we shall probably be detained two or three months repairing, during which time, unless ordered to another vessel, I shall have nothing to do but visit. Where shall it be? At home? Or will you come east again? However this may be counting our chickens a little too soon. We'll wait & see what turns up. Perhaps they will need my services no longer, so that my visit home will be a long one.

I am glad you had so pleasant a time at your festival. It seems too that it was a decided success which is better still. I wish I could have been there. I think I could have contrived to have enjoyed myself. At any rate I should have made love to the strawberries & cream—it is so long since I have seen any that I have almost forgotten how they taste.

This kind of life does not suit me. I don't care how soon I get home. I don't think I could ever get used to it. I was talking with one of the old sailors to day.† He has been on a man of war *48 years*, was in the *Brandywine* when

---

* Violent protests in New York City by working class whites, primarily Irish immigrants, who opposed the new conscription law. Over the four days of rioting from July 13-16, more than 100 people were killed.

† Possibly James Sancston (~1806-1867). He served on the *Florida* from March 1863 to October 1863 when his three-year term as seaman expired. Born in Baltimore, he died on the USS *Lackawanna* and was buried at Hanalei, HI.

OFF WILMINGTON (MARCH TO SEPTEMBER 1863)

she carried Lafayette home.* His experience has been a varied one. Hardly a part of the globe but what he has visited. I wish you could hear him talk. He says "when he gets on shore he always feels so lonesome that he's glad to get on a ship again, it seems so like home." So much for training.

We have a motley collection for a crew—from all parts of the world—England, Ireland, France, Spain, Portugal, Russia, Austria, Poland, Norway, Sweden have representatives on board. Besides those we have a Lascar, a Mexican, Sardinian, Italian, one from Maderia, one from Manilla, another from Peru &c. Almost all the different trades & occupations are here—we have a good barber on board, we can have our shoes mended or clothes made.

Of course among so many we have every kind of character & disposition. Many of those who shipped as landsmen are hard cases, deserters from the army, & it is only the strictest discipline that keeps them in subjection. The real old "men of war's men" (of whom we have some fine specimens on board) are characters well worth studying.

Among the smaller fry we have a son of one of the celebrated bank note engravers of New York—Rawdon, formerly of the firm of "Rawdon, Wright, Hatch & Co."† His father is dead & his mother wanted he should go into the Navy that he might do something for his country. Mr. Greene shewed the boy some kindness when he first came on board & his mother sent Mr. Greene, in one of her boy's letters, a very pretty note containing "a Mother's thanks for his kindness to her fatherless sailor boy."

Then we have a little contraband, formerly the property of Senator Yulee‡, rejoicing in the name of "Columbus."§ He is only about 13 years old & a perfect monkey, eternally grinning or cutting up some shine. A few days ago the Chief Engineer went into his room & found the boy there with his (the Eng'r's) uniform coat & sword on & mounted on the top of his bureau admiring himself in the glass.

Some of the men have seen service in the war between France, England & Russia—some on one side, some on the other. One of our officers was in the *Westfield* when she was blown up.** Another (Wagstaff) whose father

---

* The Revolutionary War hero sailed home to France after touring America in 1824-25 in a ship renamed the *Brandywine* to commemorate the battle in which he was wounded.
† Frederick W. Rawdon (1847-1916). His name appears on the *Florida*'s muster rolls up to and including April 1864. In September 1864 he entered the U.S. Naval Academy but resigned three months later.
‡ David L. Yulee, U.S. Senator from Florida from 1855-1861.
§ Columbus Hibbard (~1848-1889). He enlisted at St. Simons, GA as a 3rd class boy in May 1862. He appears on the *Florida*'s muster rolls up until October 1863. The following year he served as a 1st class boy on the USS *Massachusetts*, and was discharged in July 1865. He was married in Brunswick, GA (near to where he enlisted) in 1874 and appears in the 1880 Federal census in Brunswick where he was employed as a stevedore.
** In January 1863 the sidewheel steamer USS *Westfield* ran aground during the Battle of Galveston and was blown up to prevent from falling into the hands of the rebels.

commanded one of those large fine steamers between Detroit & Buffalo, was on one of the mortar schooners & assisted in taking Forts Jackson & [St.] Philip at New Orleans, then went up the river & shelled Vicksburgh for a time. Another (McGowan) is the son of the person who commanded the *Star of the West* when she attempted to provision [Fort] Sumpter just as the war broke out.* He has been on the Potomac through the war & has seen some service there. He is a nephew of the notorious Ned McGowan† of California & who has recently made himself conspicuous by the capture of the *Maple Leaf* from our folks. Mr. Greene I suppose you know is a son of Brig. Gen. Greene who has just distinguished himself at Gettysburgh.‡ Mr. G. has just rec'd a letter from him giving an account of the fight—it is very interesting— he says that the removal of Hooker gave universal satisfaction to the army.§ Our Chief Engineer Ziegler has been in the naval [service] of some of the South American republics where he has seen some hard fighting. Another of our officers went with McClellan up the peninsular, was in all the battles before Richmond & in the retreat, was at Antietam, South Mountain, Bull Run &c—has been in 14 battles & any number of skirmishes, has been wounded four times.** So you see we have some good fighting material on board. As to the old *Monitor* officers, I never hear their courage doubted.

Tuesday evening 21st—The *Victoria* has just returned bringing the mails. I found your welcome letters of the 2nd & 9th, also one from Henry & a paper from him. I have just written a reply to his in which he made some enquiries about going to Ridgebury†† & my hour for which I have permission

---

* On January 5, 1861 the commercial steamer *Star of the West* commanded by John McGowan, Sr. sailed from New York with supplies and re-enforcements for the besieged Federal garrison at Fort Sumter. The vessel was driven back by the batteries in Charleston Harbor on January 9 and was unable to accomplish its mission.

† The Philadelphia lawyer, who went to California during the Gold Rush after having been kicked out of the Pennsylvania House of Representatives for brawling, had become a Confederate army officer. Captured in the bayous of Louisiana, he was held in a New Orleans prison cell for several months. In June 1863, while being transported North on the prison ship USS *Maple Leaf*, he and another Confederate officer took over the vessel, ran it ashore in Virginia, and returned to Louisiana.

‡ From 7 pm to midnight on the second day of the Battle of Gettysburg George Greene's lone brigade defended a half-mile stretch of Culp's Hill against an entire Confederate division. An engineer by training, the strong defensive works he ordered built enabled his men to hold off multiple attacks until reinforcements arrived.

§ While in pursuit of Lee's army as it advanced toward Pennsylvania, Hooker resigned his command of the Army of the Potomac. The army's faith in him had been greatly diminished after his stunning defeat at the Battle of Chancellorsville two months earlier.

** Possibly Acting Master's Mate William H. Knowlton (1828-1908) who was a private in the 1st Massachusetts Infantry from May 1861 to October 1862. Knowlton must have embellished his fighting record, for his Navy pension application mentions that he was wounded only once (by a falling tree when he was helping to build their winter quarters at Budds Ferry, MD).

†† The village in Connecticut where Keeler's father was born.

for a light has nearly expired. I must try & finish my sheet to send off by the *Chocura* which leaves for Beaufort to morrow morning.

We have just heard that the *Calypso* has been sold to gov't for $40,000, about one third of what she cost. Of course we do not feel very well pleased at such proceedings. Her cargo was not included, that will add somewhat to the sum. We are expecting to go out cruising in a few days & hope to add to our list of prizes.

When at Newbern I searched through all the hospitals but could find nothing of Chapin. We shall go up to Beaufort again in two or three weeks & if I go to Newbern will make another search.

I am glad to hear that Father & Sarah are enjoying themselves so well. I have written your Mother & am going to write to Uncle Brush.

Love & kisses to yourself & the children.

Wm

[Marginalia] Tell Eddy he is a good boy to send me the drawing. A terrible thunder storm is raging. The Capt. of the *Chocura* who goes up tomorrow was with Strain on the isthmus.* I send something for the children.

No. 15—

U.S. Steamer *Florida*
Off Wilmington, N.C.
July 24th, 1863

Dear Anna,

It is as beautiful a moonlight night as one might wish to see. A heavy gale is blowing, bringing in the heavy rollers over which the *Florida* is rising and falling at her anchor with a motion which I suppose would soon *disgust* a landsman, but our appetites I find are no ways impaired by it. If it was a good cool refreshing wind from "way up north" it would be most gratefully received, but as it happens to come from the opposite direction, bringing with it the heated air from the Gulf Stream, we do not feel very much refreshed thereby.

I have been so long accustomed to the sound of the waves as they dash, dash night after night & day after day against the side of the vessel that I don't know as I could sleep without their sounding in my ear. Through my open air-port (which I suppose you remember, though I presume you would call it window) their murmur and dash is the last thing I hear at night & the first sound that greets me in the morning.

When I sometimes contrast my situation this summer & last I wonder how I ever lived through it, shut up as we were in that close iron box, no

---

* The ill-fated 1854 U.S. Navy expedition led by Lieutenant Isaac G. Strain that explored a route across the Isthmus of Panama. Six of the 27 men died of starvation. William T. Truxton, the USS *Chocura*'s captain, was a midshipman on the expedition.

ventilation or air, but little light, in an atmosphere at times fairly suffocating, the heat enough to drive out a salamander, our rooms swarming with flies & mosquitoes & as if all that was not enough a brute of a captain who seemed to make it his study how to add to our discomforts. Rebel bullets & sharpshooters I make no account of as they were the least of the evils. Nothing but pure patriotism would ever tempt me to go through with the same again.

Those "harbingers of summer" you speak of (mosquitoes) have not made their appearance here nor do I think we will be troubled with them. We lie so far from the shore that I hardly think they will find their way to us. For fear they should however I have just put up a nice mosquitoe bar I got from the *Calypso*. The dozen or two flies we have in the Ward Room realy look lonesome as they hover around the table in search of company.

How I wish I could spend some of these beautiful moonlight evenings chatting with you on the front steps. I believe too I could appreciate a dish of raspberries. However there's no use in wishing, but it does begin to look now as if the end [of the war] was approaching when all of us could return home once more. The news is cheering & we are all feeling anxious to hear from Charleston.* It is not impossible that I may get there before my friend Dr. Kennifick, for I believe they have him with the rest of the prisoners we took from the *Calypso* shut up still in Fort Delaware.

You must have had quite a dry season from what you say. I suppose the garden has felt it. I am glad you are going to have an abundance of grapes. Hope there will be no early fall frosts.

Tell my friends not to give me to[o] much prize money. They must bear in mind that the expenses attending the disposition of them is large, then half of the nett proceeds goes to government, the other half being divided among the captors. The *Calypso* & cargo have been sold. What they brought we do not know exactly, but hear the vessel brought $48,500. & the cargo about $31,000. Government took the vessel at their appraisal, which is less than half what she is worth & far less than what they are paying private individuals for vessels not as good as the *Calypso*. There has been "gouging" somewhere. The vessel cost but a short time since 25,000 pounds & put up at auction would in all probability have brought from 75 to $80,000. The cargo was sold during the [draft] riots in New York & the fall of gold, all operated to bring down prices so that it did not bring what it should. Our schooner we have not heard from yet except of her safe arrival in New York. It may be the mob there burnt her up. I think between the two I shall get enough to make up for my loss in the *Monitor* & I hope some more.†

---

* The cheering news was the huge Union victories at the Battle of Gettysburg on July 3 and the fall of Vicksburg on July 4. However, Union forces had not fared so well at Charleston: Gillmore's second assault on Fort Wagner on July 18 was repulsed with heavy loss.

† Half the total sale value of the *Calypso* less court costs was $37,667. Since prize money was divided among the officers and crew in proportion to their salaries, Keeler's share equals his salary ($1,300) multiplied by the ratio of the prize money and the combined

Off Wilmington (March to September 1863)

Tell Mrs. Hough I have just one of my photographs left, but of course I couldn't think of such a thing as offering it to a lady unsolicited. She might think I was vain & desirous of intruding my phiz among her collection of friendly countenances uninvited, which I know would lessen me very much in her estimation. It is contrary to etiquette, which I know she regards too highly to suppose that I would infringe.

So you think when the mails come in I sit down & quietly read the war news before I "turn to the gossip of home"—not a bit of it. I don't realy believe you think so. Home letters are always first & foremost & I assure you are always thoroughly read before a newspaper is looked into. Perhaps this don't appear very patriotic but it is none the less true.

July 31st—The *Chocura* has just arrived from Beaufort with the mails, bringing your welcome letter of the 16th. If you are suffering from drouth [drought] we are not. Showers are of almost daily occurrence & the air is hot & sultry, making one long for a snuff of your cool northern atmosphere.

One of our men died on the 28th, the first death we have had on board.[*] We ran out to sea some 40 or 50 miles & buried him the same day, the Capt. reading the burial services of the Episcopal Church.

Evening—We are now at sea on our way to Beaufort. I wish you were on board for the ride. It is delightful, the poetry of "life on the ocean wave" & you could not help but enjoy it. The sea is as smooth & calm as a mill pond & the moon looks out bright from a clear unclouded sky. We are gliding along against a cool gentle refreshing breeze, a grateful contrast to the heated current from the Gulf Stream we have been lying in for a month or two past.

I am acting as Caterer of our Mess which adds somewhat to my work and responsibility, but not much, as we have a capital steward.

Aug. 1st—This is a clear bright & refreshing cool morning. Beaufort is in sight & in a few hours we shall be at anchor in our old spot under the walls of Fort Macon. If Chapin is in the hospital there I shall see him. I have been in the hospital a number of times every time we were at Beaufort but made no enquiries for him supposing him at Newbern.

I will try & write to the children next time. Kiss them for papa & accept much love from

William

---

salaries of all the men on the *Florida*. The combined salaries of the commanding officer, the eight wardroom officers and the 159 men listed in the July 1, 1863 muster roll is $46,565. Assuming $10,000 for the salaries of the steerage officers, who are not listed in the muster roll (noting that Keeler said there were 184 men on board the *Florida* in his May 8, 1863 letter), Keeler's share of the prize money would therefore have been roughly $900. Half the sale value less court costs of the *Hattie* and *Emily*, the two other blockade runners captured by the *Florida*, totaled $36,722 which would have yielded Keeler roughly $800 in prize money. Salaries are taken from the pay table in the *Register of the Commissioned, Warrant, and Volunteer Officers of the Navy of the United States to Jan. 1, 1864.*

[*] 23-year old Ordinary Seaman Alonzo Bennett from Hancock, ME.

Civil War Years: USS *Florida* (1863-1865)

No. 16—

U.S. Steamer *Florida*
Beaufort, N.C.
Aug. 1st, 1863

Dear Anna,

We got in here last Saturday morning [August 1] & in the evening our boat came off with your letter mailed July 24th, only *eight days* from home—the quickest time yet. The next morning, Sunday, I went ashore & hunted up Chapin at the hospital. I found him without any trouble. He was glad enough to see me, the first one he had seen from home since he had left there. It seemed strange to meet in this distant part of the country & coming by such different routes. I staid with him through the forenoon, talked over old times, home matters &c, took dinner with him, looked through the hospital & then in company with two of our officers got a carriage, the only one in Beaufort, & went out five or six miles beyond our pickets to a *farm* (by courtesy) after some fruit.

The ride seemed pleasant after being shut up so long on ship board. It was over a somewhat sandy road which "meandered" through dwarfed pines & scrubby underbrush, a splendid lurking place for the secesh of which we were told they sometimes took advantage & gobbled up the unsuspecting seekers after peaches or melons.

"Boy," says I to the *intelligent contraband* who guided our *gothic* steeds in the way they should go, "are there any secesh about here?"

"Well I spec thar be sometimes massa."

"What would you do if you should see some?"

"Golly dis nigger'd cut & run," a wise conclusion on his part undoubtedly but not particularly gratifying to us in a labyrinth of crooked roads & cart paths, winding in all directions among the dense undergrowth.

We however arrived at the "*farm*" without interruption. As no other house was in sight it was undoubtedly of large extent but the greater part being hidden by the "dense tangled wildwood" it was difficult to tell its exact dimentions. We however set the proprietor down as a "large landed proprietor" who in the generosity of his soul was allowing dame nature to cultivate his extensive domains without artificial aid from man. The house straggled about in separate bits something like a rail road train off the track & seemed to have been built & hitched together as increasing wants or a growing family rendered necessary. In architectural appearance it was a combination of the latest improvements of an "illigant pisant" and a backwoods saw-mill.

Constituting myself the spokesman of the party I made known our errand to a rather good looking elderly lady who answered my summons at the open door, who refered me to "her man." "Her man," after scan[n]ing our uniforms as if calculating the amount of brass we carried, came to the conclusion that we might accompany him to the orchard & pick some peaches for the moderate sum in old times represented by a coin now unknown but which in years gone by was called a "nickel" each.

He professed to be an ardent Union man, so of course we expressed our gratitude & was profuse in our thanks for the distinguished favour shewn us. We could not suppose it was for the filthy lucre which he expected to be transfered to his possession that he should submit to such a sacrifice, but pure & unalloyed love for the great American eagle.

His "*orchard*" of a dozen or so of scrofulous looking trees was scattered about in the odd angles of a dilapidated Virginia worm fence, whose protecting arms was the only defence they had against browsing bovines & had proved an effectual guard against any spasmotic attacks of horticultural industry on the part of the proprietor. Nature must have degenerated vastly if his peaches were the test. What a pity that the same power that starts the germ & gives it an impulse can't go around afterward with a budding knife & follow that up with a spade & a little fertiliser.

A careful reconnoisance in a thicket of weeds brought to light a vegetable production in which melon, squash & gourd were so intimately mingled that it was a hard matter to tell which predominated. We tested a number by applying to them the venerable "Father of his country," beautifully done in green paint at the expense of "his country" & surrounded with the mysterious characters of 50, 50, 50, also in green*. As they had some resemblance to watermelons we decided to call them such, & eat & relished them accordingly. We invested some green backs in a lot of *chickens* at 75 cents each, which were probably young once, but that time must have been "beyond the memory of the oldest inhabitant." As relics of antiquity they would have been valuable to the antiquarian, but as to food for human beings, a life time wouldn't have sufficed to masticate one. Then we were favoured with some small, knurly, crosseyed looking tomatoes at 15 cents per quart & some measly field corn at the paltry sum of 5 cents per ear, for all of which of course we were duly thankful.

In our settlement with our liberal entertainer for his unexampled generosity we discovered a deficiency in our finances, or rather an inability to make change which left us his debtor a few cents. This we made up by giving him the latest news from Charleston, to wit—that our iron clads had smashed fort Sumpter & our troops had taken the city which they had razed & transformed into a watermelon patch—that a lot of Massachusetts yankees were on their way down with [a] Bunker Hill monument which they were going to set up as a land mark to shew future generations the site of a secesh city. He expressed himself gratified at the news but hoped he wouldn't be "*conscriptionised*" as he didn't want to fight in neither army.

---

* The fifty-cent "postage currency" Federal bank note.

Civil War Years: USS *Florida* (1863-1865)

Such things as I have mentioned we get here in moderate quantities by paying immoderate prices. But fruits & vegetables are all of the poorest & most worthless kinds owing to want of cultivation & good pure seed. But we relish them I assure you & are not at all disposed to be fastidious. It is but a few days that we are here & then for can'd fruits & meats which are hardly enough like the original to claim relationship.

Sunday, 2nd—The rebel steamer *Kate*, the same one which I wrote you about* was run ashore by our vessels three weeks ago to day & which was shelled all that Sunday, came in to day in tow of the *Iroquois*. It seems that after running her ashore we attempted to destroy her with our shells (by "we" I mean our vessels on the north side) and also sent some boats to try & get her off or if they could not to burn her. They went on board, all hands got drunk, had a fight & came off without accomplishing their purpose. The vessel laid where she was, the rebels taking everything out of her even her machinery, leaving nothing but her bare hull & that they got off & was taking it in when our vessels mustered up courage & took her from them. They stripped her right under the guns of our fleet, a most disgraceful thing.

But I must close with love to all.

William

No. 17—

U.S. Steamer *Florida*
At Sea
Aug. 9th, 1863

Dear Anna,

We left Beaufort to day & are now on our way to our station "off Wilmington." While lying at Beaufort Capt. B., who had nearly recovered from his previous illness, was taken severely sick again with inflamation of the bowels & it was deemed prudent by the Fleet Surgeon that he should be taken out of the vessel, which was done & we left him behind in the hospital in the care of Dr. Ainsworth† of the army who has the care of the hospital (the one to which Chapin is attached).

I went ashore in advance of him & had a room made ready in a vacant building next to the Dr.'s. It was fitted up as well as circumstances would allow but I could not help contrast the place with the comforts & conveniencies of a nicely furnished room at home. The walls were entirely bare, no looking glass, pictures or ornaments of any kind, the plaster broken off in many places, no carpet on the bare floor, the room destitute of furniture of any kind except the iron bedstead, a small stand for medicine & a wooden

---

* See letter of July 12, 1863.
† Frederick S. Ainsworth. The Harvard Medical School graduate was in charge of the Hammond General Hospital in Beaufort.

chair, no curtains at the open windows which perhaps was better as they admitted the cool fresh sea breeze, that is when there was any, for part of the time there was no wind & it was "*awful hot.*"

Capt. B. had his servant with him & a nurse was detailed to take charge of him, so I think he will be well taken care of. He is not one of those who will miss the many little kind attentions of a home as he has never been used to them. Born in *Fort Moultrie*, his whole life from infancy up has been passed in the army & navy. He was a strict disciplinarian, exacting obedience & respect from both officers & men and according to each their due. But while he was a model officer he never forgot he was a gentleman. His officers he always expected to do their duty & while they did, were always treated with the greatest courtesy & consideration. To those of us who stood by him on the *Monitor* he seemed particularly attached. For myself I have nothing but the most pleasant recollections while under his command.

I was not present when he left the vessel, but was told that he seemed much affected when parting with his officers. As the boat which carried him left the ship's side the rigging was manned & three rousing cheers given which I heard distinctly at the hospital, miles distant. Just before I left him he says to me, "Paymaster, when I get well & have another command I shall wish you were with me." If the Dept. had sent more such men down here in the room of the old fogies to whom they have given the control of matters, much more would have been accomplished. Lieut. Greene has charge of the vessel & will remain in command till some one is ordered to us to take Capt. B's place. Who it will be I do not know, but it will be a difficult matter to fill it in every respect.

August 13th—My letter has lain unnoticed till now. The weather has been awful. "Hot" does not convey any idea of it. It has been impossible to write. If ink & ideas would flow as fast & freely as perspiration I should have had a ream ready for you by this time, but ideas evaporate before I can get them on paper. I can't say that under such circumstances it is much of a pleasure to write. I am doing it now as a duty. While this weather continues don't expect very lengthy epistles nor much in them. I shall as heretofore try & have a letter to send by every opportunity.

We have recently had a change made in our supply boat. Instead of the *Massachusetts* which used to supply both squadrons, we have the *Newbern* running from New York to supply this squadron exclusively. It enables the vessel to make the trip oftner, so that now we can have our ice, fresh beef, vegetables &c every fortnight instead of once a month as heretofore & besides in case any of my friends wants to send to me, anything directed to the care of the Naval Lyceum will come directly to me. I only wish you could jump on board & make me a visit. Her paymaster, Cushing[*], was Comman-

---

[*] Edmund H. Cushing (1838-1869). The Harvard graduate and lawyer served as principal clerk for the Mississippi Squadron in 1862 and 1863. In June 1863 he was appointed acting

dant's Clerk for some time at Cairo [Illinois] & knows Laning, Bennett & Pratt, besides a good many other of our Illinois folks.

Another very agreeable change has been made on board our vessel, or rather is to be made. Our M.D. [Weeks] is to be sent home & a Dr. Park* from Boston is to take his place.

A more miserable specimen of a man or a greater abortion of an M.D. I never saw.† He has exhausted the patience & excited the contempt not only of the Ward Room Mess but of the whole ship & to avoid being dismissed [from] the service is going home on a sick leave. It would take too much time & paper to give an account of our trials & troubles with him, but things finally got to such a pass that Capt. B. sent for him one day & told him that he must pursue a different course, that if he (Capt. B.) had been one of the Mess he would have kicked him out on deck long ago, that it was only owing to the forbearance of his brother officers that he remained where he did. Capt. B. thinks & so do the rest of us that it was owing to his (the M.D.'s) want of skill & inattention that brought Capt. B. down so low.

Dr. Parke is now on board & has been for a few days. We hope to find him a pleasant agreeable companion. Thus far we are much pleased with him.

Tell Hough that my opinions of negroes hasn't changed at all since I was cooped up in the *Monitor* up James river. I considered them then as I do now, human beings, but I never felt inclined, nor do I now, to place them as high in the scale of social existence as the whites. I speak in general terms. Only in one respect has my opinion changed. I never thought that they could be made into soldiers. Now I think they can & will fight too.

My opinions of McClellan have not changed unless to esteem him still higher is a change. It is only wasting words for anyone to attempt to depreciate McC. in my estimation. My opinion of him is not based upon newspaper reports or idle rumour but upon what I saw & heard for myself in my daily intercourse with his officers & camp while at Harrison's landing. There is one question I would like to ask Hough. Who should be the best judge of McC.'s military skill & genius, his officers & soldiers who fought with him through all the battles of the Peninsula, or those who have remained quietly at home whose only means of information has been the public prints?

Speaking of negro regiments reminds me of what I was told by Capt. Bowen‡, the Quartermaster at Beaufort who is a strong believer in negro

---

assistant paymaster and served on the supply ship USS *Newbern*. He joined the regular Navy after the war and died of yellow fever on board the USS *Tuscarora* off the west coast of South America.

* John G. Parke, Jr.*
† Keeler is referring to Grenville Weeks.
‡ John J. Bowen (1819-1901). The native of Brighton, NY was commissioned captain and assistant quartermaster of volunteers in June 1862. He served successively at Morehead City, New Berne and Beaufort until 1864 when he was transferred to the James River where he assisted in landing the Army of the James at Bermuda Hundred.

Off Wilmington (March to September 1863)

soldiers. He said that he thought that the slave regiments raised at the south would make better soldiers than those from the north for the reason that they had thoroughly instilled into them the most essential [trait] for a soldier—strict obedience & subordination.

Aug. 14th—I had just finished my sheet last evening & was thinking about "turning in" when the distant report of a gun, followed immediately by our alarm rattle calling all hands to quarters, induced me to change my mind & I rushed on deck to see "what was up." Another gun as I reached the deck & a rocket whizzing off to the south indicated a blockade runner & the course he was taking. Our chain was slipped at once & we took the course indicated by the rocket.

A couple of miles brought us up with the *Victoria*, who had made the signals, who hailed us that "a large side wheel steamer had just passed out" [and] that she came very near running the *Victoria* down, coming within two ships' lengths of her when the *Victoria* fired her first gun. The vessel then stopped, thundering off to the south, the *Victoria* giving her another gun & firing the rocket to let the other vessels of the fleet know the course she had taken. We could see nothing of her, but started in pursuit & kept it up till daylight revealed to us "old ocean," but nothing upon its surface but ourselves. We turned back & reached the fleet about noon. What a pity it is at such a time that the idea of the ancients wasn't true & the earth a flat surface where your vision could extend for miles instead of being bounded by a watery horizon but a short distance from you. The convex surface of our globe has proved a most convenient hiding place for many of the blockade runners & has saved many of them.

This evening another steamer came down the river apparently with the intention of running out & lay until dark under the guns of the Fort [Caswell]. Instead of remaining at anchor we are cruising about hoping to stumble upon her should she come out. This cruising about in the dark, uncertain whether you are to stumble upon friend or foe, is not the most agreeable or safest thing in the world but it forms a part of our blockade life & duty. Every light is most carefully guarded that it does not reveal our position & we plod slowly along through the thick darkness, every ear open to catch the faintest sound & every eye strained for the first view of an approaching vessel. The loaded guns are surrounded by their crews with cutlass & pistols in their belts, a slow match burning in the armoury with a row of rockets & signal lights ranged according to their numbers ready for instant use—white, red & blue lanterns burning, but their light concealed by canvass covers till required for use.

So we go. Every eye peering into the surrounding darkness. "Sail ho," cries the look out. "Where away?" "On the starboard beam." "Man the starboard battery." "Train your guns right abeam & be ready to fire." "Quartermaster, challenge her," & the colored rays of a red lantern stream out into the darkness for a brief period, then for a moment they are hidden, then again they are momentarily visible to be finally extinguished.

Civil War Years: USS *Florida* (1863-1865)

Now follows a brief period of suspense & wonder who she may be. Is she a friend? Will she answer our challenge? Or is she a foe ready to sweep our decks with grape & canister as soon as she can make us out? Or is she an unarmed blockade runner anxious only to escape the vigilance of our cruisers? The brief interval allowed for an answer is an anxious & exciting one.

There is no reply & the dark object looms up dimly in the darkness. "Stand by to fire." "Are you all ready?" "Aye, aye sir." "Hold, there she goes." A white light, & all is right, but a moment more & three one hundred pound shells would have gone crushing through her sides.

Now a gun lights up the horizon from some of our more distant vessels, then a rocket mounts up into the darkness, followed by a signal light giving a most beautiful crimson glow to the vessel & the surrounding water. This changes to a green so intense that it blinds the eye to look at it & calls for a response from some vessel of the fleet. These all have their signification & it requires the use of every faculty to see & read them quickly & correctly.

Tuesday, 18th—I fully realised the truth last night of what I have just written. Just before dark a strange steamer was seen outside and one of our smaller gun boats (the *Victoria*) was sent after it to see what it was. The night came on intensely dark before she got back. Occasional flashes of lightening lit up the sky & now & then a slight rain squall drove across the water. We could see but a very few feet from the ship's sides. "A light on the port bow," "light on the starboard quarter," "light right astern" came in succession from the lookouts.

"Sail ho." "Where away?" "Bearing down on our starboard beam." "Stand by your guns." "Ahead full speed." "Hard a port." "No. 4 gun fire."

A blockade runner! Yes & she's gone as quickly as she came. Had she kept her course & we ours, she would have run into us.

But here's another sail. "What is she?" "Can't make her out." "No. 3 gun all ready?" "Aye, aye, Sir." "Hold, I think it's the *Sacramento*, challenge her." "Yes, all right." "We're challenged, sir, right ahead." "Answer quick." "There's the *Victoria*'s signal. She's got back & is looking for us." "Answer her."

Lights were continually seen in different directions, first here, then there, appearing & disappearing as if by magic. It seemed as if the Flying Dutchman & Will O' the Wisp were playing hide & seek around us. To add to the excitement the *Victoria* on her return reported having got near enough to the strange sail, which acted very strangely, made her out to be a large armed vessel, much too large for the *Victoria* to cope with. The Capt. of the *Victoria* set her down for the *Florida* or *Alabama*. I assure you we were glad for daylight to shew us where we were & by what surrounded. Nothing was in sight but the other vessels of our fleet & the distant shore & fort.

An *armed* vessel ran in on the north side two or three days ago & day before yesterday a blockade runner went in, in broad daylight. The Admiral is there now in his flag ship (the *Minnesota*) so I suppose he sees just how it's done.

It has been blowing a gale from the north-east all day. We are lying at anchor under the lee of the land enjoying the refreshing coolness of the air.

Mr. Dunham's or Durham's or Daskam's (for I have never yet been able to make his name out yet from your letters) "physic" reached me safely.* Many thanks to him. I hope to make his acquaintance in a more physical manner one of these days.

Mr. Flye had none of his photographs with him & at his request *I sent mine to his wife* & requested her to send one of his to you. I am glad it reached you safely.

Wednesday, 19th—It still continues to blow from the north, cool & comfortable. The "Wilmington" blockade is about raised. Only three vessels on this side & one of them (the *Victoria*) is as good as none at all as she can't steam over six miles an hour. On the north side is the same number, including the flag ship which is always an incumberance & productive of more evil than good. Vessels are going out & in with impunity. We are daily looking for the *Florida* & *Alabama*. Then there will be a scattering, as we can't fight them with any hope of success.

I meant to have written to the children by this mail, but have no time as the *Sacramento* has just come down & the *Victoria* will leave in a few minutes. I have rec'd your No. 3. Good bye with love to all. Have just rec'd a letter from Hen at Ridgebury.

[unsigned]

[Marginalia] I enclose Act. Master McGowan's photograph.

No. 18—

U.S. Steamer *Florida*
Off Wilmington, N.C.
August 26th, 1863

Dear Anna,

Everything since my last has been quiet as possible—nothing doing—no excitement—nothing that will serve as a text for a letter. Tuesday [August 25] we paid the fleet on the north side a visit, returning the next day. On our way around [Frying Pan Shoals] we sighted "a suspicious looking steamer" burning black smoke &c. We made after her full speed & were soon near enough to give her a hint from one of our rifles that she'd better stop, but she paid no heed, keeping quietly on her way till our third fire when she ran up the French colors & proved to be a french man of war, so our dreams of more prize money soon "vanished into thin air."

---

* Henry Durham*, minister of the La Salle Congregational Church who had recently arrived in La Salle. In addition to having a degree in theology, he also had one in medicine.

Civil War Years: USS *Florida* (1863-1865)

Upon getting around to the Flag Ship [*Minnesota*] our new Captain came on board & took command—Lieut. Commander Jas. Parker.* How we shall like him of course we can't tell. He appears to be a still, quiet man but I don't think he will be the disciplinarian that Capt. B. was. He messes with us in the Ward Room for the present & is quite sociable & pleasant at the table. There was always something about Capt. B. which repelled any attempt at familiarity. This one on the contrary seems rather to invite it. Besides he does not rank as high as Capt. B.—two or three of us in the Ward Room ranking with him. Having the command ensures for him a certain degree of respect, otherwise it would be "How are you, Parker, old fellow?" &c &c.

He [Parker] tells us he was never under fire till last Sunday when the *Minnesota* went in to destroy a blockade runner that had been driven ashore. The rebels brought down some Whitworth guns to drive them off, but were themselves driven off by the *Minnesota*, their guns captured & brought away & the blockade runner destroyed. Capt. P. resigned from the Navy some years ago & studied law with Sec'y Chase†, but again entered the service upon the breaking out of the war.

In one of my recent letters I mentioned how little reliance could be placed upon most of the newspaper reports & what a miserable foundation they were upon which to base an opinion—in their statement of facts they *sometimes* commit *slight errors*. The slip of paper I enclose is a case in point.

You remember the blockade runner *Kate* of which I have spoken in some of my previous letters? It has been highly amusing to read the different accounts of her in the various papers which we have had on board & no two of them at all alike. No. 1 has it that she was run ashore by the *State of Georgia* who, finding it impossible to get her off, took out her cargo & destroyed her. No. 2, that she was run ashore while running in by the *Penobscot* who burned her. No. 3, that she was completely riddled by shells & destroyed by the *Iroquois*. No. 4 attributes it to the *Victoria* (which was on this side & never saw the *Kate*). No. 5 informs us that she was captured by one of our vessels while running out, having on board 15,000 bales of cotton. No. 6, that she was on her way from England direct with a full & valuable cargo of arms, which the veracious writer tells us he has been on board & seen.

The facts of the case I have given you before, but they are briefly these. The *Kate* ran ashore in the night while endeavouring to steal by our blockaders & was discovered by them at daylight the next morning (Sunday) whereupon they all commenced a furious cannonade which they kept up the greater part of the day & succeeded in striking her *twice*. So much for being completely riddled as Capt. Case‡, the senior officer, reported to the Department.

---

* James Parker* had been assigned only temporary command of the *Florida*.
† Secretary of the Treasury Salmon P. Chase.
‡ A. Ludlow Case. The 51-year old former fleet captain of the North Atlantic Blockading Squadron commanded the USS *Iroquois* off New Inlet.

OFF WILMINGTON (MARCH TO SEPTEMBER 1863)

Finding that they were not likely to destroy her in this way they sent some boats ashore with instructions to burn her. The officers & men upon getting on board found an abundance of liquor & all hands got drunk & went to fighting among themselves. Of course, no effort was made by them to accomplish their mission but they returned on board beastly drunk. By this time the rebels had succeeded in getting one or two small field pieces down from Fort Caswell & our vessels were driven off & the vessel with her cargo remained uninjured on the beach. The rebels then went to work without molestation & in about two weeks' time took out & carried off all her cargo & her entire machinery, completely stripping her of everything that could be detached from her hull, leaving nothing but a mere iron shell. This they worked at till they got it off & was towing it under the guns of the fort when the old granny of the fleet (the Flag Officer [Case]) got desperate & allowed some of our more enterprising & daring commanders to go in with their vessels & take her out, which they did. I saw her at Beaufort & went all over her. She appeared just as I have described her above—a mere iron shell, everything taken out. This is the way blockade duty is done, but what does the country know of it?

I saw a statement a few days since that seventeen vessels had run in in the last few days. I don't doubt it.

Friday, 28th—This has been the stormiest day we have experienced since we have been on the blockade. When I awoke in the morning the rain was coming down in torrents & a furious gale blowing from the north west which continued to increase till noon when it began to ease up & now (evening) it is comparatively quiet once more although the clouds look black & threatening. Below decks one would hardly know that there was a storm, the ship lay so still & quiet. I have been writing in my office through the day, unconcious most of the time of the furious storm raging about us. The northerly wind has lessened the temperature & I am writing now with my airport closed to *keep out the chilly breeze.*

It seems as if there wouldn't be much of LaSalle left by & by after a few more fires—how desolate it must look under the bluff. I was sorry to hear of the destruction of the mill as it will be an injury to the place, but I was still more sorry to hear that friend Hough was so heavy a looser. It has caused me a good many anxious hours but I regret to have it destroyed. Tell Mrs. Hough that I am not surprised to hear that she wants to leave the place. I wonder she has endured it as long as she has.

I believe if Hen hadn't gone to Ridgebury I should have sent for him to come down here. He could have come down on the *Newbern* from New York, stopping at Hampton Roads a few hours & then on down here. He could have remained on board with me about 4 hours when he would have started back. The trip would have cost him nothing, been very pleasant, taking 8 or ten days which I know he would have enjoyed much. I had a letter from him at Ridgebury a few days since. He appeared to be enjoying himself. My love to all friends, not forgetting my wife.

                              William

[Marginalia] I am so sorry to hear that Dave's eyes trouble him again. Poor fellow how much he has to try him. Any one else would have been discouraged long ago.

No. 19—

                              U.S. Steamer *Florida*
                              Off Wilmington, N.C.
                              Sept. 2nd, 1863

Dear Anna,

Here it is nearly a month since I have heard from home—your last being Aug. 6th & the latest paper we have seen was one of Aug. 19th, not because letters nor papers have not been sent us, but no boats have been down from Beaufort to bring them. There must be a large mail there for us & if we don't get it pretty soon we shall do something. I don't know what unless it be to go in & capture Fort Caswell, get possession of the telegraph & so send home for news via the wires. That solitary minded individual who longed so ardently "for a lodge in some vast wilderness"* should have tried the blockade for a short time & I think a change would have "come o'er the spirit of his dreams."†

I dispatched a letter for you to day & one for Hen which I hope will reach you in due time. I want to hear from Hen what kind of a time he had at Ridgebury & how he enjoyed himself. I have also written to Uncle Brush & Sarah. The latter was a terrific epistle.

Our cool weather still continues much to our satisfaction. The nights are so cool that I am glad to sleep with my air port closed & crawl under a blanket.

Last night Mr. Craft made a boat expedition in towards the fort to sound the channel & watch a large steamer that is lying under the guns of the fort waiting to run out. I had a pressing invitation to accompany him but as I could not perceive any particular pleasure to be derived from passing a dark, cool night in an open boat, tossing about on the water, with the chance of getting a grist of grape or canister from the guns of Fort Caswell, I politely declined. I imagine he returned in safety, as I met him at the Mess table the next morning looking as *salubrious* as usual. He is the "Mrs. Partington" of the Mess.‡

---

* William Cowper's *The Task* (1785).
† Lord Byron's *The Dream* (1816).
‡ A person of indomitable spirit. After the English anecdotal character Mrs. Partington who tried to keep back the Atlantic Ocean with her mop.

OFF WILMINGTON (MARCH TO SEPTEMBER 1863)

Sunday, 6th—No vessel or mail yet. We got desperate yesterday for the want of news, or excitement, or something to eat, or may be a combination of the whole, so Mr. Greene & myself took one of the boats & started across the [Frying Pan] Shoals to see what had become of them all there. We were met on the opposite side by the *Niphon*, but found they were as badly off as ourselves. They however had been able to get up an excitement, though with a serious result to themselves—the loss of two boats & their crews, in all 20 officers & men. They had forced the *Hecla* [*Hebe*], one of the blockade runners ashore & sent in the boats to get her off if possible & if not to des[t]roy her. In trying to effect a landing the boats were by some means capsized in the surf & while the men were struggling helpless in the water a company of rebel soldiers made their appearance out of the adjoining brushwood & commenced firing upon them. The officer in charge of one of the boats was seen to reach the beach when he was fired at by the rebels & fell. He rose & was fired upon again & fell the second time. He rose once more & was seized by the collar by a cavalry officer & dragged off. The officer in charge of the other boat succeeded in reaching the *Hecla* [*Hebe*] & fired her amid a storm of bullets. He then jumped overboard & swam ashore where he was shot by the rebels.*

By this time the rebs had got down a couple of pieces of artillery with which they opened fire upon the *Niphon*. The *Minnesota* & other vessels of the fleet came up to their assistance & the rebs "skedaddled," leaving their guns behind which were brought off by one of our boats which was sent for them. This little diversion however cost the rebels dear as well as ourselves, for in order to retreat they were obliged to run along a narrow sand spit under the fire of the *Niphon* which steamed steadily along paralell with them, exploding her shell among them at every step.

The blockade on the north side is merely nominal, the *Niphon* being the only effective vessel there. Beside[s] her there are three or four others, but nearly worn out & useless.

The Admiral found the blockade getting tedious after his ice & fresh beef were exhausted and has gone back to Hampton Roads with the *Minnesota*.

As a proof of the "effectiveness" of the blockade, the Capt. of the *Niphon*† told me that a large side wheel steamer ran in on that side in the middle of the day, that there was not effective force enough on that side to prevent it. We are nearly as badly off on this side, the *Sacramento* & ourselves being the only vessels here at present.

---

* Acting Ensign William W. Crowninshield (1833-1874). The Charlestown, MA native recovered from his ordeal, was exchanged, and later served in the East Gulf Blockading Squadron. He rose to the rank of acting volunteer lieutenant and served on the *Florida* after Keeler left. He died while serving on the Asiatic Station as captain's clerk on the USS *Monanacy*.
† Acting Master Joseph B. Breck.

Civil War Years: USS *Florida* (1863-1865)

On our way back across the Shoals we were very near being capsized in the breakers, a heavy sea coming into the boat & nearly filling her with water. We were well soaked but I have found that salt water harms no one unless taken in *too large quantities*. While the shoal is only 4 or 5 miles across it is 40 miles around from one side to the other.

Sunday evening—Just as I got to the bottom of the page, "Sail ho" came from the lookout & we started out to see who the stranger might be. She proved to be a schooner with coal for Port Royal. We sighted another from Port Royal for New York. She gave us the glorious intelligence that the Stars & Stripes were once more waving over Fort Sumpter.* On our way back we spoke the steamer *S. R. Spaulding* & got from her papers of the 1st and 3rd. So all that can get hold of them (there are only two) are deep in newspaper literature, while the rest are anxiously waiting their turn. I have just glanced over one & am now waiting for the Capt. to finish the other.

Monday evening [September 7]—"Now is the winter of our discontent made glorious summer"† by the arrival of the mail. One from Hen & No. 2, 4 & 5 from you—No. 3. I had previously rec'd. I have had no time to read them yet, though they arrived this noon. I am hastily closing this scrawl, as the mail leaves tomorrow morning & I have but little time for I want to read yours before I "turn in."

More changes—a new Capt. (Queen) & another M.D. of which I will write you at length in my next.

I'm must close, as I feel impatient to peruse my home news. Best love to all. Kisses to yourself & the children.

William

No. 20—

U.S. Steamer Florida
Off Wilmington, N.C.
Sept. 9th, 1863

Dear Anna,

Change appears to be the order of the day. Capt. Parker has been detached & his place supplied by Lieut. Commander Walter W. Queen. Dr. Parke has also been relieved by Dr. H. H. James‡.

I can't say that I was very sorry to have Capt. P. go though he was an agreeable man in his way, that is, he would come into the Ward Room & talk & laugh with us, play dominoes, discuss politics & war measures &c. He was a rabid war democrat (I believe they are termed) & prided himself upon having voted for Douglass.§ He was down on the Republicans & particularly

---

* False news.
† William Shakespeare's *Richard III*.
‡ Hiram H. James*.
§ Stephen A. Douglas, the Democratic Senator from Illinois who lost to Lincoln in 1860.

OFF WILMINGTON (MARCH TO SEPTEMBER 1863)

bitter on Massachusetts, whose Governor he denounced in the strongest terms. Of course we used to have some pretty warm arguments & at times we would get quite excited. He boasted of hailing from Ohio, & was bearing down on Dr. Parke, who is a Boston man, one day at the Mess table (he messed with us). Well says I, "Dr., admit all the Capt. says about Gov. Andrews[*] is so, how would you trade him for the candidate in Ohio, Vallandingham?"[†] It raised a shout at the table & the Capt. didn't get over it in all day. He was a warm advocate of McClellan as nine tenths of the army & navy are. The old adage is true "that familiarity breeds contempt" & I believe it would have been exemplified had he remained with us.

Dr. Parke was a very pleasant companion & associate & we all felt sorry to have him leave. He was ordered back to the *Victoria*. His successor will not wear as well I fear.

Our new Captain is a fine looking man & appears very different from Capt. Parker. He formerly commanded a division of the mortar schooners at New Orleans & has the reputation of being a good officer.

I rec'd a letter from Mr. Flye a short time ago telling me that he was ordered to the *Kensington*, a much finer command than the vessel he leaves. Mr. Crafts has just been promoted to Acting Master & of course feels quite elated.

I have just been reading "Our Contraband" in one of the late numbers of *Harpers*. We have her match on board of the opposite sex—"Columbus"—as mischievous a black ape as was ever invented. We have long since given up punishing him as we found it entirely useless. The Steward sends him on an errand & finds him playing checkers forward with the men. Mr. Greene sends him to his room for a cigar & waiting till his patience is exhausted goes after him & finds him coiled up in one corner on the floor fast asleep. I believe I wrote you of his trying on Mr. Ziegler's uniform. There is no end to his tricks. He breaks more crockery & makes more trouble & mischief than a dozen of them are worth. I hope some benevolent quaker will take compassion on him.

We have been amusing ourselves for some time past watching the rebs building a new battery about a couple of miles from fort Caswell. They have had a large force at work & have apparently been urging the work to completion as rapidly as possible. It looks as if it was designed to be to Caswell what Wagner is to Sumpter.

It would be a severe joke on the industrious rebs if our forces when they made an attack should land forces up the beach towards Masonborough inlet

---

[*] John A. Andrew, the Republican governor of Massachusetts.
[†] After having been exiled to the Confederacy in May 1863, Clement Vallandigham, the leader of the Peace Democrats, made his way to Windsor, Ontario where he declared himself a Democratic candidate for governor of Ohio. He won the nomination in absentia but lost the election to the National Union candidate in October 1863.

out of the reach of all the forts. This can easily be done & at present there is nothing to prevent them making a landing there and marching up to Wilmington or entrenching themselves between the river (which runs nearly paralell with the shore and about two miles distant) & the beach.

The almost incredible range & accuracy of artillery was shewn last evening by a Whitworth bolt being thrown from Caswell & striking within a hundred feet of the vessel, a distance of very nearly five miles.

However this is no further than Gen. Gilmore is throwing his shells into Charleston. From what we hear our troops are making good progress there.* I sincerely hope they will meet with no reverses. With Charleston ours it seems as if that "backbone" [of the Confederacy] would once more be "broken."

Friday, 11th—Well here we are on our way to Hampton Roads for coal & repairs. It seems like a long step towards home. I wish it was but I have no expectation of getting there now. We will probably remain a week or ten days for temporary repairs & then back once more to our station.

Should our forces at Charleston be successful, the iron clads will not be needed there & we shall then look for an attack on Wilmington. I hope to be there to take part in it, though if it does not take place soon it may be delayed till spring, if the iron clads are used, as there is no shelter for the Monitors from the frequent severe gales of the winter months around Cape Fear, & they could not live in the open ocean.

We left our station yesterday morning, stopping on the "North Side" to take up the mail &c. While there we learned the cause of the heavy firing we heard a day or two since. Two large steamers in attempting to run the blockade in *open day* got ashore & a furious fire was opened by our vessels, with the usual result—the escape of the blockade runners, who after remaining aground 48 hours got off & went up the river.

The *Montgomery* on her way down from Beaufort yesterday morning chased one 5 or 6 hours but loosing on her gave up the chase. It is no exageration when I say that Wilmington has a larger foreign trade to day than she ever had before. They are getting bolder & bolder every day as our blockade grows weaker & weaker, for it has grown weaker till it amounts to almost nothing.

One of those "romances in real life" that we sometimes hear of has just come to light on board. One of our men by the last mail had a letter from Germany stating that his uncle who was Sec'y of War in one of the free cities of Germany had died, leaving this person his property which was bringing an

---

* On September 7 Quincy Gillmore's troops finally captured Fort Wagner after a 60-day siege. The bombardment of Charleston, which began on August 22 when the "Swamp Angel" started lobbing incendiary shells 7,900 yards into the city, continued for the next 600 days. The city did not fall until February 1865 when Confederate troops evacuated.

income of $80,000.00 a year. Of course he is very anxious to leave the service & get home.

Saturday night [September 12]—We are pushing steadily along. Cape Henry light [house] just in sight. Tomorrow morning if nothing prevents we shall be at anchor in Hampton Roads. So good night.

Sunday morning [September 13]—Here we are in the old familiar locality of Newport News. I have just returned from a visit to the *Sangamon* (one of the Monitors) & the three turreted *Roanoke*.

The mail is closing & I have no more time to write. You will hear from me again soon. With love to[o]

W—

[Marginalia] Father's photograph is good—am much obliged to him for it.

Norfolk Navy Yard (September to October 1863)

We are now tied up alongside one of the docks, amid the charred, sunken wrecks of our vessels, the cracked walls of long rows of once fine brick shops & warehouses destroyed by fire, a splendid dry dock blown up, huge piles of rubbish, tangled masses of machinery bent & ruined by heat & tall monumental like chimneys standing like sentinels to mark the ruins of one of the largest Navy Yards of the world. (19 September 1863)

On September 10 the *Florida* left the blockade for the Norfolk Navy Yard for repairs. Since the yard was in ruins, having been destroyed by the Confederates when they evacuated Norfolk in May 1862, facilities existed for doing only minor repairs. Compelled to remain there to pay off the crew members whose terms of enlistment had expired, Keeler was unable to obtain a leave of absence to go home to La Salle or to visit New Haven and made do by enjoying dinner parties on board the *Florida* and visits to Norfolk and to Old Point Comfort.

Leaving them at Norfolk was Samuel Dana Greene, who was granted a leave of absence to get married and was subsequently placed on special duty inspecting ironclads at the New York Navy Yard. Replacing Greene as executive officer was 23-year old Acting Lieutenant Edgar Merriman, who had entered the Naval Academy in 1857 but resigned due to ill health in 1860. He enlisted in late 1861 and served on one of the mortar schooners in the attack on the forts guarding New Orleans in April 1862 and later on the USS *Santiago de Cuba* in search of the Confederate commerce raiders *Alabama* and *Florida*. Keeler described him as "full of fun & frolick" and "the best hand at telling a comic story that I ever saw."

Letters of special note: September 20 (a military execution); September 24 and 26 (visits to Old Point and Fort Monroe); September 29 (duties as paymaster and caterer of the mess).

Civil War Years: USS *Florida* (1863-1865)

No. 21—

U.S. Steamer *Florida*
Norfolk Navy Yard, Va.
Sept. 19th, 1863

Dear Anna,

We arrived at Hampton Roads last Sunday [September 13] & proceeded immediately to Newport News from which place I sent a letter to you by first opportunity. Since then I have not written as it has been undecided what to do with the vessel—whether to send her north for repairs or repair her here. The Department have finally concluded to make temporary repairs in this yard. It is needless for me to say how greatly I am disappointed as I had not only anticipated a visit to New Haven but home also.

We shall probably be detained here from four to six weeks during which period the term of enlistment of a large number of the crew will expire & I am compelled to remain here to pay them off & discharge them—a portion of my work which I cannot delegate to any one else.

Though if I had not that to detain me it is extremely doubtful if I could obtain leave of absence, the Department having heretofore refused to grant any from this station & I have come to the conclusion that I must forgo even the satisfaction of a day or two in New Haven.

Capt. Queen has sent for his wife & she is now *living with him on board*. Mr. Craft has sent for his wife. She will probably be here to-morrow. So also have some of the other officers. How I wish you were in New York or New Haven. I should have you here as soon as possible. But that cannot be, so I will not dwell upon it. If your parents were not so much opposed to having Henry out of school I should send for him. It seems hard to have to give up my contemplated visit home but I see no other way at present.

You will all feel the disappointment as well as myself I know. If it was necessary I would not say a word, but it is not, and that makes the disappointment greater. If Capt. Bankhead was with us I think I might be able to effect something, but our present Commander is a different man from Capt. B. Well, as I cannot go home I will do the next best thing & that is write home.

We lay at Newport News all day Sunday, giving me an opportunity of visiting the *Roanoke*, one of our monster iron clads with three turrets, having on[e] of those huge 15 inch guns that you saw in the [New York] Navy Yard & a two hundred pounder rifle in each turret. She is a wooden frigate of the size of the *Minnesota* cut down & plated. One wants to go aboard to realise her monstrous proportions & size, for like the Monitors she is mostly below water.

I also made a visit to the *Sangamon*. It seemed like going home, so much did she seem like *the Monitor*. My mind was carried back to the scene of a year

Norfolk Navy Yard (September to October 1863)

ago & it seemed as if Capt. Jeffers & my old Messmates of that famous little iron clad must every moment make their appearance from the hatchway.

So far I have seen all the different kinds of iron clad vessels built by government—the *Monitor, Naugatuck, Galena, Keokuck, Ironsides, Roanoke*—all different, most of them in very material points. The *Ironsides* presents the most formidable appearance, as indeed she has proved herself to be at Charleston. I wish we had more like her in the navy. Her battery is the most powerful in the navy—14 eleven inch guns, such as [we] had on the *Monitor* and two 200 pounder rifles. She throws between 16[00] & 1700 weight of iron at a broadside. No wonder they dread her at Charleston.

The person who led the unsuccessful boat attack on Sumpter was Capt. Stevens* who commanded the *Monitor* for a time—just the person to lead such an expedition. He is an acquaintance of John Rockwell's†.

We remained at anchor Monday & I made a visit to Old Point, found my friends there well & glad to see me, the place looking very much as it did when I last saw it—alive with officers from the army & navy, mule teams, negroes, army wagons, soldiers, ambulances, shot, shell & cannon & all the appliances of war. The next day to my great disappointment it was decided to send us here for repairs instead of letting us go north.

On our way up [to the Norfolk Navy Yard] we passed the never to be forgotten batteries at Sewell's point, Craney island, & through the obstructions placed in the river by the rebels—could see the ripples in the water caused by the sunken wreck of the *Merrimac*. Many things tended to remind me of that bright May morning when we forced our way by & through all these things to the hastily vacated nest of rebels at Norfolk & the smoking ruins of the Navy Yard.

We are now tied up alongside one of the docks, amid the charred, sunken wrecks of our vessels, the cracked walls of long rows of once fine brick shops & warehouses destroyed by fire, a splendid dry dock blown up, huge piles of rubbish, tangled masses of machinery bent & ruined by heat & tall monumental like chimneys standing like sentinels to mark the ruins of one of the largest Navy Yards of the world. The extent of the vandalism and the

---

* On September 8, 1863 Commander Thomas Stevens led a daring nighttime boat attack on Fort Sumter. Towed to within 800 yards of the fort, the men rowed the rest of the way, but were unable to scale the walls due to overpowering resistance from the defenders. Writing about the attack twenty years later, Stevens described the air being "filled with hissing, shrieking missiles from the James and Sullivan's Island batteries," with a rebel ironclad "pouring grape and canister into the boats" and "the parapets and crown of Sumter ... filled with men pouring a murderous fire down on our defenceless party." Several boats managed to land, but their crews and officers were taken prisoner; the remaining boats withdrew to the safety of the Union fleet. Of the roughly 400 sailors and marines who participated in the attack, 124 were killed, wounded or captured. ("The Boat Attack on Sumter" by Thomas H. Stevens, *Battles and Leaders of the Civil War*, Vol. 4, 1884).

† Stevens met Keeler's friend in the 1850s when they were both serving in the U.S. Coast Survey.

completeness of the destruction cannot be realised till one has spent some hours in the yard & made the circuit of its high brick wall, which is nearly three miles in extent & loopholed the whole distance for musketry by the rebels. Beside the wall is a large water front. A few slight wooden buildings have been put up in the yard to enable them to make slight repairs upon the vessels sent here & workmen are now engaged in cleaning out the dry dock (a larger & finer one than you saw in New York) & repairing it for use.

Norfolk has more of a business look than when I last saw it. Most of the stores are open & there is considerable stir & bustle in the streets but I am told that it is still full of secesh & as bitter as ever but more quiet & still. They still delude themselves with the idea that the rebels are again to have possession.

We are living on the fat of the land—plenty of melons, tomatoes, cucumbers, oysters, crabs. Of fish we had a surfeit while on the blockade. Then we have an abundance of the finest sweet potatoes & I have discovered a new article of food—*figs* & *milk*—very much like, but superior if anything, to baked apples & milk. Fruit appears to be quite abundant & of fair quality. As you may suppose we are making up for lost time on the blockade & can appreciate these things the better from having been so long without them.

I have more to say but will send that along in another sheet. With much love to yourself & all.

W—

No. 22—

U.S. Steamer *Florida*
Norfolk Navy Yard, Va.
Sept. 20th, 1863

Dear Anna,

The day after our arrival here I witnessed a new phase of military life—a military execution. The culprit in the first place deserted from one of the Georgia regiments & joined a cavalry regiment from Penn. from which he deserted in a short time & was taken. He deserted again & committed a highway robbery to a large amount, was taken again & lodged in the Norfolk jail from which he escaped & was captured by some of our pickets in company of some guerillas, was tried & sentenced to be shot.

The place fixed upon for his execution was a short distance out of Portsmouth & in company with a number of others I went to witness it. The troops were drawn up in the form of a parallelogram, a regiment of infantry forming each of the sides, one end composed of a battery of artillery & two or three squadrons of cavalry. The other end at which the prisoner was to be placed was of course left open.

Norfolk Navy Yard (September to October 1863)

A short time after I reached the ground the procession with the prisoner arrived. First came the Provost Marshall* with other officers, then a band playing a dead march, followed by four soldiers carr[y]ing the coffin. Behind these came a carriage containing the prisoner, three or four ministers & the surgeon. Then came the guard detailed as executioners.

The procession came into the square at the upper end, marched to the open end where they halted. The coffin was set down, the prisoner got out of the carriage & was seated upon it, with his back to his executioners & the square. He was a young man only 18 years of age, tall & well formed, very muscular, but with one of the most villainous looking countenances I ever beheld.

The Provost Marshall rode up & read his death warrant to him when the ministers made a long address to him, then prayed with him, all kneeling around the coffin. He was then seated on the other side of the coffin facing his executioners who were drawn up in a line about 30 feet from him. The Provost Marshall rode up & shook hands with him, a bandage was tied over his eyes, the Provost Marshall raised his hand & the muskets were levelled. When it fell they fired. The man fell back across his coffin seeming to die instantly. The troops were marched around the body as it lay on the ground & then all left the field. I understood he had a father & mother living in Georgia.†

I believe I could be willing to be shot in battle if necessary but such a death as his—'tis horrible. I believe he died a thousand deaths while they were talking and praying with him around his coffin.

Yesterday I made a visit to the Naval Hospital, a very large beautiful building fronting on the river, a fine large lawn interspersed with shade trees in front & in the rear an extensive garden & a very large grove of heavy pines.‡

---

* Major Hiram B. Crosby, 21st Connecticut Infantry.
† William D. Benton's sad story was recounted by Rev. Ferris Scott, chaplain of the 148th New York Infantry, who met him at the Norfolk jail several weeks before his execution. According to the chaplain, Benton invited the chaplain into his cell room, offered him the only chair, sat on the edge of his cot and proceeded to tell him his story: "[I] was living at the beginning of the war at Griffin, Georgia. I have not been home or seen my folks since the war, and I don't want any of my family to know of my sad end. I was but eighteen when the war broke out, but was crazy to enlist and joined the first battalion of Georgia infantry. I was wild and reckless as I always had been. My mother was a pious, good woman, and tried hard to bring me up right, but I took after my father and was head-strong and reckless." He went on to say that he had enlisted and deserted numerous times before crossing Union lines and enlisting in the 11th Pennsylvania Cavalry, where he "tried to desert again but was caught, tried and am now to be shot." The chaplain later escorted him to the place of execution, which took place on September 17, bowed with him by the side of the coffin and "offered a prayer for the peace of his soul." (*Neighbor's Home Mail: The ex-soldier's Reunion and National Campfire*, Phelps, NY, November 1874, p. 166). The 1860 Federal Census shows Benton living in Griffin with his father (a cabinet maker), mother and two younger sisters, who presumably never learned of his fate.
‡ The handsome three-story granite and freestone building still serves as a naval hospital.

I had my fill of grapes & figs in the garden. The building is some four stories high, built of brick & stone & presents a very beautiful & imposing appearance from the river as you approach Norfolk. For comfort, convenience & good attendance it presents a great contrast to the army hospitals. The rebels would have destroyed it when they did the Navy Yard had it not contained some of their sick. As it was they stripped the large handsome parlours & reception rooms of their expensive carpets & furniture.

To day our M.D. (Dr. James) & myself concluded for a novelty to go to church. We first brought up at a Catholic [church], then at an Episcopal church (a slight improvement). At the door of the next we addressed ourselves to a venerable ethiopian, who stood hat in hand, to know what church it was—"Dis massa *ossifers* am de cullerd persons church. I speck you find de Union church round dat corner dar."

So to the "Union" church we went & found a small building used by the 21st Conn. The attendance was light, but quite as large as the quality of the preaching and singing would warrant. The preacher was an old man and undoubtedly as good as he was aged, but he lacked very many very essential things to make a sermon either useful or ornamental. He was a second edition of Uncle Burton[*] without any improvements. Next Sunday I think we will try it in Norfolk or else down to Fortress Munroe.

In the afternoon I went to call on the Col. of the Conn. 21st (Col. Dutton[†]). I found him [to be] a distant connexion of your family. [He] was a classmate of Melzar's[‡] & had been at your father's house & was acquainted with the family. I think he told me he was from Wallingford & had graduated at West Point.

Mrs. Crafts arrived this morning & her husband has taken board for her at a short distance from the gates of the Yard. I have just returned from a call on her. I told her I was very glad to see her. I only wished it was Mrs. Keeler I was shaking hands with instead of Mrs. Crafts. She said she left all the folks well at New Haven. Mr. Ziegler's wife came at the same time.

Monday 21st—I had some business at Old Point to day & as it is not always convenient to shape your time & business to suit the steamboat I thought it would be better to have a steamboat to myself. So I applied to Capt. Goodwin[§], the Quartermaster, to know if he would give me a boat. "Certainly," he said & gave me a card to the Master of transportation [that read] "place a tug at the disposal of Paymaster Keeler U.S.N. for the day." I had a delightful ride, taking with me for company two or three of our officers. There are quite a number of these small steamers here under the control of

---

[*] Nathan Burton, minister of the Congregational Church in Ridgefield, CT and the second of three husbands of Keeler's father's sister Rachel.
[†] Arthur H. Dutton[*].
[‡] Dutton attended Yale before switching to West Point, but was not a classmate of Melzar's.
[§] Hollister E. Goodwin (1842-1899). The 21-year-old son of a Methodist minister from Lima, NY was assistant quartermaster of volunteers with the rank of captain.

the Quarter Master & it is much more convenient when you can obtain one as you can come & go when you please without any risk of being left.

Wednesday 23rd—We have had great times on board to day. Mrs. Col. Biddle & Miss McGowan came on yesterday to see their brother, Mr. McGowan.* To day we gave a dinner party to the ladies & had a very pleasant time. We had Mrs. Queen, Mrs. Crafts, Mrs. Ziegler & their husbands, Mrs. Biddle, Miss McGowan & the officers of the vessel—fifteen in all. Being caterer of the mess you might accuse me of vanity if I should tell you how nice our dinner was, but I must tell you we all enjoyed it & had a right merry time. *I did so wish you were here.* It was all that was wanting to complete my enjoyment.

Mrs. Biddle is quite young & has been married only a few months, having gone out to camp in Indiana for that purpose. Her husband is with Gen. Burnside. She is a trainer I tell you. To morrow they are "coming down to darn my stockings & sew the buttons on my shirts," which service they say they are going to do for each officer whose wife is not here—don't you feel obliged?

I haven't heard from you since we left the blockade. I suppose they [the letters] have gone down there. Our weather is not only cool but cold. I crawl under two or three blankets nights to be comfortable. If it is as cold [up] north you must have frost. I hope not. How the evenings are lengthening. I wish I could spend some of them at home. Kisses to yourself & the children & love to all.

W—

No. 23—

U.S. Steamer Florida
Norfolk Navy Yard
Sept. 24th, 1863

Dear Anna,

I mailed a letter to you this morning telling you what first rate times we are having here and how much I wished you were here with us. How pleasant it would be. I have hoped for a long time that you might sometime be able to visit this part of the country. There is so much to see here that would interest you. You would enjoy it all so much but not more than I would having you here & going about with you. If you was only within reach. But I don't see that it does any good to wish.

The ladies were all on board this afternoon. Buttons were sewed on & stockings mended, though as I contrive to keep my wardrobe in pretty good order I don't think that many repairs were found necessary. Mrs. Crafts sends

---

* Ellen Biddle (1841-1922), wife of Colonel James Biddle of the 6th Independent Cavalry, and her then unmarried older sister Kate A. McGowan (1838-1920).

her love & says that she regrets so much that you are not here. Mr. McGowan's sisters will leave in a few days & as they are all boarding at the same place it will make it rather lonesome for her through the day while Mr. C. is away, though she will probably spend a considerable [amount] of her time on board the vessel.

We took a stroll around the Yard this afternoon among the ruins as they were left by the rebels. They alone are well worth a journey to see.

The days are delightfully cool & makes our rather thick uniforms feel quite comfortable & paper collars last somewhat longer than they used to in hot weather. Then they used to *wilt down* about as soon as they were put on. I saw "steel collars" advertised & thought they would be just the thing till I saw them. They would make a splendid collar—for a dog. But as I am not canine in my habits I declined to purchase. Though if I remain in the service much longer I believe I shall get one & have the name of my owner, "Uncle Sam," engraved on it, with a chain attached.

Have you ever read "Parson Brownlow's" book? Mrs. Biddle has lent it to me & I have just been glancing over some of its pages. The old man seems determined to give some of his secesh neighbors the benefit of notoriety. I don't wonder at his using such severe language after the experience he relates. He must have been a thorn in their side while among them.*

Friday, 25th—I applied to the Commandant of the Yard ("Commodore Livingston"†) to day for a leave of absence for seven days, intending to go up in the *Newbern* on her return north from the blockading fleet & return here in her when she came back. This would enable me to spend a day or two in New Haven & New York. He wouldn't grant it, although he has been authorised by the Dept. to grant leaves of absence at his discretion to the officers of vessels repairing in the Yard, but he "didn't like to take the responsibility." So I have made up my mind to go back on the blockade without *seeing any one.*

It amuses me to see what dodges & artifices are sometimes resorted to to shift responsibility from one to another. It is the great bug bear of the navy—none, or very few at least, are willing to assume any respo[n]sibility where by any possible means they can contrive to get rid of it. Capt. Bankhead was an exception—when satisfied that he was right he did not hesitate to act. If there was anything he abominated & detested it was *"red tape."* The meaning of that term I fully realise I assure you after nearly two years' experience. Does it

---

* William G. "Parson" Brownlow was a newspaper publisher and Methodist minister from Tennessee, who railed against secession in the years leading up to the Civil War. Imprisoned at the start of the war, he was released and exiled to the North where he became a much sought-after speaker. He described his experiences in *Sketches of the Rise, Progress, and Decline of Secession; with a Narrative of Personal Adventures among the Rebels*, which was published in 1862.

† John W. Livingstone. It is unclear why Keeler put his name in quotes.

seem as if I had been from home so long?—nearly two years. How fast the time has slipped away.

I cannot but think that I shall be with you next spring, for I cannot now see what will keep me longer, unless it be a war with England, which I almost hope may be the case—then I will remain in the service if I work for nothing. I have the greatest desire to see that set of hypocritical scoundrels receive a thrashing, & we are fast accumulating strength & means to do it. It would be almost entirely a naval war & notwithstanding all her boasts, England is to day far behind us in iron clads & guns. Gilmore's artillery practice at Charleston has thrown them all into a fever & as to iron clads they haven't one they can send across the sea & if they did our Monitors with their 15 inch guns would effectually prevent their return.

Saturday, 26th—A party composed of Mrs. Craft, Mrs. Biddle, Miss McGowan, Mr. McGowan & myself started this morning for Old Point & Fortress Munroe. How very much I wished you could have made one of the number. We started at 10 o'clock, taking one of our cutters to the steamboat landing at Norfolk. The morning was cool, cloudy & somewhat windy & though *we sailors* called the water quite smooth the excessive timidity of Mrs. Craft from the slight motion of the boat as we passed over the waves took away all the pleasure of what would otherwise have been a pleasant boat ride.

We took the steamboat & as we passed down the river I had the pleasure of pointing out the batteries, obstructions &c, the work of rebel hands, the battle ground of the famous fight of the iron clads & other places with which I was familiar. An hour's ride brought us to Old Point and, upon going to the Fortress, an orderly was given us as a guide. We made the circuit of the ramparts to which a person very seldom gains access and from which on one side a fine view can be had of Hampton Roads filled with shipping among which our war vessels are most conspicuous. Mingled with them was one from France & from two others floated the detestable St. George's cross.

Huge & black loomed up above all else the hulks of the *Brandywine, St. Lawrence* & others of our once fine & powerful frigates. But in these days of steam & iron clads & gigantic guns they are doomed to spend their old age dismantled & forlorn, mere receptacles for ordnance & other stores for their smaller & insignificant looking but more formidable competitors.

Numerous merchantmen lay quietly at anchor while the puffing tugs glided swiftly among them, each intent upon its mission. Numerous little sail boats were gliding quietly about, while others with the national ensign fluttering from their sterns all neat & trim & impelled by the steady, measured stroke of men of war's men told of naval discipline & drill & distinguished them from the slovenly build & lazy oar of the fishing craft & merchantmen.

Beyond them lay the Rip Raps whose lower tier of guns already frowns over the water, while further on Sewall's Point projected into the bay, the pine woods & country about Norfolk forming the background of the scene, while nearly up to the walls on which we stood the surf rolled lazily over the clean white sand.

More to the left we looked out upon Old Ocean dotted with the whitened sails of numerous arriving & departing vessels or the more impetuous steamers. As we moved along [the ramparts] the scene shifted & we looked over the many houses & buildings which the exigencies of the times have clustered beneath the sheltering guns of the Fortress.

[unsigned]

No. 24—

U.S. Steamer *Florida*
Norfolk Navy Yard, Va.
Sept. 26th, 1863

Dear Anna,

Let me continue where I left off so abruptly in my last. Beyond [Fort Monroe to the north] was the long causeway & bridge which connects the sandy point on which the Fortress is built with the main land. Further on was Camp Hamilton, its white tents glistening in the sun. Still on & in the distance the ruined walls & tower like chimneys of rebel ruined Hampton* could be dimly seen, while the dark pine woods and white sand of Newport News made up the background. Conspicuous in the landscape was the fine building where the daughters of fire-eating secessia once received their education, now used by our forces as a hospital.†

After making the round of the ramparts, which was by no means a short stroll for they enclose an area of between seventy & eighty acres, we looked through the water batteries, examined the hot shot furnaces, the big Union gun, the long rows of solid brick & stone arches forming the casemates & bomb proofs, the drawbridges & all other objects of interest our guide brought to our notice.

By this time the ladies began to feel somewhat tired so we all adjourned to my friend Kimberly's. They had done dinner some time, nevertheless he set his cooks to work & in a short time gave us a good meal. We could appreciate his kindness the more as the Hygeia [Hotel] has been torn down & there is no place on the Point where a person can find "entertainment for man or beast" unless it be from some friend living there or the government officials.

After dinner & a rest it was proposed to take a stroll on the beach to which all assented except Mrs. Crafts who we left behind tired out. We strolled carelessly along picking up shells & pebbles when my attention was attracted by

---

* On August 7, 1861 the Confederates burned the town of Hampton rather than let it be used to house the thousands of runaway slaves who had crossed the Union lines to freedom.
† The Chesapeake Female Seminary in Hampton was commandeered by Union doctors as a military hospital during the Peninsula Campaign.

Norfolk Navy Yard (September to October 1863)

a darkey shouting "Look out massa, dey gwine to fire de big gun now." I glanced at the big "Lincoln gun" which we had passed a few moments before and directly in front of which we were standing, though some distance off. A huge jet of smoke & flame belched from its mouth & the massive bolt of iron—450 pounds—passed directly over our heads & splashed in the water a long way off throwing up the spray in clouds.*

I expected to see a couple of frightened females, but upon looking I found them admiring the flight of the shot which could be distinctly seen through its whole course. I was thankful that Mrs. C. had been left behind for we should have had a *scene* had she been with us. She is either exceedingly timid or thinks it nice to pretend to be. In fact, those *unfeminine* traits spoiled half our pleasure. She was frightened in the boat lest it should capsize. She couldn't go over a bridge for the planks were a little loose. The stairs were so steep she knew they'd break down. She was sure the guns would go off if we went near them & the ramparts were so high it made he[r] head giddy to walk on them, &c till I got tired of her and would most gladly have consigned her to the care of her husband had he been there. He could not leave the vessel or would have accompanied us.

Deliver me from weak nerves & timidity in man or woman. It will do in brute beasts who have no reasoning faculties, or in man in time of real danger but to spend one's whole time in conjuring up evil when assured to the contrary by those who should know seems to me excessively foolish & silly. I don't expect a female to be coarse or masculine, that's not at all necessary— I only want her to be *feminine*, truly so.

Mrs. C. is a regular fidget & the couple are so sickeningly loving "*before folks*" that I sometimes feel qualmish. I fear she thinks we are not a very loving couple, as one day when she was on board I came down into the wardroom & found her seated on her husband's lap, her arm around his neck & his around her waist, to the evident amusement of some of the officers who witnessed the exhibition, & Miss McGowan & Mrs. Biddle who were also present. She evidently felt a little *queer* for she appealed to me as soon as I came in with, "This is nothing new to you Mr. Keeler, for I suppose your wife often sits with you in the same way?" "No," says I, "I have no recollection of my wife have [having] set in [my] lap since I first formed her acquaintance" & hesitated & was going to add, "*when we were in company,*" when she broke in with "Well that's the way her mother brought her up." I left my

---

* Forged in Pittsburgh in 1860 and installed at Fort Monroe the same year, the 16-foot long 15-inch gun was the largest artillery piece in the world when it was made. Originally named after the Secretary of War in the Buchanan Administration, John Floyd, who became a Confederate general, Lincoln's Secretary of War Edwin Stanton ordered it renamed after his boss. Following the Battle of Hampton Roads in March 1862, the Lincoln Gun was moved from the fort's ramparts to the beach near the 12-inch "Union Gun." Seven decades later it was moved to its present location overlooking the fort's parade ground.

speech unfinished & her unenlightened, but she felt mortified I could see & took the first opportunity to withdraw from her "lovyer's" embraces.

He [Crafts] is [a] regular "betty."* I was up to their boarding house the other evening & he was basting some sewing he wanted her to do for him. However he makes a tolerably agreeable messmate. There is no polish or refinement whatever about him—very fond of argument, with a little smattering, superficial knowledge of everything from the latest improvement in tin whistles to the most approved method of frying an egg. He has recently been promoted to an Acting Master & has charge of the navigation of the vessel.

But to return to my story. We had a pleasant ride back & I spent the evening with them at their boarding house.

Sunday, 27th—At the invitation of the ladies I accompanied them to church with Mr. McGowan & Mr. Crafts. The majority of the party being episcopalians we went with them to that church.† Services had commenced when we entered & we were left to find a seat as best we could, which we did not far from the pulpit in the main [a]isle. It was a small building but handsomely if not richly furnished—stained glass windows, comfortable cushioned seats & a pulpit beautifully trimmed. The ladies only had a prayer book & as I was ignorant of the church service I followed the lead of others—got up when they got up & set down when they did. While the prayers were being read, Mrs. Biddle raised her head, her cheeks red & her eyes fairly flashing. I was in the seat behind her. She turned to me & said, "I'm going out. I won't stay in a church where they won't pray for the President."‡ So we all left highly indignant. It seems that on coming to the prayer for the President, he [the minister] cooly skipped it & went on. I mention this to shew the feeling still existing here. How such a thing is to be prevented it would be hard to tell—it would be hard to compel them to pray for what they don't desire. Mrs. B. was right when she said as we came out, "My husband is with Rosecrants [Rosecrans] fighting for his country & I am not going to church to pray for Jeff Davis & the rebellion," for such in effect it was & she so considered it.

But I am [at] the end of another sheet & will send it with my love, promising another soon.

W—

[Marginalia] [March] 28th—Haven't heard from you yet. Direct to me at Hampton Roads, till requested to change.

---

* A man who occupies himself with household chores.
† Trinity Church, located at the corner of Court and High Streets in Portsmouth.
‡ The minister who refused to pray for Lincoln was John H. D. Wingfield. Three months later he was forbidden to officiate at Trinity and was later arrested and forced to clean the streets of Portsmouth, reportedly shackled to a ball and chain. In March 1864 he signed the Oath of Allegiance and spent the remainder of the war in Baltimore.

NORFOLK NAVY YARD (SEPTEMBER TO OCTOBER 1863)

No. 25—

U.S. Steamer *Florida*
Norfolk Navy Yard, Va.
Sept. 29th, 1863

Dear Anna,

We had another dinner party to day & of course a real fine time. Mrs. Biddle & Miss McGowan leave to morrow for home. I feel sorry to have them leave as their presence has been a relief to the dull routine & ceremony of man of war life. Not that I care particularly for them, though they are very pleasant young ladies & agreeable company, but the sight of a petticoat is a treat even if it is our old black washwoman.

The last of the quarter is at hand & I am up to my eyes in red tape, returns, reports & papers of various kinds. My time through the day if [is] fully occupied, but however pressing business may be I devote my evenings *exclusively* to *writing home* & glancing over the papers which we now get daily from New York but a few hours after they are printed. New orders issued from the Department from time to time keep adding to my work & this with the constant changes being made among the officers & the discharge & enlistment of men keep me pretty busy.

I am now allowed a Clerk, Steward, Assistant Steward, Capt. of the Hold & Servant, enough to do my work, but I find to have it done thoroughly & well I must see to it myself. Then as Caterer of the Mess I have the control & supervision of all the expenditures & receipts of the Mess, have the care of the Ward Room Cook & Steward & all the boys & the management of all our domestic affairs generally. If a dinner party is to be given, I must assign to each one his place, see that the table is properly arranged and the various dishes come on in proper order, must see that marketing is done—enough food in quantity & variety. Then when we leave port I am to provide the outfit for one, two, three or more months as the probable time of our absence may seem to require. But this don't require my personal attention at all times.

We have a jewel of a Ward Room Steward* & I give general directions to him which he carries out in detail. He comes to me in the evening for orders for the next day. We arrange what it is best to have & I supply him with funds to do the marketing the next morning & am called at "7 bells" (1/2 past seven) to breakfast, which is my marketing experience. The Steward brings me his expense book every evening when he comes to me for orders that I may see how he has expended his money, when we arrange for the succe[e]ding day.

He [the Steward] has the immediate care of the boys but no power to punish them. Any misbehavior he reports to me & I assign them such punishment as I think they merit. Flogging not being allowed in the Navy, although

---

* David Ellis.

it is sometimes richly deserved, we cannot administer that, but I send them up in the rigging to study astronomy two or three hours of a night & make them shoulder a good heavy musket for the same time. There are plenty of ways to punish them.

All dishes broken are reported to me by the Steward & I deduct it from the pay of the careless one. (By the way let me tell you in parenthesis as a secret just the nicest way of preparing potatoes for the table. After being boiled & mashed run them through the colander. It is the way they are always prepared by our steward & we find it very nice. All our visitors before being helped [served] want to know what it is. Try it sometime when you have company & let me know the result.) Then the getting of proper food in proper quantities for all our men on board & seeing that it is properly kept & issued in the requisite quantities & at the right times is no small task. To be sure I don't see to all this personally as these are my steward's duties, but I am obliged to have a supervision of the whole & am the responsible party. Whenever the vessel is in port the crew need a change from salt food to fresh & I am to see that fresh meat, vegetables & soft bread is supplied them.

Then a hundred times a day I am applied to for "a little money, sir, I've got liberty ashore," "a pair of shoes, sir, mine are all to pieces," "a cap, sir, mine has blown overboard" & a thousand wants like these. Usually these requests are not granted, as money & other articles are issued every month & not till the month comes 'round are the store rooms or the safe opened again unless I hear a good reason.

A sailor is never paid in full till his time of enlistment expires. I usually pay them from 3 to 5 dollars a month as spending money. Sometimes they come to me with a doleful tale of sickness, death or destitution at home & a request for 15 or 20 dollars to send to their families. "You say your wife wrote you that one of the children was dead?" "Yes sir." "Well where's the letter?" If their tale was a true one the letter is produced & I give them as I think they need. If on the contrary the letter, as is frequently the case, has been torn up or thrown overboard they meet with a pretty abrupt refusal. If they choose, they can appeal through the 1st Lieutenant to the Capt. He [the captain] however very seldom changes the decision of the Paymaster.

Wednesday 30th—Your No. 11 was rec'd to day—the first I have heard from home since I have been here. The last I had was No. 5, rec'd Sept. 7th. So there are five of your letters somewhere which have not been received—probably down on the blockade. Continue to direct to me at *Hampton Roads*, not Norfolk, for the Postmaster at the former place will forward my letters wherever I may go.

Mrs. Biddle & Miss McGowan left for home to day giving me an urgent invitation to call on them in Philadelphia.

Thursday Oct. 1st—No. 8 reached me to day, brought up by the *Newbern* from the blockade. Where are the others? I suppose I shall get them in good time. I also rec'd one from Henry.

Norfolk Navy Yard (September to October 1863)

Friday, 2nd—Mr. Greene left us to day—gone home to get married.* Mr. E. C. Merriman† takes his place. I will tell you more about him when I get acquainted.

Saturday, 3rd—Was down to Hampton Roads to day on the flag ship. Saw Gen. Foster there. Some movement is on foot from here. I don't know what. It may be towards Richmond from James river or the peninsula.

I enclose a paper dollar brought from Hayti [Haiti] by Mr. Merriman. You will observe that the act of engraving has not been brought to quite as great a degree of perfection as with us—preserve [it].

With love to all & kisses to the dear little ones & yourself.

W—

No. 26—

U.S. Steamer *Florida*
Norfolk Navy Yard, Va.
Oct. 8th, 1863

Dear Anna,

I have just finished a sheet to Henry & wish I had one completed for you, but I have been too busy for the last few days to do much with my pen besides official writing. Besides there is but little or nothing in the way of news to make a letter readable.

I have been obliged to trench even upon my evenings, which I have heretofore devoted exclusively to *private* business—the Paymaster then is laid aside for husband & father—but Muster Rolls‡, Descriptive Lists, Discharges, Pay Rolls &c have occupied my attention the last few days to the exclusion of all other matters. Clerk & Steward could of course do much, but with more important matters I trust no one but myself, or at least give it my personal supervision. I suppose for the last few days my signature has been attached to over one hundred papers of various kinds a day, most of them requiring a good deal of care in making out. I have never had as yet but one paper returned to me by the Department for correction.

No. 11 (or 10 as you had numbered it) reached me yesterday, only four days from home. It seems too bad to be so short a distance from home and not be able to go there.

Mrs. Crafts still remains here. She comes aboard and takes dinner with us occasionally. I think they don't live very high where she is boarding & she is glad to get a good dinner on board the *Florida* once in a while. I was provoked

---

* See Keeler's letter of late November 1885 in Part 3 for an amusing story about Greene's going home to get married.
† Edgar C. Merriman*.
‡ The digitized copies of the *Florida* muster rolls, which are available on-line at the National Archives, are written in Keeler's neat hand.

at her the other day. She had been spending the forenoon on board & I asked her to stay to dinner. To my invitation she replied by asking what we were going to have—not in a joking way at all, but as if she was considering where she could get the best [meal]. I told her I would give her a specimen of a blockade dinner, but she declined & went off & we sat down to oyster soup, a splendid baked fish & roast turkey.

The other ladies I think I wrote you had returned home. They seemed to enjoy their visit here very much. You ask me to "tell you about them, how they look, act &c & which I like best." The dress being the most important I will commence with that. They both dressed in black for the loss of a sister which is all that I remember under that head. Then as to looks Mrs. Biddle was about 22 (her own confession & I think not far out of the way), about the size & very much the shape & appearance of Mary Joy, light complexion, blue eyes, light curling hair very tastily arranged, fine set of teeth, could ride a horse, fire a gun, row a boat, walk a plank or anything else that it was right & proper & becoming a Col.'s wife to do, her tongue always in motion either singing or talking. Her sister Miss Kate McGowan was more fleshy & not as quick & active, hair dark & cut short, eyes dark, complexion ruddy, features regular, height—well I am not able to give a complete descriptive list. She was more sedate & less talkative than her sister. Both were well educated, intelligent ladies & I found their society very pleasant & agreeable. Can't say which I liked best. Had *another lady* of my acquaintance been here who calls herself *39*, it is very probable that I should not have given the younger ones a second thought. So much for your queries. As to their photographs, not being favoured by them with any, I am unable to comply with your request. The pen & ink one I have just made will have to answer.

I am so anxious to get your back letters as you allude to some things in those just rec'd which will be explained in those previously written. I received a letter from Henry a few days ago. I fully agree with you in the improvement made by him in composition & spelling but I have written him to take more pains with his penmanship—his writing is horrible. He writes in too much of a hurry, but his improvement is very gratifying to me. It shews that he is making good use of his time.

Saturday, Oct. 10th—I made a call on Capt. Hill*, Commissary, to day. I found his office besieged by a large number of persons, mostly females, many of them respectable appearing, well dressed. He was issuing food to them for the support of themselves & families, they having no means of support. In looking over his book in which he made a note of the circumstances of each applicant I found such memorandums as these: Mrs. H., 40 years of age, has two small children, husband in the rebel army—Mrs. L., a widow, has two sons, one in the army of the Potomac, the other in the rebel service—Mrs. G., widow 60 years of age, has living with her 3 grandchildren whose father

---

* Possibly George W. Hill.

is in the rebel service—Mrs. B., husband killed in the rebel army—Miss A., one brother in the rebel army, another supposed to be on the *Florida** (pirate)—Three girls, father killed in the rebel army at Fredericksburg &c &c, presenting one of the strange features of this war, of our feeding the families of those who are fighting against us. Many of them as I have said were well dressed but also *attended by black servants to carry their food home.*

It seems that you are receiving some additions to your society in LaSalle. I hope you will find them pleasant ones. What kind of persons are Dr. Page's father's family?†

I judge from your account that the local politics are in a rather mixed condition. I'm glad that I am not there to be in the mess.

You must have had a very pleasant party at Mr. Rockwell's. I would liked very much to have made one of the number. You must imagine me with you sometimes. I am often there in spirit, wish I could be in person.

How much I want to see the children. They must be regular romps from what you say. That's much better than paying doctors' bills. Kiss the children & remember me to all friends. "*Yours truly,*"

W—

No. 27—

U.S. Steamer *Florida*
Norfolk Navy Yard
Oct. 15th, 1863

Dear Anna,

I have just returned from Old Point from which place I sent you a note enclosing the Express receipt which I forgot to put in the day before.

Capt. Queen's wife & Mrs. Zeigler went home to day. Mrs. Craft is to remain till Monday. I am almost glad now that you were not here as we have not got to part.

Mrs. Queen is what you might call a stylish woman in manners & appearance—not handsome, but easy & pleasant in her manners, having evidently mingled a good deal in society. She has very light curly hair, but the wrinkles are beginning to shew themselves in her face. Altogether she looks as if she had some of the tartar in her composition.

Friday evening, 16th—I had got so far last evening when I was called off & of course my letter remained unfinished. I rec'd a letter from Mr. Greene to day! He was married on the 9th. He says, "I am the happiest man that ever lived." He is making a sort of wedding trip & dates from Springfield, Mass.

---

* The Confederate raider.
† John J. Page, physician and mining businessman in La Salle. In 1863 Page's father, who was a state auditor in Frankfort, KY, was convicted of corruption for embezzling $88,000 from the state.

CIVIL WAR YEARS: USS *FLORIDA* (1863-1865)

Mr. Merriman who takes Mr. G.'s place is somewhat younger than him— is full of fun & frolick & music & I think we shall get along first rate. He keeps a guitar & melodion in his room & every night before I "turn in" he sends a note by one of the messenger boys for "Pay to come up & take a smoke." So I go up & smoke while he sings. He is a capital singer & is the best hand at telling a comic story that I ever saw. He has dark curling hair, a pleasant face with fun in every lineament. He is going to have some photographs taken before we leave & I will send you one to add to _my_ collection. I enclose two of my friend Kimberly, neither of them very good.

I expected to have had the pleasure of witnessing the execution of Dr. Wright to day but he has had a reprieve of a week. I say "pleasure" for it would be a gratification to see such a cold blooded murderer hung. You probably heard the circumstances but may have forgotten them. The murder took place I think last spring. One of the negro regiments was marching through the streets of Norfolk when this fellow (an influential man of the place) step[p]ed to his store door, drew a pistol, took aim at one of the lieutenants & fired. The lieut. staggered towards the store when he fired again. It was a bold defiance of the laws. He [Wright] had previously made his boa[s]ts that he would shoot one of the white officers of the "nigger regiment" if they attempted to march through the city & his wife & other secesh females came to the store to urge him to put his threat into execution & to see it done. I only hope the ends of justice will not be defeated. He was tried by a military commission, found guilty & sentenced to be hung. As the time drew near his friends worked every dodge to get him clear but without avail. His spirit of bravado left him & he wilted down & his wife has also discovered that it is not so pleasing a diversion to have her own husband killed as to see another woman made a widow.[*]

There are some very pretty places around Norfolk. I have wished at times that I was settled in it for I think I should like to live there if it were not for the bitter feeling that will exist for some years to come. There is a good chance to make money there now. Tell Dave I wish he was there & had his health. With good judgement & some shrewdness a fortune could be realised after the close of the war when rebel estates came up for settlement.

Sunday evening, Oct. 18th—Another interruption, but my letter shall be finished to night. It will be the last from here for we are now in Hampton

---

[*] On July 11, 1863 David M. Wright shot and killed Second Lieutenant Anson L. Sanford of the 1st U.S. Colored Volunteers as he marched his company down the main street of Norfolk. The high-profile case came to the attention of President Lincoln who helped choose expert witnesses to testify to Wright's state of mind at the time of the shooting. Wright was found sane and sentenced to death. His wife made numerous appeals to Lincoln, whose only concession was a one-week reprieve in the execution date so that the doctor could get his personal affairs in order. He was hanged on October 23. His widow was left to raise their eight children ranging in age from 4 to 20 years old.

Norfolk Navy Yard (September to October 1863)

Roads, just against Fortress Munroe, ready for sea, excepting taking in the remainder of our stores which we shall complete to morrow morning.

I rec'd a paper from you to day which had the familiar look of home & also a letter from Henry wanting me to let him come out in "long tails," which I believe I shall do, especially as he mentioned (as an extra inducement I suppose) that in a few weeks he should be 16 years old. I believe the little scamp exagerated two or three years, for it can't be possible that any of our progeny is so near manhood—if he would only grow some I wouldn't care. I shall couple my consent with the condition that he has his photograph taken & send one to each of us. Have you had the children's taken yet? Don't neglect it.

I sent you a paper to day with an account of the reception of Gen. Foster here or rather at Norfolk & the review of the troops.* I had an invitation from Capt. Queen to accompany him on the Admiral's Staff, but I declined as I had business matters to attend to & besides I had no fancy for a long dusty ride, mounted on horseback. Moreover you know that I have no partiality for equestrian performances where I am the performer. Capt. Queen came back pretty much used up—lame, covered with dust, and hasn't fully recovered yet.

Mr. Crafts left for Baltimore yesterday evening on business & will return to morrow morning. His wife accompanied him.

On our return off Wilmington we expect to be employed on the "outside blockade"—that is in cruising about outside of the [Frying Pan] shoals and coast, at times running over near Nassau in the track of the blockade runners, which I hope will throw some more prizes in our way. The smaller vessels of the squadron will be kept nearer the shore as we have been heretofore.

We all feel anxious to hear that our forces have commenced again at Charleston, though no one supposes that Gilmore has remained idle all this time.

The attempt on the *Ironsides* was a bold one & inflicted more injury on her than they are willing to make public, but it is hoped that she will not have to be sent home for repairs till her work there is done. I saw the rebel lieutenant who was in command of the torpedo to day. He was landed here a prisoner on his way north. He conversed very freely on the subject but was evidently very deeply mortified at the failure of his plans.†

---

* Major General John Foster had been placed in command of the Department of Virginia and North Carolina in July 1863, with his headquarters at Fort Monroe.
† Two weeks earlier Confederate Navy Lieutenant William T. Glassell made a daring nighttime attack on the USS *New Ironsides* outside of Charleston Harbor by ramming her with a 60-pound explosive device attached to a spar extending ten feet from the bow of his small low-riding vessel. He got to within fifty yards of the *Ironsides* before being detected, pressed on through small-arms fire and exploded the torpedo against the ironclad's five-foot thick hull, causing damage enough to require lengthy repairs. The Union Navy kept details of the damage secret for fear the rebels would make further such attempts.

Civil War Years: USS *Florida* (1863-1865)

I shall write you every opportunity & hope to find something to make my letters interesting to yourself & our friends. Good bye & good night.

W—

[Marginalia] Your Mother sent me a fine photograph of "Lila."* Direct to me as heretofore "via New York." I wish I could get one more letter from you before we leave but don't expect it.

Cruising (October to December 1863)

We were between her & Nassau, her destination, & she has vainly endeavoured all day to cross our bows & we have been gradually crowding her on towards the coast. At times we would seem to gain on her & then in turn she would gain on us & so it has kept on all day, the excitement at times increasing as we seemed to gain & then dying away as the space between us widened & now night has hidden the pursuer & pursued & each is ignorant of the other's intentions. (30 November 1863)

On October 20 the *Florida* left Hampton Roads and arrived among the fleet off Wilmington with orders to serve on the outer tier of the blockade. With the exception of several trips to Beaufort and a brief stint on the blockade, they roamed the seas from early November to mid-December. Expecting more prizes to come their way, they cruised as far away as the Bahamas. However, despite several exciting chases, the "black smokes" eluded them, a result which Keeler attributed to their captain (Queen) who was "as vacillating as the wind" and who, if "dressed up in petticoats," "would make a very good grandmother to an infant school."

Queen was relieved in mid-November and replaced by 39-year old Commander Peirce Crosby, a veteran of 25 years in the Navy who was well-liked by all on board. Keeler described him as "a still, quiet man of very few words." Another departure was Samuel Crafts, who also left in mid-November when ordered to the USS *Newbern*. Joining them at Norfolk was 34-year old Acting Ensign Cornelius Washburn whose company Keeler much enjoyed. The New Yorker had served in the Navy as a seaman from 1855 to the first year of the war when he received his commission. Prior to joining the *Florida* he was on the USS *Commodore Barney*, where he was praised for "good shooting" at the Battle of Roanoke Island in February 1862.

Letters of special note: October 24 (Colonel Dutton's stomach); November 3 (description of some of the steerage officers); November 6 (a blockade runner gets away; criticism of Captain Queen; observing porpoises); November 26 (a sailor drowns); November 30 (cruising north of the Bahamas); December 10 (supper at Fort Macon; an oyster roast).

---

* Keeler's two-year old niece, Elizabeth E. Watrous.

CRUISING (OCTOBER TO DECEMBER 1863)

No. 28—

U.S. Steamer *Florida*
At Sea
Oct. 24th, 1863

Dear Anna,

We left Hampton Roads last Tuesday the 20th for our old place on the blockade, taking as a passenger Col. [Arthur] Dutton* to go down to his father in law's (Capt. Sands†) vessel, the *Dacotah*. We had a smooth sea, beautiful weather & as fine a passage as could be desired.

The next evening, Wednesday, we ran in among the fleet which we found very much increased since we left. The day before our arrival they had driven a blockade runner, the *Mars*, ashore & destroyed her. A number of wrecks are strung along the beach of sailing vessels & steamers destroyed while attempting to run the blockade. Still the business is kept up, the number of vessels apparently not diminishing though so many are destroyed & captured.

We found on communicating with the flag ship (the *Dacotah*) that she had 43 cases of small pox on board so that the Col. had to remain with us.

We left the fleet at dark to cruise around outside the shoals during the night hoping to pick up a prize. We however saw nothing & the next morning ran in among the fleet on the south side.

As on the other side the fleet had been strengthened in our absence. Some of the old vessels had left, while a number of new ones had been added. Only one or two of our old acquaintances were left. The rebels had also strengthened their works & thrown up some new ones. They now have three large guns in strong casemates on Smith's island nearly opposite fort Caswell.

We lay at anchor through the day & left in the evening to cruise again outside the shoals. The next morning early we espied a schooner which upon overhauling proved to be a prize to our protege the *Calypso*‡, taken the previous night & in a couple of hours we came upon the *Calypso* herself fitted up as a gun boat & a very pretty one she makes too, as well as fast.

This morning we left for Beaufort to leave the Col. there. He has found no rest since he came on ship board. His visit to his father in law being so singularly interrupted, he has been obliged to remain with us wandering about the sea. He has not appeared to enjoy it very much, having been sea sick nearly from the time we left. So also has our M.D. (Dr. James) and the Capt.'s Clerk, a youngster by the name of Frank[s]§.

I don't like the Col. at all. He is very reserved & aristocratic in his manners, which don't tend to make friends & sympathisers on ship board. I took a

---

* Anna's distant cousin.
† Benjamin F. Sands.
‡ Following her capture by the *Florida*, the *Calypso* was purchased by the Navy and employed on the Wilmington blockade.
§ James P. Franks*.

malicious pleasure when I went on deck in the morning & found him pale and woe begone leaning over the guards looking "as if his belly had caved in & his last friend had left" in accosting him with, "Good morning, Col., beautiful weather, we are getting along finely, the vessel moves along as steady as an old wagon, won't you try a cigar?" Of course the cigar wouldn't be accepted, for a sea sick man very seldom desires an emetic. Then along would come Lieut. Merriman, "Hullo, Col., sea sick? Take a chew?," handing out his tobacco box to the Col.'s evident disgust. This *sympathy* of ours didn't seem to attach him to us very strongly. The Dr. & Capt.'s Clerk who were in the same box were the only ones whom he seemed to care to associate with & they were too much absorbed in their own troubles to express much sympathy for him.

This morning, Sunday 25th, we arrived off Beaufort harbour & sent the Col. ashore in a small pilot boat which came off to us & turning about we headed once more for the blockade.

Towards evening, when within about 20 miles of the fleet, a sail was descried which we bore down for & when near enough could see unmistakeable signs of the blockade runner, aside from the almost infallible black smoke which is always their tell tale. Of course we all felt *jolly*. Shares of prize money were quoted at various rates & a variety of speculations were undertaken on the strength of what some thought was already in the pocket. Our forward pivot [gun] was fired and dropped a shot just under the stranger's bows. Of course she stopped at such a hint & we rapidly overhauled her & saw a small American ensign run up union down*. Holders of prize shares heard "something drap."

With our glasses, as we approached, we could see an officer & men on board in uniform, but the wind was blowing a gale & a heavy sea running which rendered it impossible for them to hear our hail or for us to understand their reply. She was very low in the water—very long & sharp & very narrow—iron, side wheels & built for great speed regardless of carrying capacity. A part of her wheel houses & bulwarks had been carried away & the heavy seas were washing completely over her. It was a difficult task to board her but we lowered away a boat which approached her near enough to learn that she was the *Jupiter* and had been captured by the *Cimerone* [*Cimarron*] in Wassaw Sound.

She was leaking badly & [the prize crew] feared they could not live through the gale & requested to be taken in tow. We made a small line fast to a tight cask which we threw overboard & which they caught as it flo[a]ted by them & hauled in the line, the other end of which was made fast to a large strong hawser. After two hours' work everything was ready & we started once more for Beaufort harbour. As it grew dark the wind & sea increased & we

---

* The distress signal.

had the prospect of doing for them what the *Rhode Island* did for us of the *Monitor* off Hatteras. Their signal lights were watched with anxious hearts.

This morning (Monday [October 26]) however we arrived with her in safety off Beaufort, though the poor fellows must have been nearly exhausted with pumping & bailing all night. We sent her into the harbour with a pilot & are now (Monday evening) waiting outside for the gale to subside to return to the fleet.

If we understand the matter correctly, the salvage we are entitled to will be nearly as much as if we had made the capture. Her value will be small, as the vessel is very much injured & the cargo which cannot be a large one is badly damaged by water. However every little helps. Hope my next will give you the taking of another prize. Love to all.

William

[Marginalia] As you all seem to be in the conundrum way, let me ask why Powers the sculptor was a mean contemptible thief? Let me know if you give it up. This is original!

No. 29—

U.S. Steamer *Florida*
At Sea
Oct. 28th, 1863

Dear Anna,

Once more we are on our way to Beaufort & I suppose to remain there two or three weeks, for last night we broke a portion of our engine which we shall have to send to New York to replace & I suppose we shall be detained in that sand hole till again ready for sea. This is not very pleasant to look forward to after leaving port with our minds settled upon the conviction that we were to be out till spring when the vessel will go out of commission.

It is somewhat pleasanter & more safe to be securely anchored in good harbor than to be knocking about at sea in the gales of winter, but our chances of prize money are of course lessened & we are all anxious to "be in" if there is anything to be done.

As for the gales we have a splendid sea boat & it matters but little to us below in our cosy rooms whether it's a gale or a calm. The only evidence we have of a heavy sea or a hard blow is the increased rolling of the vessel. The watch officers to be sure don't find it quite so pleasant in stormy weather, but once below & their wet clothes off their troubles are soon forgotten.

The weather is cool enough to make overcoats comfortable on deck & we are glad to sleep in our blankets with our air ports closed.

We have escaped one torment this summer—mosquitoes. A few found their way on board while we remained at Norfolk but fortunately my mosquito bar was in readiness to prevent any intrusions at night & after we left the Navy Yard the cool weather & sea air soon caused the few that were on board to disappear.

I was very busy while we were at Norfolk & had but little time to look around, during the latter part of our stay at any rate. A good many northern people seem to have come into the place and business appeared pretty brisk. Most of the stores were open, good stocks of goods & an appearance of plenty of customers.

Many of the secesh still remain there—females especially, who though desirous of going south are not permitted to leave. How they live is a mystery to me, for though many of them were formerly wealthy & still live in handsome houses, they have no business to support them & their investments in bank, rail-road & other stocks which they relied upon for an income have been swallowed up in the rebellion, leaving them apparently with nothing to maintain them.

Many are incumbered with old worn out slaves too old & decrepid to run away & useless to hire out. Most of the blacks who were of any value to their masters have either left for parts unknown or have put on the uniform of "U.S." [Uncle Sam]. Their former mistresses wander forlorn about the streets or shut themselves up at home, gloomy & discontented & I'll warrant with some anxious thoughts for the future. You can tell them in the streets, for they either dress in black or for the want of means to purchase new materials they have gone back to their cast of[f] wardrobes & have donned the finery and fashions of other days.

Sunday Evening, Nov. 1st—I went ashore to day & found upon calling at the Hospital that Chapin had gone home on a furlough, so that I shan't see him this time.

We find upon an examination of our machinery that it can be repaired so as to make it do for a time & shall probably be able to leave here Tuesday.

We sent another of our officers to the hospital here to day, Mr. Ziegler, our Chief Engineer, sick with a disease very much like diptheria.

I meant to have attended church ashore to day but could not get a boat in time. I wanted to hear a prayer for the President of the U.S. in a Southern church & by a Southern man, & there is such a church & man here. He has been a strong Union man since the war broke out, in consequence of which his church was closed by the rebels & himself insulted in every imaginable way till our forces took the place when the order of things was speedily reversed.*

Your letters have kept straggling along till yesterday [when] I got No. 9, Sept. 18th, which completes the series to No. 12 which was the last I have received. I was very glad to have the gap filled & to get a connected narrative of events at home. What between riots, elections & fires you cannot want for

---

* David D. Van Antwerp, rector of St. Paul's Episcopal Church in Beaufort. Keeler was mistaken about his place of birth: he was a Northerner, born and raised in New York state.

excitement. Do I understand you that the works at the Kentucky shaft have been destroyed by the mob? I think the best course has been adopted, to employ an entirely new set of men.

In this I enclose the photograph of Ensign Williams who steered the *Monitor* in the *Merrimac* fight & was made a Master's Mate & at the sinking of the *Monitor* was promoted to an Ensign. You will observe his "medal of honor" given him by Congress attached to his breast. In the photograph of the crew of the *Monitor* he is sitting reading a paper.

I received a short note from Capt. Bankhead a few days ago stating that his health was still poor though he was gaining slowly. We miss him much on board. His place is filled by a very different sort of a man who is neither the officer nor gentleman that Capt. B. was. Things don't work so smoothly & nicely as when Capt. B. was on board with Mr. Greene for an executive officer. There's a jangle in the machinery which don't work with the quiet regularity it used to. However we shall know him [Capt. Queen] better by & by when I will tell you more about him.

Ever since I had anything to do with that naval abortion, *Jeffers*, I have hesitated about forming an opinion to[o] quickly. We at first thought him everything that was needed as the commander of our famous little iron clad, but we had sad reason to change our minds before we were through with him. Our present captain has a different set of officers to deal with from what Jeffers had—they have been in the service longer & know their rights. A storm is already brewing in the discordant elements, the Capt. having suspended Crafts from duty to which Crafts don't propose quietly to submit, especially as it was for no fault but merely vindictiveness on the part of the Capt. Crafts has called for a court of inquiry. The end is not yet. The Ward room of course side with Crafts & I think he will come out ahead.

But I must close with love & a kiss.

W—

[Marginalia] I feel anxious to hear if my box reached you safely & how it was received.

No. 30—

U.S. Steamer *Florida*
At Sea
Nov. 3rd, 1863

Dear Anna,

Here we are once more afloat. We left Beaufort this forenoon & are now, 8 P.M., slowly feeling our way along in the supposed vicinity of the fleet, expecting every moment to see a challenge light flash out from the darkness. Creeping in among the fleet in this way after dark is neither pleasant or safe, for the probability is that some of our vessels in their over watchfullness & anxiety for prize money may give us a gun first & challenge afterward.

CIVIL WAR YEARS: USS *FLORIDA* (1863-1865)

However as my staying on deck would have but little to do with stopping shot or shell I have concluded that I could better occupy the time in writing home.

We have had a beautiful day, just warm enough to be comfortable on deck in thick clothing. We have had our stove put up in the Ward Room to day, as we need a fire mornings & evenings. Moreover the north-easterly gales which will soon be our frequent visitors will make it cold, wet & cheerless on deck & will help us to appreciate a pleasant Ward Room & a good fire. I wish you had a few tons of our good anthracite coal of which we use about ten tons a day.

We have on board now a total of 197 souls—21 officers, 161 men & a marine guard of 15. Some changes have been made of which I believe I have not spoken. Master Nutting* and Ensign Wagstaff were detached before we left Hampton Roads & their places filled by two Ensigns, Rich & Washburn,† both good officers & I think will make pleasanter messmates than those who left. At any rate it's a change & that is something. One gets tired of seeing the same faces all the time, hearing the same "yarns" & laughing at a repetition of old jokes till they become worn out & stale.

There was also a change in the Steerage officers‡ among the Master's Mates, one being sent to the hospital & the other (a Mr. Mathews§) went home sick & was killed on the Potomac by the accidental discharge of a pistol. Capt. Queen has for a clerk a young man from Philadelphia by the name of Franks.

My clerk, a Mr. Gilbert**, I took from among the men, on trial, & like him very much. He has kept books for seventeen years & entered the navy thinking that a sea voyage would be good for his health without any idea of the kind of life it was to be. As you may suppose the change from the rough life, hard diet & still harder associates of the berth deck, to the increased pay & rank & privileges of a steerage officer is a most agreeable one to him. He writes a fine business hand & is quick & correct at figures.

It is amusing to listen to the history of the lives of some of our men & learn how they started in life—what they were once & what they now are. In most cases whiskey is the cause. My clerk I have just spoken of, though I think he is a temperate man. Ellis, my Steward, is a welchman & commenced life by studying for the Episcopal church, but I fear beer interfered sadly with

---

* William G. Nutting.
† Charles E. Rich* and Cornelius Washburn*.
‡ Steerage officers on the *Florida* comprised clerks, master's mates and assistant engineers.
§ A. P. Matthews. He was accidentally killed on the USS *Wyandank* on the Potomac River.
** William W. Gilbert. The 29-year old book keeper from Middletown, CT enlisted in New York as a landsman in February 1863. He enlisted again as a landsman for a three-year term in 1866 and served as ship's writer on the USS *Pensacola* until he was transferred to the naval hospital at Mare Island, CA in 1867, after which all trace of him disappears.

his studies, as I find it does with his duties when he is allowed to go ashore & which by the way I have vetoed altogether since we were at Norfolk.

One of our quartermasters is a descendant of Gen. Washington & bears his name & had a large estate left him in Virginia which he has squandered.* One of the firemen was once a Prof. in an Irish college. One of our boys who we shipped just before leaving Norfolk was right from Richmond from which place he escaped leaving "ole massa" to lament his loss.

The Capt.'s Steward† was on board the *Merrimac* in the fight with the *Monitor* & the other day gave me a very graphic account of it. As I have been told by others, she was badly injured & in a sinking condition when they returned to Norfolk. He gave a glowing description of their leaving that memorable morning, of the hundreds that came down to see them off, of the cheers that were given, of the flags & handkerchiefs that were shaken, of the salutes that were fired & predictions made & of the fleet of small boats that followed to see how quickly the remainder of the "yankee" fleet would be used up & how when they returned it was like a chastised canine with his caudal appendage at half mast.

A few days since one of the men received a letter from the old country informing him of the death of his uncle who had been minister of war in Bremen & had left this man his heir with an income of eighty thousand dollars a year. He will have to serve out his term of enlis[t]ment before he can enjoy his fortune. Sailors are so scarce that U.S. [Uncle Sam] don't give them up very readily when he once gets hold of them.

Thursday evening, Nov. 5th—There was a great stir among the fleet last night on the north side where we were. Guns were fired, rockets & signal lights burned at the escape, as we suppose, of some blockade runner. Nothing came of it, however, as the morning disclosed the fleet lying quietly at anchor, prizes minus. I slept soundly through it all & was first made aware of the excitement of the night by the conversation around our mess table at breakfast. I have been turned out so many times by false alarms that I have pretty much made up my mind not to be disturbed till a shot or shell walks through into my state room.

We have now just started to cruise around outside till in need of coal when we will return to Beaufort. I hope we may stumble upon a prize but with our present captain we shan't find one unless we accidentally stumble upon it. He is too cautious and careful. Then he has no self reliance nor confidence in the judgement of his officers. He is as vacillating as the wind. There is no telling one moment what he will do the next & it is extremely doubtful if he knows

---

* See footnote on Corbin Washington in June 30, 1863 letter.
† John Jones. The 23-year-old barber from Hampton, VA served first on the CSS *Forrest* in the North Carolina Squadron, then on the *Virginia*. He later deserted from the ironclad CSS *Richmond*, entered Union lines, and was sent to Washington, DC where he took the oath of allegiance and was sent home to Norfolk. He enlisted on board the *Florida* at the Norfolk Navy Yard on October 3, 1863.

himself. At one moment he will issue an order & the next countermand it. He is a worshiper of "red tape" & everything must be done with a due regard to the formalities prescribed by the venerable Grandma of the Department*. We of the Ward Room contrive to keep him in a constant state of worry & excitement. Something is always wrong that some of us does & he fumes & frets & we laugh. His sins of omission & commission are freely criticised at the Mess table & form the topic of many a laugh & joke. We are all most thoroughly disgusted with him and as to respect there is nothing to call it forth.

No letter from you yet. When shall I hear from you? Love to yourself & all,

W—

No. 31—

U.S. Steamer *Florida*
At Sea
Nov. 6th, 1863

Dear Anna,

We have been cruising about all day in the Gulf stream & have fallen in with & overhauled three or four vessels, none of them however were what we were in search of. One of them just from Port Royal told us that Gillmore had taken [Fort] Sumpter.† I hope it's so, but what advantage it will be now we have it I can't tell, beyond the men saying that it is ours.

We have had a beautiful day, the air as soft and mild as a spring morning. We have been glad to seek a shade.

Will you ask Mr. Durham when his uncle, Mr. Osborne, was ordered to the *Underwriter*?‡ It was not him who was attached to her when I spent the night on board with Mr. Flye. The Paymaster then attached to her has since been dismissed for some misconduct. It is not very probable that we will fall in with the *Underwriter* unless we should happen to see her at Beaufort, as she is a different class of vessel from this, intended for service in shoal water in the rivers & sounds.

The *Newbern* will be down while we are absent this time, so that we will loose our fresh beef & ice. We have come down to blockade fare again, canned meats & vegetables, except sweet potatoes & those I have a plenty of, of the very best which I bought at Beaufort for fifty cents a bushel. I can

---

* Gideon Welles.
† A false rumor.
‡ Marcus B. Osborn (1803-1893), a real estate broker from Rock Island, IL before the war. In October 1861, at the age of 58 he enlisted in the Union Navy and served as paymaster on the USS *Arthur* in the Gulf of Mexico. As a result of chronic sea-sickness and malaria he was transferred to the USS *Underwriter* in July 1863, but resigned the following month due to continued illness. He was Rev. Henry Durham's great-uncle.

live as long as those last. I wish you had two or three barrels of them. How the children would enjoy them. You would find them a very different vegetable from the sweet potatoes raised at home.

Saturday, Nov. 7th—I turned out this morning just before breakfast & went on deck. The sky was perfectly clear & the water smooth as a mirror. Just the faintest shadow of a haze like cloud hung over the watery level in the distant horizon. Faint & almost imperceptible as it was it had caught the eye of our lookouts & we were heading for it with a full head of steam when I went below to breakfast.

When I returned to the deck another tell tale cloud had been discovered & the first had been resolved into a vessel apparently in chase of the last discovered smoke. It was difficult to tell what to do, but from our position we could keep on a course that would bring us between the two strangers & after ascertaining their characters decide what part we should play in the game. So we kept on till we could see that the hindmost & the one first discovered was a gun boat & of course in chase of the one ahead, & that one of course must be a blockade runner. So the course of our own vessel was altered accordingly, both vessels converging to a point, & that point the black smoke ahead.

As we gradually drew near we exchanged signals & found our companion to be the *Keystone State* & now commenced one of those exciting chases you sometimes read of. At eleven o'clock we were so near that we could see the hull of the vessel & make her out distinctly. The *Keystone State* was gradually gaining on the chase, as well as leaving us behind. That she was making every exertion to overtake the chase was evident from the black smoke which would at times pour out of her pipe, caused by the tar & grease used in her furnaces.

Of course we resorted to the same expedients & an extra head of steam was raised & we watched anxiously but still they gained. Then our sand bag barricade—about four hundred bags of sand which was piled around our steam drum to protect it from shot—went overboard but with no visible result. Then down came yards & top masts & everything which could offer the least opposition to the air to check our speed but of no avail, they were slowly & gradually widening the distance between us.

Still for a time we kept on hoping "to be in at the death," or when the *Keystone State* made the capture so as to entitle us to share in the prize & so we should have been, but the Capt. from some unaccountable whim ordered the vessel put about at 2 P.M. before the prize was fairly out of sight. We turned about & made for another vessel which we sighted in the distance & which proved to be the *Grand Gulf*, another of our gun boats. We ran along side & Capt. Queen hailed them & told them that the vessel in the distance was the *Keystone State* in chase of the *Robert E. Lee* (as we had made the blockade runner out to be). "I'm going in chase," says Capt. Ransom* of the *Grand Gulf.* "No use," says Capt. Q, "I am going twelve knots & they gained on me & I go faster than you." "I don't care if I don't [do] six," says Capt. R., "I'll chase her till the last trump blows." That is the difference in the men, one irresolute & undecided & the other just the opposite. Off went the *Grand Gulf* at the top of her speed & changing his mind once more our Capt. turned about again & followed after for an hour, an unusual space of time for Capt. Q. to remain without changing his mind. We 'bout ship once more & stood off, giving up the chase altogether.

What the Capt.'s idea was in thus giving it up I don't know. We all felt sure of being up within signal distance when the *Keystone State* overhauled her, which was all that was needed to give us a share in the prize. Of course it was not for us to question the Capt.'s motives in thus discontinuing the chase, but I know that he has been pretty freely denounced in all parts of the vessel. He is very evidently not the man for the place & what is more he knows it & he knows that we know it. I should not be surprised if he did not remain with us much longer. Dressed up in petticoats he would make a very good grandmother to an infant school but he is out of his place on a man of war.

For some fancied insult he [Capt. Queen] suspended Crafts from duty & ordered me to pay him no money, in which he exceeded his authority. Crafts at once wrote to the senior officer demanding a court of inquiry. His letter the Capt. refused to forward as it was his duty to do, till Crafts wrote another which he was about forwarding through another channel when the Capt., finding Crafts persistent & determined to follow the matter up, called him into the cabin & restored him to duty & in fact, though not in matter, took back all he had said & done, though he was not man enough to come out and admit himself in error. The matter furnished us with a fund of amusement & conversation at the Mess table for the week or more before it was settled as I have related.

To my great disgust the Capt. for some reason seemed to select me for a confidant & would call me into his cabin & talk to [me] about this officer & that & relate his grievances. Of course all my sympathies were the other way & I was a cold comforter. I finally asked Mr. Merriman to tell him that I did not wish to hear him talk about my mess mates the way he did, that he criticised the performance of their duties, matters of which I was totally ignorant & knew nothing about, that he condemned them for acts which I could not, consistently, that it was my desire to have things pleasant & agreeable in the Ward Room & have all the mess meet on friendly terms, which could not be done if any of us were to espouse his quarrels with others &

---

* George M. Ransom. From October 1863 to October 1864, he commanded the USS *Grand Gulf* in the blockade off Wilmington, during which time he captured three blockade runners. Two weeks after Keeler started this letter the intrepid commander captured the blockade runner *Banshee* on her way in to Wilmington from Nassau.

Cruising (October to December 1863)

moreover I had enough to do to engineer my own difficulties & did not desire to take part in his. Whether Mr. M. repeated his message verbatim I do not know, but I find the Capt. has much less to say about others than formerly.

Mr. M. & the Capt's Clerk, Mr. Franks, both mess with the Capt. but are sick of the living. Mr. M. was telling me to day that the Capt. will allow no butter on the table at noon nor any cold meat at night. Mr. M is just the opposite of this, being generous & liberal to a fault & he despises the man as much as he detests the living. He [Merriman] comes into the Ward Room when he feels uncommonly hungry, for a meal.

Capt. Q. for some reason dislikes Capt. Bankhead very much & it is extremely disagreeable to him to have Capt. B. quoted as authority for what we may do or say, for which reason we all take occasion as often as possible, or whenever he objects to our manner of doing anything, to inform him that it was the way in which Capt. B. had it done. It is one of our schemes to annoy him & it succeeds capitally.

Last night I was sitting on the guards smoking with Mr. Merriman. The water was perfectly still & smooth & in that phosphorescent state sometimes seen at sea when a school of porpoise came up. At a distance they looked like a large luminous cloud in the water moving rapidly along. Then as they approached us the cloud seemed to burst like the head of a gigantic rocket & each huge spark pursue his individual course, wheeling, turning & zigzaging about, the course of each marked by its line of fire. Then they would unite into a cloud again & float along by the side of the ship till suddenly each would dart out, leaving behind them straight, paralell lines of waving liquid light. Then one would throw himself out of the water amid a spray of fire which would sparkle & flash like myriads of diamonds as it fell on the smooth surface beneath. Then as if at a preconcerted signal they would suddenly disappear beneath the vessel to shew themselves on the opposite side. I watched them in this way for nearly an hour, & a beautiful sight it was. Most of the time they kept close by the vessel, swimming along with equal speed & so near that we could throw a biscuit on one. One of the men finally got a harpoon with which he succeeded in striking one when they all at once disappeared.

We have passed through large quantities of gulf weed to day and a great variety of molusca including the singular bubble like "Portugese man of war," scaring up now & then a solitary flying fish.

Sunday, 8th—Another clear, still, beautiful day. Just after dinner a "black smoke" was announced from the mast head. All steam was put on & we gained rapidly on the stranger till discovered by her, when her endeavours to escape us disclosed at once her character. We did our best, gaining slowly on the chase, till she was hidden by the darkness, when ignorant of the course she would steer we gave up the pursuit. "Chased a blockade runner." How very few realise the excitement & anxiety, the hope & fear concentrated in that short sentence so frequently met with now a days.

CIVIL WAR YEARS: USS *FLORIDA* (1863-1865)

I fear the "old *Florida*" in the smooth still water we have had for the past two or three days has not sufficient speed, but give her rough weather & a heavy sea which while it would but slightly check her speed would materialy diminish that of the blockade runners, which are a very different class of vessels, intended for a high speed in smooth water but can make but little headway in heavy weather.

Wednesday, 11th—Since writing the above it has been as rough as the veriest old sea dog could desire. Last Monday morning when I turned out it was blowing a regular north-wester, the wind howling & shrieking through the rigging, carr[y]ing the spray entirely over the vessel & it still keeps it up. Now if we could but discover a "black smoke," it's ours. In what part of the world we are I have but little idea. I have been on deck but two or three times since Monday morning & found it decidedly nasty weather & no land in sight & retreated to a good comfortable Ward Room & a warm stove.

Thursday Morning, Nov. 12th—Clear, bright & pleasant. Steamer *Massachusetts* in sight ahead. We hope to overtake her & send letters home. You will get Nos. 30 & 31 together, as since finishing 31 I have had no opportunity to send. We shall be in Beaufort in a few days. Good bye with much love & kisses for yourself & the little ones.

W—

No. 32—

U.S. Steamer *Florida*
Off Wilmington, N.C.
Nov. 12th, 1863

Dear Anna,

We are back to our old place among the fleet once more. Just before getting in we spoke the *Massachusetts* & put one mail on board. In it was a good big package of three or four sheets for home which had been accumulating ever since we have been out cruising.

It would have been more profitable had we remained here, as in the seven days we have been gone, no less than *five* steamers have been captured by the fleet here in attempting to get in, all with valuable cargoes. Among them was the *Rob't E. Lee* which we chased all day last Saturday & the *Cornubia* another noted & very successful blockade runner. This will make a hole in the vessels engaged in this traffic, but the vacancy I suppose will soon be made good by our philanthropic English cousins, though I think in the end it will create a vacancy in the pockets of some of them.

Another piece of news—welcome news to us—Capt. Queen has been relieved & Commander Crosby*, formerly Fleet Captain, takes his place. You may rest assured that we do not regret the change. The universal dissatis-

---

* Peirce Crosby*.

Cruising (October to December 1863)

faction of all on board I suppose is one reason why the change has been made. Had we had the right sort of a Captain I think we might have made some valuable captures while we have been out. Capt. Crosby has the reputation of a pleasant, agreeable man & a good officer. I hope it may prove so. I have met him occasionally on the Flag Ship & elsewhere & have been pleased with what little I have seen of him. He has not got here yet. When he arrives & I have seen more of him I will tell you how I like him.

Friday, 13th—The *Tuscarora* came down to day with the mail. I rec'd by it your No. 13 & the note acknowledging the rec't of the box, also one from Hen & the two papers from Mrs. Hough & for which by the way I am very much obliged.

"O. N."* was most essentially sold. He'll never do for mayor, but I believe it characteristic of the greater part of *distinguished scientific* individuals to be easily imposed upon by such a class of persons.

A sight of the *Chicago Tribune* seemed to take me back home. I enjoyed a real treat in looking over the columns.

Another piece of news by the mail—Crafts has been detached & ordered to the supply steamer *Newbern*, a very pleasant & agreeable position, as it enables him to be home, or at least at the New York Navy Yard for three or four days every fortnight. He will undoubtedly have frequent opportunities of going home while the vessel is lying in the Yard taking in stores for the squadron. I only wish I was to be ordered to her as Paymaster. I think you would spend the winter in New York.

One of the boys while fishing to day caught a cuttle fish, one of the most singular & hideous things I ever saw taken out of salt water. You will find some engravings & a description of them in some of the old *Harpers*, some three or four years ago, which is much better than any I can give.

Just before dusk to night a small steamer was discovered standing rapidly in, along the edge of the shoals. Of course it was a blockade runner. Signals were set, chains slipped & every one gave chase, some to cut him off from land, others to prevent his getting out to sea. We were the first up with him & on sending a boat on board found it was the transport *Delaware* with Brig. General Seymour† on board making a reconnoisance. He had been on the South side during the day looking around & proposes to take a look at this side to morrow. This looks as though there was to be a move made here by

---

* Orville N. Adams, Keeler's friend in La Salle.
† Truman Seymour, division commander in the Department of the South. While recuperating from a serious wound sustained at Fort Wagner on July 18, 1863, Seymour had been asked to report on the defenses of Wilmington in preparation for a joint army and navy attack on the city and the forts guarding it. However, the 25,000 troops that were recommended could not be spared at that time, and it was not until the fall of 1864 when the requisite number of troops could be freed up that preparations for the attack on Fort Fisher began in earnest.

& by. We are now standing out to cruise again & will continue out till our coal is gone when we will proceed to Beaufort & fill up.

Tuesday, 16th [17th]—We have been cruising about since last Friday but with no success. We raised a "black smoke" Sunday just about sundown, but if it was a blockade runner darkness favoured it, for before we could trace the smoke to its origin, night had overtaken us & hidden the object of our search. We have boarded numbers of sail vessels of all kinds but all have proved to be "all right."

To whom am I indebted for Mrs. Hough's photograph? To you or herself? It is tolerable, a good likeness, but it has not her pleasant look—a little to[o] much vinegar in it, the same as the one you had taken in New York. Notwithstanding, I am under a thousand thanks & will try & keep it till I see the original (which I hope won't be long) or till I have a better.

Wednesday, 18th—We arrived here (at Beaufort) this morning & anchored just off the fort, with which & the surrounding sand & water, I am by this time pretty familiar. We found a good big mail waiting us, my share being *17* letters among them your Nos. 14 & 16. The latter I think should be 15, as only a week intervenes between the dates. I also rec'd one from Mr. Greene who has been ordered to special duty, on iron clads in New York, which is just what he desired.

How was Jas. Miller hurt? You speak of him as having been injured. Who was the Bunce who aided the escape of "O. N." quasia professor? Not ours of the firey locks, surely.

Did you ever read, *John Halifax, Gentleman*? by Miss Mulock* I believe? I have just finished it & think it capital, one of the best works I have read in a long time.

So you "give it up" do you? Didn't Powers "chisel" a poor slave girl out of her clothes!!!†

Don't let anyone else claim this—I have applied for a patent.‡

Have been ashore to day. Can't see that the sand has diminished any, though it is not so intolerably hot. The weather is delightfully cool, just enough so to make our uniforms comfortable. They have had one slight frost here but it don't seem to have affected vegetation any—roses are still blooming in the gardens.

Chapin has not returned yet.

The piece of wood of which you enquire was perforated by the torredo [teredo]§. I picked it up on the beach here. It had probably been in the water

---

* A novel about English middle-class life by Dinah Maria (Mulock) Craik published in 1857.
† American sculptor Hiram Powers' masterpiece The Greek Slave (1843), a marble statue of a young woman, nude and bound in chains. Keeler posed his riddle in his October 24, 1863 letter.
‡ This would be his patent for a governor. See letter of May 8, 1865.
§ Shipworm.

Cruising (October to December 1863)

but a short time. It is very much like a piece you saw in the Lyceum in the [New York] Navy Yard if you remember.

With much love,
William

[Marginalia] Tell Eddie that I got his letter & the pictures from him & the flag from Tibbie & that I will write to them in my next letter to you. They are nice dear children both of them. I hope you will be able to send their photographs in your next.

W—

No. 33—

U.S. Steamer Florida
At Sea
Nov. 26th, 1863

Dear Anna,

We left Beaufort last Tuesday the 24th & instead of going back to the blockade have been cruising about in search of "black smokes," so far however without success. Most of the time we have been in the Gulf Stream with pleasant weather & so warm that we have been glad to put on flannels again. At the time we left, there was some talk of the Admiral (who was at Beaufort) coming on board & for a time making this his flag ship. Fortunately we escaped by his taking the *Fahkee*.

The supply steamer *Newbern* arrived the day before we left, so that we were able to fill up our ice houses & get a supply of fresh meat & vegetables which with our ice we will make last some time. One luxury sent out by government, & which I assure you was most acceptable, was apples. These articles are not sent to us free but we can have them at the price at which they are supplied to government by contractors. This is for the officers' messes. For the men I take what I think necessary & issue it in the room of the usual salt rations.

I was ashore but once at Beaufort. After having once seen the place there is but little inducement to repeat the visit. I took a stroll over the beach in company with some of our officers & added to my collection of shells for the benefit of the children.

Mr. Crafts left us on the arrival of the *Newbern* & went on board of her. Capt. Queen also left us on our arrival at Beaufort, as I believe I have already informed you. We also received on board a Mr. Taylor from New York as coast pilot. He comes into the Ward Room Mess & proves a very pleasant & agreeable member. These are all the recent changes.

I like our new Capt. Crosby very well so far. He appears to be a still, quiet man of very few words and disposed to make the ship as efficient as possible & desires to make it as pleasant & comfortable as he can for all on board.

Civil War Years: USS *Florida* (1863-1865)

A painful occurrence took place on board to day. I was sitting in the Ward Room after dinner talking with Mr. Merriman when my attention was attracted by the engine bell ringing, "slow," "stop," followed by a quick tramp of feet overhead across the deck & the loud energetic orders of the officer of the deck to "cut away the life buoy." In company with others I rushed on deck & saw one of the men in the water but a short distance astern. The life buoy was already floating near him but he did not seem to see it, the very heavy sea which was running apparently hiding it from him. We were under sail at the time as well as steam. Before the sail could be taken in & the vessel's progress stopped we were a long distance from him but he could be seen from aloft, a black speck, as he was now & then thrown up on the top of a wave. At such a time the discipline & order of a man of war is apparent. There was no excitement, no confusion, no running about after something that could not be found. Every one had their stations & was at his post upon the first alarm. A boat was soon lowered, manned by a picked crew but they failed to reach him before he sank. Indeed the sea was so rough & so heavy a gale blowing that it was almost a miracle that the boat succeeded in getting back safely. The loss of the man, who was a good active seaman & one of the best men on board, seems to have cast a gloom over the whole ship. It seemed harder to see a man lost in that way than to have half a dozen killed in a fight. He fell from the guards while drawing a bucket of water. He swam well but the water was too rough for the best of swimmers to live long.*

I received another letter from Mr. Greene just before we left Beaufort. He has been ordered on "shore duty" at the New York Navy Yard, as a sort of assistant inspector of purchased vessels & is associated with Capts. Worden and Bankhead. He said both desired to be remembered to me & Capt. Bankhead said if his influence at Washington could be of service to me at any time that he would willingly use it. Mr. Greene wrote in fine spirits & said he had sent the Mess a box of his wedding cake but it has failed to reach us.

I hope you will be able to read this, but the seas are knocking the vessel around so that it is almost impossible to write legibly.

The fact is it is hard work to fill a sheet now when once commenced for there is so little to put in it. Our life is the same thing day after day & day after day, one monotonous round. Each of us when he *"turns out"* in the morning knows just what he has to do. His day's work is before him, all laid out—'tis the same that he did yesterday & the day before & the day before that & 'tis this constant repetition that tires one & he wearies from the sameness of his work however much he may have to do.

---

* 22-year old seaman John L. Crane. He grew up on a farm in China, ME. Prior to his enlistment in July 1863 he shipped to New Zealand for 10 months. He served on two Union Navy vessels before joining the *Florida* in October 1863.

Cruising (October to December 1863)

Saturday, Nov. 28th—Our rough weather still holds on & it alternately rains & shines & blows all the time. The sea is rough & the spray at times driving across the deck makes it wet & uncomfortable there, so we spend most of the time below. The Dr. spends his in being sea sick and apparently intends to keep it up, as he has been sick ever since we left & as he says, "Unfavourable symptoms still continue, gentlemen." I feel kind of sorry for the poor fellow, though at times I can't help laughing at him. As he came out of his state room this morning, says I, "How are you doctor?" "Oh Paymaster," says he, with the most doleful expression imaginable, "I wish I was home." He very evidently never was designed for salt water.

We shall probably be cruising about in this way for between two & three weeks more & then to Beaufort again. Nothing particularly pleasant to look forward to. I wish we were obliged to go to New York for supplies. I think we shall be obliged to go there for good by the latter part of Feb'y, but I hope we shall take two or three good prizes before that time. Mr. Merriman has between six & seven thousand dollars coming to him from two prizes, besides being interested in four or five more from which it is uncertain how much he will get, but it will be at least as much more.

I shall finish my sheet not knowing how or when it will reach you. Should we speak a homeward bound steamer I shall have it in readiness to go on board of her. If not I shall have to mail it from Beaufort when we get there. At all events I don't expect to hear from you till then. With my best love to yourself & all.

W—

No. 34—

U.S. Steamer Florida
At Sea
Nov. 30th, 1863

Dear Anna,

We have had another exciting day's chase & now while I write (8 P.M.) the old *Florida* is being crowded to the utmost, the jar of the engines & the roll of the vessel making it almost impossible to write legibly.

Just as day broke this morning a "black smoke" was seen bearing right down on us, about seven miles off. We started for her at once & she, discovering us about the same time, started off. The weather was just what we had been wishing for, a strong wind & a heavy head sea. The steamer was a large one & from the direction she was steering had evidently run out from Wilmington last night & so of course was cotton loaded & very valuable.

We were between her & Nassau, her destination, & she has vainly endeavoured all day to cross our bows & we have been gradually crowding her on towards the coast. At times we would seem to gain on her & then in turn she would gain on us & so it has kept on all day, the excitement at times increasing as we seemed to gain & then dying away as the space between us widened & now night has hidden the pursuer & pursued & each is ignorant of the other's intentions.

We have supposed that she would make straight for Nassau & have crowded all steam ourselves hoping to intercept her before she gets in. I think the chances are very strongly against us. Still there is a bare chance, a hope, & on that we are acting. I hope I may have to chronicle her capture in this sheet before it is full. Oh how we have wished to day that we were a little faster, or that daylight had held off a little longer this morning, till she had come within range of our rifle, we should all have felt richer to night.

Tuesday, Dec. 1st—Nothing visible this morning but the wide ocean. We are a little north of the Bahamas. The wind is blowing a howling gale & the seas look like rolling mountains. The old *Florida* usually so strong & quiet is pitching about in a uneasy & uncomfortable manner. Now she is deep down in a hollow & now she rises on the top of a rolling mountain. Now her bow rides gracefully up a watery ascent & her stern sinks almost as suddenly as if every support had been knocked from under, producing that peculiar sensation, if standing on it, at the pit of the stomach, that is sometimes felt in swinging on a high swing. Now her bow plunges into an apparently fearful abyss while the stern goes up, up, up till the deck presents an inclined plane not agreeable & difficult to travel over, especially to one who would give evidence of his sobriety & steady habits by "walking a crack." The gale whistles & howls through the rigging above, while below the timbers grown & creak an accompaniment, with the addition of an occasional smash of a departed piece of crockery or glassware, "departed never to return."

The motion of the vessel is a very peculiar one & trying to weak stomachs. Mr. Merriman is *slightly uneasy* in that portion of the system. So is the pilot who has been sixteen years at sea & one of our Ensigns. As for the M.D. & the Capt.'s Clerk, they were *"cleaned out"* long ago but notwithstanding *have not ceased their efforts* all day. How I wish we had Col. Dutton on board. The Dr. says "If I can only get home once you'll never catch me on salt water again." Nothing seems to disturb the Paymaster's appetite. The more the vessel rolls & pitches the more he eats & laughs at the miseries of those who can't.

Where our *friend?* of yesterday is we don't know. Certain it is if we should come across her now it would be impossible to send boats aboard. We could only keep her under our guns till the wind & sea went down.

Friday, Dec. 4th—This has been a clear, quiet, still day—the water as smooth as a mill pond, not a breath of air to raise a ripple on its surface. To economise our small stock of coal we have allowed our engines to rest & have been floating idly along wherever the current of the Gulf Stream chose to take us. While at home you have been hugging the fire, we have been glad to seek a shelter from the sun's rays.

CRUISING (OCTOBER TO DECEMBER 1863)

It seems odd to be bourn along in mid ocean so quiet & still. No banks or land marks to denote our progress. No houses or trees to glide by. No life. Nothing upon which the eye can rest for relief from the watery plane. The water, "deeply, darkly, beautifully blue"* contains not even the smallest mote as we float so quietly along, ourselves the center of a circle about twenty miles in diameter. Although we lie so still & quiet, it needs but the word of command, a black smoke or the lofty spars of the coming vessel on the distant horizon & life & animation at once take the place of listless inactivity.

What has taken place in the world during the last three weeks? For in that time we have heard nothing from it—no letters, no papers, nothing to tell us what is taking place about us. This is one of the worst features of this life out here on the ocean wave—cut off from home and the world.

Tuesday evening, Dec. 8th—Beaufort, N.C. We arrived here safely this morning. I found No. 15 from you enclosing the children's photographs. The little darlings, how glad I was to see them. I think them good likenesses, though as you say Tibbie's looks a little "thunderous."

Last Sunday morning was beautiful, but the wind kept gradually increasing till the middle of the afternoon when it blew a gale & by night it had risen to a most fearful pitch. We were in the middle of the Gulf Stream very near the place where the *Central America* went down when Fred Hawley was lost.† I went on deck about 9 P.M. but found it impossible to stand without holding on to something for support, the wind was so severe.

We were going head on to the sea & wind, & the waves were rolling down upon us like mountains. First we were high upon the crest & then deep down in the hollow &, besides, the constant working & straining of the vessel had made her leak badly. Capt. Crosby, Mr. Merriman & some of the others were up all night. I turned in & slept soundly till morning. The Doctor was so sea sick & frightened that he couldn't sleep. The next morning we had got under the lee of the land & the water was smoother, though the gale continued, but abated somewhat towards evening & the next morning we run into Beaufort.

I have just heard from Mr. Greene. His father, Brig. Gen. Greene, was shot through the head at the battle of Chickamuga, a severe but not dangerous wound & now his brother, Capt. Greene, has had his leg taken off by a shell at the recent fight with Bragg.‡

---

* Robert Southey's epic poem *Madoc* (1805), which was requoted by Lord Byron in *Don Juan* (1821) as "Oh, 'darkly, deeply, beautifully blue', as someone somewhere sings about the sky."
† Laden with tons of California gold, the steamer *Central America* sank in a hurricane on September 12, 1857. More than four hundred passengers and crew drowned, including Keeler's friend from Bridgeport, Frederick S. Hawley. Hawley's wife and two young children were rescued.
‡ Greene's father was shot in the face at the Battle of Wauhatchie, TN on October 28. The wound was so severe that he did not return to active duty until 1865. Greene's 21-year-old

Civil War Years: USS *Florida* (1863-1865)

What glorious news we get from Grant.* We did not hear of it till we arrived here. I suppose the "backbone" [of the Confederacy] has received another severe fracture.

I have just written Hen that he may spend the holidays in New York if he wants to.

We shall probably leave here in about a week & will try & write you again before we go. This time we shall probably go down on the blockade.

I enclose you some scraps from papers by which you will see that catching blockade runners is rather more profitable than chasing them.

With my best love to yourself and the darlings.

W—

No. 35

U.S. Steamer *Florida*
Beaufort, N.C.
Dec. 10th, 1863

Dear Anna,

Your No. 18 of Nov. 27th reached me to day, having been detained for want of postage *illegally* charged upon it. You may imagine my indignation— I can't describe it. I had the letter weighed by the P.M. [Post Master] here & found the stamp you put on it amply sufficient to cover all postage. I set down immediately & wrote to the P.M. General enclosing him the envelope with P.M. certificate at this place of the weight of the letter, but thought afterwards it might be better to have some one see the P.M. at La Salle & see if such carelessness could not be remedied at home. If not, I can very soon find a remedy which will prove effectual. If Dave has no objection I wish he would see the P.M. & state the case to him, tell him that it is not the first time it has happened & if it occurs again I shall report him to the P.O. Department, which I shall most assuredly do if I have occasion, as he will find to his cost. Letters are long enough in reaching me by the most speedy conveyance, but when they are detained (especially those from home) for postage unlawfully charged upon them it is a tax upon our patience which I fear our good nature will not submit to.

A large mail was sent down on the blockade for us just before our arrival here which I suppose contains a number of letters for me. We shall leave here in a few days for the blockade & upon reaching there will very likely find that all our letters have just been returned here & then they will be started back

---

brother Charles was hit by an unexploded shell that took off his right leg at the knee at the Battle of Ringgold Gap, GA on November 27.

* Union victories at the battles of Lookout Mountain and Missionary Ridge (November 24 and 25) at Chattanooga, TN, and the ensuing retreat of the defeated rebel army to northern Georgia.

Cruising (October to December 1863)

to the blockade as we have just gone down & when they get there we will have gone out cruising. When we get back here again for coal &c we will find that our mail, after having made two or three trips back and forth, is waiting us below. How provoking it is, but we cannot help it.

In my last, which I mailed to day, I mentioned the gale we encountered in the Gulf Stream but had room & time to say but little about it. I think it was the severest gale I ever saw, unless it was two or three in my California experience. But the seas beat anything I have ever seen. It seemed at times as if we should be buried, but we rode them finely & took but little water on deck. In our Ward Room brightly lighted & by the side of a good fire one knows but little about the wind or weather except from the watch officers who come down from time to time as their watch expires.

This afternoon in company with Washburn & the Dr. I went to make a call on the officers in the fort (Macon). The garrison had been changed since we were here last & they were all strangers to us. However under such circumstances it don't take long to get acquainted. We were very hospitably received in their quarters in one of the casemates. I say hospitably, for in these quarters it always includes a bottle of whiskey, which I am sorry to say is almost universally patronised. Otherwise they were a very pleasant set of officers & exerted themselves to make it agreeable.

They urged us to stay to supper but as a boat was to be sent for us at sundown we were obliged to decline. So they shewed us around the fort & then took us on the ramparts to see the sundown gun fired at the report of which the gates of the fort are closed & no one goes out or in without the countersign. This, the officer of the day, who was with us & is the only one who can impart it, utterly refused to do, so we had nothing to do but "surrender unconditionally" which we did & took supper with them laughing at the "strategic move" by which they made sure of our company. We got back to the vessel long after dark.

Friday, 11th—The pilot, Washburn, Dr. & myself, with a couple of pilots from shore for guides, started this morning just after breakfast for an island in the mouth of the harbour [Harkers Island] where clams and oysters are abundant to have an oyster roast. We took one of our boats with sails & had a splendid sail of six or eight miles, though the clear morning air was rather cool, the thermometer standing at 45°.

We landed on a low sandy beach covered with the shells of departed oysters. The island was a long narrow strip of land, or rather sand blown up in huge heaps & piles & long winrows, covered in most places with dense thickets of scrubby cedars & live oaks—what keeps them alive is a mystery I can't solve.

In places huge piles of clean white sand were heaped up like gigantic snow drifts over which the finer particles danced along driven by the wind, like as I suppose the snow is now whisling along over our northern snow drifts. It reminded me more of a walk after a heavy fall of snow where the wind had piled the fleecy chrystals into immense rounded heaps & given them the solidity to bear our weight. The thickets of evergreens peering up above the smooth wind swept surface as if to protect it from the sun's rays. All that was needed to convince me that we were plodding along over snow banks was chilled toes & an occasional slip over an icy surface.

Between the piles of sand were now & then a shallow pond or marsh where the salt water had filtered through the loose material from the sea. We c[r]ossed over the island through such scenery as I have just described to the side fronting on the open sea where the surf was rolling in with violence on the smooth sandy beach. This, for miles in length & perhaps quarter of a mile in width, was not only paved with shells (similar to those I have sent home) but mingled with the sand, which itself is comminuted shells, formed the whole substance of the beach. I added a small lot of some new varieties to my stock as we strolled along the beach & then returned across the island [to] where we had left our boat.

We found the tide had gone down leaving a large, low point of rocks bare. They were covered with oysters, which we knocked off in clusters as large as half a bushel & carried them back to our fire where we separated them as much as possible & laid them on the coals to roast. Clams were plenty if any prefered them. The oysters though not large were good, & with a basket of edibles the steward had put up for us, made us a good dinner. It was decidedly a primitive way of cooking our bivalves & we enjoyed it the more for that very reason.

Saturday 12th—We leave this evening & it is undecided whether we go cruising or on the blockade. If the former I fear my opportunities for sending home will be but seldom but I shall write as often as possible.

With much love to yourself & the little ones.

W—

No. 36

U.S. Steamer *Florida*
At Sea
Wednesday evening
Dec. 16/63

Dear Anna,

We have been weather bound in Beaufort Harbour since last Saturday [December 12], at which time we expected to go to sea, but the continuous heavy wind has raised such a swell on the bar* that we dared not attempt to cross it. The sea went down a little this morning & we seized the opportunity

---

* A deposit of sand formed at the mouth of a river by the interaction of the outgoing tide and ocean breakers. Breaking waves in these shallow waters made crossing the bar a dangerous undertaking.

to slip out. So here we are once more *bob[b]ing* about under the influence of a regular northeaster which is blowing good & strong. We realised the truth of the old adage, "it's an ill wind" &c, for the delay kept us till the *Newbern* arrived with meat, vegetables, ice, papers & *mails*.

Crafts has been detached & ordered to the *Shokokon* (what a name) as executive officer. I had a letter from him by the *Newbern* enclosing one from your Mother. He is not at all pleased with the change & has gone on to Washington with letters from Capt. Bankhead to see if he can't get his orders revoked. The *S.* is one of the old ferry boats intended for sound & river service, though she has been down on the blockade, but was found to be unserviceable in rough weather.

Last Sunday, the *Aries*, a captured steamer fitted up as a gunboat, came in towing the *Sirius* [*Ceres*], a blockade runner she had captured. The *S.* [*Ceres*] was on fire. She was run on to the beach where she lay when we left, a slow smouldering fire still burning in her.

As we passed the entrance to Bogue sound just after leaving Beaufort, we passed another rebel craft*, a fine large schooner which the *Mount Vernon* had just run ashore & set on fire. She was in a sheet of flame & her masts fell just as we were abreast of her.

As the *Newbern* was leaving Hampton Roads on her way down, a fine large three masted screw steamer was coming in with the Stars & Stripes hoisted over the English flag, evidently a capture recently made. So they go. I see by the papers that the Clyde is getting drained of steamers, bought up to run the blockade.† Let them come. There will be the more to capture.

I see by the papers rec'd to day that the *Weehawken* has gone down at her anchors off Charleston. I can't understand it, as she weathered a severe gale coming down under the command of Capt. Rogers [Rodgers], who commanded the *Galena* in the fight at Fort Darling. She was more strongly built & much better provided against such contingencies than the old *Monitor*. There must have been carelessness somewhere. It seems the loss of life was much greater than on the *Monitor*.‡

I saw Chapin at Beaufort, well & hearty. He promised to come & dine on board but failed to for some reason. He had just returned from a furlough, having left home only three days before his mother reached there.

---

* G. O. Bigelow.
† The River Clyde in Scotland was the major center for building blockade runners. At the height of the building boom in 1864 it was estimated that 27 Clyde ship yards, employing 25,000 men and boys, were involved in the illegal activity.
‡ On December 6 the monitor USS *Weehawken* sank while at anchor off Morris Island. Four officers and 26 crew members drowned. A board of inquiry concluded that the vessel sank as a result of an excessive amount of ammunition that had been stored in the forward compartments, which reduced the freeboard and allowed water to pour in through an open hatch.

Civil War Years: USS *Florida* (1863-1865)

Lieut. Greene has been ordered to the *Iroquois*, probably as executive officer. I hoped that his marriage would induce him to quit drinking, but I fear it has not.

We get along very pleasantly with Capt. Crosby, who by the way is a brother in law of Queen's but don't appear to like him any the better for it. I haven't seen a person in the service so universally disliked, unless it be that naval excrescence, Jeffers.

Your Mother, in her letter just received, makes the very modest request that I should give Henry a silver watch for a Christmas present!! What do you think of that?? I have no objections to his having one & think he deserves it, but aren't boys getting rather expensive? I have just sent him forty five dollars for clothes. At any rate if he has a watch it will be after I get back to select it for him.

I received No. 19 from you just as we were getting under way to leave this morning. So I made that much more by being detained.

You ask how I spent Thanksgiving? What I had for dinner, if I thought of home &c? Well I must confess that the day slipped by unnoticed & unknown to all on board, or at any rate to any of us in the Ward Room. But we took ample revenge the next day for we got up the most extensive & luxurious repast our larder would afford—pork & beans—molasses for those who liked. Ask Mother for the *Deacon*'s recipe that we may have a greater variety next time.

So you have had Aunt Hannah*. You may well say that you may look for your Mother next. I wish she had made her visit at a more pleasant season of the year. You must all have enjoyed her company. I wish I could have been there with you.

I am glad to hear such good news from Dave that his eyes a[re] getting better. I wish he was down here somewhere with them in good working order.

Thursday, 17th—We arrived down at the fleet this morning & found our mail that had been sent down from Beaufort. I received by it your No. 17 & one from Sarah which I must answer as soon as possible. I had a large mail which has taken all my time to day. I have written no less than seventeen letters since morning.

We shall probably [be] here for some time. I think our chances are as good here for prizes as cruising outside unless they will give us a faster vessel.

We have had an addition to our Ward Room Mess to day in the person of a Mr. McLean† who takes the place of Mr. Zeigler. Mr. Z. sent me his photograph. You will find it enclosed. I think you will have quite a collection of naval characters in your collection if you keep on, or rather if I continue sending home.

---

* Hannah A. Plant, widow of Keeler's maternal uncle James Plant from Utica, NY.
† William H. McLean*.

Cruising (October to December 1863)

I want to know if Dave has taken up checker playing. That's about as bad as dominoes with which we pass away our leisure time. Cards are not allowed on ship board.

Do you know when your subscription to the [New York] *Times* expires? I have a mind to order the [New York] *Herald* for you for the year to come unless you prefer the *Times*. The *Herald*'s maps are quite a feature & make the paper much more valuable & interesting.

What shall I write to Sarah in the way of a "sensible" letter? Do tell me for I am at a loss to know. I shall invent a letter mill as soon as I get home.

I hope to have an opportunity to send this up by the *Newbern* on her return to morrow morning. Good night.

W—

Off Wilmington (December 1863 to March 1864)

I stood on the guard of the vessel preparing to get into the boat when I heard a crash in the wheel house (by the side of which I stood), an explosion & at the same instant received a severe crushing blow in the back. For an instant all was blank. I sank to my feet & should have fallen overboard had I not had hold of the line which surrounds the guard. I knew I was wounded. I put my hand to my back, found my clothes torn away & the flesh raw & bloody & I am free to confess I was frightened. I knew not how badly I was injured. I felt but little pain but I did not know but it was the deadening insensibility which sometimes follows a mortal wound. (3 March 1864)

For the next three months the *Florida* was back on the blockade off Wilmington where they destroyed or helped destroy three blockade runners. On February 2 they came upon the *Wild Dayrell*, which had run ashore some 50 miles northeast of Masonboro Inlet. While they were trying to get her off the beach, Keeler was placed in charge of a boat carrying orders back and forth between the *Florida* and land. Failing to float the vessel, Commander Crosby ordered her destroyed and placed Keeler in charge of ensuring that the vessel was thoroughly fired. Once the sailors had finished plundering the vessel, Keeler and fellow officers McGowan and McLean set her on fire and returned to the *Florida* as a Whitworth bolt went whizzing past their heads.

One week later they chased a steamer which ran ashore near Masonboro Inlet. It proved to be the *Fanny and Jenny* commanded by the "notorious Captain Coxetter," as he is characterized in the Official Records. As Keeler was preparing to board a boat to take possession of the vessel, a Whitworth bolt fired from a distant shore battery exploded in the *Florida*'s wheel house a few yards from where he was standing. A fragment of the shell struck him in the back, ripping a deep furrow in the muscles next to the spine. An inch to either side and the wound would have been fatal. Not wanting to go to a hospital and unable to withstand the long journey home, Keeler elected to remain on board the *Florida*. For the first two weeks he suffered intensely. Unable to write long letters, he sent brief notes to Anna letting her know how he was getting on. It was during this time that he received the sad news that his father had died following a one-month illness.

Leaving them in early January was their seasick surgeon Hiram James who was replaced by Howard Vose, a "very pleasant appearing young man" who attended to Keeler during his convalescence. Shortly before the *Florida* headed to Norfolk for repairs, their captain Crosby was detached and command of the vessel passed temporarily to Lieutenant Merriman.

Letters of special note: December 18 (a call to battle stations); December 25 (Christmas dinner on board the *Florida*); January 1 (how Washburn busted up the salt works; Mr. Fader's exploits); January 11 ("Sail ho, black smoke"); January 28 (a call on Aunt Peggy); February 4 (plundering and destruction of the *Wild Dayrell*); March 3 (Keeler's wounding; demise of the *Fanny and Jenny*).

No. 37—

U.S. Steamer *Florida*
Off Wilmington, N.C.
December 18th, 1863

Dear Anna,

I wonder if the moon shines as bright & clear & the air is as calm & still at home as it is here. I have just returned from the deck where it is cool enough to make the fire feel comfortable when one returns to the Ward Room.

We are lying just far enough from the coast to be out of range of artillery should it be sent up from Fort Fisher. Not much chance for blockade runners these bright moonlight nights. They seem to prefer darkness rather than light, for the reason I suppose that their deeds are evil. Their skeletons dot the shore along here pretty thickly & every few days is adding to their number.

Last night was dark & rainy & one of our gun boats coming near us in the gloom was mistaken for a blockade runner by the officer of the deck. The rattle was sprung & everything was hurry & bustle for a few minutes—men tumbling up on deck, just out of their hammocks, half asleep & half dressed, hurrying to the armoury for their arms—officers rushing from their rooms, buckling on their side arms—a hasty unrolling of fire hose across the decks— the uncoiling of ropes & casting loose the battery—the hurried roll call by the officers & the rush of each & every one to his station before roll call is over—the hurried tread of many feet over the decks—the rattle of ropes & blocks—the creak of the heavy guns as they are run out—the low but earnest orders of the officers & the response of the men. [It] would seem to the uninitiated like a scene of the wildest & most disorderly confusion when it is

Off Wilmington (December 1863 to March 1864)

just the opposite. Not a man on board from Captain to boy but what has his post and duties assigned him for any emergency which may arise, & he is drilled in those duties till they become familiar to him. Whether it is a call to arms, an alarm of fire, to make or shorten sail or man the boats, he must know his post & be familiar with its duties.

As for myself, my peculiar duties being to see that no evil disposed shot finds its way into pork or beef barrels or money chests, I have made up my mind not to be disturbed by these night alarms unless I find some stray shot coming into my state room. While I had charge of a division I was out as soon as any one, but now I simply turn over & go to sleep again & trust to mess table gossip the next morning for the news & cause of the alarm.

Saturday evening, 19th—Another fine moonlight evening. To night we are lying in so close to the shore it seems as if we could almost throw a stone on the beach.

Our curiosity was a good deal excited this morning by seeing a small boat with a white flag coming off to the vessel. Upon a near approach we found it to contain two persons, one of them a young man of 18, a deserter from the rebel army. He stated that he had been compelled to enter the cavalry in which he had served about 16 months when he lost his horse & was given a month's furlough with orders to procure another. The other was an Englishman of about 30 who had had charge of some salt works* on the shore & for that reason had been exempt from military duty, but the more thorough enforcement of the conscription law, compelling all between 16 & 60 to enter the service, forced him to shoulder a musket or quit rebeldom. He chose the latter & came off in company with the youngster, who was his brother in law, leaving behind his wife & family to the tender mercies of the rebels. It seems a picket guard is kept up along the shore, not so much to prevent our landing as to stop those on shore from coming off to us.

They eluded the guard upon the pretence of coming off the beach after oysters, but after getting out of the range of the sentry's musket made for the vessel. The man was quite an intelligent sort of a person, but the boy looked as if Topsey like he never had any parents, but "growed."† Neither of them could give us information of any value & both seemed to be of that kind who didn't care which side they fought on so long as they were well paid & kept, but had a little rather keep out of harm's way & not fight at all. We wanted them to enlist but they declined. So we have got them to feed & clothe till we can make some disposition of them, for it won't do to send them back again.

---

* A crucial commodity during the Civil War, salt was produced in coastal regions by evaporating seawater. While many of the salt works along the North Carolina coast had fallen into Union hands early in the war, those near Wilmington remained in rebel control until near the end.
† Topsy, the young slave girl in Harriet Beecher Stowe's *Uncle Tom's Cabin*, who when asked whether she knew who made her replied, "Nobody, as I knows on. I spect I grow'd. Don't think nobody never made me."

Civil War Years: USS *Florida* (1863-1865)

Sunday evening, 20th—Last night was the coldest weather we have had, ice forming on pails of fresh water on deck.

One of our boats was sent in last night towards the shore to take soundings. They went in to one of the wrecks which are scattered along the beach & returned having accomplished their object without seeing a person or being molested.

I see by a slip from a paper you send me that Gen. Barnes[*] has had *our* President prayed for in the churches of Norfolk & Portsmouth. It was quite time. The rebels had prayed for their President (for it amounted to that in substance) about long enough, and I believe would be doing it now had Gen. Nagley[†] remained there.

It was realy shameful when I was at Norfolk [to] see our officers both of the army & navy sit quietly & allow the prayer for the President to be cooly & and impudently omitted & no notice taken of it. I am glad that Gen. Barnes has given his attention to the matter & corrected the evil. I think such churches would be less desecrated by using them as hospitals for our soldiers. The first time McGowan writes his sisters, I am going to send the slip you sent me.[‡]

Mr. Merriman was on the *Santiago de Cuba* & comes in for about $7,000. prize money. She was a fast vessel & was very fortunate in her captures. Had the *Florida* been faster I have no doubt but what I could have counted on $10,000. as my share from the vessels we have chased & most likely double that.

Tuesday, 22—This has been a clear still warm day. All hands have been practising with small arms at a barrel placed about 300 yards off in the water. I beat all the officers with a musket & revolver except the Captain. Mr. Merriman did not shoot.

We are lying in so close to the shore to night that we can plainly see a house a little back from the beach with a light shining from the window. We were going to put a shell into it which we could easily do but desisted when one of the refugees on board told us that it was occupied by Union folks, though the rebels make a picket station of it.

With much love,

W—

---

[*] James Barnes, military governor of Norfolk from October to December 1863.
[†] Henry M. Naglee, commander of the District of Virginia from August to September 1863.
[‡] Keeler is referring to McGowan's sister's indignation at the omission of the prayer for the President at the church service they attended in Portsmouth. See letter of September 26, 1863.

OFF WILMINGTON (DECEMBER 1863 TO MARCH 1864)

No. 38—

U.S. Steamer *Florida*
Off Wilmington, N.C.
December 25th, 1863

Dear Anna,

How many absent ones have wished themselves at home to day & how many of those at home have wished that the absent ones were with them to enjoy with them a Merry Christmas. On the blockade we have kept the day as well as we could, wishing each other a "Merry Christmas," which with the exception of a semi-holiday to the men and a Christmas dinner constituted our sole observance of the day. We are stationed some ways up the coast away from the rest of the fleet doing sort of picket duty, consequently have had no friends to visit nor calls to receive.

We got up a tolerable good dinner to which we invited Capt. Crosby. Just as it was coming on the table a strange sail which we had started for some time before was made out to be the *Farkee* [*Fahkee*], with the Admiral's pennant flying, on her way down from Beaufort. She was soon abreast of us & signalised for Capt. C. to come on board which deprived us of his company at dinner.

As you may have some curiosity to know what a Christmas dinner on the blockade consisted of, suppose I give you our bill of fare. I wish I could find the one our Steward made out in regular hotel style, unpronouncable french & all, but as I can't I shall come down to plain english: Oyster & tomato soups, boiled & baked fish, boiled ham & tongue, roast turkey, roast beef, chicken pie, broiled chickens, roast ducks, clam pie, quails on toast, giblet stew, beets, sweet & irish potatoes, onions, green corn, & peas, asparagras, cranberry sauce, currant jelly, claret, sherry and catawba wines & ale, plum pudding, corn starch do. [ditto], blanch mange—apple, cranberry, cherry & raspberry pies—fruit cake, can'd peaches & grapes, apples, raisins, figs, chestnuts, almonds, hickory nuts, coffee & chocolate & some good sweet fresh Orange Co. butter with better bread than is often found on ship board.

So you see that Christmas was duly kept as far as eating was concerned. Not that this is our every day fare—by no means—but we always keep a few delicacies in our store rooms for company or extra occasions like the present. Then for our turkey & quails we were indebted to McGowan's sisters who sent them down by the last trip of the *Newbern*. They also sent another box of brandy peaches, cakes, confectionery, pickles &c which failed to reach us. For a very nice fruit cake we were indebted to our pilot who had just received it from home. Our wines were from the private stores of the officers who had them, as we have no wine fund in the mess—each one supplying himself as he sees fit. Our meat we got from the *Newbern* when last here & our chickens & ducks we got at Beaufort just before leaving there & kept them as well as our meat in one of our ice houses of which we have four & usually fill them all at each trip of the *Newbern*. Most of our Mess stores we now order from New York to come down in the supply ship. We get a much better article & cheaper than can be had from the sutlers in Beaufort.

We were sorry to loose Capt. Crosby's company at dinner & he seemed loath to leave us just as we were going to sit down. He however had his Christmas dinner with the Admiral (though I don't believe it was any better than ours) & returned on board late in the evening bringing quite a large mail with him—the most welcome gift we could have had.

I rec'd your No. 20 & a LaSalle paper which seemed quite homelike. I also had one from Henry enclosing his photograph, one of which I suppose you have rec'd by this time. How the dress [clothes] alters his looks—makes him look so much older & manly. I hope he has gone to New York to spend the holidays. He will be there long enough to get acquainted & I think will enjoy himself.

Three more refugees came off to us a few evenings since in a small leaky boat. They seem to be rather more intelligent than the last batch we received but are evidently some of the "poor white trash." The enforcement of the Conscription has driven them off & they tell us that many more would like to follow if they could get away—rats it is said will quit a sinking ship. When asked if they would enlist, they said that they "didn't want to fight for the Confederacy nor against it." They want to go to Beaufort, hoping to get some employment till the war is over.

We have just heard that a blockade runner was driven ashore a few nights since on the south side & one captured. Just before we came down here the last time, the *Howqua*[h], one of our gun boats, saw a vessel running in & running up alongside of her fired a few times till they exploded a shell in her side, when the night being dark & the smoke of their guns obstructing their view they could see no more of her till next morning they could see a little of her masts above water. The shell in her side had sunk her and it is supposed that all on board went down with her. It was the *Bureguard* [*Beauregard*] & thus ends another chapter in blockade running.*

More changes have been made in our Mess. A 1st Asst. Engineer, Mr. McLean, has been ordered to us to take Mr. Ziegler's place. He is a still, quiet man & I think will make a pleasant messmate. With the exception of the pilot I am the only married one in the mess.

A week or two ago the Dr. wrote to the Dept. telling them that in consequence of continued sea sickness he found it almost impossible to do duty at sea & asking to be detached & ordered to some vessel on the sounds or rivers where the water would be s[m]oother. In a short time I rec'd a communication from the Dept. to the effect that his appointment had been revoked & that another Surgeon had been ordered to fill his place. He arrived to day—

---

* The rebels destroyed the blockade runner *General Beauregard* after salvaging her cargo.

OFF WILMINGTON (DECEMBER 1863 TO MARCH 1864)

a Dr. Vose* from Calais, Me., a very pleasant appearing young man & I hope will prove an agreeable messmate.

Sunday 27th—The *Houqua* [*Howqua*] came down to day bringing a small mail. I rec'd your No. 21, only nine days from home—no[t] so bad that.

I was sorry to hear of Capt. Pratt's death.† It will be a terrible loss to his family.

From the way you speak I think you cannot have rec'd all the letters I have written & fear that one or more have been lost in a steamer which was recently wrecked off Hatteras. Look over the numbers & see.

My best love to yourself & the children.

W—

[Marginalia] Tell the children that I got their letters. They are very good for writing to me. I will send them a letter by & by.

No. 39‡—

U.S. Steamer *Florida*
Off Wilmington, N.C.
January 1st, 1864

A Happy New Year my dear friends one & all & you may be assured that this wish is sincere and heartfelt. I only regret that I cannot express it in person instead of employing pen & ink.

The day has been a busy one with me, as my returns for the last quarter are to be made out for the Department. But often through the day my mind has been at home & I have visited you in imagination.

What have you all been about to day? Where is "our circle" met to night? For I take it for granted that you are in conclave assembled somewhere—is the absent member thought of? It has seemed but little like New Year's with us—the usual routine of shipboard has gone on uninterruptedly.

My calculations of stores expended, provisions required & "red tape" mysteries were pleasantly interrupted in the forenoon by a message from Capt. Crosby requesting the pleasure of my company to dinner at *5 o'clock*. This is a compliment not often paid to Ward Room officers, so of course is to be appreciated the more. Dr. James (who is still on board) was invited with me. At the appointed time the Dr. & myself were duly seated at the Capt.'s table & did full justice to his roast turkey &c. His table is furnished with about the same fare as our own, so that we did not expect anything better in the way of eatables than what we could furnish from our own store rooms. We

---

* E. Howard Vose*.
† Keeler's friend from La Salle Oscar Pratt died on board the USS *New National* on the Mississippi River on December 13, leaving his 37-year old wife and three children fatherless.
‡ The sheet marked No. 40 was included in this letter.

passed a very pleasant evening for Capt. C. though not much of a talker can make himself very agreeable.

He [Capt. Crosby] is liked very well on board. Everything goes along smoothly & without trouble. Like Capt. Bankhead, & very unlike Capt. Queen, he is satisfied to give his orders & let the officers having charge of the different departments of the vessel carry them into execution in their own way—though each is expected to see that his department is in the highest state of efficiency.

There is the Paymaster's department, whose peculiar duty it is to see to the clothing, feeding & paying those on board; the Engineer's department, relating to the engines, fuel & machinery of the vessel; the Gunner's department, who has charge of the guns, small arms, & all ammunition on board; the Master's department, pertaining to the navigation & sailing of the vessel & the Medical department, having charge of the physical well being & sanitary regulations.

With a good Captain & good officers at the head of each department, with good regulations well enforced, which it is the duty of the Executive officer to see to, everything moves harmoniously & without trouble. But there is sometimes a clash between the different departments which causes a good deal of ill feeling—this has seldom if ever been the case on board of us.

We have as pleasant & agreeable a Ward Room Mess as can be found on any of our vessels. None of the members very highly educated nor refined, but all good sound sense, practical men. Most of them, with the exception of the Dr., Engineer & myself, men who have followed the sea for years, some as captains or officers of merchantmen, others old men of war's men who, like Ensign Williams, have been promoted for bravery & valor during the war. Nearly every part of the world has been visited by them & the relation of their adventures at various times & places are really entertaining.

They have seen a good deal of this war too, at different places along the coast from Hampton Roads to Texas. The parts they have played at different fights & skirmishes where no witness could doubt their bravery & valour forms a most interesting page in what will in all probability be the unwritten history of the war.

"Washburn," says I the other evening to one of our Ensigns, "let's know about your destroying the salt works on the coast above here."

"Why," says he, "there's nothing about it, only Capt. Cushing sent me ashore one night to help 'em bile salt & I did it & busted up the salt works."*

"How did you do it?"

"Well, in the first place some contrabands came off & told Capt. Cushing that there was some large salt works ashore just abreast the vessel with only

---

* The saltworks that Washburn described were possibly those at New Topsail Inlet which were destroyed on October 29, 1862. If so, Lieutenant William Cushing made no mention of Washburn in his report of the action (ORN, I:8, p. 174).

Off Wilmington (December 1863 to March 1864)

about a dozen workmen to see to them. Capt. C. asked me if I thought I could destroy them. I told him I would try if he would let me. He told me to be ready to go that night.

"The works were not immediately on the beach. To get to them you had, after landing through the surf, to cross a strip of land covered with brush, logs, stumps, sand & swamp for about a mile & a half. Then we came to a strip of water or sound about a mile wide, on the opposite side of which were the works. This strip of water communicated with the sea a few miles above where we lay & we could easily have gone up the coast in our boat & then down the sound to the works but sentinels were placed at the entrance of the sound to prevent any such expedition & give notice of its approach. So I thought I wouldn't attempt that but land on the beach opposited the vessel.

"So after dark, I started for the beach with a boat's crew of ten men. In tow of our cutter we had a small light boat. After landing I left four of the men in charge of the cutter & with the other six started across the strip of land taking with us the small boat.

"The night was as dark as it could well be & I guided my course by occasional glimpses of the fires at the salt works & by a small boat lantern & compass. We made a straight course, partly draging, partly carrying our boat through the brush & over the sand, sometimes tumbling over logs & stumps & then up to our knees in mud & water. We had a time of it, no mistake.

"Well, after nearly two hours' work, we finally reached the sound, on the opposite side of which were the works. Our boat was soon in the water and we pulled silently across, landing a little distance below the fires which were burning brightly. Leaving the men by the boat I started on a reconnoisance to see what kind of a job I had on hand. Wasn't I astonished, after I had crawled up through the brush to where I could get a good view of their camp, to see not only the ten or dozen workmen but a lieutenant and six soldiers.

"I made up my mind that the job was a bigger one than I had contracted for & at first I rather wished I was safe back [on board ship] again. The soldiers were seated around a camp fire playing cards, two or three of the workmen being with them, their muskets stacked a few yards from them. The rest of the workmen were busy about the works. I took a good look to see just how matters stood & concluded I would play my hand at any rate. If I trumped over them I should take the trick, if not then the 'Libby'*.

"In getting back to my men I made my plans. Each of us had a musket, revolver & cutlass but I couldn't bring my mind to stealing up around them & shooting them down in cold blood. It seemed too much like murder. When I got back to the boat I told the men just how matters stood & what they had before them & says I, 'Boys, I'm going in. Will you stand by me?' They all agreed they would. 'Now' says I, 'we will crawl up to them as close as we can & when I give the order, first section charge, 'go in' & yell like so many devils,

---

* The Confederate prison in Richmond.

make for the muskets—(we had left our muskets by the boat & had only our small arms). If the soldiers get them first & show fight, lay out as many of 'em as you can.'

"We crept up as near as I thought we could without being discovered. I took a good look to see if everything was right, then I yelled out, 'First section, charge,' & we all 'went in' with a rush & a yell. I trumped that trick & I reckon I took it. With three or four jumps & before they had dropped their cards & got on their feet we had their guns. I pointed my revolver at the Lieutenant's breast & says I, 'Come down, Secesh. I've got the biggest trump. It's no use, you're surrounded.' So he gave me his sword & said he surrendered.

"Some of the workmen started to run. I sang out, 'Capt. Smith, see that your company surrounds the camp. Shoot the first one that attempts to go through your lines.' In this way I led them to think they were surrounded by two or three hundred men.

"I set the boys to watch the Lieut. & his men while I looked about with the workmen. 'Got any tar or turpentine, old fellow?' says I to one of the men. 'Yes, sir, in the shed yonder.' 'Well, roll it out, let's see how it looks, & two or three of the others just take those logs & punch the bottoms out of the salt kettles. As I'm going out of the business I shan't want them any more.'

"Well, I made them knock the bottoms out of the kettles & roll the [barrels of] tar & turpentine around all the buildings, knock in the heads and set them on fire & as they began to blaze up I thought of getting back to the vessel.

"The query was what should I do with my prisoners. It would not do to expose my weakness, so I kept up the deception. I told the Lieut. that I had my own boat with me—the gig—& would take him & two of his men with me, which was all my boat would carry. 'The rest of you keep along this path till you come to the river, you'll find 8 or 10 boats there, you can come off in them' & then I hallooed out, 'Capt. Smith, I'm sending the prisoners down to you. I want you to bring them off in your boats.'

"I threw the prisoners' guns into the fire & then told the Lieut. & his two men to start. We soon reached my boat & wasn't long in getting in & rowing across to the opposite side, for I expected, between the prisoners I had turned off & the fire which was burning up furiously, the whole country would be raised.

"We dragged the boat up into a thicket of bushes & hid it, for I had no time to spare to get it across to the beach. I crossed over to the beach & found the cutter & four men as I had left them & was soon on my way to the ship once more & it was not till I was well off from the beach that I told the Lieut. my real strength & that Capt. Smith with his hundred men & dozen boats only had an imaginary existence. A more mortified individual I never saw. It was nearly morning when I got on board & that's the way I busted up the salt works."

Off Wilmington (December 1863 to March 1864)

This is a sample of what is told us by those who have taken part in the scenes which they describe. I could fill quires of paper with just such "yarns" but they loose by repetition & on paper too. It needs the actor to relate it.

One of our Master's Mates, Mr. Fader[*], was "spinning me a yarn" a few days since in which he didn't give your cousin, Col. Dutton[†], the credit of a great deal of bravery. Mr. Fader says he was sent by Admiral Lee one day on an expedition up the Nansemond [River] with sixteen men & a howitzer. Gen. Butler sent Col. Dutton with between four & five hundred men with him as an infantry support. When they got in the neighborhood of where the enemy were supposed to be the Col. was very anxious that Fader should post his piece in a hollow. It was a *safe* place & out of sight but didn't suit Fader who said he came to fight & kept moving on till he could see the rebs scattered among the trees.

The Col. kept advising him to halt but he continued to advance slowly, giving the enemy an occasional grist of grape & cannister. He drove the enemy before him till sometime in the afternoon he came upon a small earthwork they had thrown up & where they had a small field piece. At the first fire two of the Col.'s men were killed when he & his men started for the river, some four miles, on a full run, leaving Fader with his gun & sixteen men to get off as best they could. The Col. probably expected Fader would follow, but he ain't that sort of a man. Fader said he stopped & gave them a couple of rounds of cannister when a shot broke both legs of one of his men & he made up his mind he might as well go too. It took four of his men to carry the wounded one. The rest dragged the gun, loading as they went, the enemy following. When they got too near & he was afraid they would charge, he would let them have some cannister. In this way he reached the river where the vessel lay, bringing off his gun & wounded man.

There are many such men as these we meet with, who are hardly known or heard of outside their circle of acquaintances but are heroes none the less. They may not have been mentioned in official dispatches nor their deeds found their way in print, but are deserving credit far more than many of the

---

[*] David Fader (~1837-1897). Born in Halifax, Nova Scotia, he served in the American merchant marine and U.S. Coast Survey in the 1850s. He enlisted in the Navy as a seaman in May 1861, serving on the USS *Roanoke*, USS *Commodore Barney* and USS *Shokokon* before being transferred to the *Florida* on which he served until August 1864. In November 1864, while on shore leave at the New York Navy Yard, he got drunk and assaulted a superior office. He was court-martialed, found guilty, and sentenced to one year in prison, but was granted executive clemency on account of past good behavior, sobriety and gallantry. From January 1865 until his honorable discharge four years later, he served on five more vessels. He re-enlisted in 1870 and served for 15 months in the North Atlantic Fleet before being forced to resign on account of having smuggled liquor on board ship.
[†] Arthur Dutton.

paper heroes whose glory has been made for them by just such men as these I have been speaking of.*

Friday evening, Jan'y 8th—We have been anxiously [waiting] for the *Newbern* which has now been due for three or four days. We want to hear from home once more. We want the mails & papers & some fresh meat & vegetables, for our larder is getting low.

The last two or three days have been quite cool—the coldest I have experienced since I have been here. A cold north west wind blowing. A thin scale of ice covered the decks this morning.

With my kind regards to all. Yours truly,

W—

No. 41—

U.S. Steamer *Florida*
At Sea, Sunday evening
Jan'y 11th, 1864

Dear Anna,

When anything unusual or of an exciting nature takes place it seems almost invariably to occur on Sunday. To day has not been an exception.

The day was ushered in by, "Sail ho, black smoke," from the mast head, followed by the quick ringing of the "Go ahead fast" bell in the engine room, the hurried hoisting of signals to the fleet below & the roar of the *9 inch occupant of the floor above me* to call their attention.

My morning nap was thus interrupted by a sort of vague impression that something had happened, I couldn't tell what. For an instant it seemed as if there had been a general smash of everything & the decks above were coming down on a visit to my room. But after a moment's pause, hearing the oft repeated & well known order, "serve, vent & sponge," I at once comprehended the origin of the uproar and then hearing the hail, "How does she bear?," I knew its cause. So I turned over to finish my nap till "John's" knock at my door & his "Seven bells, sir" once more roused me to get ready for breakfast.† I must say that being suddenly startled from a sound sleep by the explosion of 10 or 12 pounds of powder in a shotted gun, directly over one's head with only a few inches of wood intervening, is not the most agreeable of sensations.

Upon going on deck after breakfast to take a look at the prize (in prospective) I could see just the faintest trace of a small shadowy cloud on the far off horizon which to unaccustomed eyes would have been undiscernable. We kept up the chase till towards noon, the small cloud growing "smaller by

---

* Although neither men's exploits are mentioned in the official reports, Fader's are described in detail in his testimony at his court martial in December 1864.

† Possibly 1st class boy John Mulligan, the 17-year old butcher from New York City who appears on the *Florida*'s muster rolls starting March 1863.

degrees & beautifully less,"* a very conclusive indication that, to say the least, we were not gaining on it, so we returned to our station.

While at dinner the cry of the morning from the mast head was repeated & in a little while another sail was reported by the same lookout as apparently being in chase of the first. We were soon under way & carried the news down to the fleet who were soon all in chase.

In a short time still another sail was descried & in a position (should it be one of our vessels) to head the blockade runner off from the sea, in which direction he was endeavouring to escape. The respective positions & courses of the different vessels soon brought them all in view from our decks, the last discovered & seaward one proving to be the *Newbern* on her way around from the "South Side."

This placed the chase in our power, for the *Newbern* cut her off from sea, the *Mount Vernon* was behind her preventing her escape in that direction, while the remainder of the fleet kept her from running on the beach or under the forts & ahead of her was the "Frying Pan Shoals" extending out to sea some twenty miles from the extremity of Cape Fear.

It was by this time a little dusk & we all felt jolly enough over our prize money & counted ourselves some dollars richer, certainly. We were now about four miles nearly astern & the chase had changed her course so as to bring the *Newbern* on one side (or as sailors say on her port beam) while the *Mt. Vernon* was on the other side but further astern.

The *Newbern* had got within range & opened fire which was soon echoed by the *Mt. Vernon*, the three vessels running in nearly parallel lines slightly converging to a point—the edge of the shoals. The rest of the fleet were all still behind & out of range, we being the headmost.

A dense cloud of black smoke floated above the chase, in the midst of which & over her decks & on all sides of her, the flash of bursting shells, which were poured into her from each side, could be plainly seen. She was evidently having a hot time of it & we expected every moment to see her heave to in token of surrender.

It was now so dark that we could see nothing ahead of us but the flash of the guns and bursting shells & still steamed on followed by the fleet. In a little while the firing ceased but whether from the surrender of the chase or her escape in the darkness, of course we could not tell.

We stood out to sea followed as it seems by the most of the fleet & it seems were mistaken by them for the blockade runner for they all bore down on us during the night burning challenge lights.

The *Newbern* came in this morning & reported that the chase had escaped her when escape seemed impossible by running across the [Frying Pan] shoals, or through a passage which has never been used by our vessels being deemed difficult & dangerous. The *Newbern* at the time was within 1200 yards

---

* Misquoted line from *Henry and Emma* by English poet Matthew Prior (1709).

Civil War Years: USS *Florida* (1863-1865)

of her & kept on after her through the passage but slackened her speed for fear of getting aground, so that the chase was soon hidden in the increasing darkness. After getting through the shoals, the chase was no where to be seen & of course nothing more was to be done. The *Mount Vernon* in essaying to follow through the shoals run aground but was got off.

I was very much disappointed in not getting letters from home by the *Newbern*, my latest date from you being Dec. 17th which was rec'd Dec. 27th. I think you must have written but for some reason it has failed to reach me. I rec'd one from Henry containing no news of consequence. He did not go to New York to spend the holidays, as he did not hear from Uncle Brush in reply to his enquiry if it would be convenient for him to come.

Tuesday, 13th—The Flag Ship *Minnesota* with the Admiral came around from the "South Side" to day bringing the news that the chase of Sunday night had been run ashore & destroyed by our vessels, also that three others during the week had shared the same fate, one of them a large new side wheel steamer with a very valuable cargo.

The *Iron Age*, one of our gun boats, in attempting to get off one of the blockade runners, got ashore & after three or four days of fruitless attempts to get her off we were obliged to destroy her. We saw the explosion of her magazine last Sunday night but did not know at the time what it was.

Thursday, 14th—The *Tuscarora* came down to day with a small mail. No letters for me however from home. I am getting anxious to hear from you all. The *Minnesota* goes up to morrow & I shall send this by her.

We expect to go to Beaufort in about a week. You will hear from me from there. With love to you all. Good bye.

W—

No. 42—

U.S. Steamer *Florida*
At Sea
Jan'y 16th, 1864

Dear Anna,

Nothing I believe has happened to day to disturb our Sunday quiet. We are now on our way to Beaufort for coal & provisions. I don't know how true it is but many of us think that this will be our last visit to that land of sand & "snuff dippers." The opinion is that we shall soon be ordered home for repairs, in which case the vessel will go out of commission and I hope the Paymaster as well as the other officers will have an opportunity to see home & friends once more.

A year will soon be up now since we left New York & all on board are beginning to look forward to our return. Only two of our Ward Room officers, besides myself, are left of those who left New York in the vessel.

Off Wilmington (December 1863 to March 1864)

The others have been detached at different times & ordered elsewhere or have been sent home sick.

I did hope, & do now, that we shall be here long enough to "lend a hand" in taking Wilmington & its defences, though appearances do not promise an early movement in this direction.

The blockade now is something besides a "mere paper one" as the numerous wrecks scattered along the beach, both on the north & south side, can attest. We know of but one vessel getting in in the last month & she run in last Sunday night while we were in chase of another, an account of which I gave you in my last and as I have nothing of a very exciting kind to fill my sheet with this time I will give you an adventure of Paymaster Clarke* of the *Shenandoah* [*Tuscarora*] on that night.

The day (last Sunday) being pleasant he thought he would take a boat & cross the [Frying Pan] shoals to visit some of the vessels which lay on the south side. He had got nearly across when some of them, the nearest ones, got under way. But he continued on, hoping to reach some of those farther off, but they too moved off, leaving only one or two, but too distant to reach, it being then late in the day. He headed his boat around & recrossed the shoals to go back to his ship. This was just as the blockade runner hove in sight & every vessel had just started after it, his own among the rest, so that nothing was left him but to retrace his way across the shoals once more & endeavour to get on board some of the vessels lying there.

It was now dark & by the time he had got across no vessels were to be seen, so he had no choice but to pass the night in his open boat which could not have been very agreeable for he had eaten nothing since breakfast & the water was quite rough & the night cold. Moreover an open boat is not the most convenient place to dispose of one's body for sleep, with nothing but the ordinary clothing to keep off spray & wind.

Towards morning he said he heard a vessel coming and, as he was out of the track of our gun boats, knew it could not be one of them. It bore right down for him & it was only by skillful management of the boat that he was not run down by the blockade runner, for such she was & got safely in—the only one for a long time that we know of. Mr. Clarke crossed the shoals once more in the morning & got on board his vessel satisfied with his first night's experience in an open boat at sea.

Wednesday evening, 20th—Beaufort. We have been lying outside the bar here ever since last Sunday morning, the wind blowing a gale & raising so heavy a swell on the bar as to prevent our crossing it. We are now in & lying

---

* Ambrose J. Clark (1836-1892). Son of a Republican Congressman from Watertown, NY, he was a private in the 35th New York Infantry before being appointed assistant paymaster in the Navy in September 1861. He served on the USS *Tuscarora* for three years, searching for Confederate raiders off the coasts of England and France from December 1861 to October 1863. Clark's postwar career saw him rise to the rank of pay inspector.

quietly at anchor once more under fort Macon. Quite a number of our vessels are here, among others the *State of Georgia* with the small pox on board.

We found quite a large mail here waiting us which I assure you was welcome enough, though I felt sad to hear of Father's sickness. Among other matter I received a LaSalle & Chicago paper from you.

What a winter you have had. While I am sorry for your sakes I cannot but feel glad that I have escaped such a fall of mercury. In looking over the log of the vessel I find the lowest the thermometer has been is 28°—this is taken every hour, night & day. What a time they have had on the railroad, blocked up with snow & ice. It must have occasioned severe suffering in many parts of the country.

I see by the papers that Gen. Wild has been making a raid through some portions of North Carolina with some portions of his colored troops.* They must be some of those I saw at Newbern last summer, & from the accounts I read in the papers have fully justified the opinion I then expressed of them. I find that the opinion of army officers is very much changed in regard to negro troops the last year. Many who a few months ago would have scouted† the very idea of a black soldier would now be very glad to lead them into battle.

Sunday evening, 24th—I went ashore to Beaufort this morning & attended church in company with some of the other officers. It was the Episcopal service & I can't say that I found it very interesting, but I heard a good union man pray for the President, one too who had continued to pray for him from the commencement of the war till turned out of his house by the traitors, but he remained true to the Union notwithstanding all their persecutions till our flag was again raised here & gave him protection.‡ The congregation was not very large, composed mostly of northern people—officers of the army & navy, merchants, sutlers &c with their wives.

Yesterday we gave a dinner party to the officers from the fort & had quite a pleasant time. It is a Mass. regiment quartered here, most of the officers being from that state. We find them very agreeable companions & moreover it is very convenient to have an acquaintance at whose quarters you can loaf a while when on shore & time begins to hang heavy on our hands.

---

* Brigadier General Edward A. Wild. The 39-year abolitionist commanded a brigade of African-American soldiers that included the 1st North Carolina Colored Volunteers led by Keeler's friend James Beecher. After losing an arm at the Battle of South Mountain in September 1862, Wild returned to Massachusetts where he recruited his brigade. In the winter of 1863-64 they freed hundreds of slaves in eastern North Carolina, many of whom joined the brigade. Based in Norfolk his troops went as far south as South Mills, NC, and occupied Elizabeth City for a week, terrorizing the white inhabitants as they went.
† Rejected with disdain.
‡ St. Paul's Episcopal, built in 1857 and still in use. David D. Van Antwerp, the church's first rector, was the "good union man" Keeler was referring to.

Off Wilmington (December 1863 to March 1864)

We expect to leave here in two or three days for the blockade once more. That our fleet are not idle there you will see by the slip of paper which I enclose. There are many more vessels which should be added.

Good bye. My love to all.

Yours,
William

[Marginalia] I wrote you a short note immediately upon the rec't of yours informing me of Father's sickness. I hope this will find him living.* Remember me to him with my kindest love—to mother & all. A kiss to yourself & the children.

No. 43—

U.S. Steamer Florida
At Sea
Jan'y 28th, 1864

Dear Anna,

We left Beaufort this morning and are now once more on our way to our station. We had beautiful weather during our stay there, more like our early summer weather than anything else I can compare it to. I hoped to have heard from you again before I left but did not, but shall look anxiously for a letter by the next steamer that comes down.

Transports were arriving loaded with troops while we lay at Beaufort & it is the opinion of the army officers there that the movement on Wilmington of which I spoke in one of my former letters will take place as soon as settled spring weather will admit, if indeed the Union persons in North Carolina don't take it into their own hands before that time & so save us the trouble.† A body of our troops were sent out yesterday towards Swansborough on a reconnoissance as a sort of feeler in that direction.

If the papers which we received to day on our way down here from the *S. R. Spaulding* are to be believed, things look gloomy enough in rebeldom. It seems as if they were preparing to make one last de[s]perate effort in the spring, which I hope will be their dying struggle. After that the war will probably degenerate into a guerrilla warfare. How welcome the news of peace will be both north as well as south. But however gladly it may be received & how welcome it may be, I have no desire to hear it proclaimed till the last vestige of rebellion has disappeared.

I am reading *Gen. Butler in New Orleans* which I find one of the most interesting works upon the war I have read. It relates to his administration of affairs while commanding that department & of course eulogises him highly

---

* His father died on February 9, 1864. Keeler would have been notified about his death when he was recovering from his wound and unable to write.
† The movement on Wilmington did not happen until late in the year.

but I cannot help but think that he was the right man in the right place.* I wish I could send it to you to read when I am through—you would like it I know. I have quite a number of good books which I mean to send home the first chance I have. I only wish you had them now to help you pass away the long winter evenings.

I took advantage of the fine weather one day before we left Beaufort to go with a number of others on a clam roast to the same sandy island [Harkers Island] that we went to for the same purpose once before.† This time we landed on the beach some miles from the scene of our former visit. The island seems to bear the same general appearance here as elsewhere. The only peculiarity about our visit on this occasion was a call on "Aunt Peggy" & I wish you could have been a witness to it.‡

The house was made of rough board from the common yellow pine of the country, with cracks on all sides through which the chickens could almost run—one room which answered for kitchen, chamber & parlour for the family, which I should have said were some of the "poor white trash" of the country & consisted as far as I could see of "Aunt Peggy" & two daughters, one of whom was married & her husband & three children went to make up the occupants of the single room. Two rough bedsteads, three chairs & a rough pine table comprised the furniture.

Upon showing ourselves at the door, Aunt Peggy invited us to "walk in gentleman" & take some chairs. As I found that five of us couldn't comfortably be seated in three chairs I was upon the point [of] seating myself upon one of the beds when Aunt Peggy rushed up with "Oh don't set on the baby," to which very reasonable request I of course assented & turning down a corner of the quilt brought to light a very pretty plump blue eyed baby. The women however like most all others that I have seen at the south were thin, pale & sallow—nothing like beauty about them.

The two beds, which looked as if they had been "slept in forever & never made up," occupied one end of the room. Opposite was the rude fire place, the hearth strewn with a motley collection of pine chips, dead embers, live coals & oyster shells, flanked by an old iron teakettle & a lazy dog.

An application to "Aunt Peggy" for some water brought forth a reply something after this fashion—"Reckon there ain't any. Dis yere tide's so low it's all gin out, but I kin give yer some right smart yaupon," at the same time catching up§ the aforesaid teakettle & a bowl no ways remarkable for cleanliness. "Yaupon" is a tea made from a shrub of the same name which grows in great abundance in the sandy soil. My curiosity to taste the beverage was

---

* James Parton's 650-page book was published in 1864.
† See letter of December 10, 1863.
‡ Aunt Peggy is none other than Margaret Lewis. Born in about 1812, she lived on Harkers Island. She was illiterate and poor; her personal estate in 1860 was $25. Living with her in 1860 was her 20-year old nephew(?) and his wife, who were also illiterate, and two others.
§ Grabbing.

OFF WILMINGTON (DECEMBER 1863 TO MARCH 1864)

conquered by conscientious scruples against consuming more than "my peck of dirt." Some of the others who were not detered by *trifles* declared it tasted like a mingling of sage, catnip & boneset, flavored with quinine.

I suppose they were fair specimens of the poor whites of the south. They declared themselves good Union folks, & I think truly so.

Sunday evening, 31st—Here we are back on our station once more & here we will probably remain for six weeks to come unless something unforeseen should occur. The weather is clear, warm & beautiful, so summerlike that we need no fires.

A boat load of refugees came off to us night before last & another instalment last night—driven out by the conscription which I should think from their description was dragging every man into the army who can carry a musket. They brought off the previous day's Richmond & Wilmington papers from which we got *later news from New York than any we have received through our own papers.* By these papers I see that the most stringent measures are taken to prevent any one leaving the shore or escaping in any way. An advertisement warns any person against going out in a small boat without a special permit, under penalty of being shot as a deserter.

They bring off with them considerable sums with them in specie—from 200 to 1000 dollars—some small amounts in green backs & some of them have from 1000 to 3000 dollars in No. Carolina bank notes. They all knew enough to dispose of their Confederate rags before leaving, exchanging it at the rate of from 20 to 25 dollars for one of gold—a valuable currency that. One party came off armed with two double guns & a number of pistols, declaring that they intended to fight their way through the guards if necessary.

No letter from home yet. I am anxiously looking for one & hope I shan't be disappointed when the *Newbern*, which is now overdue, arrives.

My best love to all friends & many kisses to yourself & the little ones.

William

[Marginalia] Tuesday evening, Feb'y 2nd—A blockade runner, *Wild Dayrell*, hard & fast ashore. We are trying hard to get her off. Will send particulars in my next.

No. 44*—

U.S. Steamer Florida
Off Wilmington, N.C.
Feb'y 4th, 1864

Dear Anna,

As I hinted in my last, which I sent you yesterday by the *Newbern*, I have something to write about, some material from which to make a letter without cudgeling my brains for something to say.

---

* The sheet marked No. 45 was included in this letter.

Civil War Years: USS *Florida* (1863-1865)

Day before yesterday our lookout aloft reported a sail a long distance up the coast. It was just as a thick fog cleared away which had been hanging over the water for the last two days, so dense that objects twenty feet from the vessel were scarcely discernable. Only one of our fleet was in sight, the *Cambridge*. We signalised to her, "strange sail in sight," & started in chase.

We found upon coming up with the stranger that it was one of our gun boats, the *Sassacus*, lying near the shore & close by on the smooth sandy beach another beautiful side wheel iron steamer whose peculiar build & shape & John Bull look betrayed at once her business.* For a long distance up & down the shore the beach was strewn with boxes, bales & packages of various sizes. She was lying partly on her side & the heavy swells rolling in dashed against her with sufficient violence to send the spray over her in sheets. The *Sassacus* had a hawser fast to her & was trying to pull her off.

Our great draft of water prevented our approaching her as near as the *S*. which drew about half as much as ourselves. Our boats however were soon lowered & a hawser run out to the *S*., an operation by the way consuming a good deal of time & requiring some hard labour. At dusk everything was ready & both vessels started. A good steady strain was on the hawser & every one was looking to see the stranded vessel start for deeper water, when snap went one of the hawsers measuring ten inches in circumference. The tide was falling & it was too late to do anything more that night so our anchor was let go & all turned in, whose duties would allow, to plan for to morrow & dream of prize money.

At the earliest dawn our anchor was up. We had taken a new position & all hands were engaged in running new lines for making fast to the prize once more. After breakfast, much to my gratification, Capt. Crosby gave me charge of one of the boats for the purpose of carrying orders back & forth between the vessels & rendering such other assistance as might be necessary.

My first effort however to reach the prize, on which we had already placed about one hundred men, came near being disastrous, for in crossing the bar, over which the surf rolled heavily, & on the other side of which lay the prize, the boat struck heavily & was only prevented from being swamped & capsized by the men jumping overboard & dragging her across the bar.

It appears that the *Wild Dayrell*, for that was her name, had run ashore in the fog (of which I have spoken) the day previous & when discovered by the *Sassacus* had thrown overboard & landed a large portion of her cargo & otherwise lightened her & were endeavouring to get her off. Upon the approach of the *S*. her crew all left her. A fire which they kindled in her to destroy her went out before she was boarded by the *S*. She was a new iron steamer, of beautiful model, built for the express purpose of running the blockade, this being her first trip.

---

* This was the *Wild Dayrell*. Built on the River Mersey in north-west England in 1863, she was run ashore about nine miles north of Masonboro Inlet.

Off Wilmington (December 1863 to March 1864)

Upon getting on board I found as I have stated that a large part of her cargo had been thrown overboard & lay scattered along the beach. Still a large quantity of goods remained on board, consisting mostly of coarse army shoes & blankets & writing paper. All our efforts were at once directed towards lightening her by throwing overboard her coal & the least valuable portion of her cargo & making fast to her with large heavy hawsers, hoping to be able to pull her off at the next high tide. The vessel lay on the smooth sandy bar in three or four feet of water, the surf rolling by her in swells which made it dangerous for our boats & occasionally breaking over her side.

I was looking into the water watching the huge hawser as our men hauled it slowly in, when the thud thud of rifle balls against the iron side of the vessel & the shrill shriek of a Whitworth bolt over our heads gave us the first intimation that there were interested spectators on shore. We could just see the slight puffs of smoke from their guns as they rose from behind the distant sand piles.

A boat's crew from the *Sassacus* who were on board instantly jumped into their boat & made for their vessel, the officer in charge remarking that their orders were to return instantly if the enemy opened fire on them. Our men never flinched nor was the hawser checked in its slow progress. Our vessels in the meantime opened with their heavy guns, but I think with no other effect than to make the sand fly right merrily, for those piles of sand afford the best protection against the shell from our large guns. At any rate the enemy managed to get in a shot now & then, notwithstanding our shells [which] were bursting among the sand piles which sheltered them.

I took my boat & returned to the ship for orders, a rifle ball every now & then whistling over our heads or spattering into the water alongside. I made three or four trips back & forth in this way till finally just as I was leaving the ship the last time, the *S.*, to which one end of the hawser was made fast, for some reason unknown to us started ahead & the other end of the hawser not being sufficiently secured on board the prize, it parted again but not till she [the prize] had been started a number of feet towards deeper water & all thought she was once more afloat, but of course as soon as the hawser parted her progress was checked.

The tide was just beginning to fall so any further effort then was considered useless. Capt. Crosby made up his mind to destroy her & gave me orders to that effect, telling me to see that she was well on fire in every part before leaving her, adding to let the men bring away anything that they considered of any value to them. Of course this was free license to plunder & it was amusing to see them go at it, nor were the officers much behind. The *S.* however had had the start of us, her crew having been stripping her of everything they considered of any value all the previous day.

Civil War Years: USS *Florida* (1863-1865)

The scene of waste & destruction on board exceeded if possible that of the *Calypso* at the time of her capture.* Boxes, barrels & casks were smashed open with axes & iron bars, bales of calicoes & blankets ripped open with knives, each one helping himself to what he wanted of the contents, scattering them over the decks, throwing them in the water & crushing them under foot.

Here a jack tar is rushing across the deck, his arms full of pieces of calico when his eye is caught by an unopened box just thrown out of the hold. Down goes the dry goods upon the deck among coal, water, oil and molasses & catching up a heavy hammer he brings it down upon the box with a force which not only crushes in the top but drives it to the bottom through bottles of quinine with which the box is filled. Catching up a bottle—"damn the medicine"—& in he jumps half up to his knees in quinine, completing the destruction which the hammer had commenced.

Another has slashed open a bag of coffee & catching it by the corners is draging it about the deck making a liberal outpouring of its contents, while another follows with a barrel of crushed sugar which he has summarily unheaded & is "putting in the sweetning." Others are pelting each other with oranges from some barrels which they have discovered, while another party are smashing bottles of preserved fruits on the ship's bell.

Here are some who have got a huge box of shoes upon the deck & are scooping them out by armsfull & throwing them over the side, some falling into the water & a portion into the boats & others having ripped open bales of blankets are tossing them in confusion over the side, the water and boats each getting an allowance. Another exhibits his destructiveness by hammering away upon the machinery with a heavy sledge, filling up intervals of time by smashing windows, looking glasses and crockery, winding up by making a wreck of the steam whistle.

Another has discovered a box consigned to some unlucky secesh milliner & has ornamented his cap with wreaths of artificial flowers, while ribbons & laces are fluttering about his neck. Here are some who have dragged to light some boxes of choice perfumery & breaking the bottles against each other are showering a comrade whom *spirits* have made incapable of resistance. Tired of this they pitch into boxes of guava jelly, distributing the contents with a liberality only equaled by the abundant supply.

Other parties in the holds are tossing up through the open hatches packages of pins, tape & threads, reams of writing paper, buttons, felt hats, braid, pieces of calico, percussion caps, cans of preserved meats & vegetables, hams, packages of shirts, cheeses, boxes of sardines & matches, bottles of pickles & sauces, & all apparently without any care or expectation of their being saved from the wreck.

---

* See letter of June 12, 1863.

Off Wilmington (December 1863 to March 1864)

The constant tramp of many feet over all these articles as they are thrown up & scattered about the deck is working them up in one confused, mixed, & indistinguishable mass which it is impossible either to imagine or describe. Another party in the cabin are making the plate glass mirrors a target for cut glass tumblers & decanters, the jingle of broken glass mingling with shouts of laughter at a "splendid shot."

Others again more careful & prudent are hastily gathering up what they consider the most valuable & throwing them into the boats which are pitching & tossing alongside, searching every part of the vessel for unopened boxes or packages of undiscovered treasures.

The sharp shooters from the shore have not forgotten us as an occasional whistle of their leaden messengers attest, accompanied at intervals by the shriek of the Whitworth bolts from the more distant sand hills. They are replied to by the deeper roar of the guns of our two vessels & the crash of their shells as the[y] burst among the piles of sand which shelter the foe.

All this may seem to you unnatural & exagerated, but I assure you I was a witness to it all & instead of being overdrawn it seems only to convey a faint picture of the reality.

The boats were in a short time loaded as deep as was safe, a few drunken ones were deposited on the top of their assorted cargoes. The crews [were] ordered in to return to the ship, leaving only Mr. McGowan, our Chief Engineer [McLean], & myself with my boat's crew to complete the work of destruction. Fires had for some time been burning in the furnaces to destroy the boilers from which the water had been allowed to escape. I took some boxes of matches, gathered up some of the loose quires of paper with which the deck was strewed & went into the cabin as the point at which my fire was to be started, others selected such other parts of the vessel as they thought most fit. I broke up some rosewood chairs & the arms of a sofa & piled them up against a mahogany sideboard as kindling wood. Over & around this I piled sperm candles & over all poured a liberal supply of oil.

When every preparation was made the word was passed, "Are you all ready?" "Then fire," & the ill fated vessel was fired in six or seven different places simultaneously. At first, faint blue colums of smoke floated lazily up, then growing whiter and thicker & more & more dense, then a tongue of flame shot out from an open door, a broken window or a hatchway, quickly followed by another & another & another till a huge column shot up roaring & crakling as it fiercely licked up the more combustible parts. My boat's crew were all ordered into the boat as soon as the torch was applied & with the other two officers I waited only to see the Capt.'s orders executed, that she was "thoroughly fired in every part," before we left. The flames crept rapidly over her & in a short time she was blazing fiercely nearly her whole length. We crept to the outermost edge of the guard, underneath which our boat was tossing on the rollers, to escape the heat. Just as we shoved off, the shrill shriek of a Whitworth bolt mingled with the roar of the flames as the missile passed through the paddle box just over our heads.

As soon as we were well clear of her, both vessels opened on the burning wreck with their heavy guns, & shot & shell went crashing through the iron hull scattering the fragments & effectually completing the work of destruction. We remained at anchor till near midnight when her wood work was mostly consumed, & the iron hull a bright glowing red & out of it a bright tongue of flame & a cloud of sparks would occasionally shoot up as the remaining cargo smouldered & burned.

The next morning found us down to the fleet to make a report of our proceedings & talk over with numerous visitors from the other vessels the events of the two previous days. We found the *Newbern* there with fresh meat and vegetables & what was better, with a mail. But no letter from home. What is the matter? My latest date from you is Jan'y 5th & I know you have written, or if not that you have some good excuse. But I do so want to hear from home. Love & kisses to all.

Will

[Marginalia] I haven't done with blockade runners yet, as you will learn by my next.

No. 46—

U.S. Steamer *Florida*
Beaufort, N.C.
March 2nd, 1864

Dear Anna,

After this long interval, with only now & then a note to let you know how I was getting along, I know that you will be glad to see that I have once more resumed the pen.* I must try & go back & take up the train of events where I left off, risking some repetitions, for I have almost forgotten where I was when a rebel shell obliged me to drop my correspondence.

I think I closed with the destruction of the *Wild Dayrell*. We got but little out of her that would be of use in a family as she had been pretty thoroughly overhauled by the *Sassacus* & but little was left in her except coarse army blankets & shoes, cheap mourning calicoes, paper & a few other articles. Yes, there was one other thing—liquor. Officers went on board and broke over 100 five gallon demijons of choice liquors before the men were permitted to go on her decks. It was the only way to keep it away from them. Liquors pay a very large profit to the blockade runners & most of them carry large quantities of it.

---

* Keeler had been unable to write since he was wounded on February 10. The brief notes he sent to Anna saying how he was faring, which were penned by his clerk, have not survived.

OFF WILMINGTON (DECEMBER 1863 TO MARCH 1864)

After seeing the destruction of the *Wild Dayrell* complete we left for the fleet to make a report of our proceedings. We remained there all the next day & then received orders to cruise between our former station (off Masonborough inlet) & Bogue inlet (which is 22 miles below the entrance to Beaufort harbour) through the day, lying off Masonborough inlet through the night.

The next morning we started early for the upper end of our station, reaching the wreck of *Wild Dayrell* a little after sunrise. Capt. Crosby thought he would run in & fire a shot or two at her & see how she looked. I stood on the hurricane deck with a number of the officers watching the effect of our shells when a shrill shriek just over our heads, a ringing blow & scattered pieces of metal made us all look up to see a hole about the size of my arm through our smoke stack made by a Whitworth bolt fired from a field piece a long distance back from the beach. One of the men standing a little ways behind me was struck on the breast by a rivet head knocked out of the smoke stack. It penetrated to the ribs & glanced downwards about two inches. Of course we didn't remain long in that position, as nothing was to be gained by staying there a target for their long range guns—our mission had already been accomplished.

Towards noon another sail was raised up the coast which proved to be the *Sassacus* again with another blockade runner ashore—the *Nutfield*. The *S.* had a hawser fast to her & was trying to pull her off. Of course she was a prize to the *S.* & we could not interfere unless our assistance was asked by them. They told us they could not get her off & were going to destroy her—their boats were already passing back and forth loaded with plunder. Capt. Crosby asked them if they would let him try & get her off. No, she was their prize & they intended doing as they pleased with her. They wouldn't even give us a chance to send our boats to her to get anything, but applied the torch & she was soon in flames when both vessels opened on her with their guns.

She had on a heavy head of steam & when one of our shot struck her boilers the effect was grand. She was instantly enveloped in a dense white cloud from out of which was projected sticks & timbers & pieces of the wreck falling in a shower upon the water on all sides of her. Slowly the enveloping vapour passed away & disclosed the naked hull with decks, spars & the lighter portions of her wood work shattered by the force of the explosion which had strewn the water with fragments of the wreck. For a time it seemed as if the dense body of steam had extinguished the fire but the flames in a little while raged more furiously than before & when we left her, a little after dark, the iron hull was a bright glowing red.

We all thought she might have been got off had proper exertions been made, but the *Sassacus*, as I have said, claimed her as her prize & would allow us no opportunity to try & save her. She was a large, iron, side wheel steamer—new, this being her first trip & had a very valuable cargo of Enfield rifles, field pieces & a large amount of valuable merchandise. She undoubtedly would have proved one of the most valuable captures of the war.

We all felt provoked at such a "dog in the manger" operation—they would neither get her off themselves nor allow us. I think the Department will hear of it. I suppose her officers really made more in the way of plunder than their prize money would have amounted to had they got her off & this may be the reason why they were so anxious to destroy her. From what I have heard they must have got a large quantity of rich silks & cloths & other valuable articles from her.

In capturing a prize the law allows nothing whatever to be taken from her unless it is for the better preservation of the articles or unless they are required for use on the vessel making the capture. Any on[e] breaking this law forfeits his prize money. If for any reason we are obliged to destroy the vessel we get nothing in the way of prize money, but most of the commanding officers will in such cases allow the officers & men to take what they want. Some however will allow nothing to be taken but destroy vessel & cargo.

But to return. We got down to Masonborough inlet towards morning & found the blockade runner *Dee* burning. She had been chased ashore & fired by the *Cambridge*. This is making quick work with the property of our *neutral* English cousins. Some of them will come to grief through our operations of the last few days. I have "more of the same sort" to tell, but will reserve it for my next. Till then with much love. Good bye.

W—

[Marginalia] My back is getting along finely. The Dr. says in a few weeks the wounds will be entirely healed. Remember me to Mother, Sarah, Fan & Dave & a kiss to the little ones.

No. 47*—

U.S. Steamer Florida
Beaufort, N.C.
March 3rd, 1864

Dear Anna,

When I mailed my last we were expecting to leave here that day or the next but here we are still. The rebels are said to be in great force in the vicinity of Newbern & are daily expected to make an attack on that place & also [Little] Washington & Plymouth.† If successful they will probably make an attempt here. Their number is variously estimated from 20 to 35000 to

---

* The sheet marked No. 48 was included in this letter.
† Confederate forces attacked the Union garrison at Plymouth, NC on April 17. After a four-day combined operation, which included use of the ironclad ram CSS *Albemarle*, the garrison surrendered.

Off Wilmington (December 1863 to March 1864)

oppose which Gen. Peck* has but about 4000 men at Newbern but he is very strongly intrenched & has the aid of the gun boats in the Trent & Neuse rivers. The rebs are no doubt very anxious to repossess themselves of this place & Fort Macon & should they be successful at Newbern they will make a strong effort here.

We are kept here, in daily or rather hourly expectation of a fight coming off, to aid the fort & land forces in their defence. There is a "big scare" in Beaufort. Women are seeking shelter in the fort, merchants have their goods packed up, the streets are barricaded. Every man capable of carrying a musket has the choice given him to drill a certain number of hours every day or be locked up in the guard house. I am not able to leave the ship but I frequently hear our officers laughing at the motley crowd forced out to drill. Merchants, sutlers, idlers, loafers, gamblers, whiskey sellers & whiskey drinkers all have come to the "shoulder arms."

At night all our gun boats send out their boats with armed crews & howitzers on picket & guard duty. We lie with our guns trained on the railroad above Morehead city from which direction it is supposed the attack will be made. I hope the rebs will "try it on" while we are here. I want to see the style of their reception. We have the means of making it a warm one.

So much for the present, now for the past. On the 10th of last month (a day or two after the events related in my last) with the first dawn of morning I was awakened by the springing of the rattle, followed by the hurried tread of feet over my head & in a few moments by the discharge of our howitzer. I felt sure that work was on hand & I was soon up & in my *working dress* on deck. Sure enough, on the beach close by us but barely visible in the early dawn was a blockade runner. Our boats were soon lowered. One proceeded immediately to her to take possession while the others were running a hawser to pull her off.

As it grew lighter we could see the wreck of the *Dee* about 300 yards above the *Fannie & Jennie*, for that was her name, but better still & to our surprise there was another blockade runner, the *Emily*, beached about 300 yards above the *Dee*. Some of our boats were instantly dispatched to her to ascertain her situation. They soon returned with the information that she was deserted & could easily be got off. By this time it was broad daylight. We knew that what we did must be done quickly for we should soon be discovered by the rebel batteries & sharp shooters ashore. We had just given a pull on the hawser made fast to the *Fanny & Jennie* & parted it without starting her. Capt. Crosby told me that I could take a boat to the *Emily* to take possession of her till he could get a hawser to her to pull her off.

I stood on the guard of the vessel preparing to get into the boat when I heard a crash in the wheel house† (by the side of which I stood), an explosion

---

* John J. Peck, commander of the District of North Carolina.
† The structure holding *Florida*'s paddle wheels.

Civil War Years: USS *Florida* (1863-1865)

& at the same instant received a severe crushing blow in the back. For an instant all was blank. I sank to my feet & should have fallen overboard had I not had hold of the line which surrounds the guard. I knew I was wounded. I put my hand to my back, found my clothes torn away & the flesh raw & bloody & I am free to confess I was frightened. I knew not how badly I was injured. I felt but little pain but I did not know but it was the deadening insensibility which sometimes follows a mortal wound.

The Dr. happened to be standing by me & with him I went down to the cockpit where my clothes were taken off & I soon had the comforting assurance that it was "a severe flesh wound but no internal injuries." The shell exploded inside the wheel house within five or six feet of me, the fragments flying on all sides of me. Had my position been varied two or three inches in any direction I should have been killed. Splinters from the wheelhouse were thrown against the side of my face, scratching it some, but the only severe injury was on my back. The piece of shell just passed over the spine & entered the flesh on the left side ploughing out a furrow about an inch deep, one & a half wide & four inches long. Just below the cut was a bruise about the size of the palm of your hand & another of about the same size on the right side of the spine. They were the most dangerous & painful. The flesh sloughed off & the suppuration weakened me very much. They were deep but are now rapidly filling up & I hope in two or three weeks' time to be as good as new.

For the first week or ten days I suffered intensely. The jar of the engines & the motion of the vessel as it rolled from side to side gave me the most excruciating pain—& oh the long, long nights with no one but my boy John to watch with me & him snoring on the floor, I would most gladly have skipped them. I must either sit bolt upright or lie stretched out on my face & the change of position was like passing a knife through me. Sleep for the first few nights was out of the question, & those nights seemed lengthened into years. I assure you I have no desire to repeat my experience. My friends here try to console me with the idea of honorable scars &c but I think I paid pretty dear for the whistle. I don't want any more at the same price. What followed after I was hurt I only know from others.

Capt. Crosby saw that it was only risking life to attempt to get the vessels off &, very properly considering that both of them was not worth one life, very properly gave the order to destroy them. Our lookouts from aloft could see boat loads of sharp shooters crossing the inland sound which runs paralell with & but a short distance back from the beach, & every few minutes the Whitworth shells were either plumping into us or the blockade runners or passing over our boats. We were struck four times.

Our boats were hurried to the *Fanny & Jenny* & twenty five prisoners remaining on board of her were speedily transfered to us when she was fired. Another boat in the meantime had boarded the *Emily* & she too was speedily

Off Wilmington (December 1863 to March 1864)

in flames. Her crew had all escaped to the shore or had been drowned in the attempt, their bodies were tossing in the turf.

The sharp shooters had reached the sand heaps back of the beach & as our last boats shoved off they were saluted with a shower of balls. Fortunately no one was hurt, though there were many narrow escapes.

The *Cambridge* by this time had come up & lowered her boats, thinking they could put out the fire & get the vessels off. Our retreating boats met them on their way to try the experiment & cautioned them against making the attempt. They only laughed at us—knew the vessels could be got off & would shew us how it was done. They kept on in spite of our caution & received a volley from the sharp shooters which wounded every man in the foremost boat—all slightly but one who was shot through the chest. They wasn't long in getting back to their vessel & we saw just "how it was done."

Of course in such a haste there was but little time for plunder or even to examine to see what the cargo was. However while some were firing the vessel others hastily ransacked the cabins where the most valuable articles are usually found. They secured a small quantity of silks, velvets, cloths, some silver ware & one found five hundred sovereigns & another was said to have come across a large amount in bank of England notes; if he did he kept it to himself. One of the engineers which we took from the *Fanny & Jenny* told us there was a splendid sword on board sent by some English nobleman to Gen. Lee at a cost of $2500. He told us that as soon as the vessel was beached the Capt. ordered his boat lowered, went into the cabin & got the sword, remarking as he passed the engineer, "I have got to go to hell anyhow & I might as well go now as any time." In attempting to get into the boat he lost the sword overboard & the boat was soon after swamped & every one in her lost, most of them were the officers of the vessel. Some of their bodies had been drawn up on the beach, others were rolling about in the surf. A letter from the Capt.'s wife in Wilmington was found directed to him in Nassau wanting him to bring her a nice black silk dress & 5 or 6 yards of velvet. He complied with her request but I fear it will be some time before "Mrs. Coxsetter" will get her dress & velvet, for it was brought on board of us. I tried to get it for you but could not succeed.*

The *Fanny & Jenny* was an iron side wheel vessel & has been captured once before under the name of the *Scotia*. She was sold & run on the New

---

* The captain of the *Fanny and Jenny* was the "notorious" Louis M. Coxetter (1818-1873), as he was styled by Admiral Lee. Over the course of the war, he commanded a dozen different privateers and blockade runners, the first being the privateer *Jeff Davis* which captured nine merchant ships in the summer of 1861, another the blockade runner *Herald* which he renamed *Antonica* after his wife. Although Crosby's report of the destruction of the *Fanny and Jenny* states that Coxetter drowned (ORN, I:9, pp. 474-76), Southern newspapers stated that he survived. The sword he was bringing to Robert E. Lee was never found, and, if the story is true, lies several hundred yards off the Wrightsville Beach where the wreck of the *Fanny and Jenny* lies.

Civil War Years: USS *Florida* (1863-1865)

England coast for a time under the name of the *Gen. Banks*. Those engaged in running the blockade managed to get hold of her again & started her in her old business, but her career is ended now & her bones lie washing in the surf by the side of the *Emily* & the *Dee*.

Her cargo appeared to consist principally of liquors & *bacon* which proves very conclusively to my mind that food of the latter kind is not so plenty in the south as their papers would have us believe. Blockade runners are not in the habit of carrying anything but what pays them the very highest profit & government certainly would not be importing bacon if there was plenty of it in the Confederacy.

The *Emily* was a large iron screw steamer—new, this being her first trip. Her cargo seemed to be mostly salt, but after burning awhile she blew up with a heavy explosion which leaves us to think that she had a large quantity of powder on board. The salt was most likely covered over it to protect it from fire in case she was struck by a shell.

Besides the five blockade runners whose destruction I have related, we hear of the destruction & capture of three others on the "South Side," making eight in all inside of a week. It is their custom to take advantage of the absence of moonlight nights to run in, which accounts for the presence of so many of them at one time. Their deeds being evil they prefer darkness to light. With a bright moon we do not expect them.

The rebels have constructed a road running from Wilmington to Fort Fisher paralell with the beach & from two to four miles from it. At different points on this road they keep field pieces of great range [Whitworths] ready to start out on a moment's notice. The road follows the sound (of which I have spoken before) on the *inland* side which would prevent our landing a body of men at any time to take possession of them, as we would have to cross the sound to reach them.

When any of our ships drives a blockade runner ashore these guns are started out. As soon as our vessels get within range, they fire & immediately change their position so that it is impossible for us to tell where to direct our fire as we cannot at that distance discover them among the trees till a slight puff of smoke tells of their whereabouts, when their position is again changed, while we offer a fair target for them plainly seen on the water. We were struck at a distance of four miles. For reasons given above we made no attempt to drive them off but contented ourselves to do our work & get away as soon as possible.

I hope the length of this letter will make amends for my long silence. With love & kisses to yourself & the children—

W—

[Marginalia] March 4th—We left Beaufort to day. No fighting yet. As we left another prize was going in—the *Cumberland*, a prize to the *De Sota* [*De Soto*].

Off Wilmington (December 1863 to March 1864)

No. 49—

                                      U.S. Steamer *Florida*
                                      Off Wilmington, N.C.
                                            March 6th, 1864

Dear Anna,

    Sunday is noticable down here as a day of excitements. Something or other seems to "turn up" on that day if on no others. To day the *Monticello* ran into the *Peterhoff* (a prize fitted up for a gun boat), sinking her in a few minutes. It was early in the morning, just light & the vessels were on their night stations under Fort Fisher (about a mile & a half from it). We were about a mile from the vessels at the time of the accident & immediately steamed up to them & sent our boats to their assistance. The officers and men barely had time to get into the boats when the *Peterhoff* went down in five fathoms of water. Fortunately no lives were lost. We were within easy range of the guns of the fort & batteries but they did not open on us. Why [not], we can't imagine.

    We have all the crew & some of the officers [of the *Peterhoff*] on board of us which adds about 120 to my family. They will stay but a few days, till they can be transfered to other vessels. Mr. Dunham*, the Paymaster, had but just entered the service. He thinks it a pretty hard start.

    I fear that Henry's expectations in his letter you sent me about my coming home in a week or two will not be realised. We have got to go somewhere for repairs soon, but I fear they will send us to Norfolk & patch us up as they did last fall & then send us back here for five or six months longer. This however is only a surmise. No one on board really knows anything about it.

    In my present state I could go home at any time on a sick leave by simply making the request, but I haven't strength at present to reach home & where else should I go unless to a hospital, which I don't care to do. Then when able to do duty again I might be ordered to some small uncomfortable vessel. Now, our vessel is large, comfortable, with pleasant mess-mates & every facility for doing the duties connected with my department. I fear I should make nothing by the exchange.

    Monday, 15th—My letter was laid by to be completed the succeeding evening. In the meantime a slight touch of fever put a veto on it & so it has remained till now. I don't like to have two things on my hands at a time & so concluded, with the Dr.'s assistance, to put off the fever till I could give it my whole time & attention—my back is about all that I can care for at present. I don't feel in very good writing trim yet, but my letter has been delayed so long that I feared you would feel worried at not hearing from me.

---

* Josiah F. Dunham (1833-1917). Son of wealthy cordage manufacturer from Boston, he was a book keeper in that city before the war. He enlisted in November 1863 and was honorably discharged in December 1865.

Civil War Years: USS *Florida* (1863-1865)

My back continues to gain slowly but surely, I hope. When I get so that I can put on a pair of suspenders & dress up I shall begin to realise that I am making some progress. At present I can bear nothing on my back but my shirt & with my pants buttoned about my hips I can't see that I am either useful or ornamental.

Your Note (No. 6) reached me yesterday with the paper containing the notice of Father's death.

I don't wonder that you felt somewhat alarmed when you got my letter directed in a hand new to you. I tried to direct it myself but after spoiling two or three envelopes in vain attempts to produce something legible I gave it up & had my clerk do it for me.

I had to laugh to see how philosophically Hen, the little scamp, took the news of my being hurt. The "honorable scars" he tells about, that are produced by sub-soiling the flesh with ragged pieces of iron are harrowing to the feelings, as any one will find who will try the experiment.

You[r] "share of the spoils" shall be forthcoming in due time. You will laugh when you see the medly of which they are composed. I wanted to send them by this trip of the *Newbern*, but after packing up a little box of shells which I want to send with them I found "the spirit indeed was willing but the flesh was weak"* & was forced to give it up. I will send with them a suit of clothes which, having been *ventilated* by the rebs in violation of every scientific principle, I have discarded [it] in disgust.

I confess to a slight affection for the coat although the back may be dilapidated. It has served its time & I will keep it as a memento of the past. I wore it at the fight with the *Merrimac*, at Sewall's Point, Fort Darling & when the *Monitor* went down I threw it off on her deck whence it was washed into the launch which carried me to the *Rhode Island*. It was stuffed into the holes in the boat to keep out the water, where it remained till it was found in cleaning out the boat & recognised as mine by some letters in the pocket. It was left at Kimberly's for me where I found it when at Hampton Roads one day. Couldn't it tell a story if it could speak?

As I "plundered" a suit of clothes from the *Wild Dayrell*, I am content to call it an even trade with the rebs & give them the credit of spoiling an old suit which I have replaced with a new one. The suit I got was nicely put up & directed to some one in Wilmington. I intended to have kept the name & [to have] sent the person a letter, through the Provost Marshal at Beaufort, acknowledging the receipt of them & telling him that they were doing good service in the Union cause.

The cold spell you mention while staying at Rockwell must have extended down here. We had the only snow about that time that I have seen this winter, & this I only heard, as it served to muffle the heavy tread of the watch on deck while I lay in the Ward Room below cogitating on the disagreeable

---

* Matthew 26:41.

effects of rebel shells. The snow fell to the depth of two or three inches, but under a bright sun the next morning every trace of it soon disappeared.

How much I would like to be home with you all & have a good chat—see how you all look & what you are about.

I fear the children will grow out of my recollection unless I get home soon. Kiss the little darlings for me & give my love to Mother, Sarah, Fan, Dave & all Friends, reserving a large share for your own use.

William

No. 50—

U.S. Steamer Florida
Off Wilmington, N.C.
March 18th, 1864

Dear Anna,

Many changes have taken place on board since the date of my last. The time of a large number of our crew who came out from New York with us a year ago has expired, they having enlisted for one year only. We sent home by the *Newbern* 50 of our crew, among them our Ward Room Steward & all our boys. Their places we have tried to fill from the crew of the *Peterhoff* but I fear after the experience of a day or two we shall not fare as well in the Ward Room as formerly.

Capt. Crosby has also been detached & ordered to the command of the *Keystone State* & the command of the *Florida* turned over temporarily to Mr. Merriman, a change with which none of us are at all pleased.

My Steward [Ellis] also got homesick, so I let him go home & took the Paymaster's Steward* of the *Peterhoff* in his place.

The slip, which I have cut from a stray paper which found its way on board, by no means tells the whole story, with the circumstances of which I am familiar.† Capt. Cushing‡ of the *Monticello* took his boat one evening after

---

* J. B. Woodhouse. Born in Ogdensburg, NY, the 27-year old book keeper enlisted as a landsman for a two-year term in late November 1863. He served as Keeler's steward until September 2, 1864 when he deserted.

† The clipping which is pasted into Keeler's letter book reads: "Complaint of Rebel Negligence. From the *Richmond Sentinel*, March 7. The *Wilmington Journal* of the 2d says that on Monday night last a boat load of Yankees from one of the blockading vessels slipped in over the main bar, past the forts and up to Smithville, from which place they carried off Captain Kelley, of General Hébert's staff, and also a negro man. Captain Kelley was General Hébert's Chief of Engineers."

‡ William B. Cushing (1842-1874). Expelled from the Naval Academy in 1861, he enlisted as an acting master's mate at the start of the war. He served as executive officer on the USS *Commodore Perry* and then commanded the tug USS *Ellis* and the gunboats USS *Commodore Barney* and USS *Shokokon* before commanding the USS *Monticello*. Famed for his bravery and resourcefulness, he carried out numerous reconnaissance and raiding missions. His crowning achievement was the destruction of the ironclad ram CSS

Civil War Years: USS *Florida* (1863-1865)

dark & rowed up over the bar to Fort Caswell, a distance of four miles—succeeded in passing the fort & passed on up the river to Smithville, a distance of three or four miles further. Here he landed & walking up into the place stopped at the barracks where there were some hundreds of soldiers & cooly enquired where the General [Hébert] was. The soldiers pointed out his head quarters. Cushing walked in but found the Gen. had just stepped out, so he took the Capt. mentioned in the paragraph & succeeded in getting to his boat with him. He passed the fort safely on his return by compelling his prisoner to give the countersign. It is looked upon here as a rash, foolhardy exploit, but as it was successful nothing is said. Had he failed he would have probably been dismissed [from] the service.

I rec'd yours of March 4th No. 7 to day. It was as welcome as home letters always are. As to my coming home, I am quite as anxious to do so as you are to have me, but the time when I can do so is quite uncertain & it is this state of uncertainty that makes it all the more aggravating.

First there is a rumour that we are going immediately to Norfolk for repairs & then back on the blockade again for six months longer. Then we are told that in a few weeks we are to go to New York. I have come to the conclusion that no one here knows anything about it & so don't allude to it in my letters to you.

Whenever it is known to a certainty what we are to do or when we are to go you shall hear from me. As I have said before I could go home at any time on a sick leave & would do so had I strength to travel. It is a hard thing for a Paymaster to get detached from his vessel as it involves a good deal of work besides expense. All the officers & men have to be transfered to his successor & stores of all kinds invoiced & turned over to him, requiring considerable time.

I have somehow set my heart upon going home this spring & shall feel greatly disappointed if I do not. It may not be in time to "trim & prune & make garden," but in time to see it after it is done. I shall see then how good a gardener you are, so you had better get some one to "dig, prune & plant," whoever you think the most suitable.

Tell Dave to reserve his "blowing up" till I have recovered from the effects of the one I have just had—then I will receive it with all due humility. Tell him to see all my taxes paid. I have been studying over the matter of back taxes for a long time. It is my impression that some 3 or 4 years ago I went to the collector (either Neustead or Cogswell)* & could find nothing of my property on the tax books—it had not been returned by the assessors, & I was told by the collector that I had thus escaped the payment of my taxes,

---

Albermarle in a daring nighttime raid in October 1864 for which he received the Thanks of Congress and a promotion to lieutenant commander.
* Morris Neustadt and Robert Cogswell, La Salle constables who did double duty as tax collectors.

Off Wilmington (December 1863 to March 1864)

& I think I mentioned it to Dave at the time, congratulating myself upon my good fortune, for dimes were not very plenty then. This is the only explanation I can give of the matter. If Dave will only see the thing straightened out he may "blow me up" & welcome, or if it will be more satisfactory we'll have a fight as soon as I return.

The Alapaca I have is of fair quality. There is about fifty yards of it. "Plundering" don't pay as well as capturing, as you would have found could we have got the vessels off that we have destroyed. The few articles that we are able to get from a vessel run ashore is but a very small fraction of the value of the vessel & her cargo, that would be divided among us could we save them.

In your last you allude to some article you have seen in the papers from Capt. Rowe claiming the credit for the destruction of the *Wild Dayrell*.[*] You must bear in mind that it is but seldom we get a paper down here, perhaps two or three a month, dailies at that, so that we know but little of what is going on in the world about us & it is only by chance such an article as you allude to would be seen by us. The account I have already given you of the destruction of that vessel is correct in every particular. None of her officers or crew were on board the *W. D.* when she was fired. I had charge of the firing party myself & know it was composed entirely of our own officers & men. A party from the *Sassacus* was on board the *Wild Dayrell* plundering, while our own folks were working hard to get her off, but they took french leave with the first bullet that whistled over us from the sharp shooters. All the *S.* did was to fire into the blazing wreck after we had left it. So also did the *Florida* & we made by far the best shots. They are welcome to make what capital they can out of it.

I have had no opportunity of sending No. 49 since writing it & so will enclose it with this, so you will get double allowance. I don't think I will send any kisses in this since they are treasured up against.

W—

---

[*] In his report of the destruction of the *Wild Dayrell* (ORN, I:9, pp. 438-39) Lieutenant Commander Francis A. Roe, the captain of the USS *Sassacus*, gave proper credit to the *Florida*.

Civil War Years: USS *Florida* (1863-1865)

Norfolk Navy Yard (April to May 1864)

Our mess is hard up. The time of our cook, steward & boys having expired, they have been discharged & sent home so that each of us is left to shift for himself, the Paymaster to night being obliged to crawl into an unmade bed & several others I think in the same fix. We shall probably get board in some private boarding houses near by or hire some of the coloured women to keep house for us. (7 April 1864)

The *Florida* arrived at Hampton Roads on April 1 and made her way to the Norfolk Navy Yard for repairs. The vessel was in desperate need of new boilers and her hull needed cleaning. Hoping they would be sent to New York for major repairs, they were once again disappointed to learn that the vessel would only be patched up at the yard and sent back out on the blockade.

To Keeler's great relief, his wounds had nearly healed: the last plaster was removed from his back the month after their arrival in Portsmouth. Able to get around, he had the chance to visit the headquarters of a brigade in the Army of the James, located a short ride from Norfolk, and to Old Point where huge amounts of military hardware were being amassed for the upcoming campaign. Ever the frugal yankee, he also sent home some of the "plunder" from the *Wild Dayrell*, which included a 166-pound sack of coffee, a bale of blankets, several dozen shirts, calico, braid, buttons and more.

While the *Florida* was being patched up, their new commanding officer 36-year-old Lieutenant Commander Samuel Magaw arrived. On leave in Italy where he had gone with his family to recover his health, he returned home at the start of the war and served first on the Potomac River before being transferred to the North Atlantic Blockading Squadron.

Big changes had occurred in the Union armies. Having proven himself in the West, Ulysses Grant was now in command of all Union armies. Grant's overall strategy was to attack the Confederacy simultaneously on different fronts. The Army of the Potomac would advance towards Richmond from the north, with the goal of destroying the Army of Northern Virginia. Benjamin Butler's Army of the James would cross the James River at City Point and threaten the rebel capital from the south. William T. Sherman would advance into Georgia, capture Atlanta and wage total war.

The military situation along the North Carolina coast had also changed: the rebels had taken back some of the territory they lost back in early 1862. In a combined operation involving a 7000-strong Confederate force and the ironclad ram CSS *Albermarle*, the Union garrison at Plymouth on the Roanoke River was captured on April 20. After the loss of Plymouth, Union forces also abandoned the town of Washington.

Letters of special note: April 29 (visits a camp of the Army of the James); May 2 (Ensign Rich's wedding).

Norfolk Navy Yard (April to May 1864)

No. 51—

          U.S. Steamer *Florida*
          Gosport Navy Yard*, Va.
          April 7th, 1864

Dear Anna,

 I suppose you have been looking for some time for a letter from the Paymaster and Eddie has trotted down to the post office day after day & returned empty handed. The fact is I have been putting off writing from day to day hoping to be able to tell you I was coming home or else say that I could not & thus end all suspense. But I can do neither yet. I think the chances are against us. It is *barely possible* that I may be able to make you a visit this spring but I do not allow myself to think it probable. We were all confidently expecting to go to New York when we left Beaufort to come up here for a survey on the vessel, but the Admiral, fearing he would loose the vessel if he allowed us to go out of his domains for repairs, sent us up here.

 We got to Hampton Roads last Friday evening [April 1] just as a terrible storm commenced & it has continued till to day. We felt well content to be safe in a good harbour for the gale was a furious one accompanied by rain, sleet & snow in turns. This morning it cleared off & the frogs to night are making merry music in the swamps on the opposite side of the river.

 How long we shall be here I cannot tell as the vessel & machinery have not yet been inspected to see what repairs are needed. I think it probable that they will patch us up temporarily & send us back on the blockade for three or four months longer when new boilers for the ship will be completed & we shall then have to go to New York, where they are building, to have them put in.

 I think I can get "leave of absence" long enough to go to New Haven but it is doubtful if I can go further—still I shall continue to hope. You cannot feel any more disappointed than myself & I feel sometimes that if it were not for the name of it I would resign & come home for good.

 I rec'd your letter enclosing your Father's & have written him to the effect that I should probably be in New Haven this spring & would see him about Hen's going home. I shall regret very much his leaving a good school after getting so nicely started in his studies, but he will be of great assistance to you & I hope as you propose he may be able to continue them at home with Mr. Durham's† assistance. I had hoped he might remain long enough in New Haven to go through the [Yale] Scientific School which would fit him for almost any station in life except a profession.

 The Navy Yard here presents the same scene of ruin & desolation which it did last fall when we were here—the same cracked, blackened walls &

---

* Keeler was using the former name of the Norfolk Navy Yard.
† Rev. Henry Durham.

roofless ruins that we saw then. But little has been done towards repairing them. A small force is at work at the Dry Dock which may be ready for use sometime during the present century.

We have a new captain, Lieut. Comdr. Magaw*. He has the reputation of a good officer and a gentleman. I saw him this evening for the first time.

Our mess is hard up. The time of our cook, steward & boys having expired, they have been discharged & sent home so that each of us is left to shift for himself, the Paymaster to night being obliged to crawl into an unmade bed & several others I think in the same fix. We shall probably get board in some private boarding houses near by or hire some of the coloured women to keep *house* for us.

Saturday, 9th—I meant to have finished this last night & wrote till eleven o'clock but was too sleepy to complete it & besides I got out of material.

I commenced boarding to day at the place where Mrs. Crafts & Mc-Gowan's sisters boarded last fall while we were here. The fare is plain but everything looks clean & neat. Board at $6.00 per week seems like a good price, but when you come to pay 60¢ per pound for butter & $1.80 per pair for chickens, high prices are accounted for.

Dr. Vose left us to day having resigned. He soon got sick of the service, having been in it only four or five months. His relief, Dr. Brooks†, is from New York [and] has just entered the service & is the greenest & most homely specimen of the genus homo that I have seen in a long time.

Our old Dr. (James) is on the Mississippi. I had a letter from him the other day giving an amusing account of his entree into Cairo [Illinois] in the night & his navigating the mud in search of a hotel. He is very tall, his lower limbs "long drawn out," a wise provision of nature he thought when he came to sound the depths of the Illinois mud.

Capt. Magaw came on board to day bringing his wife with him. She is on board to night but how long she is to remain I don't know. He is as bad off as our Mess, as he has no cook or steward, so that they will be obliged to board off the vessel.

We had information from the Navy Department a few days since that the *Nutfield* & cargo, which was destroyed by the *Sassacus* in company with ourselves, "cost over *one million of dollars*, being the most valuable cargo sent onto the coast since the commencement of the war."

I have sent all the men we took from the *Peterhoff* to Baltimore for the *Iroquois*, which is supposed to be fitting out for some foreign station. Mr. Greene is on board of her as Lieut. & Executive officer.

A good many of our other men have been discharged, their time having expired, which has reduced the size of my family to less than one hundred. Some of our officers went off on short leaves of absence to day, the Commo-

---

* Samuel Magaw*.
† Robert F. Brooks*.

Norfolk Navy Yard (April to May 1864)

dore* having refused to grant them longer than one week. I have not applied yet as I have not arranged my affairs so that I can leave but I have no hope of getting further than New Haven. How I wish I was going to meet you there, but if you were there I should have you come down here. You won't feel the disappointment any more than I do. I try not to think of it but look forward to the latter part of summer or fall when I hope we may all meet again.

My back keeps gaining slowly. It will be some time before it is entirely healed.

My love to all & kisses to yourself & the children. Tell Eddy he is a good boy to send me such nice pictures. I send him & Lizzie a present & one to you of one of the new Treasury notes.

William

No. 52—

U.S. Steamer *Florida*
Norfolk Navy Yard, Va.
April 19th, 1864

Dear Anna,

Since I last wrote you I have rec'd two letters from you, Nos. 10 & 11. The latter No. reached me first, as No. 10 was sent down to the blockade & had to be returned from there while No. 11 was stopped here. I have delayed writing from day to day expecting to date my next from New Haven, for I had given up the idea of getting home as I found that no "leaves of absence" were granted by the Department for 30 days except under very peculiar circumstances, in which category I knew I would not be placed, so consoled myself with the "half loaf" of visiting New Haven.

When we arrived here my work had got a good deal behind owing to my wound, so I worked hard for a week to get everything up square & in good shape to leave for fifteen days, the greatest period for which leave was granted. I made my application & carried it to the Commodore (Livingston) who after a good deal of "huming & hawing" concluded he could grant leave for 10 days. After a good deal of argument pro & con he "didn't know but he could extend it to 12 but would consider the matter till next morning when I could call again." I was on hand the next morning & after going over the whole of the arguments of the previous day received 15 days leave & upon getting back to the ship found I had been ordered to a Court Martial as President, so my plans were all frustrated.

I immediately set down & wrote to your father telling him that I should be unable to go home this spring & desiring him if not inconvenient to let Henry remain till fall. I sent Henry $15.00 & told him that he could spend his

---

* John W. Livingston.

vacation (which is about to commence) where & how he pleased provided he had good associates, but rather advising him to go to New York as there he could provide himself with spring and summer clothing. I told him he had better write to Uncle B. first & see if it was convenient & that if he went down he could spend part of the time at your uncle Frank's if they did not object.

I am going to be revenged for my disappointment by sending for you when we go to New York & we (you, Henry & myself) will all go home together. Our new boilers which are building in New York will be done in July or August when we will go there to have them in, which will take two or three months. The repairs making on us now are temporary, merely to make the vessel last till the new boilers are completed. So you may make up your mind to be *ordered* east in the latter part of the summer, & have my company home, making a stop at Utica, Hudson &c.

I am glad you find such a pleasant companion in Mrs. Rockwell. It will make up for Mrs. Hough's absence. I wish they lived nearer to you so that you could see her oftner. I am glad to hear that there is a prospect of their remaining in La Salle, on the principle I suppose of misery loving company. Our new Captain (Lieut. Comdr. Samuel Magaw) was acquainted with Mr. Rockwell on the coast survey & desired to be remembered to him when I was writing home. Please mention it to Mr. R. when you see him.

I have sent on to the *New York Times* & renewed my subscription. I would have done so sooner had I not expected to go to New York & I disliked to send money by mail. I have also renewed my subscription to the *Sci. American*.

I hope you continue to take *Harper*. I see an occasional no. & I like it as well as ever. The "Monthly Record of events" makes it more valuable & interesting. I was surprised that the editors should publish Read's *Very Hard Cash*.* I have been reading it & a more worthless piece of trash I haven't met with in a long time. Some of his expressions are anything but elegant. I should think something far superior could be found without going across the water.

Tell Dave I will write him before we leave here & send him the power of Att'y as he desires, if I can find any of the legal fraternity in this place. Gen. Butler I believe has *squashed* all the secesh ones.†

I am glad that you had that old flag staff taken down. I have often thought of it & hoped it was down but it did not occur to me while writing home. Tell Mr. Chapin that I am under many obligations to him.

I sent from here to day by a schooner going to Philadelphia *your* share of the plunder from the blockade runners we have destroyed. I gave the Capt.

---

* *Hard Cash, A Matter-of-Fact Romance* by English novelist Charles Reade (1863). The novel was serialized in *Harper's Weekly* under the title *Very Hard Cash*.
† From November 1863 to April 1864 Butler commanded the Department of Virginia and North Carolina, with his headquarters at Fort Monroe. In December 1863 he ordered all public officials, which included lawyers and justices, to take the oath of allegiance to the Federal government in order to continue in their positions.

Norfolk Navy Yard (April to May 1864)

directions to ship from Phila. by some freight express or ordinary transportation Co. as it would cost too much to send by the regular express. I could not prepay the freight here so you will be obliged to pay it. Ask Dave to keep a look out at both depots as I don't know which one they will go to. Let me know as soon as you receive them as I feel anxious to hear that they reach home safely.

I wish there was more that was realy useful at home & could be used in the family to save buying. There is a sack of coffee of 166 pounds. How good it is I don't know but I don't think it is of the very best—let Dave look at it when you get it. Then there is a bale of blankets which I suppose will be acceptable cold nights when you use *linen* sheets. The dark coarse ones are from the *Wild Dayrell*, the others are from the vessel here. A portion of a bale I had over, two pair of them I have slept in & will probably need washing.

In the same bale is my "Pea Jacket" I had on the morning I was hurt. As the back is gone it is of no further use to me. You can see where the piece of shell went in on the right side coming out through the left.

The box contains a variety. Some things of no use to you such as the parchment, locks &c you can put up till my return. Also the signal lights, do not let the children get them as they have caps on them which a blow would explode & I suppose you do not want fireworks in the house. In the bottom you will find a number of books, some have been given to me, some I have bought—some are good, others good for nothing.

When "our circle" meets you can bring out the guava jelly & marmalade & think of me when you eat it. I wish I had something more for the children—there is a pink dress for Lizzie but I could get nothing for Eddie. The contents are all yours to use as you please but I would like to give Mother & Fan each a pair of white blankets & Mother an alapaca dress if it is worth taking. I don't know as the calico is worth making up but you will probably find something to do with it.

I feel ashamed to let so long a time pass without writing you & shall not do so again. Remember me to all friends. Love to Mother, Sarah, Fan & Dave & an *unlimited* supply of kisses to yourself & the dear little ones.

W—

My back is so far healed that I apprehend no further trouble with it. I get around now without difficulty. I will write you again *soon*. Will send "*that money*" before we leave here.

William

Civil War Years: USS *Florida* (1863-1865)

No. 53—

                                        U.S. Steamer *Florida*
                                        Navy Yard, Norfolk, Va.
                                        April 25th, 1864

Dear Anna,

    Since my last I have received two letters from you—Nos. 12 & 13. The last one reached me to day & also one from Henry. I could imagine your disappointment on learning that I was not coming home this spring. But you are no more disappointed than myself for I had looked forward to it with so much pleasure & had to come to regard it as almost a certainty. I wanted to see you all so much & the children especially—while they were children with all their cunning ways. I am glad they talk of me & look with pleasure to my coming.

    I wish some one could tell me how much longer this war will continue, for if it is going to last two or three years more I think I should do as you say my friends say I am going to & hire a place east & have you move there where I could make you an annual visit at least. I have seriously thought of it a good many times & nothing but the expense involved in buying furniture &c & the uncertainty of the duration of the war deters me from doing it now. I hope this summer will bring it to a close, at least as far as the volunteer officers of the navy are concerned. I can't see what they are going to want of our large fleet of vessels when the seaboard is once in our possession. I hope this season will see the stars & stripes waving over the most if not the whole of it. I have got tired of it & long to settle down quietly once more with my family & friends around me.

    You see I make no calculations upon leaving the service till the war is over. I entered it so near the beginning that I desire to see the end. I have a pride in being able to say that I was in the service during the war & I think you share in it, don't you?

    I presume you have learned by this time that I shall not get even to New Haven. Henry of course feels quite disappointed but he will be the more glad to see us both in the fall & go home with us. In his letter rec'd to day he thinks he will take his walk to Middletown [Connecticut] & on his return go to New York. I think after he has walked to Middletown he will be glad to take the cars back. I hope he will find time to go to New York as I want him to get his summer clothing, as I think he can do better there than in New Haven.

    I see that the schooner in which I shipped your things has not left here yet so that you must not get impatient if there is some delay. I think I told you that there were three packages—a box, a bale & a sack of coffee.

    Most of the books in the box have been given me from time to time by acquaintances, a good many of them by officers leaving the vessel who did not care to carry them with them, others I have bought. I think you will find something readable among them. I want you to read [*General*] *Butler in New Orleans*. The writer was partial no doubt, but it gives one a very good idea of what New Orleans was [like] when the Gen. went there & how he managed the sesech. His measures were summary no doubt, but I think no one can say but that he was the right man in the right place. The books, such as they are, will make something of an addition to our library. The Southern history of the war I read with a good deal of interest, to see how differently the same events were viewed from the opposite side.

I have kept half a dozen shirts & send home the rest—three dozen & a half. If you can get for them what the wife of one of our officers did who sent his home ($3.00 each) I think you had better sell a couple of dozen of them, as the remaining two dozen will last me a long time—you may do as you think best however.

Of tape & braid I think you will have a supply for some years to come. If you think best you can trade off what you don't want, at the stores. I should like to know the value of the articles I send just to see how much my plunder counts up. Such calico as I sent was selling at Beaufort for 25 & 30 cents per yard. If you want more porcelain buttons I can send them, as I have about a hundred more packages which I thought I would send to New York & sell, supposing I had sent you enough to button up all the children the rest of their lives. I have also quite a quantity of paper such as I send which I thought I would dispose of in New York. Let Mother, Sarah, & Fan have some of the tape, braid, buttons & the smaller things if they want, if you have them to spare. I think I asked you to give Mother an alapaca dress if it is suitable & she likes it.

I think you will laugh when you come to the quinine. It is a bottle the Dr. gave me—he got about a hundred bottles of it. It is a medicine frequently used in a family & won't come amiss. With it you will find a bottle of nice perfumery for yourself. I had a bottle of bay rum* but could not make room for it.

I wish you would send me the size of shoes, gloves & hose you wear, as if I have another chance I shall know what sizes to send home for we frequently exchange with each other on board when we want different sizes.

Put the percussion caps, fuze & signal lights out of the way of the children for they might get hurt with them.

I wish I could be behind the door when the box is opened & hear the remarks that are made. A number of articles for my own use I have not sent home—the suit of clothes, which at the rate some of our officers have paid for clothing are worth $60.00, a number of pairs of boots, some felt hats &c.

Since our arrival here, till the last three or four days the weather has been dismal. A cold northerly wind with an almost continuous rain has made it very disagreeable getting about & has tended to reconcile me to my

---

* A cologne made from distilled rum and the leaves and berries of the bay tree.

disappointment, as if I had gone to New Haven I could have run about but very little & this tramping about in the mud, especially when one is visiting, is not the most pleasant thing in the world.

I cannot tell how long we shall remain here. The mechanics are still at work upon the boilers & after they are done we are to go into the dry dock, the repairs on which are not yet complete.

Remember me to all my friends. I hope they won't forget there is such a person as myself in existence.

William

[Marginalia] Direct to me on the blockade as formerly, only *via Baltimore*, as our letters are stopped at Fortress Munroe & sent up here & when we leave for the blockade our letters will follow us down immediately, instead of lying in the office here for a while.

No. 54—

U.S. Steamer *Florida*
Norfolk Navy Yard, Va.
April 29th, 1864

Dear Anna,

For a few days back we have had most delightful weather—clear, bright skies & a warm sun, too warm in fact for our thick clothing. When we first arrived here the earlier spring flowers, the flowering almond & such, were in full bloom & now most of the trees have come out in spring fashions of the brightest green. Fruit trees are in full blossom & everything looks fresh & fair.

We are supplied at our boarding house with a plentiful allowance of shad, radishes & lettuce & will soon have green peas. Oysters are on the table every meal, so that I begin to tire of them. I wish you were here to help me eat them.

On the second warm day our stove was taken down, as we supposed summer had commenced in earnest. But we found our mistake this morning, for on going on deck a raw cold north wind was blowing, making us covet the well remembered comforts of our departed stove.

Boiler makers are still at work on the vessel & our departure from here seems as far in the future as ever.

Yesterday I made a visit to Old Point for the first time since I have been here. I found my friends there all glad to see me & everything there looking about as usual. Many things seem to indicate vigorous movements this season on the peninsular.* A number of our large ocean steamers were lying in the

---

* The plan was for Butler to head up the James River, cut the railroad between Petersburg and Richmond and threaten the rebel capital from the south, while Grant advanced on Richmond from the north. The staging area for Butler's attack was Fort Monroe.

Norfolk Navy Yard (April to May 1864)

Roads coaling, on their way to Hilton Head to bring up troops & a number of river steamers were on their way for York river filled with soldiers.

An immense quantity of ordnance stores has been accumulated at Old Point. Camps in all parts of the country have been broken up & their inmates seem to be concentrating in different places on the peninsular. Boats are coming in loaded with huge army wagons with their four, six & eight mule teams, heavy iron siege guns & lighter ones of bronze, ambulances, horses & all the et cetra of an abandoned winter camp.

In every direction there is an unusual bustle & stir which one cannot help but notice. Richmond I think will be attacked from a number of different points. But the opinion seems to prevail here that the real attack will be made by Grant, all the rest will be feints. I suppose however but very few if any here *know* anything about it.

A few days since Gen. Heckman's[*] Adjutant sent an ambulance in from the camp for McGowan, McLean & myself with an invitation to come out & make him a visit. Of course we did not refuse. We had a delightful ride out to the camp over a good road, a distance of six or seven miles, through pine woods with occasional patches of maples, elms & white woods.

We passed an hour or two quite pleasantly visiting around among the officers of the General's staff, winding up with a half hour's call on the Gen. himself. Although full of business he was very pleasant & sociable. He has under his command five brigades numbering about twenty thousand men— infantry, artillery & cavalry. They however were breaking up their camps & embarking in transports for Newport News.

I told the Gen. that I hoped he wouldn't have to spend the summer in the Chickahominy swamps.[†] He seemed to have no fears of that & expressed an opinion that there *might* not be any hard fighting around Richmond. What he meant I did not enquire—it may be that they expect to force Lee to evacuate the place without fighting by cutting off his supplies from the south & thus starving him out. I think it is the intention to move a heavy force up the south bank of the James as well as up the peninsular, but of course this is all a mere surmise as I have not conversed with the "reliable contraband."

I fear the loss of Plymouth will operate against us if the rebels are allowed to hold it but I do not think they will be able to keep it long.[‡] It was gross negligence on our part that we did not have a monitor up there to meet their iron clads which we knew positively months ago were preparing to come out. It was a subject of conversation among all naval officers.

---

[*] Charles A. Heckman, a brigade commander in the Army of the James. His camp was located near Portsmouth, VA. Major Robert S. Davis was his Assistant Adjutant General.
[†] As McClellan did two years before.
[‡] The 2800-strong Union garrison at Plymouth, NC surrendered on April 20 after a four-day attack involving Confederate ground forces and the ironclad ram CSS *Albemarle*. Six months later Union forces recaptured the city after sinking the *Albemarle* which guarded the approaches to the city.

Civil War Years: USS *Florida* (1863-1865)

Gen. Heckman told us if we would like to visit the defences he would furnish us with horses & orderlies & the Adjutant would accompany us as a guide. My back was not in a condition to allow me to display my equestrian accomplishments so Mr. McLean & myself were furnished with a buggy & McGowan mounted a horse with the Adjutant for a companion & we started off with two mounted orderlies bringing up the rear.

The defences extended for miles through heavy pine woods, across open patches, through swamps, cleared land, cultivated (or what had been cultivated) fields & farms, a fine smooth military road running paralell with them. At every favourable point heavy earthwork forts had been built up, mounted with guns of various calibers. These were being dismounted to accompany the troops & long trains of field artillery filled the road at various places—all converging to the place of embarkation.

At short intervals we came upon the camps of the different regiments composing the brigades, at each of which, of course, we made a stop & made the acquaintance of the officers, visiting around from house to house or tent to tent for that purpose. Many were living in tents, others had built snug, comfortable houses from the pines with which they were surrounded & not a few *confiscated* chairs, tables & sofas added to the comforts of camp life. A few had gone still further & had added their wives to the list of *luxuries*. We had a "splendid" time & I enjoyed it exceedingly. We took dinner with a portion of the Gen.'s staff & our ambulance set us down at the Navy Yard gate at sundown.

I saw great quantities of the yellow sweet scented jessamine & am pressing a flower or two of it for you. How I wish you could have taken the ride with us. You would have agreed with me that the day had been very pleasantly spent. It gave me a better idea of camp life in winter quarters than I had before.

We received cordial invitations to "come out again," but I have since met many of the officers on their way to the peninsular & imagine their deserted camps must present a rather uninviting appearance. I hope we shall hear good news from them before the summer is over.

Remember me to all friends. With much love & *many* kisses to yourself & the children. Affectionately yours,

William

[Marginalia] I suppose the [military] news I give you here is "contraband." Don't let it find its way into print.

Norfolk Navy Yard (April to May 1864)

No. 55—

U.S. Steamer *Florida*
Norfolk Navy Yard, Va.
May 2nd, 1864

Dear Anna,

I was made glad to day by the arrival of your No. 14 & to learn by it that you were all well at home. What a dismal wet spring you have had. I suppose when summer comes it will be with a jump.

I am glad to see by your letter that you keep up the garden. I would give a good deal for the privilege of a stroll through it in your company. It may cost something, but even if you derived no benefit from it is worth all the expense in the innocent amusement & gratification it affords you all, the children especially.

I suppose the reason you have not heard from Henry is that he has been off spending his vacation. I hope he will write when he gets back & let us know what kind of a time he has had.

There is some talk of our getting off from here in about a week. I shall be glad when we do, for I want to get to sea again for a change. Anything to make the next two or three months pass away as speedily as possible, for I do so long to get home once more & see you all.

I hope in a week or two more to have the good news to tell you that I am out of the Dr.'s hands. One of the places on my back is healed over, the others are healing but require dressing daily which is not always very convenient. The wounds are no longer painful or troublesome in getting about. I assure you that I shall be glad enough when I have done with them.

An agreeable episode in our every day life occurred to day in the shape of a wedding—the marriage of one of our Ward Room officers (Mr. Rich) to a young lady of this place.* We were all invited of course, & of course we all went, as did Capt. Magaw & his wife. They were married & took the boat for Baltimore.

The wedding was to come off at 1/2 past eleven, at which hour we were all on hand, when we were informed that the ladies were not ready & the ceremony would not take place till half past 12. The company was not large, the gentlemen being mostly naval officers & the ladies, acquaintances of the family of the bride, & of course mostly unacquainted with each other.

As the different parties arrived & were introduced into the parlour they ranged themselves around the walls—ladies on one side, gentlemen on the other, in that most embarassing silence which no doubt you have sometimes seen & *felt*. It reminded me somewhat of Ridgebury on a similar occasion. I

---

* The young woman was Emma J. Butcher, daughter of an English-born stone mason who died in the 1855 yellow fever epidemic in Norfolk and Portsmouth that killed an estimated 4,000 people. Her stepfather, a painter in Portsmouth before the war, enlisted as a private in the Confederate army in 1861 and was mortally wounded at Antietam in 1862.

made a desperate effort to break the spell by engaging the minister who sat on the opposite end of the piano from me, opening on him with the weather—that failed—then I tried the war, the army, the navy, Norfolk, its inhabitants & the surrounding country, but failed to elicit a response except now & then by skillful cross-questioning the briefest kind of a reply. So I gave it up & Mrs. Magaw & myself kept up a sort of desultory fire across the room doubtless to the edification of the company for they did nothing but listen. Mrs. Magaw is a very pleasant, lady like little body, quite easy in her manners & in conversation.*

After a while there was a stir & a bustle & in walked the matrimonial candidates with their four attendants—two of our officers acting as grooms & one of the bride's sisters & another young lady as bridesmaids. The minister arose & drawing from his pocket an ancient looking & somewhat soiled, leather covered memorandum book, I thought he was endeavouring to extricate his handkerchief from the depths of some hidden receptacle & in his efforts had brought to light his grocery-man's pass book. My doubts on that point were dispelled however when he opened the book & commenced reading the marriage service.

To have the knot firmly tied the parties deemed it necessary to use a ring. Now the proper use of the said ring was a somewhat difficult operation while the digits of the users were invested in white kids. So it had been arranged beforehand that at the proper time the bridegroom was to present his hand to one of the bridesmaids who was to divest it of its covering while one of the groomsmen performed the same office for the bride, an operation requiring no little skill with a tight, neat fitting kid glove. The bridesmaid did her part quite cleverly, but the groomsman with a *paw* but a trifle smaller than the Belgian giant's† fumbled away among laces & ribbons in his efforts to loosen the wrist & then his awkward attempts to disengage the glove were excruciating & would have been in vain without the assistance of the bride. I confess to an audible smile about that time which I did my best to disguise with a severe fit of coughing.

The ceremony through, the customary congratulations took place when we were invited below to refreshments. With my *acknowledged* discrimination (?) I selected the best looking, disengaged female in the room who readily accepted of my escort.

The table was very nicely set out with cold chicken & turkey, pickled oysters, tongue, nuts, ra[i]sins, cake mottoes‡ &c. Everything passed off nicely

---

* Margaret H. M. Magaw (1833-1917). Born in Virginia, she was the daughter of Navy Lieutenant Commander Archibald S. Campbell who died in Macao in 1836. She married Samuel Magaw in Portsmouth in 1849. After his death she moved to a farm in Prince William County, VA where she lived the rest of her life.
† Jean Bihin, the Belgian-born giant who was purported to stand over eight feet tall. He was a play actor at P. T. Barnum's American Museum in New York City.
‡ Sweets wrapped in fancy paper together with a short phrase.

notwithstanding there was considerable stiffness & formality. I felt in just the mood to enjoy myself & make others do the same if possible & exerted myself accordingly & I think I can say without being thought vain that I have heard through a number of different sources that I was complimented by the ladies. They "didn't know what they should have done if it hadn't been for the Paymaster" &c. You see what it is to have had good training!!!

All the officers were in uniform & the ladies were dressed well, then I am at fault—but as near as I can remember the bride & bridesmaids were dressed very much alike—in brown merino dresses, long sleeves, high in the neck, with a wreath of white artificial flowers around their heads—that I believe includes all, don't it? At any rate it's all I can recollect.

Wednesday evening, May 4th—Just returned from Old Point where I have spent the day in a vain search for Cook, Steward & Ward Room boys. On my way up I made the acquaintance of Capt. Dutton, a brother of Col's.[*] Found him [to be] a very pleasant agreeable person, very different from his brother. He is on Gen. Shepley's staff.[†]

Preparations are being made on the most gigantic scale for the movement upon Richmond. Gen. Gilmore is here with his whole command on his way up the peninsular & a fleet of monitors & other iron clads are waiting at the mouth of the James [for] the proper time to ascend.[‡] The force on the south bank of the river will be mostly if not entirely of cavalry.

Everything has been done so quietly that the country has but little idea of the numbers now advancing upon Richmond. The opinion prevails here that in a short time we will hear of the severest fight of the war or of the quiet evacuation of the Rebel capital.

Those who know the extent & magnitude of our preparations talk confidently of our success. I hope it may be so. Our tactics have been changed & "concentration" made the order of the day till many important points have been left almost defenceless. This is the case with this place, a regiment of cavalry could ride through it without opposition.

But it is getting late & I must say good night. With much love.

Will

---

[*] Clarence E. Dutton (1841-1912), a distant relative of Anna's. A brilliant young man, he attended Yale College where he won the Yale Literary Prize in his junior year. He did postgraduate work at Yale until 1862 when he enlisted in his older brother Arthur's infantry regiment. In 1864 he was transferred to the Ordnance Corps of the regular army and in 1865 commanded the ordnance depot of the Army of the Potomac. After the war he kept his army assignment while pursuing his interest in geology, publishing more than 30 scientific articles. His most important work was the principle of isostasy, in which the gravitational equilibrium between the Earth's crust and mantle is such that the lighter crust floats on top of the heavier mantle.
[†] George F. Shepley, commander of the District of Norfolk and Portsmouth.
[‡] Gillmore's X Corps had been transferred to Virginia and merged into the Army of the James.

Civil War Years: USS *Florida* (1863-1865)

[Marginalia] I sent you a *"Peculiar"* book yesterday & *Cudjoe's Cave* to day by mail.* Let me know if you receive them.

No. 56—

U.S. Steamer *Florida*
Norfolk Naval Station, Va.
May 8th, 1864

Dear Anna,

Here we still are, but making preparations to leave which we shall probably do in the course of two or three days. I have been hoping to hear from Henry for the last few days as I want to know how he spent his vacation. I have heard from him however in the form of a bill for clothes from New York to the amount of $50.00. I suppose from that that he has been to New York, but I can't see why he don't write.

It has been very warm here for the last few days, the thermometer standing most of the time at 94°. Most of the trees are in full leaf & the gardens (where there are any) are bright with flowers.

All are anxious to get to sea again where we can breathe the cool fresh air. All the officers have returned from their leaves of absence—the bride & bridegroom getting back to day. I find that the lady I was so *attentive* to at the wedding has a husband, an officer in the rebel army. I have not seen her since the wedding. If we were going to remain here long enough I think I would make a call on her & see what she says of the war.

There is a great anxiety here in regard to the movements of our forces. No one seems to know anything & everyone is asking everyone else for news. I think it can't be said but what this movement has been kept still since it was first contemplated. Gen. Butler it seems has made a move which I have long wondered has not before been attempted—approaching Richmond by way of City Point on the James River. His ruse of landing his forces at Yorktown is regarded by military men here as a most masterly move.† The news as far as we can learn is most encouraging. Butler will cut the rail road south of Richmond destroying Lee's communication with the South, leaving him the alternatives of being beaten by Grant on the Rapidan [River] or of retreating to Richmond & being starved into a surrender there.‡

---

* *Peculiar, A Tale of the Great Transition* by Epes Sargent and *Cudjo's Cave* by John T. Trowbridge were anti-slavery novels set during the Civil War.
† To hide his true intention, Butler had sent the steamers carrying his troops up the York River. At midnight they turned back, and by daylight were far up the James River. They seized City Point and Bermuda Hundred early in the day of May 6, without loss and to the great surprise of the Confederates.
‡ Butler's attempt to threaten Richmond from the south had stalled. He failed to cut the railway between Richmond and Petersburg and missed the opportunity of striking Richmond with overwhelming force. He was defeated at the Battle of Drewry's Bluff (May 12-16) and soon after bottled up at Bermuda Hundred by a much smaller Confederate force

Norfolk Navy Yard (April to May 1864)

Monday, May 9th—I took the boat from here to Old Point to day to bring up a draft of men for us from the *Minnesota*. As soon as we reached Old Point the boat was taken by the Quartermaster & sent up to City Point with troops & I was left to find my way back to Norfolk as best I might. After working a long time amid the stir, bustle & confusion of arriving & departing steamers, the loading of artillery & stores & embarcation of troops, I finally succeeded in borrowing a small tug with which I went to the *Minnesota*, took on my men (to the number of 54 who had been transfered from the army to the navy) & returned in season for supper.

We hear to day that two of our gun boats have been blown up. One, the *Commodore Jones*, was an old ferry boat, a good boat for river service, carrying a heavy battery, but of not much value for aught else. She was destroyed by a torpedo, which raised her bodily in the air blowing her into fragments. A large number were killed & wounded.* The other, the *Shawsheen*, was disabled by a shot in her boiler & was obliged to surrender. The rebels being unable to retain possession of her, blew her up. She was a small river craft & not of much value.

Mr. Crafts is up the river in his vessel, the *Shokokon*. I don't envy him his position as his vessel is one of that kind kept in the advance of the fleet as a picket boat.† His wife must feel anxious. I have no desire to spend another summer up that river, but I wish it had fallen to my lot to have had a part in the present movement there.

Wednesday, May 12th [11th]—We left Hampton Roads last night. I was so busy that I could find no time to finish this sheet for you, but sent a note telling you that we were on the point of leaving—all well. We cannot remain out long, as our hull which needs repairs badly had nothing done to it. A few repairs were made on the boilers and we were sent off till our coal is gone when we expect to return to be patched up again, or, we hope to be sent to New York. A month or six weeks will decide the question of where we are to go.

The wounds on my back have healed. The Dr. took the last plaster off yesterday—just three months from the time I was hurt. It will be sometime I imagine, if ever, before the scars disappear. As my *market is made* however it does not occasion me much uneasiness.

We are right glad to exchange the heated air of Norfolk for the cool refreshing breezes of old ocean.

---

under Pierre G. T. Beauregard. Meanwhile, Grant had started his bloody march southward following the inconclusive Battle of the Wilderness on May 5-7.

* On May 5 the USS *Commodore Jones* and six other Union gunboats were sent up the James River past Bermuda Hundred to clear the river of mines in preparation for the landing of Butler's army at City Point. The following day the old ferry boat was blown up by an electrically fired mine that killed and wounded 69 of her 88 men.

† The USS *Shokokon* was one of the vessels sent up the river in search of mines.

Civil War Years: USS *Florida* (1863-1865)

There has been a sad falling off in our Ward Room table. As I have said in some of my previous letters our cook, steward & all our boys have left, their time having expired. We were unable to obtain others & were obliged to pick up such as we could find & have a cook who knows nothing about cooking, a steward ignorant of his duties, & two stupid, sea sick, young Americans of African descent as Ward Room boys. Our potatoes come on the table parboiled, the ham fried crisp, dishes unwashed, unleavened bread & unmade beds. Growling & grumbling appears to be the only luxuries indulged in. The sooner we see home the better.

There is a good stiff breeze blowing with some considerable sea. Our green Ohio M.D. is about as sea sick an individual as is often seen. I think as we become acquainted with him we will find him a very pleasant mess-mate.

Friday, 13th—We reached the familiar locality of the fleet early this morning. Everything on shore looked as of old, through a glass, but we could plainly see that the rebels are continually strengthening their defences. Blockade runners still continue to find their way in. Only now & then one being caught.

We stopped but a short time on the north side of the shoals. The flag ship or senior officer being on the south side, we went around there to report our arrival, deliver dispatches, receive orders &c. The same station has been assigned us as formerly—on the north side, extending between Masonborough & Bogue inlets, for which place we are now on our way.

How I wish I could accompany this letter home. You must imagine it filled with love & kisses for you all.

William

Off Wilmington (May to August 1864)

I have been sitting on the guard under the awning enjoying our fine cool sea breeze & thinking of home & its dear ones. I have been imagining you all on the way to church & wishing I were with you. When I can be so in reality is very uncertain. The return of our vessel to New York seems as far or further off now than ever. We are now anticipating seeing home next fall but I have been disappointed so many times that I don't allow myself to fix upon any time. Only one thing reconciles me to staying here as we do—the hope that an attack will be made on Wilmington sometime in the course of the summer in which we will participate. (26 June 1864)

Relieved to exchange the stifling heat of Norfolk for the cool breezes of "old ocean," Keeler was glad to return to the blockade off Wilmington and back on their station on the North Side. Cut off from communication with the outside world, they waited anxiously for news of the Army of the Potomac which had commenced its bloody advance toward Richmond.

Off Wilmington (May to August 1864)

Leaving them in July was Lieutenant Merriman, who by then was not well liked. As Keeler stated, he was "one of that kind who don't wear." Replacing him as executive officer was John McGowan.

As the spring and summer of 1864 dragged on, hopes for a quick Union victory faded. With no seeming end in sight to the war, Anna's letters grew more despondent. Adding to her despair, no doubt, was Lincoln's call for half a million more men and the huge increase in the cost of living. Keeler tried to buoy her spirits by encouraging her not to "believe all the dismal forebodings which are so dolefully croaked out on all sides" and reminding her of times past: "If our heart[s] fail us now, what would it have done had we been living in the times of the Revolution?"

Letters of special note: May 15 (the demise of the ironclad ram CSS *Raleigh* and the "smell of mutton"); June 5 (refugees from Little Washington and Plymouth); June 12 (a trip on the USS *Newbern*; Paymaster Wood's adventure); June 26 (visit to the hospital garden at Beaufort); July 9 (another daring exploit by Lieutenant Cushing); July 14 (a poor white farmer's home; muster of the crew).

No. 57—

U.S. Steamer *Florida*
Off Wilmington, N.C.
May 15th, 1864

Dear Anna,

I wonder if you have got as beautiful a bright, clear, moonlight night as we have & I wonder too what you are all doing at home & how you are. How I would like to spend Sundays with you, if nothing more. It always seems a dull lonesome day to me & I cannot help but feel a little homesick at times as I sit quietly on deck & think of home & its dear ones. How many are longing for this war to be over that they may get back to their quiet homes once more & how many there are who will never see their quiet homes again.

How anxiously we are waiting for a mail with news from our armies. It seems harder now than ever before to be cut of[f] from all communication with the world just as we are on the eve of great events. By the next mail we shall hope, rather than expect, to hear that our forces have possession of Richmond. It cannot be that another summer will have to be spent uselessly before that place. If it falls, the limits of rebeldom will be a good deal contracted & should Wilmington & Mobile be taken a good many of the vessels now doing blockade duty will be laid up & of course their officers will then have *leave of absence*—an extended one, too, I think.

Wednesday, May 18th—My letter has lain along day after day partly for the reason that I have had considerable to do & partly that I have had but little if anything to write about. Our life here is one monotonous round, day after day about the same thing—now & then an excitement of which you are always notified.

A day or two before we came down here, the *ram* which has so long been building in Wilmington & about which so much has been said finally made its appearance.* It came out among the fleet in the night, but notwithstanding "wolf" had been cried so often & so long that many had grown careless & affected to laugh at it, it did not find our vessels unprepared —— to run†, which they did, all but two small gun boats which hung about the ram through the night giving her an occasional shot from their guns, which were small rifles. One of them received a shot from the ram through her smoke stack, the only damage done by the ram. With the morning light the *Tuscarora*, having recovered from her panic of the previous night, came in from seaward with the intention of attacking the rebel. The ram however having accomplished her purpose or fearing the *Tuscarora*, started to go in, but with the same ill luck which seems to follow all the rebel rams & iron clads she run aground on a bar at the mouth of the river where we have since seen her, through our glasses, surrounded with tugs trying to get her off. Refugees who came off to the *Fort Jackson* to day say that she has broken in two & will be a total loss. If this information is correct, & we have reason to think it is, it is to be hoped that it will tend to allay the *"ram fever"* which has run high ever since we have been down here. It has been "ram, ram, ram," till, as one of the officers remarked the other day, the very atmosphere was impregnated with the smell of *mutton*.

The *Newbern* came down to day bringing dates of the 12th & also a mail. I rec'd your No. 15 & also one from Henry.

The news from our armies is quite as good as we could reasonably expect. Grant is pushing on, though Lee makes a more stubborn defence than we supposed he would.‡ From the way in which you write I fear you have some croakers at home which tinctures your views of the future. We have met with some reverses to be sure, but could we look for uninterrupted success? For my own part I feel thankful that we have done so well & look forward with hope & confidence to the future. When reverses come it will be time then to mourn over them, but I don't like to anticipate them—let us hope for the best. Should this season's campaign be a failure, for the first time I shall feel

---

* On the night of May 6 the rebel ram CSS *Raleigh* steamed out of the Cape Fear River and attacked the Union blockading fleet. The sluggish ironclad steamed blindly through the fleet, almost unnoticed, exchanged shots with several vessels, but inflicted no serious damage. On her return to Wilmington, she ran aground on the bar and broke in two when the tide receded.

† To emphasize his disgust Keeler has drawn a long dash between "unprepared" and "to run."

‡ As Keeler was writing this, Grant and Lee were engaged in the bloody Battle of Spotsylvania Court House.

discouraged & begin to fear for the future, but I believe the right will eventually triumph. It cannot be that the Union is destined for such a future.

You mention an idea which has often occured to me—taking a boarder. I have often wished you had a man about the house but have never mentioned it as I did not know as you desired it. Besides I was at a loss to conceive where you would put him or who it would be. If you could arrange it so as to take Mr. D. [Durham] without too much inconvenience I should feel much better satisfied as to your safety & security & as you say it would probably save you many annoyances from the [neighborhood] boys. You must consult your own feelings in regard to it. Whatever you may do I shall feel satisfied with. If Henry & myself should come home we could get along somehow during my short stay.

Henry at any rate will be home sometime during the summer or fall. Should I be again disappointed in coming, you had better make some arrangements to have him meet some of the LaSalle merchants when they go east after their fall stocks & have him come on with them. It seems from what he writes me that the greater part of his vacation was a rainy one, only giving him an opportunity to spend two or three days in New York. I hear nothing from your Father in regard to his remaining there during the next quarter, but I suppose if it was not convenient he would have written me.

Notwithstanding all our efforts, vessels continue to run the blockade, out & in. Now & then one is taken but a dozen seems to take her place. Night before last the lightning during a heavy thunderstorm disclosed one which had just run out loaded with cotton. She had broken down & was "gobbled up" by the *Kansas*—a valuable prize.

Kiss our little ones for me & remember me to all our circle. With my best love & many kisses. Yours,

              W—

No. 58—

            U.S. Steamer *Florida*
            Off Wilmington
            May 21st, 1864

Dear Anna,

By one of our vessels from Beaufort to day I received an ever welcome letter from yourself—No. 16, mailed the 11th & only ten days from home. Getting news so soon from home seems to bring it nearer to me. I wish it did in reality. Since the date of my last "all has been quiet on the Potomac"[*]— nothing to get up an excitement—nothing to write about.

---

[*] A phrase used by McClellan in his telegraphic bulletins reassuring Northerners after the defeat at Bull Run. It soon became a phrase of derision aimed at McClellan due to his inactivity. The phrase was also used in a Civil War poem by Ethel L. Beers, published in 1861 and made into a popular song in 1863 called *All Quiet Along the Potomac Tonight*.

Civil War Years: USS *Florida* (1863-1865)

The weather is getting uncomfortably warm & we are glad to seek shelter in the cooler parts of the vessel.

What a late, cold, wet spring you have had. I suppose when summer comes it will do so all at once and everything will be behindhand. Farmers had ought to make money this season at the present prices for grain although labour is high. I am glad to hear that the grapes have suffered so little injury through the winter & shall hope for an abundant crop in the fall & also that I shall help you eat them if I do not get home before.

I shall be glad when you get Henry home that you may have the benefit of his assistance about the house. I think you must have your hands full with the house, garden, committies &c. It seems as if everything about the house had taken advantage of my absence to give out, break down, or something of the kind. I think you are in a fair way to learn the value of "a man about the house."

What has become of the cow? You have made no mention of her recently. I am sorry you have neighbors to be troubled by the hens & I fear from the *kind* that they are not the best sort of neighbors. How about the doves? Do they still increase & multiply? I would not let them increase to[o] much for they will be a greater trouble to yourself & neighbors than the hens.

Have I ever told you that I came across Col. Dutton's brother while at Norfolk? I liked him much better than the Col.

That *gray hair* reached me safely, for which I shall think of you with all due *veneration*.

I do not desire you to preserve the *Army & Navy Journal*. I sent it thinking you might find something interesting in it. I have been reading *Mistress & Maid* by Miss Mulock* & like it very much. I don't believe any one could read her writings without being the better for it.

What has become of Laning?† The Navy Register for this year does not contain his name. It is either accidentally omitted or he has left the service. How many changes the two & a half years that I have been absent from home have brought about in LaSalle. What with deaths, removals, fires &c it will hardly seem like the place I left, but home is left me yet, though change has reached even there. Send me a LaSalle paper occasionally. It serves to fill up the chinks in your letters & I sometimes gather from them things you omit to mention.

---

* Dinah Maria (Mulock) Craik's *Mistress and Maid: A Household Story* (1863).
† Keeler's friend from La Salle James Laning was in command of the USS *Rattler* on the Mississippi River. Several months earlier he had devised a plan to re-float the ironclad USS *Indianola*, which had sunk on the Mississippi south of Vicksburg a mile from the main channel. In November 1864 his plan was approved and he was detached from the *Rattler* and detailed to refloat the *Indianola*. He succeeded in refloating the ironclad in January 1865, but at the cost to his health. He resigned one month later and returned home to La Salle a very sick man, never regaining his health according to the statements in his Navy pension application in 1879.

Off Wilmington (May to August 1864)

By the papers received by to day's mail we get but little news from the army, but that little seems favourable. Butler as I thought has cut the rail road communication south of Richmond which will deprive Lee of further supplies or reinforcements.* What had previously been accumulated at the Rebel capital does not appear to be known, but I judge from the tone of the rebel papers that their supplies there are not very abundant, but I think that nearly the whole rebel force has been concentrated at that point.

Lee is making an obstinate defence & our losses have been fearful—the rebels have probably lost in proportion. Grant seems to hold on with a bulldog resolution which I trust foreshadows his success. Capt. Magaw prophecies a ten year continuance of the war, but I cannot see it so. One party or the other must be annihilated before that.†

Thursday, May 26th—I am doing my best to spin my letter out of nothing & have written down everything promiscuously as it entered my mind. You will find it a queer mixture. To day we are out on the fishing banks & shall have a nice mess of black fish for dinner, for they are being hauled in rapidly over the side. Our coal is nearly out & we shall soon have to go to either Beaufort or Norfolk for a fresh supply.

Sunday, May 29th [at Beaufort]—I have just returned from church (Episcopal). The building is a small neat one, made of the yellow pine of the country with which it is finished off inside & varnished, giving it a neat pretty appearance. The congregation was not very large—quite as large however as the abilities of the speaker.

Your No. 17 mailed the 20th inst. reached me yesterday—only *eight* days from home. I was happy to learn by it that you all continued well & that my "plunder" had been safely received—you must have had a time opening it. I wish I could have been an unobserved spectator. I thought Eddie would be disappointed at not finding anything for him, but I had nothing to send which I thought he would care for. I am glad you gave the little fellow the book. Tell Lizzie to call her dress, "her blockade dress." She must take good care of it, for I want her to look pretty in it when I come home. I fear if you put those blankets in the barn the moths will destroy them unless looked at frequently—they will come in play in cold weather.

Where do you get all your bad news from the army? You always write in the most desponding tone. In the few papers I get, everything appears to be moving on well. We can't expect a great victory every day, nor can we look for uninterrupted success. A reverse now & then must be sustained.

---

* Although Butler had launched several attacks on the vital railway link between Richmond and Petersburg, the railway line was successfully defended by Confederate General Beauregard. By May 20 Butler was bottled up at Bermuda Hundred and unable to advance.
† The Union losses incurred since Grant crossed the Rapidan River on May 4 were a staggering 36,000 (5,000 killed). The Confederate losses were about a third less. Grant's bulldog resolution stemmed from the grim calculus that Lee would run out of soldiers before he did.

Has Dave received the power of attorney I sent him? I should think his children would get through the catalogue of diseases by & by—every letter you write they seem to have some new trouble.

I hardly expect another letter from you before we leave here, much as I would like it. Many thanks for your "avalanch" of kisses. You may consider a like quantity enclosed with much love to yourself, children & all

William

[Marginalia] We arrived here yesterday morning. Shall take in coal & leave as soon as possible, probably on Wednesday. I think active operations will soon be commenced on the coast off Wilmington.

No. 59—

U.S. Steamer *Florida*
At Sea
June 5th, 1864

Dear Anna,

We left Beaufort this morning at sunrise, having been there about a week taking in coal & stores. While lying there a plan was concocted in connexion with the land forces for the capture of Fort Fisher & the batteries above it on the banks, by which we should control the river & effectually prevent any more running the blockade. When we went up from here we carried with us a complete plan of the fort & the adjacent works, furnished us by some of the Union persons on shore, with a statement of the number of troops in the different defences. Our manner of obtaining this information is rather singular. We were told by one of the refugees who came off to us that he had female friends ashore who would furnish information of what was going on in the rebel lines if we desired it & that the letters containing it would be deposited from time to time in a certain part of a wreck of one of the vessels we had driven on shore & destroyed. We send a boat in dark nights for mail from this novel post office. In this manner we sometimes get valuable information in regard to blockade runners, the disposition of forces &c. The plan refered to above was to carry down with us fifteen hundred troops, land them on the beach from which they were to make a rapid movement & take the fort in the rear or river side where it is entirely unprotected, while we drew their attention by a cannonade in front. All the rebel defences here are but poorly manned, every available man being sent to Richmond.

Refugees have been brought into Beaufort from Little Washington & Plymouth to the number of four or five hundred, mostly women & children who left their homes in those places when they were abandoned by our troops.* They have been crowded into the hospital & churches & now they are being placed in a camp in the outskirts of the place. All or nearly all are destitute of everything & all their wants have to be supplied by government, though private charities furnish them with many things which cannot be had from the Quartermaster or Commissary.

It realy makes one's heart ache to see them as they wander about sick, destitute, forlorn & spiritless, women with children in their arms & a little flock about them, their husband dead or forced into the rebel army, no one to care for or see to them & without a shelter except such as government provides & that is of the poorest kind. What makes it worse is their homes were mostly destroyed by our own forces when they evacuated those towns—it is an act which will ever stain our flag.

For the last few days the deaths among them have averaged nine a day. Many are now sick & are without any of the delicacies which those so situated should have, being furnished by government with soldiers' rations only. There are some noble spirited folks here who are doing what they can for them, but with so many to do for & so few to do, it is impossible to prevent much suffering. When the camp now making for them is completed & they get into the tents with the ground for a floor it is a chance if the sickness & mortality among them is not greater than it is at present.

I was very much interested in your account of the garden in your last (No. 17), the more so as it was so much in detail I could almost see everything before me. I realy hope the boys & vagabonds will allow you to enjoy the fruits of your labors, but I fear they will trouble you. I wish you had "a man about the house." Can't you make room for the *minister*?

You desire me to give the folks in New Haven a present. What shall it be? You know I am a poor hand at selecting for such a purpose.

We have had an engineer on board this vessel by the name of David M. Lane. It may be one of the cousins of Mr. Blanchard you enquire about. He resigned lately on a pretence of sickness & the last we heard from him he had gone to Nassau, as we suspect to offer his services to blockade runners.†

I am very glad to get Henry's letters you send me, though they are sometimes a repetition of what I hear from him direct. But it annoys me exceedingly that he takes no more pains with his penmanship. I have written him about it but dislike to say anything more for fear I shall not hear from him as

---

* Following the Confederates' capture of Plymouth, NC on April 20, 1864, Union troops garrisoned in the nearby town of Washington were evacuated and transferred to Fort Monroe and to New Bern.
† David M. Lane (1831-1898). The Connecticut native was working as a machinist at the outbreak of the war. He enlisted as a first-class fireman in October 1861 and served on the *Florida* from that date onward. His Navy pension application indicates that his health was ruined while serving on the *Florida*: severe rheumatism, nervousness and malaria. It therefore seems highly unlikely that he offered his services to the blockade runners after he resigned.

often. He has improved vastly in spelling, style & composition for which he deserves credit. Do tell him when you write to take more pains. If he was a good writer I could give him an appointment as clerk at $800. per year, though of course I should not do so unless I found he was determined to enter the service.

Friday, June 17th—I have just returned from Beaufort. While there I wrote you (No. 60) & now go back to finish 59. While there I rec'd No. 20 from you & on my return Nos. 18 & 19 which were, as they always are, the dearest & most highly prized of anything which reaches me on the blockade.

I was inexpressibly shocked at hearing of the death of little Maggie. It was so sudden & unexpected. Assure Dave & Fanny of my sincere sympathies in their bereavement. We know by experience what their feelings are & can more truly sympathise with them.[*] I regret I could not have been with them in their aff[l]iction. It would have given me pleasure to have repaid in some small degree their kindness to us on a similar occasion.

A continuous storm prevailed during my stay at Beaufort, depriving me in a great measure of what little pleasure I might otherwise have had during my absence from the vessel & while free from the discipline & routine of our every day man-of-war life. I returned on the *Mercedita* & had a very pleasant trip down without any occurrence worthy of note.

I have rec'd an Ottawa paper, from Sarah I think by the writing, & also a LaSalle paper with a notice of Maggie's death. I am sorry to see you are to be so troubled with thieves about the premises. I think you had better have slats *securely* nailed over the barn windows & see that the doors have proper fastenings. I am the more anxious as all my tools are there which I should not like to loose. The door between the *old* hen house & the barn should be kept hooked & be particular to see that *all* the doors are locked at night. Be careful of the back door of the barn. If any new locks or fastenings are needed, buy them. I mention all these precautions, though I don't suppose it is necessary.

With kind regards to all and much love to yourself & the little ones.

William

No. 60—

U.S. Naval Warehouse
Fort Macon, N.C.
June 12th, 1864

Dear Anna,

We left this place (Beaufort) last Sunday (a week ago to day) for the blockade. The following Tuesday the *Newbern* came down & finding it necessary to return to Beaufort on business I took passage in her. She first made a visit to the "South Side" to supply them with beef &c which gave me an opportunity

---

[*] Keeler is referring to the death of his three-year old daughter Minnie in 1857.

OFF WILMINGTON (MAY TO AUGUST 1864)

to see how things looked there. Found everything pretty much as it was when we were blockading there except that the rebels had continued strengthening their defenses & a large blockade runner which lay aground under the guns of Fort Caswell where she had been chased by the *Victoria,* who set her on fire & made prisoners of her crew. The fire was afterwards put out by the soldiers from the fort, so I suppose they will save the greater part of the cargo which was said to be valuable.

The accommodations on the *Newbern* I found to be much inferior to ours on the *Florida*, the vessel, which is a propeller, rolling badly in the sea, breaking crockery & furniture & making it very disagreeable eating & sleeping. Any one who supposes it is an agreeable sensation to a child to be rocked or that it is an extra inducement to sleep I would advise to try a sea voyage in this class of vessels.

The next morning after leaving the blockade for Beaufort I was suddenly awakened by a cutlass which had been stuck up over my bed, slipping out of its sheath & falling across my head simultaneously with the firing of one of the guns. It cut quite a gash which bled profusely for a time. As soon as I could check it I dressed & went on deck & found them in full chase of a blockade runner* from three to four miles off.

The second shell fired exploded on her deck [but] still she kept on. It was uncertain whether we were gaining on her or not. Both vessels kept gradually working in nearer the shore which we sighted about seven o'clock when the chase headed directly for it having apparently given up the idea of escaping, either as we supposed because they were out of coal or did not know where they were.

We kept on after her & at about half past eight she struck on the beach. We ran in as near her as we could & were just lowering our boats to send on board when she blew up. Masts, smoke pipe & pieces of the vessel shot up into the air from out [of] a cloud of steam & when it had passed away we could see her crew running across the beach into the bushes.

Boats were soon sent on board & found the boilers had exploded, completely destroying the midship section of the vessel. But one person was found on board of her who said he had been left asleep in the cabin when the others abandoned the vessel. He represented himself as her second mate.

There was a heavy surf running at the time so that it was with the greatest difficulty that the boats could go back & forth, so but little was brought off.

A short time after she struck, a squad of [Union] cavalry was seen coming at full gallop down the beach from Fort Macon, for we were within sight of the fort & we knew that her crew would soon be "gobbled" up by them, as afterwards proved to be the case.

---

* The *Pevensey.*

Civil War Years: USS *Florida* (1863-1865)

A tug from the harbour & the *Cherokee* shortly after made their appearance for the scene of action. Capt. Dove*, the senior officer of the station, came down in the tug & ordered the vessel (the *Newbern*) to Beaufort so that we were obliged to leave the prize after one or two ineffectual attempts to get her off.

We went up to the entrance of the harbour & found so heavy a sea on the bar that we could not get in & were obliged to lie at anchor all that day & the following night when the sea went down & we succeeded in getting in. We found that the cavalry had captured most of the officers & crew. In fact it was a difficult matter to escape, as they were on the same island as Fort Macon from which it was no easy matter to get off without a boat.

Paymaster Wood† who has charge of the naval stores at this place went down with the cavalry & was riding through the brush when the Captain of the blockade runner & six of the crew came out of the bushes & enquired how far it was to "the fort." "Eight or ten miles," says Wood. "Well," says the Capt, "I have blown her up so she won't do the cussed yankees much good" & this style of conversation was kept up for some time, Wood riding along on his horse & they walking by his side. They finally came to our pickets & Wood says, "Well, you have probably taken me for a Confederate officer but you are mistaken for I am a 'cussed' yankee one. Here are our pickets & you are on your way as my prisoners to Fort Macon." They were, as a sailor says, taken completely aback and tried to take back their *compliments* to the yankee nation. Wood took them to the fort & turned them over to the commanding officer. The Capt. said he did not know where he was but supposed he was in the vicinity of Fort Caswell & thought after running his vessel ashore they would be able to make their way to the Fort. The person who was left on board & who claimed to be the second mate has turned out to be the chief of Magruder's staff & others who passed as firemen &c have proved to be persons of consequence in the Confederacy.‡

She had been chased the previous day by one of our vessels & had thrown overboard all her weighty cargo consisting of lead & bacon but had a good deal of value left, cloth, silks, arms &c. The vessel which was a side wheel iron steamer of about six hundred tons & called the *Pevensey* is fast breaking up on the beach. A portion of the cargo has been taken out & part of the balance may be saved in a damaged state.

---

* Benjamin M. Dove.
† Samuel S. Wood (1837-1898). The native of Peekskill, NY was appointed acting assistant paymaster in 1862 and served on the USS *Freeborn* and store ship USS *William Badger* before becoming naval storekeeper in Beaufort in June 1863. He later served as assistant paymaster in the regular Navy and resigned in 1868.
‡ The "second mate" was in fact the real captain of the *Pevensey*, a New Yorker named Joseph Long, who was an "habitual violator of the blockade" according to Admiral Lee (ORN, I:10, p. 138). The "chief of Magruder's staff" was probably Captain Stephen D. Yancey, Magruder's adjutant general.

Off Wilmington (May to August 1864)

I shall leave here next Wednesday or Thursday in the *Mercedita* for "*home*" again. I left a letter on board [the *Florida*] for you partly finished which is numbered before this but will not reach you till after this one.

I did not go on board the *Pevensey* & got nothing from her but two or three little articles as momentoes. The *Dacotah* sent in a boat for plunder & loaded her so deep that she swamped in the surf & lost all they had in it & one of the officers was drowned. He was buried yesterday.

I shall finish my other letter as soon as I return so you may expect to hear from me again soon.

Another prize is lying in the harbour while I write, the *Syren*, a little steamer yatch [yacht] sent out as a present to Gov. Vance of No. Carolina.

I am staying with Paymaster Wood at his quarters in the warehouse & find it very comfortable & an agreeable change from shipboard life.

With love & kisses to you all, I remain your affectionate husband.

W—

No. 61—

U.S. Steamer *Florida*
Off Wilmington, N.C.
June 26th, 1864

Dear Anna,

I have been sitting on the guard under the awning enjoying our fine cool sea breeze & thinking of home & its dear ones. I have been imagining you all on the way to church & wishing I were with you. When I can be so in reality is very uncertain.

The return of our vessel to New York seems as far or further off now than ever. We are now anticipating seeing home next *fall* but I have been disappointed so many times that I don't allow myself to fix upon any time. Only one thing reconciles me to staying here as we do—the hope that an attack will be made on Wilmington sometime in the course of the summer in which we will participate.

We are all feeling joyful over the news from Grant's army & most heartily wishing him continued success. How singular that he should adopt the very same route to Richmond that I have always advocated as you will find by refering to some of my old letters. Had McClellan been allowed to do the same while at Harrison's landing I sincerely believe that he would have taken the city. At that time the road from Petersburgh to Richmond was almost defenceless. Now, on the contrary, every step is covered with almost impregnable defences. Grant will have to fight his way step by step & he will only succeed at a heavy loss of life. But succeed he will I am firmly convinced.*

---

* On June 12 Grant disengaged from Lee's front and six days later slipped across the James River to City Point, with the goal of capturing the railway hub of Petersburg. There he got

CIVIL WAR YEARS: USS *FLORIDA* (1863-1865)

I have just received a letter from our old Surgeon, Dr. James, who was with the Red river expedition*, which I enclose thinking you may find it interesting.

While at Beaufort the last time I hunted up Chapin. He has charge of the hospital garden about a mile out of the place & is engaged in raising vegetables for the use of the hospital—a much safer & more pleasant business than fighting & marching. He has some eight or ten acres under cultivation—peas, tomatoes, beets & "garden *sass*"† generally. I took dinner with him & had some cucumbers—knowing my fondness for them you can imagine what a treat they were.

I took quite a walk out into the country with him, stopping occasionally at the farms or plantations as they term them here, small ragged looking patches of ground, cultivated in a manner which would set one of our northern farmers distracted.

They seem to have no idea of progress or improvement in anything relating to their mode of life or manner of cultivation, seeming to lay it down as a rule to follow in the footsteps of their ancestors. I asked one how long he had lived on his "plantation."

"I was born here & so was my father & my grandfather."

"What are you growing on your land this summer?"

"Corn & cotton."

"Do you think it will pay you as well as other things would have done?"

"Well I don't know, it didn't last year, but I had a few beets & onions the woman planted in the garden that we didn't use. I carried them to town for the ships & they paid right smart."

"You found they paid so well last year, why didn't you plant your whole farm with garden stuff this spring instead of cotton & corn, the army & navy here would have been glad of all you could raise at big prices?"

"I didn't know as they would be here all summer. Besides my father always raised the same as I am & he got along." And that was just it, his father did so & so he must. The total want of enterprise & what a yankee would call management is surprising.

When Chapin was ploughing his land preparatory to planting he had a quantity of manure hauled out from the cavalry stables to enrich the exhausted soil. The neighboring "planters" told him he was destroying the soil & would "burn up his crops." They seemed to look upon it as a specimen of yankee folly. Thinking there might possibly be something in what they said Chapin left a strip through the field without manure. As might have been expected the manure wrought wonders. The difference between the veg-

---

bogged down and the siege of Petersburg lasted until April 1865, by which time Grant's army had suffered a staggering 42,000 casualties.
* Keeler's old messmate was serving in the Red River Campaign in Louisiana.
† Garden vegetables.

etables grown where the ground was manured & where it was not was astonishing, the former being twice & in some instances three times as large as the latter. But I doubt if his neighbors will profit by his example. The contrast between these plantations here & the small snug fields of our northern farmers is very great & almost forces one to believe that he is in another portion of the world, not in our own country.

They seem to live from hand to mouth, content to do & get along as their fathers did before them. They contrive to locate their dwelling near the sound or some arm of it so that they can have access to the town, to their neighbors or to market by means of their boats, two or three of which in various stages of decay & dilapidation are drawn up on the sand in front of almost every dwelling. Not but what this is for them an economical arrangement, since it enables them to dispense almost entirely with wheel vehicles & beasts of burthen & consequently with the use of the roads, which thanks to the sandy soil, need but little care.

Of course I speak of only what I saw. Of plantations in reality, the large estates of wealthy planters in this section of the country I know nothing, not having seen them.

But the yuccas growing wild in their native soil, I wished you could see them & at the same time I was glad you could not. Glad, because you would be disgusted with our miserable, little, dwarf specimens at home & gladly consign them to the tender mercies of the first root beggar whom the spring should bring along. Great pyramids of white blossoms rising four or five feet about my head—they were beautiful indeed. Blackberries were just beginning to ripen by the roadside & will probably be abundant the next time we go to Beaufort.

I meant to have answered some of the enquiries in your last three or four letters, but shall have to defer till my next for want of room. The collars I sent home I intended for Henry & myself. You may give Mr. Durham half a dozen of the shirts if you wish & Mrs. Hough a pair of the white blankets if she wants them, with my compliments.

Has Dave rec'd the power of attorney I sent him from Norfolk? You have not mentioned it in any of your letters. I rec'd your No. 21 yesterday, as acceptable as ever.

Kiss our little ones for me & remember me to all friends. With my best love as ever. Yours,

W—

Civil War Years: USS *Florida* (1863-1865)

No. 62—

U.S. Steamer *Florida*
Off Wilmington, N.C.
July 3rd, 1864

Dear Anna,

Very little if anything has taken place since the date of my last worthy of note. We continue to eat, drink & sleep & perform our usual routine of every day duties. The weather is warm & would be hot were it not tempered by a most grateful sea breeze. As yet we have had none of those insufferable hot days we experienced last summer when not a breath of air ruffled the water or moderated the rays of a scorching sun whose heat was thrown back by the mirror like surface of the sea making all shades & awnings alike useless. We are expecting to go to Beaufort some time this week for coal & will probably find it much warmer there than here.

In some of your last letters you have made some enquiries which I will try & answer as it will help fill up my sheet which otherwise I fear would be blank paper.

Lieut. Flye's letter you sent me was received & I would have written him myself if I had known to what vessel he was attached. I was much surprised to hear of his being ordered to the Mississippi as the last I heard from him he was in command of the *Kensington* where I supposed he would remain for a time, but constant changes are being made by the Department in all officers but Paymasters.* They are seldom detached from a vessel till the expiration of the cruise. All the stores of the vessel & the accounts of the officers & crew being in their charge renders a great deal of work necessary if a change is made in them. They are seldom detached unless for sickness or some similar reason. Should you find out where Lieut. Flye is I wish you would let me know.

I should like to drop in upon you sometime unawares when you were using the hoe & Mother acting as "carpenter & tinker to the establishment." It is a capital thing to have a minister who can "make himself generally useful."†

I will endeavour to make a collection of shells for him [Rev. Durham] but I fear it will not be as complete as those I have sent you, as different kinds are found at different seasons of the year & in different localities. Of some kinds, cart loads can be shoveled up off the beach at any time. Others are much more rare, as it is only now & then one that is thrown up by the waves & even then the more delicate ones are broken. Some of those you have came from "Shackleford" island some miles from Beaufort where a few of us went one day for a sail. No pretty sponges can be found now but I picked up the

---

* Flye was briefly in command of the ironclad USS *Osage* which had run aground on the Mississippi. Prior to and following that he was assigned to the Navy Yard at Memphis, TN.
† Rev. Henry Durham was boarding at the Keelers' house.

last time I was on the beach some very pretty specimens of sea weeds. I wish Mr. D. could accompany me & gather some himself.

Has Moore* got the nomination for clerk of the Circuit Court again? If the republicans have given it to him I hope they will be defeated. What a convenient deafness he had—to get him home just in time to win [and] pull for his nomination again. I suppose Hough is opposed to him. I know he has good reason to be.

I think I told you in my last of the Yuccas I saw back of Beaufort—they were so beautiful. Ours looked so insignificant in comparison.

I must beg leave to differ with yourself and Waters about the grapes. The trouble is not that they are carried out to[o] far but that they are carried out that distance too soon—before the vine had formed roots enough & had a body of sufficient size to nourish all the branches. It should have been cut back each year within a few feet of the previous year's growth. I was well aware of this when I did it but was in a hurry to get the arbour covered.

I hope both Henry & myself will be home in the fall to taste the grapes with you, but I have been disappointed so many times myself that I shall make no more promises. Of one thing you may be assured, I shall go there just as soon as possible.

I suppose Henry by this time must be looked upon more as a man than boy. Notwithstanding it will do no harm & be much pleasanter for him to have some good company [on his way] home. I only wish I could be ready to go when he does.

I hope to be at home to vote for *Mr. Lincoln.* I would like very much to see him President for another four years. Political considerations aside, the country needs his services & they are worth more to the country now & will be through the war, in the Presidential chair, than those of any other man.

What you will do with Henry when you get him home I don't know. I wish I was there to plan for you & him. If Mr. Nixon will take him in the bank I wish he would do so even if he gets nothing for it. I don't want he should get into habits of idleness & loafing about to pass away time. I wish to do all I can to foster habits of industry in him. I have formed no definite plans for him & cannot till I see you & him. Being in the bank would probably lead him to pay more attention to his penmanship & give him some knowledge of bookkeeping & it would also give him considerable time at home to help you. I shall have to leave it all with you till I come home.

I would like very much to have been with you at the social gathering you mention in your last. I am glad I was not forgotten. How often I think of those I used to meet at those pleasant little gatherings & I hope before many months to be able to make one of them again. I am sorry, though not

---

* Absolom Moore, the La Salle County politician and former colonel of the 104th Illinois, whose ineptitude led to the capture of a brigade he commanded at Hartsville, TN in December 1862.

disappointed, that you did not think more of the guava jelly. For myself I would much prefer some of your currant jelly. From your description you must have had pretty lively times after Mrs. Hough's return & can well imagine how you all must have enjoyed it.

I believe I told you in my last about having the barn well secured. It is better to spend a little in extra fastenings than have everything in it stolen.

Send me a LaSalle paper once in a while. I sometimes pick up an item of news in it that I do not find in your letters.

Has Dave heard from Ham lately? Is John still with him?

I am writing in great haste, for we are expecting a mail to leave to night & I want to get this ready. I sometimes have to keep my letters nearly a week before an opportunity offers to send.

Kiss the children for me. Remember me to Mother, Fan, Dave & Sarah & all enquiring friends. We hope soon to be in Beaufort & get some fresh vegetables. With my best love & kisses I am yours affectionately,

W—

No. 63—

U.S. Steamer *Florida*
Beaufort, N.C.
July 9th, 1864

Dear Anna,

We are back here once more, having arrived the day before yesterday. I found your No. 22 waiting me at the P.O., also two from Henry. He acknowledged the receipt of $15.00 I sent him a short time before & also protested very strongly against "being treated like a baby & being sent home in charge of a LaSalle merchant." He said something about spending a few days at Branford [Connecticut]. I wrote him that I thought he had better do so if he wished & that he could also stop a short time at Bridgeport, Ridgebury, New York & Utica, as it might be a long time before he would have another opportunity. I sent him twenty dollars for *contingent* expenses which had ought to be sufficient. I sent nothing for his fare, as you had written me that you would send a check for that purpose & I did not like to trust any more by mail, neither did I like him to travel with too much money about him. What you will do with him when you get him home I don't know, but I hope you will find something to keep him busy.

This is Lizzie's birth day—I send her a present. It came from one of the prisoners we took from the *Calypso*. Tell Eddie that he shall have a present too when his birth day comes around.

We spent the 4th on the blockade. It was a fine pleasant day with a fine cool sea breeze blowing. All the vessels were decked out with their flags & signals, presenting quite a gay appearance. At noon each vessel fired a salute of twenty one guns, all commencing at the same time & firing as rapidly as possible, making of course a good deal of noise & more smoke. What the rebs ashore thought we were doing—keeping the 4th or pitching into some of their blockade runners—I don't know—they preserved a dignified silence. In the afternoon we had a regatta, Capt. Howell* of the *Fort Jackson* putting up $200.00 for the men of the different vessels to row for. Thirty one boats containing about 300 men started on the race which was an exciting sight. The day closed with a heavy thunder storm & continued raining all night.

Lieut. Cushing of the *Monticello* of whom I wrote you some time since as having gone up under the guns of fort Caswell and brought off a rebel captain as prisoner†, has performed another exploit. He landed one night some miles below the fort [Caswell] with a boat & its crew, procured some horses, had his boat dragged some distance across the country till he reached a stream running into Cape Fear river. Here he launched his boat & went down to the main stream, up that to within three miles of Wilmington & then down the river, passing all the forts & batteries unobserved. He was gone three days & nights & returned with four or five prisoners, all that his boat would carry in addition to its crew.

How the black troops fought at Petersburg. I wonder if there are any doubts now about their making good soldiers.‡

The *Alabama* it seems has at last come to a fitting end. It's a pity that her John Bull officers & crew had not gone down with her. Capt. Winslow is blamed by many of the naval officers here for parolling his prisoners instead of bringing them home.§

The *Keystone State* has just come in from a cruise outside. She reports having chased no less than twelve blockade runners at different times, but owing to their superior speed she took but one. I believe there are more of them now than ever. The proportion of them who are caught or destroyed is very small compared with those who get safely in.

You ask me what I think of gold at 235. I think it is higher than I ever expected to see it, but I consider it no indication of the successes or defeats of our armies nor of the feeling of the public mind. It is the result of the operations of the gold speculators. With gold at 235 I am working for about

---

* John C. Howell. He commanded the USS *Nereus*, not the *Fort Jackson*.
† See letter of March 18, 1864.
‡ On the evening of June 15 two brigades of U.S. Colored Troops successfully stormed five heavily guarded Confederates batteries in front of Petersburg. Their baptism of fire came at a heavy cost, however, for they suffered nearly 500 casualties (55 killed, 400 wounded, the rest missing). A newspaper correspondent who witnessed their attack on one of those batteries praised their performance: "With a shout and rousing cheers they dashed at the redoubt. Grape and canister were hurled at them by the infuriated rebels. They grinned and pushed on, and with a yell that told the Southern chivalry their doom, rolled irresistibly over and into the work." (*Evening Post*, New York, NY, June 21, 1864).
§ The commerce raider CSS *Alabama* was sunk off the coast of Cherbourg, France on June 19, 1864 by the USS *Kearsarge*. Her commander John A. Winslow's decision to parole the 70 prisoners earned him a severe rebuke from the Secretary of the Navy.

$42.00 per month.* How long it will take to get rich at that rate I leave you to calculate.

I was very glad indeed to hear from Mother. Tell her I shall try and write to her soon. I think the "barn department" is in very good hands. The report was very satisfactory & interesting.

A survey was called on our rudder yesterday which has been out of order for some time. It was condemned as being unsafe at sea. What the result will be I don't know. It is possible it may send us to Norfolk to be patched up again, but I hope not for I have no desire to spend this hot weather there & besides should we go there it would probably be the means of keeping us out here till next spring, whereas now we have a fair prospect of going home in the fall.

Tell Mother & Sarah if they go east I shall hope to see them there. Should we go to Norfolk & I be unable to obtain leave to go home (which is quite unlikely) I think I shall send for Henry to come down & stay with me while the ship remains in the Yard. I should enjoy the visit quite as much as himself. If we go it will be in the next two or three days.

What a dry spell you are having. But dry as it may be, I think you can count on the well & cistern holding out.

We are having new potatoes, blackberries & water melons here, but at present they are high [expensive] & not very abundant. I am some expecting to go up to Newbern to morrow if we do not go to Norfolk. I sent you a Newbern paper a few days since printed on coarse wrapping paper shewing to what straights the printers are reduced here sometimes.

Most of our officers have gone to church to day but I did not accompany them as I did not feel first rate. Besides I don't like the preacher.

I suppose your father & mother will soon be leaving so that Hen will be without an abiding place. But he seems to think he knows enough to take care of himself. I hope it may be so.

I send much love to yourself & the children, as well as kisses. Remember me to all who enquire for me which you say is many.

W—

[Marginalia] Fearing that Eddy might think me partial I enclose something for him. Tell him to write to me again.

---

* "Gold at 235" meant that it took 235 paper dollars to purchase 100 gold dollars. Since Keeler's assistant paymaster's annual salary of $1,300 was paid in paper dollars, Keeler's annual salary in gold dollars was $553, or $46 per month (Keeler's math was a bit off). The depreciation of paper currency, which reached its peak in July 1864, lessened as Union victories mounted, until one month after Lee's surrender in April 1865 140 paper dollars cost approximately 100 gold dollars.

Off Wilmington (May to August 1864)

No. 64*—

                              U.S. Steamer *Florida*
                              Beaufort, N.C.
                              July 14th, 1864

Dear Anna,

In my last I think I said something about the vessel being ordered to Norfolk. It is still uncertain whether we go, but the probability is that we will not. The Admiral is expected down here in a few days when the matter will probably be decided.

Since my last your welcome letter of June 29th has reached me with the good news that you were all well at home. I hope to hear from you again before leaving here.

Last Monday the Dr. [Brooks] & myself took a walk out to the Hospital garden where we found Chapin. Everything looked flourishing about the grounds. He gave us some very nice sweet corn (Stowel's evergreen), cucumbers &c. Watermelons are just beginning to ripen but he had none that were quite fit to pick. I am told that the season here is about a month later than usual.

The place occupied by the Hospital for a garden belongs to a person in Beaufort who while the Secesh held the place was as bitter as any of them & although a member of the Episcopal church assisted in turning his minister out of it because he (the minister†) persisted in praying for President Lincoln notwithstanding the reiterated remonstrances of his sesech church members. After getting him out he [the minister] was made the object of persecution & insult by this man and others. After our forces took possession here this man, Hall, like thousands of others through the south, took the oath as prescribed by the President's proclamation in order to keep his property.‡

On his [Hall's] farm, now used by the Hospital, he kept his negroes, he residing in town & going out to his plantation as he saw fit. A small rough frame house was his negro quarters which is now occupied by Chapin. A fine large blackwalnut tree stands in front, to one of the large arms of which he used to tie up his slaves to flog them. Chapin told me that a fine looking yellow girl who was formerly one of his slaves came out there one day to see the old place. She described to him how she had been tied up to the limb & flogged till her back was so cut up that when they let her down she fainted.

The minister, Mr. Van Antwerp, whom he turned out of the church was appointed Post Chaplain when our forces took possession of the place with

---

* The sheet marked No. 65 was included in this letter.
† David D. Van Antwerp.
‡ The owner of the land on which the hospital garden was located was Richard S. Hall, a farmer and landlord from Beaufort. The 1860 Federal Census lists him as owning eight slaves, including a mulatto woman who may have been the one who was tied up to the black walnut tree and flogged as Keeler recounts here.

a salary of 1200 dollars a year. He was also put in possession of his church in which he now preaches.

While we were out there the hospital team came out & the driver offered to give us a ride back through the country, an offer which we very gladly accepted. He drove us out some ten or twelve miles, the country through which we passed resembling very much that immediately back of Beaufort. We made occasional stops at the houses or rather shanties along on the road. All were very similar in appearance, inside & out, so that a description of one will answer for all. Very few men were to be seen. Some had been forced into the secesh army & some had gone voluntarily.

The houses are rudely built of lumber made from the pitch pine of the country. They are of one story and one room, which answers for dining room, parlour, kitchen & bedroom no matter how numerous the occupants. From two to four beds generally occupy as many corners of the room, one or two of them sometimes separated from the others by a screen of ragged shawls or quilts.

The building is raised some two or three feet above the ground on pine blocks at each of the corners. The space underneath serves as a general rendezvous for the pigs, poultry, dogs, little niggers & other animals belonging to the establishment who revel here in undisturbed enjoyment—a happy family whose possession Barnum* himself might covet.

The floor is of boards, loosely laid, for the purpose I suppose of allowing the sand which is tracked in by every comer to filter through. It certainly allows the broom greater intervals of quiet repose. Moreover it affords greater facilities to the fleas, ever numerous in a sandy country, whenever they desire to change their base of operations from the possessions below to the possessors above or vice versa.

A fence made of staves split from the pines & curiously interwoven for the want of nails encloses this architectural effort of southern chivalry, taste & refinement which is generally screened from the rays of the sun by a pine or two, a mulberry or a magnolia. In the corner of this enclosure devoted to a garden (if such a use of the term isn't a profanation) is a few straggling stalks of corn & many of weeds, potatoes of which it might well be said they are "small & few in a hill," not enough even to excite the rooting propensities of the hungry grunters under the house, a half dozen hills of water melons whose jaundiced looking arms seem eagerly stretching out as if anxious to escape from their bed of weeds into the open air & sunshine. This is a tolerably fair photograph of one of the houses I visited.

Two lank, scraggy, cadaverous looking elderly women were occupied, one carding cotton with small hand cards, the other spinning with a rude attempt at the old fashioned spinning wheel. I enquired if that wasn't rather a slow

---

* New York City showman P. T. Barnum.

way of getting along. "Oh, no, they got along right smart. It was just the way they had always done."

On one of the three beds a dog was curled up, on another was a half naked girl of 16 or 17 fast asleep in the sun which shone in hot through the door—bare feet, bare legs—bare of all covering but dirt—water very evidently had formed no portion of her toilet for a long period of time.

On one side of the room the fragmentary remains of a hoop skirt hung entangled with the barrels of a couple of old rusty flint lock guns, flanked by a pair of butternut unmentionables. On the opposite side, a dilapidated fish net, two or three gourds, an ear or two of corn, a pair of shoes that had *traveled*, & an old tin pail contended for the possession of a wooden hook, while at convenient places was suspended the odds & ends of the well worn wardrobe of the family.

The fire place occupied the greater portion of one end of the room. On the long shelf over it was a broken teapot, a tumbler or two in like condition & in fact the sum total of the crockery of the establishment, no two pieces of the same shape or pattern & last not least the pot of snuff for family use. The whole interior was black & dingy from the smoke of the pine fuel.

"Wall, stranger," says one of the women, "I reckon ye kin tell us some news fur ye's got a paper in yer pocket."

"What news do you want to hear," says I.

"From the army."

"Well, which side."

"Why, your side. You needn't think I'm a rebel, stranger, fur I ain't. I want to have em whipped, dam em. When they were in Beaufort they troubled me powerful & told me I was an *aberlishener* & a nigger lover & they came to conscript my boys, but I druv em out of the house & told em my boys would fight for tother side."

Her language was more forcible than pious & I came to the conclusion that she was putting on Union most too strong. However I gave her the paper (a *Herald* of the 4th) & told her she could read the news for herself. She went out & brought me in some half ripe pears & brought forth some honey from some hidden store which she urged me to eat. But the surroundings and the honey itself was anything but inviting & I declined. I found afterward that she was a strong Union woman & had really driven the secesh officers from her house when they came for her sons, who are now in the Union army.

All these persons seem to bear their poverty with a kind of stoicism & without any attempt or idea of bettering their condition in life. But poor as they may be it is no excuse for the dirt & filth in which they live. At all the places at which I stopped & asked for water I could not drink it when brought—it was so filthy, not only the water but the vessel which contained it. I except one place where there was a family of negroes. They brought me a clean glass of good cool water.

Civil War Years: USS *Florida* (1863-1865)

I got my fill of blackberries as we passed along from around the fences of the cotton fields. Whortleberries were to be found in the woods in small quantities but we didn't go far from the road to pick them for fear of the ticks which abounded. As it was I found a number on me at night when I came to "*turn in.*"

The next morning I sent a boat ashore for Chapin who came off & dined with us. I took pains to shew him about the vessel & he seemed to enjoy his first visit to a man of war. He brought with him a basket of corn, beets, squash &c which made his visit doubly acceptable. All the company to which he belongs were taken prisoners at Plymouth or Washington, so that he was very fortunate in being detailed for special duty at the Hospital.*

The *Fort Donelson* came in to day with Paymaster Dunham, who was on the *Peterhoff* when she was sunk off Wilmington by the *Monticello*. I went on board & dined with him. Capt. Pickering† had two foxes, two dogs & three cats running about the decks. He said he was fond of pets & had the promise of a "*coon*" which he thought would complete the assortment. I was on board the *Dacotah* a few weeks since & saw a bear running about the decks. Sailors are proverbially fond of pets. They aid in passing away a good many leisure hours at sea.

Mr. Merriman received leave of absence with permission for an extension to day & left for home. We are all hoping that he will not return as he is not very well liked by any of us. He is one of that kind who don't wear.

Sunday, July 17th—I wish you could have seen our crew at "muster" to day. It is a sight but seldom if ever seen ashore & to a person who has never witnessed it, it is both novel & interesting.

At the beat of the drum, at about 10 o'clock, all the crew quietly take their places on the port side of the quarter deck dressed as the executive officer thinks the weather requires. To day each one was dressed in blue pants, white shirt with blue collar & cuffs embroidered with white, & straw hats.

The officers assemble on the starboard side dressed in their usual uniform (white pants to day) after the men have taken their places. The executive officer then goes into the cabin & informs the Captain that the officers & crew are mustered & the vessel ready for inspection.

The Capt. then comes on deck accompanied by the executive [officer], the officers & crew making the usual salute which is returned by the Capt. when the pair proceed to various portions of the vessel to see that all is neat, clean & everything in proper order. On their return to the quarter deck the

---

* Chapin's regiment, the 24th New York Independent Battery, along with the rest of the Union garrison at Plymouth, NC were captured on April 20, 1864. He was indeed fortunate to have been detached, for many of his comrades died in the infamous rebel prison at Andersonville, GA.
† Thomas Pickering.

Off Wilmington (May to August 1864)

articles of war are read, all new orders received from the Department & when the Capt. directs the Episcopal service is also read.

After all this the muster roll is called by the Paymaster's clerk, each man as his name is called crossing over to the starboard side & taking off his hat passes in review before the Capt. & other officers & woe betide him if his shoes are not well brushed, his white shirt without a spot, his neckerchief properly tied & all his "rigging" without a fault. The drum beats the retreat which ends the *formalities* of the day & the watch off duty is at liberty to pass the time as they please.

Mr. McGowan takes Mr. Merriman's place [as executive officer] in the absence of the latter. We find it much more pleasant & things move along more smoothly.

I wish you could have some of the rain with which we have been so abundantly supplied of late. We have had real dog day weather—first a hot scorching sun, then a heavy pouring rain, then sun again & so on alternately for some days.

Saturday, 23rd—You will find I think that my last sheet [No. 63] breaks off rather abruptly. My intention was to have had this finished to send with it but an unexpected offering [arose and] I sent what I had written, trusting that your patience would allow you to wait for the conclusion.

I feel concerned that I have not heard from Henry in reply to mine enclosing him $20.00 dollars. I fear it was an investment for the benefit of the rebs, as I see by the papers that they managed to intercept one or two mails between Washington & New York & if you should miss a letter also you may attribute it to the same cause.

We have been amusing ourselves by imagining the scare they must have had in Washington.* I hope Grant did not have to detach any portion of his force to protect the place—it isn't worth it—there has been too much of that already during the war. If those who choose to take it easy at home can't muster the spirit to defend their Capital, let it go. Its destruction might give a good many a realising sense that we have a civil war on our hands, which they don't seem yet to have discovered.

But the bottom of the page warns me to close, which I do with love & kiss[es] to you & our little ones.

W—

---

* In mid-June Lee sent Jubal Early on a diversionary offensive to the Shenandoah Valley and then on to Washington in an attempt to force the withdrawal of some of Grant's troops at Petersburg. Early's raid ended at the outskirts of the capitol at the Battle of Fort Stevens on July 11 and 12 where he found the city's defenders too numerous and was compelled to withdraw.

Civil War Years: USS *Florida* (1863-1865)

No. 66—

U.S. Steamer *Florida*
Off Wilmington, N.C.
Sunday July 31st, 1864

Dear Anna,

I have been looking anxiously for a letter from home for a number of days. Day before yesterday a mail arrived from Beaufort, but nothing in it for me, much to my disappointment as you may well imagine.

This morning however I fared better, receiving yours of the 15th (No. 25), enclosing Henry's of the 11th. Your previous letter (No. 24) is still missing, which accounts for what I considered your long silence. I hear nothing from Henry yet in acknowledgment of the $20.00 I sent him. I fear that [letter] as well as your No. 24 have fallen a prey to the rebels—much good may they do them.

Henry, I see, expects to start on the 25th for home. So I suppose before this reaches you, you will be rejoicing in his presence. I hope he will find something to employ his time as seems to be his desire in his letter. I am sorry to see that he takes no more pains with his penmanship—the same hasty, careless style as heretofore. He should bear in mind that whatever he may find to do, the use of a pen will be more or less necessary & a plain neat hand will always be of benefit to him in whatever business he may be.

How I wish I could have accompanied him home. It would have been so pleasant for us all. I still allow myself to hope I may be able to gratify you in coming home to eat some of your melons—they would have a peculiar flavour all their own I assure you.

We want a new rudder, new boilers, one of our magazines leaks so that our powder is spoiling. All of which combined I hope may have some influence in sending us home. The Admiral is daily expected down when we expect to have it definitely settled. As soon as it is determined that we are going & where we are going I shall write you.

How everything is rising with you? At this rate I shall soon have to do as Dave says & go home & do something to support my family.[*] I have had some good offers made me at Beaufort & have felt strongly tempted at times to leave the service & stop there. But it is too far from home & I never could have the conscience to ask you to take up your residence there unless it was for a very brief period of time.

---

[*] Over the course of the war the consumer price index in the North nearly doubled, while Keeler's salary remained unchanged.

Off Wilmington (May to August 1864)

You speak of seeing Laning. Has he left the service?* The Stoddard of the *Kearsa[r]ge* is not my old messmate of the *Monitor*.† He is in command of the *Adela* in the S.A.B. [South Atlantic Blockading] Squadron.

Our life is just as tedious & monotonous as ever. You have no idea what hard work it is to find something to write about.

Has Lizzie got her gold dollar? I wish I had more of them for you all.

I am glad to hear that my letter afforded old Mr. Chapin so much pleasure.‡ I supposed that he heard from his son frequently.

I shall hope to meet Mother & Sarah in Brooklyn. When do they leave?

Monday, Aug. 1st—Another mail this morning by the *Kansas* & two letters from home—Nos. 24 & another 25. You can't imagine how glad I was to get them.

What a fearful drought has prevailed all through the west. I am rejoiced to learn from your letter that the [dry] spell is at last broken as far as LaSalle is concerned. Your good *luck* in raising melons & cucumbers will make me fearful of trying my hand again lest I should not succeed so well.

You seem to write in very desponding terms about the war—our want of success—the new draft—the frightful increase in the cost of living &c. Do look on the bright side sometimes. Don't believe all the dismal forebodings which are so dolefully croaked out on all sides & if the same sort of ill favoured vermin chose to croak through the papers rest assured that you are just as well able to form conclusions as they are. We can't reasonably expect to carry on war without meeting with an occasional reverse. If our heart[s] fail us now, what would it have done had we been living in the times of the Revolution? I see no reason to be discouraged. On the contrary our prospects seem as fair & bright as at any time since the commencement of the war. All the season thus far we have had an almost uninterrupted series of success.

The recent raid in Virginia resulted in nothing excepting a severe fright of the Washington politicians (no harm in that) & the robbery of the surrounding country to the extent of some two millions of dollars. It failed to accomplish its main object after all—to draw Grant off from Richmond. Sherman is victorious in every engagement & will soon have Atlanta.§ Grant has obtained a position before Richmond from which he cannot be driven & will eventually have possession of that rebel stronghold. We have had many successful raids, skirmishes &c. What is there in all this so disheartening?

---

* See the footnote about Keeler's friend in the letter of May 21, 1864.
† Eben M. Stoddard, acting master on the USS *Kearsarge* which sank the commerce raider CSS *Alabama* off the coast of France in June. Keeler's mess mate from the *Monitor* who was serving on the USS *Adela* was Louis Stodder.
‡ This would be Keeler's letter of June 26, 1864 in which he describes his visit to the hospital garden at Beaufort with Mr. Chapin's son.
§ Sherman had crossed into Georgia in May 1864 and forced the Confederates to withdraw towards Atlanta. He lay siege to the city, which fell on September 2, 1864.

Civil War Years: USS *Florida* (1863-1865)

The President has called for half a million more men—a good omen for it shews that he is resolved to "strike till the last armed foe expires"* to which every true patriot will say amen. Were our currency in a better condition there would really be nothing with which the veriest grumbler could find fault. I hope our new Sec'y of the Treas. will find some way to relieve us.† We can't better matters by grumbling, but we can look forward to a bright future which I *know* is before us.

In one thing I have the advantage of you. We are shut out from the multitude of false rumours so constantly in circulation & when news reaches us the truth gets sifted from the falsehood. Besides I hear all these matters discussed by military men who can see the different movements of the armies in their true bearings.

Now you must submit to this *scolding* with the best possible grace as it is accompanied by best love & kisses to yourself & the children. Tell Henry to write me.

W—

No. 67—

U.S. Steamer *Florida*
Off Wilmington, N.C.
August 7th, 1864

Dear Anna,

When I wrote my last I thought I should be able in this to tell you something definite in regard to the vessel—what is going to be done with us &c—but things are still in status quo. For the last week we have been on the "south side." The Admiral came down a few days ago in his flag ship, the *Malvern*, & is still here. Rumour has it that he received a severe reprimand from the Department for spending all his time up the James river where he wasn't needed & neglecting the blockade where they seemed to think his presence was necessary.‡ But of what use he is here no one that I know of has yet been able to discover. All under his command dislike him & wish him

---

* *Marco Bozzaris* by American poet Fitz-Greene Halleck (1825).
† William P. Fessenden was appointed Secretary of the Treasury following Salmon Chase's resignation on June 29, 1864.
‡ Samuel Philips Lee's days as commander of the North Atlantic Blockading Squadron were numbered. On July 26, 1864 Gideon Welles informed the Admiral that his squadron would be broken into four divisions, with the squadron's headquarters at Beaufort, NC, and bluntly added that "you will visit Hampton Roads only when the public emergency requires it, giving your principal attention to the blockade, which has latterly become very inefficient" (ORN, I:10, p. 307). Dissatisfied with Lee, the Navy secretary had in fact been searching for a new squadron commander for some time, eventually settling on David Porter, who would lead the naval forces in the attack on Fort Fisher later in the year. When his replacement arrived in October 1864, Lee was sent to command the Mississippi Squadron.

Off Wilmington (May to August 1864)

away—their visits on board the Flag ship are no more frequent than duty demands.

The *Newbern* was here & left day before yesterday bringing mails, ice & fresh meat—that is meat as fresh as it could be after having been killed a week & kept in ice.

Blockade runners still continue to slip out & in, notwithstanding the Admiral's presence. No recent captures have been made that I know of. Alarms are of nightly occurrence. Rockets, guns, blue, red & white lights & challenge signals greet us on every side through the night. We really are in more danger from friends than enemies. The *Vicksburgh*, one of our own vessels, fired into us three times night before last mistaking us for a blockade runner, she not understanding our answer to her challenge. Fortunately she missed us, though her last shell just passed over our quarter deck.

Mr. Rich was sent to the Norfolk Hospital by the *Newbern*. He has been sick for some time with a disease of the throat. Fortunately as he resides in Norfolk he will go home.

In your next I shall hope to hear of Henry's safe arrival home. Unless he finds something to do time will soon begin to hang heavy on his hands. I want he should write me frequently.

I am glad to hear that Dave is doing so well. He certainly deserves it after undergoing as much as he has with his eyes. When he moves down on his farm he will want to have some one to superinte[n]d, for which place he may consider me a candidate, though what he wants to leave LaSalle for to move out on the open prairie I can't conceive & I don't think he will. I wish you would ask him about my Ottawa property, if it is increasing in value any & what he thinks I had better do with it, sell it or hold on.

We were all disappointed that our pay was not raised at the last session of Congress, as we had been given to think it would. At the present cost of living & value of gold, our pay, especially for those who have families, is but a very small sum & compels pretty close economy. In view of this I don't wonder that you ask what you are to do. I hope there will be a change for the better ere long. In the mean time we must make the most of what we have. Use your own judgment as far as all household expenses are concerned. I shall feel perfectly satisfied with whatever you may do.

Monday morning, 8th—One of our vessels, the *Lilach* [*Violet*] (a tug) got ashore last night on the bar close under the fort [Caswell], through the man in the chains giving wrong soundings. It was found impossible to get her off, so she was set on fire to prevent her falling into the hands of the rebs and abandoned. She blew up shortly after all had left her & no vestige of her is now to be seen.

I am told that the Admiral finds the blockade "very tedious, tiresome & monotonous" as he calls it to those who go on board to see him. To the question of "How he supposed others found it?" "Oh they get used to it." He misses his fresh meat, fruits, vegetables, ice &c just from market every morning, as he had them while lying in Hampton Roads. We are all hoping that he will be obliged to remain here for the next six months. Probably by that time he will also "get used to it" & can appreciate it as well as the rest of us.

We have had an addition to our mess of an Ensign to take Mr. Rich's place—Mr. Stoddard*, the Capt. of the tug destroyed last night. We have also two more engineers. They however go into one of the steerage messes.

Friday morning, July [August] 12th—No mail has left us for the past week & my letter has lain unfinished, partly for the want of something to say & partly because there was no chance to send. I fear till I have something more to write about you will find a long interval now & then between my letters & even then they will be wanting in interest. I still have the hope that before long my communication will be verbal. Still it is not by any means certain. We shall probably go to Beaufort in a few days, when I hope the matter will be settled. This state of uncertainty is worse than all. The Admiral has gone there & when we go up I suppose we will learn what his decision is. I will write you from there what we are to do unless we go north when I shall be the carrier of my own letter. In case we go to New York I will write you from there as I shall be detained there some days before I can get leave of absence, settling up my accounts.

It has been a long time since we have had a mail (for I had nothing by the *Newbern*). I shall hope for letters when we reach Beaufort. Should we go north I shall hope to meet Mother & Sarah there. Let me know when they leave home & where they are to visit.

We sighted a blockade runner going in this morning & managed to head her off & drive her off again & gave chase which was kept up for about two hours when finding that she went two miles to our one we gave it up & returned to the fleet. For two mornings in succession we have seen two large vessels ashore on the bar under the guns of the Fort [Caswell] but out of reach. They got off & went in.

The mail leaves in about an hour. So good bye with love and kisses.

W—

---

* Thomas Stothard (~1827-1894). Born and raised in New York City, he enlisted as a master's mate in August 1861. He commanded the tug USS *Violet*, which ran aground on the Western Bar at the mouth of the Cape Fear River in August 1864 and purposely destroyed. Following his brief time on the *Florida*, he was acting master on the USS *Eolus* and took part in the attack on Fort Fisher in January 1865.

To Halifax (August to November 1864)

> *I can imagine you all looking for me very anxiously by every train but I am sorry to say that we "have met with a slight reverse," or in other words my visit home has been postponed for a short time by orders from Washington to leave here in search of the* Tallahasse *and we are now, at daylight in the morning, getting under way. We shall probably be out 8 or 10 days, going up in the vicinity of Halifax.* (31 August 1864)

On August 6 the Confederate raider CSS *Tallahassee* slipped through the Wilmington blockade and commenced the most destructive raid by any warship during the Civil War. Over the course of her 19-day hunting spree, the *Tallahassee* captured or destroyed thirty-three merchant and fishing vessels while cruising between Long Island and Halifax. When word of the raider got out, Navy Secretary Gideon Welles ordered all available vessels to go in search of her and any other commerce raider rumored to be out and about.

While the *Tallahassee* was wreaking havoc along the Atlantic coast, the *Florida* was slowly making her way back to the New York Navy Yard to have her boilers replaced. After receiving the engineer's report, the yard's commandant Hiram Paulding notified Welles that owing to her defective condition the vessel was ready to go to sea in search of the *Tallahassee* but only for a short period of time and with little speed. As they were awaiting further orders, news arrived of an impending attack on Long Island Sound passenger steamers by other Confederate warships. To counter that threat, the *Florida* was ordered to New London, Connecticut on September 4 where she waited for an attack that never came.

On September 22 the order finally came for the *Florida* to go to sea. Their destination was Halifax, which blockade runners had been temporarily using as their base due to a yellow fever epidemic in Bermuda and Nassau. Arriving off Halifax on September 28, they passed the time fishing and cruising about until invited to come into port. Offended by the tone of a letter from the senior British Navy officer there, Keeler, who as usual on such occasions, was asked by Captain Magaw to help draft a response, which Keeler delivered the next day. Following that, Keeler headed into town to pay his respects to the American consul and the Lieutenant Governor, accompanied by a British naval officer who helped keep at bay the "secesh rowdies" who were "gathered at the street corners & at the grogeries."

On October 3 the *Florida* left Halifax for Boston, and from there to the New York Navy Yard where the vessel was laid up for four months for major repairs. Keeler remained in New York long enough to "give a good Union vote" on election day, which saw Lincoln win a second term as president, before heading to Utica, New York to visit family. Two months before that Anna's gloom deepened when she learned that her sister Mary Graves had been diagnosed with a terminal illness (most likely cancer) and given six months to live. Anna arrived in Connecticut in late October to say her good byes and remained out East with Keeler while the *Florida* was laid up.

Letter of special note: September 27 (trip to Halifax).

U.S. Steamer *Florida*
New York Navy Yard
August 31st, 1864

Dear Anna,

I can imagine you all looking for me very anxiously by every train but I am sorry to say that we "have met with a slight reverse," or in other words my visit home has been postponed for a short time by orders from Washington to leave here in search of the *Tallahasse*[e] and we are now, at daylight in the morning, getting under way. We shall probably be out 8 or 10 days, going up in the vicinity of Halifax. I hope we may meet her, but there is not much probability as she is so much faster than ourselves.

I shall hope to see Mother & Sarah here on my return. I received your No. 27 to day, via the blockade, telling me that they would leave home on the 5th of Sept., so that they should be here about the time we get back. Tell Sarah when they get here to write me a note where to find them, directed to U.S.S. *Florida*, New York Navy Yard.

I wish Henry was here. I would take him out with me.

I will drop you a line on my return telling you what the prospect is of a speedy visit home. Till then good bye. I have but a moment to spare as the boat is just going ashore with the mail. My best love to you all.

William

U.S. Steamer *Florida*
New London, Conn.*
Sept. 12th, 1864

Dear Anna,

I took the boat from here to New York last Thursday evening [September 8] on business & have just returned (Monday evening). Friday night I spent at Orange, N.J. with Birdsey Blakeman & his family. It is one of the pleasantist places I find to visit.

The next day I made a call on your uncle Frank, whose family are still in the country, & on uncle & aunt Brush who had just returned. I was hoping to hear or see something of Mother & Sarah there but was disappointed. Aunt B. looks miserably. I should not be at all surprised if she did not live long. Uncle looks much as usual.

---

* On September 4 the *Florida* was ordered to New London to counter an anticipated attack on the Long Island Sound passenger steamers.

To Halifax (August to November 1864)

I had the pleasure of meeting Capt. Worden for the first time since he was taken wounded from the *Monitor*. He gave me a very pressing invitation to spend a few days at his home in Greenwich, Conn.

Saturday afternoon I finished up my business & took the boat for New Haven, arriving there about 8 P.M. The folks were both surprised & glad to see me. I found your Aunt Mary Joy there, looking about as she used to. Your father & mother are both well, but time has left his footprints on your mother's face—she is growing old.

You have heard before this probably of the sad news of Mary's situation, as I was told you had been written to.* I first heard it from your uncle Frank. It seemed to send a chill all through me. It was so startling, so painful I could not realise it. Your parents had just returned from there [Litchfield] & confirmed what your uncle Frank had told me. They feel very bad, but more cheerful than I had expected & talk very calmly of Mary's approaching end—for I suppose there is no hope for her. Your Aunt Nancy is there now taking care of her & when she leaves your Aunt Mary is going up.† Geo. tells me Henry feels very badly.‡ He has drank nothing since last Jan'y & Mary thinks him reformed. I hope it may prove so. I think it will while Mary lives but I fear for him afterwards.

I tried to find some nice fruit in New Haven to send up to Mary but was unable to & so left some money with Geo. to buy some when it came up from New York & send it up with a note I left for Mary, telling her of my sympathy & love. I should have gone up to see her but it was necessary I should be back to the ship to day. I shall try & go up there next Saturday & remain over Sunday. Geo. will go with me. I wish you were here to go also.

You have been written to, to come on I am told. I am sorry that Mother or Sarah are not at home to see to the children & take care of the house, but don't let that interfere with your coming if you wish to. I cannot advise you as I do not know just how you are situated. Should you wait for me to come home, to return with me, it will probably be two months before you will be here, as it is doubtful if I can get away from here short of a month & then there will be my month's leave before I come back.

From what your father tells me Mary may be expected to live five or six months. I want you to come just when you think proper & remain as long as you desire & I hope you will be able to make such disposition of the house & children that they will not deter you from coming or compel you to return sooner than you would otherwise wish. I do not speak of bringing the children with you, much as I would like to see them, because it would be too much

---

* Anna's sister had been diagnosed with a terminal illness (most likely cancer) and given six months to live. She died in Litchfield on February 5, 1865.
† Anne (Nancy) Tuthill and Mary P. Joy, Anna's mother's sister and half-sister.
‡ George Watrous and Henry B. Graves, Keeler's brothers-in-law.

for you to travel with them & you could not take them to Litchfield & they would interfere sadly with your going about. As I have said before I cannot plan for you. I wish I could. I can only say don't let anything stand in the way if you desire to come. Come prepared to stay with Mary if desired & if you wish to.

What will become of her children?* Anna is at New Haven. She is a sweet girl, just what I imagine Minnie might be were she living now. I wish we could afford to take her into our little family circle & give her a home, that she might fill Minnie's place—that is as much so as a sweet loving disposition could ever fill it. She won my heart, the little I saw of her at New Haven.†

I need not say dear Anna how much I sympathise with you in this approaching affliction. As time sunders the ties of the loved ones about us let us love each other the more & be the nearer & dearer to one another.

Hattie & Geo. are well, though complaining of slight colds. They have a beautiful little girl & a great fat bouncing boy. Little Geo. is as thin & fragile looking as ever.‡

Write to me when you get this. Direct to New London, Conn. Kiss our dear little ones for me & tell Henry I want to hear from him. With my best love & kisses I am your affectionate husband.

W.

[Marginalia] Allow me to introduce you to an old acquaintance of yours. It was taken on board the ship standing behind one of our 9 inch guns. A store of grape, cannister & a 9 inch shot are in the foreground.

U.S. Steamer Florida
New London, Conn.
Sept. 22nd, 1864

Dear Anna,

Your letter of the 18th inst has just been handed me. In reply to all your enquiries about my coming home I can only say that it is uncertain—in fact that I know nothing about it, that is as to the time, nor does our Captain. Both of us are just as ignorant of the matter as you are.

You know, for I have already written you, how we were sent home for repairs, how I was expecting to get leave of absence on our arrival at New York to go home, how we were kept there day after day waiting orders from the Department to go to sea, how we were finally sent up here as was supposed for but a short time. How long we are to be kept here none of us knows. I do long to see home and all its dear ones (as all my letters tell you)

---

* Keeler was concerned that Henry Graves, who was an alcoholic, would not be able to care for his two daughters after Mary was gone.
† Mary's youngest daughter, 9-year old Anna Dutton Graves, lived with her Dutton grandparents in New Haven for several years following her mother's death.
‡ Hattie's three children George, Lila and baby Charles.

quite as much as you want to have me. But are you quite reasonable when you give me to infer that my coming & going is at my own option? You must bear in mind that we are the mere tools of the Department, that all our movements are regulated by it. Were it left to myself alone the first train that left here for the west would bear me along in it.

I fear that you are sick or surrounded by a bad atmosphere, your letters of late are so dismally dolorous. If the latter, I would much prefer meeting you away from home & its gloomy surroundings. If the former, why have you not told me. If you are in trouble of any sort why not confide in me. If I cannot be with you to assist you I will do what I can to advise & counsel you. If home is gloomy & the atmosphere depressing the sooner you leave it & come east the better. I am at a loss to know what gives you such gloomy forebodings of the future. I am sure it never looked brighter or more promising, but you don't seem to see any of our successes while you treasure up every defeat or disaster. Has Sherman accomplished nothing, or Farragut, or Sheridan, or Grant?* Your news must reach you through a very different channel from what it comes to me.

Don't let the hopes of my coming home delay your visit east one moment, for the Department may keep us here all winter, or tomorrow morning a telegram may come ordering us to New York for repairs where we will go out of commission, when I can go home. As you say "the *Florida* may be fitted up & leave for another two years' cruise," but it by no means follows that I shall go in her. It will take from four to six months to repair her & should I remain attached to her I should have a long play spell in that time.

I have just had a letter from Sarah in New Haven. She & Mother arrived two hours after I left last Wednesday. I shall try & go over on Saturday to see them & prevail on them to make me a visit here & go up to Norwich with me to see some of our cousins there.

We have had beautiful weather for the past few days but to day it is as dismal as your letter, with a promise of a continuance.

Mary Joy with a sailing party from Stonington in a yatch [yacht], passed close alongside of us a few days ago without either of us being aware of the other's presence.

I hope you will be able to arrange it so as to leave home soon. Make such disposition of the children as you think best. Leave Henry at home to take care of the house as I said in one of my previous letters.

It is late & I must close with love & kisses.

William

---

* The future did indeed look bright: David Farragut's warships captured Mobile Bay on August 5, Sherman's troops took Atlanta on September 3, and Phil Sheridan's cavalry won a string of battles in the Shenandoah Valley, the most recent being September 22. Although Grant was still bogged down at Petersburg, it was only a matter of time before that city fell, and with it Richmond.

Civil War Years: USS *Florida* (1863-1865)

Friday morning, 23rd—You can see now how very uncertain our future movements are. The Capt. has just rec'd an order from the Department to proceed to sea immediately & we leave tomorrow morning. We shall remain out till our coal is gone, probably about three weeks, till then good bye.

If I have opportunities I will write. Write & direct your letters to the *Florida* at this place.

Excuse my grumbling letter. I didn't mean to be cross but I did feel hurt when you seemed to think I could go home if I wanted to.

With my best love & a thousand kisses to yourself & the children.

William

[Marginalia] I shall hope to see you east on my return. You have plenty of money in the bank to draw on.

No. 69*—

U.S. Steamer Florida
At Sea
Sept. 27th, 1864

Dear Anna,

If you or my friends have ever "wished me to Halifax" you are in a fair way now to have that wish gratified, for we are bound for the land of the "blue noses." I do not think we shall stop there unless circumstances compel us, but cruise about outside in company with the *Vanderbilt* in search of the cotton loaded blockade runners from Wilmington which are running in to Halifax in considerable numbers.†

It is quite cool or I might say cold, for we have got on our winter clothing & a stove up in the Ward Room. We feel the change the more having so recently come from the "sunny south." I think I am in a fair way to become acquainted with our North American coast & will be competent for a pilot to the more ignorant ones when the war is over.

We left New London early last Monday morning [September 26]. I was sorry to go for we had found it very pleasant there. Moreover it gave me a chance to see my New Haven friends occasionally & I was in hopes of seeing you soon & giving you a welcome on board the *Florida*. Mrs. Col. Biddle & two other of Mr. McGowan's sisters had come on. Capt. Magaw's wife had come from Minnesota, where she had been spending the summer, & the wives of two or three of our other officers were also there & we were having very pleasant times.

In fort Trumbull was a very agreeable set of officers some of whom had their wives with them & we were just getting acquainted with the New

---

* Letter No. 68 is missing from the collection.
† Blockade runners were using Halifax, Nova Scotia as a base due to a yellow fever outbreak in Bermuda and Nassau.

To Halifax (August to November 1864)

London folks, numbers of whom visited us from day to day.* We had had one or two dinner parties on board & had been invited to the fort in return. Our officers used to go there frequently evenings with their ladies to hear the music—there being two fine bands in the fort. The friday evening before we left we were to have a "hop"† on board—one of the bands from the fort was to furnish music for the occasion—a rainy night spoiled it all. One of the wealthy citizens was getting up a party for us, but our departure spoiled that. You see that time did not hang heavy on [our] hands while we were there.

The friday before we left I had some business which took me to Norwich & so spent a portion of the day with Cousin Mary Norton.‡ I got there just before dinner & remained till 9 in the evening. They are living in very pretty style in the pleasantest part of the city. They had a good deal to say of their visit to La Salle & the ride out to Starved rock§. After dinner Mary had her horse & carriage brought out & drove me all over the city, which is a beautiful one & contains many fine residences. The fair was in "full blast" a few miles out of the city. We went out there, remained an hour or two, saw the races, driving through cemetery on our way home. She pointed out Judge Rockwell's former residence, a large fine house with extensive grounds well laid out.**

Wasn't it too bad that I could not see Mother or Sarah in New Haven. I left there tuesday about two hours before they arrived. I telegraphed to Capt. Magaw on Monday for permission to remain till next day that I might see them but was disappointed after all.

Did I tell you that I met your uncle Frank & wife & Mary while there? A few days before Mary had been close along side of us in a yatch [yacht] with a sailing party from Stonington. Neither of us was aware of the other's presence. She is just as light hearted & pretty as ever.

Here I am on "No. 69." I very little expected that a month ago when we were coming in through the narrows. I was looking so confidently to laying aside the pen for a while & using my tongue—& when we were kept day after day in the Brooklyn Navy Yard waiting orders to go to sea, none of us had any idea that this was our destiny. It was a great disappointment to us all I assure you, to none more than myself.

---

* Fort Trumbull is located at the mouth of the Thames River in New London, facing Long Island Sound.
† A dance.
‡ Keeler's second cousin Mary E. (Plant) Norton.
§ A popular tourist site, the large sandstone bluff is located on the south bank of the Illinois River about 5 miles south east of La Salle.
** John A. Rockwell (1803-1861), lawyer, judge, politician and businessman from Norwich, CT, and uncle of Keeler's good friend from La Salle. In 1836 he and his older brother Charles founded the Rockwell Land Company with the purpose of developing land in La Salle County.

CIVIL WAR YEARS: USS *FLORIDA* (1863-1865)

Of all our mess who left New York in the vessel in March 1863 only Mr. McGowan & myself returned in her. The others have been transfered from time to time or have resigned.

When our coal is out we are going to Boston to fill up. Whether we will be sent back here again or not it is impossible to say. If it were warm summer weather I would not care so much about it, but I don't fancy spending the winter so near the north pole.

Sunday evening, Oct. 3rd [2nd], off Halifax—We arrived here last Wednesday about noon & have passed the time cruising about, now & then sending one of our boats to some of the surrounding fishing smacks* for bait with which we supplied ourselves with plenty of fresh codfish.

Yesterday afternoon an English man of war, the *Jason*, came down to us out of the harbour. The Capt. of her came on board & left a copy of the port regulations & a letter from himself which our Capt. did not consider quite as courteous as he would have liked, so he determined upon a reply asking for explanations &c. As usual on such occasions I was called in to his aid & we sat up till 12 o'clock Saturday night concocting a reply to Johnny Bull's manifesto. Of course as it was an official document every word had to be well weighed & considered.†

I was to be the bearer of it to Halifax the next morning at which place the *Jason* was lying. So this morning after breakfast I took a twelve oared cutter & with Mr. Washburn for a companion we started for Halifax, a pull of some ten miles over a heavy sea & a raw, cold, strong wind.

As we got up into the harbour among the shipping we counted no less than six blockade runners, with the Confederate flag flying at the fore and the English at the mizzen. We passed along through them all with our boat ensign flying & of course attracted a good deal of attention, for a boat from one of our men of war is not often seen in the harbour now a-days. As we pulled along by the blockade runners we were hailed from them in terms neither choice nor complimentary, but as I had expected all that I was not disappointed nor do I think my feelings were very much injured. The boys & others pulling about the harbour in small boats were not much behind the others on the vessels in their reception of us. However it only went to prove the truth of the old adage that "words never break bones."

---

* Single-masted sailing vessels.
† Magaw's short reply to Captain Edward P. B. Von Donop, composed with Keeler's help, is as follows: "Sir: I have the honor to ask an explanation of this clause in your letter of October 1, 1864: *The vessels of war of the United States which may visit the port of Halifax in a becoming manner.* My Government would censure any of her ships of war that behaved in friendly ports or waters in an unbecoming manner. I am sorry we had so short an interview yesterday, and hope to be able to pay my respects to you soon, and must again apologize for not having been on deck to receive you, but the report made me was that *an English officer was coming alongside with no pennant flying in his boat.*" (ORN, I:3, p. 296).

To Halifax (August to November 1864)

We pulled up to the Navy Yard & alongside the *Jason* & found them at [Sunday] service. It is not customary to go on board our own vessels at such a time much less those of another nation, but having in mind the long pull back I went on board without hesitation & was received by Capt. Von Donop on his quarter deck very cordially & invited below to his cabin.

I delivered my dispatches which of course before they could be answered required a lengthy consultation with Admiral Hope* who was near by in his flag ship. Giving the Captain to understand that I intended to comply with the etiquette of the service & pay my respects to the Admiral before I left I intimated that in the mean time I would go ashore & make a call on our consul. He said they were "full of blackguards & blockade runners" ashore and if we went in our own boat & alone we might get into trouble. He advised us to let our boat's crew remain on board, where he would provide them with a good dinner & he would send us ashore in his own boat with one of his officers to shew us about. His offer we of course very gladly accepted, the more readily as it relieved us of the care of our men & we could leave them without any danger of their getting drunk or running away.

We were landed in the Captain's gig in company with one of his lieutenants. Passing through the Navy Yard we had a long walk through the streets before we reached the American Consulate. I was very glad of a companion as well as guide for our walk, for I very soon became satisfied that his presence only restrained the secesh rowdies from the blockade runners, who were gathered at the street corners & at the groceries, from open insult & abuse if not from personal violence. Their threats were but half suppressed as we passed by them.

I do not suppose we saw the best portion of the place but the streets we passed through were quite narrow & dirty with very narrow walks. Most of the buildings were low & small & but very few made any pretensions to architectural display or elegance.

We found our Consul (Judge somebody I have forgotten his name)† at home. We got from him what late papers & news he had & what he knew of the movements of the blockade runners. We had an invitation from him to dinner & a glass of wine. His wife he said was in New York.

Learning from him that etiquette required that we should pay our respects to the Governor‡, we left the Consulate for his residence. You very well know that official & diplomatic visits are not my forte nor to my taste or liking— perhaps you will say, "You are too matter of fact for that." However I found I was in for it and so put a bold face on the matter. We were ushered into his presence by a footman & very cordially received by a "fine old english gentle-

---

* Rear Admiral James Hope, commander-in-chief of the North America and West Indies Station.
† Mortimer M. Jackson.
‡ Sir Richard Graves MacDonnell, lieutenant-governor of Nova Scotia.

man" in a well furnished parlour, in a fine large house surrounded by nice tastefully laid out grounds. I apologised for calling on Sunday & explained the object of our visit of which he seemed to be aware. We conversed on general topics for a short time when we took our leave. Although his treatment of us was very cordial & gentlemanly, I got the idea that our yankee way of talking to him was not altogether pleasing—that is, our plain "Yes, sir" or "No, sir" did not suit as well as the John Bull "Yes, your Excellency" &c.

We returned to the *Jason* to find that the Admiral's reply, which we were to take back, was not ready, but he had sent us word that he would excuse us from calling on him as he knew we had far to go & was [were] anxious to get off as soon as possible, at which I was not sorry for I was getting sick of *diplomacy* & wanted a dinner, to which we had been invited by the Ward Room officers. It was as english as roast beef, plum pudding, & *ancient* partridges could make it & concluded by drinking "to the health of her majesty, the Queen" which they said was always customary with them at their Sunday dinner, adding that they supposed we did the same thing for our President. I assured them that we very seldom or ever thought of it unless it was at a public dinner, which they seemed to think was very singular. They have been gone from home *four* years. The Paymaster told me that he had been married but a short time when he left & was going home to find a boy three & a half years old. They are looking for the arrival of their relief every day when they will return. They were the pleasantest set of English officers I have yet fallen in with, with less of those John *Bullisms* which usually make them so disagreeable.

The cabins & ward rooms of the English vessels are much more plainly fitted up than our own & their ships, I do not think, are kept as neat & clean as ours, but I think their discipline is better.

We had a rough cold ride back to our ship which we reached about nine o'clock at night. The Captain congratulated me on my *diplomatic* efforts but I hardly think I shall make another trial unless compelled.

Thursday evening, Oct. 6th—We have been lying off Cape Sable since last Monday morning but are now headed for Boston which we hope to see Saturday morning. We have passed the time fishing for cod with sufficient success to furnish all on board what they wanted. It has been fresh cod in every style at every meal, baked, boiled, fried, chowders, "cod head *muddles*"* &c till I have got sick of it.

We have for a pilot an old fisherman we brought from New London & there is nothing comes out of the sea in this part of the world but what he knows just what it is & just how it should be cooked. He is in his element with a fish at one end of a line and himself at the other.

---

* A stew made of cod heads.

TO HALIFAX (AUGUST TO NOVEMBER 1864)

The weather for the most of the time since we have been here has been boisterous & disagreeable, the vessel rolling & pitching about breaking our chairs & smashing what little crockery we had left.

If we are to remain out much longer we shall have to fit out anew. We are all hoping that when we reach Boston we shall be ordered to New York to be laid up for repairs. Still we have been disappointed so many times that we don't allow ourselves to count to[o] confidently upon it.

Saturday morning, Oct. 8th, Boston—We have just got in from our *codfishing excursion* & I found your letter of the 1st inst. waiting my arrival, also one from Sarah & Mother. We are waiting to hear from the Department what they will do with us. I think we will go to New York. Still it is uncertain. If we do I shall probably be there about the time you get there or in New Haven. Fearing you may be gone when this letter reaches home I enclose it to Henry to for'd to you.

I am looking forward with *much pleasure* to meeting you soon. But how our little family will be scattered. It seems to[o] bad that we cannot meet together. I will write to Henry soon.

I dread the tedious ride from home for you but I hope you will get through safely. Should you stop in Brooklyn you will hear from me at Uncle B.'s or if you go direct to New Haven I will fix it so that you will hear from me there. With my best love to you all,

W—

U.S. Steamer *Florida*
New York
Nov. 2nd, 1864

Dear Anna,

I have just rec'd yours of Oct. 31st & was glad to hear of your safe arrival at Litchfield & that Mary [Graves] was so comfortable.

I was up to your uncle Frank's & took tea last evening. Found him & Harry keeping batchelor's hall, Mrs. Joy being in Stonington where she will remain two or three weeks longer & Mary [Joy] visiting in Brooklyn.

Last Saturday evening Mother, Sarah & myself made a very pleasant call at Mrs. Warner's*. They (mother & Sarah) have gone to New Jersey to spend a few days, will probably return sometime this week.

I am still at work on shipboard, too busy to realise whether it is "dismal" [out] or not. I hope to get through this week. Then what I do will depend upon what you say. Mother is going to Utica about that time & wants me to go with her. Shall I go there & see Lizzie† or go to Litchfield first? At all events I do not want to leave here till after election, for I am going to give a

---

* Keeler's mother's first cousin.
† Anna left Eddie in La Salle with Keeler's sister Fannie and Lizzie in Utica with relatives.

Civil War Years: USS *Florida* (1863-1865)

good Union vote here if I cannot send home. I am expecting to hear from Hough in reply to my letter to him about the matter in a day or two. My plan would be to go to Utica immediately after the election, make my visit there & then go to New Haven & Litchfield. I will however arrange my movements to suit you. Let me hear what you would like me to do.

I believe I wrote you that all the officers had been detached from the ship except the Capt., Chief Engr. [Exec. Officer] & myself. I expect to remain by the vessel till we are ready for sea again, which will be in from two to three months. After getting through my present work I shall have but little to do but run about. My occasional presence here will be all that will be necessary.

I think when you come to look over *all* your things you will find both your cuffs, as I am pretty sure I put them both in. I will enquire however at Mr. Joy's [Uncle Frank's] the next time I go up.

So you would not "*swap*" your incumberance of a husband—well that is strange—no accounting for tastes, women's tastes at any rate.

Don't be alarmed, the Democrats, or rather traitors, won't prevail. Mr. Lincoln is to be our next President. You may set that down as a fixed fact.

Unfortunately the *Old Helmet** is packed up with all the rest of my books. Tell Mary [Graves] that I am very sorry. If the boxes were not so strongly nailed that I should have to break the boxes in pieces in unpacking I would open them & take it out.

I met Col. Cannon in Wall St. to day & received a very cordial invitation to come up to his house & "talk over old times."† Mrs. Deforest [Cannon's wife] was disappointed that you did not call on her before you left. All are well at Aunt Brush's. Aunt remains about the same. During the past pleasant weather she rode over to New York & made a call on Mrs. Deforest.

Don't you think it would be better for me to do as I have said—go to Utica & make my visit, then return & go to Litchfield? From there you could accompany me to New Haven (stopping at Waterbury if you choose), make our visit there & then lay plans for the balance of the time, after finding out what time will be. As far as my duties will allow I will make my plans conform to yours.

Another thing. Had I better take Henry with me when we go out again? I mention the matter now that you may think it over. When we meet we will discuss it. In the meantime don't mention it to him, I do not think it will be best till we have decided.

I feel anxious to hear from the children & shall wait impatiently for Mother's return to see your letter to her. I wrote Henry a long letter night before last, which I suppose the *young man* will think contains more good advice than needed. However I don't think it will hurt him. Shall I get any-

---

* A novel by American evangelical writer Susan B. Warner published in 1864.
† Wealthy businessman Le Grand B. Cannon. He was John Wool's chief-of-staff at Fort Monroe from 1861 to 1862. His wife was Keeler's father's first cousin Mary B. DeForest.

To Halifax (August to November 1864)

thing to take to Lizzie & shall I give the girls any money? If so, how much? Let me hear from you & be sure & answer all my questions. I don't think that New Haven *air* was *prejudicial to your health*. Remember me with much love to Mary & Lillie [Graves] & accept as much as you desire for yourself from your

Husband

[Marginalia] Be careful about directing your letters to *U.S.S. Florida, New York Navy Yard*.

U.S. Steamer Florida
New York
Nov. 9th, 1864

Dear Anna,

Yours of yesterday reached me this morning with Henry's enclosed. I was right glad to hear from you both. The past three days have been stormy & disagreeable, confining me mostly to the vessel. The weather however don't seemed to have dampened the ardour of the loyal voters. What splendid news we have. I felt sure of it before. Now I know & can *feel* it, it is tangible. McClellan meets with no better success as a politician than as a general. Well when he undertakes to lead an army of traitors, renegades, copperheads & such like on a raid against his government he deserves no better fate, to say the least. He is laid out now with Buchanan* & with him will become a by word for posterity. I did respect him when he led our armies against the armed foes of the country but when he comes to marshall the secret foes of the country against it he has my utter loathing & contempt. Such men find their level. He has found his & there we will leave him.

Last Sunday morning I went to the *performances* at Trinity church in the afternoon with mother & Sarah to hear Dr. Robinson† & took tea at Mr. Joy's [Uncle Frank's] & have now just returned from supper there. All are feeling good over the splendid news which the telegraph still keeps bringing. Next to the defeat of the traitor McClellan, they regard that of Seymour & Ben Wood as the most important.‡ Their joy is not boisterous, it seems too great & deep for utterance.

Your aunt Ann is still absent.§ It is uncertain when she will return.

---

* President James Buchanan.
† Charles S. Robinson, minister of the First Presbyterian Church in Brooklyn from 1860 to 1868. Keeler's parents were members of that congregation when they lived in Brooklyn in the 1820s.
‡ Horatio Seymour, Democratic governor of New York from 1863-64, who narrowly lost re-election to the Republican candidate. He was opposed to many of Lincoln's policies, in particular the draft. Benjamin Wood, Peace Democrat congressman from New York, who, facing almost certain defeat, did not run for re-election in 1864. He was the owner of a pro-Southern newspaper in New York City that was suspected of passing on secrets to the Confederates, and so was viewed by many as a traitor.
§ Uncle Frank's wife.

CIVIL WAR YEARS: USS *FLORIDA* (1863-1865)

Last Saturday Mary [Joy] heard a ring at the door & expecting one of her companions opened it when in rushed a young man enquiring for Harry whom Mary called down stairs. The stranger informed them that their father had been run over by an omnibus down street, was seriously hurt & had been taken to the hospital. His clothes had been badly torn & dirtied & it was necessary for Harry to go to him immediately & take with him some clean clothing, which Mary in great trepidation got together. Harry started off with him carrying the bundle. At the first corner he left Harry, telling him he had an errand a short distance off & would join him at the hospital. As is supposed he hurried around the block & made his appearance again at the house, telling Mary that there were some articles which had been forgotten which Harry had sent him back for, such as an overcoat, underclothing &c. Mary went to work to get them together, the stranger telling her how much he thought of Mr. Joy [Uncle Frank], how he used to be in his Sunday School class & administrating doses of pious consolation—Mary all the time expressing her gratitude for his kindness. He got the bundle & started & that is the last that has been seen of him or of the bundle. Harry of course made all haste to the hospital where the fellow told him his father was lying with a compound fracture of the skull. Of course his father wasn't there, but was advised to go to his office & see if he was there. He found Mr. Joy writing at his desk with a sound skull & unconcious of what had taken place at home. Of course it gave them a terrible fright at the house, Mary particularly. It was a pretty sharp dodge.

I have my things all packed & shall vacate the old *Florida* to morrow. I have three boxes of odds & ends packed to send home, also a barrel of our Ward Room crockery, some of which you may find of use. My trunk of clothes, which I intend to use while on shore, I shall send to Watrous at New Haven to keep till I return from Utica.

I hope to start next Monday but may be obliged to remain till Wednesday. I hope to hear from you before I go [to Utica]. Direct to Uncle Brush, 99 Henry St. I wish you were going up with me—we would have a fine time, but it seems to be our fate to go poking about alone. I hope Lizzie will know me but I cannot really expect her to.

I am sorry that Henry feels so discontented & still more sorry to see such a horrid scrawl. I was in hopes that after all I had said to him he would take more pains. Do write to him about it. I am tired of it. He certainly cannot expect to do much in a business way till he is a better penman.

I have given you all the news I know of & so will close with a kiss & good night. Remember me with much love to Mary & Lillie.

William

[P.S.] I have sent you quite a number of papers recently, thinking you might want a slight mixture of truth with copperhead lies.

Gulf of Mexico (March to November 1865)

> *We have on board the President's murderers (the unhung ones), taking them to the Dry Tortugas where government is to furnish them (except Spangler) with a residence for the rest of their lives. Spangler goes for six years. I only regret that these didn't go with Mrs. Surratt to keep her company. We should have been saved this trip down here.* (17 July 1865)

On January 15, 1865 while Keeler was out East with Anna on his four-month furlough, Fort Fisher was captured, closing the port of Wilmington for good. The attack commenced with a massive bombardment by Union warships, followed by a ground assault by marines, sailors and infantry. Keeler, no doubt, was greatly disappointed not to have been able to participate in the ground assault, for he would surely have volunteered. However, he could count himself lucky, for the sailors were beaten back with heavy casualties.

The land war, too, was winding down. Grant was close to breaking through Petersburg's ever weakening defenses. Sherman had devastated Georgia in his March to the Sea and was rolling through the Carolinas where he planned to join up with Grant for a final assault on Lee.

With the dangers of the blockade finally over, Anna agreed to letting Henry join his father on board the *Florida*. Henry served as Paymaster's Clerk. Quiet, still and unobtrusive, he gained the esteem of all on board. Always addressing his father as Paymaster, it was some time before others knew there was a relationship between the two. With most of the ship's officers little to their liking and a brute of a captain, William Budd, the two spent most of their free time in Keeler's cabin.

From March to June, the *Florida* delivered sailors and fresh beef, vegetables and fruit to the squadrons along the Atlantic and Gulf coasts. In April, while they were on their way to New Orleans where Keeler was tasked with delivering more than one million dollars to the Gulf Squadron, he learned of the fall of Richmond and the assassination of President Lincoln. After delivering the greenbacks to the treasury in New Orleans he witnessed the rebel ram CSS *Webb* steam down the Mississippi past New Orleans in an attempt to get into the Gulf of Mexico and on to Havana, Cuba where they hoped to continue the war. In July the *Florida* was tasked with transporting four of the Lincoln assassination conspirators to the Dry Tortugas, a desolate island off the south tip of Florida, where they would serve out their long prison terms. One of the prisoners whom Keeler had ample time to observe and talk with was Samuel Mudd, the doctor who treated John Wilkes Booth's broken leg when he was on the run after shooting the president.

Upon returning to New York, Keeler expected that the *Florida* would be put out of commission and the officers and crew discharged. However, Navy Secretary Welles had other plans, and it was three more months before Keeler saw home. After towing two light-draft monitors from New York to the

Civil War Years: USS *Florida* (1863-1865)

Philadelphia Navy Yard and transporting the contents of the Naval Academy back to its pre-war home in Annapolis, the *Florida* was sent to Aspinwall (now Colón) to deliver 300 men to the Pacific Squadron. Their last trip was made more pleasant by the absence of their captain (Budd), who had been relieved of command for a drinking incident in Newport. It also gave Keeler the chance to see the Pacific Ocean one last time.

In November, Keeler's request to be relieved arrived when he was in Philadelphia. Expecting to take the first steamer to New York, he and Henry instead remained on board the *Florida* when she was ordered to tow two old hulks from Norfolk to New York. Visiting the Norfolk Navy Yard for the last time, Keeler was stirred by the sights around him: the remains of the USS *Congress*, which was destroyed by the *Virginia* on the first day of the Battle of Hampton Roads, and fragments of the *Virginia*, which had been taken out of the waters off Craney Island. Upon arriving at the New York Navy Yard, Keeler packed up his books and papers and mailed them back home. On November 13 he and Henry paid short visits to relatives in Connecticut before heading home to La Salle. His sea-faring days were over. On April 25, 1866 he received his well deserved honorable discharge after having served his country faithfully for nearly four years.

Letters of special note: March 18 (a distant view of Fort Fisher); April 14 (Key West and points along the Gulf coast); April 27 (New Orleans; the dash of the CSS *Webb*); July 27 (delivering the Lincoln assassination conspirators to the Dry Tortugas); August 6 (description of New York harbor); October 10 (Aspinwall; across the isthmus to the Pacific Ocean).

No. 1—

U.S.S. *Florida*
New York Navy Yard
March 5th, 1865

Dear Anna,

Here we are still & with less prospect of getting to sea than when you left here. Week ago last Saturday [February 25] we took in our stores & supplies for the squadron in great haste & hauled out into the stream & the next day (Sunday) our crew of some 200 men came on board, making it like anything but Sunday for me, for there was the usual confusion & disorder attendant upon getting a new crew on board.

We got up steam the same night to be in readiness to leave the next morning but found our new boilers leaked so badly that we were obliged to blow the water out & set the boiler makers to work & they didn't get through till last night & now our chief engineer tells me that they leak as bad if not worse than ever, making extensive repairs necessary which will consume a good deal of time. Still they may send us off as we are, for among other supplies for the squadron we have on board some 20,000 pounds of fresh beef

& 500 bbls. of potatoes, onions & apples which of course won't improve by keeping. If we are detained much longer the beef, which is packed in ice, will spoil if not taken out & shipped by some other vessel.

This is a sample of the way in which things are managed here. Instead of letting us make a short trial trip to test our boilers and machinery as common sense would dictate they must rush everything on board, taking it for granted that all was right. It proves the truth of the old adage "the more haste the more waste." However it has given me time to get matters well arranged in my department before getting out to sea. I would not be at all surprised if all hands were detached & the vessel was laid up again. If this should happen I shall wish you were back here again. We shall know what we are to do in a day or two, as engineers are coming on board to morrow to hold a survey.

Henry & myself have been pretty busy through the week & will be for some days to come. I have had a bad cold which has made me almost sick for a day or two but feel much better to day.

I went up to your uncle Frank's this morning & went to church with them to hear Dr. Hitchcock.* They were all well except your uncle F. who still suffers from his cold & his wife & Mary feel a good deal concerned about him. He seems to be disposed to brave it out.

Yesterday was to have been a great day here but it rained in torrents all day long. The celebration comes off to morrow, if pleasant which appearances now indicate. It will be a great day here. I hardly think I can get away to witness the display but I want Henry to see it. Harry Joy has kindly offered us a window in the medical college in front of which the procession is to pass.† I send you a *Herald* containing the programme, also a notice of our sailing on Tuesday last—Mem[orandum], don't believe all you see in the papers.

I saw Nathan Keeler‡ a day or two since. He was down from Waterbury in a great stew, hunting up a substitute, as he had been drafted. What success he met with I don't know as I have not seen him since.

I don't think that we are going to have as pleasant & agreeable messmates as on the last cruise, though it is difficult to say on so short acquaintance, but they appear to be more rough & less refined. Capt. Magaw I see has been detached from the *Lenapee* & given a sick leave. I wish we might get him back here again.

---

* Roswell D. Hitchcock, Congregational minister and professor of church history at the Union Theological Seminary in New York City.
† The 7-mile long procession, which celebrated Union victories and the expected successful conclusion of the war, extended from 14th and Broadway to Union Square. Led by major generals, admirals, as well as state and city politicians, the parade included exotic animals from P. T. Barnum's menagerie. The grand finale was a re-enactment of the Battle of Hampton Roads, which included a representation of "the little Yankee cheese box, commanded by gallant Worden." (*New York Herald*, New York, NY, March 4, 1865, p. 1).
‡ Presumably a relative of Keeler's but not a close one.

Civil War Years: USS *Florida* (1863-1865)

The Capt. we have is a perfect bear.* None of us like him. He objected very strongly to our having a stove up in the Ward Room & did all he could to prevent it. We slept for a number of nights in our rooms, cold & damp till pretty much every one in the mess had a cold when they deputed me to see the Admiral†. I told the Admiral that we were sleeping on board without a fire, with our holds full of ice & found our rooms very cold & damp & that the most of us were suffering with colds. We had a stove the same day. One big enough to heat a church.

I have not heard from you since you left Utica & feel much concerned about you, but cannot help but think that you reached home safely but that your letter notifying me of it has failed to reach me. Write at once & let me know. If you have not time for a long letter a short one will do, so that I know that you are safe at home.

I have heard nothing from New Haven or Litchfield since you left. Geo.‡ wrote me that he had sent me a boy but he failed to reach me. I have managed to pick up a very good one however.

I have not time to finish my sheet, as I have two or three other letters to write to night, & have nothing to fill it if I had the time. I have been trying to get Henry to put in a note but he says he has nothing to say so he sends his love. Give him a scolding when you write, for he has no excuse for not writing you.

You must imagine the rest of the page filled with love & kisses for yourself & the children & regards to all our friends. I am looking anxiously for a letter from you by every mail. Direct to me here—U.S. Steamer *Florida*, New York Navy Yd.

Did I send my napkins home? I can't find anything of them among my things here & think I must have packed them up in the boxes I sent home, by mistake.

I shall keep my letter open till to morrow, as I may be able to tell you more of our future.

Tuesday morning, 7th—We are getting in readiness & will probably leave soon. It is a beautiful bright clear morning. Just such a day as yesterday—a splendid day it was for the celebration. I could not get away to see the procession. Henry went & had a fine view of it from the Medical College. No letter from you yet. Do write. You can't think how anxious I am to hear from you. Good bye. With love,

Will

---

* Acting Volunteer Lieutenant Commander William Budd*.
† Hiram Paulding, commandant of the New York Navy Yard.
‡ Keeler's brother-in-law in New Haven.

Gulf of Mexico (March to November 1865)

No. 2—

U.S. Steamer *Florida*
Chesapeake Bay
March 11th, 1865

Dear Anna,

After having been detained for two days at anchor off Sandy Hook in consequence of fogs & bad weather we left there yesterday about noon & hope to reach Hampton Roads sometime this afternoon. The weather down has been stormy, cold & disagreeable. We were treated to a three or four hours snow storm yesterday afternoon and you may be assured that I considered myself fortunate not to be plodding about the streets in New York up to my ancles in filth & sposh.

We have had a tolerably smooth sea, but rough enough to try the stomachs of some of the "green horns." Henry however has escaped thus far & seems to consider himself proof. I think Hatteras will put him to the test.

It is now *two weeks* since my meat was put into the hold. How it will come out I don't know, but I imagine some of it will be rather *ancient* despite the ice in which it is packed.

I hear nothing from you yet, but hope to get a letter at Hampton Roads. If not, I shall imagine that you are sick or some mishap has befallen you. I feel very anxious indeed, the more so that I know that you would not neglect to write as you promised as "soon as you reached home."

I don't like to send a sheet partly filled but shall have to once in a while, partly because I am too busy to write more & partly for the want of something to say. But as an offset I hope you will hear from me more frequently than when on the blockade.

I have my office nicely fitted up. Henry has a good berth in it. I wish you could drop in upon us some evening as we are seated writing or chatting—a bright lamp burning and everything cheerful & pleasant, while outside the storm is howling. The heat from the boilers makes it warm & comfortable (our thermometer marking 70°), but in summer I fear the heat will be intolerable.

I don't find many pleasant associates among the officers & spend most of my time in the office with Henry. The Capt. contrives to render himself more & more disagreeable & is hated more & more by all on board every day.

I have just thought that I owe Eddie a letter. Tell the dear little fellow that papa will try & write to him in your next.

With the balance of the sheet filled with love & kisses to yourself & the children I am affectionately,

W—

Civil War Years: USS *Florida* (1863-1865)

No. 3—

U.S. Steamer *Florida*
At Sea off "Hatteras"
March 18th, 1865

Dear Anna,

We left Hampton Roads early last Monday morning [March 13]. I had no opportunity while there of going or sending ashore for a letter from you, so I am still in ignorance of you since you left Utica. We reached Hampton Roads on Saturday afternoon & immediately ran up to Norfolk where we spent Sunday. It was a beautiful day & I longed to improve it by a walk ashore but could not, as I was kept busy all day issuing provisions to the vessels in the Navy Yard. I merely went ashore in the Yard on duty. I saw Crafts a few minutes. He has his wife in Norfolk and is expecting his promotion to a lieutenancy. I suppose his wife will be his *vice*.

We ran down to Beaufort but could not go in as we drew too much water, so I was prevented from seeing my friends there. A tug came out to meet us & we sent the mails & supplies in by it.

We arrived off fort Fisher Wednesday the 15th where we lay till yesterday afternoon. You may imagine my anxiety to go ashore & take a view of the place we had been nearly two years blockading & see the effects of the late terrible bombardment & fight, but I could not.* Had Capt. Magaw been in command I could easily have arranged matters so as to have left the vessel for a short time. But with our present Captain I knew I could not & so did not make the attempt.

We however lay close enough in to the beach to enable me to get a pretty good view of fort Fisher & the adjacent works with a good glass. The fleet here had dispersed, only one vessel (the *Alabama*) being outside on our old blockading ground. Five or six of the smaller class of vessels are in the Cape Fear river between Fayettville & the mouth. The others are, some of them laid up in the different navy yards repairing, some up the James river, others sent off to join other squadrons.

I saw a number of our naval officers who had been at different points up the river from Smithville to Fayetville. They give a very interesting account of what they have seen. They represent a good deal of Union feeling at the different places & contrary to what we have been led to believe, plenty of provisions.

---

* On January 13 a fleet of more than 60 warships carrying more than 600 guns opened up a massive bombardment which silenced Fort Fisher's guns. Two days later a ground force comprising nearly 10,000 infantry and 2,000 sailors and marines advanced on the fort. Carrying pistols and cutlasses, the sailors were cut down by heavy musket fire and failed to get into the fort. However, that assault distracted the fort's defenders, enabling the infantry to enter the fort with relative ease. Six-hours of brutal hand-to-hand fighting ensued. At 10:00 pm the Confederates surrendered.

Gulf of Mexico (March to November 1865)

One who is stationed at Wilmington with his vessel said that they wanted a place for a club house while ashore, to loaf & smoke in & so took possession of a fine house there which had been deserted by its rebel occupants who went off leaving the house with all its furniture, library, paintings, &c which are being used more freely than their original owners would approve.

Sherman's army when they passed through Fayettville had scarcely drawn a ration since leaving Savannah, having lived almost entirely on the country & were leading & driving horses & mules loaded with poultry &c.*

One of our pilots who went ashore to fort Fisher says that one cannot imagine the effect of the fire from our vessels without going over the ground. The strip of land between the sea and the river for half a mile above & below the fort is covered with shot & shell of all sizes, mingled with grape & cannister & fragments of exploded shells, while the ground is ploughed & torn as nothing but such a fire could do. Broken & dismounted guns lie scattered about, all of them bearing the marks of our "neutral English friends."

One cannot appreciate the magnitude of the task undertaken by our forces in the capture of this work till he has seen its strength & the preparations made by its defenders to resist such an attack. Now it lies, as I have said, its guns broken & dismounted & all the works bearing full evidence of the strength and accuracy of our fire. The rebel rag is hauled down from the flag staff & the place is deserted except by an occasional curiosity seeker.

The fleet, as I have said being dispersed, there was but little call for the fresh beef with which we are loaded, so that now we are on our way back to Hampton Roads & "a market," the market being up James river in all probability. I don't at all object to making a trip up there among places which became so familiar in the summer of '62.

We expect to get in to night & shall probably know to morrow morning where we shall go. The meat has now been on board over three weeks but has kept better than I should suppose, being well packed in ice. I threw overboard 2000 pounds yesterday which had spoiled & the rest I think won't keep much longer.

We took down to Wilmington with us, from Norfolk, two of the correspondents of the [New York] World. They were quite good company & had many amusing stories to tell of the war of which they had seen a good deal in their capacity.

Our executive officer is from Greenfield Hill, Conn. His name is Staples†, a nephew of your old acquaintance of that name in Bridgeport. He is acquainted with a good many of the Bridgeport folks.

---

* Fayetteville, NC fell to Sherman's forces on March 11.
† Acting Volunteer Master William E. Staples (1832-1891). He was the son of a wealthy lumber merchant, banker and ship owner from Westport, CT. Family lore has it that he ran away to sea at a young age to serve as a cabin boy. By the age of 18 he was a full-fledged mariner, and by 28 a sea captain. He enlisted in 1861 and served on the USS *Tuscarora*,

Civil War Years: USS *Florida* (1863-1865)

Another of our Ward Room officers was with Price* when he captured Lexington. He afterwards deserted the rebel ranks & joined the Navy, was captured & confined about a year in a prison pen in Texas. He makes a good deal of sport for us.

Sunday morning [March 19]—a chance to send ashore. So good by & a kiss.

[unsigned]

No. 4—

U.S. Steamer *Florida*
New York Navy Yard
March 22nd, 1865

Dear Anna,

We have just reached here from Hampton Roads, in twenty two hours, after a very pleasant trip. I think I mentioned in my last that there was a probability of our going up James River. We did not, as we received orders to proceed immediately home.

I was much gratified on reaching here to find by your *note* that you had reached home safely. This was the first intelligence I had from you since you left Utica. Had you kept your promise & complied with my request when you left New York, by sending me a line immediately on reaching home, I should have received it before we left here & should have been spared many anxious moments. I was disappointed in getting nothing more than your little note of the 13th, but the knowledge that you had reached home safely more than compensated for my disappointment. My idea was, & I thought I so expressed it, that you should write me a line or two at Old Point to assure me of your safety in case I should have access to the mail there, but that all your *letters* would be directed to me here. I was unable to go ashore at Old Point & so did not get your letter or Dave's. I have written to the Postmaster to forward them to me & hope to have the pleasure of reading them soon.

We left Norfolk Monday evening [March 20] with the thermometer at *90°* & we find it here cold & blustering—real March weather. I let Henry go ashore there Sunday to see the place. He came back in the evening apparently well pleased with the green grass, flowers & budding trees. I *ordered* him to sit down & write you a good long letter. I hope the result of my order has been apparent to you before this. I saw Crafts again in Norfolk. His wife is still there. He is expecting a new command.

We brought up with us from the Norfolk Hospital fifty of the wounded from fort Fisher sufficiently recovered to be sent North. One had had five

---

searching for Confederate raiders off the coast of England and France. He served briefly on two more vessels, doing blockade duty in the Gulf of Mexico, before joining the *Florida*.
* Confederate Brigadier General Sterling Price.

balls through him, others without legs & arms &c. They presented a sad spectacle.

I know nothing of our future movements. I hardly think we shall be sent to Wilmington again on the same errand, as I now have some eight thousand pounds of beef spoiling in the holds. I would not be surprised if we were to be sent down to the gulf. As soon as anything definite is known I will let you know.

We have had a case of the small pox on board or rather variolvia. He has been lying in his hammock within three feet of my office door so that I probably passed within that distance of him a hundred times a day. I congratulated myself that I had been vaccinated while in New Haven.

Saturday, March 25th—We are now preparing for a trip to the gulf & will probably be gone about a month visiting Key West, Pensacola, Mobile (or the fleet off that place), New Orleans & Texas, and the rumour is that on our return we are to be employed in convoying mails & treasure to & from Aspinwall*.

We are having real cold raw March weather and I long to get into a warmer & a pleasanter climate.

A number of the purchased vessels which have come north for repairs are either being laid up or sold, but I think after the extensive repairs just made on us we shall be kept in the service for some time longer & then for home. How I do long to see us all at home once more. How pleasant it will seem. I don't care how soon it comes about.

Sunday evening, 26th—I have just returned from a call at your uncle Frank's. Found them well as usuall. His cold still hangs on to him & his family seem a good deal concerned. They want him to make a trip to Aspinwall. I got there in time to go to church with them this morning & heard Dr. Hitchcock.

Mary [Joy] told me that they had had a letter from you, which she promised to let me read before I left but she went out to Sunday school & forgot it. She mentioned that you met with a good many delays on your trip home & was obliged to remain in Chicago over Sunday & was unable to find Mr. & Mrs. Dikeman†. It must have been a long lonesome day for you. I hope I shall get your letter from Old Point giving the particulars. If not, you must send me a duplicate of it. Let me hear from you as soon as you get this. Let me know how you found everything at home & how you get along.

Mary [Joy] tells me that you think Eddie has grown a good deal. How I wish I could see him. I send him a letter with this which I want you should have him answer some time when you are writing.

---

* Aspinwall (now Colón) is on the Caribbean Sea side of the Isthmus of Panama.
† Fannie Dikeman, daughter of Anna's mother's sister Nancy Tuthill.

Civil War Years: USS *Florida* (1863-1865)

I also enclose $20. counterfeit Confederate note from Fort Fisher. It has passed through one of the Wilmington banks & has been stamped by them to prevent its being passed again.

What good news we get from our armies.* It does seem as if the end was near at hand. Gold I see continues to decline but prices do not seem to go down with it. I was told that Stewart† had been selling cotton cloth for 15 & 18 cents—that is a decline truly.

Should we be here another Sunday I shall try & go up to New Haven if possible. Now do write me a good long letter at once. Only think of the one little note I have had since you left Utica.

With love & kisses yours as ever,

W—

[Marginalia] Monday morning [March 27]—Yours of Mch 1st & March 20th just rec'd, also Dave's. Tell Dave I will write to him to day to go by next mail.

No. 5—

U.S. Steamer *Florida*
New York Navy Yard
March 31st, 1865

Dear Anna,

My heart was rejoiced & my eyes made glad by the receipt of yours of March 1st & March 20th, both arriving the same day, & again yesterday by the one of the 25th to Henry.

We are preparing for a trip to the Gulf. How long we shall be absent I don't know, but I think from four to six weeks. We shall touch at Key West, Pensacola, New Orleans, off Mobile (I hope to the city) & Galveston. We carry out ice, fresh beef & vegetables for the squadron.

I do not expect to hear from you till I return. It will seem a long, long time—worse than the blockade. If an opportunity presents itself I will mail you a few lines from New Orleans—perhaps they may find their way up the river to you.

What a time you had getting home. It is tedious at the best traveling in the winter, but I think you had more than your share of accidents & delays. What a pity you could not find any of your acquaintances in Chicago. It must have been a pretty long Sunday to you.

It is a comfort to know that you reached home safely at last, even if it was as disconsolate in its appearance as you represent. By this time you must have

---

* On March 21 Sherman defeated Confederate General Joseph E. Johnston at Bentonville, NC, the last battle those two armies would fight. Four days later, Lee's last attempt to break the siege of Petersburg failed, leaving the Union lines unchanged and the Confederate lines much weakened.

† A. T. Stewart & Co., a department store in New York City.

GULF OF MEXICO (MARCH TO NOVEMBER 1865)

everything "put to rights." How I would like to drop in upon you & spend the evening. It is fortunate that you have a good girl.

Tuesday, April 4th—My letter has lain these last few days untouched. I have been very busy, I was going to say day & night.

Last Saturday I spent in New York in company with a couple of detectives, hunting up some property which had been stolen from the ship while we were repairing—our cushions, mirrors &c. I think you have heard me speak of it. I got out a warrant by Admiral Paulding's order & searched a house where I found a small portion of them. We were after the man all day but he managed to elude us. I got back to the ship about nine at night, having eaten nothing all day & about as tired as I could well be.

The next morning, Sunday, I was just leaving the ship to go up to your uncle Frank's when I was sent over to the Police court in New York on the same business. I got up there just in time to take tea with them. Mary [Joy] was bright as ever. Harry [Joy] was in Philadelphia. Watrous had been down, or rather through the city, on one of his flying visits—I saw nothing of him.

What great, glorious, splendid news the telegraph is bringing us.* I hope it will not be shadowed by any reverses. It is so great & important that I cannot begin to realize it, nor do I believe the public does, in all its magnitude and its consequences. I feel as if I wanted to shake hands with every one I meet—too happy to contain myself. "Othello's occupation's gone"† or very soon will be I cannot help but think.

Who knows but what this trip to the Gulf will be our last—then for home. But I do not allow my mind to dwell too much upon it—something may turn up to delay that happy time, but I cannot think that it is very far distant.

I take out with me over *one million* of dollars for distribution to the Squadron in the Gulf & I was told to day that I was to receive *nine million* more to take to New Orleans for the army. Ask Dave if I hadn't better forfeit my bonds. I could "make a *pile*," but I fear "it wouldn't pay." Should I take it all out with me it will be more than has been entrusted to any one Paymaster during the war.

We have now & then a spring like day, but most of the time the weather is cold, sour & disagreeable. I suppose we shall soon be where it will be too warm.

I received a letter from Capt. Magaw a few days since. He was on sick leave at Milwaukee.

Wednesday, April 5th—Yours & Eddie's of March 31st reached me to day. Tell Eddie he is a splendid little fellow & a good scholar & his letter was a real nice one & that I liked it very much.

---

* News of the fall of Richmond on April 3: After the Union army's breakthrough at Petersburg on April 2, Lee told Jefferson Davis and his cabinet to leave the Confederate capitol.
† William Shakespeare's *Othello*. Keeler is referring to the end of slavery.

Civil War Years: USS *Florida* (1863-1865)

If Dave can get $1500. for my Ottawa property I think he had better sell. Has he struck ilo [oil] yet? I hope he will succeed but I think it doubtful.

Mother is at Uncle Brush's. I have not seen her—have made two or three unsuccessful attempts. My time while I have been here has been pretty fully occupied, giving me but little time to run about.

Write me a little note at New Orleans—I may get it. Don't fail to write to me here [New York Navy Yard] every week. The news will neither be old or stale.

If I could only get home in June when everything is fresh & fair how I would like it.

I have been busy the greater part of the day with money matters in the Sub Treasury New York. To morrow I expect to get my money on board & leave for the sunny South. I will leave a small space for a post scrip just before sailing.

Thursday evening [April 6]—This has been a busy day with me. I got on board my "greenbacks," between one & two millions. I have been relieved of the care of the other eight million by an army paymaster who goes down with us for that purpose.

We sail to morrow afternoon. Henry is writing. Good bye. With love & kisses to all.

W—

No. 6—

U.S. Steamer Florida
Key West, Florida
April 14th, 1865

Dear Anna,

We arrived here yesterday after a very pleasant & quick trip, this being our first stop since leaving New York, being just seven days making the passage.

After making the Florida coast we skirted along the coral reefs in water of the most beautiful blue colour, shading into a light pea green as it shallowed over the reefs. Its transparency was surprising, equaled only by some parts of the Pacific. As we came into the harbour we crossed some of the coral ledges, the water alternating from a deep, dark blue to a light green as it varied in depth, at times seeming to shoal so that one could wade ashore, so clear was the water & so distinct & apparently near the coral bottom.

We passed under the guns of Fort Taylor* & came up alongside the dock among quite a crowd of vessels all decked out in their gayest colors from trucks down, in honor of the capture of Richmond, the news of which reached them the previous evening. At noon a salute was fired from the fort

---

* The fort located at the southwestern tip of Key West.

Gulf of Mexico (March to November 1865)

& from each of the different vessels & the day ended with bonfires, illuminations &c &c so that we have had a double celebration, in New York & here.

A number of our passengers leave us here, for we brought down quite a number of officers for the squadron, some eight or ten in the Ward Room & 25 or thirty in the steerage, with one hundred seamen.

We find it very hot & feel it the more from having so recently left a northern climate.

Henry & myself have spent a short time ashore, two or three hours, long enough to see the place & make us wish to leave, for I assure you there is but little that is desirable here. It is a narrow sand spit or island, with a small settlement upon it. But who or what the inhabitants are I cannot say, as I came in contact with but few if any except at the small shops where they appear to be a sort of mongrel spanish, possessing all their vices with none of their virtues (if the spaniards have any of the latter).

The streets are wide, sandy, hot, dry & dusty. The buildings are small & like all others in hot climates built open so as to admit the air as freely as possible & surrounded with cool, comfortable looking verandahs, shaded by cocoa nut & tamarind trees. They looked inviting from the dry hot streets as we passed along gazing over the white picket fences at latticed doors and windows.

We lounged awhile in some of the miserable little shops hunting up shells & coral to send home. A few miserable looking oranges, bannanas & mangoes brought from Havanna was all the fruit we could find except a few cocoanuts grown on the island, all of which could be bought much cheaper & better in New York.

Except for a military station I cannot see what there is about Key West to make it desirable. Plenty of fish & green turtle are to be had here. We had some of the former for breakfast & found them very fine.

The most pleasing feature to me was the flowers—few if any annuals, but large beautiful shrubs covered with flowers of various bright hues, red of different shades predominating. It was so long since I had seen flowers that it was a treat the rarity of which enabled me to appreciate it the more.

In all my acquaintance with tropical countries I never saw flowers blooming so profusely & in such variety. The oleander was the only kind with which I was acquainted. I found four or five varieties of it, of various shades of red, double & single, the bushes growing in clumps & from 10 to 15 feet high, the tops one mass of blossoms. Almost every house had more or less of them & mingled with a bright yellow shrub & a species of intensely crimson alathea, gave the streets a gay appearance. I brought on board a huge bouquet gathered over the fence tops as we sauntered along, which I wish you could see. You will have to be content however with some of them in a dry state.

Civil War Years: USS *Florida* (1863-1865)

Mobile bay, April 20th—Here we are a few days after the capture of the place.* As our draft of water is too great we cannot go up to the city and are at anchor some thirty miles below it. We arrived at daylight this morning, but my duties I fear will prevent my visiting the city.

But to go back a little. We left Key West on the 15th, skirting along the coast, most of the time being within sight of it, & stopping whereever there was one of our blockading vessels to be supplied. How welcome we were you can infer from the fact that some of them had been without vegetables, papers or news of any kind for over two months. In this way we stopped at Indian River, Charlotte Harbour, Tampa Bay, St. Marks, East Pass, West Pass, Apalachicola, St. Joseph, Cedar Keys, St. Andrew, St. Vincent, arriving at Pensacola Navy Yard yesterday morning. At none of these places save the latter did we go on shore, sometimes going barely within sight of the land & at others running close in to it & a more dreary desolate forbidding coast I think I never saw. If the country back [of the coast] is like it, it's hardly worth fighting for.

As I saw the solitary blockaders watching this dreary stretch of naked sand, cut off from the world for such long periods of time, not even blockade runners to chase or rebel batteries to watch to relieve the monotony of their life & too far apart for an occasional visit to each other, I felt thankful that my lot had been with the N.A.B. [North Atlantic Blockading] Squadron where dull as I used to think it we used to have an occasional excitement of a blockade runner or shelling the rebel batteries & were near neighbors enough to exchange at times a grumble or growl at our out of the world condition & anathematise the whole Navy Department.

The whole coast along which we passed as far as I could see it was a low, level, dreary waste of white sand fringed in the background with pine & live oaks. Capt. Budd who has formerly been on the coast survey here says most of the interior is a vast interminable swamp & that the coast along which we have been steaming swarms with mosquitoes & sand flies, which latter are by far the worst as they are so small that no net can keep them out & their bite makes them more annoying if possible than the mosquito.

At some of the vessels at which we stopped they told me they would occasionally go on shore to hunt, game being plenty in their vicinity, such as deer, bear &c. Green turtle were plenty & fish abounded all along the coast. Eggs of the water fowl were also plenty in some places. Other vessels were stationed near some small settlements or some farming district from which they supplied themselves. If the inhabitants were loyal they were paid, if not they got no pay.

---

* Mobile surrendered on April 12 following a siege by Union troops. The city had been cut off from the Gulf of Mexico since August 5, 1864 when Farragut's fleet gained control of Mobile Bay.

Gulf of Mexico (March to November 1865)

Numbers of refugees are scattered along the coast where they can be protected by the gun boat stationed in the vicinity, living in miserable huts hastily constructed by themselves or deserted by the rebel owners, subsisting on game & fish. Numbers came off to me begging for a few potatoes, flour, sugar, coffee & tea which some of them said they had not tasted for months.

The same scene of havoc & destruction is presented at the Pensacola Navy Yard as at Norfolk.* It has been a large fine yard but there [are] but few buildings remaining in it entire. The yard is some six or seven miles from the city. Consequently I did not visit it as I had no desire to walk or ride that distance throught [through] hot sand ankle deep. The walks & avenues running through the Yard are shaded by rows of the Palmetto & Pride of China, the latter a mass of lilach colored blossoms giving an agreeable perfume. A cloudless sky made their shade desirable, but a delightfully cool breeze from the water tempered the heat and rendered it far more endurable than Key West.

I left about two hundred thousand dollars here & one hundred men.

We got under way towards evening & before dark had passed out into the Gulf between forts Pickens & Barrancas, the former bearing many marks of the present great struggle.†

As I have already said we reached here [Mobile Bay] early this morning & are lying at anchor between Fort Morgan & Fort Gaines with[in] hailing distance of the *Richmond* & just above the obstructions placed in the river by the rebs to prevent our passing the forts. Fort Morgan still shews the marks of the terrible fire from our vessels in the great fight in the bay here.‡ Through some of the holes in the walls made by our fifteen inch shells I believe a horse & carriage could be driven.

At Pensacola we received the cheering news of the surrender of Lee & his army.§ It was not unexpected to me, as from the position of the respective armies when we left New York I considered Lee's capture or the destruction of his army inevitable. But I feared there would be another bloody fight first & was most agreeably disappointed to learn to the contrary. I cannot see what there is now to prevent a speedy peace, one which will be honorable to the north.

Friday evening, 21st—We have just got under way for New Orleans where we have been ordered in haste in consequence of the news of Mr. Lincoln's death.** I cannot bring myself to believe the truth of this report, but it is very generally credited here & all the flags have been at half mast in

---

* The Confederates had set fire to the yard when they evacuated on May 9, 1862.
† Forts guarding the entrance to Pensacola, FL.
‡ One of the forts guarding the entrance to Mobile Bay which was attacked by Farragut's warships on August 5, 1864.
§ With his westward path of escape cut off by Union cavalry and his rear facing the mass of the Union army, Lee had no alternative but to surrender which he did on April 9.
** Lincoln was assassinated at Ford's Theatre by John Wilkes Booth on April 15.

consequence of it. It is too horrible to be true. But after all it would but be in keeping with the spirit of the rebellion from the outbreak to the finale which I believe to be near at hand. Had this taken place a year or two ago when the rebels might possibly have turned the temporary derangement of our national machinery which the President's assassination would occasion to their advantage it would seem probable, but now when all is lost, when there is no hope, it staggers belief.

Such a deed cannot have the countenance of the sober thinking men among the rebels—for I believe there are many such still among them. It would be more like[ly] to be rejoiced over by northern secessionists, sympathisers & copperheads. A heart black enough to sympathise with Southern traitors would not hesitate to gloat over the murder of the President.

Should Mr. Lincoln be dead I am of the opinion that the rebels will not be dealt with by his successor as kindly or as leniently. If I do not mistake Mr. Johnson* he will be easily bought up by the South or he will turn upon them to revenge the injuries & insults which he feels they have been the means of bringing upon him as a Southern man & as such they will find that there is a spice of vindictiveness in his disposition which perhaps he will not care to conceal altogether & which they will be made to feel.

Trouble is anticipated at New Orleans & we are under orders to reach there as soon as possible.

Before we leave there I will try & let you hear from me again. I shall hope to find a letter there from you. Henry & myself are both well & send lots of love & kisses to you all.

Will

No. 7—

U.S. Steamer *Florida*
New Orleans
April 27th, 1865

Dear Anna,

My last left us hastening to this place from Mobile bay in consequence of the sad intelligence of the President's death. What I had hoped was a mere rumour was confirmed upon our arrival here. Trouble was anticipated here in consequence of this sad & unexpected change which might make our vessel with its heavy battery needed. Fortunately however we found every thing quiet & the whole city manifesting every outward sign of sorrow.

We passed up the river in the day time giving me a fine opportunity to view the country adjacent to the stream. I was much disappointed in its appearance. Few if any of those large splendid plantations of which I had

---

* President Andrew Johnson.

heard are to be seen. We enter the river from the Gulf through rows of coarse grass & half submerged willows which border the stream on either side & beyond them is a vast expanse of shoal water & swamps, interspersed with half sunken logs & stumps floated down from the interior.

As we proceed up the stream the narrow strips of half submerged vegetation gives place to swamps with an occasional dead cypress and these in turn to an occasional patch of firmer land (I can hardly say dry ground). On some of these a venturesome darkey has built his cabin, set out perhaps one or two orange trees & tries to cultivate the little patch of ground.

As we proceed up stream the ground becomes firmer & has larger portions under cultivation with larger buildings, sometimes a little cluster of them. Then comes the sugar plantations, some of them large in extent to be sure, but wanting that air of elegance, taste & luxury which I imagined was to be seen. For the most part they occupied somewhat narrow strips of land extending along the river, shut in in the background by the dark walls of evergreens which appeared to form their boundary. On a few of them the buildings for the manufacture & storage of sugar were of brick, large & expansive.

There was the little cluster of negro quarters, on some of the plantations, laid out in streets & blocks, neat little one story, whitewashed, wooden buildings with fences enclosing a garden patch & a short distance from them the more pretentious house of the owner or overseer usually surmounted with a bell for calling the hands to work, very few if any of them that I saw displaying much architectural taste or elegance & were wanting in that comfortable home look which is so common about our northern dwellings.

Groves of orange trees & clumps of beautiful oleanders hid many defects. Every thing had a neglected appearance & a sort of tumble down look as if things were left to take care of themselves. This was no doubt owing in part to the war. All the plantations seemed to be nearly deserted, but few persons could be seen about them, black or white.

We passed a number of large orange groves, the fruit being probably raised for market, the trees being set out with the regularity of an orchard, not bearing however perpetually as in tropical climes but having an annual crop, in the fall.

The levees instead of being the large embankments I had supposed were mere slight ridges of earth thrown up along the river side which seemed as if the swash of our [paddle] wheels would wash away.

We anchored for the night four or five miles below the city & early the next morning, Sunday, were under way again & came to anchor in the stream at the upper end of the city.

Civil War Years: USS *Florida* (1863-1865)

I went ashore for a stroll in the course of the day & spent an hour or more seated in the verandah of the "St. Charles" gazing up & down the streets.* All the stores & public buildings were closed & there was not the stir & bustle in the streets I had been led to suppose I should see. All or nearly all the buildings, public & private, were draped in mourning. On some of them it was very tastefully arranged & with a good deal of expense.

I think the city has become a good deal *yankeeized* since it has come into our possession. There are many fine large expensive buildings, but their Canal street will bear no comparison with Broadway in the expense or style of architecture.

The next day I came across some of my James river acquaintances who furnished a fine carriage & took me out over the famous shell road to Lake Ponchartrain. This once celebrated drive has been taken possession of by Uncle Sam who has occupied more than one half of its width with a rail road track & the balance is badly cut up by the frequent passage of heavy army wagons. So for the time [being] its glories have departed.

Starting off at right angles with the river we are soon through the city, which is stretched along the stream. The country is low, flat & in many places wet & marshy. Nothing of notice presents itself if we except the cemeteries which differ from ours, their interments being made above the surface & the bodies being enclosed in masses of solid masonry surmounted by the usual varieties of sculptured figures & ornaments, whose snowy whiteness contrasted with the dark green foliage of the orange & the brighter magnolia mingled with the oleander & other gay flowers.

A few miles out from the city is the "half way house," an eating & drinking establishment, much frequented by pleasure parties. It was surrounded by a handsomely laid out garden filled with a variety of flowering shrubs. From there to the lake the road was bordered on one side by the canal & on the other by a low level swamp covered with coarse grass, stunted palmettoes, live oaks & cypress, the landscape rendered still more gloomy if possible by the masses of dismal colored moss trailing from the branches of the trees. The lake is a vast expanse of turbid looking water. Nothing but the coarse grass to indicate its boundaries or that of the swamps by which it is surrounded.

New Orleans I think must be a good location for ducks, darkies (acclimated ones) & yellow fever. I think I could find a more desirable spot for a residence.

The tuesday following our arrival I was on my way from the Treasury, where I had been to make arrangements for delivering the funds I carried out, when I met the Capt. [Budd] who told me that a rebel ram was on her way down the river & he wished I would get the money ashore as soon as

---

* A large hotel on the edge of the French Quarter at the Common Street bend of St. Charles Avenue.

possible. Now I had heard "ram, ram" so much since being in the service without seeing it that I had come to regard it as a myth & so found my way very leisurely to the dock where I hired a boat (none from our vessel being there) & went on board [the *Florida*]. I found our crew at quarters and everything in readiness for action.

Maj. Mann* who had charge of eight millions for the army had just got a tug alongside & had his money on deck, in twenty six iron safes. To this I added mine & persuaded him to see it safe to the Treasury with his own, though the Capt. wished me to go on shore with it, but my desire to see a rebel ram overcame my anxiety for the safety of the money. The safes went over the side into the tug in a hurry I assure you.

She was hardly shoved off from us when as I was joking one of our officers about "the ram" I heard a gun fired by one of the vessels lying in the river above us, followed by another & another. At first I took it to be a salute till I heard the howl of the missiles when I glanced up the stream & just turning a bend I saw a comparatively small steamer coming at a furious rate of speed, the American ensign at half mast at her stern.†

Her speed, going with the current, was so rapid that as she passed one vessel after another they could only fire a shot or two at her. First one of the bales of cotton piled up on her decks went spinning into the river, the loose material flying in all directions, then the splinters flew from her bow as a shot passed through it, then the stays to her smoke stack tumbled onto her deck, but she kept bravely on.

She still kept up the American flag & many seemed to hesitate to fire into it, but I expected when she came opposite us to see her receive the contents of two of our nine inch guns which were trained directly upon the path she had to take. But our Capt. like others seemed to hesitate to give the order, fire, fearing it might possibly be one of our own boats & so the favourable opportunity was lost.

Our vessel was much the highest out of the water & as I stood upon our deck looking down upon the ram to note the effect of our expected shot I saw but one person upon her. He was behind some cotton bales lying flat on his face pulling down the American flag & running up the rebel which was boldly displayed just as they were astern of us.

She passed nearer to us than to any other vessel, so close in fact that I could have thrown my hat on board. It was impossible to have missed her

---

* James Mann, paymaster in the Union army with the rank of major. He was a state legislator in Maine in the 1850s. After the war he remained in New Orleans as a Treasury agent, and in 1868 was elected as a Democrat to the U.S. House of Representatives from Louisiana's 2nd congressional district, but died at the start of his term.

† The CSS *Webb* had broken through the Red River blockade on April 23 and steamed down the Mississippi towards the Gulf of Mexico with the intention of becoming a commerce raider.

had we fired. She passed the other vessels lying below us in the same way, not a shot being fired from them, till she came abreast of the *Fearnought*, a large sailing vessel used for storing ammunition & having on board three thousand barrels of powder. Here she hesitated for an instant & headed for the vessel but turned again & kept on her way down the stream.

We were ignorant at the time of her intentions, but the Capt. of the *Webb* has since told us that he took the vessel for the *Portsmouth*, which it was his intention to blow up with a torpedo he had attached to his bows. Fortunately for all the vessels in the river & the city too, as well as the rebels themselves, they found upon attempting it that the torpedo was disarranged & so gave it up. Had they succeeded they would have destroyed everything for a mile around as well as themselves.

Of course everything in & about the city was excitement. The first one to give chase was a small tug, the *Hollyhock*. Then as soon as the Admiral* could collect his scattered senses he signalised for us to follow, but with two anchors out & a large quantity of chain it was not so speedily done. One anchor & chain we slipped & lost, the other was hove up & we were off, but not until the *Webb* had got a good start of us & was entirely out of sight. We followed for about twenty five miles when we all at once saw a dense black smoke rising from behind a wooded bend in the river which the *Hollyhock* returning said was the ram ashore & in flames.

It seems they kept down the stream, supposing that all obstacles but the forts were passed when an unexpected opponent presented itself—the *Richmond*, one of our large frigates carrying a very heavy battery. Not daunted at this & knowing it to be their only chance they determined to ram her & might have succeeded, but the *Richmond* was anchored behind a bar which projected from the river bank, making it impossible to reach her without first going down stream & then heading up again by which manoeuvre they would not only have exposed themselves to a broadside from the *Richmond* but have lost their momentum as a ram. Their hearts failed them here—they turned the *Webb* to the river bank, ran her aground, fired her & then made for the woods whence they were hunted out by cavalry sent down for the purpose.

The *Webb* was a New York built boat & was used on the river here for towing till the war broke out when the rebels seized her & fitted her up for a ram. She was the one, I think, which sunk the *Indianola*.† She was commanded by Lieut. Read of the Confederate navy, the same one who took the *Tacony* out of Portland harbour & made such havoc among the fishermen.‡ He

---

* Acting Rear Admiral Henry K. Thatcher.
† On February 24, 1863 the ironclad USS *Indianola* was rammed on the Mississippi by the CSS *Webb*. Badly damaged, she ran aground and was captured and later partially burned. The ironclad was re-floated in early 1865 by Keeler's friend from La Salle James Laning.
‡ Charles W. Read. In June 1863, the 24-year old Confederate Navy lieutenant went on a three-week raiding spree that ravaged merchant shipping along the North Atlantic coast. Starting off in command of the CSS *Clarence*, a brig captured by the CSS *Florida* on May

boldly avows his object to be, in case he got out of the river, to make for Havanna, burning & destroying everything that fell in his way. He with five of his officers are prisoners on board—candidates I hope for fort Lafayette. They don't consider the war as ended by any means, for "they can fight us for years in the bush."

We asked Reed what he thought when he saw the *Hollyhock* after him. He said it was just what he desired, as he intended after she had pursued him a little further down the river to capture her (which he could easily have done) & putting the most of his crew in her & keeping up our flag would have gone by the forts who if they had fired at the *Webb* would not at her pursuer, as they would have supposed the *H.* to have been.

The most badly scared persons in this affair were those living in Algiers opposite this city, the shot from the guns passing through & through their houses. Fortunately no persons were injured. One or two cows I heard were killed.

There was great rejoicing among the secessionists at the carrying [of] the rebel flag past New Orleans & by all our gun boats as well as by all the vessels & forts above. It is one of the boldest & most audacious exploits of the war.

New York, May 6th—We arrived here early this morning after a very pleasant & short passage. Found the weather cold, sour & disagreeable—a great change to us. Yours of the 14th & 27th were waiting me. Many thanks for not forgetting my request to write. You shall hear from me again soon. With love to all.

W—

No. 8—

U.S. Steamer *Florida*
New York Navy Yard
May 8th, 1865

Dear Anna,

I am ever so thankful to you for the two letters I found when I got here. They did not seem old or stale by any means. They had but one fault, they wasn't long enough.

This is a dismal rainy night & the rain is pattering on the deck over my head, but it is dry & comfortable within my room. We got here last Saturday

---

6, he captured the bark *Tacony* on June 12. Finding the *Tacony* better suited to raiding, he transferred his command to that vessel and captured or destroyed fifteen more ships. Knowing that the Union Navy was in hot pursuit, he destroyed the *Tacony* and transferred his command to the schooner *Archer* which they had captured on June 25. Two days later they sailed into Portland harbor disguised as fishermen, boarded the revenue cutter *Caleb Cushing* which was docked at the federal wharf, and sailed out of the harbor at dawn. They were captured soon after when their vessel was becalmed. Read was imprisoned at Fort Warren, MA and exchanged in October 1864.

morning after a very pleasant trip. In fact in some respects it seemed a sort of pleasure excursion, though rather long drawn out. The change was great coming from the almost furnace heat of Key West to the sour, cold, disagreeable weather we have experienced since we reached here. From the thinest kinds of summer clothing we have once more crept into our winter garments; white linen pants have been laid aside for overcoats. We found in the markets in New Orleans *blackberries*!, *strawberries*!, new potatoes, green peas &c. Here the trees are just well leaved out.

The rebel officers [from the *Webb*] are still on board of us. To morrow they are to be turned over to Gen. Dix, I suppose as candidates for Fort Lafayette.

Yesterday was a passably fair day. I went up to your uncle Frank's but did not get there in time for church. Your Aunt Nancy & Aunt Mary are both staying there for the present. How long they are to remain I don't know. The family are going to Fairfield [Connecticut] the first of next month. Your Uncle Frank has just bought another horse for their use during the summer. Harry will remain at Fairfield with Mary & his mother, going to New York occasionally. Aunt Mary I could easily see is tolerated, nothing more. When she is going, or what she proposes to do I did not learn.

Henry Graves has let his house & has taken board for himself & Lillie at the hotel.* Your mother is going to take Lillie, but I fear she hasn't counted the cost, though it will undoubtedly be a good thing for Lillie. I mean to go up to New Haven next Saturday if I can, to remain over Sunday.

Nancy Tuthill† has been married, quite unexpectedly & unknown to her friends here & I think to her mother as well, though she tries to make the folks here think she was anticipating it. Nancy did not write to her mother till after she was married & then only a few lines. Unfortunately they were sent to New Haven & your mother opened the letter & read it. I suppose poor Aunt Nancy caught it, not because Nancy got married but because she was not informed of it. I could not learn who her husband was, only that he was a soldier & was stationed near Washington. I hope he will prove a good husband.

What is to be done with us I don't know. There is some talk of our carrying the mail between here & Havanna. We shall find out I suppose in a few days when I will let you know. A good many of the purchased vessels like the *Florida* are being sold off, but they are mostly those needing extensive repairs. I should not be surprised if they kept us going for some time yet, but I look forward to getting home in the fall with a good deal of confidence as well as pleasure. What I shall do when I get back I have not yet determined. What is your advice?

---

* Husband and eldest daughter of Anna's late sister Mary.
† Aunt Nancy's daughter from Utica, NY.

Gulf of Mexico (March to November 1865)

I think Dave made a very good sale of my Ottawa property and feel obliged to him for it. It would be well I think to turn the money over to Mother. I will write Dave about it.

May 10th—Was over to New York to day & got my patent papers from Washington.* Munn & Co. did the business for me. My expectation for making a *fortune* out of it are not very sanguine. However I mean to endeavour to do something with it here, while I have an opportunity, as I have more or less leisure while the vessel is here.

I can't say that our Capt. improves any upon a longer acquaintance. He is disliked by all on board.

I stopped at Mr. Warner's office to day & found him & his wife. William they say is sick at Utica. Frank has bought out a book store in Utica & is going into the business. He is now, or soon will be, in New York. I shall try & see him.†

Our rebel prisoners left yesterday. Gen. Dix sent a small steamer along side of us & they were transfered to her under a strong guard, to be taken to the Fall river boat & from there to Boston, where they will be allowed to meditate for a while, in Fort Warren, on the instability of all Confederate things, particularly *rams*.

It seems to me that the greatest enemy of the rebel cause could not wish it a more disgraceful or ignominious end than that which has just been brought about. After all their vain boasts & threats about "the last dollar," "the last man" & "the last ditch" to be compelled to such humiliating surrender of their different armies to the "cowardly Yanks" and to see their "Christian President" flying a fugitive from justice, branded a traitor & a murderer with a price set upon his head, must have been rather humbling to Southern chivalry.

I heard while in Mobile bay a circumstance which has been suppressed so that it should not find its way into the papers. One of the forts at Mobile (Blakely I think) was garrisoned by Mississippi troops who participated in the massacre at Fort Pillow.‡ A couple of regiments of black troops got permission to attack the fort & carried it when the garrison surrendered, but were all or nearly all killed by the infuriated blacks. The few who escaped were saved by being surrounded by some of our white troops who kept the blacks from them. Officers got down on their knees & begged for quarter—their

---

* While running the LaSalle Iron Works Keeler invented an improvement to the governor, the apparatus that regulates the speed of a steam engine. His patent (No. 47109) was finalized on April 4, 1865. Orson D. Munn, the publisher of *Scientific American*, ran the patent firm that did the paper work for Keeler.
† Samuel E. Warner, assistant secretary of the American Tract Society at 150 Nassau St. in New York City. His wife was Keeler's mother's first cousin Helen Potter. William was presumably Helen's brother. Frank was possibly Keeler's first cousin Francis W. Plant.
‡ The massacre of nearly 200 black troops at Fort Pillow, TN on April 12, 1864.

answer was the bayonet—a most righteous retribution. I cannot vouch for the truth of this but I had it from pretty good authority.*

I think you can't complain for the want of variety in my letters but I fear you will not find that variety very interesting. However I give you the best I have. It may be a little better than blank paper. I hope wherever we go to find something to write about that may prove of interest to you all.

Friday evening. May 12th—Well we are to go to the Gulf once more with supplies, as we were informed yesterday from Washington. Hen & myself have just been out providing ourselves with straw hats for hot weather when we get south once more. We found our caps rather uncomfortable when we were last there. It don't seem much like straw hats here—every one is buttoned up in an overcoat. Our trip this time I think will be extended as far as Galveston.

I rec'd a letter to day from my *friend* Mrs. Crafts saying that her husband had been transferred to the West Gulf Squadron in command of the *Clematis*. She wants to send down to him.

I am expecting to go to New Haven tomorrow to remain till Monday. Will drop you a *line* before we leave. Write me at New Orleans. You shall hear from me from there. Tell Dave I will write him about the money for the Ottawa property before I leave. Yours of the 8th enclosing one for Henry was rec'd to day. Kiss our little ones for me. With love to all, yourself particularly.

W—

U.S. Steamer Florida
Off Carysfort Reef, Florida
May 22nd, 1865

Here we are again, my dear Wife, nearly down to Key West once more. To morrow morning early we shall probably be off there but do not intend to go in. But what we have to leave there will be sent off in the pilot boat.

These few lines I shall send ashore there, but they most likely will not reach you till after you have heard from me at New Orleans. They will probably go to New York via Havanna & will be some time getting to LaSalle.

We have had fine weather & a pleasant passage. To describe it at any length would be a mere repetition of my previous letters—so you must

---

* Although the official reports of the attack on Fort Blakely say nothing of a massacre, eye witness accounts say otherwise. Walter A. Chapman, a second lieutenant in the 51st U.S. Colored Infantry (one of the regiments involved in the attack), said that African-American soldiers "did not take a prisoner, they killed all they took to a man." According to Chapman many of the Confederate soldiers ran to the white Federal troops "to save being butchered." The number of Confederate soldiers who were massacred is unknown. (*Confederate Rage, Yankee Wrath: No Quarter in the Civil War*, George S. Burkhardt, Southern Illinois University Press, 2007, p. 238).

Gulf of Mexico (March to November 1865)

imagine everything going as happy as the marriage bell. Even the Capt. had a laugh with me to day!

I hope you will be able to read this. The engine produces such a jar of the vessel that I find it a very difficult matter to write very legibly.

Our next stop will be at Pensacola & from there we shall skirt along the coast to New Orleans & I hope will have to go no further west.

We brought down 8 or 9 passengers in the Ward Room, most of whom will leave us at Key West to morrow morning. They have been a very agreeable set fortunately & have added much to the pleasure of the trip.

It is very warm & even the thinest clothing is uncomfortable.

Henry is well & seems to enjoy it as much as any of us. I don't know how often he writes home. I frequently tell him that he should, but whether he does so or not you can tell better than myself.

How I would like to drop in upon you to night. What a joyful time it would be. What are you all doing now adays? How does the garden look? How do you get along? How are the children? & a thousand things I wish I could hear you answer personally.

It seems lonesome when I get to New York not to find you there & I find but little pleasure in remaining or in going around, so I leave for sea again without regret & without caring how soon.

Now that your Uncle Frank's family are gone it will seem doubly lonesome—no one to see or call upon. They were all very anxious to have me come up to Fairfield on my return & [I] may do so.

I am beginning to look forward to the time when I shall leave the service & be "homeward bound" for good, with much impatience. What a happy time it will be when I once more open the door, won't it.

I shall not attempt to fill my sheet for reasons which I have previously given. That you will hear from me first by way of New Orleans. But what my letter from there will be or what it will contain that will prove of an interest to you or any one else I am sure I can't tell. I know of nothing now to put in it. Something perhaps may turn up before I get ready to write—another rebel ram, a blockade runner—something to make an item or furnish a text.

I shall hope to find a letter from you at New Orleans & also *quite a number* at New York on my return there & I hope too that our letter writing will soon be over. It isn't very satisfactory is it? when our tongues would do so much better.

Did you get the pamphlets I enclosed you in a paper? I think your mother said she wished one given to Mrs. Hough & one to Mrs. Rockwell. How are they? You often speak of them. I long to see them once more & hear them speak for themselves. I hope I shall find my friends have not forgotten me when I return. I am sure I often think of them.

You must imagine the rest of the sheet filled with what you would most like from me. I should not have written at all but I desire to improve every chance for sending home, though as to time I consider this dubious.

Civil War Years: USS *Florida* (1863-1865)

How are our little ones? Give each of them a hug & a kiss for me. Our *big* one as I told you is well & is making himself quite useful to me.

With love & a good night kiss.

W—

U.S. Steamer *Florida*
Mobile Bay, Alabama
Saturday evening
May 27th [1865]

Dear Anna,

Here we are thus far on our journey to the westward. We left Pensacola this forenoon and reached here about 2 P.M. We are to leave here early tomorrow morning for Galveston & from there to New Orleans which place we hope to see in a week from to day when we shall be homeward bound, touching only at Pensacola & Key West.

I wrote you a short note and a has[t]y one just before getting to Key West & fortunately as we were going in met one of our gun boats coming out on her way to Hampton Roads. She sent a boat on board for late papers & I embraced the opportunity to forward your letter. Hope it reached you safely & found you all well. If you didn't get it you lost nothing, as like this one it had nothing in it of interest or importance.

Henry & myself [are] both well & are enjoying ourselves as well as could be expected under the circumstances. I find him of great assistance at times. At Pensacola I was obliged to send him ashore in charge of between 30 & 40,000 dollars worth of stores. He did the business promptly & correctly and much to my satisfaction. He is quiet, still & unobtrusive on board & seems to have gained the esteem of all the officers. He always addresses me as "Paymaster" & had been on board some time before it was know[n] that there was any relationship between us.

Thus far we have had a very pleasant trip, fine weather, good company, a smooth quiet sea & a pleasant time generally. I hope our stay in New Orleans will not be long as I feel anxious to get back to New York, hoping that Government will be able to dispense with our services, especially now that that great bug bear, the *Stonewall* is out of the way.*

We are lying at anchor in Mobile bay, not being able to get up to the city on account of our drawing too much water. So I shall not be able to see the place, though I have not a great deal of curiosity that way. The fact is I am

---

* Built in France and acquired by the Confederates in December 1864, the ironclad CSS *Stonewall* was armed with a 300-pound rifle, two 70-pound rifles and a ram at the bow. The plan was for her to break the Union blockade off Wilmington, capture gold steamers running between Aspinwall and New York, and disrupt shipping in the North Atlantic. However, she left France too late, and in March 1865 headed for the South Atlantic, getting as far as Havana, before her captain learned that the war was over.

about tired of sight seeing & would give more for a sight of home than any place I know of & hope I shall be gratified before long. Only think it is going on three years since I have been there. What changes have taken place since then.

You must remember me kindly to all my friends. Tell them I often think of them all & imagine I am occasionally remembered by them at the social gatherings. For I hope when I return that I shall find that I have not been entirely forgotten in my long absence.

It has just struck four bells (10 o'clock) & the Master at Arms will be around in a minute or two to let me know that my light must be out. So good night to you & the dear ones with love & kisses. Don't feel neglected because I don't fill the sheet. I only heard a short time since that there would be a chance to send a mail to morrow & I have improved the time since. Good night once more.

W—

No. 9—

U.S. Steamer *Florida*
Off Galveston, Texas
May 30th, 1865

Dear Anna,

We arrived here to day after a very pleasant passage, touching at Key West, Pensacola & Mobile bay. Galveston and its defences are in plain sight through our glasses, the place looking much larger than I supposed it to be. Our fleet were lying quietly before it, though it had been evacuated some days since. Why they do not go in and take possession I do not know. Flags of truce are daily running back & forth, so that it was well know[n] that there were but few if any rebel forces in or about the place.

The rumour is that the forces of Magruder who was in command here were included in Kirby Smith's surrender.[*] At any rate Magruder has acknowledged that any further continuance of hostilities on the part of the rebels would be fruitless & productive of no good result.

Refugees who come off represent that all is disorder & confusion in & about the place. Robbery & plunder by those who acknowledge no law but might is the order of the day & neither life or property are safe. They are urging our naval forces to go in and take possession that they may have their protection.

---

[*] Smith's force of 40,000 men was the last main body of Confederate troops still at large. Although some of the fugitive members of the Confederate cabinet had hopes of reaching Texas and continuing the war with his troops, Smith realized that it was a lost cause and on May 26 opened negotiations with his Union counterpart, which led to the formal surrender of his army on June 2. John Magruder, of Yorktown fame, was under Smith's command.

Civil War Years: USS *Florida* (1863-1865)

The *Denbigh*, one of the most successful of the blockade runners, succeeded in getting in from Nassau a few days since & was boarded by a mob who plundered her of a portion of her cargo when she succeeded in getting off, but in attempting to get out again run aground and was set on fire by one of our gun boats & destroyed, a needless destruction, as the battery near which she grounded was deserted & there was nothing to interfere with our taking possession of her & getting her off. It is however in keeping with many similar things to which I have been a witness while I have been in the service.

I had the pleasure of meeting Capt. Stevens who for a time was in command of the *Monitor*. He is in command of the *Oneida* here. He is a very fine man & a good officer & stands next to Capt. Magaw in my estimation. He was very urgent for me to visit him on board his ship & insisted that if I ever went through Erie, where he resides, that I shall stop & see him or if he is not at home his wife.

It is not as warm here as I expected to find it—a good cool breeze blowing in from the sea, & I am told that there has been but very little hot weather here this season.

It is a month since they have had a vessel here from the north. You may imagine the eagerness with which letters, papers &c are sought for. My past experience on the blockade will allow me to feel for them.

Our supplies of fresh beef, ice & vegetables were most welcome I assure you after being so long without those articles.

New Orleans, June 1st—We left Galveston on the 30th and reached here to day about noon.

President Johnson's proclamation* seems to be pretty generally observed both on the plantations lying along the river & here in the city.

It was amusing as we steamed up the river to watch the groups of darkies passing from one plantation to another or to some point where a little church served as a center about which to gather & observe the day. The only roads between the different plantations and points on the river seem to lead along the levee, so that we had a good view of all that was passing. All seemed well & comfortably clad & very many, especially the females, dressed with a good deal of taste & show, doubtless a good many of them in the abandoned wardrobes of their former mistresses. Head dresses of the most fantastic shapes & gayest colors & hoop skirts of the largest diameter were abundant & the dignified walk & consequential air of some of the young bucks as they strutted along under the shade of a huge umbrella, white gloves & cane in hand as they did the agreeable to their *fair?* companions, was extremely ludicrous. Only on one or two plantations did I observe large gangs of them

---

* The proclamation of amnesty for Confederates who took an oath to disclaim slavery and uphold the Constitution.

at work among the sugar cane which has grown rapidly since we were last here.

Many of the plantations we pass belong, or did belong, to those whose names stand prominent among the list of traitors to their country. Of course they are confiscated & are being worked by those who have hired or purchased them from government.

We passed one large one belonging to Benjamin, the rebel Sec'y of War, now gone from him forever by his own foolishness.* How far this confiscation Act† is to be carried out I do not know, but it will doubtless be productive of very great changes all through the South, and many once quiet & happy homes & elegant residences & extensive possessions will be lost to their former owners forever & the despised "Yanks" & "greasy mechanics" & "northern mudsills" will occupy their places & teach Southern chivalry what true chivalry is.

We feared to find the yellow fever here upon our arrival but it has not yet made its appearance, though a sickly season is being predicted by many.

It is very warm, dry & dusty. A long time has passed since any rain has fallen & most of the cisterns, upon which the inhabitants rely for their supply of drinking water have given out, the turbid water of the river being the only substitute. We hope to get away from here in a week or ten days. I don't care how soon, for the heat here is excessive.

May [June] 5th—I have kept my letter till now hoping to be able to give you some further information as to our future movements. We shall probably leave here on Friday or Saturday next, touching at Pensacola & Key West. I am told that we are to have 50 officers in the Ward room for passage home. Where they will all stow I cannot imagine.

We have just rec'd on board 20 men just released from some of the Texas prison pens. Some of them have been there from two to three years. They have evidently had better treatment than those at Richmond, Millen‡ &c.

Henry & myself are both well & send lots of love to all the dear ones at home. We hope to give you an ocular demonstration of it before long.

W—

---

* Bellechasse Plantation, which Judah P. Benjamin had sold a decade before.
† A proposal by Radical Republican Congressman Thaddeus Stevens to confiscate land holdings in excess of 300 acres and re-distribute them to freed slaves and poor whites. The proposed legislation never passed.
‡ The prison camp at Millen, GA was opened in October 1864 to relieve congestion at the notorious Andersonville Prison located 160 miles away. Two months later the camp was closed when threatened by Sherman's advancing army. Despite the brief time it was opened 700 prisoners died there.

Civil War Years: USS *Florida* (1863-1865)

U.S. Steamer *Florida*
New York Navy Yard
June 19th, 1865

Dear Anna,

We arrived here this morning ten days from New Orleans, stopping a short time at Pensacola & Key West. Our usual good luck of fine weather has attended us the whole trip, though it has been excessively warm, or rather hot.

I wrote you from New Orleans just before we left & hope it has been received before this. I should have mentioned in it that I rec'd your letter while there. Many thanks for it & the assurances that all were well at home & the absent ones not forgotten.

We brought up over a hundred passengers with us, some of them just released from some of the prison pens in Texas, others sick & wounded from the Hospitals in New Orleans & Pensacola. One died on the passage & was buried at sea.

I assure you we were all glad when we were by Hatteras & could exchange the heated air of the Gulf Stream for the cool invigorating atmosphere of a more northern clime.

Among our passengers home was a Dr. Sargent who formerly taught school in Bureau Co. near Mr. Lovejoy's[*]. He has been in the Gulf Squadron for over two years and comes north on sick leave to recruit.

We had quite a number of passengers down with us, among them a brother of Admiral Porter—an Acting Master & a poor miserable drunken vagabond.[†] We had also a Dr. Plant from some part of New York state & a connexion of the Branford Plants[‡]—also a Paymaster Duane[§] from Kansas, making with others quite an agreeable company.

We found it excessively hot at New Orleans, as well as in the gulf & at the different places at which we stopped, though at none of them was there any epidemic so that we escaped quarantine upon our arrival here.

Our Captain rather improves upon acquaintance, & a few days before we got in actually invited Messrs. Staples, Sampson[**], McLean & myself to dinner with him. We had a new dish—*gophers*, a species of large land turtle found in the neighborhood of Pensacola. The[y] make a very fine soup & stew.

---

[*] Acting Assistant Surgeon Fernando C. Sargent of the gunboat USS *Penobscot*. Owen Lovejoy was the Republican Congressman from Keeler's district from 1857 until his death in 1864.

[†] Henry O. Porter, second youngest of Admiral David Porter's six brothers.

[‡] Keeler's maternal grandfather was a Plant from Branford, CT.

[§] Martin Duane.

[**] Acting Ensign L. Granville Sampson (1834-1894). Son of a customs inspector from Duxbury, MA. In the mid-1850s he ran passenger packets between Boston and Liverpool. In 1863 he was master of the ship *Ceylon* in the Australian and New Zealand trade. He served on the *Florida* from January 1865 to January 1866.

Gulf of Mexico (March to November 1865)

On our way down the Miss. we passed the wreck of the *Webb* or rather the remains of it where we had left it burning on our last trip. Forts Morgan [Jackson] & St. Philip, which I do not remember having mentioned before, do not present from the river the formidable appearance one would be led to suppose from the part they have played in the rebellion.* As we pass them on the river they appear but slight elevations of land above the surrounding level, half concealed by scrubby bushes, from among which and over the grassy slope the black muzzles of the guns peer out over the stream. Over them waves the "Star Spangled Banner" & I trust "Long may it wave" before it will again be hauled down by a traitor's hand. I have a precious relic from Fort Fisher—a flag, said to be the first one our forces raised on that work.

On our arrival here [New York Navy Yard] this morning our first move was for the mail. I found yours of May 15th & June 1st & you can imagine how eagerly they were read. I should have had a letter written & ready to mail to you upon our arrival but the excessive heat [along] with my numerous duties prevented [it]. So you must excuse the delay of one mail.

All vessels arriving here now are put out of commission & their officers discharged and I am hoping that may be our lot, though it will probably be some days before our future is know[n]. As soon as anything transpires I will let you know. My fear is that we will be sent out again somewhere, for the reason that we are in thorough repair & good order, while most if not all the vessels arriving here are as we term it, "pretty well played out."

I suppose your Uncle Frank's folks are all in the country. I shall try & go over to his office to morrow & see him. Should I go up to New Haven while we are here I mean to stop at Fairfield an hour or two if possible.

Henry's cold of which you enquire left him long ago. I think you need not fear for him.

I saw Crafts at New Orleans. He arrived with his boat the *Clematis* just before we left. I went on board & staid an hour or two. He gave me a gun from Fort Fisher. His executive was Williams, one of my old *Monitor* shipmates & till lately a messmate on board here.

You do not know how much I want to get home & see you all, quite as much as you want to have me. I am hoping to before fall, but even if discharged now it will take me some little time to settle up my business so that I can leave for home. At any rate do not expect us till you hear from me that we are coming. I shall hope to be there before cold weather puts an end to all your picnics & rides.

---

* Located in the mouth of the Mississippi, the two Confederate forts guarded New Orleans in the first year of the war. They were bombarded and then passed by the Union Navy in advance of the capture of the city in April 1862.

Civil War Years: USS *Florida* (1863-1865)

Tell Dave that he had better keep away from Memphis or the South. I know he would not like it. I will send Eddie a *Harper* with Jeff Davis in Petticoats.[*]

With love & kisses to you all.

W—

[Marginalia] Let me hear from you as often as possible.

> U.S. Steamer *Florida*
> New York Navy Yard
> June 22nd, 1865

Dear Anna,

I have an evening before me with nothing to do & I cannot pass it away more pleasantly or agreeably than in a chat with you. When I can have a real chat is more than I can say. It looks farther in the future than when I last wrote you. Your idea that I would not be home before fall may yet prove correct.

The Admiral[†] to day rec'd a telegram from Washington saying, "Keep the *Florida* ready for sea." So it seems that they are not yet through with us—though keeping the *Florida* "*ready* for sea" does not by any means indicate that we are *going* to sea. We may be kept in "readiness" for six months & not move from our anchorage, or we may be ordered off tomorrow.

I think we are to be kept ready for any emergency which may arise—perhaps to tow home some of the iron clads from the southern ports. It is doubtful if we go out with supplies again. There are no squadrons now to be supplied, our large fleets having dwindled down to a few scattering vessels here & there along the coast. Our vessels are fast coming north & are filling the different Navy Yards. Many of the purchased ones are being sold off but a good many will be retained for some time yet.

A large squadron is fitting out for the Mediterranean & other foreign parts. I was asked yesterday by the Admiral's Sec'y how I would like to go to the Mediterranean. I told him, "I shouldn't like it at all. I had stronger attractions the other way." I don't think there is any danger of my being ordered there unless I desire it, which I most assuredly do not.

When we are to go & where, I will let you know as soon as I know myself. I was expecting to go to New Haven to morrow, stopping a few hours at Fairfield, returning on Monday & had got permission, but afterwards received orders to hold myself in readiness to go to Philadelphia to attend a Court Martial in case I was wanted, which I fear will spoil my visit.

---

[*] The Confederate president was purportedly wearing his wife's dress and shawl when he was captured. The Northern press ridiculed him as a coward, alleging that he had disguised himself as a woman in order to evade capture.

[†] Acting Rear Admiral Charles H. Bell, who replaced Hiram Paulding as commandant of the New York Navy Yard.

Gulf of Mexico (March to November 1865)

I saw your Uncle Frank yesterday. He says that they are all well & at Fairfield. Aunt Mary is keeping house for him in New York. I am going up to call on her some evening—don't be jealous!! I wish you could call with me.

I find the weather here very pleasant—cool & comfortable, after my experience "down south," though folks here try to make me think it very warm.

Almost all our officers are [gone] to Philadelphia on Court Martial, only four or five on board & about a dozen of our crew, the rest having been sent on board the receiving ship for safe keeping & to prevent desertion, 18 of them having left last night. Seven or eight got into one of the boats this morning & succeeded in crossing over to New York where they escaped. The officer of the deck fired on them a number of times ineffectually. I suppose the "shell backs"* feel a good deal as I do—the war is over [so] what's the use of keeping us any longer.

As Dave says perhaps I should resign, which I could do & receive as a reply, "Your resignation is hereby accepted"—very short but not very gratifying after three years & a half service, or what would be worse, "Your appointment is hereby revoked," or worse still, "You are hereby dismissed." &c. Unless you object too strongly I mean to stay till I receive an "Honorable Discharge," which is being given to those who are considered deserving. I don't think they will keep me much longer.

Won't you come on board & dine with us tomorrow? Mr. Sampson, our caterer, is in Philadelphia & I am acting ad interim. I have just been ashore & spoken for some fresh blue fish for breakfast & some clams for a chowder for dinner with the proper vegetables &c &c to which I will add, if you will come, some strawberries, cherries &c &c which are very plenty here in the market. If we are sent off again I hope it will be to some fruit region. You will not be forgotten if I can contrive to get some to you.

I rec'd yours of the 10th a few days ago which was as welcome as your letters always are. I wish Dave & Fan were coming east instead of going south. I think he will soon recover from his southern fever. Why can't he settle down upon something?

I don't see why my LaSalle friends desire me to come back there to live. None of them seem to be fixed there permanently or have any intention of remaining, while I desire to settle in some place for good where I can remain at anchor the rest of my days.

But 10 o'clock has come around & my sheet is unfilled. I shall send it as it is however, as I know you will prefer it to nothing.

I believe I owe Eddie a letter & must try & write him in your next. How I want to see the dear little fellow. It will soon be three years since I saw him. No wonder the girls tell Lizzie that she hasn't any papa. It wouldn't take much

---

* Veteran sailors.

Civil War Years: USS *Florida* (1863-1865)

to make either of them believe it. Kiss them both for me & believe me with much love and kisses.

Affectionately yours,

W—

U.S. Steamer *Florida*
New York Navy Yard
July 15th, 1865

Dear Anna,

We have suddenly rec'd orders to sail for Port Royal & Charleston, S.C., and are now getting under way. We will tow one of the monitors from there to Philadelphia & will probably be gone two or three weeks when I hope you will hear from me at length. In the haste & confusion of getting under way I have only time to scratch these few hasty lines to let you know where we are going. It seems too bad to send such a short scrawl but I can't help it this time. I hope the mail will get in & bring me a letter from you before we leave the dock. My best love & kisses to you & the children. Hen & myself both well.

Affectionately,

W—

U.S. Steamer *Florida*
in the "Narrows"*
July 15th, 1865

Dear Anna,

I will scratch off these few lines to send ashore by the pilot when he leaves us. Your letter of the 10th reached me very opportunely—just as we were shoving off from the wharf.

Dear little Lizzie, I didn't forget her, though I had forgotten that it was her birth day. I should have sent her something when I sent Eddy's book but did not know what to get. I have nothing now, but send her fifty cents with which to get something to please her.

How often my thoughts turn homeward & how often I wish I were with you. The time seems more & more tedious. I hope we will meet soon.

With my best love to your own dear self & the little ones,

W—

---

* The narrow strait between Upper and Lower New York Bays.

Gulf of Mexico (March to November 1865)

> U.S. Steamer *Florida*
> At Sea, Sunday Evening
> July 17th, 1865

Dear Anna,

I sent you a hasty scrawl just as we were leaving the Navy Yard & another by the Pilot, written while we were passing through the Narrows. My conscience accused me for not having a good long letter for you, ready to send in an emergency as I usually have. But the fact is I find it *awful hard* work to write—not but what the will is good but our life has become so dull & monotonous it furnishes us with no material.

Now that the war is over it seems as if there was nothing more to do. There is no more fighting to be done, no more blockade runners to chase, nothing to give interest or excitement to our life. All has settled down to one unvarying round of red tape & routine.

The only subject of discussion among us now is, "When will they be done with us & how long before we will be allowed to go home." You have no idea how slowly the time passes. Every hour seems a day & every day a month when I think of home. I never left port so unwillingly or with so little anticipation of pleasure or enjoyment as on this present trip. I had so fixed my mind on going home, hoping that something might turn up to prevent our going to sea & put us out of commission—hoping thus in fact when I felt convinced it was of no use, for the fact was before me that we were going to sea again & were daily preparing for it. But after all, I felt disappointed when we left, though I had no reason to hope for anything else, and then as if two years & a half from home was not enough the Department had the *impudence* to ask me if I would like to go with the squadron now fitting out for the Mediterranean. It was no doubt intended as a compliment but "I couldn't see it in that light" & I gave them to understand that my first great wish was to leave the service & go home as soon as they would let me.

The fact is I am getting homesick. I cannot summon the energy necessary to go through with my daily routine of duties, for I no longer find any interest in them & I can hardly gather the courage to commence a letter home. I get the paper before me & commence thinking about you all, how you all are & how you are looking & where you are & what [you are] doing & an hour passes & I have not touched my pen to the paper. It seems as if I must be with you to talk & I haven't the patience to communicate my ideas with pen & paper.

I have just learned from the Capt. that we are to stop for a short time at Hampton Roads & will mail this from there. We expect to go from there to Port Royal and Charleston to tow one of the Monitors to Philadelphia. What we are to do then I don't know—go home I hope. It seems as if we were kept to do all the odd jobs, pick up all the odds & ends which have been scattered about during the war.

Civil War Years: USS *Florida* (1863-1865)

A great many officers are daily leaving the service with honorable discharges. My turn must come before long. I only hope I shall be able to reach home before cold weather sets in. What a grand time we will have.

Your letter of the 10th came in the best of season, just as we were leaving the dock. It is unnecessary for me to say how welcome it was & how glad I was to learn you were all well at home.

You will miss Mrs. Rockwell. You must have become quite intimate. You mention her so frequently in your letters. I saw so little of her before leaving home I hardly feel acquainted. However I hope to know her better on my return. I certainly feel thankful to her as well as all our other friends at home for their kindness to you during my absence.

I bought *Christian's mistake* by Miss Mullock to read just before we left. I shall probably read it through before we return & will mail it to you. If it is as good as some of her other works it will pay well for the reading.

How are Fan & Dave & what new project has he got? Tell Dave I wish him success in his Petroleum operations. Hope he will strike the "biggest well out." I will be home one of these days to see how it's done. I often think of Fan's children & Eddy & wonder how they look. They must have altered much in the years I have been away.

I shall reserve the rest of my sheet till we get in to Hampton Roads to morrow, hoping to find something of interest to fill it. There certainly is nothing in what I have already written—you will learn from it that I still live & love & that is about all that it does contain. Good night.

Port Royal, S.C.
July 19th, 1865

We have just dropped anchor here to remain long enough to take in a hundred tons of coal & will then be off again. We reached Hampton Roads about two o'clock Monday afternoon [July 17] & left at sundown. None of us except the Captain had any communication with the shore, so my letter was not forwarded from there.

We have on board the President's murderers (the unhung ones), taking them to the Dry Tortugas[*] where government is to furnish them (except Spangler[†]) with a residence for the rest of their lives. Spangler goes for six years. I only regret that these [men] didn't go with Mrs. Surratt[‡] to keep her company. We should have been saved this trip down here.

As I said we go from here to the Tortugas & leave our prisoners & then back to New York. That is the plan now. What changes will be made I don't

---

[*] A chain of small islands in the Gulf of Mexico about 70 miles west of Key West. The prisoners were taken to Fort Jefferson on Garden Key, one of the islands in the chain.
[†] Edmund Spangler, a carpenter and stagehand at Ford's Theatre where Lincoln was shot.
[‡] Mary Surratt, owner of the boarding house in Washington, DC that was frequented by John Wilkes Booth. She was sentenced to death for her involvement in the assassination and hanged on July 7, 1865.

Gulf of Mexico (March to November 1865)

know. There is a Monitor here [and] we may have to return here to tow her north, but I hope not. It's too warm here for comfort & I have no desire to return. My only desire is to get home as soon as possible.

I will give you the details of our trip in my next. Till then good bye with my best love & *a* kiss.

W—

No. 10—

U.S. Steamer Florida
Key West, Florida
July 27th, 1865

Dear Anna,

We left New York, as I have previously informed you in a brief note, on Sunday 16th. We had been ordered to be ready for sea a number of days previously & had been given to understand that we were to go to Port Royal to tow one of the Monitors to Philadelphia.

When final sailing orders came we were taking on naval stores for Port Royal & carpenters & painters were at work repairing damages caused by the falling of a large derrick across us & which came very near sending us to the bottom. Mechanics were hurried ashore leaving their work half done, the remainder of the stores were soon on board & we were off.

It seems however that the orders for Port Royal &c were only for a blind & to conceal the real purpose in sending us off. Just as we were leaving the dock a telegram from Washington was received ordering us to call at Hampton Roads.

We reached there the next day about noon & dropped an anchor opposite Fortress Munroe, the familiar scenery on all sides reminding me of the eventful occurrences at the outbreak of the war. Of course we were all ignorant of the cause of our being sent there & many speculations were ventured as to the why & wherefore. We had not long to wait however for a steamer, which we saw coming down the bay as we came into the harbour, came up and anchored near us.

Brig. Gen. Dodd[*] with a portion of his staff came on board in a small boat & were soon followed by Dr. Mudd, Arnold, McLaughlan [O'Laughlen] & Spangler, the unhung ones of the President's assassins, & a guard of 30 of the veteran reserves in charge.[†]

The mystery was now solved & our real destination was found to be the Dry Tortugas. The prisoners were brought on board in irons closely guarded, nothing about them to attract particular attention, though their crime had

---

[*] Levi Axtell Dodd.
[†] Samuel A. Mudd was the doctor who set John Wilkes Booth broken leg when he was on the run after assassinating Lincoln. Samuel Arnold and Michael O'Laughlen were involved in two failed attempts to kidnap the president in March 1865.

given them a notoriety which made them objects of curiosity to all on board. They had been gazed at I suppose till they ceased to regard it as anything strange & seated themselves quite composedly in some chairs which had been placed for them on the quarter deck.

None of us were allowed any communication with the shore. We were under way again before sundown & were probably many miles at sea before the curious public knew but what the murderers were safely housed as for weeks past in the old capital prison. They were taken from Washington in the middle of the night, none but the President & his Cabinet being aware of the transaction except the guard who accompanied them. The prisoners had seen in the papers that they were to be sent to the Albany penitentiary & supposed they were put on board of us for the purpose of being conveyed to New York. It was not till they had been on board for forty eight hours that they began to mistrust their real destination. They appeared a good deal dejected when they learned the truth. The Dr. wanted to know "how long a person would proba[b]ly live at the Tortugas."

Like most all criminals they all claimed that they had been found guilty upon false evidence. Dr. Mudd had a good deal to say about the trial, pointing out the evidence where it clashed as he thought, giving the character of various witnesses, calling attention to points which he thought had been overlooked or had not received sufficient attention from the court. He had had the evidence in his case, pro & con, published in book form & produced a copy which he commended to our careful perusal.

He [Mudd] is about 30 years of age, though he looks much older. He leaves a wife & four children. He is said to be a sharp shrewd man but I saw nothing about him to indicate it. He has a sort of cunning, foxy look, as if possessed of plenty of low cunning & a desire for concealment. The officers in charge of them & who have had a good opportunity of knowing say that "Mrs. Surratt & him furnished the brains for the party" & they think that he should have accompanied her to the gallows, that her fate was just & merited they have no doubt & that she had any claims, as a woman, on executive clemency they deny.*

---

* In January 1869 Keeler learned that President Johnson was planning to pardon Mudd. Concerned that the president was unaware of Mudd's true relationship with Booth, Keeler wrote the following letter to his congressman Burton C. Cook: "Dear Sir: I learn by yesterdays *Chicago Tribune* that efforts are being made to procure the pardon of Dr. Mudd. The U.S. Steamer *Florida* to which I was attached conveyed him & his associates from Hampton Roads to the Tortugas. In conversation with myself, & I think with others on our passage down, he admitted what I believe the prosecution failed to prove at his trial–viz– that he knew who Booth was when he set his leg & of what crime he was guilty. I have thought it might be well to have these facts known if they are not. Very truly yours, W. F. Keeler" (Richard D. Mudd Papers, Georgetown University, Washington, DC). Although Keeler's letter was forwarded to the attorney general, it had no effect, for Mudd was pardoned in February 1869.

Gulf of Mexico (March to November 1865)

Spangler is a coarse, rough, uneducated, unprincipled man. His bull neck, bullet head & brutish features mark a villain, but without sufficient nerve & steadiness to carry out the villainy his heart would prompt. He appears to take his punishment (six years) quite stoically & appears at times quite light hearted. He protests with any amount of profanity his entire innocence of the charge, but admits that he has committed crime enough of other kinds to merit the punishment so that his sentence is not undeserved.

The other two [Arnold and O'Laughlen] are young men, quiet & still, saying but little except when spoken to—men of no more than ordinary information & intelligence. With the exception of Dr. Mudd who may have the ability to plan I cannot conceive how the execution of plans of such vast consequences to the rebels could have been entrusted to such kind of persons.

With Gen. Dodd was Capt. *Dutton*[*], Dr. Porter[†] & thirty privates. The Assistant Judge Advocate General (Col. Turner[‡]) also went down with us with instructions to look into the status of all the political prisoners at Tortugas & other places South & with power to liberate such as in his judgement he might deem advisable. We had a very pleasant company, the Gen. & Col. going into the [captain's] cabin to mess & the Dr. & Capt. coming into the Ward Room.

The hand irons were taken off the prisoners after they came on board, but the leg irons were kept on for the first two or three days, [and] after that they were removed during the day but put on at night. The first two nights they were kept on the orlop deck below the Ward Room, but they complained so much of the heat & closeness they were allowed to spread their mattresses on the quarter deck but were closely guarded. They were fed the same as the sailors—the regular ration. I was in hopes they would send us Jeff Davis from Fortress Munroe—it needed him to make the assortment of scoundrels complete.[§] They appeared much more contented & resigned than I should suppose persons leaving behind them everything that could make life desirable, to be shut out from the world the remainder of their lives, could be. Though that they realised their condition was shewn by a remark of the Dr.'s one day that "if it were not for his dread of an hereafter he should jump overboard."

We arrived at Port Royal on Wednesday the 19th & left for the Tortugas on the 21st. During our stay there [Port Royal] we lay at the docks of the naval station across the harbour from Hilton Head. General Dodd had a tug

---

[*] George W. Dutton. See the footnote later in this letter.
[†] George L. Porter, the army surgeon who cared for the Lincoln assassination conspirators while they were imprisoned at Fort Monroe.
[‡] Levi C. Turner.
[§] The Confederate president had been held at Fort Monroe since his arrest two months earlier. He was locked in one of the fort's casemates, with irons attached to his legs, a huge American flag on the wall in front of him, and nothing but the Bible to read.

placed at his disposal during his stay & made a trip up to Beaufort, about 16 miles. Capt. Dutton & Dr. Porter accompanied him & I made one of the party by his invitation.

We had a very pleasant trip & a good opportunity for seeing the country along the banks of the [Beaufort] river, though I must say we saw but little to admire, either in scenery or productions. The land like most I have seen in the southern states is low & sandy or marshy—the timber mostly of pines or oaks, with now & then a palmetto raising its singular shaped head. I saw nothing that had the appearance of large plantations or the "lordly residences" of their proprietors. But little evidences of cultivation were to be seen except a few fields of corn owned by the "freedmen."

One of the most noticeable things was a monument of the folly, waste & stupidity of the rebellion—a breastwork of cotton bales, enclosing between two & three acres of ground, built on land sloping down to the water's edge, thus exposing its defenders to the full fire of cannister & shell from our gun boats. The bales on its water front were displaced & half buried in the sand & water & all were probably worthless.

We undertook an exploration of Beaufort, but the hot sun above & the hot sand beneath us shortened our walk & made us glad to return to the "Steven's house"* where we succeeded after some exertion in getting a homeopathic dinner of homeopathic quantities of roast beef, sweet potatoes &c. The charges I noticed wasn't graduated by the same scale. The place itself resembles, on a large scale, its namesake in N.C., the same quantities of sand, fleas, little darkies & gives one the same impression of a want of yankee thrift and energy. We were glad to leave & get back to the ship & a cool sea breeze.

A few rods from the dock was the rebel fort B[ea]uregard, a small sand work, now dismantled & unoccupied. On the opposite side, at Hilton Head, was another of their works, fort Walker—a work of greater strength & importance & now occupied by our forces. Both of these forts were taken by Admiral Dupont (I think it was) in his attack on Port Royal.

In the evening a steamer came over from Hilton Head bringing Gen. Birge†, his staff, a brass band and a number of ladies. I had retired when the band struck up & they commenced dancing on deck. I lay quiet for I knew that whiskey would play no small part in the hospitalities(?) of the evening. I think I had the best of it as I could lie & enjoy the music & not have to suffer from the whiskey as most of those who took part did. It seems strange that a person to shew his hospitality & good will to his friends must do so by making them drunk. Strange as it is however it is the practice in the service

---

* Formerly the elegant plantation house of John Joyner Smith, which was taken over by Brigadier General Isaac I. Stevens in 1861 when Federal forces took control of Beaufort, SC. The house, which is still standing, is located on Bay Street overlooking the harbor.
† Henry W. Birge.

Gulf of Mexico (March to November 1865)

& I believe has added millions & millions to the expenses of the war, if it has not doubled its cost.

I met at Port Royal Paymaster Douglass* who was attached to the *Rhode Island* when we were taken from the *Monitor*.

I could imagine the feelings of our prisoners as we approached fort Jefferson, on the Dry Tortugas, on the morning of the 24th where they were to spend the remainder of their lives. The particular island is a small, low patch of white sand on the coral reef of about thirteen acres, seven of which are enclosed within the brick walls of the fort, a good portion of the remainder being covered with sheds, shops, stables &c pertaining to the fort & its occupants, giving it, at a short distance, the appearance of a small village.

Not a particle of vegetation is visible on the island outside the fort. The only green thing in sight was a few scrubby oak bushes on another small patch of sand a half mile or so distant. Inside the fort, vegetation adapted to the dry, sandy, hot soil was nursed with a good deal of care, most of it transplanted from Key West. A tamarina, a few oaks, some banannas, mangroves, a number of varieties of the cactus (one of them producing the flower from which the night blooming cereus is extracted) were pointed out to me growing around the officers' quarters.

A false impression seems to be entertained of this place at the north. That it is dreary & desolate in its appearance you can infer from what I have already said—nothing but the "wide blue sea" can be seen from it except a few small patches of low, barren, white sand scattered at irregular intervals along the coral reefs. A sea breeze continually blowing makes it cool & comfortable & the hea[l]th must be good, as a visit with the surgeon to the hospital of the garrison of a full regiment (the 110 N.Y.) shewed but five patients & that of the 550 prisoners contained but 4. The Dr. told me that in his six years' residence there he had had but six cases of yellow fever. His wife had just left for the north after a stay of three years.

The prisoners are kept employed when there is work to do, but now there is nothing for them to do & they roam about the fort & beach at will, fishing, bathing, gathering corals, shells, mosses &c which they sell to those visiting the place or send abroad for sale, many of them realising quite a handsome sum from the proceeds of these curiosities. They are kindly treated & seem to enjoy almost unrestricted liberty. Notwithstanding the sentence of "hard labor with ball & chain" with which many of them are sent there, such punishment is not carried out & is only resorted to as a penalty for misbehavior after their arrival on the island.

Dr. Mudd is to be sent into the hospital as an assistant to the Surgeon, Arnold is to be employed as a clerk & Spangler will be kept to work at his trade [carpentry]. I have no doubt but what they are glad by this time that they were not sent to the penitentiary as was at first intended.

---

* Richard H. Douglass.

Civil War Years: USS *Florida* (1863-1865)

I got some beautiful corals which I will send home the first opportunity—hope I will be able to bring them myself.

The Capt. & some of our officers had another drunken spree here in which they *were ably assisted* by some of the officers from the fort. Such things are deg[r]ading to the officers & disgraceful to the Service & could it be shewn to the Department in its true light would undoubtedly subject the offenders to dismissal, for drunkeness is strictly forbidden. There is but little use however in bringing such a complaint against a commanding officer by an inferior, as it has been tried a number of times & by some species of legerdemain has resulted in the acquittal of the offender & the dismissal of the complainant, so that all we can do is to look quietly on & inwardly condemn them.

There seemed to be a contrived plan to get the Gen. [Dodd], who is very abstemious, though not strictly temperate, drunk. He was brought on board & put to bed, the Capt. glorying in the success of his plot. The Gen. came on deck the next morning & says "Gentlemen, you saw last night what no one ever saw before." "What's that Gen.?" "You saw me drunk."

We left the next morning for Key West, about sixty five miles, & arrived here [Key West] about noon & are now just passing out the harbour after a stay of two days.

There has been a repetition of the drunken orgies at Port Royal & Tortugas. Our Capt. has not the first qualification of an officer or a gentleman about him & the sober thinking ones among us are thoroughly disgusted with him & his proceedings. If I am to remain any longer in the service I shall pray for a change.

We found Key West the same dry, hot, dusty place it was on our former visits & left it without regret. As an illustration of the peculiarities of the "peculiar institution," I had my washing done at Key West by a daughter of the Sec'y of the rebel Navy, formerly Senator Mallory. She was a few shades darker than her sister, Mrs. Bishop of Bridgeport, & probably not as well educated.*

We find Col. Turner a very pleasant companion. He has resided at Washington during the war in charge of the political prisoners, or rather superintending all proceedings in relation to them. He was well acquainted [with] Mr. Lincoln & is full of anecdotes of him as well as of other public characters in Washington. In a two or three hours' conversation with him last night he gave me an account of the secret history of the rebellion, how mails & letters were opened, detectives employed & other secret measures taken to detect &

---

* In the 1850s Stephen R. Mallory, then a U.S. senator from Florida, owned a plantation in Key West where his slave daughter was presumably born. His 23-year old white daughter Margaret was married to a wealthy young man of leisure named Henry Bishop from Bridgeport, CT.

ferret out the traitors in our midst. Many he says who are now esteemed loyal would tremble if they knew the record against them at Washington.

Capt. Dutton is from Boston. I cannot find that he is related to your family. He is full of fun & makes a good deal of sport for us in the Ward Room.*

One of our men managed to get hold of some whiskey here & of course got drunk. The Capt. had him put in double irons on bread & water. Such is the difference between Cabin & forecastle, Captain & jack. Capt. gets drunk & the safety of the ship & all on board is endangered [and] nothing is said. Jack does the same & injures no one but himself & is dicted[?]† in double irons with ample leisure to reflect on the evil of his ways.

The Gen. [Dodd] is a quiet, modest, retiring man with a broad, good humoured face ever ready to light up with a smile. All on board like him. He was promoted for gallantry at Petersburg.‡ This is his first trip to sea & of course everything is new—the source of an endless variety of questions which are always asked with a good humoured smile.

Monday evening, July 31st

"Home again!" I wish it were so. We have just taken on board a Sandy Hook pilot, which seems a step in that direction. Early to-morrow morning we shall be passing up the Narrows—the most delightful ride in the world. I wish you were on board to enjoy it with me. By eight o'clock we shall be at anchor off the Battery. There we will all be longing to know what the future has in store for us—whether the *Florida* goes out of commission & we go home or are to be sent off again—quien sabe?

The length of this letter must make amends for the brevity of some of my previous ones. It will also prove to you (if proof is necessary) that my letters are lengthy when there is anything to make them so. I shall hope to find "a pile" of home missives waiting me at the [New York] Navy Yard. Am I to be disappointed?

---

* George W. Dutton (1836-1925). He commanded the Old Capitol Prison in Washington, DC where the Lincoln assassination conspirators were held. A machinist in Stoughton, MA before the war, he enlisted in April 1861 and was commissioned a captain in the 9th Massachusetts Infantry. He participated in all of the battles of the Peninsula Campaign and was severely wounded at the Battle of Malvern Hill on July 1, 1862 when a minie ball shattered his left leg. Never fully recovering from the wound, he resigned in March 1863 and was transferred to the 10th Regiment Veterans Reserve Corps where he held the rank of captain. He and Anna Keeler were both descendants of Thomas Dutton from Chester, England who emigrated to Massachusetts in the 1600s.

† Possibly "indicted," although that is an odd use of the word.

‡ Levi A. Dodd (1833-1901). On April 2, 1865 the 31-year-old colonel of the 211th Pennsylvania Infantry, an oil speculator in Brookville, PA before the war, led his men on an attack on Fort Mahone, which formed part of the defenses of Petersburg. They captured the fort, turned its guns around to face the enemy and repulsed multiple fierce counterattacks. For his actions he was breveted brigadier general of volunteers.

Civil War Years: USS *Florida* (1863-1865)

Good night, with love & kisses to yourself & our little ones, if they can be still called such—nearly three years (long ones) since I have seen one of them. I suppose he can scarcely be called small now. How much I want to see him.

William

U.S. Steamer Florida
New York Harbour
Sunday Eve, Aug. 6th, 1865

Dear Anna,

I have just been driven from the deck by a shower which threatens to continue all night so I have all the evening before me to chat with you. The *Florida* lies at anchor in the harbour just at the mouth of the North river between Jersey City & Gotham. In one direction we have a beautiful view up the Hudson, bordered on one side by the Pallisades & on the other by a forest of masts, shipping & buildings. In another we see Bedlow's & other islands with the Narrows in the distance. Tall chimneys & church spires & manufactories & princely residences towering up above the trees or peeping out from among the foliage are scattered along the shores on either side. Turning again we see Gove[r]nor's island with its little circular brick fort, built for artillery of years gone by—the barracks snugly ensconced among the greenest of trees & surrounded by the greenest of well kept lawns. Beyond, the East river opens, fringed on either side by a tangled maze of shipping & solid brick walls, while on every side of us is busy life & activity.

The chimes of Trinity reach us amid the shrill whistle, the roar of steam, the puff, puff of the tugs, the clang of bells, the dash of wheels, & the softened din & clamour of the great city. Huge steamers move steadily by us as they arrive or depart for various portions of the globe, while the more stately sailing vessel glides smoothly on, or if the wind is not auspicious, held fast in the embrace of some spiteful, diminutive tug whose quick, vicious puffs seems impatient of its task. Swarming upon the decks of many of these are emigrants from the old world gazing with curiosity & anxiety upon the busy scenes opening to them in the new. Vessels bearing the flags of nearly all nations dot the water as they ride quietly at their anchors while smaller craft of every kind from our home ports are hastening to discharge their cargoes of the necessaries or luxuries of life into the lap of this great mart.

Among all these the busy ferry boats ply back & forth from shore to shore, bridging the waters which separate the city from its neighbors. Noticeable too are the numerous steamers running to Long Branch, Coney Island, Shrewsbury, the Fishing Banks &c &c filled with a living mass of pleasure seeking humanity. One wonders how in the midst of all this stir & bustle & money seeking & money getting a person's thoughts can to turn to pleasure seeking or time can be given to gratify the desire. (By the way I went to Coney

Gulf of Mexico (March to November 1865)

island & can tell you my *experience* when I return home.) Such is a free city of the north in contrast with the slave cities of the south—free they are now I know but years & years will elapse before they recover from the blighting effects of slavery & rebellion & then it will be brought about mainly by the energy & thrift of yankee "mudsills & greasy mechanics."

I didn't find my "pile of letters" here when I arrived but rec'd yours of July 24th which perhaps was all I deserved after the very brief epistles I had been sending you, but I trust I made amends on my return, though how "graphic" you found my "description" you can judge better than myself. I only want to say that if my letters are heard or read by others than "our folks" that they are not written for criticism nor is it expected that they will be subjected to the test. They are intended to give you some idea of what I see, hear & do & are written without any attempt at style or composition & many of them are sent off without any attempt at revision or correction.

Your last was a real news letter—giving me more LaSalle news than I have had for a long time. I wish I had some of the beets, peas &c you mention. We do our marketing at the Catherine market* (the best in the country I suppose) but a mess of good fresh vegetables just out of my own garden & of your own raising too would be a luxury indeed. Fruit & melons are abundant here now, but not very cheap—good peaches can be had for two dollars per basket. The market here is well worth a visit. I have got up at 5 two or three mornings to go with our Steward to do his marketing just from curiosity. The quantities of meats, poultry, fish, fruit & vegetables exposed for sale are enormous & one wonders where such piles of everything eatable finds purchasers—but there are many mouths to feed in this city & its vicinity. I know it takes money to do marketing—I have tried it. Five dollars just buys us a steak for breakfast & a small roasting piece for dinner. *How* the poor live here I can't imagine nor can I see the reason *why* they live here, unless it be that they cannot get away.

Are you going to have any grapes this fall? I hope so for it seems as if some from my own garden would be of a better flavour than those raised elsewhere. I often get thinking at sea what I would like most from home & singular as it may seem the preference is usually given to a glass of good cool clear water just out of the well—especially if we are out of ice & are using our condensed water which is warm & insipid & not very palatable in warm weather.

Nothing more about our leaving here. We are loafing about the decks in the shade of the awnings enjoying the busy scene about us. Most of the time we have a fine cool breeze making it much more comfortable & pleasant than if we were lying at the dock, though it is not as convenient communicating with the shore. But our boats run back & forth at fixed times so that we

---

* Located on Catherine Slip in Manhattan.

always know when we can come & go & can regulate our motions accordingly.

Have you read *Christian's Mistake* I sent you & what do you think of it? I do not like it as well as some of her other works. If the manner of bringing up children in England is correctly represented, I think I shan't send mine there to get there *"broughten up."*

We are both well & send love & kisses to all of you.

W—

No. 11—

U.S. Steamer *Florida*
Navy Yard, Philadelphia
Aug. 15, 1865

Dear Anna,

Here we are in the Quaker city, with the probability of remaining a few days—long enough to look about a little. We have just dropped our anchor so that I can say but little about the appearance of the place except what can be seen from the river as I have not yet been on shore.

On Friday last [August 11] we received orders to tow the two Monitors, *Naubuc* & *Modoc*, to this place. They are two of Stimer's failures—intended for light draft Monitors, but from some miscalculation they cannot carry their turrets, so they have been altered into what are called torpedo boats, but of what use they can ever be I cannot conceive as they can scarcely stem the current of the river—and there are about twenty "more of the same sort."* On Saturday morning we left with the *Naubuc* in tow, reaching the capes of the Delaware about noon the next day, Sunday. Here we left our tow to find her way up to the city on the flood tide the best way she could, & started on our return to New York. We reached there daylight the next morning & found the *Modoc* waiting us under the walls of fort Lafayette. She was soon made fast to us & and we were once more outward bound.

Early this morning we entered the Delaware bay, passed the breakwater, & were headed for this city, one hundred & three miles. The first half is up to the bay which is wide, the channel running in the middle, the banks on either side are visible but not distinct enough to give one a general idea of their appearance. After we pass fort Delaware the bay narrows or rather we

---

* Alban Stimers, who assisted John Ericsson with the design of the *Monitor* and served on board her during the battle with the *Virginia*, had been placed in charge of constructing twenty light-draft monitors for use in shallow inland waters, two of which were the USS *Naubuc* and USS *Modoc*. When it was discovered that Stimers' modifications to Ericsson's original design were fatally flawed, he was removed from control of the project and Ericsson brought in to fix the damage. However, the changes that Ericsson was forced to make rendered the vessels unusable for the purpose for which they were designed. Stimers' design mistakes torpedoed his career.

enter the river, both banks with the country for some distance back are in plain view.

The right, or the New Jersey side, is rather low, flat & level, though I should think not swampy. A large proportion of the land, perhaps one half, appeared to be cultivated, mostly in corn & pasture lands, but everything had a sort of shiftless appearance, the houses small & unpainted. No neat, nice yards with flowers & shrubbery—for I consider these sure indications of taste, refinement & good, prudent management. Their fences were down & outbuildings had a sorry dilapidated appearance. Although in a free state it seemed as if "slavery" was stamped upon it.

The other, or the Delaware side, presented a most remarkable contrast. The country rose gradually from the river in gentle knowls and was covered with splendid country seats, good substantial farm house[s], well fenced fields of corn, groves of timber from behind which the church spire marked the village site. Large well kept orchards & tastefully laid out grounds went to make up a panorama which I think a person would have to travel far & long to find its equal. I have seen nothing in this country to compare with it. There is no grand or beautiful natural scenery, but a constant succession of fine farms, tasteful residences, quiet homes & cool shady groves which could not fail to attract the attention of a lover of these things.

Thursday 17th—I spent yesterday travelling about the city seeing the lions[*] &c in company with Mr. Swift[†] one of our engineers. I got up at *half past four* & took the market boat ashore with the Caterer to have a look at the market & found that a sight at the market & early Philadelphia hours repaid me for the sacrifice of two or three hours sleep. There are two days in the week when the country folks drive in & and sell their own produce from their wagons. This morning was one of them. There was a long row of wagons stretched along the street, many of them in the care of women, loaded with fruit & vegetables. It was amusing to go from one to another pricing their fruit &c & listening to their talk after once getting them started. I asked one woman who had a load of water melons if she raised them herself.

"Sartin mister."

"Well how far do you come with them?"

"Nine mile down the Jarsey & we grow good peaches & melons there too mister. Don't you want some of 'em?," & if all the melons were like the two she sold me for ten cents each & sent down to the boat by her *terrier* haired boy they were splendid. Fruit & vegetables are much cheaper & better here than in New York, being bought as it is right from the producers.

---

[*] Sightseeing.
[†] Robert B. Swift (1835-1922). Acting second assistant engineer on the *Florida* from January 1865 to April 1867. A farmer's son, he was born in Bensalem, PA. He was an assistant engineer in the U.S. Coast Survey from the late 1850s to 1864, and survived the sinking of the survey ship *Robert J. Walker* off the coast of New Jersey in June 1860 in which 20 of her crew died.

Civil War Years: USS *Florida* (1863-1865)

After breakfast I went ashore again & in company with some of our officers visited Independence Hall, saw the old cracked bell &c &c &c. From there to Fairmount & the far famed water works.* It is a beautiful spot, tastefully laid out, shady walks, fine old trees, rocks, rustic bridges, fountains, statuary, with a fine view of the Schuylkill, all on a small scale however when compared with Central park. We were too late to get into the mint. They however graciously permitted us to take a view of the exterior at our leisure.

A large number of iron clads are lying here, most of the Monitors, some of them pitted with shot marks from Charleston, Savannah, Mobile & other places. Then there is the *Ironsides, Monadnock* (with my old friend Ziegler on board), a number of Stimer's failures, the torpedo boats & the captured rebel iron clad *Atlanta*†. This latter I visited to day & was surprised to find a vessel of such strength, size & power. Had she had anything but a Monitor to contend with she would have proved an ugly antagonist, but fifteen inch shot were more than a match for her. She still bears the marks of the conflict but is in good fighting order should there be an occasion.

The weather since we have been here has been cool & comfortable. We have enjoyed it as well as the abundance of fruit.

Sunday morning [20th]—We have just arrived in New York. What our next move will be I can't tell. Our trip to Havanna has been given up on account of the prevalance of the yellow fever there.

Love to all.

W—

No. 12—

U.S. Steamer *Florida*
Newport, R.I.
August 24th, 1865

Dear Anna,

For our *distinguished* services, or for some other good reason, the Department has sent us to this noted watering place to enjoy ourselves for a while. Our "season" here however I am inclined to think will be somewhat brief as the evenings are growing cool and the fashion (the elite) are already leaving, so we shall not linger long.

We left New York yesterday afternoon and this morning our anchor was dropped in Newport harbour. I have spent the afternoon, the greater part of it, at the Ocean house‡ seeing the sights, watching the fashions, & gazing at the lions—*the* lion appearing to be "Fighting Joe Hooker." There was a find band of music, a promenade in the Hall, wealth, dress, fashion, carriages &

---

* Fairmount Water Works, located three miles from Independence Hall on the Schuylkill River.
† The ironclad was captured in Wassaw Sound, GA in June 1863.
‡ One of Newport's largest and most fashionable hotels.

Gulf of Mexico (March to November 1865)

turnouts of almost every imaginable description, & everything one would expect to find at such a place except handsome women. Of this latter *article* I don't know that I am a competent judge, but in my humble opinion a greater collection of plain, homely & ugly women, both young & old, it would be difficult to collect. They would "draw" if Barnum had them on exhibition. Shoddy & oil may put silks, diamonds & laces on misshapen forms & hideous features but the forms & features are there still—nor can they conceal the want of refinement which was too evident in many.

The beach looked dwarfed & insignificant in comparison with some of the beaches on the southern coast. The "rock bound coast of New England" cannot boast of the fine sand beaches of the south, nor does the low sandy shore of the south present such beautiful ever changing scenery as the rugged coast of the north with its background of rough wooded hills & cultivated slopes.

The day was cool so that the long row of bathing houses were untenanted & the surf rolled in unopposed. Among other things, we visited the old *tower*. It stands in the middle of a handsomely laid out green & is covered over with the Virginia creeper & other vines. Our visit here has less to do with fashion, pleasure or amusement than the removal of the Naval School to Annapolis, for which place we will leave in a few days.*

I had a very narrow escape just before leaving New York. I do not wish to alarm you unnecessarily but as it has passed I may as well tell you how near I came to—going home. Three or four days after getting back from Philadelphia the vessel was ordered to be put out of commission. I was preparing to discharge the crew, transfer my stores &c & had a letter written telling you that you might look for us home in about a fortnight when the order was countermanded & we were sent up here. We are to go from here to Annapolis & return to New York which will consume about a fortnight, when I hope we will go out of commission, but I consider it very uncertain. I shall not count on it as sure till I see everything & everybody out of the vessel & our pennant down, then I shall write you that we are coming.

I could keep this till to morrow night & fill the sheet but prefer sending it off as it is & writing again before we leave here.

So with love & kisses to you all & a good night.

W—

---

* The Naval Academy had been moved to the safety of Newport, RI at the beginning of the Civil War.

Civil War Years: USS *Florida* (1863-1865)

No. 13—

U.S. Steamer *Florida*
Annapolis, Md.
Sept. 2nd, 1865

Dear Anna,

We have just arrived here from Newport, having left there on the 31st, having had a very pleasant trip. When we left there, and during our stay, the weather was so cool as to make thick clothes comfortable, especially in the evening. To day we have been sweltering in the shade & this evening, while writing, the perspiration is starting from every pore & the mosquitoes are as thick as they can conveniently be.

Very unexpected & very welcome was the return of our boat from the shore bringing a large mail for me, among the number your letter of the 21st & one from Geo*. So you delay writing out of revenge. Well I should write oftner if had anything to say, & I don't like to send a sheet partly filled as I think all my letters home will testify. I have come to regard my return home as so close at hand that it seems sometimes as if there was no need of writing & I cannot get myself in the mood. I hav'nt the patience to set myself down to a letter when it seems that I shall see you so soon.

As I have said we have just reached here. I have not been ashore so cannot tell you anything about the place. Tomorrow I shall try & get to church. I understand that peaches & melons are abundant & cheap so that we shall feast the three or four days that we will probably remain here. We expect to go from here to New York, from there to Newport & then return here again, so we have a two weeks' job before us at any rate. After that we are hoping to go out of commission.

As I have said in one of my previous letters we seem to be reserved to do up all the odd & ends left at the closing of the war. We have brought down from Newport a *full load* of furniture, housekeeping articles & "other things too numerous to mention" belonging to the Professors & others of the Naval Academy, which at the commencement of the war was moved to Newport & now has been moved back here. We are to return for another load including the band & *their families*, so that we shall have plenty & a variety of music on our next trip. We had a very pleasant time while lying at Newport—fine cool weather—passing the time sailing, fishing, boating, watching the "*shoddy*" & criticising the fashions.

Our noble(?) Capt. [Budd] as usual was on an almost constant drunk while there, getting into a fight at the Ocean house for which he was brought up before the Police court & fined, which coming to the knowledge of Commodore Blake† he reported the Capt. to the Dept. The Capt. leaves to morrow

---

* Keeler's brother-in-law.
† George S. Blake, superintendent of the Naval Academy.

morning for Washington to see about it, hoping to get his resignation accepted & not be dismissed. I don't care which so long as we get rid of him. "More anon."

Yours,
W—

No. 14—

U.S. Steamer *Florida*
New York
Sept. 8th, 1865

Dear Anna,

We have just returned from Annapolis & have not yet learned what our future is to be, but it seems to be the general opinion that the vessel is to go out of commission. The order was received by the Admiral* here before we left for Newport and our detachments had been sent him by the Department. But being in want of a vessel to send to Newport he sent us off, instead of obeying the orders of the Dep't, as he had a right to do, he having discretionary power in the matter. I am so far convinced that we have made our last trip that I am packing my superfluous *traps* to send home. I hope the barn is empty, for you will not have room in the house.

Our "*noble Budd*" started for Washington as soon as we reached Annapolis & was forced to resign to save being dismissed, so that we returned here under the command of the Executive officer, Act. Master Ira Bursley.†

We feasted on peaches while at Annapolis, a large orchard being across the river from which we helped ourselves whenever we wanted, by permission of the owner. Most of his early fruit had been gathered, but some were remaining on the trees—enough for us both in quantity & quality. They were delicious—the very perfection of that kind of fruit. How I wished you could have enjoyed them with us. I thought we got good ones in the market here but they will not compare with the ripe fruit picked from the trees.

I see by the *Army & Navy Journal* which I send you that the vessel is noticed as going out of commission on the 21st of last month on which date we were all detached. The *Memphis* has been sent to Newport so that we shall not have to return there.

The mail is just leaving, so good bye with love.

W—

---

* Charles H. Bell.
† See Biographical Notes.

Civil War Years: USS *Florida* (1863-1865)

U.S. Steamer *Florida*
New York
Sept. 12th, 1865

Dear Anna,

"Things is workin." After waiting with Micawber-like patience for a number of days in a discouraging state of suspense & uncertainty something has turned up. This morning a coal barge was sent alongside us with orders to coal up & get ready for sea immediately. All hands set to work & by sundown about 50 tons of coal was aboard, when another order was received to the effect that we were to cease coaling, put everything out of the vessel (which includes the coal just taken on board) when we are to go out of commission. To morrow we commence by sending out our powder & loaded shell, other things will speedily follow & unless the order is revoked, of which I think there is not much probability, a week will see our pennant down, the *Florida* out of commission & the Paymaster & his clerk homeward bound or making preparations to speedily start that way. Day before yesterday I started four boxes homeward filled with superfluous traps. Whether they will reach you by "Central" or Rock Island R.R. I don't know, but when they come pay the freight & have them stored in the barn unopened till I get home. I think neither of us will be disappointed this time, but I shall be able to say with more certainty in a few days.

Our incipient blossom [Capt. Budd] has been forced to succumb to bad whiskey & the pressure of the Department. His place is more worthily filled by Act. Vol. Lt. Wm. H. Maies*, a sort of unpolished diamond. I think he would make a pleasant commanding officer were we to go to sea under him.

In yours of the 5th which has just reached me you ask about getting in the winter's coal. I hardly know how to advise you. Do as you think best. I hope I shall be home in time to see about it myself.

I saw your uncle Frank to day. He says that your Mother & Aunt Mary had been over to Fairfield to make them a visit. Your Father has been out to Sandusky & stopped at your uncle Frank's office on his return. All are well.

I met a cousin of yours to day—a Mr. or Rev. Mr. H. D. Noble† from Brookfield. I had but a few moments' conversation with him & learned nothing of importance.

It is useless to send love or any of that sort of nonsense in a letter when I am coming so soon to bring a large lot of the genuine article. But lest you may feel slighted I will enclose just one kiss each.

W—

[Marginalia] I shan't forget your dress.

---

* See Biographical Notes.
† Henry Dutton Noble, rector of St. Paul's Episcopal Church in Brookfield, CT. His mother was an older sister of Anna's father.

Gulf of Mexico (March to November 1865)

No. 15—

U.S. Steamer *Florida*
Sunday evening, at Sea
Sept. 24th, 1865

Dear Anna,

Two weeks ago when I wrote you I fully expected to be spending this Sunday evening quietly at home. Man prop[o]ses Gideon disposes.* At any rate he has done so in this case. When we arrived in New York from Annapolis we had settled upon the belief that the vessel was to go out of commission and that we would all soon be at our respective homes and began laying our plans accordingly, for we knew that the vessel had been ordered out of commission by the Department before we were ordered to Newport and that our detachments had been waiting us in the Navy Yard ever since.

How great was our chagrin a few hours after dropping our anchor off the Battery to receive orders to get ready again for sea. Of course we had no choice but to obey. A coal barge was sent alongside & we commenced coaling. Fifty tons had been taken in when orders came to cease coaling, take out our powder & loaded shell, bring the ship to the Yard, discharge all our stores, transfer the crew, & the ship to be put out of commission. Our spirits rose accordingly. We considered the matter settled & never did an anchor come up with a more hearty good will than ours with the promised land of home before us. Well we got to the Yard & before our anchor was let go for the last time, as we were fondly believing, were met by an order from the Admiral† to resume our anchorage off the Battery, complete our coaling & prepare the ship for sea as soon as possible.

Grumbling and growling was of no more avail than the Pope's bull against the comet—orders must be obeyed. Two of our officers were expecting to take command of fine merchantmen which were then waiting them & called on the Admiral to represent their case to him, telling him among other things that they had permanent employment offered them & good wages & that their duties to their families made it necessary that they should accept, that the country was welcome to their services during the war but that was now over, &c &c. The Admiral told them "that he cared nothing about it, neither for them nor their families, [and that] if their families were dying they should go." One of them, Mr. Bursley, immediately telegraphed his resignation to Washington but heard nothing from it till we were getting up anchor to leave when he received a telegram that his resignation was accepted & he left us with a light heart but the vessel was detained till his place could be filled. In the meantime our M.D. had managed to get detached & another (a Dr.

---

* A play on "man proposes but God disposes," but with God being the Secretary of the Navy.
† Charles H. Bell.

Civil War Years: USS *Florida* (1863-1865)

Bowen*) was ordered in his place. One of our other officers was suddenly taken sick & was left behind so that our Mess now only numbers six or I might say five for the Dr. has been sea sick since leaving port & has not left his room.

We have on board 300 men for the Pacific Squadron, which with our own crew makes about 500 persons I have to feed & provide for, but as I have a good Steward the labour is not much, though the responsibility is. Many of them are landsmen & are as sea sick as they can well be. We have been speeding through the clear blue waters of the Gulf stream all day, just sea enough on to make the sea sick ones feel no better.

Sunday evening Oct 1st—Another week has passed rapidly by & it finds us still widening the distance between ourselves & home. This has been a still, quiet sabbath with but little variation from our every day life except the usual monthly muster of the crew & the reading of the "Articles of War."

Our ship has been urging her way through the calm blue waters of the Caribbean Sea, the north east trades tempering what would otherwise be an extremely heated atmosphere. As it is we find it hot & close below but cool & comfortable on deck, where most of our time is spent.

Yesterday we passed along the eastern end of Cuba & within sight of Hayti [Haiti] & Jamaica. By the aid of a glass we were able to form a tolerable idea of the appearance of the former island, or that portion of it along which we skirted. The shores were rough & rocky, the waves breaking against a low rocky bluff. As the eye swept back towards the interior it passed over a succession of rocky precipices & sloping table lands covered with scattered masses of loose rocks whose weather stained points & angles were raised above the vegetation which appeared sparse & stunted. Deep rocky ravines intersected these plateaus, running from the interior, their rough ragged mouths opening upon the sea. The eye was finally lost in endeavouring to penetrate the clouds above which rose the mountains farther inland. No habitation, no cultivated fields, no sign of a human being was to be seen. All seemed still, deserted & forsaken, very different from what I had pictured Cuba to myself. This description applies however only to the extreme eastern point of the island. The two latter islands were too far from us to be seen distinctly, nothing but a rough ragged outline being visible against a bright tropical sky.

---

* William S. Bowen (1844-1907). He abandoned his medical studies in 1862 and enlisted as a private in the 11th Rhode Island Infantry. In January 1865 he was appointed an acting assistant surgeon in the Navy and was honorably discharged the following year. After completing his medical studies at Harvard in 1867 he was commissioned an acting surgeon in the regular navy, but was court-martialed in 1873 and forced to resign. After practicing medicine in New England for a decade he became a roving newspaper correspondent for the *New York Herald* and *New York World*, reporting on events around the world. In 1903 he was selected as the consul general of Guayquil, Ecuador, but the appointment was rescinded due to his 1873 court martial.

Gulf of Mexico (March to November 1865)

We have had one or two days of pretty rough weather on our trip, the ship rolling about more than I have ever known her [doing] during the three years she has been my home. Many ludicrous incidents occurred during one of the nights while we were rolling in the trough of the sea by the water forcing its way through the air ports which had been left open for ventilation in the different state rooms.

We expect to be at Aspinwall in twenty four hours if nothing happens & I am to take charge of our men across the isthmus which will give me a chance to see Panama & a view once more of the mild Pacific. I hope to find a steamer ready to go north & have this sheet ready to send. I will tell you of the isthmus in my next. Good bye till then with love & kisses.

W—

No. 16—

U.S. Steamer Florida
Aspinwall, New Grenada
Oct. 10th, 1865

Dear Anna,

We arrived here on the 2nd inst., nine days & fifteen hours from New York. An error in our chronometer gave us a landfall some 50 miles too far down the coast, thus delaying our arrival five or six hours. We skirted along the land to our destination, with the connecting link of the great ranges of mountains which traverse both continents in easy view. High broken hills with conical peaks covered to their summits with dense tropical forests, partially hidden by patches of low fleecy clouds resting on their tops & sides, made a beautiful back-ground, in front of which & scattered along the water's edge was now & then a cluster of native huts peering out from groves of palms.

We had hoped for pleasant weather during our stay here but found it the midst of the rainy season which does not close till about the first of December. This however is one of the pleasantest of the wet months; the fore part of the day being clear & hot; heavy showers coming up towards evening & raining heavily the greater part of the night.

Aspinwall cannot be said to be very preposessing in its appearance. It is situated on the island of Manzanilla & is the Atlantic terminus of the Panama R.R. which has given birth to the city.* The Company's offices, depots, club & mess houses & residences of its employees, together with one or two hotels & a few stores, comprise the best appearing portion of the place, & are stretched along the water front, while back of them are congregated a collection of small, dirty, wooden buildings in the front part of which are exposed

---

* The city was founded by Americans in the 1850s as the terminus of the Panama Railroad which was built to provide a fast route to the California gold fields.

Civil War Years: USS *Florida* (1863-1865)

for sale the fruits & productions of the country, cheap liquors from abroad, monkeys, parrots & native wares, displayed to tempt the eye & empty the purse of the passing sailor, while in the rear the Jamaica wenches, by whom the places are mostly kept, have their dens.

The narrow, filthy passages running through this portion of the place rejoice in the suggestive & not inappropriate names of "bottle lane," "monkey alley," "parrot corners," &c &c. Expensive docks extend out into the bay, built on iron screw piles & covered with metallic roofs. Wood being so soon destroyed by the torredo cannot be used below water. A stone church of somewhat imposing exterior has been erected by the R.R. Co. but the pulpit I believe is not now filled.

The day after our arrival myself & some of the other officers took our draft of three hundred men across the isthmus to Panama, a distance of forty seven miles, in a special train furnished by the Company for that purpose. After a pleasant ride of a few hours I was afloat on the Pacific in a small steamer furnished to transport the men from the dock at Panama to the U.S. Frigate *Lancaster*, to which vessel they had been sent out.

My late papers & home news insured me a welcome in her Ward room where I dined with the mess. Among them I found an old acquaintance of the Wilmington blockade, Lieut. Com'dr Cushing of *Albermarle* fame.* I also found another on this side in the person of the commander of the U.S. Steamer *James Adger*†, who gave me a pressing invitation to accompany him to Carthagena, about three hundred miles down the coast where he was going with his vessel on account of one of the local disturbances or outbreaks which seem to be of periodical occurrence in these countries. I found a good table & bed at the "Aspinwall Hotel" kept by a Spaniard in his country's style.

The city of Panama is rich in historic associations connected with the early days of the Spanish rule in this country & presents a striking specimen of one of the old cities of the new world gradually crumbling to decay. Standing as it does at the foot of high hills from which the buccaneer Morgan made his descent on the ancient city nearly two hundred years ago‡, it projects boldly out into the sea, it's high, massive & turreted walls being washed by the waters

---

* Using a small steam launch fitted with a spar torpedo, Cushing sank the ironclad ram CSS *Albemarle* which had controlled the Roanoke River and the approaches to Plymouth, NC through the spring and summer of 1864. On the night of October 27-28, 1864 Cushing worked his launch upriver to where the *Albemarle* lay docked at the Plymouth waterfront, rolled it up and over the log boom surrounding the ironclad and rammed her with the spar. The torpedo blew a gaping hole in the *Albemarle* which sank in minutes. Cushing and his crew of 13 were blown overboard by the explosion. Cushing and one of his men escaped, two were killed and the rest were captured. The next morning Cushing stole a small skiff and paddled down the river to safety. Cushing's daring exploit made him a national hero and earned him a promotion to lieutenant commander. See Keeler's letter of March 18, 1864 for another of Cushing's daring exploits.

† Thomas H. Patterson.

‡ Sir Henry Morgan, the Welsh privateer who plundered the city in 1671.

of the Pacific, whose surges have dashed in vain for so many years against their solid base. But their glories have departed; grim cannon no longer bid defiance from the ramparts, the bugle blast has long since died away, & the flaunting colors of the Conquistador have with the bearers crumbled into dust. They are monuments at once of the pride, wealth & power of haughty Spain & her subsequent decay. One solitary, rusty gun sunken in the midst of its decaying carriage lies with its muzzle projecting over the ramparts, powerless but defiant in its dotage. It is related of these walls that when the Queen of Spain was asked to sign the appropriation for their construction that she enquired if they *were made of silver.*

Within the walls the high tiled roofs of the present occupants are mingled with pearl shelled spires, dilapidated towers, ruined edifices & crumbling arches of the past—deserted, grass grown & decaying. The streets are narrow, the projecting balconies from the buildings on either side seeming to almost meet over them. The pavements put down by the founders of the city still remain, but Spanish poverty & indolences forbid much needed repairs. Happily for them nature ever mindful of their necessities has furnished them with scavangers, in the rains & buzzards, by which most of the paved streets are kept tolerably clean. The lower story of most of the dwellings is used as stables, offices or storerooms, the windows being strongly grated as a security to the inmates above in the revolutions so common here. But little change seems to be made in the place by the immense traffic & travel so constantly passing through it. There is so little to mark the progress of improvement & so much of the old Spanish forms & customs still remain that one can easily imagine it to be the same sleepy, quiet place it was in by gone ages.

The Cathedral fronting on the Plaza & one or two of the churches which I visited were open for morning service but the priests were repeating their prayers to unappreciative walls & cold stone floors. In the Cathedral two old Spanish senoras were at their devotions but not so much engrossed but what they, as well as the priest, would occasionally turn & give us a curious stare. Enough remains of their former costly magnificence to give one some idea of what they were in the palmy days of the empire, but their splendor has faded out. Precious metals which once adorned their altars have given way to cheap, gaudy tinsel & the gilt work & costly finish which decorated their walls are covered with the coarse paint daubs of later & poorer days.

But little besides the Spanish language is spoken & I had great difficulty in making my wants known at the hotel & at the stores where I endeavoured to make some purchases. The universal, "no entende Senor," is the almost unvarying reply to all your inquiries. In one store I found a French woman, "fat, fair & forty" who with a pretty daughter were the presiding deities. A few Spanish words of which I was the fortunate possessor & a little English on their part enabled me to supply my wants. In another large wholesale establishment a good-natured red-headed Irish woman, for twenty years a resident of Panama, seemed to possess all the energy & animation of the concern. The owner, a sleepy, dreamy old Don, gazed at her as she bustled about with a vacant, listless stare as if wondering how so much life & activity could be concentrated in one body.

The morning after my return from Panama our commander (Capt. Maies), Henry & myself started on a pleasure trip for the same place. The train left in the cool of the morning & we were soon whirling along through the varied vegetation of perpetual summer. The ground for the first few miles was low & swampy. The few feet on either side of the track from which the original growth had been cut was thickly covered with a variety of huge lillies & aquatic plants, whose broad shining leaves were spread over the slimy ooze beneath. Beyond this low & recent vegetation rose the wall of the primeval forest, dense, dark & impenetrable.

Then the land became more elevated & drier & the character of the vegetation was somewhat changed. Tall & graceful palms rear their heads from amid the feathery foliage of the bamboo, huge clusters of bright red & yellow fruit ornamenting their pinnated crowns. Then we pass a small open space dotted with clumps of guava bushes, the ground beneath covered with their ripe yellow fruit. Clusters of broad leaved banannas overshadowed by the more lordly cocoanut & pawpaw. Now we are walled in by a leafy barrier whose density the eye fails to penetrate. Bright hued flowers of many colors, & fruit with whose names & character we are not familiar abound in great profusion. Interlacing vines with innumerable shoots & branches weaving & interweaving among the close & crowded undergrowth bind the whole together in a close compact body, while palms in great variety lift their heads as if struggling for the light & air of heaven & anxious to free themselves from the crowded mass below.

A hundred feet above all rise the giants of the forests, their bodies covered with thick growing creepers & parasites. Parasitic vines stretch themselves from their wide spreading arms & without throwing out branch or shoot reach the ground taut & straight as cordage, giving the tree the appearance (to use a nautical phrase) of being "guyed up." Trailing vines & blossoming creepers are on every side in great profusion & luxuriance, enwrapping the trees & festooning the branches.

Convolvulus of many varieties enrich the scene. Among them the morning glory with its many pleasing home associations shines out beautiful & blue among the dark green foliage, like amethysts in emerald setting. Leaving this we pass along low ranges of hills whose open sloping sides are dotted with dun colored cattle quietly feeding beneath clumps of bamboos, palms & guava bushes.

Then by a sudden turn we find ourselves upon the banks of the Chagres, in years gone by the highway of the hardy California adventurer, whose vexations, mishaps & adventures as he ascended the small turbid stream in the bungoe* of the native or camped upon its muddy banks he now recalls with interest as he passes over the route in three hours which he was once a fortnight in accomplishing. We caught an occasional glimpse of an alligator dozing in the sun on the slimy ooze of the stream & gave one patriarchal looking fellow a passing volley from our revolvers but failed to disturb his slumbers.

Now the warning whistle gives notice of a short delay at a station around which is clustered a native village, & as we stop between rows of bamboo huts the scantily dressed women come flocking to the sides of the cars with the fruits & productions of the country for sale, carried in large wooden trays or the more capacious calabash. Groups of naked children sport about the doors or stare at us with curious look, while those too young to walk are carried astride the hip of the mother, who with a calabash of fruit balanced on her head traffics with the passengers.

Leaving this we pass between high mountains covered to their tops with the densest verdure. A clear mountain stream which murmurs along beside us is half concealed by festoons of over hanging vines. An occasional gap in the luxuriant screen discloses groups of naked females bathing or washing. Their mode of washing, which is done by selecting a rock with a flat, smooth surface in the stream, upon which the articles are pounded with a club, I would not recommend to our folks at home. It is efficatious in removing dirt but my experience proves that it is as effectual in removing buttons to the great annoyance of those unfortunates forced to lead bachelor lives.

When within sixteen miles of Panama & a mile above Obispo station our tender ran off the track & as it promised to be a lengthy job to get it [back] on we concluded to return to the station. Our way lay through the woods & along a small mountain stream whose sides were covered with a low, dense undergrowth from which we started up several iguana—a large green lizard from three to six feet in length whose flesh is said to afford most excellent eating—our revolvers failed to secure us a specimen. The woods about us rang with the sharp screech of innumerable parrots, the harsher cry of the toucan, the melodious whistle of the turpiale & the cooing of the turtle dove.

The heat of the sun was intense & our mile seemed a long one before we reached the station where we introduced ourselves to the agent whom we found to be a generous, warm hearted St. Louis Irishman. He immediately set his cook to preparing our breakfast after which we took a look about his place. Like most of the others on the line of the [rail]road it consisted of a good sized, two story, wood house surrounded by cool, pleasant looking verandahs. Two or three acres of land set out with the fruits & flowers of the tropics spread out around the house, the whole surrounded by a neat, white picket fence. Limes, lemons, oranges, pineapples, guavas, cocoanuts, pawpaws & other tropical fruits were growing over beds of radishes, lettuce, beets

---

* A dugout canoe.

&c from our more rigorous clime, and northern roses mingled with the bright hued flowers of the tropics. I was shewn here the "Flor del Espiritu Santo," or the Flower of the Holy Ghost, so named by the early Spaniards from the image of a dove to be seen in the cup of the pure white, tulip shaped flower.

Our kind entertainer took us on his handcar to Matachin, the next station below where was a native village & where we spent the remainder of the day till the return of the train from Panama, rumbling over the hills & making ourselves acquainted with the manners & customs of the natives. Their houses are usually of a single room, constructed of bamboos set upright in the ground & thatched with leaves of the same plant, the bare earth forming the floor. Hammocks are slung inside or in the shade of the neighboring trees in which the indolent natives lounge away the day. Dogs, pigs, children, chickens, parrots and monkeys sport promiscuously together in all the freedom of unrestricted nature.

Children till six or eight years of age go naked. The women are dressed in a skirt of thin, gay colored fabric, heavily flounced at the bottom, which is allowed to drag on the ground behind in the most approved northern style. The single remaining garment partially covers the upper portion of the body, hanging loosely off the shoulders, which on dress occasions are covered with a lace cape or shawl whose delicate tracery is displayed to advantage over the dark ground. A coarse grass or palm hat is sometimes worn but they commonly go bareheaded.

The natives are indolent & improvident to the last degree. Content with what generous nature has so profusely lavished upon them, they bestow no thought for the morrow. Their wants are few & easily supplied. The bamboo furnishes their house with but slight labor. The neighboring calabash tree supplies them with dishes & most of their culinary utensils, while the nutritious yam takes root & twines over their huts which are sheltered beneath trees whose tops are loaded with fruit. How much nature has done for this country but how little has been done by man.

In a ride over this pathway of civilization through the tropics one meets with much that is new, strange & novel but for beauty of scenery, for evidences of progress & improvement, for charming landscapes, for much that adds to human happiness & enjoyment, give me a trip along the hill-sides of New England or across the garden prairies of our State. Here one soon tires of the monotony of uncultivated wilds & looks in vain for the country school-house, the village church, the quiet hamlet, for cultivated fields, the snug farm house with its tasteful surroundings, for all the evidences of taste, wealth, education, refinement & enterprise so characteristic of "Our Country."

Everything about the Panama R.R. is built in the most substantial manner & evinces the greatest liberality in the management of the road & care of the employees. The rails are laid on lignum vital ties which are as durable as the iron itself & the track is kept in the best of order. The larger bridges are all of iron & stone arches span the smaller streams. A telegraph wire extends

Gulf of Mexico (March to November 1865)

from ocean to ocean supported by light, well proportioned concrete columns. The fare ($25.00 for 47 miles) would be thought rather extravagant on our northern roads, but it is not so much out of proportion to the first cost of the road & the expense of maintaining & running it.

Letters from the Sec'y of the road in New York to some of its officers here insured me a welcome, & their kind attentions have added much to the pleasure of my short visit. We have had the freedom of the road to go & come when we pleased, the free use of their library, club room & billiard tables, with a standing invitation to the officers' mess when ashore at meal times & last but not least a daily gratuitous supply of ice.

The Steamship *New York* has just arrived, bringing her cargo of living freight on their way to the western shores of the continent. We will soon leave for the north so I must close, having already "spun my yarn" to an unexpected length.

Affectionately yours,

W. F. Keeler

U.S. Steamer *Florida*
At Sea off Absecomb[*]
Sunday Morning, Nov. 12/65

Dear Anna,

I believe I wrote you from Philadelphia that I had been relieved at my own request.[†] My detachment was sent to me at New York but as the vessel had left for Phila. it was for'd to that place where I found it on my arrival. Upon the reporting of my relief I was to turn over to him all the stores & accounts in my possession after which I was to consider myself detached from the *Florida*. Mr. Chenery[‡] who relieved me did not reach Phila. till just previous to our leaving there so that I was obliged to go to Norfolk in the ship that I might make the necessary transfers during the trip. Upon our arrival at Hampton Roads Capt. Maies found orders to go to Norfolk to have the ship fitted out for a six months' cruise.

At the latter place I got all ready to take the first steamer to New York when orders were received from Washington for the *Florida* to go to New York taking in tow two of the "stone fleet," bought to sink in Charleston

---

[*] The lighthouse at Atlantic City, NJ.
[†] That letter is missing from the collection.
[‡] Charles E. Chenery (1841-1876). Born in Wisconsin, he grew up there and in Massachusetts. In the early 1860s he moved to San Francisco to live with his father who moved there during the Gold Rush. He enlisted in March 1863 and was appointed to the USS *Narragansett* in the Pacific Squadron before joining the *Florida* on which he served until April 1867. He served in the regular Navy until September 1868 when he was dismissed following the findings of a court-martial.

harbor at the commencement of the war.* A portion of them were sunk when it was found the experiment was a failure. The remainder of the old hulks (for they were little else) were used at different points on the coast as store ships. The two we have (the *Roman* and the *Ben Morgan*) were kept at Norfolk filled with ordnance stores. We towed the old sloop of war *Dale* from Philadelphia to Hampton Roads loaded with the same description of stores.

While stopping at Norfolk I met my old messmate Dr. Brooks & took dinner with him on the frigate *St. Lawrence* to which vessel he is attached. He is desired to be remembered to you & mother.

In the Norfolk Navy Yard at the present time are many objects of interest. Among them in the dry dock are the remains of the *Congress*, destroyed by the *Merrimac* the day previous to our fight in 1862. Then there are the fragments of the *Merrimac*, as they are being taken out of the water at Craney island. The *Albermarle*, sunk by Lieut. Cushing, is tied up at the dock there too & also the boat used by him in the exploit. Near the *Albermarle* are two more of the rebel iron clads, the *Columbia* & the *Lady Davis*, captured at Charleston. Besides these are the remains of the old frigates *United States* & *Brandywine*. We left Norfolk last Thursday evening [November 9] & hope to be in New York early to morrow morning. I shall be detained there two or three days & a short time in New Haven & Waterbury when we will leave for home direct.

It is a beautiful bright clear Sunday morning & you may imagine us quietly gliding along with the two old hulks rolling & tumbling after. We have just got through "general muster" & the reading of the "Articles of War," a farce which I hope I have witnessed for the last time. The thermometer stands at 46° on deck with very little wind, making it quite comfortable in the sun. We are passing a wreck about a mile off lying on her beam ends—no appearance of any one on board.

I hope to find letters from you on my arrival in New York but shall not write again unless something occurs to require it, & will release you from further duty in that line as it is doubtful if your letters would be found by me, or if you must write you can direct to La Salle, Ills., but I want you to keep your tongue in good talking order so that it can be used when I get home. Till then good bye with love & kisses.

W—

I shall send by Express from New York two boxes filled with my books & paper (official) which I wish extra care taken of as they contain accounts amounting to over three million of dollars. Allow me to introduce to you my successor, Mr. Chenery.

---

* A fleet of old ships, mainly whaling vessels from New England, filled with stones that were sunk in Charleston Harbor to prevent blockade runners from going in and out. The exercise was a failure for the shipwrecks sank deep into the sand or broke up and floated away.

Part 3
Mayport Years

On the opposite shore are the cottages of Mayport, around which the eddying winds pile up huge banks of sea sand, which at night have a strange resemblance to snow-covered hills. The name of this settlement commemorates the original name of the river, which was the River of May, afterwards changed to St. Matthias, and again to St. John's. It is associated, too, with the memory of the young and promising botanist, Henry D. Keeler, who found an untimely grave beneath the snows of New England. His father, Major Wm. F. Keeler, has a fine mansion a mile out on the old road to St. Augustine. It is a sylvan home embosomed in grand forests of palmetto, which open eastward and allow a fine view of the ocean. Great natural beauties and art skillfully directed conspire to render it a home worthy of its cultured occupants. (botanist Allen H. Curtiss, 11 August 1884)*

The Keelers remained in La Salle for five years after the end of the Civil War. Ed and Lizzie attended public school there. (Henry was in Chicago where he kept the books for his uncle Dave Brown's wholesale tea business.) Living with the Keelers were also his sister Sarah and his mother—his father had died in 1864 when Keeler was on the USS *Florida*. Anna's father too was gone. He retired from the bench of the Connecticut Supreme Court in 1866, but was still active at Yale law school at the time of his death in 1869.

By 1870 Keeler's business ventures were doing poorly. His iron works had long since closed, and he was a partner in his brother-in-law's tea

---

* Clipping from the *The Florida Dispatch* (Jacksonville, FL, August 11, 1884) in Keeler's *Mayport Journal*. Allen H. Curtiss (1845-1907) was a botanist from Jacksonville, FL and a friend of Keeler's son.

business. The 1870 census lists his occupation as "miscellaneous dealer." In November 1870 the Keelers packed their bags once more and headed to Mayport, Florida, a tiny village at the mouth of the St. John's River thirty-five miles downstream of Jacksonville. What led them to this backwater is lost to time, but one could imagine it was Keeler's love of warm weather, tropical vegetation, pristine beaches, and "old ocean." His sister Fannie and her family also moved to Florida in 1870, settling near Jacksonville where Dave was a dairy farmer. Six years later they moved to Lake Worth near West Palm Beach.

Keeler built a two-story house a mile east of Mayport on the old road to St. Augustine, and named it Thalassa after the Greek goddess of the sea. Scattered nearby and also with a fine view of the ocean were a dozen or so summer cottages which were used by Jacksonville residents and Northerners. Standing tall among the cottages was Thalassa, which by all accounts was a majestic place. Many years after they were gone, the "Keeler place," as it was called by the locals, was purchased by a wealthy Northerner who was developing a tourist resort nearby. While looking for a place to stable her horses she came upon the abandoned property, which she described as "a perfect paradise . . . huge oak trees with branches hanging to the ground, cedars, bay, magnolia and holly. . . . On a hill stood an old two-story mansion house, down below a tenant house and off to the other side, large roomy stables."* The house and the outbuildings are long gone, presumably demolished by the Navy when they built a naval base there in the 1940s, but its location, at least its latitude accurate down to 100 feet (30°23'35"), is noted in the astronomical journal Ed Keeler kept in the 1870s. This places the house on a line due east of the old Mayport lighthouse (located on the east side of the village and still standing) and close to Ribault Bay (now Mayport Basin).

Keeler served as the deputy collector of customs from 1871 to 1880 and on occasion inspector of elections. For reasons long forgotten, he referred to himself by the military honorific, Major, preferring to keep his naval background secret. Commencing in 1883 he was the Mayport correspondent for the *Florida Times-Union* newspaper in Jacksonville. His short, offbeat weekly column entitled "Mayport Mention," written under a variety of different pseudonyms (Leslie, Silex, Monitor and K) reported on ship arrivals and other happenings in Mayport.† Most of his time, however, was spent working around the house, in his shop, and tending his orange groves, the latter being his primary occupation. The peak yield was in 1884 with 6,664 fruit from 59 trees, with one tree producing a whopping 550 oranges. Regarded as an authority on orange growing, he was also an expert in budding pecans on hickory trees, as seen by the newspaper clipping of a letter he wrote on the subject which is pasted into his journal.

---

* *Story of Mayport, Site of the Great Modern Naval Station*, Elizabeth Stark, 1961, p. 27.
† Appendix C contains several of Keeler's "Mayport Mention" columns.

On account of his wartime injury, Keeler received a Navy pension of $10 per month commencing June 1875.* The physician's report included in his pension application states that his "back is so weakened by the injury that he is unable to perform any severe labor that requires the motion of the back in bending" and "is laid up with it at times, so that he is confined to the bed." A hired hand did the heavy work outdoors, while a maid helped Anna with the domestic chores indoors.

Henry joined his parents not long after they moved to Mayport. He helped his father build their house and tutored his two younger siblings. Never having attended college, he was nevertheless a talented botanist and roamed the Florida countryside collecting rare plants which he would send to scientific institutes up North. In a letter to his grandmother in early 1873 he said that he would be leaving for Jacksonville in a few days. He was "sorry to leave the folks, but now that the house is completed and they are so comfortably situated" he wanted to move on.† Three years later he moved to New York City where he was a clerk for the Equitable Trust Company. While on a botanical vacation in the Connecticut River Valley he fell violently ill at Branford Point and died several days later on August 22, 1877. He was 29.

Keeler's second son was a brilliant boy who went on to become one of America's leading astrophysicists. According to his biographer, Donald E. Osterbrock, Ed's interest in astronomy developed from the practical side of surveying which he learned from his father. His prowess in building astronomical instruments and his love of science were also nurtured by him. Spending untold hours in his father's workshop in Mayport, Ed built a surveyor's cross which he used to lay out lands for neighbors, an experimental windmill, and a telescope from parts he ordered from Philadelphia. Ed kept a small journal, whose cover was adorned with the large title in block letters, "Mayport Astronomical Observatory," below which appeared "J. E. Keeler, Director!" (his exclamation mark). In it he documented his projects, in particular his telescope which he finished in 1875: "Saturday, at work completing my telescope. The other day I tore a postage stamp into quarters & put one up on the lighthouse and saw it easily with my telescope." His excitement a few days later when he was finally able to view the heavens is palpable: "Directed my telescope to the stars and saw the rings of Saturn for the first time . . . Saw the annular nebula in Lyra, one satellite of Saturn. Divided the double star Castor with 108 . . . saw all four of the stars in the trapezium in the Great Nebula of Orion. . . ." Another one of his journals is filled with beautifully detailed pen and ink drawings of celestial bodies, as well as detailed calculations of their positions.‡

---

* Navy Survivors' Certificates (Certificate No. 2177), NARA M1469.
† H. D. Keeler to E. E. Dutton, February 15, 1873 (Henry Dutton Family Letters).
‡ Photocopies of Ed's two journals are in the James E. Keeler Papers (MS 271), Special Collections and Archives, University Library, University of California, Santa Cruz, CA.

Ed's unique talent was discovered by Charles Rockwell, a wealthy amateur astronomer from Tarrytown, New York and a friend of the Keelers from their days in La Salle. Keeler's daughter Lizzie, who was attending a private school in Tarrytown in the 1870s, happened to be visiting Rockwell's private observatory and, while looking through his telescope at Saturn, remarked that she had often seen the planet in her brother's telescope back home. Intrigued, Rockwell inquired more about her unusual brother and not long after brought him north, helping to finance his education at Johns Hopkins University in Baltimore. After graduating in 1881 he worked as an assistant to Samuel P. Langley at Allegheny Observatory in Pittsburgh. He went on to become director of that observatory and of Lick Observatory in California.

It was in 1878, the year after Henry's death and Ed's departure for Johns Hopkins, that Keeler started the journal in which he noted in short, terse phrases his daily activities, work in his orange groves, vegetables and crops planted, fruit trees harvested, frost and ice days, and monthly precipitation, as well as birthdays and his wedding anniversaries. A sampling of his journal gives a glimpse into the daily routine of this hard working and energetic man: "finished transplanting Henry's seedlings" (written six months after his son's death), "fitting up shop over the stable," "budded Japan persimon, mulberry, plum, grape &c," "plowed out the corn in front of the old house site," "making chicken coop on the island," "repairing saddles & harnesses," "putting in sink & fitting up pumps." His daily routine was not without hazard, however, as the entry for October 8, 1880 reveals: "To day while forging a drill it slipped from the tongs & struck me in the right eye totally destroying the sight." Back to work a month later he never again mentioned the loss of an eye. And, as with his dry goods stores in Bridgeport in the 1840s, fire again took a toll, burning down his workshop in 1878.

Scattered throughout Keeler's journal are newspaper clippings of Ed's growing scientific achievements, obituaries of friends and relatives, and Keeler's articles to the *Florida Times-Union*. Also noted are the frequent visits of sea captains, colonels, generals, lawyers, doctors and clergymen from Jacksonville and other nearby locales, as well as family and friends from up North. His unmarried sister Sarah made extended visits to Mayport to escape the cold Illinois winters. His brother-in-law George Watrous, who by then was one of New Haven's leading lawyers, was another visitor. Suffering from Bright's disease and overwork, he came south for a month to recuperate. Living not far away was Keeler's old friend from La Salle, Samuel Carter, who had lost two brothers in the Civil War. He too had come south on doctor's orders. Employed as the chief engineer of the Jacksonville, Tampa and Key West Railroad, he was a frequent visitor at the Keelers' house.

Also noted in his journal are sad remembrances. Each year the anniversary of Henry's death was duly recorded, and on occasion that of their infant daughter Minnie who died in 1857. In September 1883 Anna's mother's obituary appears, followed a month later with the entry that "brother Melzar's portrait from New Haven" had arrived. This would have been a treasured photograph of her son that Eliza Dutton had kept by her side since his death at the Battle of Cedar Mountain in 1862.

For the last two years of his life Keeler suffered from heart disease and other issues relating to his wartime injury. With the realization that his days were numbered, his thoughts turned back to the *Monitor*, spurred in part perhaps by the sad news of the suicide of his old friend and shipmate Samuel Dana Greene, whose obituary he pasted into his journal in December 1884. On March 8, 1885, the day before the twenty-third anniversary of the battle between the *Monitor* and the *Virginia*, he signed his newspaper column "Monitor," a clue perhaps to his neighbors of his true identity. In April he applied for an increase in his Navy pension on account of increased disability (vertigo and kidney problems)* and in June was declared totally unfit for manual labor. Starting in July, "sick, nothing done" are his journal entries.

Two months later his thoughts of the *Monitor* were stirred up again, this time by a letter from a Connecticut collector named Frank H. Pierce who was corresponding with the officers and crew of the *Monitor*. He penned two letters to Pierce before sickness prevailed, and Anna took over the writing. His letters to Pierce, along with Anna's two follow-on letters, are a fitting end to Keeler's life story in which the USS *Monitor* played such a big part. Those letters are included in the next section.

Keeler's last journal entry was December 27 after which Lizzie picked up the pen and continued the writing until mid-February 1886. Keeler's last two "Mayport Mention" columns, signed "K" and dated mid-January and early February of 1886, must have been dictated, for by then he was too ill to write. Friends and acquaintances from Mayport and Jacksonville came to pay their last respects, and possibly learn his real Civil War story. His sister Sarah from Illinois arrived in early January to be with her brother. Ed Keeler, who was in Pittsburgh preparing to head to Lick Observatory, where he had been hired as a junior astronomer, was informed of his father's worsening condition, and left for Mayport on March 2. He never got to say goodbye to him, for the next day he learned from a newspaper he purchased while his train was in Charleston that he had died.

William Keeler died on February 27, 1886, followed two days later by his 85-year-old mother, who was unable to bear the loss of another son. Taking up the pen in her husband's journal for the first time Anna noted "Wm buried Feb. 28th" and "Mother buried March 3rd," along with the names of their pall bearers. Pasted on the next page is a short announcement of their deaths from a local newspaper, as well as an obituary from the *New Haven Evening Register* (see Appendix D).

---

* It is unclear from his pension records whether Keeler was granted an increase in his pension. However, he did apply for an accrued pension and was paid in arrears at $10 per month starting the day after his honorable discharge date of April 25, 1866 to June 1, 1875.

Final Letters

> *Although it is a matter of small consequence I would like to correct a slight error of Green's in his* Century *article where he speaks of Toffey & myself as landsmen &c. I had seen two years of sea life before being ordered to the* Monitor, *having gone to California around "the Horn" in /49, a passage of 255 days. From thence home as a passenger in one of our clipper ships around the Cape of Good Hope, so that I was familiar with all sea terms & phrases.* (15 November 1885)

As soon as the smoke of battle cleared from Hampton Roads on March 9, 1862 questions arose as to why the *Monitor* had not vanquished the *Virginia*. Since Worden never wrote an official report of the battle, blame had fallen squarely on the lap of executive officer Samuel Dana Greene who was accused of cowardice for breaking off the fight after Worden was injured. Two years after the end of the Civil War, Worden tried to remedy the situation in a letter to then Navy Secretary Gideon Welles in which he defended Greene. However, the war of words was reignited six years later when Catesby ap R. Jones, the commanding officer of the *Virginia* in the fight with the *Monitor*, stated in a letter to former Assistant Navy Secretary Gustavus Fox that the *Monitor* had run away in defeat. John Ericsson, the proud and prickly inventor of the *Monitor*, then jumped into the fray and placed the blame entirely on Greene, whom he referred to in a letter to Fox as a "miserable executive officer who in place of jumping into the pilot house when Worden was blinded ran away with his impregnable vessel."[*] Ericsson did not stop there but also blamed the sinking of the *Monitor* on alcohol and questioned whether an executive officer older and more experienced than Greene could have saved the vessel. Greene, who by then had risen to the rank of Commander, defended himself in a letter to Fox in 1875 and in an article in the *Century Illustrated Monthly Magazine* a decade later.[†] However, the damage to Greene's psyche could not be undone and he killed himself with a bullet to the head at the Portsmouth Navy Yard in December 1884 soon after preparing his article, which was published posthumously.

Not long after Greene's death, Connecticut collector of *Monitor* memorabilia Frank H. Pierce began a correspondence with the officers and crew of the *Monitor*. In late September 1885, Keeler's first letter from Pierce arrived at the Mayport post office, along with a note from his brother-in-law George Watrous in New Haven endorsing Pierce. Although Pierce's letters have not

---

[*] *War, Technology, and Experience aboard the USS* Monitor, David A. Mindell, Baltimore, MD, 2000, p. 138.
[†] In the *Monitor* Turret, S. D. Greene, *The Century Illustrated Monthly Magazine*, Vol. 29, New York, NY, March 1885, pp. 754-63.

survived, his main point of enquiry appears to have been Greene's actions during the fight with the *Virginia*.

In his typically clean and crisp prose Keeler defended his old friend Greene and questioned the veracity of statements made by several *Monitor* crew members who had written to Pierce. He also touched on the subject of drunkenness, stating that it was not the cause of the vessel's loss. In his last letter, which he never finished, he countered the criticism of poor gunnery levelled by John T. Wood, a lieutenant on the *Virginia*,* by giving a clear and detailed explanation of the difficulty in aiming and firing the *Monitor*'s guns. That letter closes with an amusing anecdote about Greene's request for leave to go home to get married when he was serving with Keeler on the *Florida*.

By late November Keeler was too ill to write, and Anna continued the correspondence. Realizing that the end was near, he decided to send Pierce a box of artifacts that he had collected after the Battle of Hampton Roads, with the request that the contents be donated to a historical society. This was in addition to a scrapbook of newspaper and magazine clippings, much of it pertaining to the *Monitor*, which was destined for his daughter Lizzie. In Anna's last letter to Pierce, dated a month after Keeler's death, she wrote:

> *The packing of the box was the last work Mr. Keeler ever did. The letter announcing its safe arrival reached him a day or two before his death and I told him of its contents. The keys of the safe of the* Monitor *that he had in his pocket when the vessel went down he left to our son and son in law.*

The key to the safe that was given to their son is long gone, lost perhaps in the fire at my great-grandmother's house in Berkeley, California in 1923. The whereabouts of the scrapbook, which was presumably returned to Lizzie, and the relics that were sent to Pierce are also unknown.

Mayport, Fla.
Sept. 27/[18]85

F. H. Pierce, Esqr.

Dear Sir,

Yours of the 22nd inst. accompanied by one from Mr. Watrous is rec'd. The latter I return herewith as you requested.

I have not had a photograph taken since the war. I send you two taken during war times, not very good ones however. If Brady's† photograph rooms are still in existence in New York, you should find there a number of views of the *Monitor* taken shortly after the fight, which may be of interest to you. The engravings in the March number of the *Century* [*Magazine*] pages 755 & 760 were taken from some of them.

---

* The First Fight of Ironclads, J. T. Wood, *The Century Illustrated Monthly Magazine*, Vol. 29, New York, NY, March 1885, pp. 738-54.
† Civil War photographer Matthew Brady.

I was attached to the *Monitor*, as Paymaster, from the time she went into commission till she sank off Hatteras & consequently should know something of the vessel & its inmates. At the time of the fight with the *Merrimac*, Captain's clerk, Toffey*, & myself transmitted all communications between the pilot house & the turret, consequently were as well posted as to what was going on as any one could be who was not an actual spectator. If you have plans of the vessel you will see that the only access to the pilot house was by means of a step ladder from the Captain's cabin. The duties of none of the crew took them to that, so considered, sacred place, & I think that the cabin & wardroom were without occupants during the fight, till Capt. Worden was wounded, unless it was by the Surgeon & his assistants.

I mention all this in consequence of what you say Durst† has written you. Every one on board a man of war has a certain station & duties assigned him in time of action, & it is imperative that he be found there in the performance of those duties. Now Durst was in the Engineer's department — a coal heaver. His duties would confine him to the engine room or coal bunkers which were in the other end of the vessel from the cabin, & were separated from all other parts of the vessel by an iron bulkhead which ran across the vessel just in front of the boilers, cutting off all communication with all other parts of the vessel. To be stationed "near the pilot house" Durst would have to be in the cabin & what he would be stationed there for it is difficult to conceive. I don't believe he saw or heard Worden or Greene from the time the action commenced till it ended.

As to the man Viall‡, he was rated a seaman & as such his station & duties were as the executive officer, Greene, would assign him. Possibly in the turret to aid in working the guns, if not, then on the berth deck in or near the magazine or shell room to pass ammunition. If in the turret, he had a good opportunity of observing Greene; if on the berth deck below, he could see nothing of him.

When Worden was injured I assisted in taking him from the pilot house & laying him on the cushions of his cabin, then notified Greene who was soon by the Captain's side. Worden told Greene that he feared that the vessel as well as himself was seriously injured & that he (Capt. W.) would have to turn the command over to him. Green climbed into the pilot house to examine into the extent of the injuries there & came down saying he "guessed it would hold together." Something was said about continuing the fight — all said go on. Green certainly did not shew the least sign of personal fear or cowardice, nor did I hear any one urge him not to retreat. When the *Merrimac* turned to leave us, something was said about following her up. Greene said,

---

* Daniel Toffey.
† William Durst.
‡ Thomas B. Viall.

no, our orders are to stand by the *Minnesota* & that he intended to do. If he had shewn any emotion of fear it could not have escaped my observation.

I consider Greene a brave man. He was young, inexperienced, impulsive & without the judgement of mature years. His messages which I conveyed to the pilot house during the fight shewed that he was acting cooly, cautiously & with deliberation. I think he told me that he sighted every gun himself as long as he remained in the turret, instead of leaving it to the captain of the gun as is always the case in action. Greene certainly had an immense responsibility placed upon his shoulders when he took Worden's place in the pilot house of the *Monitor*. It seems as if the existence of the nation, just at this time, almost hinged upon the result of this fight between these two vessels.

But I saw Greene in more trying circumstances than these, where greater coolness & presence of mind were required if possible — it was when the *Monitor* went down. That night has been burned into my memory. After most of the crew had been swept off the deck or carried off in the boats, Greene approached me as he crossed the top of the turret in the darkness — "Is that you, Pay?" "Yes." "Well why don't you get into the boat? Now's your chance, jump in." Forgetting himself in his anxiety to get all others safely out of the sinking vessel.

Capt. Bankhead, as brave a man as ever lived, who was in command of the *Monitor* when she went down, had Greene & myself ordered with him to the gunboat *Florida*. This in Greene's case he would not have done had he ever shewn the white feather. So much in defense of my old friend Greene. We were intimates more so than any two on board the vessel. I knew him well & I know full well that there was nothing like cowardice about him. Who or what has started these rumours I don't know, I only know them to be false. I cannot help but think that this rumour had reached him & was one of the causes of his untimely death.

I have a few little items of interest of some of our prominent men of those war times which I think have never found their way into print. I will gladly furnish them to you if you desire, as I can find time to write them out.

I should not have written thus freely, or perhaps not at all, had it not been for Mr. Watrous' letter which I consider an endorsement of your request. I have no idea what use you intend making of my letter, but I have to request that it will not be used so as to bring me into any quarrel or dispute there may be between Worden, Stimers or others. During my five years in the naval service I kept all my experiences written up in the form of letters to my wife. These were all preserved & I now have them bound in book form to refer to.

Very truly yours,
W. F. Keeler

Mayport Years

Mayport, Fla.
Nov. 15/[18]85

F. H. Pierce, Esqr.
Dear Sir,

I beg to acknowledge the rec't of yours of the 2nd inst. & the accompanying photographs which reached me in good order; many thanks for them. I am not as you think I may be a native of New Haven, tho' I have spent many very pleasant days there — I consider it one of my homes. Tho' not yankee born I pride myself upon my yankee parentage, pure & unadulterated. My mother (still living) being a native of old Branford & related to the Plants & Frisbees of that region, & my father from near Danbury. Mr. Watrous & myself married sisters, daughters of the late Gov. Dutton. I was born in Pearl Street, New York City some 60 odd years ago & lived there & in Brooklyn the first 13 years of my life. There's my pedigree — you know all about me now.

As to Durst's letter you so kindly offer to send me, I don't know as I care about seeing it. I suppose you have given me the gist of what it contains. The more I think it over, the more I am inclined to believe that the fellow is trying to impose upon you. I should receive his statements with a good deal of caution. But more of this by & by.

You say you have it "from first class authority that Green told Erricsson that the men were drunk on the night of the sinking." If he had said *some* of the men were drunk &c I think he might have been correct. There was nothing approaching insubordination or demoralization among them, & the drunkeness of a few of the men had nothing whatever to do with the loss of the vessel. The facts are briefly these. When I was ordered to the *Monitor*, liquor was allowed on board men of war & was daily issued by the Paymaster to the crew of the vessel as a part of their ration. In the fall of 1862 the liquor ration was abolished by an act of Congress & the men received in lieu thereof its money value added to their monthly pay. At this time I had on hand, to the best of my recollection, about two barrels of whiskey for which of course I had no further use & was at a loss to know what disposition to make of it. Applying to the Navy Department for instructions, I was directed to turn it over to the Medical Department of the vessel. Our dispensary was a very small one, so at the Surgeon's request I kept the liquor locked up for him in one of my store rooms which opened off the berth deck, & so was accessible (the door) to any or all the crew. On the night in question I had occasion to pass this store room a few times & noticed something peculiar about the door, but suspecting nothing wrong did not stop to examine what it was. The deck was dimly lighted by a single lantern & was filled by the steam, gas & smoke from the half extinguished fires of the furnaces, moreover I am quite near sighted. The matter was forgotten by me till called up by Green on our passage home on the *Rhode Island*. He said he believed that some of the men had broken in a panel of the door & got at the whiskey. At any rate some of our best & ablest seamen were lost with the vessel, a loss I can account for in no other way. I would like very much to see the copy of the *Army & Naval Journal* alluding to this matter, but I have not their office of publication. If you can send me a copy you will place me under obligation.

So pilot Howard* thinks that "the truth of that engagement will never be known." You very naturally ask, "Why not? What is there to conceal?" This is the first time I have heard that there was anything requiring secrecy about the movements or management of the vessel. Howard was shut up in the pilot house with Worden & Quartermaster Williams. There certainly could have been nothing requiring concealment there, & that is as far as his observations extended. He had no opportunity of knowing what was going on in the vessel below him. His duties required him to watch the *outside* movements of the vessel & I think his duties were well & ably performed. I have no desire to arrogate to myself any special credit for anything I did, or any part I took in the fight, but I fully believe that the position I occupied gave me an opportunity of knowing as much, if not more, of the little details of the fight & the inner workings of the vessel than any one on board. I have yet to learn that there was anything done or said on board the vessel by any of the officers which they would desire to have concealed. This man whom you quote (you give no name) who was ordered to the *Monitor* after the fight & who says, "I have heard the story of the *Monitor*'s fight as told by every person who was on board her at that time" &c &c. He probably means that he had heard the old salts spin their yarns about the affair. Of course he had no means of sifting a little truth from a good deal of untruth & exaggeration. Could anything be more absurd than his statement that a man taken from civil life & placed on board one of our gun boats as pilot should assume the command & management of her for half an hour. What I think the man means is this—in the interval intervening between the wounding of Worden & the assuming the command by Green, Howard & Williams both remained at their posts in the pilot house & controlled the movements of the vessel so as to prevent her from running aground. Whether they did this or not I am unable to say as I do not remember. Green says in his *Century* article that during that interval "the *Monitor* had been moving without direction." I will not venture to dispute him.

After the wounding of Worden, a few of us, I am unable to say who, gathered about him & assisted him from the pilot house down the step ladder into his cabin below, where he laid down on a transom cushion till Surgeon Logue came & directed him carried to his state room, but a few feet off. Worden was in full possession of all his faculties (except sight) & his physical strength & required but little assistance except to guide him where we wanted him to go. A few men might have been called in from the powder division

---

* Acting Master Samuel Howard, who was pilot during the battle with the *Virginia*.

on the berth deck, only a short distance off, the ward room only intervening, thinking their assistance might be needed.

Viall's statement that he was No. 1 of No. 2 gun's crew is probably correct. I know of nothing to the contrary. If he was, he was shut up on the turret & knew nothing of what was going on in the body of the vessel, or outside. As to Stimer's & Stodder's manipulations of the turret, more hereafter.*

Although it is a matter of small consequence I would like to correct a slight error of Green's in his *Century* article where he speaks of Toffey & myself as landsmen &c. I had seen two years of sea life before being ordered to the *Monitor*, having gone to California around "the Horn" in /49, a passage of *255* days. From thence home as a passenger in one of our clipper ships around the Cape of Good Hope, so that I was familiar with all sea terms & phrases.

I have a collection of scraps cut from papers & magazines published during the war, north & south, pasted into an old account book. Much of it relates to the *Monitor* — her fight with the *Merrimac* & other engagements, from both sides — her loss &c. Also quite a variety of clippings from Southern papers during war times. You may find something of interest in it in regard to the *Monitor*. I have heretofore refused to let it go out of my possession as I value it highly. I would not trust it in the mail. If you will pay the expenses each way I will send it to you by Express if I can be assured of its safe return.

There are quite a number of other matters I want to touch upon providing you wish it & your patience don't give out — if it does just cry "hold enough."

Very truly yours,
W. F. Keeler

[Draft of Keeler's letter that was enclosed in Anna's of February 9, 1886]

Mayport, Fla.
[late November 1885]

F. H. Pierce, Esqr.

Dear Sir,

So much by way of prelude, now let us examine into this matter of poor gunnery of Green's brought up by Lieut. Wood of the *Merrimac* in his *Century* article & by others. I have heard Green's skill in the use of big guns while a cadet at the naval academy & also at target practice at sea highly commended by naval officers who were competent judges. To understand Green's perplexing & novel position in the *Monitor* turret one must make himself

---

* See next letter.

thoroughly acquainted with the construction & working of the vessel, especially the turrett.

Green very truly says in his *Century* article, "The conditions were very different from those of our ordinary broadside gun, under which we had been trained on wooden ships." Never before had a person been called upon to manage a gun under such singular & perplexing circumstances. Read that portion of his article carefully on page 759 & imagine yourself in his place. Here is a huge revolving cylinder 20 feet across & some 9 or 10 feet high containing 2 heavy guns & their complement of men (I have forgotten how many) — all revolve together, top, bottom, sides, men & guns. A bomb proof grating overhead admits all the light & air they have. Through the sides not an opening through which to search for an attacking foe if we except a small hole in each iron port shelter or pendulum, immediately in front of each gun, through which the iron handles of the rammers & sponges are run when loading. Midway between the guns & near the breech of them are one or two iron levers by means of which the person in charge controls the rotary motion of the turret. Now comes an order from the pilot house, "I'll bring the foe to bear on the port quarter, fire as quickly as possible." Now the query arises which way is port & which way is starboard, where is stem, where is stern. Now the ponderous iron cylinder is started on its travels to bring the ports to what is thought to be the port quarter of the vessel, the pendulum is swung aside & the gun run out. "Yes there she is, hold on." But if the turret don't hold on, the momentum has to be overcome, & the turret turns too far. "Back a little," but now the inertia delays the movement & the foe is out of the line of fire. And so it was. You can readily see the difficulties Green had to contend with.

Stimers who was called a skillful & able mechanical engineer was probably as conversant with the working [of the] vessel & turret as any one on board. He controlled the motions of the latter but unable to see the *Merrimac* had to be governed entirely by the directions of Green to find the foe, so of course was unable to make anything like accurate calculations as to the starting & stopping of the turret. The carriages of the guns run on tracks immoveably fixed to the floor of the turret. This was one of the defects of the vessel. You will very readily see that the *horizontal* training of the guns was done by the one standing at the levers above mentioned. He not seeing the object sought for revolved the turret according to directions from the person standing at the breech of the gun for the purpose of searching for the foe & aiming & firing the gun. For *vertical* firing, the guns were trained very much as other heavy guns are except that in searching for the foe it had to be done through a small opening between the muzzle of the gun & the top of the port, *after* the port was opened. In the floor of the turret was a small hatchway & in the deck of the vessel underneath a similar one. When these were made to coincide they formed an opening though which ammunition was passed into the turret & through which we had access to the interior of the turret by means of an iron ladder from the berth deck below.

The question has been asked why wasn't the *Merrimac*'s water line sought by our shot as her weakest point. How should we know her weakest point. With us our water line was our strongest part, being 5 inches of iron & about 3 feet of solid oak. But I was told by two persons who were on board her during the fight that she was struck at her water line. That they heard a message from the carpenters of the *Merrimac* delivered to her lieutenant to the effect that she had been struck twice at her water line in nearly the same spot, abreast the boiler & that another shot in the same place would go through & into the boiler & that she was leaking badly. See also Capt. James Byers' statement in Swinton's *Twelve decisive battles of the war*. Capt. Byers commanded a rebel tug during the fight & took a party from Norfolk to witness it. His statement is too long for me to copy here. Wood however in his *Century* article denies having been struck at the water line but from what I have heard from other sources I cannot help but think she was.

I think I have been told by Green that we fired but 41 shot during the conflict, but of this I am not positive. If this was all we fired, many of them could not have gone wide of the mark. The truth of this could readily be ascertained by applying to the Ordnance Bureau of the Navy Department where a report of ammunition expended should be on file. If this was all the number of times our two guns were fired there was hardly any necessity of our "turning away from the enemy to allow our guns to cool" as some reports of the fight say we did. I remembered but 3 cessations of the conflict & each of these were brief. Once to get ammunition into the turret, again when Worden was wounded & one brief interval when a shot got stuck in one of the guns. This is a circumstance I have not seen alluded to in any published account of the fight. I very well remember conveying the message from Worden to Green — "She's right abreast of us, why don't you fire?" (delivered to me in a rather impatient tone of voice). The reply was "can't do it sir, the shot is stuck in the gun & I can't ram it home" — "depress the gun then & let it roll over board." Our firing ceased for a few minutes, the ports turned away from the enemy & one of them opened through which two or three men jumped out on the open deck & by vigorous use of the rammer the shot was sent home & our firing commenced again. It was a shell by which Worden was hurt & such was the nearness of the two vessels at that time that the Quartermast[er], Williams, who had the wheel looked into the muzzle of the *Merrimac*'s gun as it was being rammed home & called Worden's attention to it by the exclamation, "Captain, they are training that gun on us." Worden put his eyes to the lookout crack or crevice just as the gun was discharged, filling the pilot house & cabin below with fire & smoke. This is Williams' statement of the matter. I have no reason to doubt its correctness.

We called the duration of the fight, from the time we fired the first shot till our firing ceased, four [three] & one half hours, though I see Jones &

some other writers lengthen the conflict considerably. What I say here about Green is not said in his defence. I don't think he needs it if any one will *carefully* read his article in the *Century*. He gives the cause of the "poor gunnery" there if there was any. I wish he had written that part of his article with more care & more in detail. Green at the time of the conflict was but a boy, only 22 years of age & never before had heard a gun fired in earnest. He had seen about three years sea service in the Pacific & the East Indies in the frigate *Hartford*. He was generous, impulsive, excitable, somewhat reserved & unsocial in his disposition, but an agreeable messmate, a good disciplinarian, never familiar with the men & rarely addressing them except in the line of duty, consequently not popular with them. After the fight Worden received the thank[s] of Congress by name, which admitted him to its floor. He was promoted ten numbers, was feted & feasted & made the recipient of costly presents &c of which we all felt proud & pleased. Green however received but very little attention which I know he felt deeply.

During the summer of 1863 we were doing blockade duty off the mouth of the Cape Fear river in the gun boat *Florida*. Green was engaged to be married to a young lady in Rhode Island & the wedding day was fixed & fast approaching. Twice he made application to Sec'y Wells for leave of absence & was both times refused. Green was nearly frantic. One evening in talking the matter over with him I suggested that he write once more to the Sec'y giving his reasons for making the application. He did so & the next mail brought a document detaching him from the vessel & granting him a short leave of absence. Never was a trunk packed quicker than his.

[Portion of the draft of another letter]

I have frequently been solicited by friends & acquaintances to write a history of my *Monitor* experiences for publication. This I have neglected to do for a variety of reasons. I am not accustomed to writing for the public, consequently am not fitted for the task & could not do it justice. Then I have no taste for writing & avoid it whenever I can. Moreover, I have not the facilities for gathering from other survivors of the *Monitor* their statement[s] & comparing them with my own, which would be necessary. I have always hoped that some competent person would take the matter in hand before the few remaining survivors were called to the stage, to gather & collate their experiences & give them to the public. The sooner this is done the better. Any help I can give such a person will be cheerfully furnish[ed]. You do not say what use you intend making of this matter you are collecting, whether it is for your own personal gratification or eventually for the public.

Mayport
Dec. 4th, 1885

F. H. Pierce

My dear Sir,

Your letters have been received but my husband is too feeble to answer them. He has been suffering from heart disease for the last two years with other troubles brought on, we suppose, from wounds he received in the back from pieces of a rebel shell fired from a battery two miles away as he was getting into a boat to board a blockade runner.

He has been much interested in the correspondence he has had with you and had commenced another letter to you when he grew worse. The book he promised to loan you I will send you some time this winter as your time is occupied at present, and you can retain it for several months if you wish. Mr. Keeler is willing you should use any information he has given you. His only objection was that he had not written and revised the style as he would have done for publication. He has taken great pains to have his statements accurate, not trusting to his memory, but referring to the papers, documents &c he possesses.

When the *Monitor* was sent to the Norfolk Navy Yard for repairs after the fight, the fitting of the state rooms &c, which were a present to the officers from Captain Ericsson, were taken down. Mr. Keeler having a great fancy for collecting Mementoes sent his home. I have still some pieces and if you would value one will place it in the book when it is sent to you. I can vouch for its being the original article that went through the battle.

I remain with respect

Yours &c
Anna E. Keeler

Mayport
Feby. 9th, 1886

Mr. F. H. Pierce

Dear Sir,

I am obliged to take my husband's place again as your correspondent as he is still unable to either read or write and will probably remain in that condition. The delay in sending the promised book [of clippings] &c has been caused by his desire to attend to the matter himself. With the book he sends several mementoes of the fight in Hampton Roads. The articles he collected personally and can vouch for their authenticity. He has always preserved them with great care and does not think there is another such collection existing as he knew of no one that made use of the opportunities they had for obtaining them. As his health is failing and you have shewn so much interest in the subject, he sends them to you with the desire that at some time in the future you will leave them to some Historical Society. The labels show from whence they came. Our ignorance of the parts of a gun, with his imperfect speech, prevented their being as fully labelled as he would have liked. If any explanation is desired we will endeavour to furnish it. He had planned a series of letters to you, giving you his own personal experience on board the *Monitor* but fears now he shall never be able to carry out his plans.

A very interesting relic Capt. Jeffers secured when the gun boat *Teazer* (Confederate) was blown up July 4th '62 by the *Maratanza* and *Monitor* in company, being the private memorandum book of Hunter Davidson who was in command. He was one of the *Merrimac*'s officers and in this book were drafts of the *Monitor* and sketches of the mode of her capture as they intended to attempt it. It was minute in all the details. The *Monitor* was to be boarded from four tugs at the same time, one of them the *Teazer*, by men carrying ladders, turpentine, fire balls, wedges, sheets of metal, chloroform &c &c. The names of the men were given, just what article each one was to carry, the part of the *Monitor* to which he was to go, even the men who were to carry matches and sand paper upon which to rub them.

The signature of Oliver Wolcott[*] may be of interest to you. It was found among some old papers in Litchfield, Conn.

Can you give us any further information respecting the slip enclosed in your last letter in regard to the bill for prize money?[†] It is of course of great interest to us and we have seen nothing else respecting it.

Mr. Keeler is very sorry to send the book in such a dilapidated condition. He was not aware of it and is not able to attend to it now. Will you be kind enough to fasten it in some inexpensive way so that the leaves may not be lost? As I said before there is no need of haste in returning it. Keep it to read at your leisure. We hope it may prove of interest to you. Our nearest Express Office is at Jacksonville. We will send it from there C.O.D. prepaying the (15 lb) boat charges from here to that place. I hope the weight of the box may not make it too expensive.

I also enclose the letter Mr. Keeler had commenced to you thinking there might be something of importance in it. Mr. Keeler has been much interested in the correspondence and will always be happy to hear from you.

Hoping that the box will reach you safely,

I remain yours &c
Anna E. Keeler

There are some old papers in the box Mr. Keeler put in by mistake. They are of no value.

---

[*] A signer of the Declaration of Independence.
[†] In 1874 Rear Admiral John Worden unsuccessfully petitioned Congress for prize money for the officers and crew of the *Monitor*. The matter was brought up again in 1882 and 1884 when further prize bills were introduced to Congress. However, those bills went nowhere due to Southern opposition and other factors.

Mayport
March 23rd, [18]86

Mr. F. H. Pierce
Dear Sir,

Under the circumstances you will I know excuse the delay in acknowledging the pamphlets and your letters. I read parts of the articles to my husband. He was much interested in the account written by Capt. Catesby ap R. Jones* and said it was a very fair statement from a rebel point of view. As you have doubtless noticed he gives the same particulars in regard to the projected capture of the *Monitor* that Mr. Keeler had already given you. The timidity of Goldsborough which prevented the *Monitor* from accepting the challenges of the *Merrimac* was a source of great mortification to her officers and crew.

The disposition you propose making in the future of the relics is perfectly satisfactory. We resign all claim to them unless, as my husband expressed, a wish after they were sent, our son, now of the Lick Observatory, Mt. Hamilton, Cal. should ever desire a piece of the turret of the *Monitor*. In that case it is to be cut off and given him and you have the same privilege for yourself. The *Monitor* curtain was intended for you alone and the paper enclosed if it is of any interest to you.

The packing of the box was the last work Mr. Keeler ever did. The letter announcing its safe arrival reached him a day or two before his death and I told him of its contents. The keys of the safe of the *Monitor* that he had in his pocket when the vessel went down he left to our son and son in law.

The book [of clippings] you need not bother yourself to have bound. It now belongs to my daughter. Keep it as long as you wish and then please direct it to

> Dr. David T. Day
> 153 McCulloh St.
> Baltimore, Md.

Thanking you for your kind words of sympathy and also for the interest taken in my husband's past career as connected with the *Monitor*.

I remain yours truly
A. E. K.

Mr. Keeler's letters to me during the war I have bound. Should any point arise up which you need information, I shall be happy to look them over at any time for anything that will assist you.

---

* Commanding officer of the *Virginia* during the fight with the *Monitor*.

Epilogue

Anna Keeler remained in Mayport for eight months after William's death, busying herself writing letters to family and friends, and arranging for the sale of their property. A bright spot in her bereavement was daughter Lizzie's marriage to Ed's best friend and classmate at Johns Hopkins, David Talbot Day. The wedding took place at the Keelers' house in Mayport.

Anna's last entry in William's journal is dated October 25, 1886. Not long after that, she left for her daughter's home in Washington, DC where she lived for the rest of her life. She enjoyed the company of Lizzie's children Elizabeth and David, as well as Ed's children Henry and Cora when they visited from Pittsburgh where Ed was the director of Allegheny Observatory. However, in 1900 tragedy struck one more time when Ed died of a massive stroke in San Francisco. He was only 42 and was director of Lick Observatory at the time of his death.

For the last few years of her life Anna suffered from severe facial neuralgia. To relieve the pain, she sought treatment in Philadelphia, but died there on January 19, 1901 from complications arising from the operation. Her body was brought back to Washington and a private funeral service was held at Lizzie's home.

Found among Anna's possessions shortly after her death was a handwritten will dated three days before her death. Opening with "as I may be taken away at this time," she goes on to direct that money from the sale of land in Mayport be used to pay for the removal of William's body from the cemetery in Mayport and its interment at Arlington National Cemetery.[*] Together once again, Anna and William are buried in plot 784 of Section 1 at Arlington. The epitaph on their black granite gravestone reads:

WILLIAM FREDERICK KEELER,
ASSISTANT PAYMASTER U.S.S. "MONITOR"
BORN JUNE 9, 1821, DIED FEBRUARY 27, 1886.
ANNE ELIZA KEELER,
WIFE OF WILLIAM F. KEELER,
BORN OCTOBER 15, 1824, DIED JANUARY 19, 1901.

---

[*] Probate Records (District of Columbia), 1801-1930, Register of Wills, Washington, DC.

Appendix A: Letter to *Scientific American*

An avid reader of *Scientific American*, William Keeler sent the magazine the following letter about the effect of the *Virginia*'s shot on the *Monitor*. The letter was published in the March 22, 1862 issue (Volume 6, Number 12).

> U.S. Steamer *Monitor*,
> Hampton Roads
> March 11, 1862.

Messrs. Editors:

As it may be some time before the official report of Chief Engineer Stimers is made public, I have thought that the effects of the shot on our vessel in the late engagement with the *Merrimac* might be interesting to you. The details of the fight, which lasted three hours and a half, have already been made public, so that I will confine myself to the effect of the shot upon us. The *Merrimac*'s projectiles were mostly percussion shells, fired from ten or eleven-inch rifled pieces. Twenty-three shot struck us, including two from the *Minnesota*, which, during the engagement, fired over our heads. The deepest indentation on our turret was two and one half inches, produced by a 150-lb. percussion shell fired at a distance of twenty feet perpendicular with the side. Our deck received four shot making slight depressions. One shot struck us on the angle formed by the deck and side, tearing up the iron plating about one-third the width of a sheet, starting the bolts and splintering the wood a little. Three or four others struck us just above the water line, with no other effect than making indentations of two inches. The pilot house received one shot on one of the upper corners, nearly battering it down. A little later in the action, however, a heavy shell was thrown from a distance of about fifteen feet, against the front, at an angle of about thirty degrees, striking the two upper bars just at the lookout crack, the main force being on the lower of the two, forcing it in about an inch, and opening a crack of one-fourth of an inch on the opposite side. She twice attempted to open a hole in our side with her ram, as she did the *Cumberland*, once striking us squarely on our beam, nearly abreast of the turret, jarring us somewhat, and leaving a small dent on our iron side. Our hull remains perfectly tight, and the turret, notwithstanding the severe hammering, revolves as accurately and easily as when we left New York.

We experienced a severe gale on our way down, coming through it safely. That, and our trial with the *Merrimac* proves the *Monitor*, we think, a success.

> W. F. Keeler,
> A. A. Paymaster.

APPENDICES

Appendix B: Letter to *New York Times*

Three weeks after the Battle of Hampton Roads, William Keeler's father-in-law Henry Dutton combined portions of letters that Keeler had written to him and to Anna and sent them to *The New York Times* for publication. The combined letter appeared on the front page of the March 30, 1862 issue, much to Keeler's consternation as he explained in his letter to Anna of April 3, 1862.

THE FIGHT IN HAMPTON ROADS.
Interesting Particulars by one on Board the *Monitor*.

The following extracts from a private letter from one on board the *Monitor* in the recent engagement with the *Merrimac* furnish some interesting particulars of that memorable affair not before published:

We had a disagreeable and rough, not to say dangerous, passage down. We experienced a severe gale, in which our craft proved an excellent sea-boat; still, defects in some of the minor details nearly proved fatal to us. The smoke-stacks and blower-pipes were too low; the seas rolling over us, poured down them, wetting the blower belts. This stopped the blower, and filled the engine-room and the whole lower part of the vessel with smoke, steam and gas from the furnaces. We dragged out the firemen and engineers exhausted and insensible, and retreated to the top of the turret, where we put up an awning for our protection. With the exception of the hatchway in the top of the turret, all the hatchways had been battened down, and heavy seas were continually sweeping across our decks with almost irresistible force. We were obliged to hoist our colors Union down, to call the two gunboats which accompanied us to our assistance, but the heavy sea rendered help from them impossible, and things for a time looked rather blue. We managed after a while to get the ventilation started below, and our blowers going once more. My knowledge of machinery came in play, and I took charge of the engines till next day, when the engineers were sufficiently recovered to resume their duties.

We reached here (Hampton Roads) the next morning (Saturday) in time to witness the blowing up of the burning *Congress*, and share the intense excitement prevailing among the shipping, which was leaving the harbor like a covey of frightened quails. We were ordered to protect the *Minnesota*, which was aground off Newport's News, and steamed up and anchored alongside. The morning broke upon the *Minnesota* surrounded by tugs, into which they were tumbling the bags and hammocks of the men; guns were being thrown overboard, and every effort made to get her off. If this could not be done, the Captain, Van Brunt, said he should destroy her, notwithstanding Lieut. Worden told him he had been ordered to his assistance, and would stand by him to the last. But so puny and insignificant did we look, that the offer to protect our huge friend seemed simply absurd, and I am inclined to think they so regarded it.

We went into the fight entirely unprepared; the men had never been drilled at the guns, and consequently were not trained to act in concert. All of us were exhausted before the fight began, having worked hard the night before we arrived; and on the night of our arrival, the report every half hour that the *Merrimac* was coming kept all hands to quarters. We had only time to take a cup of coffee in the morning before the fight began. We went into it without knowing our own powers, offensive or defensive, and in total ignorance of those of our opponent, except his terrible destructive powers, exhibited the previous day. The fierceness of the fight has not been overstated. It continued from 8 ½ A.M. till ten minutes past 12 o'clock, most of the time within very short range, and a part of the time with the vessels in contact. We were struck with 23 heavy shot, including two from the *Minnesota*. They first fired with grape and canister, which rattled on our iron deck like hailstones. The shell by which Lieut. Worden was injured, was fired at the distance of only 15 feet, exploding within ten inches of his eyes. The old Quartermaster, who stood at the wheel, coolly looked into the muzzle of the gun, saw it loaded, trained and fired without any apparent emotion, merely saying to the Lieutenant, "Look out, Sir, they are going to try us now."

I think the public give us more credit for the mere fight than we deserve, as it requires no great amount of courage to fight behind impenetrable iron defences. Men have fought quite as well behind wooden walls, and with none at all. The daring to make the passage here, and offer battle to our huge antagonist, in an untried experiment, in our unprepared condition, is where the credit lies, if anywhere. Of Lieut. Worden, too much cannot be said. His daily intercourse with us showed him a perfect gentleman, and the fight proved him a hero. I acted as his Aid during the fight, and all his orders were passed through me. They were given with coolness and deliberation. When he was hurt, I assisted him down from his position by the wheel, he remarked, "Never mind me, my lads; save the *Minnesota*."

After the conflict, Gen. Wool and staff, Gen. Mansfield and Secretary Fox came on board. We were each introduced to, and very handsomely complimented by them. Gen. Wool said: "Gentlemen, you have made heroes of yourselves." He said that "the safety of Gen. Mansfield's army, of all the shipping in the harbor, and even the fortress itself, was due to us, as they were at the mercy of the *Merrimac* till our arrival." Secretary Fox, as he was leaving, turning to us, said: "Gentlemen, I want you to remember that millions of [dollars of] property are intrusted to your care."

We are making some slight repairs to our pilot-house, when we hope to have another chance at the *Merrimac*, which we regard as our game. We have been visited by any quantity of foreign nobles, who are serving in our army. Among them were a number of Swedes, who, being countrymen of Capt.

Ericsson, feel a pride in his invention and its triumphant success. Yesterday, on our return from our search after the *Merrimac*, as we passed close to Newport's News, the whole army came out to see us; thousands lined the shore, covered the decks and filled the rigging. Their cheers resembled one continuous roar. Each regiment had its band, the nearest of which, as we approached, struck up, "See, the conquering hero comes," then the Star Spangled Banner; and so it passed from one band to another, as we slowly steamed along in front of them. All our national airs were given. When a lull in the tumultuous cheering took place, it was laughable to hear the great variety of names applied to us by the soldiers, for we passed so near that we could readily converse. Says one: "Your're the boys," another, "Bully for you," "No sand-bag batteries there," "You're our saviours," "Iron sides and iron hearts," "No back down to you," "Your're trumps, every one of you," &c.

I sent by Col. —— [LeGrand B. Cannon] the end of an exploded shell, which I picked up on our deck at the close of the fight, to President Lincoln in the name of the officers of the *Monitor*. Our deck was covered with fragments of shattered shells, of which I have saved some as mementoes. While gathering them up, one of the *Merrimac*'s shells went about twenty feet over my head, bursting about one hundred feet beyond me. One of the men who had been working the guns, touching his hat, said very coolly – "Paymaster, there's some more pieces." I confess I looked rather anxiously to see if any more were coming.

The English war steamer *Rinaldo* came into the harbor the day after the fight, and before her captain ascertained our character, he went on shore and saw Gen. Wool. In a conversation with the General, he pointed to the *Monitor*, and asked what kind of machine they had out there, and whether it was not for raising wrecks. "No," said the General, "it is not for raising wrecks, but making them."

APPENDICES

Appendix C: The Mayport Correspondent

From September 1884 to February 1886 William Keeler was the Mayport correspondent for the *Florida Times-Union* newspaper in Jacksonville. Over the course of that 17-month period he wrote 91 short columns for the paper which he pasted into his *Mayport Journal*. This appendix includes three of them.

MAYPORT MENTION.

(Special Correspondence *Times-Union*.)

MAYPORT, March 9, [1884]

Southerly winds and warmer weather.

Mosquitoes are presenting their bills. The innocent and unsophisticated are cautioned against them.

Mr. and Mrs. C. L. Robinson, accompanied by their Vermont relatives, Mr. and Mrs. Brown, have been making a brief call. Mr. Robinson's summer cottage is one of the finest on our beach.

Improvements are the order of the day. Major Keeler's residence, Thalassa, is receiving a new coat of paint. Sidewalks are being laid in our village, and a number of small, neat houses are going up.

A little experience has convinced the writer that the laboratory of a properly manipulated skunk will produce more perfumery to the square inch than any other known source of odors.

Numbers of visitors are finding their way here—some, piscatorially inclined, others on a concological expedition, while others enjoy a stroll or drive on our unequaled beach, with its invigorating sea care. Moral—don't leave Florida without visiting Mayport.

The following vessels, outward bound, with cargoes of lumber, are in port waiting for favorable tides to cross the bar: schooners *Emma S. Briggs*, *Dione*, *T. H. Livingston*, *Mary Graham*, *Meyer & Muller*, *Twenty-one Friends*, *Melissa Trask*, and the British schooner *Pioneer*.

Mr. Birdseye Blakeman, of the well-known publishing house of Iveson, Blakeman, Taylor & Co., New York City, accompanied by his daughter, Mrs. Lewis, has been looking in upon his old friend Major Keeler. Mr. Samuel Plant, of Branford, Conn., has also been making the Major a visit.

General Ledwith, with a large party of Jacksonville's dames and damsels, was down on a fishing expedition last Tuesday. The general is an incorrigible old fisherman, and if the strings of fish which lay piled upon the deck of the *Water Lily* is any indication, his mantle must have fallen upon his fair companions.

SILEX.

APPENDICES

MAYPORT MENTION.

(Special Correspondence *Times-Union.*)

MAYPORT, May 31, [1885]

Mr. A. P. Taft and family, of Norwalk, have just moved into their summer cottage.

Mean temperature for this place for the month of May, 74.08°; maximum 88°; minimum 64°; rainfall for the month, 8.53 inches; prevailing wind south.

Our Pilot Town neighbors are about extending their dock out into deeper water to enable the Charleston steamers to make a landing there, which they cannot do with the dock in its present condition.

Some 225 persons availed themselves of the excursion trip of the *Fred. de Bary* to this place last Friday evening. A flood of soft, silvery light from a clear full moon, plenty of good music, an abundance of the best of edibles and wit, mirth and humor, all combined to make the rosy-hued hours pass joyously and rapidly away.

By the advice of his physician Colonel S. B. Carter is spending a few days on our beach recuperating. He is a guest at Thalassa with his old friend Major Keeler. The medical fraternity are beginning to realize the fact that our beach with his concomitants are worth more to their patients than pills and powders.

One of our Pilot Town neighbors is the somewhat unenviable proprietor of a curiosity and nuisance combined, which would be a valuable auxiliary to a band of Texas cowboys. This combination is a masculine bovine who seems to ignore barbed wire in any form. He has been known to go through a five-wire fence at a single butt. Strong butter he is!

A copious fall of rain yesterday. The same may be said of nearly every day for the past week or two. Frogs are rejuvenated, ducks become more animated, mosquitoes have predominated, the soil is liquidated, bangs and frizzes dilapidated, cuffs and collars deteriorated, our temper is irritated, and our faces elongated as our rheumatism is aggravated by our clothing being saturated because our umbrella has been confiscated.

The schooner *Narraganset*, discharging a cargo of stone for the jetties, is the only vessel in port.

MONITOR.

APPENDICES

MAYPORT MENTION.

(Special Correspondence *Times-Union*.)

MAYPORT, July 22, [1885]

I send a paper picked up on our beach last Sunday just after the departure of three or four steamboat loads of visitors. It is well for the perpetrator of this diabolical effusion that he effected his escape before his "musings" come to light.

MONITOR.

MAYPORT MUSINGS.

No, sir, no Mayport beach for me;
No piles of sand, no sea,
No rowing off to fish just to be whaled about—
Why I might get myself tipped out
Of that cranky little boat,
Then how could I keep afloat
      In the salt, salt sea?
      No sir-ee, not me.

Now, don't forget, I don't yet
Feel any hankering to get wet.
Then where's the fun? I can't see that
Of soaking in the water like a drowned cat,
What's more, I've got no taste
For wallowing 'round in any watery waste—
      Be it the salt, salt sea—
      No sir-ee, not me.

No, nor I don't care
For getting sand and water in my hair
'Cause Ledwith, Wallace and the rest
Say such diversions are the best;
Then, moreover, it's all gas
The sport in taking channel bass
      Out of the salt, salt sea—
      No sir-ee, not me.

And then the girls they want to sail
Out in a small boat but I fail
To find it jolly; so you see
You can't come that little game on me;
The wind gives out and a white ash breeze
Blisters my hands; then the girls teaze
      As I pull thro' the salt, salt sea—
      No sir-ee, not me.

There's Doctor Q., who with his gun
In salt-marsh kills a tip-up, calls it fun;
Mosquitoes, sand flies and all that
Ringed, streaked, speckled, lean and fat
Charge him in front, on side, in rear;
His pills and powders they don't fear
        Right by the salt, salt sea—
        No sir-ee, not me.

I don't take stock in such a circus, no, not me,
I don't want camping by the sea,
But you just bet your bottom dollar
When I get back I'll make Rome holler;
Why, I'm hungry, tired and thirsty too
And there's no chance for mountain dew
        Out of the salt, salt sea—
        No sir-ee, not me.

Appendix D: Obituary

Pasted into William Keeler's *Mayport Journal* on the page following Anna's short note of his burial is the following letter to the editor of the *New Haven Evening Register*. The writer of this obituary is not mentioned, but based on some of the statements it is without a doubt the Connecticut collector of *Monitor* memorabilia, Frank H. Pierce, with whom Keeler corresponding in the last few months of his life.

New Haven Evening Register, New Haven, Connecticut, 18 March 1886:

"To the Editor of the *Register*: By the Jacksonville (Fla.) *Times-Union* we learn of the death of William F. Keeler, February 27, at Mayport, Fla., in the 65th year of his age. He had been suffering for the past two years from heart disease, brought on as he supposed by wounds received during the war from pieces of a shell fired from a rebel battery two miles away, as he was getting into a boat to board a blockade runner. Mr. Keeler was born in New York city, where he passed his boyhood days. Later he spent some time in this city [New Haven] and always considered it one of his homes. He married one of the daughters of the late Governor Dutton—Miss Anna E., who survives him. At the time of the breaking out of the war he was a resident of La Salle, Ill., from whence he was commissioned as acting assistant paymaster, December 17, 1861, and honorably discharged April 25, 1866. He was attached to the United States iron clad battery *Monitor* from the time she was launched to the night she foundered off Hatteras. During the famous fight between the *Monitor* and *Merrimac* he transmitted Lieutenant Worden's orders to the turret and was commended for that service in Worden's official report of the engagement. In this connection it may be proper to state as Commander Greene in his article in the *Century* for 1885 said: "Keeler, being a landsman, technical communications sometimes miscarried." Mr. Keeler informed the writer that he had seen two years of sea life before being ordered to the *Monitor*, having gone from New York to California around Cape Horn in '49 and from thence came home via Cape of Good Hope, and that he was familiar with all sea terms and phrases. At the time the *Monitor* foundered, on being ordered by Commander Bankhead to "lead the men to the boats" he found the ladder on the outside of the turret which led to the deck full of men hesitating to go down on account of the heavy sea which constantly broke over the ship. Seizing a rope which hung from one of the awning stanchions above the turret, he slid down the deck. At that instant a wave engulfed him, tearing loose his grasp on the rope, and washed him overboard, carrying him away from the ship ten or twelve yards. Another wave fortunately dashed him back against the vessel's side, and grasping a life line he worked his way along the rescuing boat, by which he was taken to the *Rhode Island*, the convoy of the *Monitor*. In a short time he was ordered to the *Florida*, on the recommendation of Commander Bankhead, and cruised in search of the privateer *Alabama*. Latterly he has been inspector of customs at Mayport, Fla. Shortly before his death, feeling that the end was near, he sent his valuable collection of relics to an acquaintance in this state. The collection embraces mementoes of the *Monitor* and the other vessels engaged in the two days fight in Hampton Roads, March 9 [8] and 10 [9], 1862. A brave, able officer, a kind husband and father has gone to his long rest."

Biographical Notes

The information about the people listed here and in the footnotes was compiled from a variety of different sources. These include Navy pension applications, muster rolls, Navy registers, court martial records, regimental histories, military records, census records, church records, city directories, newspaper obituaries, college records (catalogues, obituaries) and genealogies. The following websites were also of great help: ancestry.com, FamilySearch.org, Fold3.com, readex.com.

Adams, Orville N. (1823-1882) – Merchant and coal agent in La Salle, IL. Engaged in lead mining in Galena, IL before moving to La Salle where he helped develop the region's coal deposits.

Atwater, Norman K. (1830-1862) – Born in New Haven, CT, son of a shipmaster. Mariner before Civil War. Appointed acting ensign in September 1862. Assigned to *Monitor* in November 1862. Drowned when the vessel sank. A landsman on the *Monitor* described the scene: "I hung dangling in the air over the bow of the *Rhode Island,* with Ensign Norman Atwater hanging to the cat-head, three or four feet from me, like myself, with both hands clinching a rope and shouting for someone to save him. Our hands grew painful and all the time weaker, until I saw his strength give way. He slipped a foot, caught again, and with his last prayer, "O God!" I saw him fall and sink, to rise no more."*

Bankhead, John P. (1821-1867) – Born at Fort Johnston, SC. Entered Navy as midshipman in 1838. Chief of staff for his father Brigadier General John Bankhead in Mexican-American War. Served in Mediterranean Squadron from 1855-58. Commanded a schooner in U.S. Coast Survey from 1858 to start of Civil War. As executive officer on USS *Susquehanna*, participated in bombardment of forts guarding Hatteras Inlet, NC in August 1861. Subsequently commanded USS *Pembina* in attack on Port Royal Sound, SC in November 1861. Commanded *Monitor* from September 10, 1862 to December 31, 1862. Suffered from exposure when *Monitor* sank. Commanded *Florida* from March 1863 to August 9, 1863, and three other vessels for remainder of the war. Later served in East India Squadron. Resigned due to poor health and died at sea off coast of Yemen on his way home.

Beecher, James C. (1828-1886) – Born in Boston, MA, son of a Presbyterian minister. His half-brother was the famous Congregational minister and anti-slavery activist Henry Ward Beecher. His half-sister Harriet Beecher Stowe was the author of *Uncle Tom's Cabin*, the anti-slavery novel that

---

* The Loss of the *Monitor*, Francis B. Butts, *The Century Illustrated Monthly Magazine*, Vol. 31, New York, NY, December 1885, p. 302.

hastened the path to the Civil War. Suspended from Dartmouth College for assaulting a student, but readmitted on account of the family name, graduating in 1848. Served as a ship's officer in East India trade, which is where Keeler first met him on his trip home from California in 1850. Returned home in 1857 and graduated from Andover Theological Seminary. Seaman's chaplain in Canton, China until start of Civil War. Enlisted in 67th New York Infantry (1st Long Island Regiment) as chaplain. Resigned in September 1862. Commissioned lieutenant colonel of 141st New York Infantry in October 1862. Discharged in March 1863; returned home to care for his sick wife who later died. Rejoined army and organized 1st North Carolina Volunteers, an African-American regiment, which later became the 35th U.S. Colored Troops. In 1864 he and his second wife ran a school for freed slaves in Jacksonville, FL. Congregational church pastor in New York state after the war. Suffered from mental illness later in life. Died by suicide in Elmira, NY.

Bennett, William C. (1836-1916) – Born in Brownsville, PA, son of a steamboat captain. Moved to La Salle, IL in 1856 where he co-owned a hardware store. Telegraph operator in La Salle at start of Civil War. Commissioned acting 3rd master in Western Gunboat Flotilla in May 1862. Assigned to construction department in St. Louis, MO where he helped build ironclad rams USS *Lafayette* and USS *Choctaw*. Promoted to acting ensign in October 1862. Served on *Choctaw* after its completion. Transferred to USS *Champion* in February 1864. Resigned shortly after to take care of family business. Based in Rock Island, IL from 1865-69, working as a steamboat captain on Mississippi River. Moved to Moline, IL in 1869 where he was treasurer and later president of a company that manufactured flour-milling machinery. Once mayor of Moline. Married three times. Died in Moline.

Blakeman, Birdsey (1824-1894) – Book publisher in New York City. Lived in Brooklyn, NY. Keeler got to know him when they were both living in Bridgeport, CT. Died at his country home in Stockbridge, MA.

Brooks, Robert F. (1839-1899) – Born and raised on a farm near Oxford, OH. Graduated from Miami University in Oxford in 1858. Attended medical school at University of Michigan in Ann Arbor from 1861-62. Medical degree from Bellevue Medical College in New York City in 1864. Appointed acting assistant surgeon in March 1864. Served on *Florida* from April 1864 to October 1864. Subsequently served on USS *Western World* and USS *St. Lawrence*. Honorably discharged in 1869. Moved to Carthage, MO where he practiced medicine. Never married; lived with his unmarried sister. Said to be a highly cultivated man—a lover of books, music and gardening.

Brown, David (1825 – after 1900) – Keeler's brother-in-law. Born in Pennsylvania, eldest of five children of Irish immigrants. Grew up in St. Louis, MO. Moved to Illinois in 1840s and to La Salle in early 1850s where he had a grocery business. Married Fannie Keeler in 1856. Wholesale tea merchant in Chicago, IL after Civil War. Moved to Florida in 1870, settling first in Jacksonville where he was a dairy farmer and then near West Palm Beach where he was a tomato grower. Died between 1900 and 1910, presumably in Washington state where he and Fannie were living in 1900.

Brown, Frances E. (1834-1912) – Keeler's sister. Born in Auburn, MI. Lived in Utica, NY and Newtown, CT before moving to La Salle, IL in 1853. Married David Brown in 1856. Lived in Chicago, IL from 1867-70. Moved to Florida in 1870. Six children: Anna L. (~1858-1900), Jarvis Brush (~1859-~1877), Margaret (~1861-1864), Roswell Keeler (1864-1943), Elizabeth (Lida) Plant (1865-1952), and David Edward (1868-1952). In 1890s moved to Washington state, where four of her children lived. After her husband's death, she lived with her daughter Lida in Port Angeles, WA, where she died.

Brush, Jarvis (1797-1883) – Keeler's paternal uncle. Born in Ridgebury, CT. Had a crockery business in New York City in early 1820s. In 1840 he co-founded the American Howe Pin Company, which manufactured solid headed pins which previously had to be made by hand. Over the next decade the company manufactured nearly all of the pins sold in the U.S. In 1845 he perfected a machine for inserting sewing pins into paper holders ready for sale. Lived in Brooklyn, NY. Retired from management of the company in 1850 but remained a director until his death. Married three times. First two wives died in New York City: the first in 1822 (possibly in child birth), the second in 1825 (of yellow fever). Third wife was Keeler's father's sister Sarah whom he married in Ridgebury in 1827. Son Joseph (born 1828) was a merchant in Brooklyn. Other son George (born 1831) was a professor of minerology at Yale College. Following his wife's death in 1865, Jarvis moved to New Haven, CT where he lived with son George. Died in New Haven.

Budd, William (1829-1907) – Born in either Ireland or Canada to Irish parents. Grew up in New York City. Served in U.S. Coast Survey in 1850s. Detached and commissioned acting master in May 1861. Commanded USS *Resolute* in Potomac Flotilla from May to September 1861, earning nickname "Terror of the Potomac." Assigned to South Atlantic Blockading Squadron in October 1861. Promoted to acting volunteer lieutenant in May 1862. Captured a number of blockade runners including cotton-laden *Memphis* which earned him $38,318.15 in prize money, largest single amount awarded in Civil War. His fighting prowess was so highly regarded that Gideon Welles hoped he would encounter the Confederate raider *Tallahassee* in August 1864, for he would "prove an ugly customer for the pirate."[*] Promoted to acting volunteer lieutenant commander in November 1864. Ordered to command

---

[*] *Diary of Gideon Welles, Secretary of the Navy Under Lincoln and Johnson*, Boston, MA, 1911 (August 18, 1864 entry, p. 111).

BIOGRAPHICAL NOTES

Florida in January 25, 1865. Relieved of command of *Florida* on September 2, 1865 due to a drinking incident and forced to resign. Resignation revoked and honorably discharged in January 1866. Appointed acting master in regular navy in March 1867. Honorably discharged in June 1868. Married daughter of well-to-do merchant from Georgetown, DC in 1866. Married second time in 1871. Commissioner of Docks in New York City in 1870s. Widower in Brooklyn, NY in 1900s, working as janitor and landlord. Died in Brooklyn.

Bursley, Ira (~1826-1881) – Born in Barnstable, MA, son of the town sheriff. Seaman by age of 24. Appointed acting ensign in March 1864. Promoted to acting master in November 1864. Served on USS *Sassacus* from April to May 1865 and *Florida* from June to August 1865. Honorably discharged in September 1865. Ship master after the war. Executive officer on passenger steamer *Quaker City* which took Mark Twain and other Americans on a tour of Europe and the Holy Land in 1867. Immortalized by Twain in his book about that trip, *The Innocents Abroad*: "I said to a deck-sweep, but in a low voice, 'Who is that overgrown pirate with whiskers and the discordant voice?' 'It's Captain Bursley–executive officer–sailing master.'" Died of yellow fever in San Antonio, TX where he had gone on business.

Campbell, Albert B. (1838-1867) – Born in Brooklyn, NY, son of a machinist. Studied naval engineering in New York City. Appointed third assistant engineer in 1859 after passing Navy board examination. Served on USS *Saranac* in Pacific Squadron before Civil War. Promoted to second assistant engineer in October 1861. Served on *Monitor* from February to December 1862. Missed final voyage after being hospitalized in late December 1862 due to a leg injury. Resigned due to illness in May 1863. Returned to Brooklyn where he was partner of a firm that manufactured steam pumps. Died in Brooklyn.

Campbell, Alexander (1814-1898) – Businessman in La Salle, IL and a leading Republican politician in La Salle County. Mayor of La Salle from 1852-53. Republican member of Illinois House of Representatives from 1858-59.

Cannon, Legrand B. (1815-1906) – General John Wool's chief of staff at Fort Monroe, VA. Married to Keeler's first-cousin-once-removed Mary DeForest, granddaughter of Keeler's great-grandfather Elihu DeForest. Wealthy manufacturer and businessman in Troy, NY where he became acquainted with Wool who was stationed there as commander of Department of the East. Served as Wool's aide-de-camp at start of Civil War and helped organize shipment of arms and provisions to Washington, DC and Fort Monroe, which were both under threat of attack. When Wool was given command of Department of Virginia in August 1861, with his headquarters at Fort Monroe, Cannon followed. Appointed by Wool to examine the condition of escaped slaves who had been arriving at the fort in great numbers and to determine whether they could be employed as labourers. Resigned after returning to New York City in May 1862. One of a group of 20 subscribers who in 1870 purchased John Brown's farm in the Adirondacks, preserving for posterity the farm and cemetery containing the remains of the radical abolitionist whose attack on Harpers Ferry helped ignite the Civil War. Died at his estate at Burlington, VT.

Carter, Hill (1796-1875) – Owner of Shirley Plantation on James River. Midshipman in War of 1812. Resigned from Navy in 1816 to claim ownership of Shirley which had been in the Carter family's possession since 1723. Owned 139 slaves in 1860. Between May 1862 and mid-June 1864 more than 80 of his slaves escaped to Union lines. In summer of 1862 his plantation served as a hospital for Union soldiers wounded during Seven Days Battles. Commanded a regiment at Jamestown at start of Peninsula Campaign. Three of his sons served in the war: one commanded gunboat CSS *Teaser* which was blown up on James River on July 4, 1862, another was a cavalry officer who was killed at Battle of Chancellorsville. Died at Shirley Plantation.

Carter, Samuel B. (1828-1890) – Merchant in La Salle, IL. Born in Branford, CT. Moved to La Salle as a young man. His Civil War service record could not be found, but a man by this name served as quartermaster in 14th Illinois Cavalry. However, his obituary in *The Daily Inter Ocean* (13 November 1890) states that "together with his two brothers, [he] enlisted in the army [and] received two wounds during the course of his service." Both brothers killed in the war: 24-year old Henry, a captain in 11th Illinois Infantry, at Shiloh; 18-year old Edwin, a corporal in his brother's company, at Fort Donelson. Studied civil engineering in Chicago, IL and became an authority on railroad construction. Moved to Jacksonville, FL in early 1880s where he was chief engineer of Jacksonville, Tampa and Key West Railroad. Died in Jacksonville.

Carter, Siah Hulett (1839-1892). Former slave of Hill Carter's at Shirley Plantation. According to Hill Carter's widow, he was one of their most valuable slaves and was the first to desert them.* Enlisted May 19, 1862 on *Monitor* as a first-class boy. Survived sinking of vessel and served on five other warships, including USS *Florida*, first as landsman and then as ordinary seaman. Honorably discharged in May 1865. Married Eliza Tarrow, a former slave of Hill Carter's; they had 13 children. Carpenter in Chesterfield County, VA until 1870 when he moved to Philadelphia, PA where he was a stevedore. Suffered from severe frost bite of feet during the war, which thereafter frequently incapacitated him from doing manual labor. Died in Philadelphia.

Chapin, Julius F. (1801-1884) – Painter and carpenter in La Salle, IL. Lived a few doors from the Keelers. His wife Mary helped Anna with the sewing.

---

* Navy Widows' Certificates (Certificate No. 10124), NARA M1279.

BIOGRAPHICAL NOTES

Chapin, William E. (1825-1901) – Son of Keeler's neighbor Julius Chapin. Born in New York City. Grew up in western New York state where he learned the trade of cabinet making. Moved to La Salle, IL in about 1853. In 1862 travelled to his old home in Wyoming County, NY and enlisted as private in 24th Independent Battery New York Light Artillery. Shipped to New Berne, NC as part of 18th Army Corps. Fell sick soon after arrival and sent to Hammond General Hospital in Beaufort, NC. Proved to be an excellent nurse during his convalescence and remained attached to the hospital for rest of the war, and also managed the hospital garden. Transferred to 3rd New York Light Artillery. Mustered out in May 1865. Returned to La Salle where he resumed work as cabinet maker, and later turned his hand to farming. Died in La Salle.

Coates, James H. (1829-1902) – Born in Norristown, PA. Grain merchant in Peru, IL in 1850s. Commissioned captain of Company H in 11th Illinois Infantry in July 1861; two years later was regiment's colonel. Fought at Battle of Fort Donelson, where his regiment suffered huge (60%) casualties, and at Battle of Shiloh where he was wounded. Saw action during Vicksburg Campaign in 1863 and in an expedition up Yazoo River in Mississippi in 1864. Brevetted brigadier general at end of the war and moved to St. Louis, MO where he was a grain broker. Died in St. Louis.

Collins, William H. (1831-1910) – Born in Collinsville, IL. Graduated from Illinois College in Jacksonville, IL in 1850. Studied at Yale Theological School in New Haven, CT from 1850-52. Pastor of First Congregational Church of La Salle from 1853-58. Returned to Jacksonville where he was editor of *Jacksonville Journal*. Enlisted as chaplain of 10th Illinois Infantry in August 1861. Resigned in June 1862 and returned to La Salle to raise an infantry company. Elected captain of Company D in 104th Illinois Infantry in which he served until November 1864. Absent at Battle of Hartsville where his entire regiment was captured because he had been detailed to guard a supply train. Fought at many battles in the West, including Chickamauga, Lookout Mountain and Missionary Ridge. Successful plow manufacturer in Quincy, IL after the war. Served two terms in Illinois State legislature as Republican. Co-founded Illinois State Historical Society. Died in Quincy.

Crafts, Samuel P. (1824-1910) – Born in Woodbury, CT, son of a successful manufacturer. Prepared for college but never attended, went to sea instead. Express rider in California in early 1850s. Ship master in years leading up to Civil War. Married Sarah Thomson from New Haven, CT in 1859. Appointed acting ensign in December 1862. Assigned to *Florida* in mid-February 1863. Promoted to acting master in August 1863. Detached from *Florida* in early November 1863. Later, commanded USS *Shokokon*, sweeping mines on James River and supporting army's advance on Petersburg, VA. In December 1864 given command of USS *Little Ada*, which served as David

BIOGRAPHICAL NOTES

Porter's dispatch boat during the two attacks on Fort Fisher, NC. Recommended for promotion for gallant conduct by Porter during the second attack. Promoted to acting volunteer lieutenant in April 1865. From March to August 1865 commanded tug USS *Clematis*. Honorably discharged in December 1865. After several years in merchant marine, purchased a farm near New Haven and went into the brick-making business. Later returned to New Haven where he presumably died.

Crosby, Peirce (1824-1899) – Born in Delaware County, PA. Appointed midshipman in Navy in 1838. Served in Mediterranean before attending Naval School in Philadelphia, PA in 1843, graduating in 1844. Served in Mexican-American War. Commissioned lieutenant in 1853. During first year of Civil War served on Chesapeake Bay and then on USS *Cumberland* at Hampton Roads. Participated in Burnside's North Carolina Expedition in August 1861, receiving special mention for aiding in capture of Forts Hatteras and Clarke. Commanded USS *Pinola* in attack on forts guarding New Orleans, LA in April 1862; for his actions received the Thanks of Congress. Promoted to commander in September 1862. Fleet captain of North Atlantic Blockading Squadron from February to October 1863. Commanded *Florida* from mid-November 1863 to mid-March 1864. Transferred to USS *Keystone State* in March 1864. Commanded two other vessels in last year of the war. Retired as rear-admiral in 1883. Four times married (three times widowed). Died in Washington, DC.

Durham, Henry (1836 - after 1920) – Minister of First Congregational Church of La Salle from 1863-65. Born in Ohio. Raised in Beloit, WI. Studied medicine and theology at Beloit College, graduating in 1857. Arrived in La Salle, IL in 1863. Married Keeler's brother-in-law's sister Mary Brown in November 1864. Later practiced medicine in Chicago, IL, Nebraska and Iowa. Twice widowed. Lived with his son in Bountiful, UT in 1920.

Dutton, Arthur H. (1838-1864) – Colonel of 21st Connecticut Infantry and a distant relative of Anna Keeler's. Born in Wallingford, CT. Graduated from West Point in 1861, third in a class of 34 which included George Armstrong Custer. Organized his regiment in Norwich, CT and commissioned colonel in September 1862. Served in Virginia and North Carolina. Mortally wounded while reconnoitering Confederate positions near Petersburg, VA on May 26, 1864. Died a week later in a hospital in Baltimore, MD with his pregnant wife of one year at his side.

Dutton, Elizabeth Eliot (1796-1883) – Keeler's mother-in-law. Born in Boston, MA, daughter of sea captain Melzar Joy. Paternal ancestor was Englishman Thomas Joy who came to America in the 1630s, settled in Hingham, MA and become a respected builder and architect; built Boston's First Town-House in 1658. Maternal ancestor was Andrew Eliot of East Coker, England who settled in Beverley, MA in the late 1660s, became town clerk and was a juror on the Salem witch trials. Her mother was youngest of eleven children of Andrew Eliot, a Harvard-educated intellectual and minister of Boston's New North Church. Eliza had one sister from her father's first marriage and a half-sister and two half-brothers from his second. Married Henry Dutton in Fairfield, CT in 1823. Four children: Anne Eliza, Mary Eliot, Harriet Joy and Henry Melzar. Her life was marked by great loss: mother died when she was a year old, father died on board his ship in Havana, Cuba when she was 19, son Melzar killed in Civil War at age 24, and daughters Mary and Hattie died in their late thirties. Deeply religious, she was a member of North (Congregational) Church in New Haven, CT. Invalid for last decade of her life. Died in New Haven. Her Civil War letters to her son Melzar are fraught with constant worry and anxiety for his safety and well-being.

Dutton, Henry (1796-1869) – Keeler's father-in-law. Born in Plymouth, CT and raised on the family farm near Watertown, CT. Father was a Congregational church builder and farmer who was a fifer in Revolutionary War. Maternal ancestor was Yorkshireman John Punderson, who came to America in 1638 and was an original proprietor of New Haven in 1639 and a founder of First Church of Christ on the New Haven Green. Attended public schools in Watertown. Entered Yale College in his junior year and graduated in 1818. Studied law in Fairfield, CT. In 1823 married Eliza Joy who was living in Fairfield with her stepmother and siblings. Moved to Newtown, CT in 1823, Bridgeport, CT in 1837 and New Haven, CT in 1847. Professor of law at Yale College from 1847 until his death. Judge on New Haven County Court in 1852. Judge on Connecticut Supreme Court from 1861-66. Elected five times to Connecticut House of Representatives, once to State Senate. Served one term as Governor of Connecticut from 1854-55. Whig and later Republican. Died in New Haven. His congenial nature was summed up as follows: "Keen in intellect, he was free from guile. He was bright, amiable, boyish in feeling, unsuspecting, easy of faith in others."*

Dutton, Henry Melzar (1838-1862) – Keeler's brother-in-law (Anna's brother). Born in Bridgeport, CT. Prepared for college at Hopkins Grammar School in New Haven, CT. Graduated from Yale College in 1857 and Yale Law School in 1859. At start of Civil War he was living with his sister Mary and her family in Litchfield, CT, practicing law with her husband Henry Graves. Enlisted in 5th Connecticut Infantry in July 1861. Commissioned second lieutenant and soon promoted to first lieutenant. Served with his regiment in western Maryland doing guard and picket duty on Chesapeake and Ohio Canal from August 1861 to February 1862 and in Shenandoah Valley chasing Stonewall Jackson from March to June 1862. Killed at Battle of Cedar Mountain in Virginia on August 9, 1862. Body never recovered. In a memorial written at the end of the war a fellow officer described him as "a

---

* *The New York Times*, New York, NY, April 28, 1869, p. 7.

favorite at the camp fire at night, and at our halts upon the marches by day—none could tell more amusing stories; none could repeat more snatches of poetry from ancient or modern authors; none could sing a song better; none so good a physician amid discomfort, home sickness and blues as he."*

Dutton, John (1833-1874) – Anna Keeler's first cousin (son of Henry Dutton's brother Daniel). Born on the family farm near Watertown, CT. Carpenter in Waterbury, CT. Married Anna's maternal first cousin Henrietta Tuthill in 1861. Died in Waterbury.

Dutton, William (1823-1862) – Anna Keeler's first cousin (son of Henry Dutton's brother Daniel). Born on the family farm near Watertown, CT. Moved to Mecklenburg, NY at age 14 where he farmed in summer and taught school and studied in winter. Graduated from West Point in 1846, 15th in a class of 59 which included George B. McClellan and Thomas J. "Stonewall" Jackson. Resigned immediately thereafter due to illness. Moved to Wolcott, NY and purchased a farm. In addition to farming he was also a drain tile and brick manufacturer, school principal, superintendent of schools, justice of peace, and one-term member of House of Representatives of New York. Raised and organized 98th New York Infantry in February 1861 and was elected colonel. Joined Army of the Potomac on Virginia Peninsula in April 1862 and participated in Siege of Yorktown. Contracted typhoid fever in late May 1862. At Battle of Fair Oaks he fell out of his saddle delirious with fever. Taken to hospital at Fort Monroe, VA and then to New York City where he died at a friend's house on July 4, leaving his wife and five children.

Ellis, David R. (1840-1908) – Born in Carmarthen, Wales. Abandoned his religious studies and came to America in November 1861. Enlisted in February 1862 and served on *Monitor*, first as coal heaver, then as Keeler's steward. Served again as Keeler's steward on *Florida* from February 1863 to mid-March 1864. Settled in Pennsylvania after the war where he was a lay clergyman. Died in Annville, PA.

Eppes, Richard (1824-1896) – Owner of Appomattox Manor on James River. Owned 130 slaves in 1860. Medical degree from University of Pennsylvania in Philadelphia in 1847. Enlisted as a private in a cavalry regiment and saw action on Virginia Peninsula in spring of 1862. Provided a substitute to complete his term of service. Assistant surgeon at a hospital at City Point, VA in January 1864 and later surgeon in a hospital in Petersburg, VA where his family had been living since May 1862. Died at Appomattox Manor.

Flye, William (1814-1898) – Born in Newcastle, ME, son of a cabinet maker. Graduated from Bowdoin College in Brunswick, ME in 1835. Taught school before heading to sea as a captain's clerk. Appointed professor of mathe-

---

* *The Connecticut War Record*, New Haven, CT, Vol. 2, No. 9, April 1865, p. 383.

matics in Navy in 1841 and made long cruises to Brazil and west coast of Africa. Resigned in 1857 and moved to Topsham, ME, where he served as a ship master until start of Civil War. Appointed acting volunteer lieutenant in December 1861. Witnessed Battle of Hampton Roads from USS *Roanoke*. Transferred to *Monitor* on March 10, 1862. Detached from *Monitor* in late October 1862 and given a separate command. Subsequently served on five more warships. Promoted to acting volunteer lieutenant commander in July 1865. Honorably discharged in December 1865. Accountant for a cotton and rice growing enterprise in Georgia for several years after the war. Returned to Topsham where he was a cashier in his brother's bank. Suffered from deafness which resulted from the firing of the guns of the *Roanoke* and *Monitor*. Died in Ashland, KY. A classmate later described him as "an amiable man, always cheerful, with a disposition to soften words of censure used by others, envious of no one, of scrupulous integrity, doing justice to all, without display."*

Franks, James P. (1844-1917) – Born in Lewiston, PA. Studied at Yates Institute in Lancaster, PA and at Polytechnic School in Philadelphia, PA before entering Protestant Episcopal Divinity School in Philadelphia; studies interrupted by the war. Served as fleet captain's clerk on USS *Minnesota*, captain's clerk on *Florida* (in fall of 1863) and on USS *Keystone State*. Discharged in May 1864. Completed religious studies in Philadelphia and graduated in 1866. Ordained deacon in 1868 and priest in 1869. Rector of Grace Episcopal Church in Salem, MA from 1870 until his death.

Frederickson, George (~1834-1862) – Born in Denmark. Became U.S. citizen in 1855. Mariner in Philadelphia, PA before Civil War. Appointed acting master's mate in December 1861 and assigned to *Monitor*. Promoted to acting ensign in October 1862. Drowned when *Monitor* sank. Shortly before the vessel sank he was said to have returned a watch he had borrowed from Ensign Peter Williams, saying, "Here, this is yours. I may be lost."†

Gager, Edwin V. (1833-1914) – Born in Pleasant Valley, NY, son of a carpenter. His life at sea began at age of 14. Captained steamers for Cromwell Steamship Company during decade before Civil War and was captain of steamer *Monticello* at start of the war. Appointed acting master in April 1861 and assigned to his old vessel, which had been chartered by Navy and fitted out as gunboat USS *Monticello*. Participated in rescue of an Indiana regiment at Hatteras, NC in August 1861. Transferred to *Monitor* on March 10, 1862. Resigned in early July 1862. Moved to Newark, NJ where he was employed as sea captain until his retirement in 1903. Died in Newark.

---

* *Obituary Record of the Graduates of Bowdoin College and the Medical School of Maine for the Decade Ending June 1, 1909*, Brunswick, ME, 1911, pp. 113-14.
† The Loss of the *Monitor*, Francis B. Butts, *The Century Illustrated Monthly Magazine*, Vol. 31, New York, NY, December 1885, p. 300.

BIOGRAPHICAL NOTES

Graham, Thomas (~1820-?) – gardener in La Salle who did odd jobs for the Keelers.

Graves, Mary Eliot (1826-1865) – Keeler's sister-in-law (Anna's sister). Born in Newtown, CT. Married lawyer and Connecticut state politician Henry B. Graves in 1847. Lived in Litchfield, CT. Two children: Mary Elizabeth (Lilly) (1848-1922), who married her uncle George Watrous after death of Anna's sister Hattie, and Anna Dutton (1854-1930), who married a Congregational minister. Died of cancer in Litchfield.

Greene, Samuel Dana (1840-1884) – Born in Cumberland, MD, son of an army officer who later gained fame at Battle of Gettysburg. Graduated from Naval Academy in 1859. Promoted to lieutenant in August 1861. Serving on USS *Hartford* in China Station at start of Civil War; returned to U.S. in early December 1861. Assigned to *Monitor* in January 1862 as executive officer. During battle with *Virginia*, commanded turret and its guns until taking command of vessel after Worden was injured. Commended by *Monitor*'s captain John Bankhead for his actions during sinking of vessel. Assigned to *Florida* in March 1863 as executive officer. Leave of absence in October 1863 to get married. Special assignment as assistant inspector at New York Navy Yard. Executive officer on USS *Iroquois* from April 1864 to October 1865. Promoted to lieutenant commander August 1865. Assistant professor of mathematics at Naval Academy and head of Department of Navigation and Astronomy there in early 1870s. First wife died in 1874. Remarried in 1876. Committed suicide at Portsmouth Navy Yard.

Hough, David L. (1818-1890) – Born in Middlebury, VT, son of a Presbyterian church minister. Graduated from Middlebury College in 1839. Taught school in Alabama from 1839-40. Studied law in Ohio from 1842-43. Practiced law in Quincy, IL. In late 1840s moved to La Salle, IL where he was attorney for the trustees of Illinois and Michigan Canal. Republican. Six-times city alderman of La Salle. Keeler's business partner at La Salle Iron Works. His wife Elizabeth was also from Middlebury. In early 1870s moved to Chicago, IL where he practiced law. Died in Chicago.

James, Hiram H. (1838-1885) – Born in Deerfield, NJ. Degree in medicine from University of Pennsylvania in Philadelphia in March 1863. Appointed acting assistant surgeon in April 1863 and served four months on USS *Kensington* in West Gulf Blockading Squadron. Served on *Florida* from mid-August 1863 to mid-December 1863; appointment revoked due to disabling sea sickness. Re-appointed in January 1864 and served in Mississippi Squadron. Resigned in June 1864 due to chronic diarrhea. Practiced medicine in Rahway, NJ. Never recovered from illness contracted on the Mississippi. According to his brother, "the disease had taken such a deep and permanent hold of his system that he was unable to regain his health, and after a long and patient struggle he gradually became weaker until death came to his relief."* Died at Saratoga, NY where he had gone for treatment.

Jeffers, William N. (1824-1883) – Born in Swedesboro, NJ. Joined Navy as midshipman at age 15. Graduated from Naval Academy in 1846. Promoted to lieutenant in 1855. Specialist in ordnance. Authored seven books, mostly dealing with armaments and gunnery. Commanded a patrol boat on Potomac River at start of Civil War. Transferred to USS *Roanoke* in May 1861 doing blockade duty off the North Carolina coast. Commanded USS *Underwriter* and saw action at Battles of Roanoke Island and Elizabeth City in early 1862. Promoted to lieutenant commander July 1862. Commanded *Monitor* from March 12, 1862 to August 15, 1862 when he was detached due to chronic rheumatism. Ordnance duty at the Philadelphia and Washington Navy Yards for remainder of the war. Post-war years spent in Washington, DC, mainly at the Bureau of Ordnance. Rose to rank of commodore. Died poor in Washington, DC, leaving his wife with a pension of $25 per month.

Joy, Henry DeWitt (1841-1907) – Anna Keeler's maternal first cousin (Franklin Joy's son). Born in New York City. Graduated from Williams College in Williamstown, MA in 1863. Medical degree from Columbia College in New York City in 1866. Physician in New York City. Died in New Brighton, NY.

Joy, Joseph Franklin (1811-1891) – Anna Keeler's maternal uncle (half-brother of Eliza Dutton). Born in Boston, MA. Secretary and later president of the Panama Railway Company. Lived in New York City. Two children with his first wife Anna who died in 1865. Died at Sailor's Snug Harbor, NY.

Joy, Mary Eliot (1845-1933) – Anna Keeler's maternal first cousin (Franklin Joy's daughter). Born in New York City. Married a wealthy banker in 1867 and travelled extensively in Europe. Resided in France after her husband's death. Died in Fointainbleu, France.

Joy, Mary Pyncheon (1806 - after 1891) – Anna Keeler's maternal aunt (half-sister of Eliza Dutton). Born in Boston, MA. Never married. Lived in New York City with her brother Franklin and later in New Haven, CT with Anna's mother.

Keeler, Elizabeth Eliot (1860-1926) – Keeler's daughter. Born in La Salle, IL. Moved to Mayport, FL in 1870. Attended private school in Tarrytown, NY in late 1870s. In 1886 married David Talbot Day, a chemist and geologist who was Ed Keeler's classmate at Johns Hopkins University. Lived successively in Baltimore, MD, Washington, DC and Santa Maria, CA. Two children: Elizabeth Cathcart, who was a high-school teacher who settled in Santa Fé, NM, and David Eliot, who was a petroleum engineer and oil

---

* Navy Widows' Certificates (Certificate No. 19523), NARA M1279.

BIOGRAPHICAL NOTES

executive in Los Angeles, CA. Lived with her daughter in Orcutt, CA after her husband's death in 1925. Died in Orcutt. Cremated remains interred beside those of her husband in Loudon Park Cemetery, in Baltimore.

Keeler, Henry Dutton (1847-1877) – Keeler's eldest son. Born in Bridgeport, CT. Attended public school in La Salle, IL until 1862 and private school in New Haven, CT from 1862-64. Served on *Florida* as paymaster's clerk in 1865. Bookkeeper in Chicago, IL, first for a pair of wholesale and importing companies from 1866-68 and then for his uncle Dave Brown's wholesale tea business from 1867-70. Moved to Mayport, FL soon after his parents did. Lived in Jacksonville, FL from 1873-75. Clerk for the Equitable Trust Company in New York City from 1876-77. Expert amateur botanist, he spent his spare time in Florida roaming the countryside collecting rare plants which he sent to collectors up north. It was on a botanical trip near Branford Point, CT that he fell ill and died several days later.

Keeler, James Edward (1857-1900) – Keeler's youngest son. Named after his two uncles who died in the California Gold Rush. Born in La Salle, IL. Moved to Mayport, FL in 1870. Graduated from Johns Hopkins University in Baltimore, MD in 1881. Assistant to Samuel P. Langley at Allegheny Observatory in Pittsburgh, PA from 1881-86, with a year of studies in Germany in 1882. Junior astronomer at Lick Observatory, CA from 1886-91. Married Cora Slocomb Matthews in 1891. Director of Allegheny Observatory from 1891-98. Used spectroscopy to prove that Saturn's rings were composed of particles. Director of Lick Observatory from 1898 until his death. In late 1898 he began a detailed search of nebulae (galaxies) using a large reflector telescope he had refurbished, taking long-exposure photographs to reveal their structure. Awarded Henry Draper Medal of the National Academy of Sciences in 1899 for his astrophysical research. Also a talented artist, his drawings of planets adorn the walls of the Allegheny Observatory. Died of a massive stroke in San Francisco, CA. At the time of his death he was considered to be the outstanding astrophysicist of his generation in America. Former director of Lick Observatory, Donald Osterbrock, described him as: "A skilled, intelligent research worker" who "was at the same time a successful administrator, an outstanding graduate teacher and a warm, well-loved human being, a type rare indeed in the annals of science."* Two children: Henry Bowman, who graduated from Carnegie Technical School in Pittsburgh, went to China with Standard Old Company in 1915 and died there of appendicitis in 1918 at age 25; and Cora Floyd, who married an Army lieutenant in Honolulu, HI and lived in a dozen different army bases over continental U.S. before settling in San Antonio, TX where she died in 1986 at age 92. Ed's cremated remains, as well as those of his wife

---

* *James E. Keeler: Pioneer American Astrophysicist and the Early Development of American Astrophysics*, Donald E. Osterbrock, Cambridge University Press, 1984, p. 359.

and son, are interred in the crypt beneath the Keeler Memorial Telescope at Allegheny Observatory.

Keeler, Mary Eliza (1800-1886) – Keeler's mother. Born in Utica, NY, sixth of seven children of Benjamin Plant and Lucinda Potter. Raised on her father's farm. Married Roswell Keeler in 1820. Two youngest sons James Plant and Edward died in California Gold Rush in 1850. Moved to Mayport, FL in 1870 with Keeler and his family. Died in Mayport the day after Keeler.

Keeler, Roswell (1791-1864) – Keeler's father. Born on a farm in Ridgebury, CT, second of eight children of Timothy Keeler and Lurany DeForest. Moved to Utica, NY in 1815. Dry goods merchant in New York City from 1820-34 and in Auburn, MI from 1834-39. Lived in Utica from 1840-46 and Newtown, CT from 1847-53. Employed as a railroad agent in Newtown in 1850. Moved to La Salle, IL in 1853. In 1860 was living next door to daughter Fannie. Active member of Presbyterian and Congregational churches. Died in La Salle. Re-interred at Forest Hill Cemetery in Utica.

Keeler, Sarah Emma (1841-1915) – Keeler's sister. Born in Utica, NY, youngest of Keeler's four siblings. Lived in La Salle, IL with Keeler and his family and later in Ottawa, IL with her cousin Helen Plant. Never married. Died in Ottawa. Interred next to her father at Forest Hill Cemetery in Utica.

Kimberly, William H. (1820-1898) – Born in Baltimore, MD. Co-owner with his brother Edward of Kimberly Brothers, a provisions store at Old Point Comfort next to Fort Monroe, VA which they opened shortly after start of Civil War. Known for his generosity and hospitality, he kept an open house to the survivors of USS *Cumberland* and USS *Congress* following Battle of Hampton Roads. Keeler stayed with him whenever he was at Old Point. Before the war he and his brothers had a provisions store on Pratt Street in Baltimore. When the 6th Massachusetts Militia marched through the city on April 19, 1861 on their way to defending Washington, the first person killed in the riot fell in front of their store. Died at Fort Monroe.

Laning, James (1821-1891) – Born in Bridgeport, PA, son of a cabinet maker. Apprenticed as cabinet maker in Pittsburgh, PA. Clerk on steamboats on western rivers in 1840s. Returned to Bridgeport in 1845 and worked building steamboat cabins. Moved to La Salle, IL in 1855 and opened an iron and heavy hardware store. In 1859 moved to St. Louis, MO where he was engaged in steamboating on the Mississippi until just after start of Civil War. Volunteered in Western Gunboat Flotilla in August 1861, and commissioned second master on ironclad USS *Essex*. Commanded one of *Essex*'s batteries during attack on Fort Henry, TN in February 1862 and survived the explosion of *Essex*'s boiler. Promoted to first master in April 1862 and acting volunteer lieutenant in October 1862. Unable to serve as a watch officer due to deafness that resulted from firing of *Essex*'s guns, he was ordered to St.

Louis where he superintended construction of ironclad rams USS *Lafayette* and USS *Choctaw* which were finished by April 1863. Assigned to command gunboat USS *Rattler*, he was ordered south of Vicksburg to guard ironclad USS *Indianola* which had sunk at high water a mile from river channel. Detached from *Rattler* in October 1864, he devised a plan to raise and float *Indianola*; the recovery effort took four months and was completed in January 1865. Resigned in February 1865 due to illness. Returned to La Salle where he served as a steamboat clerk, then managed a lumber dressing mill and window glass manufacturing business. Totally deaf, partially paralyzed, and suffering from a host of other health problems resulting from the war, he moved to Hot Springs, AR in 1870s. Died in Keokuk, IA.

Logue, Daniel C. (1832-1914) – Born in Otisville, NY, son of a doctor. Graduated from medical school at University of City of New York in 1856. Practiced medicine in New York City before Civil War. Appointed acting assistant surgeon in January 1862 and assigned to *Monitor* in February 1862. Resigned in October 1862. Returned to New York City where he resumed his medical practice. Died in Bellmore, NY.

Lovejoy, Owen (1811-1864) – Born in Albion, ME, son of a Congregational minister. Eldest brother Elijah Lovejoy, who was an anti-slavery crusader, was killed by a pro-slavery mob in Alton, IL in 1837. Moved to Princeton, IL in 1838 and was ordained minister of Hampshire Colony Congregational Church. Conductor on Underground Railroad; arrested several times for aiding fugitive slaves, but never convicted. Organized anti-slavery Congregational churches in northern Illinois. Member of anti-slavery Liberty Party, Free Soil Party and finally Republican Party, whose Illinois wing he helped organize. Elected to Illinois state legislature in 1854 and to U.S. House of Representatives from Keeler's district in 1857. Radical Republican. Commissioned a colonel, he served three months on General John C. Frémont's staff in Missouri in 1861. Returned to Congress where he argued for a vigorous prosecution of the war, the arming of African-Americans, equal pay for troops regardless of color, universal emancipation and more. He was one of President Lincoln's strongest supporters in Congress. Died in Brooklyn, NY.

Magaw, Samuel (1828-1884) – Born in Meadville, PA, son of a paper manufacturer. Appointed midshipman in Navy in 1841. Served in Mexican-American War. Promoted to lieutenant in 1855. In January 1860 sickness forced him to take an 18-month leave of absence, which he spent in Italy with his family. Returned home in July 1861 and ordered to Potomac Flotilla. Commanded a division of the flotilla from September 1861 to February 1864. Promoted to lieutenant commander in July 1862. Commanded *Florida* from early April 1864 to December 8, 1864. Subsequently commanded USS *Lenapee* and in late January 1865 sent up Cape Fear River for final operations against Wilmington, NC which was still in rebel hands. Detached in late

BIOGRAPHICAL NOTES

February 1865 due to illness. Promoted to commander in 1866. Resigned in 1867 due to illness. Died in Washington, DC.

Maies, William H. (1829-1881) – Born in St. Johns Parish, Barbados, son of a sugar planter. Came to U.S. in 1845 and worked as a mariner in Boston, MA and Chelsea, MA. Appointed acting master's mate in August 1861. Promoted to acting master in May 1862. Served on seven different vessels over course of Civil War, commencing with USS *Cambridge* from August 1861 to early January 1863. In November 1861, he and 12 other men were captured while trying to destroy a blockade runner that had run ashore near Masonboro Inlet, NC; paroled five days later, exchanged two months later. Executive officer on USS *Seneca*; participated in land attack on Fort Fisher, NC in January 1865; singled out for coolness and gallantry by commanding officer. Promoted to acting volunteer lieutenant in April 1865. Commanded *Florida* from September 9, 1865 to mid-January 1866. Honorably discharged in May 1866. Joined regular navy in April 1867 and appointed acting master. Served in Asiatic Squadron until resignation in July 1868. Captain on Japanese merchant ships for next 12 years; returned home only once. Suffered from liver disease for last five years of his life. In his last letter to his wife, written from Yokohama the month before he died, he stated that he was "as helpless as a child . . . swollen all out of shape" and "suffer terribly," but hoped to "get well enough to come home, for I so desire to see all my loved ones before I die."* He never made it home, and died in a San Francisco hospital.

McAlister, Alexander (~1817-1885) – Born in Ireland. Came to America as a young man. Keeler got to know him in the 1840s when they both lived in Bridgeport, CT. Moved to New Haven, CT in the late 1840s where he was cashier at the Quinnipiack Bank. In the 1870s and 1880s had his own brokerage firm in New Haven. Died at his summer residence in West Haven, CT.

McGowan, John (1843-1915) – Born in Port Penn, DE, son of a sea captain. Grew up in Philadelphia, PA and Elizabeth, NJ. Appointed acting master's mate in March 1862. Promoted to acting master in May 1862. Commanded USS *Wyandank* in Potomac Flotilla until February 1863. Served on *Florida* from March 1863 to October 1864. Ordered to USS *State of Georgia* in November 1864. Appointed master in regular navy in 1868. Retired as rear admiral in 1901. Died at Haines Falls, NY.

McLean, William H. (~1835-1908) – Born in New York City, son of Irish immigrants. Boat builder and ship's carpenter before Civil War. Entered naval service in spring of 1862 as an engineer on army transport *George Washington*, which operated on Port Royal Sound, SC and was blown up by Confederate field artillery on Cossaw River in April 1863; he escaped capture by fleeing into the marshes. Appointed acting first assistant engineer in July

---

* Navy Survivors' Certificates (Certificate No. 3138), NARA M1469.

Biographical Notes

1863, serving first on USS *Tuscarora*, then as chief engineer (ranked as first assistant engineer) on *Florida* from December 1863 to January 1866. Honorably discharged in April 1866. Marine engineer in New York City where he died.

Merriman, Edgar C. (1840-1894) – Born in Bradford, NY, son of a merchant. Entered Naval Academy in 1857, but resigned due to illness in 1860. Appointed acting master in December 1861. First served on USS *Norfolk Packet*, a mortar schooner that participated in attack on forts guarding New Orleans, LA in April 1862. In September 1862 ordered to cruiser USS *Santiago de Cuba* in search of Confederate commerce raiders. Promoted to acting lieutenant in September 1863. Executive officer on *Florida* from early October 1863 to mid-July 1864. Executive officer on monitor USS *Lehigh* for remainder of the war. Served in regular navy until 1891, rising to rank of captain. Final years plagued by mental illness, heart problems, and approaching blindness. Died in Yonkers, NY, leaving a wife and four young children.

Millward, James (1831-1892) – Born in England. Came to America as a boy and settled in New York City. Lumber dealer before Civil War. Went to Fort Monroe, VA in June 1861 as officer in Bartlett's Naval Brigade which became part of Union Coast Guard. Named captain of port and was responsible for carrying flags of truce to Norfolk, VA and Petersburg, VA. Merchant in New York City after the war. Mayor of Yonkers, NY from 1890-92. Died in Boston, MA.

Moore, Absolom B. (~1827-1879) – Born in New Jersey. Worked for Illinois Central Railroad Company in La Salle, IL in 1850s. Elected clerk of Circuit Court in Ottawa, IL in 1860. Organized 104th Illinois Infantry in Ottawa and commissioned its colonel in August 1862. In December 1862 an entire brigade he was in command of was captured at Hartsville, TN. Held at Libby Prison in Richmond, VA, he was exchanged several months later. Blamed for the defeat, he was forced to resign in September 1863. Returned to Ottawa and resumed duties as Circuit Court clerk. Owned a machine shop and foundry in Ottawa in 1870. Later moved to Chicago, IL where he held a minor appointment in Federal government. Died in Chicago.

Newton, Isaac (1837-1884) – Born in New York City, son of a steamboat builder. Civil engineering degree at University of City of New York in 1856. Assistant engineer on trans-Atlantic passenger ships. Appointed first assistant engineer in June 1861 and assigned to USS *Roanoke* in blockade off Charleston Harbor, SC. Transferred to New York where he worked with Alban Stimers and John Ericsson building the *Monitor*. Served on *Monitor* from February to August 1862. Superintended construction of ironclads in New York. Resigned in February 1865 and returned to New York City. Appointed chief engineer of Department of Public Works in 1881 and designed Croton Aqueduct. Committed suicide in New York City.

BIOGRAPHICAL NOTES

Parke, John G. (1838-1905) – Born in Groton, MA, son of a Massachusetts state politician. Graduated from Harvard University in 1858. Attended Harvard Medical School until February 1862 when appointed acting assistant surgeon. With exception of one month on *Florida* (August 1863) served on USS *Victoria* until February 1864. Subsequently served on USS *Mendota*. Honorably discharged in November 1865. Returned to Boston to complete medical degree. Later was superintendent of Worcester Insane Hospital in Worchester, MA. Died in Worcester.

Parker, James (1832-1914) – Born in Newark, OH, son of a judge. Entered Naval Academy in 1846. Served in Mexican-American War. Served on USS *Yorktown* hunting down slave ships off coast of Africa. Resumed studies at Naval Academy in 1851; graduated in 1852. Three years in Mediterranean Squadron. Promoted to lieutenant in 1855. Resigned in 1856. Studied law in Cincinnati in office of Samuel P. Chase, then governor of Ohio. Admitted to bar in 1857. Practicing law in Cincinnati at start of Civil War. Commissioned acting lieutenant in May 1861. Promoted to lieutenant commander in July 1862. Served on several ships before commanding *Florida* from August 26, 1863 to September 9, 1863. Subsequently commanded USS *Seneca* and USS *Maumee*. Executive officer on USS *Minnesota* from November 1864 to January 1865. Participated in attacks on Fort Fisher, NC. In second attack led a party of 241 officers, sailors, firemen and marines from *Minnesota* in the ground assault on the fort. Resumed command of *Maumee* in late January 1865. Placed in charge of naval stores of Confederacy after the fall of Richmond, VA. Resigned in May 1866. Settled in Perth Amboy, NJ where he practiced admiralty law and where he died.

Pierce, Frank H. (1851-1933) – Son of a screw manufacturer from Mount Carmel, CT, a small community a few miles north of New Haven. Cattle dealer in Kansas in 1880. In mid-1880s he was back in Connecticut where he began his correspondence with officers and crew of the *Monitor*. Later lived in New Haven where he was a book keeper for a trust company and a notary public. In 1900 he donated his letters and memorabilia pertaining to the *Monitor* to New York Public Library. Died in New Haven.

Plant, Helen (1841-1918) – Keeler's maternal first cousin. Born in Utica, NY, daughter of Keeler's uncle James Plant. Married in 1866 and had one son. Lived in Ottawa, IL where she died.

Pratt, Oscar H. (~1820-1863) – Steamboat captain in La Salle, IL. In 1840s and 1850s he captained passenger steamers between La Salle and St. Louis, MO. Appointed second master in Western Gunboat Flotilla after start of Civil War. Served on ironclad USS *Cincinnati* during Battle of Fort Henry in February 1862. *Cincinnati* was struck 31 times by rebel artillery and Pratt's leg was shattered by a spent musket ball. Promoted to acting master in October

Biographical Notes

1862. Died on board receiving ship *New National* in Cairo, IL in December 1863, leaving behind his wife and three young children.

Queen, Walter W. (1824-1893) – Born in Washington, DC. Appointed midshipman in Navy in 1841. Entered Naval School in 1845. Served on USS *Cumberland* during Mexican-American War. Dismissed in 1848 for fighting a dual. Reinstated in 1853. Promoted to lieutenant in 1855. Commanded a division of David Porter's mortar flotilla in attack on forts guarding New Orleans, LA in April 1862; received high praise and the Thanks of Congress. Promoted to lieutenant commander in July 1862. Commanded *Florida* from early September 1863 to October 27, 1863. Commanded USS *Wyalusing* from November 1863 to May 1864. Ordnance duty for remainder of the war. Retired as rear admiral in 1886. Died in Washington, DC. Reputed to have been one of the Navy's richest men, a claim supported by $250,000 estate left by his wife when she died.

Rich, Charles E. (1835-1880) – Born in Saco, ME. Ordinary seaman in Navy from 1859-61. Appointed acting master's mate in January 1862 and assigned to USS *Moose*. Promoted to acting ensign in April 1863. Served on *Florida* from October 1863 to September 1864. Subsequently served on USS *Eutaw* and USS *Constellation*. Honorably discharged in October 1866. Ship captain in Portsmouth, VA until 1873 when he joined regular navy as a boatswain. Died in Brooklyn, NY.

Rockwell, John (1829-1909) – Born in Savannah, GA. Grew up in Norwich, CT. Youngest son of wealthy land developer and banker Charles Rockwell from Norwich, who along with his brother John, founded the Rockwell Land Company in 1836 with the purpose of developing land in La Salle County, IL. Graduated from Yale College in 1849. Served seven years in U.S. Coast Survey charting Atlantic and Pacific coasts. Moved to Illinois in 1850s, first to Chicago and then to La Salle where he worked for the Bank of LaSalle founded by his father and uncle in 1859. Married Anne Randall from Cortland, NY in 1860. From 1862-69 he was involved in coal mining in La Salle for the Chicago Coal Company, as well as managing the large tracts of land belonging to the family. Later moved to Tarrytown, NY, where he and his wife lived with his older brother Charles who had retired from business to devote his time to astronomy. Moved to California in 1901. Died in Santa Barbara, CA.

Selfridge, Thomas O. (1836-1924) – Born in Charlestown, MA, son of a Navy officer. Graduated from Naval Academy in 1853. Promoted to lieutenant in 1860. Commanded forward gun battery on USS *Cumberland* on first day of Battle of Hampton Roads on March 8, 1862. Commanded *Monitor* from March 10-12, 1862. Transferred to Mississippi Squadron and commanded ironclad USS *Cairo*, which was blown up by a mine on Yazoo River in December 1862. Five months later took part in Siege of Vicksburg, and commanded several other gunboats on the Mississippi. Transferred east in 1864 and joined blockade off Wilmington, NC. Participated in bombardment of Fort Fisher, NC and commanded a division of sailors and marines in the ground assault on the fort in January 1865. Retired as rear-admiral in 1898. Died in Washington, DC.

Stevens, Thomas H. (1819-1896) – Born in Middletown, CT, son of a naval hero of War of 1812. Entered Navy as midshipman in 1836. Graduated from Naval School in Philadelphia, PA in 1842. Promoted to lieutenant in 1849. Participated in attack on Port Royal, SC in November 1861. In April 1862 transferred to James River, where he commanded USS *Maratanza*. Promoted to commander in July 1862. Commanded *Monitor* from August 16, 1862 to September 10, 1862. Subsequently commanded USS *Sonoma* in Caribbean. Transferred to South Atlantic Blockade Squadron and led the failed nighttime raid on Fort Sumter, SC on September 8, 1863. Commanded monitor USS *Winnebego* in bombardment of Fort Morgan, AL during Battle of Mobile Bay in August 1864 and USS *Oneida* in blockade off Galveston, TX. Retired as rear-admiral in 1881. Died in Rockville, MD.

Stodder, Louis N. (1837-1911) – Born in Boston, MA, son of a tailor. Master mariner before Civil War. Appointed acting master in December 1861. Assigned to *Monitor* in January 1862. Stationed in turret during fight with *Virginia*. Commended by commanding officer John Bankhead for his actions during sinking of *Monitor*. Promoted to acting volunteer lieutenant in January 1863. Commanded four other vessels for remainder of the war. Honorably discharged November 1865. Appointed to regular navy in 1866, rising to rank of captain. Last command was to British Columbia to quell an Indian uprising in 1883. Supervised anchorage at Port of New York from 1892 to 1901. Died in Brooklyn, NY.

Vose, Edwin H. (1838-1909) – Born in Robbinston, ME, son of a ship builder. Studied medicine at Bowdoin College in Brunswick, ME in early 1860s. Medical student in Boston, MA where he enlisted. Appointed acting assistant surgeon in early December 1863. Served on *Florida* from mid-December 1863 to early April 1864 when he resigned. Physician in Gosham, ME and Calais, ME after the war. Died in Calais.

Wagstaff, Robert M. (1835-1898) – Born in Buffalo, NY, son of a Great Lakes steamer captain. Began his career as a salt water seaman at age of seven and was a sailor on first boat carrying gold seekers around Cape Horn in 1849. Appointed acting master's mate in December 1861. Served on David Porter's mortar fleet and participated in attacks on forts guarding New Orleans, LA in April 1862. Promoted to acting ensign in January 1863. Served on *Florida* from March to October 1863. Subsequently served on three more vessels, one being USS *Tulip*, which blew up on Potomac River, killing all but 8 of its crew; he escaped without serious injury. Honorably discharged in May

BIOGRAPHICAL NOTES

1867. Settled in Detroit, MI, where he was a Great Lakes steamer captain and was later in charge of a harbor of refuge on Lake Huron. Died in Detroit.

Washburn, Cornelius (1829-1867) – Born in Ghent, NY. Enlisted in Navy as a seaman in 1855. Appointed master's mate in January 1862. Served on USS *Commodore Barney* and praised for good shooting during Battle of Roanoke Island, NC in February 1862. Promoted to acting ensign in December 1862. Assigned to *Florida* in early November 1863. In late November 1863 he sent a letter of resignation to Navy Secretary Welles stating that he did not feel competent to fulfill the requirements of the position because he knew "nothing of navigation." At the bottom of the letter *Florida*'s commanding officer Peirce Crosby wrote "Mr. Washburn is a good seaman and faithful officer, and I would be sorry to lose his services."* His resignation was not approved. Detached from *Florida* in late October 1864. Served on USS *State of Georgia* for remainder of the war. Honorably discharged December 1865. Died in Brooklyn, NY.

Watrous, George Henry (1829-1889) – Keeler's brother-in-law. Born in Bridgewater, PA. Grew up on a farm in Conklin, NY. Graduated from Yale College in 1853 and Yale Law School in 1855. Lived in New Haven, CT. Married Harriet Dutton in 1857. Practiced law with Henry Dutton from 1857-61. Counsel for New York, New Haven and Hartford Railroad Company and later its president. Also carried on a busy private law practice, occasionally taking on high-profile murder cases as counsel for the defense. Republican. Married his niece Lilly Graves after Hattie's death in 1873. Died in New Haven.

Watrous, Harriet Joy (1833-1873) – Keeler's sister-in-law (Anna's sister). Born in Newtown, CT. Married George Watrous in 1857. Lived in New Haven, CT. Six children, of which only three lived to adulthood: George Dutton (1858-1940) who became a respected New Haven lawyer and Yale law professor, Elizabeth Eliot (1861-1900) who married a Yale law professor, and Charles Ansel (1863-1899) who became a stock broker and newspaper editor in New York City. Died in New Haven.

Webber, John J. N. (1829-1909) – Born in Brooklyn, NY, son of a ship master. Commenced sea-faring life at age of three when his father took him on a voyage to China. At seventeen he was an officer on an opium smuggling brig. Three years later he owned a schooner. Enlisted in Navy in December 1861. Appointed acting master in late December 1861. Assigned to *Monitor* by February 9, 1862 when Keeler first mentioned him. In charge of powder division during fight with *Virginia*. Transferred to US Brig *Braziliera* shortly after Battle of Hampton Roads, serving as executive officer. Court-martialed

---

* Navy Officers' Letters 1802-1884, NARA M148.

and dismissed from Navy in June 1863. Returned to Brooklyn, where he was a ship master. Died at Sailors' Snug Harbor on Staten Island, NY.

Weeks, Grenville M. (1837-1919) – Born in New York City, son of a physician. Graduated from New York University Medical College in 1861. Appointed acting assistant surgeon in July 1862. Served on USS *Valley City* and USS *Brandywine* before joining *Monitor* in early November 1862. Only man injured when *Monitor* sank: right hand crushed by rescue boat and shoulder dislocated, rendering his arm permanently lame. Served at own request on *Florida* from March to August 1863 when sent home due to incompetence. Promoted by Lincoln and appointed consulting surgeon. Brigade surgeon and acting medical director in Department of Florida at end of the war. Physician in New York City in 1870s. Married three times, divorced twice. Died in Kearney, NJ. A wonderful vignette about him appears in *The New York Times* on June 16, 1916. The article describes how in 1916 he went to the White House to see President Woodrow Wilson about the design for a building. Cutting a striking appearance, he was dressed in "his Grand Army uniform . . . with his flowing white hair and beard. One arm – the right – hung limp and almost useless." The article goes on to describe his previous visit to the White House more than fifty years earlier to see President Lincoln when he was gruffly told by an officer to wait at the end of the line. On overhearing this, Lincoln told the officer, "Hereafter, whether the caller is an officer or private, Major, be a gentleman," and then turned to Weeks and said, "You are wounded, sir. There's a place for you, however, if you can use your head."

Williams, Peter (~1831- after 1867) – Born in Norway. Enlisted as seaman in January 1862. Transferred to *Monitor* on March 6, 1862, serving as quartermaster. Steered vessel during fight with *Virginia*; awarded Medal of Honor for his actions. Promoted to acting master's mate in late March 1862. Commended for his actions during sinking of *Monitor* by commanding officer John Bankhead. Promoted to acting ensign in January 1863. Served on *Florida* from March 1863 to mid 1865. Executive officer and later commanding officer of USS *Clematis*. Honorably discharged in November 1867.

Worden, John L. (1818-1897) – Born in Mount Pleasant, NY. Appointed midshipman in Navy at age of 15. Promoted to lieutenant in 1846. One week before start of Civil War he carried secret orders to fleet at Pensacola, FL to reinforce Fort Pickens. Arrested on way home and imprisoned for seven months in Montgomery, AL. After release assigned to New York Navy Yard. Assumed command of *Monitor* on January 16, 1862. Blinded during Battle of Hampton Roads on March 9, 1862 when one of *Virginia*'s shells exploded outside pilot house. Recovered from wounds in Washington, DC. Visited by Lincoln during recovery. Promoted to commander in July 1862. Received the Thanks of Congress for gallant conduct in fight with *Virginia*. Promoted to captain in February 1863. Commanded USS *Montauk* in failed ironclad attack on Charleston, SC in April 1863. Transferred to Washington, DC where he was advisor for new monitors for remainder of the war. Retired as rear-admiral in 1886. Died in Washington, DC.

Ziegler, John Q. A. (1828-1885) – Born in Philadelphia, PA, son of a coal merchant. Appointed acting first assistant engineer in February 1862 and assigned to *Florida*. Commanded a division of sailors that took possession of a plantation near St. Simon Sound, GA in July 1862. Appointed acting chief engineer in February 1863. Detached from *Florida* in December 1863 due to illness. Superintended completion of ironclad monitor USS *Monadnock* in Boston, MA. Served as chief engineer on *Monadnock* from October 1864 to June 1866, participating in both attacks on Fort Fisher, NC and making an experimental trip in the ironclad from New York to California via Cape Horn in late 1865. Ordered to USS *Monongahela* in February 1867. Spent four months re-launching *Monongahela* after it had been washed by a tsunami into the town of Frederiksted on St. Croix Island in the Caribbean in November 1867. Appointed chief engineer in regular navy in June 1868. Died in Philadelphia, where he was superintending re-construction of a monitor.

Selected Bibliography

Browning, Robert M., Jr., *From Cape Charles to Cape Fear: The North Atlantic Blockading Squadron during the Civil War*, University of Alabama Press, Tuscaloosa, AL, 1993.

Davis, William C., *Duel Between the First Ironclads*, Louisiana State University Press, Baton Rouge, LA, 1975.

Dougherty, Kevin, *The Peninsula Campaign of 1862: A Military Analysis*, University Press of Mississippi, Jackson, MS, 2010.

Frank H. Pierce papers relating to the U.S.S. *Monitor*. Manuscripts and Archives Division. The New York Public Library. Astor, Lenox, and Tilden Foundations.

Genealogy of the Dutton Family of Pennsylvania, compiled by Gilbert Cope, West Chester, PA, 1871 (appendix entitled "The Duttons of Connecticut").

Hamersley, Lewis R., *The Records of Living Officers of the U.S. Navy and Marine Corps*, L. R. Hamersley and Company, New York, NY, 1898.

Keeler, William Frederick, *Aboard the USS Monitor: 1862, The Letters of Acting Paymaster William Frederick Keeler, U.S. Navy, to his Wife, Anna*, ed. Robert W. Daly, Annapolis, MD, U.S. Naval Institute Press, 1964.

Keeler, William Frederick, *Aboard the USS Florida: 1863-1865, The Letters of Paymaster William Frederick Keeler, U.S. Navy, to his Wife, Anna*, ed. Robert W. Daly, Annapolis, MD, U.S. Naval Institute Press, 1968.

Keeler, William F., *Mayport Journal* (1878-86), Special Collections and Archives, University Library, Mary Lea Shane Archives of Lick Observatory, University of California at Santa Cruz, Santa Cruz, CA.

Keeler Family: Ralph Keeler of Norwalk, CT, and Some of his Descendants, compiled by Wesley B. Keeler, Gateway Press, Baltimore, MD, 1985.

McPherson, James M., *Battle Cry of Freedom: The Civil War Era*, Oxford University Press, New York, NY, 1988.

McPherson, James M., *War on the Waters: The Union and Confederate Navies, 1861–1865*, University of North Carolina Press, Chapel Hill, NC, 2012.

Mindell, David A., *War, Technology, and Experience aboard the USS Monitor*, The Johns Hopkins University Press, Baltimore, MD, 2000.

Navy Survivors' Certificates (Case Files of Approved Pension Applications of Civil War and Later Navy Veterans, 1861–1910), National Archives and Records Administration M1469.

Selected Bibliography

Navy Widows' Certificates (Approved pension applications of widows and other dependents of U.S. Navy veterans, 1861–1910), National Archives and Records Administration M1279.

Quarstein, John A., *The Monitor Boys: The Crew of the Union's First Ironclad*, The History Press, Charleston, SC, 2011.

Quarstein, John A., *The CSS Virginia: Sink Before Surrender*, The History Press, Charleston, SC, 2012.

Symonds, Craig L., *The Civil War at Sea*, Oxford University Press, New York, NY, 2012.

Tucker, Spencer C., *Blue and Gray Navies: The Civil War Afloat*, Naval Institute Press, Annapolis, MD, 2006.

U.S. Department of the Navy, *Registers of the Commissioned, Warrant and Volunteer Officers of the United States Navy, Including Officers of the Marine Corps and Others*, Washington, DC, Government Printing Office, 1861-65.

U.S. Department of the Navy, *Official Records of the Union and Confederate Navies in the War of the Rebellion*, 30 vols., Washington, DC, Government Printing Office, 1894-1922 (abbreviated ORN in the footnotes).

U.S. War Department, *The War of the Rebellion: A Compilation of the Official Records of the Union and Confederate Armies*, 128 vols., Washington, DC, Government Printing Office, 1880-1902 (abbreviated ORA in the footnotes).

Index

Adams, Orville N. (La Salle resident), 70, 70n, 93, 153, 403, 404; bio. notes on, 601
Adirondack, USS (sloop-of-war): launch of, 31
African-Americans: escaping to freedom on James River, 128, 133, 139, 146-47, 148-49, 151, 152, 212; bringing farm produce to *Monitor*, 137, 139, 146, 151, 154, 166; church goers in Beaufort, 318; in Louisiana, 536-37
African-American troops, 388, 430, 344-45; 1st North Carolina Colored Volunteers, 343-44; at Petersburg, 483, 483n; at Fort Pillow, 531; at Fort Blakely, 531-32, 532n
Ainsworth, Frederick S. (Surg., USA), 358
Alabama, CSS (commerce raider), 296, 362, 363; sinking of, 483
Alabama, USS (gunboat), 514
Albemarle, CSS (ironclad ram), 564, 564n, 570
Alligator, USS (submarine), 164, 164n
Almy, John J. (Cmdr., USN): Keeler's conversation with, 21
Andrew, John A. (Massachusetts Governor), 369; visits *Monitor*, 248
Annapolis, MD: *Florida* at, 558
Anna Reynolds (merchant vessel), 8, 9, 28, 81
Antietam, battle of, 239, 239n, 253, 257, 352
Appomattox Manor, VA (Eppes' house), 136, 171, 211-12, 223, 229
Appomattox River, VA, 127, 136, 142, 212, 222; gunboat expedition up, 163, 165, 166-69, 229; description of, 167
Aquia Creek, VA, 246, 262
Ariadne, HMS (frigate), 278, 279-80
Aries, USS (gunboat), 413
Army of the James: at Fort Monroe, 459, 463; description of camp near Portsmouth, 459, 460; advance on Richmond via City Point, 464; cuts railroad communication south of Richmond, 464, 471; gunboats clear mines for, 465, 465n
Army of the Potomac: arrival at Fort Monroe, 61, 63, 66-67, 68, 74; retreat to Harrison's Landing, 169, 173-75, 179; at Harrison's Landing, 177, 178, 182-87, 195; sick and wounded soldiers, 174-76,

182, 183, 184-85, 186, 188-89, 196, 198-99, 236; withdrawal from Virginia Peninsula, 207, 210
Army of Virginia, 226, 227; and Gen. Pope, 177, 196, 207
Arnold, Samuel. B. (conspirator): prisoner on board *Florida*, 545; description of, 547; employment at Fort Jefferson, 549
Aroostook, USS (gunboat), 113, 126; in attack on Fort Darling, 129, 132
Aspinwall, 517; description of, 563-64
Atlanta, CSS (ironclad ram): capture of, 347, 347n, 349; description of, 556
Atlanta, GA: imminent fall of, 491
Atwater, Norman K. (Act. Ens., USN): on *Monitor*, 253, 261; bio. notes on, 601

Bankhead, John P. (Cmdr., USN), 239, 247, 267, 268, 274-75, 292, 307, 313, 314, 316, 334, 335, 336, 337, 340, 341, 342, 355, 372, 401, 406, 413, 422; assigned to *Monitor*, 234; description of, 236, 237, 240, 270, 275-76, 299, 299n, 301, 338, 359, 364, 378, 395, 579; aggressiveness of, 237, 333, 338; and final voyage of *Monitor*, 250, 276, 283, 284, 285, assigned to *Florida*, 288; drills crew, 299; inspects crew, 301; invites Keeler to dinner, 301; illness of, 347, 358, 359, 360, 395; bio. notes on, 601
Banks, Gardner (Capt., USA), 103, 103n, 104
Banks, Nathaniel P. (Maj. Gen., USA), 36, 64, 102, 103, 158; at Winchester, 142; visits *Monitor*, 248; departure of expedition of, 261, 262, 265, 269
Banshee (blockade runner), 338
Barnes, James (Brig. Gen., USA), 418
Baxley, Catherine V. (Confederate spy), 145, 146
Beaufort, NC: *Florida* at, 316-17, 355-58, 392-93, 393-95, 404-5, 409-13, 429-31, 438-44, 471-72, 482-88; description of, 317-20; Hammond Hospital at, 318, 318n, 355, 356, 358, 478; churches in, 318, 430, 471; description of inhabitants of, 318; Union cemetery at, 319; night in a hotel at, 345-46; description of environs, 356-57, 411-12, 432-33, 478-

627

INDEX

79, 480, 486-88; refugees arriving at, 420, 441, 472-73; Federal troops arriving at, 431; hospital garden at, 478, 485; business opportunities in, 490

Beaufort, SC: *Florida* at, 294, 548; description of town and environs, 548

Beauregard, Pierre G. T. (Gen., CSA), 85, 85n, 148, 174

Beecher, Henry Ward (minister), 67

Beecher, James C. (Chaplain, USA), 67, 67n, 84, 86; as Capt., 195, 205; as Col., 343-44, 345; bio. notes on, 601-2

Bell, Charles H. (Act. Rear Adm., USN), 540, 559, 561

Benham, Henry W. (Brig. Gen., USA): visits *Monitor*, 67

Benjamin, Judah P. (Confederate Secretary of War), 151; plantation of, 537

Ben Morgan, USS (ordnance storeship), 570

Bennett, Alonzo (Ordinary Seaman, USN): buried at sea, 355, 355n

Bennett, William C. (Act. Ens., USN), 269, 326, 360; bio. notes on, 602

Benton, William D. (Private, CSA/USA): military execution of, 374-75, 375n

Bermuda, 288

Bermuda Hundred, VA, 212

Biddle, Ellen (John McGowan's sister), 377, 377n, 378, 379, 381, 382, 383, 384, 386, 500

Birge, Henry W. (Brevet Maj. Gen., USA), 548

Black, William (captain of blockade runner), 335, 337

Blair, Frank P. (U.S. Congressman): visits *Monitor*, 105; at Harrison's Landing, 189

Blake, George S. (Commo., USN), 558

Blakeman, Birdsey (Keeler's friend in Brooklyn), 23; bio. notes on, 602

blockade of Wilmington: system of, 287, 289; difficulties in maintaining, 289, 307, 314, 323-24, 348, 363, 367, 370, 469, 483, 493; monotony of, 297-98, 304, 406; nighttime on, 298, 311-12, 361-62, 416-17; dangers of, 302, 323, 367, 395, 493; daytime on, 312-14, 324, 444; supply vessels for, 325, 359; fleet dispersed after fall of Fort Fisher, 514

blockade runners: description of, 267, 288; running the blockade, 267, 288-89, 308, 416, 444; signal system for, 311, 324; cargoes of, 311, 324, 335-36, 338, 339, 435, 436, 439-40, 443, 444, 476;

financing of, 337; in Halifax, 500, 502, 503

Bogue Inlet, NC, 439, 466

Bogue Sound, NC, 413

Boston, MA: *Florida* at, 505

Bowen, John J. (Capt., USA), 360-61, 360n

Bowen, William S. (Act. Asst. Surg., USN), 561-62, 562n

Brady, Matthew (photographer), 577

Bragg, Braxton (Gen., CSA), 409

Brandon Estate, VA, 126

Brandywine, USS (storeship), 84, 277, 350; remains of, 379, 570

Breck, Joseph B. (Act. Mstr., USN), 367, 367n

Bridgeport, CT: Keeler lived in, 7-8, 11

Brooklyn, NY: Keeler lived in, 6, 580

Brooks, Robert F. (Act. Asst. Surg., USN), 457, 461, 465, 485; assigned to *Florida*, 452; description of, 452, 466; on *St. Lawrence*, 570; bio. notes on, 602

Brown, David "Dave" (Keeler's brother-in-law), 11, 571, 572; bio. notes on, 602-3

Brown, Frances "Fannie" or "Fan" E. (Keeler's sister), 11, 572; birth of, 7; death of daughter of, 474; bio. notes on, 603

Brown, Hamilton "Ham" (Dave's brother), 28, 152, 217, 280, 482

Brown, James C. (La Salle physician), 208, 243

Brown, John (Dave's brother), 217, 219, 233, 244, 247, 482

Brown, Mary (Dave's sister), 75, 109

Brownlow, William G. "Parson" (newspaper editor), 99, 99n, 378, 378n

Brush, George J. (Keeler's cousin), 38

Brush, Jarvis "Uncle B." or "Uncle Brush" (Keeler's uncle), 21; bio. notes on, 603

Brush, Joseph B. (Keeler's cousin), 25, 29, 38

Brush, Sarah "Aunt B." or "Aunt Brush" (Keeler's aunt), 21

Bry, Francis M. (La Salle physician), 97, 243, 252

Buchanan, Franklin (Flag Officer, CSN), 69, 69n, 106

Buchanan, McKean (Paymaster, USN), 69, 69n

Budd, William (Act. Vol. Lt. Cmdr., USN), 514, 543, 544; description of, 512, 513, 522, 531, 533, 538, 550, 558; assumes command of *Florida*, 512; chases CSS

INDEX

Webb, 526, 527; invites Keeler to dinner, 538; drinking sprees of, 550, 551, 558; reprimanded for drinking, 558-59; forced to resign, 559, 560; bio. notes on, 603-4
Buell, Don Carlos (Maj. Gen., USA), 177
Bull Run, 1st battle of, 199
Bull Run, 2nd battle of, 352
Burnside, Ambrose E. (Maj. Gen., USA), 90, 202, 257, 262, 377; in North Carolina, 69, 92, 105, 316, 321, 322; in Maryland, 236; at Fredericksburg, 256, 260, 269, 270, 272-73
Bursley, Ira (Act. Mstr., USN): temporarily commands *Florida*, 559; resignation of, 561; bio. notes on, 604
Burton, Rachel (Keeler's aunt), 21, 376n
Butler, Benjamin F. (Maj. Gen., USA), 425, 454; book about, 431-32, 457; at City Point, 464, 471; ruse of landing troops at Yorktown, 464, 464n
Byers, James (rebel tug captain), 584

Cairo, USS (ironclad), 279
Cairo, IL, 360, 452
California Gold Rush, 8-11
Calypso (blockade runner), 482; captured by *Florida*, 331-37, 338, 339, 436, 346; sale of, 353, 354; as Union gunboat, 391
Cambridge, USS (gunboat), 434; destroys *Dee*, 440; attempts to pull *Fanny & Jenny* offshore, 443
Campbell, Albert B. (2nd Asst. Engr., USN): on *Monitor*, 94, 191, 275; description of, 275; bio. notes on, 604
Campbell, Alexander (La Salle politician), 206, 220, 234, 244, 280; bio. notes on, 604
Camp Hamilton, VA, 380; description of, 103-4
Cannon, Legrand B. (Col., USA), 55, 101, 506, 594; visits *Monitor*, 57, 67; bio. notes on, 604-5
Cape Charles, VA, 48
Cape Fear, NC, 370, 427
Cape Fear River, NC, 298, 324, 483, 514, 585
Cape Hatteras, NC, 282, 293, 393, 421, 513, 538, 578
Cape Henry, VA, 48, 295, 371
Cape Horn, 9, 89, 282, 582
Cape Lookout, NC, 293

Cape Sable, NS, 504
Carr, Henry P. (Act. Mstr, USN), 320, 320n
Carter, Henry H. (Capt., USA): death of, 82, 82n
Carter, Hill (James River planter; Col., CSA), 139, 189; escaped slaves of, 133, 146-47, 212; plantation of (Shirley), 146, 170, 174, 176, 188, 198; description of, 170-71, 189; bio. notes on, 605
Carter, Samuel B. (Keeler's friend from La Salle), 32, 58, 153, 261, 574, 596; bio. notes on, 605
Carter, Siah Hulett (1st Class Boy, USN): escapes slavery, 133, 133n; description of, 212; bio. notes on, 605
Case, A. Ludlow (Capt., USN), 364, 365
Cavendish, Lord Edward (Lt., British Army): visits *Monitor*, 82
Cecil, Lord Adelpert Percy (Ens., British Army): visits *Monitor*, 82
Cedar Mountain, battle of: Melzar Dutton killed at, 209n, 217
Ceres (blockade runner), 413
Chandler, Zachariah (U.S. Senator), 203
Chapin, Julius F. (La Salle resident), 29, 454, 491; wife (Mary) of, 61; bio. notes on, 605
Chapin, William E. (Private, USA), 316, 316n, 327, 353, 355, 356, 358, 394, 404, 413; in charge of Hammond Hospital garden, 478-79, 485; dines on board *Florida*, 488; bio. notes on, 606
Charleston, SC: price of commodities in, 147-48; *Florida* off of, 293; failed ironclad attack on, 294, 295, 303, 303n, 304, 308; Union army attempts to capture, 347, 349, 354, 370, 379, 389; sinking of *Weehawken* off of, 413
Chase, Salmon P. (U.S. Secretary of the Treasury): 5-day visit to Fort Monroe, 112, 113, 120, 125; visits *Monitor*, 112
Chenery, Charles E. (Asst. Paymaster, USN), 569, 569n
Cherokee, USS (gunboat), 476
Chesapeake Bay, 245, 295, 513
Chickahominy River, VA, 170, 172, 173, 177, 189, 206; swamps on, 202, 203, 459
Chocura, USS (gunboat), 337, 353, 355
Cimarron, USS (gunboat), 392
City Point, VA: description of, 127, 135, 137, 162, 171; "shooting scrape" at, 135-36, 157; refugees from, 136-37, 146-47, 211; rebel artillery at, 158, 203;

629

INDEX

planned firing of, 165, 167; wounded soldiers at, 196; as base of military operations, 202, 241, 263, 464, 465

Clark, Ambrose J. (Asst. Paymaster, USN), 429

Clematis, USS (gunboat), 532; Keeler visits Samuel Crafts on, 539

Coates, James H. (Capt., USA), 29, 29n, 261, 279; bio. notes on, 606

Cockpit Point, VA, 246

Collins, William H. (Chaplain, USA), 195, 195n; as Capt., 219-20, 225, 261; bio. notes on, 606

Colorado, USS (frigate), 277, 278

Columbia, CSS (ironclad ram), 570

Commodore Jones, USS (gunboat): blown up by torpedo, 465

Congress, USS (sailing frigate), 69; attacked by *Virginia*, 41-42; explosion of, 53; remains of, 229, 236, 272, 570

Cook, Burton C. (La Salle County politician), 244

Cook, Robert (1st Class Boy, USN): description of, 242-43

Corcoran, Michael (Col., USA): expected exchange of, 145, 145n; release of, 216; as Brig. Gen., 252; brigade of, 252, 259, 260, 262, 271, 274, 275; visits *Monitor*, 274-75; description of wife of, 274-75

Cornubia (blockade runner), 402

Coxetter, Louis M. (captain of blockade runner), 443, 443n

Cozzens, Frederick S. (author): visits *Monitor*, 94

Crafts, Samuel P. (Act. Ens., USN), 298, 303, 327, 333, 372, 378, 389, 514, 516; Keeler first meets, 230, 231, 232; description of, 295, 366, 382; assigned to *Florida*, 295; in charge of *Florida*'s 100-lb gun, 299, 312; as prize master on *Calypso*, 337, 339, 346; promoted to Act. Mstr., 369; temporarily suspended from duty, 395, 400; detached from *Florida*, 403, 405; as executive officer on *Shokokon*, 413, 465; in command of *Clematis*, 532, 539; bio. notes on, 606-7

Crafts, Sarah A. (Samuel's wife), 291, 306, 372, 376, 377-78, 380, 387, 452, 514, 516, 532; Keeler's dislike of, 379, 381-82, 385-86

Crane, John L. (Seaman, USN): lost overboard, 406, 406n

Craney Island, VA: description of rebel batteries on, 124, 125; remains of *Virginia* at, 193

Crosby, Hiram H. (Maj. USA), 375, 375n

Crosby, Pierce (Cmdr., USN), 409, 418, 419, 420; assumes command of *Florida*, 402; description of, 403, 405, 414, 422; invites Keeler to dinner, 421-22; captures and destroys *Wild Dayrell*, *Fanny & Jenny* and *Emily*, 434, 435, 437, 439, 441, 442; destroys *Nutfield*, 439; detached from *Florida*, 447; bio. notes on, 607

Crowninshield, William W. (Act. Ens., USN), 367, 367n

Cumberland (blockade runner), 444

Cumberland, USS (sailing frigate), 55, 62, 106, 272, 279; sunk by *Virginia*, 41, 42, 51; bravery of men on, 72-73; sunken remains of, 223, 236

Currituck, USS (gunboat): accompanies *Monitor* to Hampton Roads, 45

Cushing, Edmund H. (Act. Asst. Paymaster, USN), 359-60, 359n

Cushing, William B. (Lt., USN), 422; daring exploits of, 447-48, 447n, 483, 564n; as Lt. Cmdr., 564, 570

Dacotah, USS (gunboat), 120, 125, 189, 488; in attack on Sewell's Point batteries, 115; smallpox on, 391; officer on drowns, 477

Dahlgren, John A. (Capt., USN), 108

Dale, USS (ordnance storeship), 570

Dancing Point, VA, 172, 206

Daniel Webster, USSC (hospital ship), 100

Darrow, Sidney (La Salle resident), 153

Davids, Garret B. (machinist at Old Point), 228, 276

Davids, Mary (Garret's wife): a sundering of Southern ties, 228

Davidson, Hunter (Lt., CSN): memorandum book of, 180, 587; wife of, 180-81, 181n

Davis, Jefferson (President, Confederate States), 214, 225, 382; as fugitive, 531; in petticoats, 540; as prisoner, 547

Day, David T. (Elizabeth Keeler's husband), 588, 589

Day's Point, VA, 125, 223

Daylight, USS (gunboat), 313

Index

de Choiseul, Count Joseph (French consul), 147, 147n
Dee (blockade runner): run ashore and burned, 440, 441, 444
de Joinville, Prince, 76; visits *Monitor*, 54, 77; article defending McClellan by, 255, 267, 268
Delaware Breakwater, 292, 554
Delaware River: description of, 554-55
Delaware, USS (gunboat), 174, 175, 403
Denbigh (blockade runner): mob plunders, 536
deserters from Confederate army, 59, 83, 141, 194, 212, 417, 433
De Soto, USS (gunboat), 444
Devil's Reach, VA, 127, 156, 158, 169
Dikeman, Fanny (Anna Keeler's cousin), 102, 103, 517
Dickey, Theophilus Lyle (Col., USA), 152
Dix, John A. (Maj. Gen., USA), 191, 530, 531; visits *Monitor*, 270; description of, 271
Dodd, Levi A. (Brig. Gen., USA): on *Florida* on trip to Dry Tortugas, 545, 547; description of, 550, 551
Douglas, Stephen A. (U.S. Senator), 368
Douglass, Richard H. (Paymaster, USN), 549
Dove, Benjamin M. (Cmdr., USN), 476
Drewry's Bluff batteries. *See* Fort Darling.
Dry Tortugas, FL: *Florida*'s covert mission to, 544-50; description of, 549
Duane, Martin (Act. Asst. Paymaster, USN), 538
Dunham, Josiah F. (Act. Asst. Paymaster, USN), 445, 445n, 488
Du Pont, Samuel F. (Rear Adm., USN), 548
Durham, Henry (La Salle minister), 363, 363n, 398, 451, 469, 479, 480, 481; bio. notes on, 607
Durkee, Charles (Lt. Col., USA): visits *Monitor*, 194, 194n
Durst, William (Coal Heaver, USN): on *Monitor*, 578, 580
Duryea, Hiram (Lt. Col., USA), 183; description of regiment of, 76
Dutton, Anna E. *See* Anna E. Keeler.
Dutton, Arthur H. (Col., USA), 463, 470; description of, 376, 391, 392, 425; as passenger on *Florida*, 391; seasickness of, 392, 408; bio. notes on, 607
Dutton, Clarence E. (Capt., USA), 463, 463n, 470

Dutton, Eliza E. (Keeler's mother-in-law), 13; anxiety about Melzar, 36; grief over Melzar's death, 218, 227; death of, 574; bio. notes on, 607-8
Dutton, George W. (Capt., USA): on *Florida* on trip to Dry Tortugas, 547, 548; description of, 551, 551n
Dutton, Henrietta "Nettie" (Anna Keeler's cousin), 22
Dutton, Harriet J. *See* Harriet J. Watrous.
Dutton, Henry (Keeler's father-in-law): legal and political career of, 8; visits *Monitor* at Greenpoint Shipyard, 26, 28, 29, 30; grief over Melzar's death, 218, 227; fails to recover Melzar's remains, 224; "abused" for opinion letter about slavery, 237-38, 237n; death of, 571; bio. notes on, 608
Dutton, Henry Melzar (Keeler's brother-in-law; Lt., USA), 8, 13, 15, 98, 157, 205, 376, 574-75; in Shenandoah Valley, 36, 36n, 64, 64n; at 1st battle of Winchester, 142, 142n, 158, 158n; killed at battle of Cedar Mountain, 209, 209n, 217; news of death of, 218, 224; Keeler offers to recover body of, 224, 227, 232, 236, 236n; bio. notes on, 608-9
Dutton, John (Anna Keeler's cousin), 22n, 201; bio. notes on, 609
Dutton, Mary E. *See* Mary E. Graves.
Dutton, William (Anna Keeler's cousin; Col., USA): sickness and death of, 177, 177n, 201-2; description of, 194; bio. notes on, 609

Early, Jubal A. (Gen., CSA): raid on Washington, 489, 489n
Elizabeth River, VA, 74; rebel defences along, 124
Ellis, David R. (Paymaster's steward, USN): on *Florida*, 295, 295n, 383, 383n; description of, 396-97; resignation of, 447; bio. notes on, 609
Emancipation Proclamation, 243
Emily (blockade runner): beached and destroyed, 441, 442-43; description of, 444
Eppes Island, VA, 205, 212; Keeler procures food from, 211
Eppes, Dr. Richard (James River planter), 136, 136n; escaped slaves of, 148-49, 151; plantation house of (Appomattox

INDEX

Manor), 171, 211-12, 223, 229; description of, 211-12; plantations owned by, 212; bio. notes on, 609
Ericsson, John, 16, 17, 18, 40, 57, 254, 576, 580, 586, 593-94

Fader, David J. (Act. Mstr.'s Mate, USN): on *Florida*, 425, 425n
Fahkee, USS (gunboat), 405, 419
Fair Oaks, battle of, 143, 143n
Fanny and Jenny (blockade runner): destroyed by *Florida*, 441, 442; crew members drowned, 443; General Lee's sword on, 443; description of, 443-44
Farragut, David G. (Rear Adm., USN), 499
Fayetteville, NC, 514, 515
Fearnought, USS (powder vessel), 528
Fessenden, William P. (U.S. Secretary of the Treasury), 492, 492n
Fingal. See CSS *Atlanta*.
flag of truce: description of conferences, 98-99, 138-39, 147, 154; and wife of Confederate officer, 141-42; and rebel privateersmen, 144-45; and Confederate spies, 145-46; and Col. Corcoran, 216
Florida coast: description of, 520, 522
Florida, CSS (commerce raider), 296, 362, 363, 387
Florida, USS: description of, 288; speed of, 288, 402, 418; tows monitor to Beaufort, SC, 292-94; Keeler's stateroom, 292, 294, 295, 513; officers' wardroom, 294, 295, 300, 303, 305, 396; number of officers and crew, 295, 396; seaworthiness of, 295, 365, 393, 402, 409, 411; daily routine on, 298-301, 305; sickness on, 304, 355, 394, 517; officers' meals on, 321, 374, 386, 414, 419, 471, 504, 541; captures *Calypso*, 331-36; captures *Hattie*, 338; struck by lightning, 349; ethnic makeup of crew, 351; at Norfolk Navy Yard for repairs, 372-89, 451-65; cruising outside Frying Pan Shoals, 391-93, 397-402, 404, 405-9; chases *Robert E. Lee*, 399-400; man lost overboard, 406; a chase in heavy seas, 407-8; Christmas dinner on, 419-20; plunders and destroys *Wild Dayrell*, 434-38; destroys *Fanny and Jenny*, 442; destroys *Emily*, 442; defective boilers, 451, 454, 458, 490, 510-11; hull needs repair, 465; defective rudder, 484, 490;

crew at muster, 488-89; at New London, CT, 496-500; at Halifax, 502-4; delivers supplies to North Atlantic Squadron, 510-15; transports wounded to New York, 516-17; delivers supplies, money and men to Gulf Squadrons, 518-29; ordered in haste to New Orleans after Lincoln assassination, 523; chases CSS *Webb*, 527-29; delivers supplies to Gulf Squadrons, 532-37; transports men to New York, 537-38; covert mission transporting Lincoln's assassins to Dry Tortugas, 544-49; tows monitors to Philadelphia, 554; assists in returning Naval Academy to Annapolis, 556-58; transports men to Pacific Squadron, 561-69; toes hulks to New York, 569-70
Flye, William (Act. Vol. Lt., USN), 280, 309, 316, 341, 342, 345, 363, 369, 398, 480; on *Monitor*, 191; detached from *Monitor*, 253; description of, 264; bio. notes on, 609-10
Foote, Andrew H. (Flag Officer, USN), 33, 87, 90
Fort Barrancas, FL, 523
Fort Beauregard, SC: description of, 548
Fort Blakely, AL: massacre of rebel troops at, 531-32
Fort Caswell, NC, 391, 448, 476, 483, 493; description of, 289, 308; flag of truce from, 336, 339; artillery at, 347-48, 365, 366, 370; blockade runners under guns of, 361, 475, 494; new battery being built near, 369
Fort Darling, VA, 120, 127, 127n, 152, 164, 181, 205, 274; gunboat attack on, 129-30, 134, 135, 137, 143, 165, 213, 241, 254, 413, 446; possible second attack on, 217, 219, 220, 222, 238
Fort Delaware, DE, 354, 554
Fort Donelson, TN: news of capture of, 29; casualties at, 35, 35n
Fort Donelson, USS (gunboat): Keeler dines on board of, 488
Fort Fisher, NC, 324, 416, 445, 514, 516, 518, 539; description of, 289, 308; construction of Mound Battery at, 304, 304n; artillery at, 416; construction of road from Wilmington to, 444; plan for capture of, 472; battle of, 509, 514n; effects of bombardment on, 515; wounded from, 516-17

Index

Fort Gaines, GA, 523
Fort Henry, TN: capture of, 25; prisoners at, 203
Fort Jackson, LA, 352; description of, 539
Fort Jackson, USS (gunboat), 468, 483
Fort Jefferson, FL: description of, 549
Fort Lafayette, NY, 64, 554; prisoners for, 529, 530
Fort Macon, NC, 316, 317, 338, 355, 430, 441, 475, 476; news of capture of, 102, 105; description of, 321, 411; Burnside's siege of, 321, 322-23; Keeler has supper at, 411
Fort (or Fortress) Monroe, VA: *Monitor* ordered to remain near, 55; guns at, 56, 74, 81, 88, 89, 278, 380, 381; Gen. Wool's headquarters at, 84, 101, 111; description of, 110-11; brass band at, 119, 191; slaves escaping to, 152; scenic view from, 379-80; prisoners at, 545, 547
Fort Morgan, AL: wartime damage to, 523
Fort Moultrie, SC, 359
Fort Pickens, FL: wartime damage to, 523
Fort Pillow, TN, 531
Fort St. Philip, LA, 352; description of, 539
Fort Sumter, SC, 80, 86, 178, 352, 357, 368, 369, 398; description of, 293; nighttime boat attack on, 373, 373n
Fort Taylor, FL, 520
Fort Trumbull, CT: social activities at, 500-1
Fort Wagner, SC, 369
Fort Walker, SC, 548
Fort Warren, MA, 531
Foster, John G. (Maj. Gen., USA), 308; description of his headquarters at New Bern, 341-42; at Hampton Roads, 385, 389
Fox, Gustavus V. (U.S. Asst. Secretary of the Navy), 16, 31, 56; visits *Monitor*, 52, 55, 57, 79, 105, 107, 110, 593; postwar letters to, 576
Franklin, William B. (Brig. Gen., USA), 102; visits *Monitor*, 101
Franks, James P. (Captain's Clerk, USN): on *Florida*, 391, 391n, 392, 396, 401, 408; bio. notes on, 610
Fredericksburg, VA, 271; battle of, 256, 269, 270, 272-73, 387
Frederickson, George (Act. Mstr.'s Mate, USN): on *Monitor*, 24, 24n, 191; promoted to Ens., 253; bio. notes on, 610

Frying Pan Shoals, 295, 363, 367, 389, 391, 403, 428, 466; description of, 289, 308, 368, 427; a night on, 429

Gager, Edwin V. (Act. Mstr., USN): on *Monitor*, 97, 160, 191, 199; description of, 97; in attack on Sewell's Point batteries, 114; in expedition up Appomattox River, 165; bio. notes on, 610
Galena, USS (ironclad), 92, 102, 110, 112, 114, 117, 126, 127, 128, 136, 154, 183, 203, 373; description of, 17; criticism of, 108, 129, 140-41, 141n; ordered up James River, 110, 113; in attack on Fort Darling, 129-30, 132, 140-41, 413; damage to from attack, 129; carnage on board of after attack, 131; in expedition up Appomattox River, 166, 169, 170; McClellan on board of, 174, 206; at Hampton Roads, 260
Galveston, TX, 518, 532, 534; *Florida* off of, 535-36
General Beauregard (blockade runner), 420
Gettysburg, battle of, 352
Gilbert, William H. (Paymaster's clerk, USN): on *Florida*, 396; description of, 396, 396n
Gillmore, Quincy A. (Maj. Gen., USA), 389, 398; shells Charleston, 370, 379; at Fort Monroe, 463
Glassell, William T. (Lt., CSN): in attack on *New Ironsides*, 389, 389n
Glendale, battle of, 171, 171n
G. O. Bigelow (blockade runner): captured and destroyed by *Mt. Vernon*, 413
Goldsborough, Louis M. (Commo., USN), 61, 62, 107, 118, 143, 144, 150, 266; visits *Monitor*, 56, 64; keeps *Monitor* near Fort Monroe, 71, 82, 82n, 83, 88, 92, 108, 113, 116, 117, 202, 266, 588; nicknames for, 92, 155; opinion of *Galena*, 108, 129; meets with Lincoln, 113, 114, 117, 120, 125, 189; criticism of, 154-55, 588; description of, 155, 163-64, 213; relieved of command of James River Flotilla, 193; as Rear Adm., 213, 223
Goodwin, Hollister E. (Capt., USA), 376
Gorman, Willis A. (Brig. Gen., USA), 193, 202

633

INDEX

Graham, Thomas (La Salle handyman), 78, 260, 303, 305, 328; bio. notes on, 611
Grand Gulf, USS (gunboat): chases *Robert E. Lee*, 399-400
Grant, Ulysses S. (Maj. Gen., USA), 90, 499; news of his victory at Chattanooga, 410; and Overland Campaign, 459, 464, 468, 471; and Petersburg Campaign, 477, 489, 491
Graves, Anna D. (Mary's daughter), 498
Graves, Henry B. (Keeler's brother-in-law), 497, 530
Graves, Mary E. (Keeler's sister-in-law), 8n, 15, 232, 271; terminal illness of, 497-98; bio. notes on, 611
Graves, Mary E. "Lillie" (Mary's daughter), 201, 507, 508, 530
Gray, Mrs, and daughters: passengers on *Calypso*, 334, 336
Greeley, Horace (newspaper editor), 238, 243
Greene, Charles T. (Capt., USA): wounding of, 409
Greene, George S., Jr.: visits *Monitor*, 101, 101n
Greene, George S., Sr. (Brig. Gen., USA), 108, 158; distinguished service at Gettysburg, 352, 352n; wounding of, 409
Greene, Samuel Dana (Lt., USN): description of, 24, 579, 585; on *Monitor*, 37, 39, 65, 129, 132, 150, 160, 191, 251; in fight with *Virginia*, 49-50, 51, 52, 55, 60, 62, 71, 578-79, 581, 582-83, 584, 585; brothers of, 101, 409; father of, 108, 158, 352, 409; in attack on Sewell's Point batteries, 114; in expedition up Appomattox River, 165, 167, 168; assigned to *Florida*, 295; on *Florida*, 298, 299, 333, 351, 359, 367, 369, 388, 395; spat with Keeler, 301; detached from *Florida*, 385; marriage of, 385, 387, 406, 585; on special duty in New York, 404, 406; on *Iroquois*, 414, 452; and drinking, 414; suicide of, 576, 579; bravery of, 579; during sinking of *Monitor*, 579, 580-81; *Century Magazine* article by, 581, 582, 583, 585; gunnery skill of, 582; bio. notes on, 611
Greenhow, Rose O'Neal (Confederate spy), 145, 145n; her conversation with Lt. Jeffers, 145-46; description of, 146
Greenpoint Ship Yard, NY, 17, 28

Gregg, Patrick (Capt., USA): released on parole, 148, 148n
Gregory, Francis H. (Commo., USN): dines on board *Monitor*, 36
Grimes, James W. (U.S. Senator), 204
Gulf coast: description of, 522

Hale, John P. (U.S. Senator): visits *Monitor*, 73, 74
Halifax, NS, 496; blockade runners in, 500, 502, 503; *Florida* at, 502-4
Hall, Richard S. (Beaufort slave owner), 485, 485n
Halleck, Henry W. (Maj. Gen., USA), 179, 239, 263, 264, 270
Hamlin, Hannibal (U.S. Vice President): visits *Monitor*, 73; description of, 73
Hampton, VA: ruins of, 380
Hampton Roads, VA: scenic view of, 66-67, 119, 379-80
Hampton Roads, battle of: March 8, 41-42, 48, 53, 72-73; March 9, 42-43, 45, 48-53, 61, 71-72, 578-79, 581-85, 591, 593; rebel sailor's account of fight with *Monitor*, 193
Hands, Robinson W. (3rd Asst. Engr., USN), 191, 191n
Harkers Island, NC, 411, 432
Harris, J. George (Paymaster, USN), 39, 39n
Harrison's Bar, VA, 174, 176
Harrison's Landing, VA, 194, 198, 239, 269; Army of the Potomac, 177, 178, 182-83, 184-87, 195, 223, 263, 360, 477; Lincoln's visit to, 189, 239
Harrison's Point, VA, 176
Hatch, Ozias M. (Illinois Secretary of State): visits *Monitor*, 248
Hartford, USS (sloop-of-war), 585
Hatteras, USS (gunboat): sinking of, 296, 296n
Hatteras Inlet, NC, 69, 97, 108
Hattie (blockade runner): captured by *Florida*, 338
Havana, Cuba, 521, 529, 530, 532, 556
Haxall's plantation, VA, 188, 188n
Hebe (blockade runner), 367
Hébert, Louis (Brig. Gen., CSA), 447n, 448
Heckman, Charles A. (Brig. Gen., USA), 342; army camp of, 459, 460
Heintzelman, Samuel P. (Brig. Gen., USA): visits *Monitor*, 54
Herring Creek, VA, 177

634

INDEX

Hewett, William N. W. (Capt., RN): commanding officer HMS *Rinaldo*, 53, 58, 594; spurns communication with *Virginia*'s officers, 86, 87

Hibbard, Columbus (3rd Class Boy, USN): on *Florida*, 351, 351n, 369

Hill, George W. (Capt., USA): issues food to destitute Southerners, 386-87

Hilton Head, SC, 293, 459, 547, 548

Hitchcock, Alexander B. (La Salle resident), 68, 69

Hitchcock, Roswell D. (New York City minister), 511, 517

Hollyhock, USS (armed tug): chases CSS *Webb*, 528, 529

Hooker, Joseph (Maj. Gen., USA), 204, 326, 352, 556

Hope, Sir James (Rear Adm., RN), 503, 504

Hough, David L. (Keeler's friend in La Salle): description of, 12; wife of, 12; and Owen Lovejoy, 63, 96; bio. notes on, 611

Howard, Jacob M. (U.S. senator): visits *Monitor*, 112

Howard, Samuel (Act. Mstr., USN): pilot on *Monitor*, 581

Howell, John C. (Cmdr., USN): celebrates Fourth of July, 483

Howland, Eliza N. (Joseph's wife): visits *Monitor*, 100, 100n

Howland, Joseph (Col., USA): visits *Monitor*, 100, 100n

Howquah, USS (gunboat), 421; shells *General Beauregard*, 420

Hubbell, Robert K. (Paymaster's steward, USN): on *Monitor*, 77

Hygeia Hotel, VA, 190; as hospital, 85; torn down, 380

Indianola, USS (ironclad): sunk at high water, 528; re-floated, 528n, 470n

Iron Age, USS (gunboat): run ashore and destroyed by crew, 428

Iroquois, USS (sloop-of-war), 309, 358, 364, 414, 452

Island Belle, USS (armed tug): destroyed by Navy, 169

Island No. 10, TN: news of capture of, 82; battle of, 87

Jackson, Mortimer M. (U.S. Consul in Halifax), 503, 503n

Jackson, Thomas J. "Stonewall" (Maj. Gen., CSA): false news of death of, 174

Jacob Bell, USS (gunboat), 158

James Adger, USS (gunboat), 349, 564

James, Hiram H. (Act. Asst. Surg., USN), 376, 411; assigned to *Florida*, 368; seasickness of, 391, 392, 407, 408, 409; detached from *Florida*, 420, 421; description of, 452; in Mississippi Squadron, 452, 478; bio. notes on, 611-12

James River: description of, 126, 127, 156

James River Flotilla (or Fleet): as separate command, 193; disbanded, 223; frustration with inactivity of, 241

Jamestown, CSS (gunboat), 81, 83, 92, 113, 117; sunk by rebels, 129, 132

Jamestown, VA, 126, 131, 139

Jamestown Church, VA: description of, 126, 223; dead from *Galena* buried at, 132

Jamestown Island, VA: rebel batteries on, 110

Jason, HMS (corvette): at Halifax, 502, 503, 504; Keeler dines on board of, 504

Jeffers, William N. (Lt., USN), 61, 65, 66, 82, 98, 102, 136, 141, 142, 150, 154, 165, 183, 208, 211, 223, 279, 341, 373, 587; assumes command of *Monitor*, 60; description of, 60, 62, 64, 69, 76, 83, 88, 101, 107, 108, 216, 230; dry sense of humor of, 76, 77, 85, 107, 115; meets with Goldsborough, 83, 88, 92, 108, 113, 114, 125; meets with Lincoln, 113, 114, 116, 189; in attack on Sewall's Point batteries, 114-15; criticism of, 117, 163; encounters with escaped slaves, 128, 139, 147, 148, 152, 212; in attack on Fort Darling, 130; rheumatism of, 132, 149, 205; conversation with rebel spies, 145-46; conversation with an overseer, 149; inspects crew, 160-61; brutality of, 175-76, 199; Keeler's contempt for, 199-200, 234, 240, 395, 414; detached from *Monitor*, 209, 216; bio. notes on, 612

Jenkins, David P. (Lt. Col., USA), 261, 261n

John A. Warner (Government boat), 193

Johnson, Andrew (U.S. President), 524, 536

Jones, Catesby ap Roger (Lt., CSN), 576, 584, 588

635

INDEX

Jones, J. Pembroke (Lt., CSN): estate of, 230
Jones, John (Captain's steward, USN), 397, 397n
Joy, Anna (Frank's wife), 26
Joy, Henry "Harry" D. (Frank's son), 26; bio. notes on, 612
Joy, J. Franklin "Uncle Frank" (Anna Keeler's uncle), 25; bio. notes on, 612
Joy, Mary E. (Frank's daughter), 26; reaction to Keeler's photograph, 29; Keeler's letter to, 137; bio. notes on, 612
Joy, Mary P. "Aunt Mary" (Anna Keeler's unmarried aunt), 27; bio. notes on, 612
Jupiter (blockade runner): description of, 392; towed to Beaufort by *Florida*, 392-93

Kansas, USS (gunboat), 469, 491
Kate (blockade runner): run ashore, 347, 358; cargo saved by rebels, 364-65
Keeler, Anna E. (Keeler's wife): early years and marriage of, 7-8; in La Salle, 11, 12; "most amiable and best of wives", 13; anxiety about William, 15, 58; financial concerns of, 159, 491, 493; death of brother Melzar, 218; in New Haven with William and Henry, 287; returns to La Salle, 309; despondency of, 468, 471, 491, 499; terminal illness of sister Mary, 497-98; visits dying sister in Litchfield, 505; at New York Navy Yard to see William and Henry off, 510; returns to La Salle, 517; letters to Frank Pierce, 586-88; final years and death of, 589
Keeler, Edward (Keeler's brother): birth of, 6; and California Gold Rush, 8, 9-10; death of, 9-10; physical appearance of, 10-11
Keeler, Elizabeth E. "Tibbie", "Tib" or "Lizzie" (Keeler's daughter), 11; education of, 574; marriage of, 589; children of, 589; bio. notes on, 612-13
Keeler, Frances "Fannie" E. (Keeler's sister). *See* Frances E. Brown.
Keeler, Henry "Hen" D. (Keeler's son): birth of, 8; early years of, 11; schooling in La Salle, 41, 97; in New Haven, 77-78, 93, 207, 235, 310, 348, 451; father's praise for, 159, 258, 386, 534; visits Litchfield, 316; visits Ridgebury, 363, 365-66; sixteenth birthday of, 389;

returns to La Salle, 470, 481, 490, 493; as Paymaster's Clerk on *Florida*, 474, 506, 509, 511, 513, 516, 521, 532, 533, 534, 566; book keeper in Chicago, 571; promising botanist, 571, 573; death of, 573; bio. notes on, 613
Keeler, James Edward "Eddie" or "Eddy" (Keeler's son): birth of, 11; scientific aptitude of, 573; education of, 574; as astronomer, 574, 588; death of, 589; children of, 589; bio. notes on, 613-14
Keeler, James Plant (Keeler's brother): birth of, 6; and California Gold Rush, 8, 9, 10; diary of, 8, 9; description of, 10; death of, 10; physical appearance of, 10-11
Keeler, Mary Ann "Minnie" (Keeler's daughter): death of, 11; Keeler reminisces about, 474, 474n, 498, 574
Keeler, Mary E. (Keeler's mother): ancestry of, 6, 580; marriage of, 6; in La Salle, 11, 12; death of, 575; bio. notes on, 614
Keeler, Roswell (Keeler's father): in New York City, 5, 6; marriage of, 6; in Auburn, MI, 6, 7; in Utica, NY, 7; in Newtown, CT, 7; in La Salle, 10, 11; sickness and death of, 430, 431, 431n; bio. notes on, 614
Keeler, Sarah E. (Keeler's sister): birth of, 7; in La Salle, 11, 12; visits to Mayport, 575; bio. notes on, 614
Keeler, William F.: ancestry of, 5-6, 580; birth and early years of, 5, 6-7, 580; dry goods merchant in Bridgeport, 7; marriage of, 7-8; California Gold Rush, 8-11; moves to La Salle, 11; watchmaker, 11; iron founder and machinist, 11-12, 13; inventor, 12, 404, 531, 531n; naval appointment, 13; character of, 14-15; responsibilities as paymaster, 23, 27, 39, 68, 80, 99-100, 247, 258-59, 295, 296, 300-1, 325, 339, 372, 384, 385, 422, 480, 562; visits *Monitor* at Greenpoint, 27, 28; as *Monitor*'s tour guide, 31, 67, 73, 77, 100, 102, 104-5; and women, 31, 73, 100, 381-82, 386, 463; on red tape and old fogies, 32, 71, 74, 84, 117, 156, 193, 197, 241, 306, 313, 359; and alcohol, 37, 71, 89, 94, 104, 168, 204, 229, 396-97, 548-49, 550; takes charge of *Monitor*'s engines, 47, 592; conveys orders in fight with *Virginia*, 49-51, 55, 57; promised a

INDEX

place in turret, 60; letter to *Scientific American*, 62, 62n, 95, 591; on slavery and race, 69, 203, 235, 238, 243, 360; frustration with *Monitor*'s inactivity, 71, 83, 88, 92, 108, 154-55, 241, 588; letter to *New York Times*, 76, 102, 592-94; physical features of, 85, 102, 159, 286, 580; emotional effects of war on, 134; close encounter with rebel soldiers, 135-36; criticism of "rose water war", 139, 171, 196; criticism of regular Navy, 156, 315, 378; on prosecuting the war, 196, 231, 492; and "ram fever", 197, 348, 468; and black troops, 205, 343-45; procures fresh food from Eppes' Island, 211; jubilation over Emancipation Proclamation, 243; suggests improvement to *Monitor*'s turret, 268; reconstructs *Monitor* pay accounts, 287; ordered to *Florida*, 288, 306-7; spat with Lt. Greene, 301; beachcomber, 322, 411-12; as caterer of the mess, 355, 377, 383, 384, 386; witnesses a military execution, 374-75; on England and Englishmen, 379, 504; and porpoises, 401; proficiency with firearms, 418; father's illness and death, 430, 431, 431n, 446; relays orders between *Florida* and *Wild Dayrell*, 434, 435; oversees destruction of *Wild Dayrell*, 435-38; ordered to take possession of *Dee*, 441; wounded, 441-42; ordered to Court Martial as President, 453; votes for Lincoln, 481, 506, 507; "diplomatic efforts" in Halifax, 502-4; delivers money to Gulf Squadron, 519, 520, 523, 526, 527; reaction to Lincoln's assassination, 523-24; crosses isthmus of Panama, 564, 566-69; moves to Mayport, 572; collector of customs, 572; orange grower, 572; newspaper correspondent, 572, 595-98; receives Navy pension, 573; failing health and death of, 575, 586, 587, 588; correspondence with Frank Pierce, 577-85; obituary, 598-99

Kenifick, Dr. John: prisoner on *Florida*, 334, 334n, 337, 339; imprisoned at Fort Delaware, 354

Kensington, USS (gunboat), 369, 480

Keokuk, USS (monitor), 373; sinking of, 308

Kernstown, battle of, 64, 64n

Keyes, Erasmus D. (Brig. Gen., USA): visits *Monitor*, 67

Keystone State, USS (gunboat), 447, 483; chases and captures *Robert E. Lee*, 399-400

Key West, FL: *Florida* at, 520-21, 532, 545; description of, 520, 521, 550

Kimberly, William H. (Old Point merchant), 55, 55n, 255, 265, 280, 388, 446; generosity of, 190, 193, 213, 227, 276, 281, 380; store in Norfolk, 256; soap factory in Baltimore, 272; bio. notes on, 614

King Philip, USS (dispatch boat): *Monitor*'s officers and crew board on, 247, 251, 252

Lady Davis, CSS (iron-hulled gunboat), 570

Lancaster, USS (sloop-of-war): Keeler delivers men to, 564

Lane, David M. (Act. 3rd Asst. Engr., USN): on *Florida*, 473, 473n; resignation of, 473

Laning, James (Act. 2nd Mstr., USN), 360, 491; on *Essex* when boiler exploded, 25, 25n; supervises construction of gunboats, 268; supervises re-floating of *Indianola*, 470, 470n; bio. notes on, 614-15

Latham, Milton S. (U.S. Senator): visits *Monitor*, 112

Lee, Robert E. (Gen., CSA), 189, 443, 464; invades Pennsylvania, 346; retreat from Gettysburg, 349; versus Grant, 459, 464, 468, 471; news of surrender of, 523

Lee, Samuel Phillips (Act. Rear Adm., USN), 267, 268, 278, 348, 367, 389, 425, 451; blockading system of, 287, 289; visits blockade off Wilmington, 362-63, 405, 419, 420, 428, 485, 490, 492, 493; reprimanded by Welles, 492; disliked by subordinates, 492-93; finds blockade tedious, 493-94

Lenapee, USS (gunboat), 511

Lewis, Samuel A. (3rd Asst. Engr., USN): on *Monitor*, 253; description of, 253, 253n

Limeburner, Joseph (captain merchant vessel), 25, 25n

Lincoln, Abraham (U.S. President), 125, 127, 128, 130, 139, 214, 234, 238, 242, 248, 268, 280, 504, 550; endorses

637

Index

Monitor design, 17; Keeler sends shell fragments to, 57, 594; orders not to risk *Monitor*, 82; 5-day visit to Fort Monroe, 111, 156; description of, 112; visits *Monitor*, 112, 116, 189; meets with his military commanders, 113, 114, 116, 117, 120, 189, 239; makes reconnaissance of Willoughby's Point, 118; visit to Harrison's Landing, 189, 239; calls for more troops, 205, 492; issues Emancipation Proclamation, 243, 329; Second Annual Message of, 262; prayer for at church, 382, 394, 418, 430, 485; 1864 presidential election, 481, 506; news of assassination of, 523-24

Lincoln assassination conspirators: on *Florida*, 544, 545-47; at Fort Jefferson, 549

Livingston, John W. (Commo., USN): commandant of Norfolk Navy Yard, 378; description of, 453

Logue, Daniel C. (Act. Asst. Surg., USN), 39, 46, 49, 65-66, 79, 88, 132, 191, 198, 230, 243; appointed to *Monitor*, 27, 27n; description of, 27, 59, 96; attends to engineers, 47; attends to Worden, 51, 581; resignation of, 253; bio. notes on, 615

Lovejoy, Owen (U.S. Congressman), 12, 31, 32, 74, 538; helped Keeler obtain his commission, 13, 96; Keeler sends shell fragments to, 60, 63, 96; bio. notes on, 615

Ludlow, Edwin (Capt., USA): assistant quartermaster in Norfolk, 192; embezzler before war, 192n

Lyons, Richard B. P. (British ambassador to U.S.), 87

MacDonnell, Sir Richard G. (Lt. Governor of Nova Scotia): Keeler meets with, 503-4

Magaw, Margaret H. M. (Samuel's wife), 452, 461, 500; description of, 462, 462n

Magaw, Samuel (Lt. Cmdr., USN), 461, 471, 498, 500, 501, 502, 504, 506, 514; assumes command of *Florida*, 452; description of, 452, 454, 536; on sick leave, 511, 519; invites Keeler to visit, 536; bio. notes on, 615-16

Magruder, John B. (Maj. Gen., CSA), 52, 231, 236, 476; at siege of Yorktown, 79, 84, 86, 109, 109n; surrenders in Texas, 535

Mahaska, USS (gunboat), 157, 170

Maies, William H. (Act. Vol. Lt., USN): commanding officer on *Florida*, 560, 566, 569; description of, 560; bio. notes on, 616

Mallory, Stephen R. (Confederate Secretary of the Navy): on board *Virginia*, 111; slave daughter of, 550

Malvern Hill, battle of, 177, 177n, 198, 204; roar of heard from *Monitor*, 173

Malvern, USS (gunboat): Adm. Lee's flagship, 492

Mann, James (Maj., USA): paymaster, 527, 527n

Mansfield, Joseph K. F. (Maj. Gen., USA), 52, 61, 114, 593; visits *Monitor*, 57

Maple Leaf, USS (prison ship), 352, 352n

Maratanza, USS (gunboat), 209; in expedition up Appomattox River, 166, 167-68, 169; captures CSS *Teaser*, 180, 587; carries sick and wounded soldiers, 188-89

Mars (blockade runner), 391

Marston, John (Capt., USN), 72

Mason, James M. (Confederate diplomat), 87

Masonboro Inlet, NC, 308, 369, 439, 440, 466

Massachusetts, USS (supply ship), 308, 325, 327, 337, 346, 349, 359, 402

Matthews, A. P. (Act. Mstr.'s Mate, USN): accidental death of, 396

Maury, Matthew F. (Cmdr., CSN), 181

Mayport, FL: description of, 571, 572

McAlister, Alexander (Keeler's friend in New Haven), 23, 272; bio. notes on, 616

McCall, George A. (Brig. Gen., USA), 202; captured, 186

McClellan, George B. (Gen., USA): removed as general in chief, 68, 68n; Keeler's defence of, 69, 89-91, 202, 203, 206, 218-19, 256-57, 264, 360; arrives at Fort Monroe, 76; visits *Monitor*, 76, 79; description of, 79; siege of Yorktown, 79, 84, 86, 102, 105, 107, 109, 110, 125; naval assistance for, 88, 92, 143, 163, 170; navy and army officers' praise for, 91, 202, 236, 270, 369; advance on Richmond, 130, 137, 140, 142, 143, 148, 158, 163, 164; retreat to Harrison's

Index

Landing, 169-74; on board *Galena*, 174, 206; camp at Harrison's Landing, 177-83, 186-87; popularity of, 187; meets with Lincoln, 189; Gen. Lee's note to regarding sick and wounded Union soldiers, 189; plan to land forces at City Point, 202, 241, 263, 273, 477; retreat from Virginia Peninsula, 207-8, 210, 213; commands Army of Virginia, 226, 236; news of victory at Antietam, 239; defeat as politician, 507; Keeler's contempt for, 507
McCook, Alexander M. (Maj. Gen., USA), 202
McDowell, Irvin (Maj. Gen., USA), 102, 148, 207, 270
McGowan, John, Sr. (John's father), 352, 352n
McGowan, John (Act. Mstr., USN), 363, 377, 378, 379, 382, 418, 419, 437, 452, 459, 460, 500, 502; assigned to *Florida*, 295; description of, 352; appointed executive officer on *Florida*, 489, 506; bio. notes on, 616
McGowan, Kate A. (John's sister), 377, 379, 381, 383, 384; description of, 386
McGowan, Ned (John's uncle), 352
McLean, William H. (Act. 1st Asst. Engr., USN), 422, 437, 459, 460, 538; assigned to *Florida*, 414; description of, 420; bio. notes on, 616-17
Meagher, Thomas F. (Brig. Gen., USA), 186, 202; visits *Monitor*, 188; description of, 188
Meckly, Thomas H. (Act. Asst. Surg., USN): on *Monitor*, 253; description of, 253
Meech, William W. (chaplain): at Newport News, 236
Melpomene, HMS (frigate): at Hampton Roads, 278
Memphis, USS (gunboat), 559
Mercedita, USS (gunboat): Keeler's trip on, 474, 477
Mercier, Henri (French ambassador to U.S.): visits *Monitor*, 105
Merrimac. See CSS *Virginia*.
Merrimack, USS (frigate), 16
Merriman, Edgar C. (Act. Lt., USN), 392, 400, 401, 406, 408, 409, 489; assigned to *Florida* as executive officer, 385; description of, 388, 401, 488; prize money won by, 407, 418; in temporary command of *Florida*, 447; leave of absence, 488; bio. notes on, 617
military execution, 374-75, 375n
Millen, GA: prison camp at, 537
Miller, Madison (Col., USA): released on parole, 148; description of, 148
Millward, James (Capt. of Port), 227; flag of truce officer, 98, 99, 137, 138, 139, 147; bio. notes on, 617
Minnesota, USS (frigate), 372, 465; aground off Newport News, 48, 592; protected by *Monitor*, 48, 49, 50, 51, 52, 71, 579; shots from strike *Monitor*, 67, 191, 254; criticism of commanding officer of, 72; panic on board of, 72; as Goldsborough's flag ship, 164, 190, 213; as Adm. Lee's flag ship, 363, 364, 367, 428; destroys blockade runner, 364, 367
Mississippi River Delta: description of, 524-25
Mix, John (Lt. Col., USA): visits *Monitor*, 105
Mix, Simon H. (Col., USA): visits *Monitor*, 104-5; death of, 104n
Mobile, AL, 467
Mobile Bay, AL: *Florida* at, 522-23, 534-35
Mobile Bay, battle of, 522, 522n, 523, 556
Modoc, USS (monitor), 554
Monadnock, USS (monitor), 556
Monitor, USS: construction of, 17, 28; description of, 17-18, 27, 58-59, 67, 254, 578, 583-84; armaments on, 17-18, 27, 34, 56, 62, 77, 80, 114; commissioned, 17, 31; planned attack on Potomac River batteries, 23-24, 27, 29; arrival at New York Navy Yard, 30; Keeler's stateroom, 33, 38, 39-40, 58-59, 254, 263; steering problems, 34, 36; officers' mess, 35, 254-55; officers' meals, 35, 36-37, 59, 197-98, 236, 239, 255, 261, 277; officers' wardroom, 35, 37, 58, 59, 254; liquor on, 37, 71, 84, 204, 229, 580-81; trip from New York to Hampton Roads, 45-48, 592; ventilation system, 47; ordered to protect *Minnesota*, 48; in fight with *Virginia*, 48-53, 61, 71-72, 578-79, 581-85, 591, 593; ordered to remain near Fort Monroe, 55; weak points of, 56, 58, 87; alterations to, 56, 61, 110, 254, 267, 268; cheered by army at Newport News, 57, 594; daily routine on, 59-60, 88-89, 274; measures taken against boarders, 59, 61-62, 106; number of men on, 60; absurd

639

INDEX

suggestions for capturing, 61; officers' leisure activities on, 65-66, 68, 96, 230, 264; in attack on Sewell's Point batteries, 114-15, 118; to Norfolk after rebels evacuate, 123-25; ordered to Richmond, 125; in attack on Fort Darling, 129-30, 140; rebel plans to capture, 140, 180, 587; engine problems, 144, 161, 244; men suffering from heat and mosquitoes, 146, 155, 184, 204, 205, 207, 353-54; farm animals on deck, 146, 151, 157; inspection of crew, 160-61; fire on, 162; in expedition up Appomattox River, 163, 165, 166-69; ordered to Newport News, 223; ordered to Washington Navy Yard, 244; at Washington Navy Yard, 247-48, 250-52; Christmas care packages, 275-76; Christmas dinner on, 277; loss of, 281-86, 579, 580-81

Monitor vs. *Virginia*. *See* Hampton Roads, battle of March 9.

Montauk, USS (monitor), 274, 278; torpedoed, 294

Montgomery, USS (gunboat), 370

Monticello, USS (gunboat), 97, 447, 483; accidently sinks *Peterhoff*, 445, 488

Moore, Absolom B. (Col., USA), 261, 481; ineptitude of, 233, 269, 271; capture of brigade of, 267, 267n; bio. notes on, 617

Morehead City, NC: description of, 320-21; anticipated rebel attack near, 441

Morell, George W. (Brig. Gen., USA): visits *Monitor*, 100

Morris, Augusta H. (Confederate spy): conversation with Lt. Jeffers, 145

Morris Island, SC: Union forces at, 347, 349

Mound Battery, NC: construction of, 304, 304n

Mount Vernon, USS (gunboat), 120, 309, 311, 328, 427, 428; captures *G. O. Bigelow*, 413

Mount Vernon, VA: description of, 246

Mount Washington, USS (gunboat): Keeler's trip on, 206, 213

Mudd, Dr. Samuel A. (conspirator): prisoner on board *Florida*, 545; description of, 546, 547; discusses trial, 546; Keeler's letter concerning guilt of, 546n; employment at Fort Jefferson, 549

Murray, Lawrence (*Monitor*'s steward), 242; dinner served by, 37, 37n; drowning death of, 229; burial of, 232

Naglee, Henry M. (Brig. Gen., USA), 418; cavalry raid of, 271

Nansemond River, VA, 425

Nantucket, USS (monitor), 292

Nassau, West Indies, 288; *Florida* cruises near, 389, 407-8

Naubuc, USS (monitor), 554

Naugatuck, USRC (ironclad), 92, 128, 373; exchanges fire with *Virginia*, 82; description of, 86-87; in attack on Sewell's Point batteries, 114, 115, 118; ordered to Richmond, 125; in attack on Fort Darling, 129, bursts gun, 132, 141; criticism of, 141

Neuse River, NC, 343, 441

New Bern, NC: Federal troops at, 319, 343-44, 430, 441; description of environs, 340-41; description of, 341-43; rebel forces near, 440-41

New Berne, USS (supply ship), 365, 378, 384, 403, 415, 426, 428, 433, 446, 447, 468, 494; delivers fresh meat and ice to squadron, 359, 398, 405, 413, 419-20, 438, 493; chases blockade runner, 427-28; Keeler's trip on, 474-76

New Inlet, NC, 289, 324, 338

New Ironsides, USS (ironclad): description of, 17, 224, 227-28, 373, 556; at Hampton Roads, 224, 227-28, 244, 260, 276; off Charleston, 293; torpedo attack on, 389, 389n

New London, CT: *Florida* ordered to, 496, 496n

New Orleans, LA: news of capture of, 99; *Florida* at, 524-29, 536-37; description of river approach to, 524-25; description of, 526

Newport News, VA: *Monitor* at, 224-44

Newport, RI: *Florida* at, 556-57

Newton, Isaac (1st Asst. Engr., USN): on *Monitor*, 37, 191; detached from *Monitor*, 217; bio. notes on, 617

New York (steamship): delivers sailors to Aspinwall, 569

New York, NY: draft riots, 350; end-of-war celebrations in, 511, 511n; description of harbor of, 552; description of Catherine Market in, 553

INDEX

New York Navy Yard, NY: *Monitor* at, 30-41; *Florida* at, 496, 505-8, 510-12, 529-32, 551-54, 559-60

Nicolay, John G. (Lincoln's secretary): visits *Monitor*, 248, 248n

Niphon, USS (gunboat): landing boat attacked, 367

Noble, Henry Dutton (Anna Keeler's cousin), 560

Norfolk, VA: rebels evacuate, 114; capture of, 117, 119, 120, 123; description of, 124, 213-15, 256, 394; defences along river approach to, 124, 125; pro-Southern sentiment in, 214-15, 374; business activity in, 214, 256, 388, 394; life in during Union occupation, 394

Norfolk Naval Hospital, 124; description of, 375-76; sick from *Florida* sent to, 140, 304, 493; wounded from Fort Fisher at, 516-17

Norfolk Navy Yard: destroyed by rebels, 120, 125, 376, 378; description of destruction to, 125, 192, 373-74, 451-52; *Florida* undergoing repairs at, 372-90, 451-65

North Carolina, USS (receiving ship), 27, 31, 33, 39

Norton, Mary (Keeler's cousin), 501

Nutfield (blockade runner): destroyed by *Sassacus* and *Florida*, 439-40; estimated value of cargo on, 452

Nutting, William G. (Mstr., USN): detached from *Florida*, 396

Octorara, USS (gunboat), 112

O'Laughlen, Michael (conspirator): prisoner on board *Florida*, 545; description of, 547

Old Point Comfort, VA: Hygeia Hotel at, 85, 190; Kimberly's provisions store at, 227; rebel prisoners at, 269; ordnance stores at, 459

Osborn, Mr. (Eppes' overseer), 149

Osborn, Marcus B. (Act. Asst. Paymaster, USN), 398

Panama City, 563; description of, 564-66

Panama, Isthmus of: description of trip across, 566-69

Parke, John G. (Act. Asst. Surg., USN): assigned to *Florida*, 360; detached from *Florida*, 368; description of, 369; bio. notes on, 618

Parker, James (Lt. Cmdr., USN): assumes command of *Florida*, 364; description of, 364, 368-69; detached from *Florida*, 368; bio. notes on, 618

Passaic, USS (monitor), 258, 278; defective boilers of, 260, 274; in ironclad attack on Charleston, 294

Patterson, Thomas H. (Cmdr., USN), 564, 564n

Paulding, Hiram (Commo., USN), 20, 21, 39; as Rear Adm., 512, 519

Peck, John J. (Maj. Gen., USA), 441

Penobscot, USS (gunboat), 310, 325, 327, 364; shelled by shore battery, 323

Pensacola Navy Yard, FL: *Florida* at, 522; wartime destruction of, 523

Perry, USS (brig), 302, 311, 324

Peterhoff, USS (gunboat), 447, 452; accidental sinking of, 445, 488

Pevensey (blockade runner), 477; chase and capture of, 475-76; description of, 476

Philadelphia, PA: market at, 555

Philadelphia Navy Yard: *Florida* at, 554-56; ironclads at, 556

Pickering, Thomas (Act. Vol. Lt., USN): keeps pets on board *Fort Donelson*, 488

Pierce, Frank H. (collector): Keeler's correspondence with, 577-85; Anna Keeler's correspondence with, 586-88; bio. notes on, 618

Pig Point, VA, 89

Pike, Nicolas (ex-U.S. consul): visits *Monitor*, 31

Pilot Bay (steamer), 330

Plant, Helen (Keeler's cousin), 96, 134, 137, 178, 225, 279, 281; bio. notes on, 618

plunder, 435-37, 439, 440, 477, 536

Plymouth, NC: under threat of attack, 440; Union loss of, 459, 488; refugees from, 472-73

Pope, John (Maj. Gen., USA), 177, 196, 207, 270

Port Hudson, LA: African-American troops at, 344; news of capture of, 349

Port Royal, USS (gunboat), 113, 126, 128, 158; in attack on Fort Darling, 129, 132; in expedition up Appomattox River, 166, 167, 168

Porter, David D. (Rear Adm., USN): mortar fleet of, 205; brother of, 538

641

INDEX

Porter, Henry O. (Act. Mstr., USN): description of, 538, 538n
Porter, Fitz John (Maj. Gen., USA), 264
Porter, George L. (Surgeon, USA): on *Florida* on trip to Dry Tortugas, 547, 547n, 548
Portsmouth, USS (sloop-of-war), 528
Portsmouth, VA, 192, 266, 418; military execution at, 374-75; churches in, 376, 382
Port Walthall, VA, 165, 168, 169
Potomac River: rebel batteries on, 23-24, 27, 29; countryside along, 245-46
Pratt, Oscar H. (Act. 2nd Mstr., USN), 25, 25n, 29, 360; death of, 421; bio. notes on, 618-19
Preston, John S. (Capt., CSA), 139, 139n
Price, Sterling (Maj. Gen., CSA), 516
prize money: for *Virginia*, 181, 266, 587, 587n; distribution of, 296n, 336; for *Calypso*, 354, 354n; sharing of, 440

Queen, Walter W. (Lt. Cmdr., USN), 372, 387, 389, 396; description of, 369, 372, 395, 398, 401, 414, 422; assumes command of *Florida*, 368; vindictiveness of, 395, 400; indecisiveness of, 397-98, 399-400; relieved of command of *Florida*, 402, 405; bio. notes on, 619
Queen, Christiana (Queen's wife), 377; description of, 387

Raleigh, CSS (ironclad ram): breaks up on bar, 468, 468n
Ransom, George M. (Cmdr., USN), 400, 400n
Rapidan River, VA, 464
Rappahannock River, VA, 207, 268, 270, 271, 277, 280
Rawdon, Frederick W. (1st Class Boy, USN), 351, 351n
Rawlings, Dr. Augustus (newspaper correspondent), 62, 62n
Read, Charles W. (Lt., CSN), commanding officer of CSS *Webb*, 528-29, 528n
refugees: escaping conscription, 141, 417, 418, 420, 433; escaping war, 468, 472-73; along Gulf coast, 523, 535
Rhode Island, USS (supply ship): tows *Monitor*, 281, 282, 580; rescues *Monitor*'s officers and crew, 283-84, 285-86, 393, 446, 549
Rich, Charles E. (Act. Ens., USN): assigned to *Florida*, 396; wedding of, 461-63; hospitalized, 493; bio. notes on, 619
Richardson, Samuel W. (Capt., USA), 103, 104
Richmond, VA: consumer prices in, 150-51; poor condition of Confederate troops in, 252; news of fall of, 519, 520
Richmond, CSS (ironclad ram): construction of, 83, 83n; *Monitor* guards against egress of, 194, 197, 200, 223, 236, 238, 239, 251, 274
Richmond, USS (sloop-of-war), 523, 528
Ridgebury, CT: Keeler's ancestral home, 5-6
Rinaldo, HMS (corvette), 53, 58, 86, 87, 594
Rip Raps, VA: Union batteries at, 52, 58, 74, 379; description of, 52n, 119; President Lincoln visits, 117
Roanoke, USS (frigate), 48, 371, 372, 373
Roanoke Island, NC, 154, 217
Roanoke River, NC, 265
Robert E. Lee (blockade runner), 399; capture of, 402
Robinson, Charles S. (Brooklyn minister), 507
Rockwell, John (Keeler's friend in La Salle), 32, 32n; description of 12; wife of, 12; father of, 32, 78; on U.S. Coast Survey, 230, 373, 454; uncle of, 501, 501n; older brother Charles, 574; bio. notes on, 619
Rodgers, John (Cmdr., USN): commands James River Flotilla, 130, 130n, 140, 141, 164, 166, 169, 172, 206; commands *Weehawken*, 413
Roe, Francis A. (Lt. Cmdr., USN), 449
Roman, USS (ordnance storeship), 570
Rosecrans, William S. (Maj. Gen. USA), 349
Ruffin, Edmund (James River planter): house of, 178, 201, 205

Sabine, USS (sailing frigate), 31, 39, 292
Sachem, USS (gunboat): accompanies *Monitor* to Hampton Roads, 45
Sacramento, USS (sloop-of-war), 296, 348, 362, 363, 367
St. George (blockade runner), 311, 335
St. Lawrence, USS (ordnance storeship), 379, 570
salt works, 417, destruction of, 422-24

INDEX

Sampson, L. Grenville (Act. Ens., USN): on *Florida*, 538, 538n, 541
Samuel Russell (merchant vessel), 10, 11, 67
Sancston, James (Seaman, USN): an "old salt" on *Florida*, 350-51, 350n
Sands, Benjamin F. (Capt., USN), 391
Sandy Hook, NY, 292, 513, 551
Sangamon, USS (monitor), 371, 372
San Jacinto, USS (sloop), 120, 125; in attack on Sewell's Point batteries, 115
Santiago de Cuba, USS (gunboat), 418
Sargent, Fernando C. (Act. Asst. Surg., USN): passenger on *Florida*, 538
Sassacus, USS (gunboat): destroys *Nutfield*, 434, 439, 452; plunders and destroys *Wild Dayrell*, 435-38, 449
Savannah, GA, 349, 515, 556
Savannah, CSS (ironclad ram), 230
Savannah, USS (instruction ship), 31
Scott, William (1st Class Boy, USN): Keeler's servant on *Monitor*, 107, 107n, 160, 242; conversation with Keeler, 242
Sebago, USS (gunboat), 234
Selfridge, Thomas O. (Lt., USN): in temporary command of *Monitor*, 55, 60, 62; description of, 62; describes sinking of *Cumberland*, 72-73, 72n; commands ironclad *Cairo*, 279, 279n; bio. notes on, 619-20
Seminole, USS (gunboat), 120; in attack on Sewell's Point batteries, 115, 118
Seth Low, USS (tug): tows *Monitor* to Hampton Roads, 45
Seward, William H. (U.S. Secretary of State), 218
Sewell's Point, VA: rebel batteries on, 48; gunboat attack on, 114-15, 118, 123; Federal forces capture, 120, 124
Seymour, Horatio (New York Governor): election loss of, 507
Seymour, Truman (Brig. Gen., USA): on board *Florida*, 403, 403n
Shawsheen, USS (armed tug): captured and destroyed, 465
Shepley, George F. (Brig. Gen., USA), 463
Sheridan, Philip H. (Maj. Gen., USA), 499
Sherman, John (U.S. Senator): visits *Monitor*, 73
Sherman, William T. (Maj. Gen., USA), 491, 499, 515
Shiloh, battle of: news of, 82, 82n, 85, 85n; casualties at, 82, 82n, 91, 91n; Union officers captured at, 148, 148n

Shirley Plantation, VA: escaped slaves from, 146; sick and wounded soldiers at, 170, 176, 188-89, 198
Shokokon, USS (gunboat), 413, 465
Sigel, Franz (Maj. Gen., USA), 272
Slidell, John (Confederate diplomat), 87
Smith, Charles F. (Maj. Gen., USA), 108
Smith, Edmund Kirby (Gen., CSA): surrender of, 535
Smith's Island, NC, 289, 308, 347; rebel artillery on, 391
Smith, Margaret (Nelson's wife), 231
Smith, Nelson (retired sea captain), 231
Smithville, NC, 448, 514
Sonoma, USS (gunboat), 240
South America (steamer), 330
Southfield, USS (gunboat), 165, 204
South Inlet, NC, 289, 330, 331, 338
South Mountain, battle of, 352
Spangler, Edward (conspirator): prisoner on board *Florida*, 544, 545; description of, 547; employment at Fort Jefferson, 549
Spinola, Francis B. (Brig. Gen., USA), 342; description of, 345
S. R. Spaulding, USSC (hospital ship), 173, 174, 183, 368, 431
Stanton, Edwin M. (U.S. Secretary of War), 92, 165; 5-day visit to Fort Monroe, 112, 113, 116, 120, 125; visits *Monitor*, 112, 116; Keeler's criticism of, 171, 179, 203
Staples, William E. (Act. Mstr., USN): executive officer on *Florida*, 515, 515n, 538
Star of the West (merchant vessel), 352
State of Georgia, USS (gunboat), 364; smallpox on, 430
Stepping Stones, USS (gunboat), 142, 147, 150, 151; carries sick and wounded soldiers, 170
Stevens Battery, 86, 86n
Stevens, Edwin A. (naval engineer), 86, 141
Stevens, Thomas H. (Cmdr., USN), 228; given command of *Monitor*, 209; arrives on *Monitor*, 216; description of, 216, 223, 230, 234, 240, 536; relieved of command of *Monitor*, 234; Keeler dines with, 240; commanded boat attack on Fort Sumter, 373; invites Keeler to visit, 536; bio. notes on, 620
Stimers, Alban C. (Chief Engr., USN), 65, 88, 579, 582, 591; description of, 60, 62, 583; in fight with *Virginia*, 60; ordered

643

to New York Navy Yard, 95; "failed" monitors of, 554, 554n
Stoddard, Eben M. (Act. Mstr., USN), 491
Stodder, Louis N. (Act. Mstr., USN): on *Monitor*, 24, 24n, 37, 191, 251, 254, 264, 265, 283, 582; bravery of, 283; bio. notes on, 620
Stone Fleet, 569-70
Stone, William M. (Maj., USA): released on parole, 148
Stonewall, CSS (ironclad ram), 534
Storrs, Richard S. (Brooklyn minister), 25, 25n
Stothard, Thomas (Act. Ens., USN): assigned to *Florida*, 494, 494n
Stryker, Stephen W. (Col., USA): visits *Monitor*, 67, 67n
Suffolk, VA, 260: Federal troops arriving at, 241
Sunstrom, Mark T. (3rd Asst. Engr., USN): on *Monitor*, 191, 191n
Surratt, Mary (conspirator), 544, 546
Susquehanna, USS (sloop-of-war), 120, 125; in attack on Sewell's Point batteries, 115
Swift Creek, VA: aborted attack on railroad bridge over, 165, 166-68
Swift, Robert B. (Act. 2nd Asst. Engr., USN): on *Florida*, 555, 555n
Syren (blockade runner), 477

Tacony, CSS (commerce raider), 528, 528n
Tallahassee, CSS (commerce raider), 495, 496
Talley, Susan A. (Southern poet), 231
Tanner's Creek, VA, 117
Tattnall, Josiah (Flag Officer, CSN), 106
Taylor, Dudley E. (Act. Mstr., USN), 28, 28n
Taylor, Mr. (coast pilot), 405
Teaser, CSS (gunboat), 117; capture of, 180; interesting items found on board of, 180, 188, 207, 238, 587
Thatcher, Henry K. (Act. Rear Adm., USN), 528, 528n
Toffey, Daniel (Captain's Clerk, USN): on *Monitor*, 27, 578, 582; description of, 27n
Toombs, Robert A. (ex-U.S. Senator), 297
Trent River, NC, 343, 441
Truxtun, William T. (Lt. Cmdr., USN), 353, 353n
Tucker, John (U.S. Asst. Secretary of War): visits *Monitor*, 67, 67n, 110

Turkey Island, VA, 170, 174, 180
Turner, Levi C. (Col., USA): on *Florida* on trip to Dry Tortugas, 547; description of, 550-51
turpentine: production of, 311, 341
Tuscarora, USS (sloop-of-war), 403, 428, 429, 468
Tuthill, Anna "Nancy" E. (Anna Keeler's aunt), 497, 530
Tyler, Bishop A. (Landsman, USN): cook on *Florida*, 295, 295n

Underwriter, USS (gunboat), 341, 345, 398
United States, USS (frigate): remains of, 124, 570

Vallandigham, Clement L. (U.S. Congressman), 329, 369
Van Alen, James H. (Brig. Gen., USA): visits *Monitor*, 92
Van Antwerp, David D. (Beaufort minister), 394, 394n, 430, 430n, 485-86
Van Brunt, Gershom J. (Capt., USN), 592-93; Lt. Worden's verbal exchange with, 49; criticism of, 72
Van Wyck, Charles A. (Col., USA), 269; description of, 194, 194n
Vance, Zebulon B. (North Carolina Governor), 477
Vanderbilt, USS (gunboat): cruises off Halifax with *Florida*, 500
Van Vliet, Stewart L. (Brig. Gen., USA): visits *Monitor*, 54
Viall, Thomas B. (Seaman, USN): on *Monitor*, 578, 582
Vicksburg, MS: false news of capture of, 330; news of attack on, 336; news of surrender of, 349
Vicksburg, USS (gunboat): fires into *Florida*, 493
Victoria, USS (gunboat), 336, 347, 350, 352, 361, 362, 363, 364, 369, 475
Viele, Egbert L. (Brig. Gen., USA), 192, 215
Violet, USS (armed tug), 350; ran aground and destroyed by Navy, 493
Virginia, CSS: construction of, 16; armaments on, 16; attacks *Cumberland* and *Congress*, 41-42, 48, 53, 72-73; in fight with *Monitor*, 42-43, 45, 48-53, 593; undergoing repairs in Norfolk, 56; reports about, 70, 83; strategies to

INDEX

destroy, 71, 82, 87, 88; appearances of after fight with *Monitor*, 81-82, 83, 106-7, 111-12, 113, 116, 117; description of, 81, 106, 111-12; absurd suggestions for destroying, 95; blown up, 120, 123; remains of, 125, 193, 373, 570; prize money for, 181, 587, 587n; rebel sailor's account of fight with *Monitor*, 193; rebel steward's description of leaving Norfolk before fight, 397; weak point of, 584

Virginia vs. *Monitor*. *See* Hampton Roads, battle of March 9.

Von Donop, Edward P. B. (Capt., RN), 502, 502n, 503

Vose, Edwin H. (Act. Asst. Surg., USN), 440, 442, 445; assigned to *Florida*, 420-21; resigns, 452; bio. notes on, 620

Wabash, USS (frigate), 294

Wachusett, USS (gunboat): landing boat attacked, 135-36; surgeon captured, 137; release of captured officers, 216

Wagstaff, Robert M. (Act. Ens., USN): assigned to *Florida*, 295; description of, 351-52; detached from *Florida*, 396; bio. notes on, 620-21

Wales, Salem H. (magazine editor), 62; visits *Monitor*, 31

Wall, William E. (Navy Department clerk), 73; pretty wife of, 73

Wardrop, David W. (Col., USA), 215

Ward's Hill, VA, 127

Warner, Helen (Keeler's second cousin), 25, 505

Warrior, HMS (ironclad frigate), 27, 27n

Washburn, Cornelius (Act. Ens., USN), 411, 502; assigned to *Florida*, 396; destroys salt works, 422-24; bio. notes on, 621

Washington, Corbin (Qmstr., USN): on *Florida*, 345, 345n, 397

Washington, DC: Confederate raid on, 489, 491

Washington Navy Yard: *Monitor* ordered to, 244

Washington, NC: rebels prepare to attack, 440; refugees from, 472-73; Union loss of, 488

Wassaw Sound, GA, 392

Watrous, Harriet "Hattie" or "Hat" J. (Keeler's sister-in-law), 8; description of, 22; bio. notes on, 621

Watrous, George H. (Keeler's brother-in-law), 22, 23, 508, 519, 579, 580; bio. notes on, 621

Webb, CSS: chase and destruction of, 526-29; prisoners from, 530; remains of, 539

Webber, John J. N. (Act. Mstr., USN): on *Monitor*, 24, 24n, 37; bio. notes on, 621-22

Weber, Max (Brig. Gen., USA), 117

Weehawken, USS (monitor): captures CSS *Atlanta*, 347; sinks off Charleston, 413

Weeks, Grenville M. (Act. Asst. Surg., USN), 268, 275, 311, 321; assigned to *Monitor*, 253; description of, 253, 259, 300, 360; injured during rescue of *Monitor*'s crew, 286; assigned to *Florida*, 295; forced to leave *Florida*, 360; bio. notes on, 622

Welles, Gideon (U.S. Secretary of the Navy), 54, 105, 160, 576, 585; Keeler's mocking of, 313, 327, 348, 398, 561

Western Bar Channel. *See* South Inlet.

Westfield, USS (gunboat), 351

Whipple, William D. (Lt. Col., USA), 147

White, George H. (Act. 3rd Asst. Engr., USN): detached from *Monitor*, 253

White House Plantation, VA: evacuation of McClellan's supply base at, 171

White Oak Swamp, VA, 188

Whittemore, William M. (Act. Asst. Paymaster, USN), 320

Wild Dayrell (blockade runner), 455; captured and destroyed by *Florida*, 433, 434-38, 439, 449; plundering of, 435-37, 446, 449

Wild, Edward A. (Brig. Gen., USA), 430

Wilkes, Charles (Commo., USN): commands James River Flotilla, 193, 197, 218, 219

William Badger, USS (storeship), 320

Williams, Peter (Qmstr., USN): on *Monitor* in fight with *Virginia*, 51, 53, 581, 584; description of, 53; promoted to Act. Mstr.'s Mate, 53, 68; Act. Ens. on *Florida*, 295, 299, 395, 422; Medal of Honor recipient, 395; on *Clematis*, 539; bio. notes on, 622

Williams, William H. H. (Paymaster, USN), 277, 277n

Williamsburg, VA, 110, 133

Willis, Nathaniel P. (magazine editor), 149-50

645

INDEX

Willoughby's Point, VA: troops landing on, 118
Wilmington, NC: importance of, 288; difficulty in closing port of, 289, 348, 363; wartime prosperity of, 308, 348, 370; rebels construct road from Fort Fisher to, 444
Winchester, 1st battle of: news of, 142, 142n
Winchester, VA, 64
Wingfield, John H. D. (minister in Portsmouth): refuses to pray for president, 382, 382n
Winslow, John A. (Capt., USN), 483, 483n
Wise, Henry A. (Brig. Gen., CSA), 154, 156; wife of, 228
Wood, Benjamin (U.S. Congressman): election loss of, 507
Wood, John Taylor (Lt., CSN): *Century Magazine* article by, 577, 582, 584
Wood, Samuel S. (Act. Asst. Paymaster, USN), 477; captures crew of blockade runner, 476
Woodhouse, J. B. (Paymaster's steward, USN), 447, 447n
Wool, John E. (Maj. Gen., USA), 52, 53, 56, 58, 61, 76, 98, 105, 150, 162, 266, 594; visits *Monitor*, 55, 57, 67, 73, 74, 112; description of, 62, 88, 111, 271; headquarters at Fort Monroe, 84, 101, 111; meets with Lincoln, 113, 120, 125
Worden, John L. (Lt., USN), 27, 31, 35, 36, 37, 39, 46, 70, 163, 236, 254, 279; accepts command of *Monitor*, 18; description of, 24, 62, 64, 69, 98; in fight with *Virginia*, 45, 48, 49-51, 55, 57, 60, 62, 71, 72, 240, 578, 579, 581, 584, 593; taken to Washington after fight, 52, 53; commands ironclad *Montauk*, 262, 274, 278, 294; receives Thanks of Congress, 268, 585; promoted to Capt., 268; supervises building of ironclads, 406; invites Keeler to visit, 497; post-war letter to Gideon Welles, 576; bio. notes on, 622-23
Wright, Dr. David M. (murderer), 388

York River, VA, 79, 88, 92, 106, 110, 154, 171, 459
Yorktown, VA, 61, 106, 133, 173, 242; advance on, 68, 125; siege of, 83, 86, 91, 92, 105; Confederate evacuation of, 105, 107, 109, 110; Gen. Butler's ruse at, 464
Yorktown, CSS (gunboat), 81, 83, 92, 113, 117; sunk by Confederates, 129, 132
Yulee, David L. (ex-U.S. Senator), 351

Ziegler, John Q. A. (Act. Chief Engr., USN): assigned to *Florida*, 295; on *Florida*, 317, 333, 351, 369, 376, 394, 420; description of, 352; wife of, 376, 377; detached from *Florida*, 414; on *Monadnock*, 556; bio. notes on, 623

Abbreviations

The following abbreviations are used in the Index and in some of the footnotes.

Act. = Acting
Adm. = Admiral
Asst. = Assistant
Brig. = Brigadier
Capt. = Captain
Cmdr. = Commander
Col. = Colonel
Commo. = Commodore
CSA = Confederate States Army
CSN = Confederate States Navy
CSS = Confederate States Ship
Engr. = Engineer
Ens. = Ensign
Gen. = General
HMS = Her Majesty's Ship
Lt. = Lieutenant
Maj. = Major
Mstr. = Master
NARA = National Archives and Records Administration
ORN = Official Records Navy
ORN = Official Records Army
Qmstr. = Quartermaster
RN = Royal Navy
Surg. = Surgeon
USA = United States Army
USN = United States Navy
USRC = United States Revenue Cutter
USS = United States Ship
USSC = United States Sanitary Commission
Vol. = Volunteer

About the Editor

Charles W. McLandress is a great-great-grandson of William F. Keeler and a life-long American Civil War buff. A retired atmospheric scientist with over 60 publications in peer-reviewed journals, he lives in Toronto, Ontario with his wife and two children. More information about William F. Keeler can be found on the editor's webpage: www.sealriverpublishing.com.

www.ingramcontent.com/pod-product-compliance
Lightning Source LLC
Chambersburg PA
CBHW071112080526
44587CB00013B/1318